A SHORT HISTORY
OF THE
BRITISH
WORKING-CLASS
MOVEMENT

1789–1947

by

G. D. H. COLE

NEW EDITION
COMPLETELY REVISED AND
CONTINUED TO 1947

LONDON
GEORGE ALLEN & UNWIN LTD

VOLUME I.   FIRST PUBLISHED IN 1925; SECOND EDITION, 1927;
REPRINTED, 1930

VOLUME 2.   FIRST PUBLISHED IN 1926; SECOND EDITION, 1927

VOLUME 3.   FIRST PUBLISHED IN 1927; SECOND EDITION, 1937

ALL THREE VOLUMES REISSUED TOGETHER IN ONE VOLUME, WITH
A NEW INTRODUCTORY CHAPTER, IN 1932

ALL THREE VOLUMES REISSUED TOGETHER IN ONE VOLUME, WITH
A FURTHER SUPPLEMENTARY CHAPTER, IN 1937

RE-PUBLISHED AS A COMPLETE WORK AND REVISED AND ENLARGED,
1948; REPRINTED, 1951, 1952, 1960

*This book has been printed in Great Britain by
litho-offset at Taylor Garnett Evans & Co. Ltd.,
Watford, Herts, and bound by them*

PREFACE

THE following study of the British Working-class Movement purports to be no more than an introductory survey of a field which needs much further research. There exist already full histories of the Trade Union Movement (up to 1920), by Sidney and Beatrice Webb, and of the Co-operative Movement (up to 1944), by the present writer, as well as many excellent studies of particular phases and periods. But no one, to my knowledge, had attempted, until this book was written, to bring within a single work a general survey of the growth of the working-class movement in all its leading aspects, political as well as industrial and co-operative. As a teacher, I had long felt the want of such a book ; for the histories of separate phases of working-class activity fail to give just that synoptic view which seems to me essential for those who begin to study the subject. When this book was first published, I hoped, at a later stage, to cover the ground far more adequately, and in a much larger work. But I venture to believe that this book as it is has been found useful, and deserves the thorough revision which I have bestowed upon it twenty years after its original publication. I have in effect re-written it from start to finish, and, I believe and hope, have made it a good deal better in the process. In addition, I have added chapters dealing with the past twenty years, and have added a number of new charts and tables designed to illustrate, better than those which they replace, the changes in working-class conditions during the period of the Industrial Revolution. I am by no means so confident as I was that I shall ever write the bigger, more comprehensive study that I had then in mind. To some extent, a part of the ground has been covered in *The Common People*, in which I collaborated with my brother-in-law, Raymond Postgate ; and I have made other specialist studies by myself, such as *Chartist Portraits*, and expect to make more. The big, definitive book I may or may not live to write : assuredly, there is no prospect of my attempting to write it now.

Naturally, this book owes a very great deal to writers who have studied, far more closely than I, particular branches of the subject—to Mr. and Mrs. Hammond, to Sidney and Beatrice Webb, to Mr. Max Beer, and to many others. They have done much to revive among British workers a knowledge of their own history, and thereby, I believe, to give them greater strength in facing the problems of the present. Nothing seems to me more important than this—that, as the working class grows towards the full exercise of power, it should look back as well as forward, and shape its policy in the light of its own historic experience. Above all, I hope this book has served a little to drive home the truth that the three great sections of the working-class movement—the Trade Unions, the Co-operative Societies, and the political organisations—are but three aspects of one single endeavour, deriving their strength from a common necessity and a common inspiration, and, though their paths at times diverge, making for a common goal.

G. D. H. COLE

OXFORD, 1947

CONTENTS

PART I: 1789–1850

PART II: 1850-1900

PART III: 1900–1947

CHARTS

PART I

Wages and Cost of Living, 1800–1860

TABLES

PART I

Wages and Cost of Living, 1800–1860

PART ONE
1789-1850

CHAPTER I

INTRODUCTORY

1. Phases of Growth   2. The Threshold of Industrialism

I. PHASES OF GROWTH

THE " Industrial Revolution " is the name which historians give, not to any single event, but to the great process of economic change in Great Britain in the eighteenth and early nineteenth centuries. That process swiftly transformed Great Britain from a mainly agricultural country into the " workshop of the world." It tore up by the roots old social relationships and institutions which had seemed to be firmly established. It destroyed the old life of the village, and created the problem of the new factory town. It compelled Parliament to reform itself, and raised the middle classes to political power as well as to affluence. And, last but not least, it created the modern wage-earning class—the proletariat which, nominally free, can live only by selling its labour for a wage. This, of course, does not mean that there were no wage-workers before the Industrial Revolution, but it does mean that only with that Revolution did the wage-earners become conscious of themselves as a class, and begin to make common cause over an area wider than that of a single occupation or industry.

In creating the proletariat, the Industrial Revolution gave birth to the Labour Movement. We can watch, during the last years of the eighteenth century and the early decades of the nineteenth, the gradual growth of a working-class point of view, and of organisations seeking to express that point of view. This is not to say that organisations of working people came into existence for the first time during the Industrial Revolution. Long before, there were Trade Unions and strikes, as well as Friendly Societies and other organisations consisting of manual workers. But until nearly the end of the eighteenth century these bodies seem to have had little contact one with another, and little consciousness of a community of view and interest. The sense of unity came only when the Industrial Revolution began to form all the workers in the common mould of the wage-system. The Industrial Revolution gave birth to the Labour Movement.

It will be seen that the Labour Movement, as I define it here, implies, in some degree, a community of outlook. It is an organisation, or, rather, many forms of organisation, based upon the sense of a common status and a common need for mutual help. A Trade Union or a Co-operative Society is not, by the mere fact of its existence and adoption of a certain method, part of the Labour Movement. To-day no one would so call the " Trade Unions " of lawyers or doctors or the Army and Navy Co-operative Society. The term " movement " implies a common end or at least a community of purpose which is real, and influences men's thoughts and actions, even if it is imperfectly apprehended or largely unconscious.

Not in a day or a year did the scattered workers' organisations of the days before the Industrial Revolution give place to, or become, a movement clearly defined and conscious of its identity. We shall watch the change coming about stage by stage ; and we shall see at the end of this book that it is still by no means complete. We shall, however, find that there are certain points at which it seems to take sudden great leaps forward. One of these occurred after the Peace of 1815, which brought the long struggle with Napoleon finally to an end. Another occurred in the eighteen-eighties, when Socialism, as a material body of doctrine, first began to exert a real influence in Great Britain. A third, perhaps, can be found about the time of the Great War of 1914-1918.

This growth of a clearly articulated Labour Movement is, however, by no means a single continuous process. We can, indeed, usefully divide the whole history of the movement from the Industrial Revolution onwards into three broadly distinct phases. First comes a period which is chiefly one of revolt—a succession of uprisings, using different means and forms of organisation, against the new industrial conditions and the new capitalist power in society. During this phase the movement was largely looking backwards, and kicking in vain against the pricks of a new system to which it felt an instinctive hostility. Up to the end of the first phase the wage-earner had not wholly ceased to be a peasant at heart. He responded most readily to leaders who, like William Cobbett, had their hearts in the country rather than in the town. He was not so much seeking to control the new capitalist order, or to build up his position within it, as he was half-consciously seeking to destroy it, and to revert to the way of life from which he had been forcibly driven. The revolts of the Luddites, the strikes and machine-breakings of 1818, the Reform agitation, the " Last Labourers' Revolt " of 1831, the Owenite Trades Unionism of 1830-1834, even the Chartist Movement, with its land schemes and its hostility to the Corn Law reformers, were all deeply penetrated with the hatred of the new industrialism. Right up to the collapse of Chartism in 1848 the working-class movement was still looking at least as much back as forward.

The second phase, stretching approximately from 1848 to the eighteen-eighties, was the period of acclimatisation to Capitalism, and acceptance of Industrialism as the basis of the social order. This explains its moderation. From revolting against Capitalism, the workers passed to the task of organising their forces within it. They built up stable Trade Unions and Co-operative Societies, and began to send a few workmen to represent their point of view in Parliament. In this period the Labour Movement, regarded as a complex of organisations, assumed something like its modern form. Trade Unions and Co-operative Societies are not so radically different in structure to-day from what they became during the middle years of the nineteenth century. But their objects have changed, or are changing ; for, during this period, the working-class movement, having made up its mind to accept Industrialism, was not yet strong enough to make an effective bid for its control. It could only fight for better wages and conditions, for recognition, and for the right to organise freely, and to build up its Unions and Co-operative Societies into strong protective bodies. It did not challenge Capitalism ; rather it accepted the capitalist system, and tried to work within it for the improvement of the workers' lot. The alliance of Liberalism and Labour, a marked feature of the mid-Victorian compromise, was the clearest expression of this transitional period in the growth of the working-class movement.

The third phase, beginning in the eighteen-eighties, was marked by the emergence of Socialism as the creed of a growing body of workers. There accompanied it, first, a great extension in the scope of Trade Unionism, which, for the first time since the collapse of 1834, began to make an effective appeal to the poorer and less skilled grades of workers, and, secondly, the rise of Labour as an independent political force. Under Socialist influence, the exclusiveness of the Trade Union movement was gradually broken down, and the idea of working-class unity found practical expression in both industrial and political affairs. These tendencies, strongly marked in the eighteen-nineties, suffered a temporary check in the early years of the twentieth century, but they were soon again active, and have remained active till the present time.

It may be that, when recent events have passed into clearer historical perspective, a new phase will be seen as beginning with the conditions created by the Russian Revolution and the first World War. Certainly there is one marked difference between present and past movements of agitation in Great Britain. Right up to 1914 British Labour, while it had certain contacts with working-class movements abroad, remained, on the whole, exceedingly insular and self-centred. This attitude, of course, was not peculiar to the Labour Movement ; it was a fixed characteristic of the British national outlook. But from 1914 Great Britain, having largely lost its exclusive and privileged position as the centre of world finance and commerce, was becoming more and more involved in international complications, economic as well as political. This change in the national situation was reflected in a similar change in the attitude of Labour, which also grew to some extent international under pressure of events, and was compelled in self-defence, and for the furtherance of its Socialist aims, to enter into closer relations with the working-class movements of Continental countries.

This tendency was, however, only half-hearted ; and it remained true even up to the Labour election victory of 1945 that the Labour Party had given much less thought to the international than to the internal aspects of its policy, with the consequence that it was relatively ill-equipped for dealing with the very difficult foreign and colonial issues which faced it on the morrow of the second World War.

While the direct purpose of this book is to study the history of organised Labour in Great Britain, one must never leave out of account the fact that the working class, and therefore the working-class movement also, is essentially an international thing. It is world-wide, just as Capitalism is world-wide ; for, wherever Capitalism exists, a working class dependent on wages is necessary to its existence, and this working class tends to feel the same need for common action against largely similar grievances, and the same aspirations towards a new order based on working-class control of the productive forces.

The modern Labour Movement, though its structure and policy differ from country to country, has thus, in all developed industrial countries, essentially the same form. This form is dictated to it by the conditions, everywhere fundamentally the same, which have called it into being. It is the child of modern Capitalism out of Industrial Revolution, and its essential basis is the modern class of wage-workers—the proletariat—among whom it arises as the expression of an essential community of class, interest and experience. Its most universal and spontaneous form is the Trade Union—the association of wage-workers for the protection and improvement of the standard of life.

Until there are Trade Unions, there is no Labour Movement. Radical, and even revolutionary organisations, largely supported by wage-earners, may exist without Trade Unions. Socialist and Communist *theories* may arise without Trade Unions. But the Labour Movement cannot exist without them, because they are the principal schools in which the workers learn the lesson of self-reliance and solidarity.

Trade Unions are, then, historically, the first form of distinct working-class organisation, as something different from the participation of workers in agitations led by other classes and expressing the ideas of other classes. They are, and they remain, the essential basis of the working-class movement.

As this movement grows it passes through a process of differentiation. As the wage-workers develop their common consciousness, they create (at first without wholly throwing off their allegiance to organisations led by other classes) political and propagandist bodies of their own, for the dissemination of working-class doctrines and for the conduct of working-class political agitation. Among these bodies Socialism gradually develops as a coherent working-class gospel. First Labour and Socialist Parties, and then Communist Parties, arise in many countries, and gradually establish international relationships. Sometimes these political and propagandist bodies are based structurally upon, or intimately linked up with, the Trade Unions. Sometimes there is no, or only a very weak, apparent link between them. But, whatever the formal structure may be, in reality working-class political organisation is essentially dependent on Trade Unionism.

In most countries there grows up, side by side with the industrial, parliamentary and Socialist organisations, a separate organisation for the purpose of mutual trade. Co-operation, like Trade Unionism, is a movement arising spontaneously among the workers for their mutual protection. It assumes many forms; but its most universal in the advanced industrial countries is the grouping of the workers, as consumers, for the common purchase of the elementary needs of life. Co-operation is not, like Trade Unionism, confined by its very nature to those who are employed at a wage or salary. It can be useful also to peasants, and to small traders and independent artisans. But in the forms which it assumes in highly industrialised areas it remains fundamentally a working-class movement, drawing its strength and coherence from the class which has learnt, through the conditions of its everyday employment, the lesson of combination. Its less-clearly-marked-off circle of patrons and its necessary engrossment in trading success tend to make Co-operation pursue, to some extent, an independent course of its own, and weaken the links between it and the industrial and political organisations of Labour. But it arises, in truth, from the same needs and aspirations; and, as these come to be more clearly understood, the unity of all these forms of working-class organisation is also seen to be necessary. The history of British Co-operation is an essential part of the story of British Labour.

Trade Unions, Co-operative Societies, political parties and Socialist organisations—these together make up the modern working-class movement. They are, at bottom, not three or four movements, but one and indivisible; for they arise out of a common need, and depend upon one and the same class, whose ideas and aspirations they seek, from their different standpoints, to express. In this book I shall be telling the story of their growth and differentiation—of the soil in which they grow, the stages of growth by which they have come to their present forms, the ideas which they have embodied. The story will be of Labour in Great Britain—the country in which modern Capitalism first emerged to full growth—the country which was, therefore, the pioneer of Labour organisation. But, though the details are different, the essentials are in other advanced industrial countries much the same. There are differences arising from causes historical and economic. The condition of the various national Labour Movements differs with the degree of industrialisation of each country, with the greater or less importance of agriculture and the peasantry, and with a hundred other things in which the nations are unlike. But everywhere, save in Russia, where a small, highly industrialised sector had come to exist in a predominantly peasant country still under despotic rule, the working-class movement developed broadly in the same way, at any rate in Europe, whatever may have been the variations in degree of development or in strength of organisation. The United States of America have indeed even now no national Labour Party and only the germ of a consumers' Co-operative Movement, and American Trade Unionism has developed in a radically different way from Trade Unionism in Europe, mainly because, save at moments of deep trade depression, labour has in most cases been a scarce commodity. For a long time, the existence of free land in the West and the rapid opening up of new communities caused the typical American worker to feel the weight of capitalist control very much less than the workman in Europe. Even to-day, the Trade Unions in the United States are engaged in an internecine conflict not unlike that which rent British Trade Unionism round about 1889. The form of the conflict is doubtless widely different : yet, when one looks beneath the surface, it seems not unreasonable to conjecture that Labour in America is, on the whole, moving along a road which Labour in Western Europe has trodden already. In a single country, whatever sharp differences may develop, there cannot really be several separate Labour movements, but only fractions of a single movement ; and, in the same way, international Labour, whatever the apparent divisions, really makes up a single movement, feeling, however feebly, for the means to international solidarity. This sentiment is some-what stronger on the Trade Union side than in politics, and in 1947 inter-national Trade Unionism, organised in the World Trade Union Federation, was stronger than international Socialism, with its sharp division between Communist and Social Democratic parties. International Trade Unionism, however, is also threatened with disruption from this cause. Nevertheless, the underlying unity exists ; and the reasons for this unity this book will, I hope, help to make clear.

2. THE THRESHOLD OF INDUSTRIALISM

There were, we have seen, Trade Unions and strikes long before there was a Labour Movement. Trade Unions and temporary combinations of wage-earners to raise wages or to prevent their reduction were common in the earlier eighteenth century, and even long before then. Isolated instances of combination can be found even in the Middle Ages ; and these became more frequent with the advance of commerce and industry in the sixteenth and seventeenth centuries. But these early combinations did not create a Labour Movement ; there was behind them no common idea of the solidarity of the whole working class, and no thought of creating a new social order based on collective control.

Nor did the rise of a Labour Movement follow immediately upon the beginnings of Capitalism. Capitalist enterprise, and especially capitalist trading, existed long before the Industrial Revolution, and was, indeed, the essential basis of that Revolution. But not until capital was widely applied to large-scale production involving the concentration of workers in considerable establishments and in industrial towns did it engender the massed discontents out of which the Labour Movement arose.

The Industrial Revolution, which is thus the real starting-point of the story of organised Labour, is generally said to have taken place in this country between about 1760 and 1830. The dates are arbitrary ; for no one outstanding event marks the beginning or end of the Revolution. But they are convenient as indicating roughly the period during which took place the great transformation of Great Britain from a predominantly agricultural country into the " workshop of the world." The corresponding changes came, for the most part, later in other countries. Great Britain, because of its island situation, its development of colonies and overseas trade, and its immunity from internal wars in the earlier eighteenth century, took the lead in the creation of modern industrialism. Even in 1830, however, the change was still restricted in scope. The railway age had barely begun, and the steamship was still in its infancy. The revolution in transport belongs mainly to the second quarter of the nineteenth century.

In order to understand how the Labour Movement arose, and how this great transformation took place, it is necessary to understand in outline the preceding conditions and the factors making both for the accumulation of wealth and for the creation of the vast mass of factory labour necessary for the growth of the new industrial system. If the exploitation of steam and machinery would have been impossible without an accumulation of capital ready for devotion to this use, the capital would have been useless without a supply of wage-labour ready for employment. Indeed, it is clear that the supply of labour was the most vital necessity; for, when once the processes of power production had been set in motion, the wage-workers themselves provided the means for their rapid expansion. In other words, the beating down of wages, the long hours of work, and the exploitation of child-labour, which marked the period of the Industrial Revolution, became the means to the extraordinarily swift accumulation of capital which enabled the Revolution to proceed with ever-increasing velocity.

We must, therefore, begin our study with a brief survey of the developments which led up to the Industrial Revolution. We must inquire what were the causes which led men, in the earlier eighteenth century, to devote their energies to the means of increasing the production of commodities and so stimulated the great inventions which were the technical basis of the new economic system.

We must inquire what stage had been reached in the development of

Capitalism before the coming of these technical changes ; how wealth had been accumulated ; and what was the condition of the " lower orders " in the days before the Industrial Revolution.

We must inquire—and this is the most important inquiry of all—whence came the supply of labour for the new factories, and the vast increase of population which accompanied the change. Who were the factory workers? Whence did they come? And what forces impelled them to seek their living in the noisome towns which grew up in the industrial districts, and to submit to the overwork and oppression of the new economic system ?

So much preliminary clearing of the ground may appear to some readers too discursive. My object, however, is not to write a detailed history of the Labour Movement, but to give a historical interpretation of its leading phases. Origins do not explain developments ; but developed movements cannot be understood without a knowledge of their origins. To begin with an unprefaced account of the Labour Movement itself would be to countenance the theory of spontaneous generation, to show it springing causeless from the head of Time. Its rise was not causeless ; and they who would understand it must understand the causes of its origin as well as of its later growth.

CHAPTER II

THE INDUSTRIAL REVOLUTION

1. THE RISE OF CAPITALISM

THE characteristic form of industrial organisation in the mediæval towns was the localised Gild. The Gild was, in essence, a combination of master-craftsmen (or master-merchants) for the regulation and government of the trade. It usually included journeymen as well as masters ; but it must not be conceived as a joint body bringing together two distinct classes. The Gild trinity of masters, journeymen and apprentices stood, at first, rather for three stages in the life of the same individuals than for a distinction of class. In theory, at least, the sole entry to the Gild was by way of apprenticeship. In due course the apprentice became a journeyman, and thereafter in time he hoped to become a master. Mastership was the completion of the process, and the government of the Gild was vested in the masters as the embodiment of this completion. The Gild was thus essentially different from either an employers' association or a Trade Union, or a joint body representing employers and employed. It was based on the assumption—at one time a true assumption in many trades—that, in due course, all good journeymen would have the chance of becoming masters.

This theory was never fully realised in fact. And it was realised less and less as time went on. Although the Gilds laid down elaborate regulations restricting the number of journeymen any master might employ, in order to prevent large-scale organisation and undue inequality of wealth from arising among their members, no restrictions did in fact prevent the rise of inequality. This first appeared in a marked form chiefly among the Gild masters engaged in trade and commerce. It was difficult to expand industrial enterprise without directly employing a large number of workers ; but a small staff engaged in merchant operations was capable of handling a relatively large turnover. Also, commerce was, in those days, mainly in luxury goods, which were expensive and realised a large surplus for the merchant, who had also the advantage of handling a far greater amount of silver and gold than came the way of the master-craftsman.

Thus the accumulation of capital took place chiefly in the hands of masters engaged in trade and commerce. As communications improved and political conditions became more settled in the later Middle Ages, there was a big growth of commercial enterprise. Economically, and also politically, the local self-sufficiency of earlier times began to give place to national organisation. "National economy," as it has been called, replaced the "town economy" of the Middle Ages. The scale of commercial enterprise increased ; and larger fortunes began to be gathered into single hands.

The mediæval Gild system, based essentially on the local unit of the town and on the assumption of approximate equality among the masters, broke down under the impact of the new conditions. Gild restrictions were felt more and more to be a burden as the opportunities for money-making increased. Greater and greater inequality between masters began to be tolerated within the Gilds. What had once been an association of equals turned by stages into a hierarchical body, in which the richer members acquired a vested right to control. The road to promotion became narrower as entrance fees and dues were increased, and mastership was limited or preference given to the sons of masters. Among the masters themselves inequality became more and more pronounced, and led to a new differentiation of class between great and small. A " Livery " of the richer masters acquired special privileges, and the smaller masters, as well as the journeymen, were often shut out of all real share in the government of the Gilds. Moreover, some whole Gilds became subordinated to others more favourably situated for access to the supply of material or to the market. Many master-craftsmen were reduced, in fact, to the position of sub-contractors and half-assimilated to the working journeymen, most of whom could no longer hope to become Gild masters at all.

Under pressure of these conditions, industry, hitherto confined almost wholly to the corporate towns, began to develop in the suburbs, market towns and country districts outside the jurisdiction of the Gilds, which commonly had authority only in the areas under municipal control. Demand was expanding, and the journeyman to whom the Gild denied mastership, or the small master whom it threatened to crush, saw prospects of better fortune in an area where he could try his hand untrammelled by Gild laws or restrictions. It often suited the merchants, who wanted a growing supply of cheap commodities, to deal with these suburban and country producers, and to foster the growth of industry outside the corporate towns. And new classes of middlemen, such as the clothiers, grew up, to act as intermediaries between the scattered producers and the merchants of the great towns and ports.

The Protestant Reformation, which threw overboard mediæval doctrines hostile to " usury," and fostered individualism in economic as well as political affairs, was, in part, a result of changes already in progress, and in part a great stimulus to their further development. Puritanism especially, with its belief in abstinence and its insistence on simplicity of living, was a powerful factor in promoting the accumulation of capital. Where his ancestor had spent on enjoyments, pageants and religious observances, the Puritan saved. And what he saved bred more.

Thus in the seventeenth century the Gild system, though it existed still, was in decay, and had largely both lost its monopoly of production and adapted its methods to the new conditions. It had become markedly oligarchical, with power concentrated in the hands of the richer masters. The journeymen had no longer any share at all in its control, though they still received in many cases certain friendly benefits from it. There are in the sixteenth and seventeenth centuries many records of attempted combinations by the journeymen, outside the Gilds, in order to enforce better pay and conditions, and many attempts by the Gilds to suppress these, either directly or with the help of Parliament. These independent attempts at combination, rather than the Gilds themselves, are to be regarded as the forerunners of Trade Unionism.

The Civil War of the seventeenth century to some extent held back the growth of Capitalism. One of the issues which accentuated the quarrel between Parliament and Crown was the objection of the Commons to the Crown's power, often abused in order to raise revenue, of granting patents and monopoly rights in the control of certain trades. The victory of the Parliament carried with it the victory of the trading interests, as the commercial legislation of the Commonwealth plainly shows. Nor did the Restoration undo the traders' victory ; the new settlement of England, confirmed by the Revolution of 1688, was based on the alliance of merchants and landowners in their common interest. The landed class retained political power, but it was essential to the settlement that this power should be used in the interests of trade. This was clearly recognised by the statesmen of the Restoration and the Revolution.

The end of the seventeenth century and the early part of the eighteenth were a period of great commercial expansion. Dutch commerce was still prosperous ; but the Dutch maritime power had waned and was passing into British hands. The wars with France expressed a deep-seated commercial rivalry. British seapower, following up the voyagings of the sixteenth and the early colonisings of the seventeenth century, pushed British commerce far to East and West. The India trade grew fast, and was accompanied by the gradual conquest of a large part of India by the privileged East India Company. The British colonies in North America waxed important as sources of supply, and especially as inexhaustible stores of timber for shipbuilding. Trade with the West Indies and with South America developed rapidly. Ships increased in size, carrying capacity, sea-worthiness and speed.

Fortunes were made fast out of the growth of enterprise. The end of the seventeenth century brought with it the beginnings of the National Debt and the foundation of the Bank of England—both directly products of the State's needs in the financing of the French wars, but both also powerful instruments for the development of Capitalism. After the wars, a long spell of peace enabled trade to increase still more rapidly. Crises, like the famous bursting of the South Sea Bubble in 1720, only marked the rapid accumulation of wealth available for investment. Landed gentry and traders alike waxed fat on the proceeds of commercial prosperity.

There was, moreover, a progressive intermingling of these classes. The gentry largely increased their fortunes by marrying into trade. Successful merchants bought landed estates or, by buying the farms of a number of yeomen, carved new great estates out of the land of England. Retired " nabobs " from India, or merchants from America, settled down as squires and Parliament men in the " Old Country."

The close alliance of landowners and business men during the earlier eighteenth century was based on a close community of interest. The great industry of England, up to the days of the Industrial Revolution, was the woollen industry. As this industry expanded the demand for raw wool, of course, steadily increased. But wool was a product of British agriculture—for in those days the import of wool from abroad was quite small. A brisk demand for wool was an assurance of profit to the landowner ; for the grazier, getting a good price for his wool, could afford to pay a good rent for land. The landowners' Parliament was therefore always ready to give legislative protection to the woollen industry, as long as it assured a good market for the products of the land. The merchants and clothiers, on their side, had no desire to upset the political control of the landowners, as long as they were given this protection, and as long as the English aristocracy maintained an open door to the successful man of business. This open door, in contrast with the closed aristocracy of France, was the secret of the British oligarchical system. Not till the new industrial employers came knocking in throngs at the gates of political power did " Reform " become practical politics. And then, where France had a Revolution, England had only a moderate measure of Parliamentary Reform.

In the eighteenth century, the growth of the woollen industry, and the general expansion of trade and wealth due to trade, steadily made land dearer and more profitable to its owners. The desire of merchants to buy land, and with it a share in social prestige and political power, also helped to enhance the value of landed property. The demand for cereals and meat grew, even faster than the demand for wool, with the rise in the standard of comfort which accompanied the economic expansion.

Thus was set on foot a powerful movement towards the concentration of land ownership and the exploitation of land as a source of profit. The Enclosure Movement, which reached its greatest intensity in the latter part of the eighteenth century, was already making rapid strides in its earlier years. At first, farms were thrown together and waste lands enclosed in order to provide more profitable units for stock-rearing or arable cultivation. Then the ancient system of land-holding in the villages was attacked, as putting fatal obstacles in the way of progressive farming.

The land of England up to this time was still largely, though by no means everywhere, cultivated under the old system of the common fields. Each owner or customary tenant had his holdings in scattered strips here and there in the fields common to the village. Each had his pasture rights both on the fields and on the uncultivated commons. In addition, many villagers, who had no land-holding of their own, or only a tiny holding attached to a cottage, exercised rights of common, recognised, or half-recognised, by law or custom, over the waste lands.

This system, standing firmly in the way of scientific agriculture, was now attacked and overthrown in the areas in which it had survived the successive waves of enclosure in previous centuries. A high return for the application of capital to the land, in the form either of drainage or clearance, or of stocking with extensive herds or flocks, could be got only where holdings could be concentrated and enclosed. Enclosure of the open fields became the necessary condition of capitalist agriculture and of the high rents which the capitalist farmer could afford to pay. Hence the swift extension of the Enclosure Movement during the eighteenth century. Between 1700 and 1760 we have records of over 200 Enclosure Acts and over 300,000 acres enclosed ; between 1761 and 1800 of 2,000 Acts and over 2,000,000 acres enclosed ; and in the first fifty years of the nineteenth century of 2,000,000 more acres and nearly 2,000 more Enclosure Acts. The increased demand for cereals, and the high prices, during the French Wars caused enclosure to proceed at an unprecedented rate during the closing years of the eighteenth and the opening years of the nineteenth century.

The story of the fearful hardships caused to the poor by this Agricultural Revolution has been often told. Its effect was a wholesale dispossession of the rural population, especially in the South of England ; for, among the peasantry, even those who were granted some land in compensation for their lost rights were, in very many cases, given it under conditions which they could not fulfil. The land had to be fenced, and often drained ; and the peasant, lacking the capital to do this, had often to sell his share to the larger owners for an old song. Moreover, many, who had held no land in the old village, but only common rights attached to a cottage, lost their means of life without any compensation at all. The cow, or the pig, or the geese, could no longer be left to pick up their keep on the common ; for the common, as well as the open fields, had passed into unrestricted private ownership and enclosure.

A great many of the peasantry therefore, even when they remained in the villages, were reduced to the status of wage-labourers. Moreover, two other factors contributed to press down their status still further. The new agricultural methods, based on larger holdings, required far less labour to the acre than the old. This was true pre-eminently of sheep-farming ; but it applied, in less degree, to arable farming as well. The Enclosure Movement thus produced at once a large surplus of agricultural workers, and this contributed to the depression of agricultural wages and accentuated the loss caused by the disappearance of auxiliary sources of income, such as rights of common.

This surplus of workers existed mainly in the South of England, hitherto the most densely populated part of the country. The new factories and mines, on the other hand, developed mainly in the North, and were far out of reach of the dispossessed "paupers" of the Southern Counties, who were liable, if they attempted to migrate to the industrial areas, to be sent back to their parishes of origin under the Acts of Settlement. Therefore, for some time, a surplus of labour in the South of England coincided with a shortage in the developing industrial areas of the North. This shortage was met partly by immigration from Ireland, with its still lower standard of living, but also largely by drawing more workers from the agricultural districts nearer at hand, which thus suffered much less from agricultural over-population than the remoter counties of the South.

The second factor, of no less fundamental importance, arose, not directly out of the Enclosures, but out of the parallel revolution in industry. The expansion of the woollen industry in the earlier eighteenth century had led to a great advance of what is usually called the "domestic system" or, sometimes, the "putting out" system. Spinning and weaving were chiefly carried on, not in factories or workshops owned by a capitalist employer, but in the homes of the workers, or in small workshops attached to them, throughout the wool-producing districts. Spinning, which was a relatively unskilled trade, was mainly in the hands of women and children, and was very widely scattered. It was carried on by the families not only of weavers and of other craftsmen but also of small farmers and of agricultural labourers. Weaving, on the other hand, was a skilled trade, practised mainly by men, and tended to be more concentrated in small towns and in mainly industrial villages. Weaving, in fact, was a main breadwinner's occupation, whereas spinning was for the most part a source of supplementary earnings to eke out the meagre income of the head of the family. The system of production in the textile areas differed from place to place, and Capitalism had developed further in the Western Counties than in Yorkshire, or the Midlands, or the East. But, generally speaking, the function of the capitalist in the woollen industry remained that of merchanting and trading rather than the direct control or oversight of production. The capitalist clothier bought the yarn from the spinner and sold it to the weaver, from whom again he bought the woven stuff. Sometimes, and increasingly, he bought the raw wool and put it out to the spinner ; and, in the West Country, he often retained ownership of the material throughout, giving it out, in turn, to spinner and weaver to convert into yarn or stuff at a piece-work price. But, save in the finishing processes, such as bleaching and dyeing, which required abundant water and a larger application of capital in order to secure the best return, and were, therefore, more and more brought direct under capitalist control, the productive workers remained, for the most part, isolated and semi-independent producers, working under their own control in their own homes. Until power-driven machinery came to be applied, there was no economic advantage in concentrating production under a single roof. It suited the capitalist better to remain a trader, and to leave the control of the productive processes in the hands of the producers themselves.

Under this system a great cottage industry grew up over the greater part of the country. Spinning normally, and weaving sometimes, were combined with small-scale agriculture by the same household. The weavers, indeed, were regular industrial workers, though some of them worked also on the land, and most lent a hand at harvest time. Where they had some land in their occupation, they had something to fall back upon when industrial demand fell off; but this was commoner among small masters, who combined farming with weaving, than among ordinary journeymen. The spinners, for the most part, earned very little, but even that little helped to raise the family income, and when industrial work was slack most of the households affected were not left wholly destitute, unless the main bread-winner also lost his job. The peasants and the industrial workers were still not two quite distinct classes, but closely inter-connected. The purely urban workers, skilled craftsmen or operatives in the few factory trades, were an insignificant minority of the whole population. London was the only really big city. Gregory King, in his estimate of the occupations of the people at the end of the seventeenth century, put the total number of artisans, including their wives and children, at only 240,000, out of a population of 5,674,000, or 4.2 per cent.

As trade and production expanded during the eighteenth century, the class of town workers, of course, expanded too. But the bulk of the increase went to swell the ranks of the domestic producers, and to add to the amount of their industrial earnings. Expanding production, under the old system, meant a rise in the standard of life for the domestic producers.

The twin revolutions in industry and agriculture destroyed the basis of this growing prosperity. The peasant household, depending partly on its industrial earnings to supplement its income from land work, found the latter either greatly reduced or wholly taken away by the Enclosure Move-ment. At the same time, or rather beginning later, but then proceeding with rapid parallel strides, came the Industrial Revolution. At the first stage, during the closing decades of the eighteenth century, spinning passed rapidly from the cottages into the factories, sweeping away the supplemen-tary earnings of the women and children in the agricultural districts and of

the families of the handloom weavers. Women and children who lived
near the new factories were driven to seek employment outside the home,
and pauper children were also imported from a distance in order to supplement the local sources of child labour. Then, in the opening decades of the
nineteenth century, the revolution spread to weaving with even more
devastating social effects. Power-driven machinery began to compete with
handicraft weaving and to reduce the cost of production with extraordinary
speed. Moreover, cotton, a cheaper substitute, to which the new machines
were first extensively applied, began to oust wool from its predominant
position. The handicraft worker could not stand up to the machine. His
earnings dwindled fast ; he was thrust more and more into the position of a re-
siduary producer, and given only what work was left to do when the machines
were fully employed. The burden of trade fluctuations fell even more heavily
upon him ; and he could no longer turn to agriculture as an alternative
occupation—for there, too, his services were no longer needed. The agricultural workers migrated perforce, when they could, in their thousands to
the new industrial districts, to seek work in the hated factories. But there
remained behind in the countryside in the southern half of England vast
numbers who could not move, and were left to scramble helplessly for jobs,
and to bring down still further the standard of real wages in agriculture.

The long war with France between 1793 and 1815 greatly accentuated the
evils attending this double economic revolution. It led to a huge rise and to
rapid fluctuations of prices, to which wages were slow to readjust themselves. It dislocated markets, and caused extreme fluctuations in the demand
for industrial labour. It hugely stimulated agricultural production, and left
behind it in the countryside an inevitable aftermath of depression and re-
adjustment. Above all, it put into the hearts of the rich a panic fear of the
poor. Fearful that the English people might follow the revolutionary
example of the French, the richer classes became callous to the sufferings of
the poor, and far less inclined to remedy even the most glaring abuses of the
new economic order than to treat the cries of suffering as dangerous signs of
popular disaffection. Thus the hardships of the economic revolution were
made far worse by the political troubles of the time. Patriotism became a
cloak for exploitation of unprecedented severity ; anti-Jacobinism was used
to cover a multitude of sins.

Under these conditions the modern proletariat came to birth. Out of
these conditions sprang the Labour Movement.

2. THE INDUSTRIAL REVOLUTION

In the light of the preceding section, what is called the " Industrial
Revolution " appears as the culmination of a long process of economic

development. We are apt to think of it as the almost personal achievement of a group of brilliant scientists, inventors, and business men, who, after long ages of groping, suddenly found the means of harnessing and developing the forces of Nature so as to produce wealth in abundance hitherto unimagined. Genius doubtless played its part ; but, if the analysis given in the foregoing pages is right, the inventors and exploiters of the new machines were themselves rather products than producers of the new conditions. The inventor might invent in vain until the world was ready for his invention. Or, rather, it would be true to say that, in the realm of applied chemistry and applied mechanics, which made the greatest contributions to the transformation of industry, the inventor seldom invents at all save under the stimulus of a strong demand for his invention. Many of the principles on which the new inventions were based were known to learned men for centuries before the Industrial Revolution ; but they were not applied to industry because the incentive to apply them was lacking. When conditions were ripe—when wide new markets were being opened up and a supply of wage-labour was being made available—the great technical inventions came about as a matter of course.

This view of the Industrial Revolution is borne out by the fact that there is hardly a single invention of this period that can be confidently attributed to a single author. Watt did not invent the steam-engine or Stephenson the locomotive : they both improved on previous models and made them more suitable for industrial use. Almost every one of the great textile inventions is of disputed authorship ; it is to this day very doubtful whether Richard Arkwright, the most famous innovator in the cotton trade, ever really invented anything at all. Most of the discoveries were made, not by great geniuses working from first principles, but by ordinary people experimenting on the basis of their predecessors' work. Inventions were so many and so great because the rapidly expanding markets and prospects of profitable production set many minds to work on the problem of increasing the output of commodities, and making labour more productive.

Only a very few outstanding instances need be given in order to make this point plain. In domestic industry on a family basis, children could spin but could not weave. The family supply of yarn tended to outrun the capacity of the weaver to make it into cloth. There was need for a speedier process of weaving. Kay's flying shuttle (1733) not merely met the need, but, as its use spread gradually over the country, caused the weavers to outrun the supply of yarn. Inventive minds turned to the problem of spinning ; and soon the new machines of Hargreaves and Arkwright again reversed the position. The evolution of the power-loom, and further improvements in the spinning processes, at last established equilibrium early in the nineteenth century.

Again, the demand for coal caused a need for deeper mine-workings.

The engines of Newcomen and Watt were the response. But more coal could not be hauled over the bad roads or taken by the inadequate waterways. New roads, canals, finally locomotives, met the need. It is true that each of these inventions had results far transcending the immediate want it was designed to meet ; but the mother of each invention was economic necessity. The Industrial Revolution is not explained by the great inventions. The inventions have themselves to be explained by the economic situation.

This is not the place for any technical account of the inventions or of the new productive methods to which they gave rise. It is enough here to point out briefly their effect on the situation of the workers. This was threefold. In the first place they greatly increased the productivity of labour, so that vastly greater markets were required to afford employment to the same number of persons. They did not necessarily cause unemployment, save on their first introduction ; but they made the maintenance of employment depend on the ability to secure an ever-widening market.

In the second place, they largely undermined the position of the skilled workers in the trades affected by them, much of whose work could now be done by machines operated by unskilled women or children. They thus called into employment a large competing supply of labour which, having less power of resistance or a lower standard of life, was used both to beat down wages and to extend the hours of labour to an inhuman length. Children were worked, in many cases, as much as sixteen hours a day, and twelve hours became the lowest standard recognised under the new system.

Thirdly, the machines revolutionised the actual methods of production. Power-driven machinery cannot be operated economically by scattered workers. Water power, and, much more, steam power, demand the concentration of labour in factories. Moreover, power and machinery first made " overheads " an important element in the cost of production. The cost of power must be spread over the greatest possible quantity of labour ; the machine, which costs money, must earn its keep by being kept fully in use. Therefore the workers are not only congregated in factories, but also speeded up, and worked hard and long, in order that the machines and the power may achieve their maximum utility. The productivity of labour is increased not only in proportion to the greater efficiency of the machine, but also in proportion to the greater incentive to use it to the full. In Marx's phrase, not only the productivity, but also the intensity, of labour is increased.

The power to produce vastly more goods thus became, under the conditions of the Industrial Revolution, a means, not to the lightening of labour, but to a great increase in its severity. The price of the goods made by machinery certainly fell very fast ; but the cost of living did not fall, both because agricultural production could not be increased in anything like the same measure as factory production, and because, after the outbreak of the war with France in 1793, war demands and inflation caused a rapid rise of prices, especially for foodstuffs. Wages, meanwhile, wholly failed to keep pace with the rapid changes in the purchasing power of money.

Despite these adverse conditions of the new factory system, the workers might have made better headway and have maintained better their standard of life had not the supply of labour increased by leaps and bounds. During the eighteenth century there was, according to all authorities, a great increase in the rate of growth of population. The first Census was not taken until 1801, and no accurate figures exist for earlier times. But, though estimates differ, they agree on this point: Between 1500 and 1600, and again between 1600 and 1700, the growth of population did not exceed a million in the century. Between 1700 and 1800 the increase was nearer three millions, and between 1801 and 1831 another five millions were added. These figures, moreover, are for England and Wales alone. Thus, to the greater productivity of the individual worker, to the greater intensity of labour, and to the increased industrial employment of women and young children, was added a most powerful fresh factor—the immensely rapid increase of population.

Now, population is influenced by three factors—birth rates, death rates, and migration. And, with respect to all three, we are sadly hindered by lack of exact knowledge from forming accurate estimates of their effects. There seems, however, to be little doubt that migration, while it counted for something, was the least important factor, and that the decline in death rates, and, above all, in the rate of infant mortality was the most important. The large immigration into Great Britain from Ireland certainly far more than balanced the emigration, chiefly directed towards the New World ; but this balance was no more than a small factor in the general increase.

Falling death rates were almost certainly, in the period from the mid-eighteenth century to about 1815, the decisive factor. For during this period there seems to be little doubt that better sanitary provision and increasing medical knowledge were steadily increasing the expectation of life. Up to the Napoleonic Wars a rising standard of living was also certainly contributing to a fall in the death rates, and even when the standard fell in the bad years during the war, the Speenhamland system prevented the fall from causing a rise in the infant death rate. It seems possible that, up to about 1815, the entire increase in population, apart from a very small part due to migration, can be explained by the falling death rates, and, above all, by the improved prospects of infant life.

This seems at first sight to contradict flatly the generally received view that the period of the Industrial Revolution was one of increasing misery for the workers. But it does not really contradict it at all. Even in 1815 the factory system was still in its infancy, and the rise of the modern factory town was only beginning. The really swift transformation of industry to a factory basis was brought about in the decades immediately following Waterloo ; and it seems clear that at this point the fall in the death rates was sharply checked, as the appalling sanitary problems of the new factory towns altogether outran the capacity of the sanitary reformers and doctors to cope with them.   We must look for the real social effects of the Industrial Revolution after, and not before, 1815.

Yet even these terrible conditions did not pull back the death rates to the point at which they had stood in the earlier part of the eighteenth century. The adult's expectation of life was probably shortened by urban conditions ; but the fall in the infant mortality rate, thanks to medical knowledge, was permanent.   It is, however, impossible to explain the rise of population after 1815 purely, or even mainly, in terms of death rates.   Conditions after 1815 were not getting better in these respects.   It seems, therefore, reasonably probable that at this point a rising birth rate became a really important factor in causing population to increase.

Why, under these apparently adverse conditions, did population increase with unprecedented rapidity ?   An explanation is often given purely in terms of conscious motive.   The Industrial Revolution created a great new demand for child labour in the textile factories.   Often the children could find work, at exceedingly low wages, when the father could find none.   There was thus, in the factory districts, an economic motive for increasing the size of the family.   Moreover, over a large part of the country, from 1795 onwards, Poor Law relief was being given on the Speenhamland system, under which inadequate wages were made up to a bare living standard according to the size of the family.   More children meant increased poor relief.   The agricultural labourers also had thus an economic motive for increased fertility.

Both these causes doubtless counted ; but it is very doubtful whether, even after 1815, they were the most powerful factors in stimulating the growth of population.   Through the greater part of human history, population has been kept in check mainly by custom and by high infant mortality, and has remained relatively stable.   But throughout the world the past 150 years have brought a rapid increase.   In countries which have developed " great industry," the change from agricultural to industrial methods has been commonly accompanied by a big growth of population, even where the economic motives just described have not been at work, or have been far less powerful.   It is at least plausible to put forward as the reason for this growth, not so much any conscious adaptation of the size of the family to economic opportunities, as improved medical knowledge, and also the withdrawal or destruction of institutions and customs tending to limitation.

The peasants, during the Industrial Revolution, were torn from the land, and driven to live in the noisome factory towns.   Even where they remained in the country the old life of the village was destroyed and the old customs were broken up. The result was a breakdown of the largely un-conscious checks on population which had existed under the old system. Men married sooner, and there was no custom or idea of a customary standard to restrain the indefinite multiplication of the people.

Thus, despite starvation wages and evil sanitary conditions, population grew faster and faster, piling up in the new towns and industrial districts as economic pressure drove the labourers out of the villages. The geographical distribution, as well as the number of the people, was radically altered. In 1700 the areas of greatest population were in the West and the South Midlands. As the century advanced, population shifted northwards into Lancashire and Yorkshire and the coalfields of the North-East Coast. Towns such as Manchester grew by leaps and bounds. In 1770 Manchester and Salford, with their suburbs, had, perhaps, a population of 40,000. In 1801 this had risen to nearly 95,000 ; and in 1831 to nearly 238,000. Glasgow, Birmingham, and other great manufacturing centres underwent a similarly swift expansion.

It was this sudden leap forward in the growth of population that caused Malthus, as early as 1798, to frame his famous theory, which, in a vulgarised form, dominated orthodox economic thinking for a whole generation. Malthus saw, in the unrestricted growth of the people, the danger of a pressure on the means of subsistence which would make impossible any rise in the standard of life beyond the barest subsistence level, and might easily pull up the whole social system by the roots. Whether it was true or false, his teaching produced disastrous results on the attitude of the rich towards the poor. Every child born in a workman's household came to appear as part of the universal menace—as an unwelcome fresh mouth to be fed. Instead of inquiring into the causes of the growth of population, and so devising fundamental remedies, statesmen and economists tried rather by forcible deterrents to prevent the poor from breeding. The new Poor Law of 1834, with its withdrawal of outdoor relief to the able-bodied and its segregation of the sexes in the workhouse, was the embodiment of that popular " Malthusianism " which became the scientific cloak for the rich man's fear of his poor neighbour.

However rapidly population may increase, or change its location, these processes are bound to take some time. From the standpoint of the supply of labour the Industrial Revolution falls into two phases. During the earlier phase, extending to about 1800, there was a surplus of workers, owing to enclosures, in the country, but often a shortage in the factory districts. Migration had not yet taken place on a sufficient scale. This was the period during which occurred one of the worst, and most often described, abuses of the Revolution—the employment of " parish apprentices " in the factories, virtually as bond slaves of the factory owners. The " parish apprentice " was a child who had fallen, owing to the destitution of its parents, into the hands of the Poor Law authorities. These, eager to rid themselves of the burden of the child's maintenance, virtually sold it, under indentures for a period of years, to the factory owner, who was experiencing a shortage of labour for the running of the new machines. The owner worked the child what hours he pleased, and made for its upbringing and education only what provision he pleased. The Poor Law authority, having got rid of the burden, washed its hands of the whole affair. Doubtless a few masters, such as David Dale at New Lanark, treated these unfortunate children fairly well according to the low standards of the time. But most employers did not, justifying excessive hours and evil conditions on plea of the intensity of trade competition. This was the situation which Sir Robert Peel the elder, himself a big factory owner, meant his Health and Morals of Apprentices Act, passed in 1801, to do something to ameliorate.

But by 1801 the system of "parish apprentices" was already beginning to die a natural death. The Industrial Revolution, in consequence of the growth and migration of the people, had entered on its second phase, and the supply of labour had already caught up with the needs even of the swiftly expanding industries. It no longer paid to employ "parish apprentices" when cheap child labour could be had for the asking in the factory districts. The serious decline in the position of the adult workers set in at this point. There was a scramble for jobs, and adults were increasingly displaced by their own children. Naturally, the standard of living fell.

These highly adverse conditions were made much worse by the commercial uncertainties due to war. From 1793 to 1815, with only a brief interval in 1801 and 1802, Great Britain was engaged in its struggle with France. For some time this did not prevent trade from expanding, and it even helped greatly the growth of the industries directly ministering to war requirements. But it caused great uncertainty and fluctuation in the textile industries, especially during the latter years, when, first, the war of blockade between Great Britain and Napoleon, waged by means of the Berlin Decrees and the Orders in Council (1806-1807), seriously dislocated British trade with Europe, and then the war between Great Britain and America (1812-1814) affected both markets for finished goods and the supply of materials for the cotton factories of the north. The long war caused great destruction of wealth and great fluctuations of employment ; and, by draining away money for the prosecution of the war and the enrichment of those who made fortunes out of contracting and stock-jobbing, it forced down the working-class standards of living to the lowest possible point.

The period of the Napoleonic war, and of the economic crises which succeeded it, is the blackest chapter in the whole history of the British working class. Driven from the land by enclosures, made redundant or exposed to the competition of child-labour by the new machines, exposed to relentless persecution because of the fears engendered in the mind of the governing classes both by their misery and by the " awful portent " of the Revolution in France, and enwalled in the hideous, stinking purlieus of the new factory towns, the workers underwent a long agony, from which they emerged at length, exhausted and docile, into the Victorian era.   In this age of misery, and as the child of this misery, the British Labour Movement was born.

BOOKS

The Rise of Capitalism

Karl Marx.   *Capital*, Vol. I, ch. 13, 14, 15, and 23–33 (especially ch. 14, 15, and 27).
M. H. Dobb.   *Capitalist Enterprise and Social Progress*, Part II.
M. H. Dobb.   *Studies in the Development of Capitalism.*
R. H. Tawney.   *Religion and the Rise of Capitalism.*
K. Polanyi.   *Origins of Our Time.*
W. Sombart.   *Der Moderne Kapitalismus.*
W. Cunningham.   *Growth of English Industry and Commerce.*
J. L. and B. Hammond.   *The Village Labourer.*
G. E. Unwin.   *Industrial Organisation in the Sixteenth and Seventeenth Centuries.*

The Industrial Revolution

P. Mantoux.   *The Industrial Revolution in England in the Eighteenth Century.*
A. Toynbee.   *The Industrial Revolution.*
J. L. and B. Hammond.   *The Town Labourer.*
M. D. George.   *London Life in the Eighteenth Century.*
M. C. Buer.   *Health, Wealth and Welfare.*
A. Redford.   *Labour Migration.*
A. Redford.   *Economic History of England, 1760–1860.*
D. Marshall.   *The English Poor in the Eighteenth Century.*
S. and B. Webb.   *History of the English Poor Law.*
A. M. Carr-Saunders.   *The Population Problem.*
J. H. Clapham.   *Economic History of Modern Britain*, Vol. I.

CHAPTER III

THE FRENCH REVOLUTION IN GREAT BRITAIN

THE outstanding event of English, as well as of French, history in the eighteenth century was the French Revolution. When the people of Paris captured the Bastille ; when the peasants took the land of France ; when, at length, the monarchy gave place to the republic, the change was not one affecting a single country alone. For France had been the head and forefront of the European State system, and the fall of the French monarchy and the French nobility threatened every dynasty and every aristocracy in Europe. The peasants seized the land of France, and burnt the title-deeds of the nobles just when the English peasantry were being successfully dispossessed of what had been left to them of the land of England. Republicanism triumphed in France ; and all the governing classes of Europe trembled, for none knew when its turn would come. " Liberty, equality, and fraternity," echoed menacingly over the world as the watchword of a new era.

In England the ruling classes were, on the whole, slower to respond to the challenge of the Revolution than elsewhere in Europe ; for the most oligarchical of all countries rather prided herself on the liberalism of her institutions, and was used to contrast her happiness under a limited and constitutional monarchy and an unlimited and aristocratic Parliament with the misery and financial prostration of autocratic France. Englishmen were used to celebrating the " glorious Revolution " of 1688, on which was based the supremacy of the Protestant religion and of the land-owning classes. At first, there were Englishmen, even in the governing classes, disposed to hope that the French Revolution might be only another 1688, and that France might settle down to constitutional monarchy on the English model, based on the fullest security of property and on the firm ascendancy of the " better part " of the nation.

But as the Revolution in France passed, under the menace of foreign interference, to more extreme courses, as the landowners were expropriated, as Jacobin ousted Girondin and aristocracy and king were swept away by the rising tide, all " respectable " opinion joined the chorus of denunciation. The governing classes of Europe entered into a holy league against Jacobinism and revolution. By 1793 Great Britain and France were at war, and the struggle lasted, with changing features and changing character, until the final defeat of Napoleon in 1815.

Here we are concerned, not with the French Revolution in itself, but with its influence on British opinion. It did two things. It gave British

Radicalism a philosophy ; and it caused the governing classes to adopt a repressive policy which, for a generation, kept all forms of Radicalism firmly in check. The first attempts of the workers at independent political organisation arose directly out of the events in France ; the speed and severity with which they were crushed were directly due to the fear which those events had inspired. The " Corresponding Societies " in England and Scotland in the last decade of the eighteenth century were the first political bodies, as distinct from Trade Clubs and Friendly Societies, created mainly by workers under their own leadership and for their own ends.

This is not to say that there was no Radical movement before 1789. There had been, for a long time past, popular discontents and movements of revolt against the aristocratic ascendancy. The Dissenters, and especially the Unitarians, led by Price and Priestley, were largely Radical, demanding that equality in political and social affairs which they were denied for themselves, and, after the manner of repressed groups, liberally claiming fair treatment for others as well. The farmers and smaller landowners in the counties had long been discontented with the corrupt Parliament, which, packed by the nominees of the owners of rotten boroughs, failed to represent adequately even the landed classes. They had started many county movements for " economical reform," and, for a few years round 1780, had conducted, under Christopher Wyvill's industrious leadership, an active movement for the reform of Parliament itself. In this movement the freeholders of the counties were for a time associated with the Reformers in the City of London ; but the two groups had not much in common, and they fell apart after a limited measure of " economical reform " had been granted in 1782—that is, after some check had been given to the growth of official corruption, though nothing had been done to reform parliamentary representation. In the 'sixties John Wilkes and his friends had stirred the people of London and Middlesex with the cry of electoral freedom, and in 1769 some members of the same group had started the Society of the Supporters of the Bill of Rights, with an advanced programme of parliamentary reform. About 1776 Major John Cartwright, most faithful of Radical leaders of the old school, had begun his crusade for the reform of Parliament, and he had founded in 1780, with a keen group of middle-class Radicals, the Society for Constitutional Information. In these movements were active men who, like Thomas Day, author of " Sandford and Merton," had learnt from Rousseau and the French Encyclopædists the doctrines which formed the ideological basis of the subsequent Revolution in France. In Scotland, which suffered from much more arbitrary government than England—largely a legacy from the days when fear of Jacobites had been strong—there was a reform movement which was stirred into renewed energy by the French Revolution.

Above all, but a few years before 1789, another revolution had sharply stirred political feeling and Radical sentiment in Great Britain. The Declaration of Independence issued by the American Colonies has many points in common with the French Declaration of the Rights of Man, and the American Revolution anticipated in some measure the controversies and the Radical doctrines which the French Revolution more decisively aroused. There was strong sympathy in England for the Americans ; and two great names in English Radicalism link the two Revolutions together. Richard Price's "Discourse on Civil Liberty" and Tom Paine's "Common Sense" were the two great English manifestoes in the American cause. Price's sermon on the "Love of Country" and Paine's "Rights of Man" were the first great English utterances of sympathy with the Revolution in France.

But the American Revolution seemed far away, and the French very near at hand. The former, too, was the insurgence of a developing nation against external domination ; the latter was the rising of a people against its rulers. The French Revolution involved the more fundamental issues, and made by far the sharper break with the past. It aroused, therefore, much more vehement controversy, much deeper sentiments, and much greater fears.

Burke, in his "Reflections on the Revolution" (1790), raised early the cry of panic. In Paine's phrase, he "pitied the plumage and forgot the dying bird"—pitied the fine ladies and fine gentlemen whose power fell with the great change ; forgot the starving people of France who had provided that finery. His book, written in the fervour of a revelation, is an inspired plea against the whole idea of revolution, and even of political change. It is a worship of things established because they enshrine a tradition ; a panic denunciation of all who would touch institutions hallowed by age, whatever sufferings and injustices may be entwined in them.

Burke's book, itself an answer to Dr. Price, called forth a host of answers. Mary Wollstonecraft was among the first with her "Vindication of the Rights of Man" (1790) ; William Godwin's great "Enquiry into Political Justice" (1793) came later, to serve as the intellectual inspiration of generations of reformers to come. But the popular answer, which swept through the country and became the political Bible of Radicalism, as Burke's "Reflections" became the Bible of the old order, was Tom Paine's "Rights of Man" (Part I., 1791 ; Part II., 1792). Paine spoke a plain language, easily understood. He, who had been the greatest pamphleteer of the Revolution in America, became in England the protagonist of the French Revolution and its ideas.

Nowadays, Paine's book seems mild enough. Godwin's anarchistic gospel of human perfectibility went far deeper. But Paine said just the things that were most calculated to rouse the ordinary man, and to put Radical thoughts into his head. His defence of France was a simple plea, such as he had spoken earlier to the people of America, for full democracy, for equality between man and man, and for the spirit of fraternity among equals.

To Paine belongs the credit, under the inspiration of the Revolution in France, of setting on foot the first unmistakable movement of working-class Radicalism in England. The battle of pamphlets, set going by Burke's and Paine's books, soon became also a battle of organisations. Major Cartwright, Horne Tooke, and the middle-class Radicals revived the Society for Constitutional Information, which had been inactive for some years. The more aristocratic Whigs, followers of Charles James Fox, who still defended the French Revolution, founded the more moderate Friends of the People. And in 1792 appeared the London Corresponding Society, the first distinctively working-class political body in English history.

The London Corresponding Society was founded by a little group of skilled workmen, including some master-craftsmen and shopkeepers as well as journeymen. Its leader and secretary was Thomas Hardy, a shoemaker from Stirlingshire. The subscription was a penny a week, and as the society grew it was divided into groups of thirty members each, and governed by a meeting of delegates from the groups. Its object was to secure parliamentary reform and adult suffrage.

The L.C.S. set to work, by leaflets, pamphlets, and correspondence with workmen in other parts of the country, to create a national movement for reform. It disavowed violence, and its methods were, in fact, largely educational. It entered at once into friendly relations with the " Constitutional Society," and both Cartwright and Horne Tooke gave it some help. Very soon its efforts began to bear fruit. Societies sprang up all over England, and in Scotland a largely similar movement made immense headway. Meanwhile, in Ireland, the Society of United Irishmen, started as a reforming body, which aimed at the union of Catholic and Protestant on a basis of common nationality, was fast goaded into becoming an organised revolutionary movement, mainly of Catholics, which saw no escape from oppression save by a violent upheaval and an alliance with the French Republic.

The societies which sprang up in Great Britain were of many different types. Some were purely or mainly working-class bodies ; some included a substantial middle-class element. In Scotland, it seems, the movement, on the whole, was led by middle-class men, but was largely working-class in composition. In London, as we have seen, the middle-class Constitutional Society and the working-class Corresponding Society were in regular touch with each other.

During 1792 most of these bodies freely exchanged addresses with the revolutionary clubs in France or with the French Convention, urging the need for an alliance of the two countries on a basis of free institutions. They also showed, in many cases, their sympathy with the French by adopting

French forms in their discussions, addressing one another as "Citizen," and talking of calling, not a conference, but a "Convention," as after 1917 rebels in England spoke of "Soviets" or of "Soldiers' and Workers' Councils." Already in 1792 a Scottish Convention, representing eighty societies, was held in Edinburgh.

The growth of these movements caused great alarm in governing-class circles. A certain John Reeves, with Government help, formed a "Society for Preserving Liberty and Property against Republicans and Levellers" as a counter-revolutionary organisation, which held "loyal" meetings up and down the country, published "loyal" literature, and intimidated licence-holders from allowing their premises to be used for Radical gatherings. A great campaign of espionage was set on foot, and informers and police agents were planted in most of the Radical bodies. This method was practised most extensively in Scotland; but it soon spread over England as well.

Meanwhile in France the Revolution was passing swiftly from stage to stage. The Republic was proclaimed in September, 1792; Louis XVI. was executed in January, 1793; and in the following month England and France were at war. The Revolutionary Tribunal was instituted in March, and the Committee of Public Safety in April. At the end of May the moderate Girondins fell, and Jacobin ascendancy was assured. Soon, the "Terror" was in full force.

These events had swift reactions in Great Britain. Paine, who had fled to France, was tried and outlawed in December, 1792; and one bookseller after another was imprisoned for selling his and other Radical works. Daniel Eaton, the leading Radical publisher and bookseller, editor of *Hog's Wash*, was, indeed, twice acquitted by London juries; but in the provinces many convictions were secured.

Early in 1793 the Government delivered a more serious blow. Thomas Muir, a young Scottish advocate, and the Rev. Thomas Fysshe Palmer, a Unitarian Minister of Dundee, two of the chief leaders among the Scottish Radicals, were arrested, and, after ludicrously unfair trials, were sentenced, the one to fourteen and the other to seven years' transportation. With these trials the *régime* of repression seriously began.

The arrests did not daunt the Radicals. The Scottish Reformers called a further Convention for the autumn of 1793, and an adjourned session in November was attended by three delegates from the London Corresponding Society. In Ireland, a special Act had just made such Conventions illegal, and there were rumours of similar legislation preparing in Great Britain. The Scottish Convention passed a series of resolutions deciding that, in this event, or if the Habeas Corpus Act were suspended, or if an invasion took place, a further Convention on a national basis should be immediately summoned.

The Government at once responded to this defiance by dispersing the

Convention and arresting the principal leaders, including William Skirving, the secretary, and Maurice Margarot and Joseph Gerrald, two of the London delegates. All three were sentenced to transportation for fourteen years. The Scottish movement for reform, save for a futile and abortive insurrectionary plot, devised by a handful of the remaining delegates under the leadership of the former Government spy and agent, Robert Watt, was effectively crushed. Watt's conspiracy was discovered before anything had been done beyond the procuring of a few weapons. It is still a moot point whether he did not deliberately hatch the whole affair in order to betray it, and so restore himself to favour with the Government. Whether or no, he was hanged. Lord Braxfield, the original of Stevenson's " Weir of Hermiston," distinguished himself by his brutal conduct on the bench as the leader of the Scottish repression.

Having terrorised the Scottish Radicals, Pitt's Government turned its attention to England, and made up its mind to strike one great blow at the two societies which were leading the agitation. Warrants were issued in May, 1794, against most of the principal leaders of both the Constitutional and the Corresponding Societies. Cartwright, rather surprisingly, was let alone ; but Horne Tooke, with Thomas Hardy and the chief working-class leaders, was put in gaol. At the same time both Houses of Parliament appointed " Committees of Secrecy," which, on the evidence submitted to them by the Government, professed to detect a widespread revolutionary conspiracy to overthrow the Crown by violence and subvert the rights of property.

The prisoners were left some time in gaol before their trial, and all sorts of brow-beating were employed in order to extort incriminating confessions. But there appears to have been, in reality, very little to confess. There is nothing at all to connect the English Radicals with Watt's conspiracy, and nothing to back up the charges of the Committees of Secrecy that an insurrection was in the making. There had been fiery speeches, of course, and adjurations to follow the French example. But of action, or preparation for action, there seems to have been hardly anything. The Radical movement of this time was never nearly strong enough seriously to consider trying armed conclusions with the powerful and firmly-seated British aristocracy. Despite all the endeavours of the Government, Hardy, Horne Tooke, and John Thelwall, the leading orator of the Corresponding Society, whose cases were taken first, as the strongest from the Government's point of view, were, in turn, acquitted by London juries, which were apt to be radically inclined. After Thelwall's acquittal, the Government accepted the setback, and released the remainder of the prisoners. But though London, with its strong Radical traditions of more than a century, did not provide juries which, like those of Scotland, could be relied on to do reaction's work, in most other parts of England, except Manchester, the Reformers got short shrift. The acquittal of Thomas Walker, a merchant who was the leader of the Manchester Reformers, was a notable exception.

The London acquittals, however, profited the movement little. The Radical societies had already been deprived of many of their best leaders, and their more timid followers had been frightened away. The emergency powers, including the suspension of Habeas Corpus, which Pitt had obtained from Parliament, remained in force. There was no guarantee that the next batch of prosecutions would not be more successful. Moreover, events in France, from the time of the Terror, were steadily alienating moderate opinion, and later, as the Revolution turned gradually into a military despotism, many Radicals as well as moderate Reformers ceased to look to France for inspiration. The Constitutional Society died at once ; the Corresponding Society, though it lingered on until it was suppressed in 1799, did nothing noteworthy after 1794. It passed into the hands of a small group of extremists, some of them Irish, who worked underground but could exert only a very limited influence in Great Britain. Francis Place, who became chairman, resigned this position in 1796, and left the society in the following year.

Indeed, after 1794 the centre of Radical interest shifted to Ireland, where the United Irishmen were growing stronger and eagerly invoking French help. The naval mutiny at the Nore in 1797, which roused the Government to fresh measures of repression, was almost certainly led largely by impressed Irish sailors, under the influence of the United Irishmen. In the following year came the "Ninety-Eight," the abortive rising in the north, and the landing of a small French force in Ireland. When this movement had been easily suppressed, the French Revolution had exhausted its direct influence in these islands. Robert Emmet's abortive rising in Dublin in 1803 was but a final flicker.

The mutiny at the Nore, following upon a smaller mutiny at Spithead, arose over purely economic grievances ; and such political significance as it took on was probably due to Irish influence. But the dying Radical societies in Great Britain got the blame. One at least of their leaders, John Binns, was concerned in the attempt to procure French help for the Irish rising of 1798, and, with his brother, in trying to organise a Society of United Englishmen on the Irish model. The events of these years stimulated the Government to fresh measures of repression. By the Corresponding Societies Act of 1799, national associations with branches and corresponding relations between local associations were made illegal. In the same year, and again in 1800, general Combination Acts were passed, and all forms of Trade Unionism were suppressed by law.

Thus the first political movement of the British workers ran its short course, and died out under the influence of war and repression. It is not easy to measure the power or influence which it had when it was at its height.   Certainly the " scare " conclusions about the planning of a general insurrection, drawn by the House of Commons and by some of the newspapers under the influence of panic, must be heavily discounted.   The movement never, in fact, got far enough to consider seriously whether its intentions were revolutionary or pacific.   Nor did it get far enough to introduce any precision into its aims.   It was still at the stage of passing declaratory resolutions when the Government swooped down on it and broke it into fragments.   It is most improbable that, outside a few towns, it influenced appreciably even the main body of working-class opinion.   It was not the houses of the leading " loyalists," but those of the Radical Dr. Priestley, and his dissenting friends, that the mob of Birmingham burnt down in 1791.

There is a plain reason for this failure.   The French Revolution came at a time when Great Britain, under the influence of the swift changes in agriculture and industry, was in a stage of transition.   There was in 1789 the necessary basis neither for an agrarian nor for an urban revolutionary movement.   The peasantry, under stress of enclosures, had already lost its independence, and was too weak to stand up to its masters.   The Corresponding Societies seem to have had little contact with the countryside, save in a few areas such as Norfolk.   It is true that the outbreak of war in 1793 was followed by a movement among the labourers for redress.   High prices caused acute distress ; and in 1795 the Norfolk labourers, at a mass meeting at Heacham, decided to organise a national petition for higher wages.   But this rural movement never got on its feet.   It was crushed out in the repression which followed the defeat of the Corresponding Societies.   For a generation of increasing misery, the labourers, save for a few localised disturbances, suffered in silence.

While the countryside was thus prostrate, the mass of the new factory workers had not yet gained the cohesion or confidence needed for any movement more ambitious than a bread riot.   The factories, indeed, were staffed at this stage largely by women and children ; and the miners, save on the north-east coast, had barely the rudiments of any organisation and were subject to fierce repression whenever they attempted to combine for the assertion of their grievances beyond a single village.   The backbone of the Corresponding Societies came from neither of these classes, but from the artisans and small tradesmen in the older towns ; a keen and intelligent body of men, long accustomed to small-scale Trade Unionism and capable of coherent action, but far too weak by themselves to make a revolution.   Their middle-class allies, very differently situated socially from the middle classes in France, wanted, not a revolution, but a reform, and were not prepared to go the length of revolution when reform was denied.   They were inclined, like the leaders of the middle-class Revolution Society in 1789, to regard the English Revolution of 1688 as having set on foot a process which only needed completion by constitutional reforms in order to make Great Britain a happy and thoroughly well-governed country. The middle classes were too comfortable, and the paupers and factory hands and miners much too weak to make a revolution. The skilled artisans, many of whom were fairly comfortable themselves, and could still step up fairly easily into the lower middle class, were, in any case, too few and too isolated to make one by themselves. But, in face of the panic of the ruling classes and the repressive policy of the Government, no Radical movement could live save by re-volutionary success. Accordingly, the short-lived Radicalism provoked by the French Revolution was crushed, and no great new popular movement appeared in Great Britain until after the Peace of 1815.

BOOKS

Max Beer. *History of British Socialism*, Vol. I, s. 2.
G. S. Veitch. *The Genesis of Parliamentary Reform.*
P. A. Brown. *The French Revolution in English History.*
H. N. Brailsford. *Shelley, Godwin and their Circle.*
H. W. Meikle. *Scotland and the French Revolution.*
C. Gill. *The Naval Mutinies of 1797.*
B. Dobrée and A. Manwaring. *The Floating Republic.*
J. Connolly. *Labour in Irish History.*
T. Paine. *Rights of Man.*
E. Burke. *Reflections on the French Revolution.*
W. Godwin. *An Enquiry into Political Justice.*

CHAPTER IV

WAR AND PEACE

1. Trade Union Struggles—The Years of War   2. Unemployment, Revolt and Repression

I. TRADE UNION STRUGGLES—THE YEARS OF WAR

TRADE Unions, we have seen, existed long before the Industrial Revolution. We can trace their working throughout the eighteenth century by references in parliamentary debates, periodicals, and other contemporary documents, even though no continuous record of their activities remains. We can see from these references well enough what these early Trade Unions were and did. In the first place, they were mostly local, though on occasions they corresponded over wide areas, and gave one another help in strikes. Secondly, they existed mainly among the skilled craftsmen in the older towns—printers, bootmakers, tailors, and the like—or in those sections of the woollen industry in which the capitalist had intervened as employer, and not merely as merchant—e.g. wool-combing. The majority were quite small ; but they seem often to have been powerful in relation to the crafts which they represented, and to have been successful both in negotiating collective agreements and in restricting employment to their members. In many cases they appear to have acted as Friendly Societies as well as Trade Unions, and to have possessed a strong social and convivial side. The line between Trade Unions and Friendly Societies was still not clearly drawn ; some of the early Lodges of Oddfellows (i.e. miscellaneous workers) appear to have been in part Trade Union bodies.

These types of Trade Society were fairly lasting : much more ephemeral were the combinations of the weavers and of other workers under the domestic system, who from time to time formed Unions over quite wide areas to demand higher wages, or to ask Parliament to legislate on their behalf. It was never long before such combinations either fell to pieces of their own accord or were suppressed by the law.

The eighteenth century Trade Unions and Clubs had very limited objects, and little sense of common solidarity between trade and trade, or of a distinctive political outlook. There was no organised link between the societies of different trades, or, usually, between those of the same trade centred round different meeting places, which were usually inns. Their aims were mutual help within the craft, and the protection of the craft and of craft standards of employment. Sometimes they struck work ; more often they sought to negotiate satisfactory agreements with the employers, who were, in most cases, small masters, little removed from the status of journeymen. Failing such agreements, they often petitioned Parliament for legal protection, or asked the justices to enforce the old Elizabethan statutes for the fixing of wages and the regulation of apprenticeship. They were often pre-pared to join with their employers in asking for State protection for their trades ; and probably they felt at least as close a unity with the small masters of their own trade as with the journeymen of other trades. Save in those sections of industry which, like the woollen industry in the west of England and the coal industry in the north-east, were already developing on a basis of large scale Capitalism, there is no sign of any acute class-struggle in industry before the Industrial Revolution. There were bickerings and disputes ; but there is no evidence of sustained hostility, or of any permanent ranging of employers and workers in opposite camps.

As the Industrial Revolution advanced, this situation changed, not so much at first by an alteration in the status of the workers in the older urban crafts as by the rise, side by side with them, of new types of industry and of a new working class recruited from the dispossessed peasantry. For some time the old Trade Unions and Clubs went on much as before, until they were affected by the growing fear of the workers in the mind of the ruling classes after the French Revolution, and by the rise of new types of working-class organisation in the textile and mining industries of the north of England. During the eighteenth century a number of special Acts were passed, usually on the petition of the masters, forbidding combination in particular trades ; and, apart from these Acts, the judges tended increasingly to regard all workmen's combinations as criminal conspiracies under the common law. These prohibitions, however, were not often invoked against purely local Trade Clubs of skilled workmen. We have seen how, by the two general Combination Acts of 1799 and 1800, all forms of Trade Unionism were specifically declared to be illegal, and the Pitt system of repression was extended from the political bodies, such as the Corresponding Societies, to all forms of working-class industrial organisation. The purpose of these new Acts, which provided for trial of workmen by summary jurisdiction before magistrates, was mainly that of rendering possible easier and speedier ways of proceeding against combinations; for the older procedure had been cumbrous and had often involved so much delay that employers were unwilling to make use of it. The new measures, though they were part of the general repression which followed the mutiny at the Nore and the rebellion of the United Irishmen, were prompted chiefly, not by fear of the older Trade Clubs, to which most of the Corresponding Societies' members probably belonged, but by the beginnings of Trade Union organisation among the miners and factory workers in the northern and midland counties. A move-ment confined to the older crafts could easily be kept in check ; but if, under the leadership of the minority of intelligent artisans, it spread to the growing mass of half-starved and violently discontented miners and factory workers, the danger of revolution might become real and imminent.

It must be remembered that the French Revolution and the outbreak of the anti-revolutionary war against France came swiftly on the heels of the first great onrush of industrial change. The last quarter of the eighteenth century was a period of furious industrial activity. Watt perfected his steam engine in 1776 ; the rapid spread of factory spinning in the cotton industry began between 1770 and 1780 ; road-making and canal-building were being pressed swiftly forward in order to deal with the increasing volume of merchandise ; the demand for coal, for both household and industrial purposes, was growing fast ; the Enclosure Movement was at its period of greatest intensity ; the new proletariat was thronging into the factory and mining districts, and creating there a social problem which presented itself to the upper classes chiefly in the guise of a social peril.

Mr. and Mrs. Hammond, whose book, " The Town Labourer," graphically reveals the mind of the new industrial age, the helpless kicking against the pricks of the factory workers, the panic repressiveness of the ruling classes, have described, in " The Skilled Labourer," the many attempts at organisation made by the factory operatives, framework knitters and miners during this period. We can see in their books how the lead in organisation had almost always to be taken, not by the new types of wage-slaves, but by the older established craftsmen, whose status and standards were menaced by the Industrial Revolution. In the cotton industry these revolts were led first by the wool-combers and hand-loom weavers, as successive changes in machinery overthrew their old monopoly of skill. A little later, after the end of the Napoleonic Wars, the spinners began to take the lead ; but their case was different. The mule-spinners were a new skilled craft, who had taken over with the aid of complicated machinery processes previously carried out by women and children, both under the old domestic system and in the earlier stages of power-production in the factories. In the collieries, the lead was taken by the skilled miners, whose relatively high wages were being beaten down by the competition of fresh labour imported from the agricultural districts or from distressed and over-populated Ireland.

These leaders of revolt in the factory districts were men of much the same social types as the skilled urban craftsmen—builders, bootmakers, tailors, bakers, and the rest—whose standards and methods of work were not yet menaced seriously, if at all, by the coming of machinery and large-scale capitalist organisation. Indeed, for the time being, many of the skilled crafts which were not superseded by the new machines reaped an advantage from the larger market for their products created by the rapid increase in the wealth of the upper and middle classes. This caused their Trade Unions to become stronger and more militant ; and there was, in the minds of the ruling class, the ever-present fear that the Radical minority of workers, who were educated enough to organise effective combinations and to imbibe Jacobin doctrines, night mobilise the mass of unorganised factory workers in support of a national revolutionary movement.

These fears account both for the panic severity with which the movement of the Corresponding Societies was stamped out, and for the relentless war waged by the Government and the new capitalist employers against all attempts at working-class organisation in the factory and mining districts. In themselves, both working-class political clubs and Trade Unions of the old sort were relatively harmless, and would have provoked no great movement of repression. But, as the sparks that might set the factory and mining districts alight, they were quenched with all the Government's resources.

Pitt's measures for carrying through this policy of repression were skilfully designed. We have seen how he rooted out the Corresponding Societies, and killed for a generation even the middle-class movement for reform. Legal persecution, backed up by the evidence of spies and informers, and by counter-propaganda subsidised by the State, was adequate for this purpose. The factory and mining districts had to be held down by more vigorous methods. In addition to sending into every working-class body that could be found spies, informers, and even provocative agents, and so disrupting the working-class movements, because no man in them knew whether he could trust his neighbour, the Government built up a powerful armed force for dealing with all signs of disturbance. Pitt abolished the old practice of billeting troops in the homes of the people, where they might easily become contaminated with Radical doctrines. Instead, he built barracks at strategic points throughout the country, and used his concentrated military force in order to overawe the people. In addition, by creating the new Volunteers and Yeomanry, he replaced the old Militia, who could not be trusted, with a force ready to deal, not so much with possible invasion from abroad, as with civil commotion at home. The Yeomanry, especially, were an upper and middle-class force on which the governing classes could place the fullest reliance. Even where the Volunteers felt qualms, the Yeomanry thoroughly enjoyed riding down an unarmed mob to the glory of Church and State.

It must be remembered that there was at this time, apart from the small body of Bow Street Runners, no properly organised police force anywhere in the country. The Metropolitan Police, or "Peelers," did not come into existence till Sir Robert Peel created them in 1829, and the system did not begin to extend to other areas until after the Reform Act of 1832. The tiny bodies of constables previously in existence were quite useless in face of any organised movement. The use of troops to deal with disturbances, therefore, seemed to Pitt and his associates the only possible course[1] ; but it is easy to

---

[1] Special constables for dealing with emergencies were instituted under Charles II, but seldom used till well on in the nineteenth century.

see that the measures actually taken were dictated by panic fear, and were, in effect, a wholesale arming of the rich against the poor.

Overawed by military force, ceaselessly spied and reported upon by agents of the Government or the local magistrates, liable to severe sentences for conspiracy under common law or for violation of the Combination Acts if they attempted any concerted action, it is not surprising that for a long time the factory workers and miners failed to create any stable combinations. It is more surprising that they managed to combine at all. It is nevertheless true that many Trade Unions existed through the whole period during which the Combination Acts were in force, and that many temporary combinations and strikes took place even among the workers who experienced the greatest rigour of the repression.

This is only in part explained by the fact that the laws against combination were not everywhere enforced with the same severity as in the great factory districts of the North. To some extent, local Trade Clubs of artisans in the older towns were allowed to exist and to carry on their work without systematic prosecution. In some trades, employers went on negotiating collective agreements with the Unions, and strikes occurred, almost as if the Combination Acts had never been passed and the judges had never declared combinations to be illegal at common law. But this applied only to trades not yet directly affected by the Industrial Revolution, and still carried on under the old system of small-scale production. In these cases there was no fear that industrial action might lead to a revolutionary outbreak, and the Government, having no cause for anxiety, often let such movements alone. Nor were most employers at all eager to proceed against such combinations. Skilled labour was scarce, and it often suited them better to come to terms with the craftsmen than to antagonise them by sending their leaders to gaol. There was, however, always the risk that some interested persons might set the law in motion, even in such cases. For example, when, in 1798, the London printers, on the invitation of their employers, met to discuss wages and conditions, they were indicted for conspiracy and sentenced to two years' imprisonment. This was actually before the Combination Act, at the height of the panic caused by the Nore mutiny and the Irish outbreak. Again, in 1810, *The Times* compositors received a brutal sentence for the crime of combination. The older Trade Clubs, which mostly took the precaution during this time of disguising themselves as Friendly Societies, were often let alone ; but they were at the mercy of any employer or informer who might choose to take action against them.

In the new industrial districts—Lancashire, Yorkshire, the East Midlands, the north-east coast, and South Wales—persecution was far more brutal and systematic ; for here, in the view of the ruling classes, the real danger lay. Here the magistrates, with every encouragement from the Home Office, and the backing of a host of spies and informers, and of the Yeomanry and other

military forces, set to work to prevent all forms of working-class combination. The archives of the Home Office are full of the local reports on
these activities, and from these reports Mr. and Mrs. Hammond have drawn
much of the material for their books.

The Combination Acts nominally applied to masters as well as to men ;
but, so far as is known, no single prosecution of a master for the crime of
combination ever took place. The Acts were used, and were meant, solely
for the suppression of working-class movements.

Until about 1808 they were successful to the extent that no stable working-
class combinations arose in the factory or mining districts, and strikes and
riots were kept down to the scale of purely localised movements. There
were protests against the introduction of new machinery, accompanied
sometimes by sporadic machine-breaking ; there were strikes and disputes
about wages. But these seem to have been, for the most part, on a small
scale. Indeed, to a great extent the aim of the workers up to this time was
rather to secure State intervention on their behalf than to organise for independent industrial action.

It must be remembered that the old Elizabethan Statute of Artificers,
under which conditions of employment were regulated and the magistrates
were empowered to fix wages, was still unrepealed at this time. There were
also many other Acts, such as the Spitalfields Act for the silk weavers, dealing
with wages and conditions in particular trades. The Elizabethan Statute
and many of the other Acts had, in practice, fallen into disuse ; but it was
still, in theory, the business of the State to regulate wages. Thus the cotton
operatives, in the last years of the eighteenth century, were constantly
agitating for the fixing of a minimum wage by the State. Pitt passed an
Arbitration Act in 1800 ; and this was amended three years later. But it
remained, in fact, almost inoperative, owing to obstruction by the masters.
In 1805 the weavers formed a general combination with the object, not of
striking for higher wages, but of pressing Parliament by petition to pass a
Minimum Wage Act. Some of the employers supported this claim ; but in
1808 the Minimum Wage Bill was overwhelmingly defeated in the House of
Commons. Parliament had not yet quite reached the point of formally
proclaiming its *laissez faire* doctrine, and repudiating all attempts to interfere
with freedom of contract between employers and workers. But it was
moving rapidly towards that conclusion. In 1813 the clauses for the regulation of wages in the Elizabethan law were formally repealed, and in 1814
the apprenticeship clauses were also abrogated. The doctrine of *laissez faire*
was thus proclaimed, and the precept of Parliament brought into line with
what had been for some time its prevailing practice.

The rejection of the Minimum Wage Bill in 1808 brought the cotton
workers face to face with the fact that they could look for no help from the
State. It provoked the first large-scale industrial movement in the new

factory districts ; a great strike of both cotton and woollen weavers broke out all over Lancashire, and resulted, despite the Combination Laws, which were not used against the strikers, in a temporary victory. Soon, however, wages were again reduced.

Two years later the miners of Northumberland and Durham conducted their first general strike, the issue being the proposal of the coal owners to worsen the conditions of the yearly bond—for the miners were then, like the agricultural workers, usually bound for a year to a single master. All the strike leaders were imprisoned and, overawed by military force and the threat of prosecution, the men were compelled to return on the employers' terms. There is no evidence of any coherent Union behind this strike ; but delegates were chosen from the various pits to conduct the struggle, and to draw up the settlement.

In 1812 came a general strike of the weavers in Scotland. The men first attempted to get an agreed scale of wages by negotiation with the employers. When this failed, they appealed to the magistrates to fix a scale. After long and expensive legal proceedings, the magistrates were compelled to publish a scale ; but they refused to take any measures for its enforcement, and the employers accordingly refused to pay. The strike followed, and lasted for three weeks. Then, just as the employers had agreed to meet the men, the authorities suddenly arrested the entire Strike Committee, and charged the members with the offence of conspiracy—for, although the Combination Acts did not extend to Scotland, the Scottish judges also regarded combination in itself as an offence. They were sentenced to periods of imprisonment of from four to eighteen months. The strike was broken and the Union shattered.

Far more important than these occasional big strikes was the organised movement of machine-breaking which began in 1811 in the hosiery districts of the Midland Counties. There had been plenty of sporadic machine-breaking—an instinctive protest against the new inhuman competition with human labour—long before 1811. But the Luddite Movement was an organised affair, skilfully directed by leaders who, working in secret, established an extraordinary hold over the framework-knitters, whose standard of life was being beaten down by new methods of production. Framework-knitting was still carried on mainly in the workers' homes ; but the frames belonged to the employers. The trouble centred round the making of a new cheap kind of " cut up " hose at less than the recognised rates of pay, and the use of a new wide frame which both produced shoddy goods and reduced the number of workers employed. The Luddite remedy was the intimidation of the offending employers by the breaking of the obnoxious frames, which it was nearly impossible to defend, as they were scattered widely in the cottages of the workers.

The name "Luddites" arose because the machine-breakers carried out their campaign, and issued their warnings and proclamations, in the name of one " Ned Ludd " or " King Ludd," of Sherwood Forest—a mythical leader whose name linked itself up with the legends of Robin Hood as the friend of the poor. Who " Ned Ludd " was, or who were the real leaders of the movement, was never discovered. A number of machine-breakers, chiefly youths, were sentenced to transportation for the offence. But the leaders were never brought to trial, and the employers were compelled by the movement to raise wages and, in part, remedy the men's grievances.

From the Midlands " Luddism " spread to Lancashire and Yorkshire, and the name was applied to all organised attacks on machinery for some time after the original movement had died down. But in the cotton and woollen industries, where the offending machines were chiefly to be found in factories, under the direct protection of the employers, the movement encountered difficulties and led to more violent affrays, when the workers attacked mills that were vigorously defended against them. In Lancashire and Yorkshire, machine-breaking and " Luddism " were never more than incidents or auxiliaries of strike action, or spontaneous outbursts in times of serious distress. They achieved no success comparable with that of the original Luddites in the Midlands.

The scale of the Luddite movement and its initial success were, however, enough to rouse the greatest alarm. Once more the Houses of Parliament appointed Secret Committees, and fresh repressive legislation was hurried through. The measures taken against the Luddites in 1812 prepared the way for the more far-reaching repression of the years following the Peace of 1815.

Luddism and a few of the strike movements of the war period have been described in outline in order to give an idea of the difficulties which the pioneers of Trade Union action had to face. We have seen the workers first trying to persuade a hostile Parliament or a hostile body of magistrates to come to their help, on the old principle that it was the State's business to regulate the affairs of industry and to secure to each his appointed status and reward. We have seen the governing classes and the employers, under the influence of changing economic conditions, repudiating this old theory, asserting the new doctrine of *laissez faire*, and supporting their action with quotations from the writings of Adam Smith and the political economists of the new school. Finally, we have seen the workers, as they realised the hopelessness of appeals to the law, and especially during the years of sharp fluctuations in trade and prices towards the end of the Napoleonic wars, turning in despair to mass industrial action as a means of redress.

Undoubtedly the war was a very powerful factor, especially during these latter years, in depressing the workers' standard of living and in sharpening the conflict between the classes concerned in large-scale industry. War drained away wealth and dislocated trade. It caused tremendous fluctuations in the cost of living, which changed from year to year according to the

state of the harvests ; and underlying these immense short-period fluctuations
was a sharp persistent rise in prices, which was ceaselessly beating down
real wages. War accentuated the struggle for the means of life. Historians
differ in the emphasis which they place on the long continuance of the war
as a cause of the prevailing misery of the times ; but all are agreed that it
was a factor which greatly strengthened the forces making for the decline in
the workers' standard of life.

As conditions grew worse, a powerful movement in favour of Peace
developed among the workers. Peace and Reform became popular cries.
Cobbett, Henry Hunt, and other Radical leaders, gained an ever-growing
body of supporters. Many employers, too, were for Peace and Reform ;
for they saw in Peace the prospect of lower taxes and the expansion of
trade, and in Reform the means to securing for their own class a controlling influence in the State. In these last years of the great war, the
virtues of Peace and the blessings which would follow it were loudly
proclaimed.

In 1815 Peace came at last, and with it the first great and general economic
depression in the history of modern Industrialism.

BOOKS

S. and B. Webb. *History of Trade Unionism*, ch. II.
J. L. and B. Hammond. *The Town Labourer.*
J. L. and B. Hammond. *The Skilled Labourer.*
F. Peel. *The Risings of the Luddites.*
Reports of Trials of the Luddites.

2. UNEMPLOYMENT, REVOLT AND REPRESSION

It has been said with truth that British Socialism was born on the morrow
of the Peace of 1815. There had been, during the long war, a great deal of
distress, especially among the agricultural workers and in the factory districts.
There had been many strikes and machine-breaking disturbances, culminating in the Luddite troubles of 1811 and 1812. There had been plenty
of persecution and repression, continuous from the days of panic which
followed the Revolution in France. There had been, too, in the later years
of the war, a marked revival of Radical agitation, and the cry of " Peace
and Reform " had provided men such as Burdett and Cobbett with a
means of popular appeal. But, on the whole, there had been no joining
of forces by the Radical reformers and the mass of the factory workers.
Radicalism had still found its chief following among the middle classes—
farmers and tradesmen—and among the relatively prosperous artisans in
the older towns. The factory workers were only just beginning to relate
their economic grievances to a political programme, and hardly at all to
express them in a social policy of their own.

In 1815 the group of tendencies which can fairly be called Socialist was represented only by one tiny sect—the Spenceans. The followers of Paine, still through his writings the greatest Radical influence, were in no sense Socialist. Cobbett was an agrarian reformer who was only just beginning to address himself directly to the factory workers, and was, in any case, as little an advocate of any sort of Socialism as of Capitalism. William Godwin, whose philosophic anarchism came nearer to a Socialist view, had ceased for the time to exert any direct influence on working-class opinion.

Thomas Spence, son of a small artisan shopkeeper who had migrated from Aberdeen to Newcastle-on-Tyne, became a school-master, and subsequently, moving to London, a hawking bookseller and editor of Radical papers. He was active in the London Corresponding Society, and served several terms of imprisonment for his Radical activities. His views, expounded in a number of pamphlets from 1776 onwards, were those of an agrarian Communist. He preached social ownership of the land, which was to be vested in the parish and let out to farmers at a rental. This rent was to be the only tax, and Society was to be organised as a federation of wholly democratic parish communes. Mere political reforms Spence held to be useless ; he pleaded for a peasant society, based on communal land ownership, and " capable of delivering us from the deadly mischief of great accumulations of wealth."

Spence's doctrine was fully developed by 1775, and was therefore wholly independent of influences derived either from France or from the Industrial Revolution. The London Corresponding Society made him known to the working-class Radicals, and after its collapse a body of disciples began to gather round him. But apparently they formed no association of their own until 1812, when the Society of Spencean Philanthropists was created by a group which included Arthur Thistlewood, leader in the Cato Street Conspiracy of 1820, and the Watsons, together with a number of London artisans headed by Thomas Preston and Thomas Evans. Spence himself died in 1814 ; but the Spencean Society continued, and played an important part in the years following the Peace. It had never more than a very small group of adherents ; but as the one body putting forward a definitely Socialist and confiscatory programme, it was the special object of the attention of " loyalists," and its doctrines and activities were chiefly quoted whenever the Government desired to prove the existence of a revolutionary plot.

When Peace came in 1815, and when Napoleon had been finally crushed and exiled, the country looked forward eagerly to a return of good times. For more than twenty years, all manner of hardships, grievances and abuses had been put down to the war, and redress had been promised on the coming of Peace. The war had drained the national resources ; for Great Britain had beaten Napoleon even more with her money than with her men. It had upset trade ; and both Continental and American markets had been, especially during its later years, largely closed to British merchandise. It had killed the movement for political reform; for military needs must not be hampered by constitutional changes. It had made repression easy, by enabling Pitt to cover the country with barracks and to provide the country with a Yeomanry force even more useful in dealing with civilian disturbances than with the threat of invasion.

So, in 1815, every one who had a claim or a grievance expected speedy satisfaction, and, above all, manufacturers and workers looked to the re-opened markets for the means of regular and profitable employment. These hopes were speedily disappointed. An agricultural depression which had begun, chiefly owing to the great increase of tillage and the abundant harvests, before the end of the war became much worse with the cessation of the abnormal war-time demand. In commerce, a feverish period of speculative export speedily glutted the foreign markets, which lacked the wherewithal to buy, and a slump of unprecedented severity followed. Agricultural wages were reduced far below starvation level, and the labourers were driven wholesale to the Poor Law for relief. Factory after factory was shut down, and the operatives flung out of work. The workers who were still under the domestic system fared even worse; for employers had more incentives to keep their machines working than to give continued employment to outworkers. Bankruptcies and bank failures multiplied in all parts of the country. Prices fell, indeed; but men soon learnt to prefer high prices which they could pay to low prices which they could not. Moreover, the fall in prices brought home, at the same time as it increased, the staggering burden of the debts incurred during the long war.

Very soon the talk was everywhere of the prevailing distress. The House of Commons set up Committees to report on the position, especially in relation to agriculture and the Poor Laws. The Government, the Church, and the Royal Dukes collaborated in reviving the National Association for the Relief of the Manufacturing and Labouring Poor, which had been originally launched during the distress of 1812. Numerous local relief committees were started and dispensed considerable sums. Proposals were put forward for the provision of employment by the State, but the Government's chief measures were designed, by lowering taxation, to relieve the distress of the farmers and employers, and so to promote the revival of trade.

The Radicals, headed by Henry Hunt, William Cobbett and Lord Cochrane, also pressed for the lowering of taxes, but added to this demands for the total or partial repudiation of interest on the War Debt, for the abolition of pensions and sinecures, and for the reform of Parliament. Robert Owen, still the successful cotton-spinner of New Lanark, and wholly untainted with Radical associations, turned from his agitation for a Factory Act to the demand that the State should find employment for all by his scheme for "Villages of Co-operation," in which the poor, settled on the land, would both provide for their own needs and create a surplus which would stimulate the revival of manufacture and commerce. Owen presented his plan, the germ of his Socialist and Co-operative doctrines, both to the Committee on the Poor Laws and to the Association for the Relief of the Poor. The House of Commons Committee refused to hear him ; and the Radicals denounced him as an interfering busybody, preaching a nonsensical doctrine of "community." Owen was already seeking a solution of the social problem in the co-operative control of the new forces of production ; the Radicals still placed their faith in the lowering of taxation and the reform of political institutions.

Before long, the increasing severity of the distress led to widespread movements of unrest. There were riots in the factory districts, and everywhere a great revival of Radical and working-class agitation. For the first time the Radicals began really to capture the mind and imagination of the factory workers, and to secure general working-class backing for their political programme. Cobbett, the greatest of Radical writers, suddenly grew to be the chief leader of the agitation. Hitherto, his famous *Weekly Political Register*, costing, on account of the Stamp and Paper Taxes, more than a shilling an issue, had circulated mainly among the well-to-do. He had been the defender and prophet of the agricultural labourers ; but to the factory operatives and to industry he had paid only intermittent attention. From 1815 his tone rapidly changed. He began to appeal directly to the factory workers, and to preach Radical Reform as a remedy for their troubles. In November, 1816, he began his famous series of "Addresses to the Journeymen and Labourers," published weekly in a special cheap *Register* at twopence a number, which evaded the Stamp Tax by the omission of news, and contained only his rousing "Addresses."

Cobbett's cheap *Register* had an enormous influence, selling 40,000 to 50,000 copies a week. A host of minor journalists and pamphleteers followed his example. The working-class press, which had been almost non-existent since the suppression of the Corresponding Societies, came suddenly to vigorous life. Wooller's *Black Dwarf*, Hone's *Reformist's Register*, and Sherwin's *Republican* (or *Political Register*), were all started in 1817. Richard Carlile and other Radical publishers reprinted Tom Paine's writings and defied the law by issuing a host of 'seditious' pamphlets and journals. At the same time, political meetings were held in all parts of the country. Old Major Cartwright, indefatigable as ever, toured the country, forming Hampden Clubs and Societies for Political Reform. Trade Unionism grew apace, despite the Combination Acts. The working-class movement began to take shape in a great outburst of activity under the leadership of the political reformers.

Meanwhile, the little Society of Spencean Philanthropists in London decided to organise a demonstration. The leaders invited Henry Hunt, next to Cobbett the greatest figure among the Radicals, to be the chief speaker, and prepared an address based on Spencean principles and advocating the Spencean plan of agrarian reform. Hunt, who was no Socialist, rejected the address, and insisted that the purpose of the meeting should be to press for the orthodox Radical programme of political reforms. The Spenceans thereupon decided to hold a separate meeting of their own at an earlier hour on the same day. They left before Hunt's meeting began, and marched off in procession through the City. A riot followed, and some damage was done to property, but the disturbance was, in fact, quite a minor affair, never in the least likely to lead to any serious result.

A riot in London, however, in conjunction with the disturbed state of the factory districts, caused the Government and the upper classes to take fright. They had spies at work within the Spencean Society, and the Spencean declaration, with its policy of Republicanism and confiscation of the land, fell into their hands. It was treated as the programme of a national revolutionary conspiracy, and the riot as the first overt sign of an impending insurrection. Four Spencean leaders, including James Watson the elder, Thistlewood and Preston, were arrested and brought to trial for high treason, and great efforts were made to secure evidence which would implicate Cobbett and Henry Hunt. Both Houses of Parliament appointed Committees of Secrecy, which produced alarming reports, recalling the days of the French Revolution, and proclaiming the existence of a widespread conspiracy, aimed at the destruction of the monarchy, " a total overthrow of all existing establishments, and a division of the landed, and extinction of the funded, property of the country."

These alarmist reports were at once followed up by special measures of repression. The Spencean Society was suppressed by name, and the old measures against " Corresponding " Societies were renewed. The Habeas Corpus Act was suspended ; all public meetings were placed under the supervision of the magistrates ; all reading-rooms were made subject to licence, which could be forfeited if they supplied undesirable literature. The penalties against treasonable and seditious utterances were stiffened up, and the magistrates were given special instructions to act vigilantly in the suppression of all dangerous movements. By the Government itself and by order of local magistrates, a host of spies was sent out into the Radical Societies ; and these, headed by the notorious Oliver, were even more active in manufacturing treason and sedition than in reporting the real activities of the Radicals.

In March, 1817, the workers in the factory districts were busy, under the influence of the Reformers, organising a great petition to the Prince Regent. This, it was decided, should be presented by a large body of marchers, who, starting from Manchester and gathering recruits as they went, were to make their way to London, each man carrying the blanket in which he would sleep by the roadside. The first serious step in the suppression of the popular movement was the breaking up of this march of the "Blanketeers." The leaders were arrested in Manchester before the start, and the few hundred men who set out were harried by bodies of troops and Yeomanry until they dispersed. Wholesale arrests were made ; and it was only after a few months in prison that the bulk of the marchers, who had committed no crime for which they could be brought to trial, were at length released.

In June the trials of the Spenceans came on at last, after long delay, during which no pains were spared in collecting evidence against them. But the "plot," which had existed only in the Government's imagination, could not be proved.; and Watson, whose case was taken first, was acquitted. There was no alternative but to drop the rest of the cases, and the remaining Spenceans were released. Thistlewood, however, was soon lodged in prison again for a year on a fresh charge—that of libelling the Prince Regent.

The great "Spencean plot" thus dissolved in smoke ; but, even while the trials were proceeding, a fresh plot was in course of manufacture. The spy, Oliver, had been actively stirring up insurrection for the purpose of betraying it. Under his influence, two small bands of desperate men were induced to take up arms. The Huddersfield party, luckily for themselves, dispersed almost as soon as they gathered ; the Derbyshire men, led by a framework-knitter named Jeremiah Brandreth, made a half-hearted attempt to march on Nottingham. A tiny body of troops caused them to fly without an attempt at resistance, and the so-called "insurrection" was over.

These petty disturbances, magnified into armed insurrections which had been barely quelled by the promptitude of the authorities, served to renew the panic. Word leaked out, indeed, of Oliver's activities as a provocative agent in Yorkshire ; but his name was kept for the time out of the Derbyshire affair, though it was almost wholly of his making. Brandreth and two other leaders were executed, and a number of their followers transported. At the same time a general round-up of Radicals was begun. Speakers addressed meetings at their peril ; both editors and hawkers of Radical journals were imprisoned right and left. Cobbett himself, realising that to remain at home would mean the certainty of a long term of imprisonment, fled secretly to the United States, whence he continued to send his writings for regular publication in England.

Though many of the Radicals went to gaol, the unrest did not die down. Unemployment remained severe, and there were renewed Luddite troubles in Lancashire and Yorkshire. In 1818 there were great strikes in the textile districts, followed by a large number of prosecutions for illegal combination and conspiracy. This year is further notable as having seen the first recorded project of a "general union" of all trades. In London and Manchester this was launched under the curious name of the "Philanthropic Hercules." In London it had behind it the organising ability of John Gast, shipwright, at this time the leader of the Metropolitan trades, and the support of his new journal, *The Gorgon*, the first newspaper largely devoted to Trade Union affairs. But the creation of big Unions was practically impossible under the Combination Laws. We hear no more of the "Philanthropic Hercules" after its first few months of existence.

The repression which accompanied the textile strikes of 1818 strengthened the following of the political Reformers. Weavers and spinners, convinced that they could do nothing by strikes in face of prosecution and military force, turned to the agitation for the reform of Parliament. Despite the Acts of 1817, known as the "Gagging Acts," great Reform meetings and demonstrations were held throughout the industrial districts. One of these meetings, held in St. Peter's Fields, Manchester, on August 16th, 1819, has come down to history as the Massacre of "Peterloo."

The Manchester meeting was designed as a great public demonstration in support of the Reformers. All the witnesses agree that it was entirely peaceful and unarmed. The demonstrators, estimated at 80,000 strong, marched to St. Peter's Fields in contingents from the surrounding districts. No proclamation was made in advance that the meeting would be regarded as illegal ; Henry Hunt, who was the principal speaker, and was wanted by the authorities on a charge arising out of a previous speech, made an offer to surrender himself voluntarily to the authorities beforehand. But those in power took the extraordinary course of allowing the vast multitude to assemble, and then telling the Yeomanry to force their way through and arrest Hunt after he had begun his speech. Despite this provocative action, the crowd managed to give way and Hunt allowed himself to be arrested without resistance. But at this point the Yeomanry began to strike out at the crowd, and the order to charge was given. Frightful confusion followed, Eleven persons, including two women and a child, were killed outright, and hundreds were injured, many by sabre cuts and many by being trampled down in the crowd. The unarmed demonstrators fled as best they could, leaving their dead and wounded behind.

The Peterloo massacre raised a fury of protest in the country, and many decent men and women, who were not Radicals, supported the protest. But the Government congratulated the authorities responsible for the affair, and treated it as further evidence of revolutionary plots among the people. Towards the close of 1819 came a further and more drastic set of repressive measures—the Six Acts. These Acts (1) equipped the magistrates with more summary and drastic powers in dealing with offenders ; (2) prohibited drilling and training in the use of arms ; (3) strengthened the laws against blasphemous and seditious libel ; (4) gave the magistrates power to search private houses, and to confiscate weapons ; (5) restricted still further the right of public meeting ; and (6) subjected the periodical pamphlets published by the Radicals to the newspaper tax, with the object of preventing the issue of cheap publications.

These measures made it finally clear that, as far as the Government's power extended, even constitutional agitation was to be ruthlessly suppressed. They were speedily followed by the one instance in which a body of Radicals really made a plot with serious intentions of violence. This was the Cato Street Conspiracy of 1820, organised by Arthur Thistlewood, who had been released after his year's sentence, and a handful of London Radicals, and aided and instigated by Edwards, a spy and provocative agent of the same type as Oliver. The plot was to murder the members of the Cabinet, who were dining together at Lord Harrowby's, and then, by proclaiming the deed, to give the signal for a rising. Edwards and another spy betrayed the conspirators' plans, which they had a large share in making. The dinner was cancelled, and Thistlewood and his followers were surprised together in a loft in Cato Street, off the Edgware Road, where they were awaiting the signal. Thistlewood managed to kill one of the attacking party, and to escape ; but he was captured a few hours later, and in due course executed, with several of his accomplices. No rising followed, though in the following month there were strikes in many parts of the country, and in Scotland especially ; and at one place, Bonnymuir, a small body of armed strikers was dispersed by force and the incident magnified into another attempt at insurrection. Here, too, several men, including an ancestor of Keir Hardie, paid with their lives for their part in the movement.

How far was Great Britain, in these years between 1815 and 1820, really on the verge of insurrection ? It is extraordinarily difficult to disentangle the grain of truth from the network of lies in which it is covered up. That discontent and hostility to the Government and the governing classes were deep and widespread is obvious enough. It is clear, too, that strikes were many and often accompanied by some measure of violence. Distress was so severe and so general that nothing else could possibly be expected. Nor can it be doubted that there were many among the working-class Radicals who would have appealed to force if they had seen in its use any prospect of success. Strikes and Trade Unions were so ruthlessly broken up, freedom of speech and writing so little allowed, that it must have seemed to many that there remained open no way of protest save the way of violence.

Yet the evidence of any revolutionary plot extending beyond one or two tiny and uninfluential coteries is wholly lacking. Nor is it possible to find a single instance in which even these little groups planned violent measures save at the direct instigation of Government agents of the type of Oliver and Edwards. The conclusion can scarcely be resisted that, although the country was indeed full of inflammable material, it was the Government itself that applied to it the few matches that set it here or there precariously alight. And these little flames the power that had made them speedily quenched in blood.

The political Radicals, such as Cobbett and Hunt, kept entirely clear of these insurrectionary movements, and were too careful to be seduced by the agents of the Government. Only a few ignorant men were deluded into believing that there was really a national plan of revolution, and into playing in it their wretched part under the stage-management of the spies who betrayed them. In fact, the main body of the workers lacked the organisation which alone could have made a revolutionary movement possible ; and the leading Radicals, who could, perhaps, have made a revolution, though certainly not a successful one, had not the will to do so. They were Radical Reformers, and not revolutionaries ; and the workers without them could not turn the chaotic stirrings of misery into an insurrection. Indeed, the Radical leaders from 1820 onwards were successfully turning the thoughts of the workers from riots and machine-breaking to political agitation. The constitutional struggle for Reform succeeded to the chaos of the years after Waterloo. As trade and industry recovered from the worst of the slump, the workers turned from riots to political organisation ; and, as the panic passed, the repression gradually died down, and constitutional agitation became easier to carry on. The troubles of 1815-1820 were not renewed until the culmination of the next phase of the struggle after 1830, and by then there had been vital changes in both the political and the economic situation.

BOOKS

J. L. and B. Hammond. *The Town Labourer.*
J. L. and B. Hammond. *The Skilled Labourer.*
M. Beer. *History of British Socialism*, Vol. I.
G. D. H. Cole. *Life of William Cobbett.*
G. Slater. *The Growth of Modern England.*
H. Martineau. *History of the Thirty Years' Peace*, Vol. I.
O. Rudkin. *Thomas Spence.*
S. Maccoby. *English Radicalism*, Vol. I.
A. W. Wickwar. *The Struggle for the Freedom of the Press.*
G. D. H. Cole. *Richard Carlile* (Fabian Tract).
G. Wallas. *Life of Francis Place.*

CHAPTER V

SOCIALISM AND REFORM

1. Socialist Origins   2. The Repeal of the Combination Acts   3. The Reform Movement

I. SOCIALIST ORIGINS

THE five years from 1815 to 1820 were a season of blind and desperate reactions to intolerable distress. The decade from 1820 to 1830 was the seeding-time of working-class ideas and organisations. In 1815 the only organised body of Socialists was the tiny sect of Spenceans, who were doctrinaire agitators, little concerned with the movement of industrial forces. By 1830 Socialism had already gone far towards taking shape as a movement aiming at the communal control of the new forces unloosed by the Industrial Revolution. On the one hand, there had grown up a body of distinctively Socialist economic doctrine, the forerunner of Marxism ; and, on the other, the Socialist policy of production for use under communal ownership and management had been clearly worked out by Robert Owen and his disciples. The word " Socialism " was, indeed, only beginning to be used, in reference to the Owenites, towards the end of the decade ; but the thing, the idea, had assumed a definite shape and substance.

Moreover, during the decade, organisation developed step by step with doctrine. There was a great growth of Trade Unionism, pointing the way to the greater movement of the years following the Reform Act. Owenism, making its appeal to the more educated section of the workers, already issued in the formation of Socialist and Co-operative Societies for both propaganda and mutual trade. And there was a great growth of working-class journalism, which became a powerful means to the rapid dissemination of the new ideas. At the same time, overshadowing all these other developments in magnitude and popular estimation, the political Reform movement grew fast in power and influence, and gave the workers both valuable experience in organisation and, as the critical days of the Reform Bill drew nearer, a keener insight into the real divisions of class and opinion in Society.

All these movements were, of course, the product less of outstanding leaders than of the powerful economic forces which were driving Society irresistibly towards a new classification of the people and a reform of institutions and re-distribution of political power. Leadership served only to clarify the movement of forces, and to mobilise opinion based upon it. Cobbett did not make the Reform movement, though his vigorous personality helped to force the issue, and contributed greatly to the awakening of political consciousness among the workers. Owen came nearer to making Socialism, which was often called "Owenism," in recognition of his influence; but it is significant that a Socialism closely resembling his developed simultaneously in France, and that there is no evidence of either development, at this early stage, influencing the other. Socialist doctrine, as well as Reform agitation, emerged among the workers because the time was ripe.

During the decade 1820-1830 Socialism and political Radicalism developed side by side, but for the most part quite independently. Cobbett and Owen had little in common save a devotion to the people's cause. Cobbett, as we have seen, was a yeoman who hated the new industrialism, and hoped by political reformation to strike down the new money-lords and bring back a golden age of prosperity to the independent yeoman and craftsman. He wanted Universal Suffrage as a means to the destruction of the power of finance and large-scale Capitalism, in order that England might be again a "Merrie England," pictured as like the free-yeoman America he had known. Every man of initiative should have his farm or his workshop, in which the few hired workers would get good wages and associate with the master on terms of friendship. Such a gospel, he knew, appealed strongly to the men of his day. The factory workers were peasants driven into industry against their wills; the skilled craftsmen were kicking against the loss of independence great industry had brought. A Reformed Parliament would surely enable the people to have its will, and restore the old order that industrialism was sweeping away.

Owen, on the other hand, was no yeoman, but a great employer—a self-made man of the new order, who had grown up among the new machines and been an active agent in the triumph of the new productive forces. He saw, as clearly as Cobbett, the evils which the Industrial Revolution had brought; but his remedy was not a return to the past, but a reformation of the new order. Increased production, the gift of the factory system, seemed to him to promise a more abundant life for all—if only it were organised aright. But the new forces had been allowed to develop uncontrolled, and to serve as the means to fabulous wealth for the few. Machinery, instead of raising the standard of life for all, had been allowed, through insane competition and private greed, to depreciate the value of labour power. This, however, was a case, not against the machine, but against the methods that had been adopted for its use. Machinery and the new forces of production must be socially controlled and organised for the benefit of all. They must be used to lighten labour and to diffuse plenty. Labour must be recognised as the measure of value, and machinery as its servant. But this could not be if the owner of capital controlled the machine for his own profit, or if each employer were driven, in competition with his rivals, to force the price of labour down. All production, therefore, must be socially organised, and capital must be made the servant of social labour. The workers must aim, not at the destruction of machinery or of industrialism, but at its control by the power of association.

Cobbett sought to use the reform of Parliament as a means to his economic ideal. Owen was distrustful of political methods for the achievement of economic ends. He believed in voluntary association of the people as the instrument of social change. While Cobbett led the political Reformers, Owen, as we shall see, became a great influence on Trade Union and Co-operative development.

We saw that, in the period of distress after 1815, Owen, known hitherto only as a great and benevolent employer and ardent advocate of factory reform, and as a pioneer of education, with some theories of his own about men's characters being made, not by them, but for them by their social environment, came forward with a plan for the employment of the poor on useful work. He was, at this time, in favour with the Government and the governing classes ; for he was no Radical and still actually opposed political reform, and few had realised that his economic doctrines were far more subversive than the most Radical political programme. His plan for the formation of " Villages of Co-operation " in which the unemployed would be set to social production, mainly on the land, but with auxiliary manufactures, was at first seriously taken up by many upper-class people. But gradually its subversive character became clearer, and it was seen that it struck at the root of the whole profit-making system, and that Owen meant it, not as a mere measure of relief for the unemployed, but as the basis of a wholly new economic and social order. His respectable supporters began to fall away, and his fellow-employers to organise strong opposition to his plan. At this stage, he alienated further support by a vigorous attack on organised religions as the greatest sustaining forces of an evil social system. Within a few years he lost nearly all his rich friends ; but, as these left him, their place was taken by working-class converts to his doctrine.

Indeed, Owenism exactly suited the younger generation of intelligent workmen who were growing up inside the new industrial order, and were learning to accept industrialism itself as inevitable. They seized hold of Owen's doctrine of Co-operation, and made it the basis of a new working-class gospel. Owen, with his abounding faith in the power of reason and goodwill, had appealed to the rich to free the poor from their dominion, and to start the new system and teach the workers to govern themselves. The younger workers, who saw that the rich were quite unmoved by these appeals, did not see why they should not, by association, make the new order for themselves. Owen still mistrusted their power, without education, to win or exercise control. They felt more confidence in the ability of their class.

From 1817 to 1823 Owen was ceaselessly active in preaching his new gospel. But he still addressed himself chiefly to the educated and the well-to-do. In 1824, seeing that the ruling classes in Great Britain would do nothing, he made up his mind to test his doctrines in the less contaminated atmosphere of the New World. In America he founded New Harmony, the first of his unsuccessful experiments in the making of Co-operative Communities.

The story of New Harmony falls outside the scope of this book. What is important here is that it caused Owen to be almost continuously away from Great Britain during the years 1824-1829. Working-class Owenism thus developed in the absence of its inspirer. The first Owenite Society—the London Co-operative and Economic Society—and the first Owenite newspaper—*The Economist*—had been founded in 1821 by George Mudie, but in neither had Owen himself any direct share. In his absence Co-operative Societies and newspapers increased and multiplied. William Thompson, the greatest of his disciples, published in 1824 his " Principles of the Distribution of Wealth," and followed this up with other works expounding Owenism in detail and giving practical guidance for the formation of Co-operative Societies. The London Co-operative Society, with William Lovett, later a Chartist leader, as store-keeper, was founded as an actual trading Society in 1826, and in 1828 Dr. William King, of the Brighton Co-operative Society, started *The Co-operator*—best and most influential of the movement's early periodicals. When Owen came back to England in 1829 he found a predominantly working-class movement, based on his doctrines, strongly established and in process of rapid growth.

To the later developments of Owenism we shall return ; but here we have to follow up certain other influences which, in the decade 1820-1830, were giving shape to the rising consciousness of the new working class. Since the days of Adam Smith Political Economy had become a great social power, and its alleged laws had come to command an almost religious devotion. Adam Smith's successors, Malthus and Ricardo, had elaborated and systematised his doctrine, and the rapid development of industrialism had given their writings a powerful sanction. The economists became, even against their own intention, the apologists of things as they were ; it became their appointed mission to demonstrate to the poor, with scientific irrefutability, the virtues and blessings of machine-production and the wage system. Political Economy, the " dismal science," was called upon to justify every abuse of industrialism, by throwing over it the glamour of scientific inevitability, and by holding out the promise of progress to all who ceased to kick against its laws.

This applies, of course, not so much to Malthus and Ricardo as to those who sought to use their doctrines in order to preach the lesson of acquiescence to the workers. Ricardo actually gave his support to Owen's proposals for the employment of the poor, and Malthus was, in private life, by no means the monster he appeared to Cobbett. But politicians, employers, and a host of lesser economists used Political Economy as a form of capitalist propaganda.   By its means, they sought to prove to the poor that low wages were fixed by an iron law, that Trade Unionism and legislation were alike powerless to amend working-class conditions, and that the best hope for the worker lay in a thankful acceptance of his lot.   Middle-class Radicals, followers of Bentham and James Mill, were as intent as hard-headed business men in seeking to combat " Socialist " ideas with the immutable laws of orthodox Political Economy.   Even Francis Place was as " orthodox " in his economics as Ricardo.   He believed fervently in Malthus's " principle of population " and in an inexorable " wages law " which no Trade Union action could affect.

Propaganda bred counter-propaganda.   It was an accepted assumption of Adam Smith and Ricardo that the source of value was to be found in labour. The measure of the value of commodities was the quantity of labour in-corporated in them.   As this view was stated by Smith, " labour " included the labour of the capitalist and the service of his capital, as well as the manual work done by hired labourers.   As it was stated by Ricardo, labour included the " stored labour " with which capital was identified as well as the present output of manual effort.   In both cases the doctrine left intact the claim of the capitalist to share in the product of labour—a claim, indeed, which it had not occurred to either writer to question.   But in the decade from 1820 to 1830 those who were in revolt against Capitalism naturally sought an econ-omic doctrine with which to combat the orthodox Political Economy of the dominant classes.   They seized on this theory of value and made it into a weapon against Capitalism.   In their hands, the labour which is the source of all value became the productive labour of the wage-worker, and upon this theory was raised his claim to the appropriation of the product, and a repudia-tion of the claim of the capitalist to interest or profit.[1]

We can see this theory taking form and substance in the years after 1820. " Piercy Ravenstone " (who may have been William Hazlitt) struck some hard blows at the orthodox economists in his " Doubts as to the Correctness of some Opinions Generally Entertained on the Subject of Political Economy " (1821).   In the same year, Owen's " Report to the County of Lanark," by far the best of his economic writings, plainly enunciated the Socialist form of the labour theory of value.   This " Report " furnished Marx with in-valuable suggestions for his theory.   Two years later, Thomas Hodgskin came to settle in London, took part in founding the London Mechanics' Institution as an educational centre, and began his series of lectures which took shape in " Labour Defended " (1825) and " Popular Political Economy " (1827).   John Gray, William Thompson and many other writers, were working simultaneously along the same lines.   Some recognised a modified capitalist claim to reasonable interest without control ; some recognised no

---

[1] The specific form of Ricardo's theory, which makes circulating capital (i.e. primarily wage-labour) the sole creator of value, lends itself to this Socialist deduction, which was subsequently the basis of Marx's theory of surplus value.

capitalist claim at all. Some, like Thompson and Owen, were Co-operative Socialists ; Hodgskin was rather an anarchist successor of Godwin ; and Ravenstone was rather an anti-capitalist Tory. Common to them all was the repudiation of orthodox economic doctrines, and the exaltation of the virtue and value of labour.

Thus two rival sets of economic doctrines, each purporting to explain industrialism, were competing for the allegiance of the working class. Orthodox Political Economy speedily stepped down from its academic throne in order to combat the new doctrines. Both sides sought to capture the minds of the people. The conflict gave the first powerful stimulus to the movement for adult working-class education.

About 1800, Dr. George Birkbeck, then a teacher at the Glasgow Andersonian Institution, had begun giving courses of scientific lectures to working men. He left Glasgow in 1804 ; but the " Mechanics' Class " survived him. Until 1823 they continued to use the Andersonian Institution as a centre ; but in that year a quarrel occurred and the working-class students split off and founded the Glasgow Mechanics' Institution as an independent body, financed wholly by their own contributions. At almost the same time, Thomas Hodgskin, and a journalist named J. C. Robertson, started in London the *Mechanic's Magazine*, and began to urge the formation of a Mechanics' Institution in London. This brought them into touch with Birkbeck, who had been elected patron of the Glasgow Institution, though he was living in London. With the aid of Francis Place, and other middle and working-class Radicals, this group in 1823 brought the London Mechanics' Institution into being.

But there were two different views among its founders as to the lines along which it should be run. Hodgskin and his group, backed by Cobbett, were all for a purely working-class Institution, entirely supported by working-class money. Birkbeck and Place, who were both members of the Benthamite Utilitarian circle, were equally intent on securing middle-class help. Behind this difference was a further issue. Hodgskin, as we have seen, was a pioneer of the new anti-capitalist economics ; Birkbeck and Place were orthodox followers of Malthus and Ricardo. Hodgskin wanted the Institution to be the means of spreading " Socialist " doctrine as well as a technical institution ; Birkbeck wanted it to be mainly technical and scientific, but also to base itself on an acceptance of the truths of orthodox Political Economy.

A struggle at once developed for the control of the Institution. Robertson was driven from the position of secretary, and a new paper was started in opposition to the *Mechanic's Magazine*. Hodgskin was indeed allowed to go on lecturing ; but the Institution soon passed entirely into the hands of Birkbeck and his friends, who had provided the greater part of the money for its development. It became Birkbeck College, and remains to-day as a constituent " school " of the University of London.

In the years after 1820, Mechanics' Institutions were rapidly founded in town after town, and most of them, whatever their origins, came before long, for financial reasons, under the auspices of the middle-class Radicals. Henry (afterwards Lord) Brougham—Lord Chancellor in the Reform Government of 1830-1832—took a very active part in the movement, which became a powerful instrument in familiarising the workers with the doctrines of Political Economy and the technical achievements of the Industrial Revolution. Directly, the influence of the Mechanics' Institutions was undoubtedly against Socialism and towards the acceptance of orthodox economics. But they did much to stimulate discussion and to kindle working-class interest, and they often applied the stimulus for the organisation of counter-activities by the working-class bodies. Their development had a good deal to do with the educational activity of the working-class movement in the following decade.

The Owenites, like the economists, were great educators. Education was, indeed, the keystone of Owen's Socialist system as well as of his factory experiment at New Lanark. Every Owenite Society carried on educational work, for adults as well as for children, as an integral part of its activity. Thus the advocates of orthodox and unorthodox economic doctrines were equally keen on working-class education, though they meant it to serve different ends. This, however, was only among Radicals. Tories and Whigs, for the most part, continued to denounce all plans for educating the workman "above his station," even when the object was to bring him to an awareness of the truths of orthodox economics. Even Hannah More and the Evangelicals, who wished to limit education for the poor to study of the Scriptures, and of the cheap moral and religious tracts which they turned out in huge editions, were often denounced as teachers of dangerous doctrines. It was a common upper-class view that the poor were much better without knowing how to read.

BOOKS

G. D. H. Cole. *Life of Robert Owen.*
G. D. H. Cole. *Life of William Cobbett.*
G. Wallas. *Life of Francis Place.*
M. Beer. *History of British Socialism,* Vol. I.
G. J. Holyoake. *History of Co-operation.*
W. Lovett. *Life and Struggles.*
A. E. Dobbs. *Education and Social Movements.*
T. Hodgskin. *Labour Defended* (Edited by G. D. H. Cole).
E. Halévy. *Thomas Hodgskin* (in French).

2. THE REPEAL OF THE COMBINATION ACTS

The gradual return of prosperity in the years after 1820 did much to alleviate the distress in the manufacturing districts ; and this, even more than the rise of organisation and the appeals of the Radicals for an orderly

and disciplined movement, accounted for the return to a comparative tranquillity. Exceptional measures of repression were allowed gradually to
lapse ; the activities of spies were relaxed ; and the law was set less freely in
motion against working-class attempts at combination. As panic subsided,
a mood of greater tolerance set in. The power of middle-class Radicalism,
directed, as we have seen, largely to the mobilisation of public opinion,
increased ; it became easier to conceive of reform as something different
from revolution.

This change of temper prepared the way for the repeal of the drastic laws
against working-class combination, which had been passed in the period of
panic after the Nore mutiny of 1797 and the rising of the United Irishmen.
The Combination Acts and the more extreme construction put on the
common law doctrine of conspiracy by the law courts had been part of the
general system of repressive legislation and administration enforced in these
years ; and, as long as the mood which caused them lasted, there was no
chance of their reversal. Accordingly, though their injustice was often denounced, there was no organised movement either among the workers or
among the parliamentary Radicals for their abrogation. Francis Place, the
" Radical breechesmaker " of Charing Cross, who had been a journeyman
but had become an employer and wirepuller-in-chief to the Westminster
Radicals, began to work for the repeal of the laws against combination as
early as 1814 ; but he had practically no following until, after 1820, the
unrest among the workers appeared to be dying down.

Then at last Place began to find supporters who not only held that the
Acts ought to be repealed, but believed repeal to be politically practicable.
He enlisted the Radical M.P., Joseph Hume, and the economist, J. R.
McCulloch, then editor of the Scotsman, and secured the full backing of
the Benthamite group. At the same time Gravener Henson, leader of the
framework knitters, began working along the same lines, with the support
of Peter Moore, M.P., and of George White. But Place soon elbowed
this group out of the way, regarding their proposals as impracticable, and
trusting for success to his own matchless power of pulling wires behind
the scenes.

The story of the manœuvres by which Place and Hume, in 1824, secured
the unconditional repeal of the Combination Acts has been told again and
again. First Hume secured the appointment of a Commons Committee of
Enquiry : then he packed the Committee with his friends—a much easier
thing to do in the unreformed Parliament than at any time since 1832.
The design to repeal the law against combination was covered up by
coupling it with the repeal of other laws against emigration and the export
of machinery. The witnesses were selected, drilled and stage-managed by
Place, who provided Hume with a full brief for their examination. Place
drafted the Report in the form of a series of resolutions, and Hume

wangled it through a committee which was barely conscious of what it was doing. When the official draftsman's Bills, based on the Report, failed to meet Place's wishes, he substituted others, apparently without most of the members knowing the difference. Entirely without debate, and without most of the Cabinet knowing what had happened, the Bill became law. The Acts against working-class combination were completely repealed, and the new Act also removed the illegality of Trade Unions at common law.

But, if the politicians were unaware of the event, the working-class leaders were quite aware of it. At once the Trade Unions came out into the open and began to organise forward movements. Prices had been rising, and, despite prosperous trade, wages had lagged behind. In 1824 and 1825 there was a great outburst of strikes in many occupations, and especially a great strike of the textile workers in Scotland.

This was not at all what Place and Hume had expected. They had argued for the repeal on the plea that it would lead to a great diminution of strikes, if not to an entire disappearance of combinations, except mere local Trade Clubs. Place believed as firmly as Ricardo in the iron law of wages, and as firmly as Malthus in the necessary tendency of population to keep wages down to subsistence level. The laws against combination, he held, encouraged Trade Unions and strikes by preventing the workers from realising their powerlessness to affect the rates of wages. Their hardships, really due to economic laws, they attributed to oppressive legislation. But give them freedom to combine, and they would realise the futility of all combinations more ambitious than the little Friendly Societies of journeymen belonging to a particular trade.

This, however, was not the workers' view. They looked to their new freedom to secure them higher wages, and to the strike as the means of forcing the employers' hands. Place and Hume managed to restrain some of the Unions by pointing out that the probable effect of precipitate strikes would be the re-enactment of the laws just repealed. But they could not prevent a sufficient movement to fill the employers with alarm. The shipowners and shipbuilders especially began to press the Government vigorously to replace the repealed laws by a new measure which would prohibit all raising of funds by bodies of workmen save under licence from a magistrate, who must also agree to act as treasurer and to control the expending of such funds. This proposal was plainly far more drastic than the old Combination Acts, in that it struck equally at Friendly Societies, political and social clubs, and every form of working-class association.

The workers, alive to their danger, formed defence associations in the various towns—forerunners of the Trades Councils of later days. They combined to send delegates and petitions to London to oppose any change in the law, and they worked up a national agitation throughout the country.

The Government, however, pressed on, under the influence of the big employers. A new parliamentary Committee was appointed to inquire into the working of Hume's Act and to propose any necessary changes, and this committee was packed as carefully by the Government as Hume's had been by the friends of repeal. Hume himself, however, could not be excluded ; and once more he and Place set to work. The committee did not propose to hear any working-class witnesses ; but under Place's management the Trade Unions showered in petitions and filled the corridors round the committee room with delegates clamouring to be heard in answer to the charges made against them. At length a few were heard.

By these means the proposals of the Government and the employers were gradually whittled down. But Hume and Place could not prevent some part of their work from being undone. Carrying the battle into both Houses of Parliament, they secured amendments to the new Bill based on the Committee's report. But in the end it fell, in several important respects, short of what had been secured the previous year. As we have seen, prosecutions against workers who struck or combined were launched, before 1824, sometimes under the Combination Acts, but also sometimes, on a charge of conspiracy, under the common law. The Act of 1824 had been designed as far as possible to give complete immunity from both types of prosecution ; that of 1825 gave much more limited protection. It merely legalised combinations for dealing with questions of wages and hours, and, at the same time, hedged round the concession with fresh penalties against " intimidation, molestation, or obstruction," and against any attempt to " coerce " either employers or fellow-workmen. It remained, indeed, lawful to form Trade Unions, but under conditions which made it very difficult for any body of workers to take effective action without incurring penalties either under statute or under common law.

Thus there were many prosecutions of workers after 1825 for virtually the same offences as while the Combination Laws were in force. Nevertheless, the victory was substantial ; for the mere fact of combination could no longer be treated as a crime, and it became possible for Trade Unions to maintain an open and continuous existence. The decade from 1824 to 1834 saw the foundation of openly constituted Trade Unions in a very large number of trades ; and many combinations which had previously disguised themselves as Friendly Societies, or kept up a secret and intermittent activity, came out into the open and adopted proper codes of rules. The Steam Engine Makers' Society and the London Shipwrights' Association in 1824, the Northumberland and Durham Colliers' Union in 1825, the Journeymen Steam Engine Makers in 1826, the Friendly Society of Carpenters and Joiners (later the General Union of Carpenters and Joiners) in 1827, are only a few of the many Trade Unions constituted, or reconstituted, as a direct result of the repeal of the Combination Acts.

3*

The strike movement of 1824-25 was launched at a time of good trade and rising prices, behind which wages had lagged. But at the end of 1825 came a financial crisis, followed by a slump in trade. The workers found themselves no longer pressing for advances, but more often resisting reductions in wages. In Lancashire, where the power-loom was now coming into general use, there were widespread riots, and much machinery was destroyed. There were also strikes among the colliers as well as among the textile workers, and a second attempt was made to create a General Union of all trades, with its headquarters in Manchester (1826). In 1825 John Gast, the shipwright, had started, in London, the Metropolitan Trades Committee, chiefly in order to mobilise working-class opinion against the attempt to reimpose the laws against combination. This body had started the *Trades' Newspaper*, the first journal actually owned and conducted by an organised body of Trade Unionists. It lasted for some years, and was a powerful influence on the side of general working-class solidarity. The ground was being rapidly made ready for the more ambitious attempts at mass Trade Unionism to be described in the next chapter.

The story of the repeal of the laws against combination has usually been told as if it had been entirely the product of Francis Place's genius for successful pulling of wires. Place's own story, which conveys this impression, has been accepted without question. In fact, Place undoubtedly deserves great credit for his work ; and it was certainly he who inspired Hume and the Radicals in Parliament to take the matter up seriously, and he who marshalled the working-class forces in support of the claim. But Place's wire-pulling succeeded in 1824-25, whereas it had failed earlier, because the conditions were then ripe for repeal. That the question was in the air is shown by the fact that another M.P., Peter Moore, prompted by another working-class leader, Gravener Henson, had also drafted a Bill for repeal, as well as by references to the question by Cobbett and other Radicals. The prohibition of all forms of combination was a panic measure, never fully enforced, and only to be maintained in face of a common belief that the working class was bent on revolution. When, after 1820, the unrest appeared to be dying down and some of the emergency measures were allowed to lapse, it was difficult for believers in *laissez faire* to argue that either the Combination Acts or the prohibition of all combinations under the common law ought to be retained. It was, moreover, believed, not only by Place but also by many other Radicals, that combination was chiefly fostered by being repressed, and that freedom of combination would soon teach the workers its futility for all save quite modest and inoffensive objects. This view was not shared by all representatives of the new Capitalism, or acquiesced in by those who regarded all popular combinations as acts of disloyalty to the classes appointed by God to rule ; but it was strongly enough held to carry the day in a Parliament where Radicals and old-fashioned gentry could still sometimes combine to teach the new cotton-lords a lesson.   Place's wire-pulling was invaluable ; but it was not the basis of the movement for repeal.

BOOKS

S. and B. Webb. *History of Trade Unionism.*
G. Wallas. *Life of Francis Place.*
J. L. and B. Hammond. *The Skilled Labourer.*
R. Y. Hedges and A. Winterbottom. *Legal History of Trade Unionism.*

3. THE REFORM MOVEMENT

Meanwhile the movement for the reform of Parliament was speedily gathering force.   The House of Commons up to 1832 not only made no pretence of being a democratic body, but was hardly, in any ordinary sense of the word, a representative assembly.   The most that could be claimed for it was that it " virtually represented " the classes which had a stake in the country—in other words, that it represented property rather than persons. The distribution of seats bore no proportion either to population or even to the number of those who were qualified to vote.   In 1780, the ninety-two members for the counties were returned by 130,000 voters—the county freeholders ; whereas the 421 members who sat for towns and universities were returned by only 84,000 electors.   Moreover, whereas the county elections did, in most cases, give at least the gentry some opportunity of expressing their views, the majority of the borough elections were pure farce. A very few boroughs, such as Westminster and Preston, had a wide franchise and a large body of working-class voters ; but many more had their members chosen by a corrupt corporation or a small body of " freemen," or were wholly under the control of some great peer or landowner.   The newer towns, such as Manchester, were entirely unrepresented ; and many so-called boroughs which returned two members had long shrunk to villages or even to a mere house or two, maintained for the sole purpose of pre-serving the right of election.   Many boroughs were " rotten " ; and many were " proprietary," so that the right to represent them could be bought and sold like any other piece of property.   " Borough for sale " was a familiar advertisement in the newspapers of the time.

The shifting of population and the growth of new towns during the Industrial Revolution made this " virtual representation " still more unreal. Cornwall had forty-four members, whereas Lancashire had fourteen, and all Scotland only forty-five.   Yorkshire returned twenty-eight borough members, but the average electorate per member was only 250.   In 1793 there were fifty-one constituencies with fewer than fifty voters, and 130 with fewer than 300.

This extraordinary system, practically unreformed for centuries, ob-viously lent itself to every form of bribery and corruption.   Where the borough-owner treated his rights as a form of property, the mere voter obviously did the same with his vote. Votes, as well as proprietary seats, were freely bought and sold. Elections were exceedingly expensive, and only rich men could afford to become candidates unless they were heavily subsidised. The constituencies with a wide franchise fell in with the common practice of selling votes. Save in exceptional cases, the only real elections were contests more of bribery than of opinion. Radicals and Reformers, as much as reactionaries, had to bribe or buy their way into Parliament.

Nevertheless, the system was strongly defended on the ground, not that it was logical, but that it produced the best results, by placing power securely in the hands of those classes which were the backbone of the country. It secured the ascendancy of the great territorial families ; but it did not close the door to the rich merchant or financier, or nabob from India, or planter from the West Indies, who could afford to purchase a seat. Until the idea that the vote was a common popular right spread, in the latter half of the eighteenth century,[1] there appeared nothing shocking in the "unrepresentative" character of the electoral machine. The system worked, and put the right people into power. The chief criticism against it came from the lesser landowning classes, who desired to increase county representation, and to decrease the royal influence, which was all-powerful in many of the boroughs.

As we have seen, the Reform Movement which arose between 1769 and 1780 was crushed by the terrors aroused by the Revolution in France. Thenceforth all proposals for reform were denounced as Jacobinism—the first steps towards a complete destruction of British institutions, which would inevitably end in the tearing-up of all property rights and the triumph of Republicanism and Revolution. The Reform agitation, recovering slowly during the later years of the Napoleonic wars, only came to command widespread support in the troublous period which followed the Peace. Thereafter it gradually gathered force until it came to a head in the decisive struggle which issued in the Reform Act of 1832.

We are concerned with this struggle here only in so far as it enters into the history of the working-class movement. The workers were by no means the only class which had reason to object to the unreformed Parliament. Though the rich merchant or financier could find a seat in the House of Commons and climb into the governing class—this openness of the English aristocracy to the infusion of mercantile elements had been for centuries the greatest source of its strength—the growing body of industrial employers and tradesmen found itself, for the most part, excluded and unrecognised. The rapidly increasing middle classes had no share in political power ; the great towns in which they lived were grossly under-represented, or not

---

[1] The idea had, of course, been preached in the seventeenth century, especially under the Commonwealth. But it had almost died out in the Augustan Age which followed the Whig Revolution of 1688.

represented at all, in the House of Commons. The tenant farmers had no share in the county franchise. And all this body of middle opinion, strongly imbued with the idea of its own growing importance, was becoming more and more critical of corruption and inefficiency in high places. The small employer who, by scraping and saving, raised himself to affluence, keenly resented the spendthrift habits of the older rich, and their little way of helping themselves, by pensions and sinecures, out of the public purse. The sharp rise in the taxes, due largely to war spending and the War Debt, roused a vigorous demand for economy and " business government."

At the same time, the demand for Universal Suffrage, as one of the " Rights of Man," had by no means spent the force acquired under the influence of revolutionary thought. Bentham and his followers, indeed, pooh-poohed the rights of man, and argued for Universal Suffrage on utilitarian grounds of common sense ; but Major Cartwright's agitation, and the continued popularity of Paine's writings, kept the doctrine alive in its more revolutionary form. Cartwright, and still more Paine, doubtless appealed chiefly to the working class ; but both Cartwright and Cobbett had also a large following among the smaller middle class, while Cobbett had, in addition, great influence with many of the farmers as well as with the labourers and artisans.

The Reform Movement from 1815 to 1832 was, indeed, essentially a popular movement in which the main body of the working class found itself in temporary alliance with the rising middle classes of the industrial towns. Naturally the latter, who had already some parliamentary influence, tended, in the main, to assume the leadership. Cobbett and Hunt, the outstanding men with influence among the workers, were both countrymen and farmers, not artisans. Gast, Lovett, Benbow, Doherty, and the other working-class leaders occupied only a secondary position. In Parliament the leader of the extreme Radicals was the millionaire Sir Francis Burdett. But none of these men really controlled the strategy of the Reform Movement. From the time when the Whig Party took up the question, the movement passed into the hands of those middle-class elements which were prepared to accept Whig leadership. Henry Brougham counted for more than Burdett in Parliament ; and most of the local Reform Associations and Political Unions were mainly dominated by middle-class men of substance. Their attitude, even when it was Radical, was far more influenced by Benthamism than by the Rights of Man.

But these different groups of Reformers, however varying their real aims might be, were at least united in desiring a reform of Parliament. They tended, therefore, especially in the earlier stages of the campaign, to work together without too close a scrutiny of one another's principles. They could all demand Reform without defining too particularly what they meant. And they could all seize occasions for putting the opponents of Reform in an awkward predicament. The political importance of the famous case of Queen Caroline lay largely in this, that the defence of the Queen against the King could be turned into an attack on George IV. and his anti-Reform Ministers. Brougham and Denham, on the one hand, and Cobbett, on the other, were equally enthusiastic in the Queen's defence. The same bodies as passed republican resolutions one day sent " loyal addresses " to the Queen the next. Loyalty to the Queen became a form of disloyalty to the King and Constitution.

The Queen Caroline case is mentioned here because it was an important factor in giving the Reform Movement a popular backing. Organised by Cobbett, a great working-class agitation sprang up in the Queen's support ; and this, when the case was over, swung itself into the Reform Movement. The creation by Daniel O'Connell and his friends of the Catholic Association in Ireland (1823) was another great encouragement to the Reformers, and Irish oppression was used as a stick to beat the Government. Irishmen were active in every section of the Radical Movement in Great Britain, and especially in the working-class societies in the older towns. The struggle which led to the Catholic Emancipation Act of 1829 did a great deal to dissolve the solidity of the Tories and to prepare the way for the return of the Whig Party to power, under conditions which made parliamentary reform inevitable.

Events abroad also influenced the growth of the movement. The Spanish Revolution of 1820 and the Greek Revolution of 1821 aroused widespread sympathy, while the French and Belgian Revolutions of 1830 were among the chief causes which precipitated the crisis of 1830-1832.

At length, in 1830, the Whigs came back to power, and their leader, Grey, at once announced that parliamentary reform would be the chief item in their policy. But what sort of reform ? The Whig leaders were by temperament fully as aristocratic as the Tories, and had certainly no intention of using their power to institute a democratic system. But they were alive to the strength of public sentiment ; and Brougham and Durham were allowed to have their way despite the protests of a section of the Cabinet. The Reform Bill which the Whig Government introduced actually went further than most people had expected, sweeping away the whole system of rotten boroughs, redistributing seats more in accordance with population, and extending the franchise to practically the whole of the middle class. As against this, it left the manual workers almost wholly voteless, and even took away the votes they had possessed in a few boroughs having an exceptionally wide suffrage. Moreover, vote by ballot, which many Reformers regarded as the indispensable condition for free elections, was not included in the Bill. At once the advocates of Universal Suffrage, and especially the working-class bodies which had been pressing for reform, had to decide upon their attitude to the Whig measure. Should they support it as a blow at the old order, and at least a step towards the new ? Or should they oppose it as merely an attempt to substitute for the domination of the landowning aristocracy the even more hostile rule of the industrial capitalists ?

In 1830 this issue was being debated in every Radical society in which the workers formed an important element. Generally, following Cobbett's lead, the main body of the workers backed the Bill, while declaring their distrust of the Whigs and reiterating their demand for a really democratic measure, including the ballot. But there was a left wing which denounced the Whig Bill, and refused to play any part in supporting a measure of " treason to the working class," Henry Hunt, who had been elected to Parliament in 1830 as Member for Preston, though he voted for the Bill, roundly denounced it in the House and moved many Radical amendments, which were, of course, overwhelmingly defeated.

The first Reform Bill was beaten in Committee in the House of Commons. An excited General Election followed, and gave the Reformers a big majority. A second Bill passed the Commons, only to be beaten in the House of Lords.

The excitement was by this time tremendous ; and the working-class Radicals were swung into the agitation, which had clearly become a national trial of strength. The main body of Radical opinion was organised in a National Political Union, headed by Burdett and largely managed by Francis Place, with local Unions in all the big centres of population. On the central committee of the N.P.U., working-class representatives were given half the seats. The more extreme section of the working classes began to organise a National Union of the Working Classes, with its own local Unions, to demand that nothing less than Manhood Suffrage and Vote by Ballot should be accepted. But the main body of working-class opinion was in favour of fighting for " the whole Bill, and nothing but the Bill," and followed the lead of the N.P.U. The Whig Government, fearful of the popular forces that had been roused, issued Royal Proclamations against the Political Unions, but was not able to prevent their growth. In Birmingham in particular, the Political Union, led by the banker Thomas Attwood, commanded overwhelming support.

Great meetings were held all over the country ; the Political Unions threatened to withhold all taxes until the Bill was passed. At Bristol rioters held the city for several days, sacking the gaols, the Mansion House, and the Bishop's Palace. Derby gaol was sacked, and Nottingham Castle burnt down. In London the King was hustled, and the windows of noted anti-Reformers were broken. A third Reform Bill passed the Commons, and was thrown out by the Lords. Grey asked the King for power to create peers, and was refused. He resigned, and the Duke of Wellington tried to form a ministry with the object of passing, against his own convictions, a Reform Bill going just far enough to divide the Reformers. The Duke failed, and Grey was recalled to power. At the close of a year of unprecedented excitement, the Lords gave way and passed the Bill. In June, 1832, it received the Royal Assent, and became law.

It had been impossible for the working-class bodies, in face of the opposition encountered by the Whig Bill, to press their own claim for a more far-reaching measure. They could only join in the popular cry for " the whole Bill and nothing but the Bill," and prevent it from being whittled down by further compromise with the opponents of Reform. Thus the identity of the main working-class groups appeared for the time to be submerged in the general agitation. But the struggle was, none the less, a big factor in rousing the political consciousness of the workers and preparing the way for the independent working-class political programme of the Chartists.

We can see this independent political movement beginning to develop during the years of agitation. In 1828 the London Irish had organised an Association for Civil and Political Liberty, and in 1829 this had developed into a Society for Radical Reform, supported by most of the advanced working-class Radicals in London. This in turn gave place, in 1830, to the National Union of the Working Classes, the body which chiefly presented left-wing Radical opinion during the critical years of the Reform struggle, and survived long enough to be the direct forerunner of working-class Chartism. In the provinces, the workers were mostly attached to the Political Unions, which were largely under middle-class leadership ; but the N.U.W.C. had its own separate Unions in a number of towns, and was in close touch with the more Radical elements in the Political Unions, and, when the National Political Union was formed in 1831 to unite the local bodies, the working-class elements were strong enough to secure half the seats on its Council.

The Reform Act was carried chiefly by working-class agitation, and by the threat of a revolution in which the workers would have played the leading part. But it left the workers voteless and detached from them the main body of middle-class support on which they had previously relied. The middle classes obtained, in 1832, their share in political power. They had only to use their opportunities in order to ensure that in the long run their interests should dominate national policy. The vast majority of the middle class accordingly dropped out of Radical agitation, and the temporary alliance of middle and working classes was broken. As we shall see, many attempts were made to revive it later, both during the Chartist period and subsequently, and in the end a new alliance was made in the Liberal-Labour compromise of the mid-Victorian period. But for the time the " betrayal " of 1832—as it was widely regarded—left the workers angry and disillusioned. They had won the battle, they felt, and yet they had none of the fruits of victory. They were left in a mood to try what they could do by their unaided efforts against a combination of the old and new ruling classes. We shall find them, in the next chapter, turning to industrial action in their mood of political disillusionment. And then we shall see them, having met defeat in the industrial field, turning back to politics, there to meet with a no less crushing disaster. For the new governing class created in 1832, though aristocrats still held most of the leading positions, was far stronger, and rested on a far broader national basis, than the old. After 1832 the outstanding poachers turned gamekeepers. Cobbett, elected to the Reformed Parliament, found himself one of a tiny minority, fighting the new power as fiercely as ever he had fought the old. Nor did he survive long to carry on the fight. He died in 1835, and the Radical group in Parliament, never strong, disintegrated fast during the ensuing years.

BOOKS

G. D. H. Cole. *Life of William Cobbett.*

G. S. Veitch. *Genesis of Parliamentary Reform.*

J. R. M. Butler. *Passing of the Great Reform Bill.*

E. Porritt. *Unreformed House of Commons.*

G. Wallas. *Life of Francis Place.*

G. M. Trevelyan. *Grey of the Reform Bill.*

G. T. Garratt. *Life of Lord Brougham.*

CHAPTER VI

REVOLUTIONARY TRADES UNIONISM

1. TRADES UNIONISM—THE LABOURERS' REVOLT

THE culminating years of the Reform agitation were also the years during which a mass industrial movement of the workers began to take shape. Politically, the workers were compelled during this time to accept the leadership of the middle classes, and to support the agitation for the Whig Reform Bill. But industrially they were under no such compulsion. The crisis of 1825 was followed by a period of bad trade and irregular employment. This arrested the strike movement which had followed the repeal of the Combination Acts in 1824. But by 1829 there had been a recovery, and the Unions, now able to organise openly under the law, were in a position to resume their forward movement. In 1829, the year of Catholic Emancipation and the year before the return of the Whigs to power, arose the great Trade Union agitation which culminated in the Grand National Consolidated Trades Union of 1834.

The movement began in the great textile districts in the north of England. In January, 1829, the Stockport spinners struck against an attempted reduction in wages. In April the Manchester fine spinners followed them, and in July the rest of the Manchester spinners came out. The Stockport men, their funds exhausted, had to return to work in June, and in October, after a vain attempt to secure arbitration, the Manchester men also went back to work. But these defeats, instead of causing discouragement, provided the incentive to stronger organisation. In December, 1829, under the leadership of John Doherty, a National Spinners' Conference of delegates from England, Scotland, and Ireland met in the Isle of Man and founded the Grand General Union of All the Operative Spinners of the United Kingdom, the first really national Trade Union of the modern type.

Doherty, an Irishman from Ulster and a Catholic, was the most influential Trade Unionist of his time. Migrating to Manchester about 1817, he had speedily become the leading figure in Trade Union circles there. He had helped to organise the movement against the Combination Laws, and, as secretary of the Manchester Spinners, had been the leader of the strike of 1829. He was, moreover, a man of ideas, a keen Owenite and a prominent figure in the agitation for factory reform. The great Spinners' Union of which he became secretary, was, in his mind, only part of a far more ambitious project. We have seen that an attempt had been made in Manchester, in 1826, to form a General Union of all trades. We can hardly be wrong in putting this down largely to Doherty's influence. At all events, he proceeded at once to follow up his success with the spinners by launching a plan for a general co-ordinated movement of the whole working class, and he was modern enough to desire that this should ultimately take shape in a general political, as well as a general industrial, organisation, each section managing its own affairs.

In March, 1830, Doherty started the *United Trades' Co-operative Journal*— the name is a clear indication of Owenite influence—as the herald of the wider movement. In July, 1830, he succeeded in launching the National Association of United Trades for the Protection of Labour, and thus realised his project of " General Union." He resigned his secretaryship of the Spinners and became secretary to the new body, on whose behalf he at once instituted a great organising campaign in the northern counties. At the same time he was working energetically with Richard Oastler, John Fielden, and other factory reformers in the " Ten Hours " Movement, and was helping to establish " Short Time " Committees throughout the textile districts to press the case for Sadler's Factory Bill, then before Parliament.

Meanwhile the Spinners' Union had become involved in a big series of strikes for increased wages. Their policy was to avoid a large-scale conflict, and to attack the employers one by one. This led to reprisals ; and in November, 1830, the masters in Stalybridge, Ashton, and Dukinfield declared a general lock-out. The Union retaliated by calling a general strike over Lancashire ; but in many places the men remained at work. Some disturbances followed, and in one of these a mill-owner was killed. Gradually the men's resistance was beaten down and they were compelled to return to work. But the Union, though weakened, was not broken. It survived to play its part in the events of the next few years. The Scottish and Irish sections, however, seem to have broken away in the course of the struggle of 1830.

The fruits of Doherty's organising work were soon apparent. Twenty trades had been represented at the inaugural meeting of the National Association for the Protection of Labour, and soon the number of affiliated societies rose to about 150. The strength of the Association lay chiefly among the textile workers, and it spread rapidly from Lancashire into the textile districts in the Midlands. But soon other trades began to join also. The Potters' Union, centred in Stoke-on-Trent, was organised in 1830 with Doherty's help. Numerous small societies of millwrights, blacksmiths, and mechanics came in. A delegate conference of miners from Yorkshire, Staffordshire, Lancashire and Cheshire, and North Wales decided to affiliate ; and the

Derbyshire miners also joined the Association. A new weekly, the *Voice of the People*, was started, and sold 30,000 copies a week, though the price was 7d. In 1831 the N.A.P.L. claimed a membership of 100,000.

Doherty made great efforts to extend his new organisation to Yorkshire and to the north-eastern counties; but though parallel movements developed in these areas, they made no contribution to the central funds of the N.A.P.L., except from a very few places. In Yorkshire indeed there grew up, parallel to the N.A.P.L., a powerful Trades Union consisting mainly of workers in the woollen and worsted trades, but with the aim of becoming a "General Trades Union" run on rather different lines. Doherty's organisation was quite open, whereas the Yorkshiremen, faced from the beginning by an attempt of the employers to boycott all Trade Unionists, resorted to secrecy. The Union leaders did their work under feigned names, and, in face of the employers' attitude, violence akin to that of the Luddite days soon made its appearance. The story of the "Yorkshire Trades Union" or the "Leeds Trades Union," or the "Clothiers' Union," as it was variously called, remains at many points obscure; but it survived to play its part in the decisive struggle of 1834, never merging its existence in any other body.

Meanwhile, Doherty's National Association had fallen to pieces. Here too the record is obscure; but the Spinners seem to have accused Doherty of neglecting their interests for his wider projects of industrial and political organisation, and the parent Lancashire section seems to have dropped away from the Association, leaving it with its main strength in the Midland textile districts and in South Wales. In 1832 Doherty started a new journal, *The Poor Man's Advocate*, as the organ of the movement, and later he threw his energies into the Owenite Society for National Regeneration, which took for its object the attainment of the eight hours day by a simple refusal to work any longer. But by 1832 the National Association had ceased to have any pretensions to rank as a truly national or inclusive body, and had broken up into a number of separate sections, most of which presently merged their identity in Robert Owen's Grand National Consolidated Trades Union of 1833.

A large number of miners' lodges, we have seen, became connected with the N.A.P.L. In South Wales a Friendly Society of Coal Mining was formed in 1831, and connected itself with Doherty's organisation. But the outstanding miners' movement, in the highly-developed coalfield of Northumberland and Durham, seems to have been independently organised. The colliers in these districts had formed a Union in 1825; but in 1830, under the leadership of "Tommy" Hepburn, this was revived and greatly extended. Some sort of informal pit organisation had long existed among the miners; but now they came together in a powerful Union, and drew up a schedule of grievances, announcing that they would refuse to enter into any "bond" until these were remedied. The system of the "yearly bond" was still the prevailing form of wage contract in the mining districts.

The strike of 1831 ended in a victory for the men, the coal-owners making substantial concessions. But in the following year the owners reorganised their forces, and the dispute broke out anew. At about half the pits work continued, and the men paid large levies in support of those involved in the struggle. At the other half the owners declared war on the Union, and began the systematic importation of blacklegs from other districts. This led to violence, which was savagely repressed. After a long resistance, the Union was broken, and the men returned to work on the employers' terms, which included in most cases renunciation of the Union. Hepburn himself, after a long struggle to maintain himself as a hawker, was compelled to give way and to accept employment on these terms. He was a great leader, active in the Reform agitation as well as in Trade Union work. But after 1832 he dropped out of the movement, the men whom he had led not daring, for fear of victimisation, to have any further dealings with him. Hepburn lived on into the 'seventies, but he took no further part in either Trade Unionism or politics. He had given his word in accepting employment, and he kept it.

London was not unaffected by the wave of Trade Unionism which spread over the country about 1830. In 1831 the London workers formed a Metropolitan Trades Union, federating the various separate Societies, and this body entered into relations with Doherty and the N.A.P.L. But, for the most part, the attention of the London workers during the years up to 1832 was concentrated on the Reform struggle, and the political National Union of the Working Classes played a larger part than any purely Trade Union body. Far less affected than the North by the new methods of production, and, as a rule, far better paid, the London artisans tended to take the lead in political rather than in industrial organisation.

The South, however, had its full share of the awakening. In the late summer of 1830 began the despairing mass movement in the agricultural districts, which has been described by Mr. and Mrs. Hammond as "the last labourers' revolt." From the beginning of the century the condition of the rural workers had been growing steadily worse. During the war the sharp rise in prices had brought no corresponding advance in wages, while the speeding-up of enclosures and the new methods of farming had caused a serious decline in the demand for labour. When it became literally impossible for the labourers to live on the customary wages, the farmers and justices, instead of raising wages, pursued the policy of supplementing them out of poor relief—the so-called Speenhamland system, named after the place at which it was first introduced. Thereafter, in the South and the Midlands, it became the practice for agricultural wages to be made up to subsistence standard by poor relief, varying with the size of the family. The poor rates naturally grew at an alarming rate, and there was strong pressure from farmers and landowners for their reduction. This was attempted, not by raising wages, but by a progressive reduction in the standard of living allowed to the labourers, who were thus steadily forced down to starvation level. Moreover, under the poor law a system of bond labour developed, and the unfortunate " paupers " were hired out in gangs, virtually as slaves, to work on the farms or the roads without wages in return for the relief secured from the parish.

For the better carrying out of the policy of beating down the poor rates, many parishes combined under a permissive Act into " Unions," and appointed paid overseers to administer the law. Naturally, these overseers became exceedingly unpopular ; for their business was both to reduce the scales of relief and to deter persons from getting it by every means in their power. Against the overseers the greatest resentment was displayed in the revolt of 1830.

There had been, in the years of distress after 1815 and intermittently ever since, a certain amount of rick-burning, and even rioting, among the half-starved workers in the rural districts. In 1830, under stress of the excitement general throughout the country, these disturbances assumed a more extended character. In East Anglia, Kent, Surrey, Sussex, Hampshire, Wiltshire, and a number of other counties, a general revolt developed. In one village after another the labourers, with no previous organisation, threw up leaders out of their own ranks, assumed control of the village, and marched forth to destroy the hated threshing-machines, to burn the ricks of unpopular farmers or landowners, to demand the remission of tithes and rents and the payment of higher wages, and occasionally to give an unpopular overseer a ducking in the local horse-pond. Apart from this last, there was a complete absence of violence to persons ; in the entire revolt the labourers appear not to have killed or wounded a single person. It is clear that a good many of the farmers sympathised with them, and a few gave them positive help.

The governing classes, however, speedily took fright, and urgent demands were sent to the Government for the suppression of the revolt. The Whigs, who had just assumed office, were intent on proving themselves as doughty champions of law and order as the Tories, in the hope of disarming opposition to their proposals for Reform. Lord Melbourne, at the Home Office, who was besides a most reluctant and insincere reformer, was as ready to use strong measures against the labourers as he showed himself against Hepburn's Colliers' Union in 1832. Troops were rushed into the affected areas and order was speedily restored, for the unarmed labourers were far too weak even to attempt resistance. Wholesale arrests were made and Special Commissions were sent down to try the offenders. Nine persons were hanged, 457 transported, and about 400 more sentenced to varying terms of imprisonment. Among those hanged was Henry Cook, of Micheldever, a lad of nineteen, whose chief offence was that he had hit Bingham Baring, the financier, with a stick and severely damaged his hat.

The savage suppression of the revolt—which did not prevent the sporadic continuance of secret rick-burning and machine-breaking—was partly the result of panic, arising in the guilty consciences of the landowners, and partly a Whig demonstration of faith in the sacred rights of property. It caused fierce resentment among the working-class Radicals, and was a means of arousing their hatred of the reforming Whigs, whom they accused of hypocrisy and betrayal of the poor. Richard Carlile, the Radical journalist, protested vigorously, defending the revolt, and was put in prison. Cobbett, though he did not defend rick-burnings, upheld the labourers' cause, and fiercely attacked the Whigs for their brutality. At the King's special instance the Government launched a prosecution against him. But Cobbett was a dangerous man to attack. His defence turned the case into " a trial of the Government more than of Cobbett," and, when the jury disagreed, the Government was only too glad to drop the prosecution. Order had been restored ; too much zeal might provoke a far more formidable revolt. Actually, after the trouble had died down, there was a slight rise in agricultural wages, and the position of the workers was slightly improved. For the moment the " last labourers' revolt " had given the governing classes a salutary fright. But within a few years the new Poor Law of 1834 ended the Speenhamland system without putting an end to the sufferings of the labourers. From 1831, through all the successive waves of industrial and political agitation, there was no important movement among the agricultural workers till the rise of Joseph Arch's Union in the 'seventies. Repression and starvation had done their work ; and the more active spirits were steadily drained away to the towns, where they could at least escape from the deadening despair of the village.

BOOKS

S and B. Webb. *History of Trade Unionism.*
J. L. and B. Hammond. *The Skilled Labourer.*
J. L. and B. Hammond. *The Village Labourer.*
G. D. H. Cole. *Attempts at General Union, 1829–1834* (International Review of Social History, 1939).

2. THE RISE OF OWENISM

This great growth of Trade Unionism was the opportunity of the Owenite Socialists. For ten years or more the Owenite gospel of Socialism or Co-operation had been making headway among small, but growing, groups of workers up and down the country. At first these groups established only propagandist societies, devoted to education—always a primary matter with the Owenites—and to the spread of Co-operative knowledge. The Owenites began, however, through these societies, to collect funds with the object of starting self-governing " Villages of Co-operation " on the Owenite principle.   Thus the London Co-operative Society, founded in 1824, started a subsidiary Co-operative Fund Association.   It also, in 1826, established the *Co-operative Magazine* as the organ of the movement.   It had already set up a store for the supply of articles of necessity to its members. James Watson and William Lovett, among the best known of the working-class leaders, were its first and second store-keepers.

The idea of opening shops appealed to these early Co-operators, not so much in itself as in relation to the larger end which they had in view.   According to Owen's doctrine, it was the mission of the " productive classes " to supersede Capitalism by Co-operation, and to establish by social action an entirely new system.   Owen had looked to the benevolent rich to provide the funds for setting up the new order ; his working-class disciples looked mainly to themselves.   A store for trading on a Co-operative basis appealed to them, first because it actually superseded one form of competitive trading—distribution—by a method based on Owen's ideas, secondly, because it offered an opportunity for craftsmen in different trades to exchange their goods by a sort of barter, dispensing with capitalist intermediaries, and thirdly because it afforded the means of raising a fund which could be allowed to accumulate and then applied to the establishment of a Co-operative or Socialist community. (The two words were used, at this stage, almost interchangeably.)   In the Co-operative Stores goods could be sold at ordinary trade prices, and the balance saved by cutting out the retailer's profit could be paid into a fund to be used for this or other forms of Co-operative enterprise.

There were intermediate stages between mere shopkeeping and the founding of " Villages of Co-operation."   Why, it was soon asked, should not the members co-operate to make for one another instead of buying from the capitalist the goods which they sold in their stores ?   As the Trade Unions grew after 1825, Owenism began to appeal to them, and especially to the skilled handicraftsmen, who were still an important element in the towns.   Groups of workers belonging to a particular craft began to set up Co-operative Societies of a different type—societies of producers which offered their products for sale through the Co-operative Stores.   Individual craftsmen, who were Socialists, or who saw a way of escape from the exactions of the middleman, also brought their products to the Stores to sell. Early in 1830 the London Society opened an Exchange Bazaar for the use of societies and individuals with products for sale or mutual exchange.

Before this the movement, as a whole, had taken a decisive leap forward. In 1827 a group of workers, previously connected with the Brighton Mechanics' Institution, formed, under the guidance of Dr. William King, a philanthropic physician and a friend of Lady Noel-Byron, who helped his enterprises, the Brighton Co-operative Society. This was successful, and other stores and productive associations soon arose out of it. In 1828 Dr. King, feeling the need to give the growing movement a clear lead, began to issue from Brighton *The Co-operator*, a practical and simply written journal of the new system. *The Co-operator* had a great success. It was read all over the country and exerted a big influence. When it ceased publication in 1830 the number of Co-operative Societies had already grown from a dozen or two to more than 300.

Meantime, in 1829, Robert Owen had recognised the failure of New Harmony, his Co-operative Community in America, and had returned to England. At first he was not quite sure what to make of the movement which his followers had created in his absence, and was inclined to mistrust the power of the workers to organise for themselves without the financial help or guidance of the " educated classes." But very soon he was swept into the stream and realised that his ideas had become the basis of a great popular movement. As the founder of the new system, he stepped naturally into a position of leadership.

In 1829 an attempt was made to link up the movement by the foundation of a central body—the British Association for the Promotion of Co-operative Knowledge—with a new journal, the *British Co-operator*, as its principal organ. A few months later, Doherty's journal, already mentioned, the *United Trades' Co-operative Journal*, became the organ of the movement in the north of England. Growth was rapid ; in 1832 the number of Co-operative Societies had risen to nearly 500. In 1831 the first national Co-operative Congress met, and attempted to launch a plan—discouraged by Owen as premature—for founding Villages of Co-operation. Thereafter, Congresses met half-yearly in various towns.

This astonishing growth of the Co-operative Movement, running parallel with the Reform agitation, but wholly separate from it, demands further analysis. The Co-operative Societies connected with the movement were of several distinct types. First, there were the purely educational and propagandist bodies, preaching the whole social gospel of Owenism, and including a great many Owenite sympathisers who were not of the working class. These were grouped round the central Owenite body which, passing through many changes of name, was best known as the National Union of the Industrious Classes. Of this group Owen was the unquestioned leader. In 1832 it created a Social Missionary and Tract Society for propaganda on a national scale ; and in many towns the local societies acquired rooms or buildings of their own, which were the centres, not only of their own work, but of the whole movement in their localities.

Secondly, there were the Co-operative Stores or Shops, mostly run by enthusiastic Owenites, but occupying an intermediate position. Thirdly, there were, especially from 1830 onwards, the societies of producers, aiming at Co-operative production of goods and looking to the Stores to provide them with a market. These naturally arose first in trades requiring comparatively little capital or plant. They appealed especially to craftsmen whose independence was being threatened by the rise of factory production or of sub-contracting through capitalist middlemen.

The most significant feature of the years we are discussing was the rapid rise of this third type of Co-operative Society and the direct entry of the Trade Unions into Co-operative production. Most of these Societies were based directly upon or at least very closely connected with the Unions of their trades, and many of them were actually indistinguishable from these Unions, which took up production as a part of their Union activity—especially for giving employment to their members who were out of work or involved in trade disputes. In London and in other towns this led to further development—the formation of United Trades Associations, which were close federations of the Societies and Unions engaged in Co-operative production. These bodies, and their constituent elements, were not necessarily Owenite or Socialist, in the sense of accepting or understanding the whole Owenite or Socialist gospel. They were bodies of workmen, attracted by the new ideas, and seeking to use them as means of mutual advancement and defence.

Indeed, one of the commonest arguments in favour of these producers' societies was that they could be valuable auxiliaries in the struggle for better conditions. Co-operative production could be set on foot for the employment of members who were out of work, especially in connection with a trade dispute, and by this means the members could maintain themselves instead of becoming a drain on the scanty funds of the Unions. This was one of the principal attractions of the proposal to the Trade Unionists ; we find Co-operative production constantly urged as an alternative to strike pay during the troublous times which began in 1830.

It was this third type of Co-operative Society that Owen set out specially to foster when he assumed the leadership of the movement. In it he saw the chance of bringing the rising Trade Unions over to the acceptance of his full Socialist gospel. Owen and the Owenites set out definitely to capture the Trade Unions for Owenite Socialism.

As soon as the workers turned to Co-operative production, there arose a far more difficult problem than any that confronted the mere shopkeeping Co-operative Store. The Store bought wholesale what its members needed, and sold it retail. The productive Society had to find somewhere a market for all its products. We have seen how, in 1830, the London Co-operators opened an Exchange Bazaar. But this was on a small scale, and the rapid growth of the movement soon made necessary a bigger agency for sales.

Out of this need arose the idea of Labour Exchanges, where workmen or producers' Co-operative Societies could directly exchange their products in such a way as to dispense altogether with either capitalist employers or capitalist merchants. The chief example of this new type of organisation, based on the labour theory of value, was Robert Owen's National Equitable Labour Exchange, which opened its doors in 1832, and was soon followed by similar Exchanges in Birmingham, Liverpool, Glasgow, and other centres. The Labour Exchange was designed to enable the various groups of producers to exchange their products one with another at an equitable valuation based on " labour time," and was also, for the time, to be the means whereby they could reach the wider market of the general public. In 1820, in his famous " Report to the County of Lanark," Owen had put forward the view that, as labour was the sole creator of value,[1] the amount of labour that went to the making of any commodity was the only fair measure of its value or price. The right way, therefore, of pricing goods was to calculate the amount of average human labour-power embodied in them.

This principle, adapted to meet the exigencies of the situation, Owen now sought to apply. Prices in the Exchanges were based on the cost price of the raw material, to which was added the sum corresponding to the " socially necessary labour-time " absorbed in production. Differences in current rates of wages were taken as measuring the differing values of differing types of labour. Pricing was done by Trade Union valuers appointed by the Exchanges[2] and a new currency of Labour Notes was issued for the conduct of transactions.

As soon as the Exchanges were opened the producers' societies began a brisk deposit of goods. These were readily bought, both by Co-operators and by the general public. Owen's Labour Notes for a time not only passed current among members of the movement, but were widely accepted by private shopkeepers in payment for goods. This is not so surprising as it sounds. The age was one in which private note issues made by small banks were a familiar form of currency, private tradesmen often issued their own copper " tokens ", and even private employers, in face of the shortage of national currency, had sometimes in emergencies issued their own notes.

For a time all went well. But the Labour Exchange system had obvious weaknesses. It was not easy for labour values and ordinary commercial values to exist side by side. Goods which the Exchange sold for less than the private tradesman were speedily disposed of ; goods for which it asked more remained on the shelves. Above all, the Exchanges could not, like ordinary shops, control their stocks to fit the demand. They had to take what was brought to them ; and this meant that they were overstocked with the products of trades in which the movement was strong, and understocked with goods which could not be produced by small groups of craftsmen, with

[1] See page 53.
[2] For a fuller account, see my *Life of Robert Owen*, pp. 252 ff. Owen's *Report to the County of Lanark* is reprinted in my edition of his *New View of Society, and Other Writings*, in Everyman's Library.

little capital at their command. In spite of this, the Exchanges met for a time with considerable success. Started originally with Owen's own money, the London Exchange was taken over in 1833 by the London United Trades Association, the federal body uniting the various producers' societies, or " Union Shops," as they were commonly called. It was carried on with apparent success until 1834 ; but by that time business had seriously fallen off, and it went down in the general crash to be described in the next section. The Birmingham Exchange, which also wound up its affairs in 1834, was able to pay all its debts and to present its surplus to the local hospital. But the London Exchange ended with a heavy deficit, which fell on Owen.

1832 was the year, not only of Owen's Labour Exchanges, but also of the Builders' Union, which is dealt with in the next section. It saw also the beginning of a new phase in the agitation for factory reform. Hitherto, the workers in the textile districts had been chiefly concerned in pressing for the passing into law of Sadler's Factory Bill, which was designed to establish the Ten Hours Day. But now, under the influence of Doherty, Owen, and John Fielden, the Radical manufacturer, they began to consider the use of industrial action in shortening the hours of work. The idea of the general strike was in the air ; William Benbow had published, in 1831, his pamphlet on the " Grand National Holiday " ; and Owen, in his lectures up and down the country, was steadily insisting that the new powers of production were amply great enough to enable all the world's work to be done in a day of not more than eight hours. Owen and Fielden were calling for a great eight hours movement, aided by the enlightened employers, and taking the form of a concerted refusal, backed, if necessary, by a general stoppage, to work more than eight hours a day. This movement, which greatly annoyed Richard Oastler and other leaders of the Ten Hours agitation, who regarded it as impracticable, took shape in 1833, in a new organisation largely under Owen's guidance. Doherty, Owen, and Fielden launched, in Manchester, the National Regeneration Society, with the eight hours day as the immediate objective, and under its auspices a great Trade Union agitation spread through the northern textile areas.

Thus, in 1833, Owen was at the head of several distinct, but closely-related, movements commanding working-class enthusiasm and allegiance. The Owenite Societies, the Co-operative Stores, the " Union Shops " or producers' societies, the Labour Exchanges, the Trade Unions, and the National Regeneration Society all looked to him for leadership. The Reform Act had become law, and the great body of workers who had been engrossed in political agitation were in a mood of disillusionment and hostility towards the victorious middle class. The main force of working-class opinion swung instinctively towards the industrial movement. Owenism became the current gospel of the working-class leaders ; political interest was for the time submerged. The way was made ready for the union of all the movements described in this chapter into a single inclusive movement, seeking, by united industrial action, to change the whole basis of society, and even to overthrow Capitalism and establish Socialism by one revolutionary industrial uprising. For a time the centre of interest was the great Operative Builders' Union, which seemed to symbolise the rising power and self-confidence of the "industrious classes."

BOOKS

G. D. H. Cole.   *Life of Robert Owen.*
G. D. H. Cole.   *A Century of Co-operation.*
F. Podmore.   *Life of Robert Owen.*
T. W. Mercer.   *Dr. William King and " The Co-operator."*
B. Potter (Mrs. Webb).   *The Co-operative Movement.*
G. J. Holyoake.   *History of Co-operation.*
R. Owen.   *A New View of Society, and Other Writings* (Everyman's Library).

3. THE OPERATIVE BUILDERS

The Operative Builders' Union came into prominence in 1832. The actual date of its foundation is uncertain, but it was probably either 1831 or 1832. Hitherto, the building workers had been organised in a number of separate craft societies, for the most part confined to a single town. The Carpenters and Joiners had, indeed, formed a national society in 1827, and probably one or two other national craft unions were in existence before the O.B.U. was founded. But, if so, these were small and weak, and in the north of England at any rate still largely secret societies. It was with the foundation of a single Union, openly organising all sections of the industry, that the builders leapt suddenly to the forefront of the Trade Union world. The membership of the new body rose rapidly to 40,000, and seems at one stage to have reached at least 60,000.

At first the Builders' Union directed its efforts to the improvement of wages, the elimination of non-unionists, and the denunciation of "general contracting," already long established in London, but in the provinces only then beginning widely to replace the older system by which master joiners, master masons, etc., contracted separately for the different jobs involved in erecting a building. In 1832 and 1833 the Union won a number of victories, successfully enforcing the greater part of its demands by local action. Members flocked in, and it became easily the leading Trade Union in the country. Its success caused widespread alarm ; the newspapers published leading articles denouncing its " tyranny " ; and with victory came wider ambitions and increasing confidence in its power.

Owen was at this time going up and down the country enlisting the Trade Unions in support of his schemes. Naturally, he and his supporters soon turned their attention to the O.B.U. James Morrison, one of the leaders of the Union and an enthusiastic Owenite, started a weekly journal, *The Pioneer*, as its organ, and there preached the virtues of the Owenite system. Owen himself addressed the builders' lodges and enlisted their support. In collaboration with Morrison and other Owenites, he drafted for the Union a comprehensive programme, which embodied the full acceptance of his schemes. At the Builders' "Parliament," the National Conference of the Union, held at Manchester in September, 1833, he secured the complete adoption of this programme. The greatest Trade Union in the country thus swallowed Owenism whole.

Nor was this merely an acceptance of the Owenite theory. What Owen put before the Builders' "Parliament" was a practical plan of action. He had been persuading many other Unions to embark on Co-operative production by opening "Union Shops" of the type described in the last section. These were appropriate to the small local Unions with which he had usually to deal ; but the Builders' Union was a great national organisation, extending over a large part of the country, and with the majority of the skilled building workers in its ranks. To it he accordingly proposed a far more ambitious plan. The Builders' Union was not merely to start Co-operative building in competition with the master builders ; it was to take over at a blow the entire building industry, and to reorganise it as a Grand National Guild under the direct control of the Union. Master builders, if they had the sense, were to be allowed to join the Union and to become its servants, subject to election by the members. Those who did not join were to be frozen out, because no one would work for them. The Guild itself was to employ all its members, paying them a regular salary in work or out, and was to undertake to carry through the whole of the building work of the country.

The Union and the Guild were to be, not two separate bodies, but one and the same. For this purpose the Union was to revise its rules, and the craft sections in which it was organised were to surrender their autonomy and to come under "universal government." The whole Union was to be organised, no longer for mere bargaining about wages and conditions, but for the direct control and conduct of industry.

So well had the preliminary work of persuasion been done that this plan was enthusiastically accepted by the Builders' "Parliament," and the Executive was instructed to launch the National Guild at once. At Birmingham, where the Owenites were strongest, plans were at once laid for the building of a great Guildhall, to serve as the headquarters of the Union and a place where educational work could be carried on. Two Owenite architects, Joseph Hansom—best remembered as the inventor of the "hansom" cab—and Edward Welsh, made the plans and raised the money needed for financing the scheme. Work on the Guildhall was begun in a fever of enthusiasm.

But the master builders were not likely to allow themselves to be superseded without a struggle. After the Union victories of 1832-33 they had set to work to organise with a view to the renewal of the contest, and at the time when the Builders' "Parliament" adopted Owen's scheme a great strike or lock-out was already in progress in the Manchester district, one of the Union's chief strongholds. The masters had made up their minds to break the Union, and to every man involved in the dispute they presented the "document"—a familiar instrument in building conflicts even in much later times—demanding renunciation of all connection with the O.B.U.

Birmingham, too, was the centre of a great lock-out, and disputes soon broke out in other districts as well. The Executive of the O.B.U. found itself facing, with quite inadequate financial resources, a whole series of strikes and lock-outs at the very moment when it was also attempting to re-organise the Union and to launch Owen's ambitious scheme for a National Guild. It had to meet, moreover, a dissentient minority within its own ranks which objected to the system of "universal government" and to the adoption by the Union of Socialist aims and policy. This group, known as the "exclusives," demanded the breaking up of the Union into a federation of autonomous craft societies. It was a small group at first; but it gained ground as the difficulties increased.

Early in 1834 the Manchester men began to give way and to sign the "document" renouncing membership of the Union. The Birmingham employers were also able to carry on with blackleg labour, and there, too, the hold of the Union was weakening. Work on the Guildhall had to be suspended for a time for lack of funds, and was only resumed under great and increasing difficulties. The Guild secured and executed a few small contracts for friendly clients; but, for the most part, those who wanted to have buildings erected showed no desire to deal with it.

London, the third strong centre of the Union, had hitherto been free from any big dispute. But in the middle of 1834 it, too, became involved. Combe, Delafield and Co., the brewers, placed a ban on Trade Union labour; and the builders retorted by placing a ban on their beer. Cubitts, the master builders, thereupon forbade the drinking of any beer except Combe, Delafield's on their jobs. The men struck, and the other masters declared a sympathetic lock-out, and presented the now familiar "document" to the men, who replied with a refusal to work with non-unionists. The dispute dragged on for several months; but here, too, in the end the men were beaten.

These defeats caused a revulsion of feeling, and the "exclusives" rapidly gained ground. In September, 1834, the masons seceded from the Builders' Union, and reconstituted their section of the Union as a separate body. This was followed by other secessions, and towards the end of the year the Operative Builders' Union ceased to exist, and fell apart into its constituent elements. The Carpenters, Stonemasons, Bricklayers, and Plumbers managed to maintain national societies, though with a greatly reduced membership ; the national organisations of Painters, Plasterers and Slaters wholly disappeared, and these trades fell back upon purely local trade clubs of the old sort. The Birmingham Guildhall was sold, unfinished, to a private buyer, who finished it and turned it into a warehouse. The National Guild, of course, went down with the Union, and left not even a trace behind.

The story of the great Builders' Union has been told here as if it had been an isolated struggle. But, in fact, the whole of its later history and collapse is bound up with the story of the greater body of which Owen and his followers designed that it should form only a single section. It is impossible really to disentangle the history of the O.B.U. from that of the Grand National Consolidated Trades Union, to the collapse of which its disintegration was doubtless chiefly due. Its significance, therefore, can only be understood in relation to the wider movement of which it formed a part. To the record of this movement we must now turn our attention.

BOOKS

R. W. Postgate. *The Builders' History.*
G. D. H. Cole. *Life of Robert Owen.*
S. and B. Webb. *History of Trade Unionism.*

4. THE GRAND NATIONAL CONSOLIDATED TRADES UNION

Owen came back from the Builders' "Parliament" of 1833, which he had persuaded to a complete acceptance of his plans and to the launching of the Builders' Guild, in a condition of fervent enthusiasm and hope. He was sure that within a few months the reign of Capitalism would be ended, and the Co-operative system be securely established by the common determination of the " industrious classes." And he was sure that the time had come for all trades to follow the example of the Builders, and to decide to take the control of production into their own hands. For this purpose a new instrument must be created. The working-class dream of a single inclusive Union of all workers must be realised in fact, and the great Union must absorb all sectional bodies, such as the Builders, and must take to itself the supreme direction of national affairs.

Owen came back in order to attend a National Conference of Trade Unions, " Union Shops," and Co-operative Societies, which had been summoned to meet in London at the beginning of October, 1833. To this gathering he unfolded his wider plan, and proposed the formation of a " Grand National Moral Union of the Productive Classes of Great Britain and Ireland." All Trade Unions, Co-operative Societies, Benefit Societies, and " all other associations intended for the improvement of the working classes " were urged to form themselves into affiliated lodges of this great Union. The plan was enthusiastically endorsed, and a provisional council was appointed to carry on the work of organisation pending a further Conference, at which formal rules were to be framed. Without any previous notice, or any direct mandate to the delegates from those who sent them, the " One Big Union " was brought into being. In February, 1834, a second Conference drew up a constitution, and adopted the title of the Grand National Consolidated Trades Union, by which this leviathan is usually known.

Thus the plan mooted in 1818, and again in 1826, and seriously attempted by Doherty in 1830, seemed at last in a fair way to realisation. But the great Union launched under Owen's influence had far more ambitious aims than any of its predecessors. Its immediate object was nothing less than the entire supersession of Capitalism and of the system of competition by a Co-operative system of workers' control. It aimed, not only at controlling industry, but at superseding Parliament and the local governing bodies, and at becoming the actual Government of the country. " There are two Parliaments in London at present sitting ; and we have no hesitation in saying that the Trades' Parliament is by far the most important, and will, in the course of a year of two, be the most influential." So wrote J. E. Smith in the Owenite *Crisis*, contrasting the democratic suffrage of the Unions with the still narrow franchise of even the reformed House of Commons.

The formation of the " Grand National " was followed by a feverish period of Trade Union activity. Countless existing Unions linked up with the new body ; and countless new societies were formed. The Owenite associations became " Miscellaneous Lodges " of the " Grand National " ; " Union Shops," local Trade Unions, and Committees of United Trades passed over *en bloc* into the larger organisation. Before long half a million members were enrolled ; and it was estimated that all the Trade Unions together had a membership of more than a million. The Builders' Union, however, refused to merge its identity in the larger body, and the " Yorkshire Trades Union," already involved in a bitter conflict with the employers in the woollen and worsted trades, maintained its independent secret organisation. Everywhere there was eager starting of new " Union Shops " and Co-operative Societies. Women workers and agricultural labourers were organised in considerable numbers. Even the Benefit Societies, then engaged in concerted action in order to secure better legal protection, were swept into the current of Owenism, and a project was launched for the formation by them of an Agricultural and Manufacturing Association, whereby they could apply their accumulated funds to Co-operative production.

But already the storm was gathering. In November, 1833, the employers at Derby, where the Trades Union had inherited a strong following from Doherty's earlier National Association, presented the " document " to their workers, and locked out all who belonged to the Union. The " Grand

National " was thus faced with the problem of financing a great dispute before it had any rules or any central fund of its own. At almost the same time the hosiery workers in Leicester were locked out for joining the Union, and similar troubles arose in Glasgow and in several other towns. Simultaneously, as we have seen, the Builders' Union was engaged in its great struggles in Manchester and Birmingham.

The " Derby turn-out " was by far the largest and most spectacular of these disputes ; and it became the test struggle to which all eyes were turned. The Union lodges in all parts of the country collected money on behalf of the Derby " turn-outs," and this was applied partly as strike pay, but also largely in starting schemes of Co-operative production. As soon as the " Grand National " had adopted a constitution it decreed a shilling levy in support of the Derby dispute ; but after four months' struggle the Union could finance the stoppage no longer, and the workers were compelled to go back to work on the employers' terms.

Meanwhile, a second smashing blow had been delivered at the Union. A group of agricultural workers at Tolpuddle, in Dorset, led by two brothers named Loveless, formed a lodge of a Friendly Society of Agricultural Labourers, designed to become one of the constituents of the " Grand National." They were promptly arrested by the local magistrates, and, after a most summary trial, were sentenced to seven years' transportation for the crime of administering unlawful oaths. This was done, despite the legalisation of Trade Unions in 1824-5, under an Act passed at the time of the Naval Mutinies of 1797—an Act certainly never intended to be used against Trade Unions as such.

At this time it was the practice of many Trade Unions to adopt an elaborate ritual and ceremony of initiation, which included the administration of an oath of loyalty. This is easily explained. It was, in part, a common form, taken over from the Friendly Societies, out of which many of the Unions had grown, and derived from a common origin with the ceremonies of the Freemasons. It was especially elaborate in the building trades, and was probably adopted by a number of sections of the " Grand National " on the model of ceremonies which had been long in use in craft societies merged in the Operative Builders' Union. It had further acquired a special solemnity during the period when the Combination Acts forced the Unions to organise secretly, and to exact from their members pledges not to divulge their proceedings, and was particularly employed by the " Yorkshire Trades Union " and by others which had resorted to secrecy in face of the employers' attempts to refuse work to known Trade Union members. Owen, from the first, disapproved of these oaths and ceremonies as " relics of barbarism " ; but he was unable to prevent their continuance.

These practices now afforded to the Whig Government a pretext for teaching the Trades Unions an exemplary lesson. Their rapid growth and extensive aims had revived the panic of the governing classes and had put them in a mood for drastic measures. The Acts against the administering of oaths by unlawful societies, passed after the Nore mutiny of 1797, had been renewed in the " Six Acts " of 1819. These laws were now invoked against the unfortunate agricultural labourers who had joined the Union formed by Loveless and his group.

The monstrous sentence of seven years' transportation, defended by the Whig Home Secretary, Lord Melbourne, as a proper application of the law, at once roused furious protests. A London-Dorchester Committee, with Lovett as secretary, was formed for the defence of the victims, and Owen headed a monster Trade Union procession to present a petition to Lord Melbourne. But the Whig Government hurried the sentenced men out of the country and refused to make any concession. Not until 1836, two years after the " Grand National " had disappeared, was the remainder of the sentence remitted, and it was two years more before the victims were actually released and brought back to England.

The Dorchester sentences, and the attitude of the Government towards the victims, showed plainly that no forces would be spared in crushing the Trades Union. The Builders' Union and the " Grand National " at once took steps to abolish the oath and the ceremonies which had made them subject to the law. But they had been heavily shaken, and fresh attacks were already preparing from all sides.

Indeed, the position of the great " Consolidated Trades' Union " was very uncertain. The delegates who had originally founded it had acted without a mandate, and even after the organising conference of February, 1834, at which a definite constitution had been adopted, it was by no means clear who was in it and who was not. The four great Unions which existed before its foundation—the Builders', the Spinners', the Potters', and the Clothiers' (or Yorkshire Trades Union)—as well as some of the groups originally connected with John Doherty's National Association, apparently regarded themselves as independent bodies, and were not, after February, represented on the Consolidated Executive. The membership of the " Grand National " consisted mainly of local societies which had declared their allegiance ; but many of these had their own rules and funds, and there had been no time to devise, or to put into effect, a common method of organisation. The Executive, shorn of some of its best leaders, such as James Morrison, by the refusal of the big Unions to join, appears to have been better at issuing manifestoes and drafting grandiose schemes than at introducing order in the administration. Recruits came in so fast, and dispute followed dispute so swiftly, that there was no time to deal even with the most pressing problems of management.

Troubles crowded thick and fast upon the Unions. The Spinners' Union had given notice of a general refusal from March 1st, 1834, to work

more than eight hours a day.   But when the time arrived the Spinners did
not feel strong enough to move, and action was deferred, first till June and
then till September, and at that point definitely abandoned.   In April there
was a brief general strike at Oldham, arising out of the murder of a Union man
by a blackleg in the course of a fracas ; but this, too, fizzled out after a few
days.   In the same month the London tailors struck for shorter hours.
The " Grand National " imposed a general levy on their behalf; but in
June the funds were exhausted, and the men drifted back to work.   Meanwhile, in May, the Leeds employers presented the " document," and the
Yorkshire Trades' Union found itself involved in a life-and-death struggle.
Here, too, the dispute ended in the defeat of the men and the breaking of
the Union's power.   In July the London building dispute, already described,
increased the strain under which the entire movement was already breaking
down.

Long before this the position had been worsened by internal dissensions.
Owen, though he had been the principal inspirer of the grandiose plan of
mass industrial organisation, was not himself a member of the Grand National
Consolidated Trades' Union until he joined it in order to head the protest
against the sentences passed on the labourers at Dorchester.   Next to Owen,
the strongest men in the movement were James Morrison, of the Builders,
editor of The Pioneer, and J. E. Smith, afterwards known as " Shepherd "
Smith, the Universalist preacher, who was editor of the Owenite Crisis.
These two were both keen advocates of a strong and co-ordinated industrial
policy, and before long they became very critical of the weakness of the
" Grand National " Executive.   Smith, moreover, held that Owen's anti-
religious views were wrecking the movement by alienating support ; for
Owen's " atheism" was being largely used by the newspapers to discredit the
Union and its work.   Owen, on the other hand, was also dissatisfied with the
way the movement was going.   He disapproved of sectional strikes, and of
class-conflict, and was by temperament unfitted for leadership in a militant
working-class campaign.   He had sought to make a union of all the " well-
disposed members of the industrious classes," and had looked to the beauty of
his Co-operative scheme to convince many employers as well as workers.   He
had hoped by the power of union to achieve a bloodless and painless revolution ; he had certainly never meant to become the leader of a mass strike
agitation.   At first he contented himself with reproving the spirit of ill-will
towards misguided persons manifested within the Union ; but soon he
launched a special attack on Smith, whose inflammatory articles were encouraging this spirit.   He got the Executive of the Union to displace The
Pioneer from its status as official organ of the movement, and to start a new
Official Gazette in its place.   Next he muzzled Smith, who had been vigorously
criticising the Executive for its inaction, by shutting down The Crisis
altogether.   The Executive had apparently no strong men upon it, and after

the crisis brought on by the Dorchester sentences it followed Owen's lead at all points.

As the year advanced Owen realised that the great movement had failed. But his buoyant spirit did not accept defeat. He merely shifted his ground. With no more mandate than there had been for the starting of the Union, he persuaded a Conference, held in London in August, 1834, to decide upon its dissolution, or rather, on a complete change in its character and purpose. In its place the Conference founded a new Owenite propagandist society—the British and Foreign Consolidated Association of Industry, Humanity and Knowledge. In appealing to force and the strike, Owen announced, the industrious classes had gone the wrong way to work. They must convince and not coerce ; they must return to their old methods of education and propaganda, and must make a purely moral appeal. Instead of the *Crisis*, Owen began the issue of another journal, the *New Moral World*. The change of name signified a profound change of method.

For a few months, some shadow of the " Grand National " survived its dissolution by Owen in August, 1834. Apparently some sort of delegate conference was held as late as October ; but Owen's overtures to the meeting were met with a refusal to hold any communication with him. The rest is silence. The great Union died away after a life of a single year.

It must not, however, be supposed that all the parts perished with the breaking of the whole. As in the case of the Builders' Union, many of the constituent groups survived, and reconstituted themselves as separate societies, living on to become the nuclei of the modern Trade Union movement. The great body perished, and with it the great plan of establishing the new society by a sudden mass movement. Trade Unions, sadly reduced in membership, took to themselves less ambitious objects. But, as we shall see, for long after the disaster a good deal of the Owenite influence survived, and plans for " Union Shops " and Co-operative production continued to figure in Trade Union policy.

Owen's direct contact with the Trade Unions ceased in 1834. Never again did he descend into the industrial conflict. Owenism, as we shall see, shaped a new course, returning, in part, to its projects of Co-operative Communities, and issuing finally in two movements which flourished greatly in the Victorian era—Secularism and Consumers' Co-operation. In the years after 1834, Owenism became chiefly a moral crusade, although the Owenites still pursued their plans for the formation of " Villages of Co-operation," or " Home Colonies," as they came to be called, and maintained their local propagandist groups and their annual Congresses of delegates. The principal Owenite settlement, Queenwood, was launched by them in 1839, and the Rochdale Pioneers' Co-operative Society of 1844 arose directly out of a local Owenite body. The mass of the workers who had followed Owen, however, turned back from Trades Unionism to political action, and devoted their energies to the Chartist Movement, which arose swiftly out of the ashes of the " Grand National."

Why did the great Trades Union Movement of 1830-34 meet with the overwhelming disaster that has been described ? The causes are not hard to discover. The Trade Unions were confronted by a class of employers full of courage and self-confidence, mostly " self-made men," who had fought their way to affluence, and were enthusiastic admirers of the system which had enabled them to rise. This class was strong and determined ; it saw infinite possibilities in the further exploitation of the new powers of production. It was also ruthless, and unmindful of human suffering. Its eyes were not on the man, but on the machine he tended. It had just won a great political victory, and had established its claim to political power and social recogni-tion. Those who kicked against it seemed to it to be blasphemers of the new powers of production and to merit the severest chastisement for the good of society.

This class, moreover, could depend on the full support of the Whig Government, which had granted its claim to political power. The Whigs had often been told that their action in passing the Reform Act would be the means of unloosing on Society every form of anarchy and disorder, and of destroying all respect for the rights of property. They were, therefore, even more intent than the Tories on showing themselves devout friends of order and property, prompt in the suppression of popular disturbances ; and they could rely on the support of most of the Tories whenever they invoked the strong arm of the law against the " lower classes."

Against this invincible alliance of aristocrats and capitalists, with its overwhelming control both of the Houses of Parliament and of the courts of law, was pitted a working class for the most part wretchedly paid and equipped, with little or no education, and with hardly any experience of concerted action. This class was swept into Owen's great Union on a wave of moment-ary enthusiasm, and was taught by Owen to believe that the social millennium could be created in a few months by the mere fact of associative action. The workers responded and were carried away so easily just because they were not educated enough to understand the difficulties in their way. They felt that they had carried the Reform Bill by a mass movement ; why should they not carry Socialism in the same way ? They did not realise the difference that the great class of employers had been with them for Reform, but was now decisively against them.

It is easy enough to point out the weaknesses in the organisation of the " Grand National," or the vacillations and incompetence of its leadership. But these were not the causes of failure ; they were, rather, the results of attempting an impossible task. The Union could not possibly have succeeded. No sooner was it founded than difficulties began to overwhelm it. Against it were forces with which it could not hope to contend. Before the workers could hope to make a great inclusive Union of all sections they had to accustom themselves to combination, and to learn the management of great forces—lessons even to-day by no means fully mastered. But, still more, before the workers could stand up to Capitalism, there had to be time for Capitalism itself to develop more fully its potentialities, and to make its contribution to history. Before the proletariat could hope to defeat Capitalism, Capitalism had to bring the proletariat to maturity. In 1834 the working classes were still weak and immature—the more capable for that reason of sporadic revolt, the less capable of sustained constructive action, such as Owen demanded of them. The movement of 1834 was a glorious failure ; but no qualities of leadership could have turned it into a success.

BOOKS

G. D. H. Cole. *Life of Robert Owen.*
R. W. Postgate. *The Builders' History.*
R. W. Postgate. *Revolution.*
S. and B. Webb. *History of Trade Unionism.*

CHAPTER VII

CHARTISM TO 1839

1. The New Poor Law   3. The Chartist Convention of 1839
2. The Rise of Chartism 4. The Newport Rising

I. THE NEW POOR LAW

THE first important social measure of the Reformed Parliament was the Factory Act of 1833, which prohibited employment in textile factories (except silk mills) at less than nine years of age, fixed a maximum working day of nine hours for children under thirteen (from 1835), prohibited night-work by young persons, and, most important of all, established the factory inspectorate. This Act, however, was really a carry-over from the days before Reform, and would probably have passed in much the same shape whether there had been Reform or not. The first great measure plainly reflecting the spirit of the Reformed Parliament was the Poor Law Amendment Act of 1834.

Reference has been made already to the condition of the Poor Law in the first part of the nineteenth century. In 1834 Poor Law expenditure in England and Wales averaged over 9s. per head of population, despite the drastic restrictions which had been made in many areas in the scales of relief. In eight counties the expenditure was over 15s. per head, Sussex heading the list with 18s. The heaviest expenditure was in the South of England, and especially in the Eastern and South Midland Counties. In the North it was comparatively light—6s. in Northumberland and Durham, 5s. in the West Riding of Yorkshire, and in Lancashire only 3s. 9d. In fact, pauperism, except in times of industrial depression, was found chiefly in the agricultural districts, and was actually worst in the most fertile areas of the country.

This heavy poor relief was, in reality, a subsidy to wages. It enabled men barely to live where they would otherwise have starved ; but it also served to keep down the wages even of those who were not receiving relief. In face of the competition of pauper labour, hired out by the parish, it was impossible for wages to rise. The labourers, as a class, were ground down to the barest level of subsistence. Yet the farmers did not necessarily profit ; for agricultural rents were adjusted to the prevailing wages, and the landlords skimmed off the surplus. Farmers and landowners combined, however, to grumble at the excessive poor rates, and to do all they could to cut them down by reducing the scales of relief. Still, the burden of pauperism grew, a seemingly insoluble problem.

There had been many projects and many committees and commissions for Poor Law Reform before the Reformed Parliament drastically remodelled the system. The Act of 1834 took the Poor Law out of the hands of the parishes and placed it under the control of a nationally appointed body of Commissioners, who rapidly reorganised the country into " Unions " of parishes, each with its Board of Guardians elected on a basis weighted heavily in favour of property and responsible to the central authority. The Commissioners, with Edwin Chadwick, thorough-going disciple of Bentham and of the orthodox economists, as secretary, set vigorously to work, beginning with the agricultural districts of the South and West. They swept away the entire system of poor relief in aid of wages, refused all forms of outdoor relief to able bodied persons, and applied to such relief as was still to be given the principles of deterrence and " less eligibility," which continued to dominate Poor Law practice for nearly a century. They were extraordinarily ruthless. Having made up their minds that the old system must go, they refused to be influenced by any consideration of the sufferings likely to be caused by its sudden abolition ; for even if, as they maintained, wages rose in consequence of the change, there was bound to be an intervening period of intense suffering for those who had relied on the rates for relief.

In the House of Commons the Act was passed by overwhelming majorities, against the fierce opposition of a tiny group of Radicals led by William Cobbett. Cobbett was no defender of the old system ; but he maintained that all the poor had a right to good maintenance out of the product of the country, and that this right the Bill proposed to take away. It was, he contended, a measure confiscating the birthright of the poor. His last act, after the Bill had become law, was to advocate a national movement for organised resistance to its application. He died in 1835, just as the struggle was beginning. Cobbett was the last of the old Radicals who looked back to the days before the Industrial Revolution.

The Poor Law Act, and the persons appointed to carry it into effect, were intensely unpopular. The Commissioners were familiarly known as the " Three Bashaws (or ' Kings ') of Somerset House " ; and they had uphill work during the early years. It may seem strange that the strongest resistance was encountered in the areas in which Poor Law expenditure had been comparatively low. But it is not really strange. The agricultural labourers in the Southern and Eastern Counties, on whom the change fell with the greatest severity, had no power to resist. There were riots in some places ; but these were speedily quelled by a show of force. The revolt of 1830 was the last widespread movement of the labourers till the days of Joseph Arch ; all power of resistance had been crushed out of them by starvation and by the migration of the more vigorous personalities to town or mining village.

The greatest resistance came actually from the factory districts. Here Poor Law expenditure had been lower because there had been no regular practice of subsidising factory wages out of the rates. But the Poor Law had been, for the workers in these cases, a last resort in times of unemployment, and such dying classes as the handloom weavers fiercely resented being driven into the workhouse—the new "Bastille," it was usually called—as a condition of relief. The segregation of the sexes in the workhouse was also deeply hated, and was ascribed to the savage disciples of the "monster, Malthus's" theory of population. The workers in the industrial districts may not have hated the new Poor Law any more than it was hated by the agricultural labourers ; but they were less under the heel of their masters, and they knew better how to organise a movement of protest.

The Poor Law question came to a head just as the great Trade Union agitation of 1830-34 was dying down. It called men's minds back from strikes and Co-operative Socialism to politics. The Reformed Parliament had brought forth this monster ; it was the reward given by the Whigs to their late allies in the struggle for Reform ; this was what came of handing over political power to the financiers and employers of labour. A savage hatred of the Whigs and of the manufacturers ran through the agitation against the Poor Law, and coloured the Chartist movement in which that agitation was speedily merged. At times Chartism almost became Tory in its hatred of the Whigs ; and men such as Richard Oastler and Joseph Rayner Stephens, who were Tories in the political sense, played for a time a leading rôle in the agitation. Disraeli, the young Tory, wrote his "Sybil ; or the Two Nations" as a Tory manifesto to the Chartists—a first essay in his favourite art of "dishing the Whigs."

BOOKS

G. D. H. Cole. *Chartist Portraits.*
S. and B. Webb. *History of the English Poor Law.*
G. Nichols and T. Mackay. *History of the English Poor Law.*
M. Marston. *Edwin Chadwick.*
G. Slater. *The Growth of Modern England.*
G. D. H. Cole. *Life of William Cobbett.*
M. Hovell. *The Chartist Movement.*
J. L. and B. Hammond. *The Age of the Chartists.*

2. THE RISE OF CHARTISM

The Chartist Movement was essentially an economic movement with a purely political programme. The Charter, in which its immediate demands were embodied, was simply a plan of democratic parliamentary reform, re-stating the claims that had been put forward by the Radical left wing from the very beginning of the Reform struggle. The groups which had fought in alliance before 1832 fell apart when the Reform Act became law ; for the main body of the middle class, having secured its own admission to political power, felt no desire to go further. Lord John Russell, who had introduced the

Whig Reform Bill, earned the name of " Finality Jack " by declaring that the Act of 1832 had settled the question once and for all.

We have seen how the working classes, angry with their late allies and disillusioned by their failure to win political power, turned away from political agitation and threw themselves feverishly into the growing Trade Union and Co-operative movement. The defeat of the Trade Unions in 1834, and the enactment of the new Poor Law in the same year, directed their attention back to politics, and caused the rapid growth of the Chartist agitation.

The men who at first assumed the leadership in this new phase of the working-class struggle were largely the same as had led the working-class Radicals in the earlier agitation for Parliamentary Reform. In London, the leaders of the National Union of the Working Classes reappeared as the founders of the new movement. William Lovett, Henry Hetherington, Bronterre O'Brien, James Watson, John Cleave, William Carpenter, and many others, were men already tried in earlier phases of the struggle. We have seen Lovett as an early Co-operator and secretary of the London Dorchester Committee. Hetherington was both an ardent Owenite and an active member of the N.U.W.C. and the protagonist in the fight against the Stamp Taxes. As owner of the *Poor Man's Guardian*, one of the best working-class journals, which Bronterre O'Brien edited for him, he suffered many terms of imprisonment for the publication of unstamped newspapers in violation of the law. Watson and Cleave had also been active in issuing unstamped journals and in the propaganda of the N.U.W.C. Carpenter's *Political Magazine*, and other writings, had made him well known as a Radical journalist. All these, and many more old stalwarts, felt, after the collapse of the great Trade Unions, that the time had come for a new move.

These men knew well that the grievances from which the workers suffered were chiefly economic, and that no purely political reform would cure them. But they looked on the further reform of Parliament as a necessary means to economic changes, holding that the capital-owning classes could not be mastered economically while they kept their hold on the machinery of government. Moreover, amid the dissensions which followed the defeat of 1834, the younger working-class leaders were seeking a cry at once simple enough and direct enough to unite all sections among the workers in its support. A plain demand for complete parliamentary democracy, based on Universal Suffrage (which meant Manhood Suffrage), seemed to meet this need ; for all the working-class groups could unite to secure this as a means to whatever divergent ends they might have in remoter view. Votes for women, though some of the leaders were in favour of them, were still outside the range of mass political agitation.

The fact, however, that Chartism was fundamentally an economic movement, and that parliamentary reform was sought only as a means, must never be lost sight of.   It both coloured the whole activity of the movement and explains the rapidity of its growth and the multitude of its followers. It helps also to account for the dissensions which soon began to arise within the Chartist body.

The story of the origin of the Charter has been often told.   After the Reform Act most of the Political Unions had been wound up, or had lapsed into inertia.   The National Union of the Working Classes had remained active till 1834, and then had broken up under the stress of that eventful year. There was, after 1834, no effective head or centre for the working-class Radical movement.   Owenism, as a mass-movement, collapsed in 1834 ; and it lived on only as the creed of a sect.   Cobbett and Hunt, leaders of the old agitation, both died in the first half of 1835.   There was acute unrest, aggravated by the Poor Law ; but it lacked unity and direction.

Under these conditions a small group of London workers decided to form the London Working Men's Association, as a purely working-class body for steady propaganda and educational work.   A few middle-class men, including Owen, were made honorary members ; and Francis Place, now an old man, acted as mentor to the new body.   But the control was entirely working-class.   Lovett, as usual, became secretary, and with him were John Cleave, Henry Hetherington, Henry Vincent, who became the orator of the movement, James Watson, George Julian Harney, and others.

The L.W.M.A. began very quietly organising small branches in London, and making a few pamphlet appeals to the workers in other towns to follow its example.   It had so far no relations with the great popular agitation against the Poor Law which was sweeping through the North of England. Early in 1837 this agitation assumed a far more vigorous shape.   The Poor Law Commissioners, for the first time, made a serious attempt to introduce the new system into the Northern Counties.   A period of bad trade and high food prices set in, and the drastic restrictions on poor relief were for the first time seriously felt by the main body of the industrial workers.   The L.W.M.A. became conscious of a rising movement of unrest over the whole country, and of this movement it sought to take the lead.   It began to send out, in the Owenite manner, "missionaries" to preach its gospel, and everywhere these touring lecturers met with outstanding success.   Working-class societies and newspapers sprang up fast in all the principal areas.   The L.W.M.A. soon found itself only one section in a great movement including many diverse elements and tendencies.

First there was, in the North and in the Midland textile districts, a great mass movement of unrest, directed principally against the Poor Law, but, fundamentally, a hunger revolt, fed on unemployment and despair.   Joseph Rayner Stephens, an excluded Methodist parson with an independent chapel of his own, and Richard Oastler, a land agent and Tory democrat, were the first leaders of this welter of protest.   Both were fiery orators, with great power of rousing the people, but no constructive programme save a juster system of poor relief. But in 1836 there appeared a new and far more powerful leader—Feargus O'Connor, who had formerly been an Irish M.P. and follower of Daniel O'Connell, but had quarrelled with his leader and had been excluded from Parliament in 1835. O'Connor had worked with Cobbett in Parliament, and had defended there the cause of the Dorchester labourers. In 1836, after a time in London, he moved to the North, and started a fiery Radical crusade. In the following year he founded at Leeds the *Northern Star*, which became by far the most influential of the Chartist journals.

O'Connor, like Stephens, was a demagogue—a powerful orator, with an immense power of stirring great multitudes of men. More than any other man he was responsible for turning the northern agitation from a campaign against the new Poor Law into a movement for Radical Reform. He became speedily the outstanding figure in the movement.

A second impetus to Chartism came from Birmingham, where the Political Union, one of the strongest centres of the Reform Movement before 1832, had been dissolved in 1834. In 1837 it was revived, and a new and vigorous agitation at once sprang up. This movement, however, was by no means exclusively working-class, and remained chiefly under middle-class leadership. Its outstanding figure was Thomas Attwood, banker and Radical M.P., but, above all, currency reformer, with a plan for ensuring universal prosperity by the liberal issue of paper money as credit against production—a plan since revived at many times and in many shapes. Attwood was a sincere Radical, who had usually voted with Cobbett in Parliament. He was exceedingly popular ; and he successfully impressed his policy of currency reform and parliamentary democracy on the new Birmingham Political Union. This body included a strong working-class section, led by John Collins ; but Attwood and his friends were, at first, the real leaders.

Thirdly, there was the movement represented chiefly by the London Working Men's Association, and by the similar societies founded elsewhere under its influence. This movement was almost purely working-class, with a small lower middle-class element of master-craftsmen, shopkeepers, publicans, and the like ; but it was also essentially moderate in tone and temper. Its strength lay, not among the starving factory workers, but among the comparatively well-paid skilled artisans of the older towns, who could better afford to wait and organise a constitutional agitation, and were not under the same temptation to break out into riot, or under the same need for immediate help in distress.

These three groups together made up the chief strength of Chartism. Of course, this is a simplification of the facts. There were middle-class Chartists in many other towns besides Birmingham, moderates in the North,

and extremists in London.   Scotland, on the whole, was a moderate centre.
Manchester was divided, but with a left-wing tendency.   In London, George
Julian Harney, one of the best of the Chartist leaders, was the centre of a left-
wing group which, in 1837, split off from the L.W.M.A. and formed the
London Democratic Association in close touch with O'Connor.   Bronterre
O'Brien, an old associate of Hetherington and his group, joined the left
wing, and became the chief writer for O'Connor's *Northern Star*.   But,
despite these cross-currents, it is in general true that Chartism was based on
three main groups—the O'Connorites, who drew their strength from the
factory operatives and formed the left ; the Lovettites, chiefly skilled artisans
in the older towns, who formed a more moderate " centre " ; and the
Attwoodites, based on the Birmingham Political Union, who sought to
keep alive the old alliance of working-class and middle-class Radicals, and
complicated the issues with their plan of currency reform.

For a brief space, a fourth group, which would have had most in common
with the third, seemed likely to play a part.   There was in Parliament a small
group of Radicals who differed from the main body of the Whigs, and
courted alliance with the workers.   Attwood was of this group ; but its
leading figure was J. A. Roebuck, a friend and collaborator of Francis Place.
In 1837 Place succeeded in bringing together this group and the leaders of the
L.W.M.A., with the object of drafting an agreed Reform Bill for introduction
into Parliament.   Out of this move grew the People's Charter.   But, having
helped to make the draft, the Radical M.P.'s dropped out of the movement,
and were seen no more, though they did vote for the Chartist Petition when
it came before the House of Commons in 1839.   They were lukewarm from
the first.

Lovett drafted the Charter, Place and Roebuck went through it, a joint
committee of the L.W.M.A. and the Radical M.P.'s passed it, and it was
published in May, 1838.   Almost at the same time the Birmingham Political
Union issued its National Petition for reform, in which almost precisely the
same demands were put forward.

There is nothing strange in this ; for there was nothing new in the
People's Charter.   Both Charter and Petition were simply re-statements of
the familiar case for full parliamentary democracy, based on Manhood
Suffrage.   Women Suffrage was discussed, and the L.W.M.A. leaders were
in favour of it.   But it was not included in the programme because they felt
it would be used to laugh the Charter out of court.   The programme thus
remained, in all essentials, what it had been from the early days of the Reform
Movement in the eighteenth century—what Cartwright and Cobbett had
preached, only put down with rather more exactness and elaboration than
in previous phases of the movement.

The " six points " of the Charter are well known.   They were (1) Manhood Suffrage ;   (2) Vote by Ballot ;   (3) Annual Parliaments Annually

Elected ; (4) Abolition of the Property Qualification for M.P.'s ; (5) Payment of Members ; and (6) Equal Electoral Districts, rearranged after each decennial census.   All these points, except the last, were also included in the Birmingham Petition.   They were the common stock of all Radical Reformers.   Differences within the Chartist Movement arose, not over the formulation of a programme, but over the measures to be adopted in order to secure its acceptance.   On this point there was room for the widest divergences of opinion and strategy.

BOOKS

G. D. H. Cole.   *Chartist Portraits.*
M. Hovell.   *The Chartist Movement.*
J. West.   *History of the Chartist Movement.*
R. G. Gammage.   *History of Chartism.*
M. Beer.   *History of British Socialism*, Vol. II.
W. Lovett.   *Life and Struggles.*
F. Rosenblatt.   *The Chartist Movement in its Social and Economic Aspects.*
S. Maccoby.   *English Radicalism.*   Vol. I.
J. L. and B. Hammond.   *The Age of the Chartists.*

3. THE CHARTIST CONVENTION OF 1839

Early in the growth of Chartism there began to be talk of a " Convention," an assembly of delegates from the Chartist membership throughout the country to work out a method of securing the acceptance of the Charter. The word "Convention," as we have seen, had associations which commended it to those who were in revolt.   It recalled the French Revolution, and it also roused memories drawn from the revolutionary history of the seventeenth century.   It suggested, not merely a conference, but an assembly claiming the right to legislate for the people.   It was, and was meant to be, a challenge to the Parliament at Westminster from a People's Parliament, based on a wider suffrage and possessing a more real popular mandate.

" Conventions " had, indeed, accompanied every phase of Radical history since 1789.   The Corresponding Societies had called their " Conventions " in the years following the French Revolution ; and the Hampden Clubs had held a Convention in 1817.   The Owenites, in 1834, had spoken rather of a " Parliament of the Industrious Classes "[1] than of a Convention ; but the idea behind their assembly was the same.   It is not suggested that any of these Conventions definitely set out to make a revolution or to establish itself as the government of the country ; but in each the element of challenge, and the claim to a greater right to govern than those actually in power could claim, was present in greater or less degree.   The issue was seldom plainly stated ; but it was constantly at the back of men's minds.

Thus, when the Chartists began to talk about holding a Convention, it was open to understand them in two ways.   They might mean merely to

[1] See page 85.

hold a Conference, and so express with greater strength and unity their demand that Parliament should pass the People's Charter into law. Or they might mean to summon an assembly which would proclaim itself as the Government and take the lead in a forcible revolutionary movement. In 1917, the Soviet Congress in Russia, until the Bolsheviks definitely secured a majority, was in much the same ambiguous position. Of the Chartists, some urged the Convention merely as a way of demonstrating the strength of their following, and some because they hoped to use it as an instrument of social revolution ; but most simply urged it, and left the question of ulterior measures to decide itself in the future.

Whatever might happen later, it was necessary, in the initial stages, to keep as far as possible within the law. This governed the form of the Convention. " Corresponding Societies " were still illegal, and the Government had further drastic powers for the suppression of seditious meetings and conspiracies. It was, therefore, thought desirable to avoid the appearance, while achieving the reality, of national organisation. This was done by choosing the delegates to the Convention, not through the local Chartist societies, but at great public meetings held in the open air in each important centre. In practice, this made no difference, for the nominations were all arranged beforehand by the local societies. But it was regarded as an advantage, both because it appeared to keep the Convention within the letter of the law, and because it made the delegates the nominal representatives of the vast crowds which attended the meetings.

During 1838 large meetings were held throughout the country, often at night by torchlight, and in connection with huge " torch-light processsions " of Chartist sympathisers. It seemed that the whole country was roused to support the Charter. At Birmingham, where the leaders had wished to base the agitation on their own " Petition " rather than on the more revolutionary-sounding " People's Charter," a great meeting adopted the Charter as well as the Petition and forced the hands of the moderates. From every centre delegates were chosen to attend the Convention ; the orators of the movement went everywhere, stirring up the people and addressing immense and enthusiastic audiences. At the same time, the agitation against the New Poor Law reached such a height that in many parts of the North its introduction had to be suspended, and outdoor relief continued for a time to be paid as before under the old system.

These measures did not pass without provoking counter-measures by the Government. News reached the Home Office from many districts that the workers were purchasing arms, and that unlawful drilling was in constant progress. The Government refused, indeed, to suppress the Chartist meetings ; but it began to organise its military forces to deal with any possible outbreak. Additional troops were sent to the most threatened districts, especially to South Wales and to the North of England, and in April,

1839, General Sir Charles Napier was given the command of the Northern District.

Meanwhile, on February 4th 1839, the Chartist Convention had met at the British Hotel, Cockspur Street, Charing Cross. It represented nearly all the industrial areas of England, Wales, and Scotland ; but there was not a single delegate from the agricultural areas. George Loveless, the leader of the Dorchester labourers of 1834, was elected for Dorset, but never took his seat. Nearly all the well-known leaders of the movement were there, and arrangements had been made to meet the expenses by means of a " National Rent," collected from loyal Chartists throughout the country. Many of the local bodies had further undertaken to maintain their delegates while the Convention was sitting. At the first meeting Lovett was appointed secretary.

The first business of the Chartist Convention was to present to Parliament the National Petition, for which signatures were being actively collected by the local bodies. This was to be done through Attwood and Fielden, the two M.P.'s who maintained the closest connections with it. But the preparations took time. The Petition, with 1,200,000 signatures, was not ready till May, and even then there were unavoidable delays before it could be debated in Parliament. The Convention had thus either to disperse or to go on talking for several months before a critical point in its career could be reached.

Protracted discussions which cannot issue in immediate action inevitably give the maximum of opportunity for disagreement. In a crisis involving action, even those who disagree in theory may be carried along together by the force of events. But, when there is nothing to do but talk, every talker has ample scope for finding points of dissent. In the present case, moreover, there was, as we have seen, a fundamental ambiguity about the whole purpose of the Convention. Those who held that it should be merely a form of peaceful and constitutional demonstration were soon appealing to the Convention explicitly to adopt their point of view, while those who held that reform would be achieved only by a show of force were soon urging the consideration of " ulterior measures," to be put into effect unless the Charter were speedily adopted by the House of Commons. The majority, standing between these two extremes, successfully avoided committing the Convention, as a whole, to either ; but within a few days of the opening the extreme right wing, headed by the younger Cobbett, withdrew because they could not secure from their colleagues a definite disclaimer of unconstitutional intentions.

By May, 1839, the Chartist Petition was at length ready to be presented. But at this point an untoward accident upset the Chartists' calculations. Lord Melbourne's Whig Government, in difficulties with the House of Commons, decided to resign. Before the Petition could be presented, it was necessary to await the solution of a Cabinet crisis. This meant a long delay, very dangerous to the Chartist cause. Uncertain as ever what course to take, the Convention first migrated from London to Birmingham, in order to be more in the midst of its own supporters, and then, a few days later, adjourned for six weeks in order to enable a Chartist campaign to be conducted by the leaders throughout the country.

Accordingly, from May 16th to July 1st, the Convention did not meet, but a series of questions, designed to form the basis of possible " ulterior measures " should the House of Commons reject the Petition, was submitted to public meetings in all the important centres. Chartist supporters were asked whether they would bind themselves to obey the requests of the Convention ; whether they would, if requested, organise a run on the banks, such as Francis Place had planned in 1832. They were asked whether they would be ready to " abstain from their labour " during a " Sacred Month " or general strike for the Charter ; whether they would be prepared to refuse payment of rents, rates and taxes ; whether they would support Chartist candidates for Parliament ; and whether they had " prepared themselves with the arms of freemen to defend the laws and constitutional privileges their ancestors bequeathed to them." To these questions were added a number of others which betrayed the Convention's doubts and hesitations about its future course of action. On the whole, the framing of the questions shows that, since February, the Convention had moved to the " left." But there was still room for more than one interpretation of its meaning.

The " Bedchamber " crisis at last ended, and the Whigs returned to power. The Petition was presented on June 14th ; but Attwood and Fielden, its sponsors, could not secure a day for debate upon it until July 12th. Meanwhile, on July 1st, the Convention reassembled in Birmingham, where excitement was already running high, and the magistrates promptly sent for police from London, having at this time no city force of their own. They had already forbidden meetings in the Bull Ring ; but these had been frequently held in their despite. The London police, on arrival in the city, found a meeting in full swing. They dispersed it with violence, and a large number of persons on both sides were injured. This led to further disturbances, and to a strong protest by the Convention at the invasion of the right of public meeting. Lovett, who signed the notice as secretary of the Convention, and Collins, the local working-class leader, were arrested. Nevertheless, without taking any action for their release, the Convention moved, a few days later, back to London, in order to be on the spot when the Petition came up for debate in Parliament.

In the debate, Attwood, Fielden, and Joseph Hume supported the Petition; Lord John Russell, for the Government, and Disraeli, in a characteristic speech, opposed it. Forty-six voted for it and 235 against. The Convention found itself, at long last, faced with the necessity for action. After two days' debate it decided, by thirteen votes to six, to call a " National Holiday," or general strike. The "Holiday" was to begin on August 12th, and the Trade Unions were to be asked to co-operate in calling it.

Thus the Convention, in a thinly attended meeting, at last determined to act. But still there were doubts. Was the "National Holiday" to be merely a cessation of work, compelling the attention of Parliament through the dislocation it would cause, or was it to be the signal for a general rising ? And, in either case, would the main body of the workers either strike or rise ? For an ordinary strike the time was obviously inopportune ; for trade was bad, and many were out of work. The Chartist bodies had no funds ; and the Trade Unions, which had still by no means recovered from the disaster of 1834, were both disinclined for great adventures and weak owing to the state of trade. These arguments would not necessarily have weighed against an insurrection. But were the Chartists ready for an insurrection, and had they the strength to carry it through in face of the armed forces in the country, and of the united power of the upper and middle classes ?

These doubts grew stronger after the motion for the " National Holiday " had been adopted. Reports of weakness and unpreparedness poured in from many centres. Bronterre O'Brien, who had been a leader of the left wing in the Convention, moved, on July 22nd, that the resolution should be rescinded. After an angry debate, his motion was carried, only six voting against it. Instead of declaring a strike, the Convention now appointed a Committee to explore the position further and adjourned again for a month. It met again at the end of August, but only to dissolve after a debate full of violent recriminations.

Indeed, the very moment the Convention attempted to act, the real weakness of its position became evident. There was a great body of middle-class as well as of working-class opinion in favour of the main points of the Charter and of constitutional agitation for political reform. There was a large mass of distress in the factory districts, where the workers were prepared for all sorts of protests and demonstrations, and were without regard for constitutional niceties. But this mass was not organised, and the organised body of Chartists did not succeed in forming an effective nucleus round which it could gather. How could it do so, when the most prominent leaders were sharply divided between " physical force men " and " moral force men," and when the leader with the greatest popular following, O'Connor, hovered uneasily between the two points of view, without committing himself to either ? The " physical force men " scorned the methods of the " moral force " advocates, but could do little without them, or, at least, without bringing over the wavering centre. The " moral force men " were not prepared, in any event, to follow the " left " into an armed rebellion which they either disapproved or regarded as hopeless.

Consequently the Convention, as a whole, could not make up its mind what it was trying to do. As long as it could it played a game of bluff, letting all sections say what they liked in the hope that, between persuasion and intimidation, the Government would be made to give way. Such strategy had been all very well in 1831, when the Reformers had powerful support inside Parliament and the whole of the middle classes behind them. It was useless in 1839, when persuasion enlisted at best only lukewarm middle-class support, and the threat of violence at once drove the middle classes almost solidly into the Government camp. The governing classes after 1832 were incomparably stronger and better entrenched against popular appeals to force than they had been previously.

The weakness of the Chartist position had been more than once clearly shown before the Convention came to an end. After the Whitsuntide campaign of 1839, the Government had begun a policy of arrests on a large scale. Benbow, the chief advocate of the " National Holiday," Lovett, Collins, Vincent, Stephens, and many other leaders, were in gaol before the " Sacred Month " was proclaimed. The Convention could do nothing for them. Then the calling off of the " Sacred Month " was a second confession of failure. Long before the Convention decided to adjourn, the moderates had left it in fear of its violence, and the extremists had despaired of it for its moderation. The real centre of interest had shifted back to the local Chartist societies, which, faced with the failure of the Convention and of the Petition, were considering what further action to take.

BOOKS

G. D. H. Cole. *Chartist Portraits.*
M. Beer. *History of British Socialism,* Vol. II.
M. Hovell. *The Chartist Movement.*
J. West. *History of the Chartist Movement.*
R. G. Gammage. *History of Chartism.*
W. Lovett. *Life and Struggles.*

4. THE NEWPORT RISING

It is exceedingly difficult to disentangle truth from falsehood in the conflicting accounts which survive of events following the break-up of the first Chartist Convention. Did, or did not, a section of the Chartists plan a general insurrection throughout the country ? If so, what leaders, and what districts, were concerned in the movement, and what form was it intended to take ? Or was there really no such plan save in the fevered imaginations of the Government and the Press ? Or was there a movement, worked up mainly by Government spies and informers, into which a few unwary Chartists were drawn as victims ?

These questions admit of no dogmatic answer. It is clear that the prospects of an insurrectionary movement were freely discussed in Chartist circles, and that a good many Chartists went so far as to provide themselves with weapons of a sort.   But it is not at all clear how far most of the Chartist groups passed from talking to actual planning, or whether there was any organised national leadership behind the sporadic efforts of the small local groups which did.   It is clear that Government spies played a considerable part in urging violent talk and preparation, which they afterwards betrayed to the authorities.   But it is not clear whether they were mainly responsible for the movement, or merely worked upon something which existed apart from their efforts.

On the whole, it seems probable that the extreme " physical force " delegates, despairing of any action by the Convention as a whole, did in its later stages get together as a secret group, and at least begin some preliminary planning for a general movement of insurrection.   John Frost, for South Wales, Peter Bussey, for Yorkshire, Dr. John Taylor, for the North, and the Pole, Beniowski, seem to have been the chief planners of this enterprise. After preliminary discussion, the leaders seem to have departed to their own districts, in order to test the state of local feeling, and, if possible, to carry the preparations a stage further by local organisation.   It appears that the more moderate Chartists were kept wholly in the dark about these plans, and it remains in doubt whether Feargus O'Connor was in any way privy to the movement.

Wales and Yorkshire, it seems clear, were the two centres chiefly concerned in the plan.   But, while in both centres the leaders made local preparations, neither seems to have known at all definitely what the other was doing.   Birmingham, where the left wing had now gained the upper hand, was also probably concerned, and was meant to serve as a connecting link between Wales and the North.

At this stage, however, the movement was still far from having assumed the shape of an organised national plan of revolution.   It is, for example, very doubtful whether any common date for an uprising was ever fixed, or whether there was any concerted national plan.   The story that the rising was to begin in Wales, and that the signal for its extension was to be the non-arrival in Birmingham of the coach carrying the Welsh mails, may conceivably have a substratum of truth ; but it is discredited by the fact that no coach at that time ran direct from Newport, the centre of the Welsh rising, to Birmingham.   This point was brought out in the course of Frost's trial.

On the whole, then, the evidence is against any serious planning of a national Chartist insurrection, but in favour of the view that such a movement had been talked about and sketched out in a preliminary way, and that there had been special communications about it between Yorkshire and South Wales, the two main " physical force " centres.   This planning, can, however, have been only preliminary ; for when the Welsh at length made a decisive move, the Yorkshiremen seem to have had no definite knowledge of their intentions or course of action.

This may have been partly due to the fact that O'Connor, apparently apprised of the plan almost at the last moment, instead of assuming the offered leadership, did what he could to stop it. His action may well account for the failure of the rising to mature in Yorkshire, his own centre, even when the Welsh rising took place. It is credibly stated that O'Connor also tried, through a special emissary, to stop the Welsh movement, but was brushed aside as too late. John Frost, the Newport draper who was the nominal leader of the Chartists in South Wales, seems to have made some attempt to call the rising off, but to have been unable to persuade his fellow-leaders, and not willing to abandon them when they determined to proceed. Even then, industrial relations were worse in South Wales than in any other part of Great Britain, and rioting was no new thing in the mining villages, which were wholly dominated by the great ironmasters and colliery-owners.

In any case, the sole armed movement of any importance made by the Chartists after the break-up of the Convention was the Newport rising of November, 1839. This affair, small enough in itself, and quickly over, is the nucleus round which legend and controversy have freely gathered. The bare facts are these.

On November 4th, 1839, some thousands of colliers, having assembled by night in the hills of Monmouthshire, marched on Newport, with the object of surprising the town. Their object seems to have been first to capture Newport, and then to march on Monmouth, where Henry Vincent, the Chartist leader in the West, was lying in prison. It had been arranged that three detachments from different areas should make the descent together. But night attacks are difficult to arrange ; and, in effect, the advance was delayed long enough to give full warning, and only one of the three parties arrived on the scene in time to take part in the critical movement. A tiny body of soldiers posted in the Westgate Hotel, on which the attack was first directed, sufficed to rout the attacking party, which had apparently expected no resistance. A number of the colliers were killed or wounded ; and within a few minutes the main body was fleeing back to the hills. So began, and so ended, the Newport rising. The other two bodies of insurgents dispersed on hearing of the fate of the first body. It remained only to arrest the leaders, and to make examples of them for the discouragement of others.

As we saw, the leader of the Newport rising was John Frost, of Newport, formerly Mayor of the town, and a magistrate until his commission was revoked on account of his Chartist activities. Frost had been one of the chief spokesmen of the left wing in the Chartist Convention. Earlier he had been a leading Reformer, and had taken an active part in aiding the coal miners' movements of the years before the rise of Chartism. In 1839 he was in close touch with Harney, Bussey, Dr. John Taylor, and the rest of the " physical force " section ; and, if a national rising was planned in London, he was evidently one of those involved in the plot. With Zephaniah Williams,

William Jones, and the other leaders of the Newport Movement, he was
arrested immediately upon its collapse, and put to trial for high treason
before a Special Commission, headed by the Lord Chief Justice.

The result of the trial was a foregone conclusion, though Chartists throughout the country raised a substantial fund for the defence, to which O'Connor
contributed a week's profits of the *Northern Star*.   Dr. John Taylor, and a
few other leaders of the " physical force " section, tried hard to force a second
rising for the rescue of the prisoners, but without success.   A secret Convention was held in Manchester, and there were tiny armed movements in a
few places in the North.   But no rescue was attempted.   Frost, Williams,
and Jones were sentenced to death, and the sentence was commuted to transportation for life.

The Newport rising was the signal for a fresh and still more extensive
campaign of arrests.   On one charge or another, nearly all the remaining
Chartist leaders were soon lodged in gaol.   Feargus O'Connor, who had
been absent in Ireland during the Newport trouble, was gaoled for libel.
Some said that his absence had been intentional, but there is no evidence of
this.   It is fairly certain that at the last moment he did get wind of what was
being planned, and that he did all he could to prevent the outbreak, and he
may have left for Ireland in the belief that his efforts had been successful.
O'Connor, from first to last, hovered uneasily between extreme left and
centre.   His speeches often seemed to rank him definitely with the advocates
of "physical force."   But, in fact, he probably realised that "physical force"
was hopeless, and was playing, at least half-consciously, a game of bluff.

Prosecution and imprisonment, however, fell on all sections alike.   By
the middle of 1840 the Chartist Movement appeared to be almost wholly
leaderless, broken, and disorganised.   It seemed to have collapsed as completely as Owen's great agitation of a few years before.   The Scottish Chartists, most of whom had seceded from the English movement in September,
1839, and had set up their own movement on moderate and constitutional
lines, held together ; but elsewhere the organisation seemed to be wholly in
ruins.   Chartism, indeed, never again looked so formidable as it had appeared
in 1839.   But the end was not yet.   Before the year 1840 was out there
were signs of its revival.

BOOKS

G. D. H. Cole.   *Chartist Portraits.*
D. Williams.   *Life of John Frost.*
M. Beer.   *History of British Socialism,* Vol. II.
M. Hovell.   *The Chartist Movement.*
R. G. Gammage.   *History of Chartism.*
The Trial of John Frost, 1839.
N. Edwards.   *John Frost and the Chartist Movement.*

CHAPTER VIII

CHARTISM—LATER PHASES

1. THE CHARTISTS AND THE ANTI-CORN LAW LEAGUE

ON the very day on which the Chartist Convention of 1839 opened in London, the Anti-Corn Law League held, also in London, its first national conference. The movement for the repeal of the Corn Laws was not new, and the system of "moderate duties" had already been introduced by Huskisson in 1823. Cobbett, followed by many of the Radicals, had vigorously opposed the Corn Law of 1815, and intelligent Radical opinion had been for a generation predominantly in favour of the free import of corn. But there had not been agreement on the point, and generally the demand for the repeal of the Corn Laws had occupied only a very minor place in working-class programmes.

The great Anti-Corn Law Movement, which began, and ran its course, simultaneously with Chartism, was not a working-class movement. Its sponsors, and financiers, were the industrial employers of the North and Midlands, and their active following came mainly from the middle classes. But, as the agitation gathered force, it appealed more and more to the workers. There was plenty of money behind it, and it had the aid of excellent leaders and organisers such as Richard Cobden and John Bright.

Inevitably, this great agitation, running simultaneously with the agitation for the Charter, came into sharp and constant conflict with the latter. The Charter itself contained, for the most part, demands which the more advanced middle-class Liberals were willing to support, or at least which they would not oppose. But the driving force behind the Charter was far less the desire for parliamentary democracy than the urgent demand for the redress of economic grievances. The middle-class Reformers might not disagree with the Charter; but they disagreed profoundly with the Chartists. The Chartist Movement was a working-class movement, seeking higher wages and better conditions, the repeal of the obnoxious Poor Law Act, the passing of a better Factory Act, and many other economic reforms, or even a social revolution. The Anti-Corn Law agitation was a movement of the employing and middle classes designed to lower prices, in order to reduce the cost of living and thereby to bring down the costs of production in industry. Thus the fundamental antagonism between Chartists and "Leaguers," as

the Corn Law repealers were generally called, was an affair, not of programmes, but of social and economic attitudes.   Even Chartists who wanted
the Corn Laws repealed in many cases hated the League, and suspected it of
being a plot to distract allegiance from the Charter.   Even Leaguers who
favoured Universal Suffrage were apt to hate Chartism as a movement
calculated to set class against class.   The League was embryonic Liberalism,
based on the collaboration of classes to get the best out of Capitalism ;   the
Chartist Movement was embryonic Socialism, based on the class struggle,
and hostile, above all, to the newly dominant middle-class industrialists.

This contrast ignores certain exceptions.   There were Chartists who were
prepared to collaborate with the middle-class reformers in order to get the
points of the Charter adopted ;   and there were Leaguers who were prepared
to make an alliance with the Chartists in order to carry both repeal and
reform.   But the main bodies of the two movements were in constant
opposition, and even those who were in theory prepared to work together
found cordial co-operation impossible in practice.   Especially did the plunge
of the Chartists in 1839 into abortive revolt scare away middle-class sympathisers, whose ideas of reform were based on a peaceful development of
Capitalism towards Democracy.

There were, moreover, divisions in the Chartist ranks, not only on the
question of class collaboration, but also on the whole question of industrialism.
Chartism inherited from earlier working-class movements a marked agrarian
tendency, which found its strongest supporters in the half-starved operatives
of the factory towns.   These men, who had been followers of Cobbett and
Hunt, were still largely peasants at heart, though enclosures and the new
farming had driven them, or their parents, from the villages into the towns.
Especially the handloom weavers and the framework knitters, who had been
used to work in their own homes, largely in the country, under the domestic
system, hated the new machines which had taken their livelihood away, and
hated the lords of the new machines.   To them the proposal to repeal the
Corn Laws appeared as a plan to complete the ruin of the countryside and the
domination of machinofacture.   Feargus O'Connor, an Irishman with an
agrarian tradition behind him, owed much of his influence, as Cobbett had
done, to his instinctive sympathy with men of this type.   He and Bronterre
O'Brien headed the anti-industrialist wing of Chartism, and were foremost in
denouncing the Anti-Corn Law League as a plot to lower wages and to force
all the workers to slave in the factories.   On the other hand, Lovett, Hetherington, and other leaders who belonged to the skilled urban crafts were more
disposed to accept industrialism as the necessary basis of Society.   While
O'Connor and O'Brien denounced industrialism, they followed Robert
Owen in seeking to devise means for its social control.   O'Brien also came
round to this view later, after his breach with O'Connor ;   but his change of
view became complete only after the Corn Laws had been repealed.

Yet it was in vain that Place urged Lovett and his group towards a real policy of co-operation with the middle classes. Place wanted the Chartists to take up the repeal of the Corn Laws and add it to the working-class programme, receiving in return middle-class support for at least some measure of political reform—perhaps Household Suffrage. Lovett, after the fiasco of 1839, was prepared—on terms—for collaboration with the middle classes ; but he was no more willing than O'Connor to fling himself into what he regarded as an essentially middle-class agitation or to modify the claim to Manhood Suffrage or surrender the name of the Charter.

Thus the two great movements went forward side by side, often in bitter antagonism and never in alliance, the one to its resounding success and the other to failure and defeat. The Corn Laws were repealed in 1846 ; the Charter has never been conceded, though several of its points have been substantially achieved. The predominantly " middle-class " movement succeeded because the social and economic forces of the country were on its side. The working-class movement failed, not so much because it was ill-led and at sixes and sevens—though it was—as because the workers were not yet powerful enough to force their will on Society. At every stage, any leftward movement among the Chartists tended to drive their right-wing supporters into the camp of the Anti-Corn Law League. The League was working with the times ; it had the immense advantage of proposing a single reform, perfectly practicable within the existing order. The Chartists, in fact if not in name, were asking for a new social order, based on a radical reconstruction of Society. But the season for that was not till the rising middle classes had time to develop and to exhaust the vast new resources which the Industrial Revolution had placed at their command.

BOOKS

G. D. H. Cole. *Chartist Portraits.*
G. Slater. *The Growth of Modern England.*
A. Prentice. *History of the Anti-Corn Law League.*
M. Hovell. *The Chartist Movement.*
J. Morley. *Life of Richard Cobden.*
G. M. Trevelyan. *Life of John Bright.*

2. CHARTISM, 1840-1842

By the middle of 1840, despite the imprisonment of many of its leaders, Chartism showed clear signs of revival. A national conference founded a new body—the National Charter Association—and, defying the legal ban on " Corresponding Societies "—which could indeed hardly be invoked against it by a Government that was not prepared to proceed against the Anti-Corn Law League—for the first time gave the movement a national organisation based on an individual subscribing membership. This membership rose to over 20,000 in 1842. New men took the place of the absent leaders ; but in the main the N.C.A. was, from the first, dominated by Feargus O'Connor, who used his journal, the *Northern Star*, by far the most influential working-class paper, to confirm his personal ascendancy. O'Connor was in prison till August, 1841 ; but from gaol he wrote articles and controlled the movement.

What he controlled was, however, only a fraction of the Chartist body of 1839. Lovett and his friends would have nothing to do with O'Connor or with the N.C.A., and were, in return, roundly denounced as apostates. Lovett and John Collins had spent their time in gaol writing their little book, " Chartism," which attempted to put the whole movement on an educational basis. Lovett had indeed abandoned hope of getting the Charter by a coup, and now wanted the movement to settle down to a solid course of education, to found schools for the children instead of conducting fiery agitations, and to rely on self-improvement as the means to social regeneration. His book is a plan for a national system of education on a voluntary basis, entirely without State aid or control. On his release he organised the National Association for Promoting the Political and Social Improvement of the People, in order to carry out his educational ideas. The Association founded one school, with Lovett at its head. But it gained no support outside the circle of Lovett's friends ; and those who did support it were ostracised by O'Connor and the N.C.A. Thus one of the three groups which together had founded Chartism practically passed out of the movement. " London is rotten," O'Connor declared.

Other Chartist moderates went off into other schemes of their own. Chartist Churches, a sort of Radical ethical societies, were founded in Birmingham, Paisley, Bristol, and a number of other towns. Christian Chartism became a rallying point for many of the more moderate groups. The Scottish Chartists kept their separate organisation, which was, on the whole, moderate in tone, though for some time the extremist, Julian Harney, was one of its paid lecturers. In short, Chartism was splitting up into a number of scarcely related movements.

The most ambitious rival to O'Connor and to the N.C.A., which had its strength among the factory workers of the North and Midlands, came from the centre which had been the third original rallying point of Chartism in the years before 1839. At Birmingham, Attwood and his friends had dropped out, and the Birmingham Political Union had died in the conflicts of 1839. But from Birmingham, which had stood from the first for an alliance of the middle and working classes, a new group of men now began to preach the old policy in a new form. Joseph Sturge, Quaker, banker and corn-merchant, connected with the Anti-Corn Law League and an honest middle-class Radical, started the Complete Suffrage Movement in 1841 as a renewed attempt to unite the classes in a demand for parliamentary reform. Sturge wanted the Chartists to drop the Charter, and all the associations of violence connected with the name, and to join with Bright and the Leaguers in a programme of reform less drastic in expression, but embodying most of its main points. He secured the backing of the Birmingham and Manchester Anti-Corn Law Leaguers, and appealed to all moderate Chartists to join him in a conference to be held at Birmingham.

Most of the discontented Chartist groups hostile to O'Connor accepted Sturge's invitation. Lovett and his friends, Collins, O'Neill, and the "Christian Chartists," even Bronterre O'Brien, who had already quarrelled with O'Connor, attended the Complete Suffrage Conference of April, 1842. The upshot was that all six points of the People's Charter were successively accepted by the Sturgeite conference. This was more than the promoters had bargained for ; but the last straw was the insistence of Lovett and his friends that the Charter itself should be endorsed by name as well as in substance. To this the Sturgeites, fearful of the violent associations of the name, would by no means agree. Finally, the conference was adjourned, in order that the whole matter might be settled later at a more representative gathering. Meanwhile, a Petition embodying the six points was sent forward to Parliament, where sixty-seven members, including all the Free Trade leaders, voted for it, and 226 against. The results of collaboration seemed to be little more hopeful than those of isolated working-class action.

The resumed Conference of the Complete Suffrage Union met in December, 1842. This time the meeting was thoroughly packed by the Chartists, O'Connor and his group attending as well as the sections previously represented. The struggle over the Charter was at once renewed. Lovett moved and O'Connor seconded its endorsement. This was carried, and Sturge and his followers at once left the hall. The Complete Suffrage Movement, based on the alliance of class, came to a sudden and ignominious end. The Complete Suffrage Union, indeed, maintained a nominal existence till 1844, but from this point both Sturge and Lovett dropped wholly out of the main stream of political agitation.

While the Complete Suffragists were organising their Petition, the National Charter Association was busy with a Petition of its own. The dimensions of O'Connor's organisation are shown by the fact that over three and a quarter million signatures are said to have been secured. Thomas Slingsby Duncombe, an upper-class Radical M.P., who was later closely associated with the Trade Union Movement, as well as with O'Connor's ill-fated Land Scheme, presented it, and a new Chartist Convention assembled to give it backing. In the House, Macaulay made his famous and trenchant attack on Universal Suffrage, and the Petition was rejected by 287 votes to forty-nine. Once more the Chartists had asked Parliament to reform itself ; and once more they had been rebuffed. Once more they were faced by the question of adopting " ulterior measures," or of acquiescing, at least for the time, in the defeat of their hopes.

Nothing, save meetings of protest, happened until August, 1842. But in that month a strike movement, beginning in Lancashire, spread rapidly through the industrial districts of the North and Midlands. A temporary recovery of trade in 1841 had been followed by a new and severe depression, and employers were generally attempting to cut wages. The strikes began in opposition to the proposed reductions, but they spread like wildfire and rapidly assumed, under Chartist influence, a political form. O'Connor at first opposed the movement, which he professed to regard as a device of the Anti-Corn Law League to discredit the Chartists ; but when he realised the strength of the popular feeling he changed his tune. A Chartist Conference met at Manchester and attempted to take the lead. Chartist speakers went everywhere among the operatives ; meeting after meeting of strikers passed Chartist resolutions and declared that work would not be resumed until the Charter became law. Bodies of strikers went round Lancashire and parts of Yorkshire stopping the mills where work was still proceeding, and removing the plugs from the boilers in order to cut off the source of power. Hence the movement is sometimes called " The Plug Plot." Chartism, because of the strike wave, had an even bigger mass following in 1842 than in 1839. But there was less real coherence behind it, and it had shed such middle-class backing as it had ever secured.

Strikes on a falling market can hardly succeed unless they become revolutions. The Government speedily posted troops throughout the disturbed areas, and made hundreds of arrests. Very soon nearly all the leading Chartists were in gaol or in hiding, or had fled overseas ; and soon the starving workers were driven back to the factories on the employers' terms. The second phase of Chartism ended, like the first, in a defeat which threatened the dissolution of the movement.

BOOKS

G. D. H. Cole. *Chartist Portraits.*
M. Beer. *History of British Socialism.*
M. Hovell. *The Chartist Movement.*
R. G. Gammage. *History of Chartism.*
S. Hobhouse. *Joseph Sturge.*
H. V. Faulkner. *Chartism and the Churches.*
T. Cooper. *The Life of Thomas Cooper.*

3. THE LAND SCHEME—THE YEAR OF REVOLUTIONS

After 1842, what remained of Chartism passed completely under the domination of O'Connor. The 'forties were a great period of transition, both in politics and in working-class affairs. While the Chartists were trying to carry on their agitation along lines hallowed by Radical tradition, the attention of the workers was already being turned to new problems and forms of organisation. Victorianism was beginning; the foundations were being laid for the economic stabilisation which marked the middle years of the nineteenth century.

In 1846 the Free Traders gained their point, and Sir Robert Peel, at one blow, repealed the Corn Laws and broke the old Tory party asunder. In 1847 the long agitation for factory reform at last secured the passing of the Ten Hours Act, and so made operative some of the changes urged by Robert Owen more than thirty years earlier. These were significant changes in national policy, marking a clear transition from the struggles of the Industrial Revolution to the smooth and secure working of the new capitalist order.

No less significant were the new departures in working-class organisation. Owenite Co-operation had nearly died out, despite many efforts to revive it. But in 1844 a little body of workmen, inspired by Owenite ideas, but seeking to realise them in a new way, founded the Co-operative store of the "Rochdale Pioneers," and set going the great modern Co-operative Movement based on the association of consumers for mutual trading. In 1845 the Trade Union revival, which had become marked as early as 1842, led to the formation of a new co-ordinating body—the National Association of United Trades for the Protection of Labour. But this body no longer planned a general strike or a sudden overthrow of Capitalism; it was rather a loose defensive alliance, the forerunner of the modern Trades Union Congress.

The old ideas, however, died hard. The revival of Trade Unionism led to a number of fresh experiments, on Owenite lines, in producers' Co-operation, including a Co-operative coal mine near Oldham. The National Association of United Trades for the Protection of Labour created a companion body—the National Association of United Trades for the Employment of Labour—of which the direct purpose was to promote the formation of "Union Shops," like those of 1832. The pure Owenite Societies, shrunk up now into a sect more concerned with the promotion of "Rational Religion" than with economic or political change, made their last important adventure in community building in 1839, when they purchased Queenwood, or Harmony Hall, in Hampshire. The Queenwood Community lasted till 1845, and thus coincided in time with the greater part of the Chartist agitation.

These various movements, except the last, will be dealt with more fully in subsequent chapters of this book, in connection with the later developments which came out of them. They are mentioned here because they undoubtedly affected the course of Chartism during the years following the defeat of 1842. The rejection of the second Chartist Petition, the defeat of the strikes of 1842, and the break-up of the movement into a number of fragments, had made it evidently hopeless to expect that Parliament could be speedily forced to accept the Charter, or to make any substantial concession to the demands for electoral reform, or indeed to the social demands which lay behind the Chartist movement. The new Poor Law, far from being swept away, was being enforced with increasing firmness. The Chartists had either to retire from the field altogether, or to reconcile themselves to a long period of propagandist activity without direct results, or to find some new course into which the movement could be deflected. As we have seen, Lovett and his friends turned definitely to educational work ; and many lesser Chartists passed over into the Free Trade movement. But neither of these was a way of holding the main body of Chartists together ; and O'Connor and his friends, influenced by the developments which they saw around them, shaped a different course.

On the one hand, from 1842 onwards, the *Northern Star*, watching the Trade Union revival and eager to secure the Unions as allies, gave more and more space to Trade Union affairs. On the other hand, from 1843 onwards, we begin to hear of plans for combating unemployment and building up a new democratic society by planting Chartists on the land. In 1845 these schemes took definite shape in the creation of the Chartist Co-operative Land Society, re-named later the National Land Company. O'Connorville, or Herons-gate, near Rickmansworth, was founded in 1846, and soon several other estates were purchased and planted with Chartist settlers, pledged to spade-cultivation on their small holdings owned by the Society, which they were to purchase on the instalment plan.

The Chartist Land Scheme, fathered and run by O'Connor from 1845 to 1848, obviously owed something to Owen. But it was essentially different from Owen's " Home Colonies " because it was in no sense socialistic. At Queenwood, at any rate in theory, the community (except some ' paying guests ') cultivated the land in common and shared in the fruit of the common labour. At O'Connorville each settler had his individual holding, for which a rent was due to the Society. The product of his labour, apart from the rent, which included an instalment of the purchase price, was his own. Owen had planned to cover the world with mainly self-supporting Socialist Communities ; O'Connor planned to cover it with peasant villages of small holders.

But if the two plans were thus vitally different, they had much in common, and they appealed fundamentally to the same land-hunger of the new urban populations created by the Industrial Revolution. This explains why thousands of workers rushed to support O'Connor's scheme, as they had rushed to support Owenism a few years before. They did feel that work on the land might be a way of escape from factory tyranny and unemployment.

Unfortunately, Owen's and O'Connor's schemes had also in common an excessive sketchiness and optimism in their financial arrangements.

O'Connor, like Owen, produced marvellous rows of figures showing the certain financial success of his settlements; but his figures were based on much too favourable estimates of productivity. Money rolled in, but before long the National Land Company was in serious financial trouble. In 1847 a great Press agitation against it was begun, and serious charges were made that O'Connor was stealing the funds. In these, some of his fellow-Chartists joined. The outcome, in 1848, was a Parliamentary Committee of Enquiry, which showed that the finances were in a hopeless tangle. It was, however, proved that O'Connor, so far from having gained by his control of the scheme, had lost a good deal of his own money, in addition to most of the £90,000 collected, mainly in small sums, from the subscribers to the scheme. In 1851 the National Land Company was wound up; but O'Connorville lasted on as a fairly flourishing little community for another twenty-five years, the settlers having been allowed to acquire their holdings individually when the main scheme collapsed.

From 1845 to 1847 the Land Company absorbed almost the entire attention of the Chartist remnant. But candidates were still nominated at by-elections, and often elected on the show of hands, though they did not subsequently go to the poll. In 1846 O'Connor was thus nominated at Nottingham; but in the General Election of 1847 he went to the poll and was elected with a good majority as the first Chartist M.P. He held the seat until 1852, when the madness which had for some years been growing upon him caused his removal to a private asylum. He died insane in 1855. But before his affliction came upon him he took the lead in the last great Chartist rally of 1848—the year in which a wave of revolutions swept over Europe, leaving scarcely any country save Great Britain untouched by armed insurrection of some sort.

From the very beginning the Chartist movement, though it was predominantly national and isolated, had held some intercourse with revolutionary movements in other countries, and some of its leaders had shown internationalist leanings. This tendency was greatly encouraged by the fact that, in the 'forties, London was the centre where large numbers of political refugees were settled, and from which many foreign Radical and Nationalist agitations were carried on. A German Communist League was formed by the exiles in London in 1840. Engels settled in London in 1844. Marx, later associated with Ernest Jones in his attempts to revive Chartism after 1848, was still abroad, mostly in Brussels; but he came sometimes to England, and was in close touch, through Engels, with British developments. Mazzini and his group of Italian exiles were in London, and had made England the centre of their revolutionary activity. Polish exiles abounded, and several, like Beniowski, threw themselves wholeheartedly into the Chartist agitation.

In 1847, the year when Marx and Engels drafted the Communist Manifesto and so began the modern phase of Socialism, there was an intensification of activity among the foreigners in London, based on an anticipation of the events then preparing on the Continent.   Chartist leaders took a prominent part in demonstrations on international affairs; Marx came over from Brussels to address a big meeting in London.   The excitement of the exiles could not but communicate itself to the British leaders.   While the Land Scheme was slowly collapsing Chartism was experiencing a revival of more directly political interest.

Early in 1848 the Revolution in France gave the signal, and revolutionary movements developed in one European country after another.   But in Great Britain there was barely a hint of revolution, and in Ireland Smith O'Brien's abortive revolt was quelled before it had time to begin.   The time had gone by when the Chartists could even start to plan an insurrection. There were, indeed, small groups of extremists, especially in London, who attempted some sort of plot, but were betrayed without being able to take any action.   Instead the main body of the Chartists busied themselves in collecting signatures for a Third National Petition in support of the Charter, summoned a new National Convention, and prepared to back up the Petition with a monster procession and demonstration which was to present it to Parliament.   The rejection of the Petition was to be met by the election of a Chartist National Assembly, which was not to dissolve until the Charter became the law of the land.

The story of the great fiasco of the Kennington Common meeting is well known.   The Government, hugely exaggerating the Chartists' strength and mistaking their intentions, placed the aged Duke of Wellington in command, and made every preparation for dealing with a formidable insurrectionary movement.   Over 150,000 special constables were enrolled— Louis Napoleon, soon to be Emperor of the French, was one.   Troops and artillery were concealed at strategic points all over central London.   The Government offices were barricaded, and the Civil Servants armed.   The Chartists had arranged to assemble on Kennington Common and to march thence to Westminster.   The Government proposed to stop this by holding the bridges with troops, and by refusing to let the demonstrators come near Parliament.   Shut away on the south side of the river they would be harmless, and their display would lose all its moral effect.

Estimates of the numbers who assembled on Kennington Common vary widely.   *The Times* said 20,000 ; the *Northern Star* 250,000.   The former is probably nearer the truth.   At all events the leaders, in face of the police prohibition, made no attempt to force the bridges ; and, after a number of speeches had been made, the Great National Petition was ignominiously delivered at the House of Commons in a cab.   It had 5,700,000 signatures, according to O'Connor's estimate ; the Officials of the House made the number less than two millions.

The great meeting of April 10th, 1848, thus dispersed peaceably without justifying either the hopes of continental revolutionaries or the exaggerated fears of the governing classes. The small groups of underground plotters were rounded up ; the National Assembly dispersed with nothing achieved. The first and second periods of Chartism had ended in defeat ; the third ended in a wholly inglorious fiasco. "Lord John Russell presents his humble duty to the Queen," wrote the Prime Minister of the day, " and has the honour to state that the Kennington Common meeting has been a complete failure." The revolutions and counter-revolutions which convulsed Europe in 1848 and the following years found no further echo in Great Britain.

BOOKS

G. D. H. Cole. *Chartist Portraits.*
M. Beer. *History of British Socialism*, Vol. II.
R. G. Gammage. *History of Chartism.*
H. A. L. Fisher. *The Revolutionary Tradition in Europe.*
A. Somerville. *Autobiography of a Working Man.*

4. THE DISSOLUTION OF CHARTISM

After 1848 Chartism was finally dead as a national force appealing to the mass of the workers. O'Connor, verging on madness, lost his hold, and there was left no leader capable of swaying the multitude as he, with all his faults, had been able to sway them. Chartism had fallen from its high estate ; but it did not easily die out. For another ten years it lingered on, surviving to the eve of that revival of working-class political activity which we associate with the names of Karl Marx and the International Working Men's Association of 1864. Many links, indeed, serve to bind the two movements together. Many old Chartists played their part in the First International ; and Chartist activity from 1848 onwards partly anticipated many features of Marx's International.

These last years of Chartism are associated chiefly with the tireless and hopeless labours of Ernest Jones. Trained for a diplomatic career, and of upper class origin, Jones became, with the gradual waning of O'Connor's influence, the leader of the movement. By one association and newspaper after another he strove to revive the dying agitation. From 1848 to 1850 he was in prison ; but thereafter his activity was ceaseless. He kept the National Charter Association alive, and practically directed its policy between the Conferences, which were still held regularly until 1858. He tried in vain, especially in the abortive " Mass Movement " of 1854, to get the Trade Unions, by then growing rapidly in numbers and power, to put their weight behind the demand for the Charter. But by 1858 the movement was finally dead. Jones himself, to Marx's great disgust, changed his views and became, in the 'sixties, an advocate of united action for Reform by the middle and working classes. Working-class political action was due to revive within a few years ; but the revival took a new form, based on the changed position and attitude of the workers themselves. Chartism, however, in its last phase, became more internationalist than it had been in its earlier period ; and the Chartist International Association prepared the way for the International Working Men's Association of 1864—which in its turn provided a link between Chartism and the revival of purely British working-class action in the late 'sixties under the leadership of men such as Applegarth and Alexander Macdonald.

Why did Chartism fail ? And why, having failed in its main objective, did it thus die gradually away, leaving no organised movement for the next generation to inherit ? The causes of its failure have been suggested already. It set out to accomplish a political change for which the time was not ripe, as the means to an economic change still less possible of immediate realisation. It was a challenge of a working class still undeveloped, uneducated, unequipped with adequate organisation or leadership of its own, to a dominant economic power strongly entrenched, ably led, and, above all, full of the self-confidence of actual and prospective achievement. Before the great alliance of the old and new governing classes, which had been cemented by the Reform Act of 1832, a purely working-class movement was bound to go down.

But Chartism was weakened, too, by the lack of any common constructive principles. The purely political programme of the Charter was a simple formula designed to enlist the support of all sorts and conditions of workers and left-wing Radicals, whatever their various ideas and policies might be. It secured unity of programme, but behind the programme there was no unity of idea or of policy. Some Chartists were Owenite Socialists, some agrarian individualists, some currency reformers, some simply rebels against the new Poor Law and the factory system, some educationists, some revolutionary nationalists, a very few in the latter days of the movement Socialists in the modern sense. Their followers were mainly the half-starved workers of the factory towns, to whom Chartism, like all other movements, was a bread and butter question. This mass might conceivably have been welded together into a solid body had the leaders agreed in their objectives as well as on a programme which merely masked fundamental differences of outlook. But when leaders led all ways at once, what hope was there for the rank and file ?

Writers about Chartism, observing the welter of conflict in policies and personalities, have been apt to colour their descriptions of the movement in accordance with their personal likes and dislikes. Many of them have idolised Lovett, because he was obviously a man of high ideals and strict personal rectitude. They have almost all abused O'Connor, because he was obviously a mob-orator and a man of most muddle-headed ideas. But the fact remains that Lovett, the ideal secretary, had no capacity at all for moving men in the mass. He was far too intellectualist and moralist to make a leader—far too much a prig to affect men in the mass with his own enthusiasm for the cause. O'Connor, on the other hand, was, with all his faults, a born inspirer of men. He could fire men's spirits ; but he could offer them no practicable plan of action. He led the Chartists to disaster ; but without him it is very doubtful whether there would ever have been the great mass movement which he led. The trouble was that, having no common philosophy, or ideal, or policy, men of these widely different temperaments and qualities were not under the compulsion of any force strong enough to make them work in co-operation. A common idea might have held them together ; the Charter, a mere common programme, was not enough to prevent them from giving their mutual dislikes free rein.

Yet even if they had worked together Chartism could not have succeeded either in its immediate programme or in its underlying economic aims. Both Capitalism and the working class had to develop further before the struggle between them could be waged on equal terms. The history of the British working-class movement up to 1848 is the history of its adolescence, which is also the adolescence of the working class. In the later sections of this book we shall be studying its gradual development to maturer forms, corresponding to stages in the development of Capitalism itself. But, before we pass on beyond this period of inchoate struggle and nascent ideas, we had best pause to make a brief estimate of the conditions under which the workers were living during the earlier half of the nineteenth century, and of the position which they had reached about 1850, when both Capitalism and working-class organisation were entering on a new phase.

BOOKS

G. D. H. Cole. *Chartist Portraits.*
J. West. *History of the Chartist Movement.*
M. Beer. *History of British Socialism*, Vol. II.
R. G. Gammage. *History of Chartism.*
T. Rothstein. *From Chartism to Labourism.*
P. W. Slosson. *The Decline of the Chartist Movement.*
S. Maccoby. *English Radicalism*, Vol. II.

CHAPTER IX

THE CONDITION OF THE WORKERS IN THE FIRST HALF OF THE NINETEENTH CENTURY

THE period covered by this section coincides roughly with what is commonly called the "Industrial Revolution." The great change in industry had, indeed, not only begun but considerably developed before 1789, at which point our survey of the working-class movement really begins. But it had hardly begun, before that time, to evoke a characteristic response. There were both Trade Unions and popular movements, strikes, and bread riots, before the opening of the revolutionary wars ; but, as we have seen, it was under the three-fold impulsion of the changes in industry, the winds of doctrine that blew from France, and the peculiar economic and political conditions created by the long war with France, that a Radical working-class movement first grew up and assumed gradually a definite shape.

If 1789 is a convenient starting point, 1848 is a convenient date for a pause and a backward glance before this narrative is resumed. For by 1848 the first phase of the great change was definitely over, and a new phase was beginning. Until nearly the middle of the nineteenth century the Industrial Revolution was still in the convulsions which attended its making ; thereafter it was not only an accomplished, but also a recognised fact. Until about 1848 a large body of opinion was still questioning, or protesting against, the new industrialism, and a good many reformers were still really trying to put back the hands of the clock. But, at least from the middle of the century, these protests nearly ceased, or ceased to command attention, and all classes alike settled down to make the best of the new conditions.

Thus, on the one hand, the repeal of the Corn Laws in 1846 completed the step first plainly taken in the Reform Act of 1832—the acceptance of the new industrialism by the old holders of political power. Sir Robert Peel's act, though it split his party, really united the new and old governing classes, by making the acceptance of industrialism a fundamental postulate of British politics. The landowner ceased to conduct the orchestra ; but he did very well for himself by playing second fiddle to the manufacturer. The country squires who cursed Peel in 1846 soon learned to acquiesce in the results of his policy—not least because the first twenty years of Free Trade turned out to be the golden age of British agriculture.

Similarly, as we have seen, the later 'forties were a turning-point in the history of the working-class movement. From 1789 to 1848 there were many successive waves of working-class revolt—the Corresponding Societies, the Luddites, the Cobbettite Reformers, the Owenite Trades Unionists, the Chartists ; and in every one of these movements, save the first (and here the parallel movement of the United Irishmen and the writings of Thomas Spence express the familiar theme), the passion for free access to the land and the revolt against machinery played a vital part. From Spence's " Plan " and Paine's " Agrarian Justice " to Owen's and O'Connor's Land Schemes, the workers found inspiration in ideas essentially hostile to industrialism and based on the preservation or renewal of a system based mainly on agriculture.

This agrarian background of working-class unrest is, of course, easy to explain. Up to the middle of the nineteenth century the main body of the workers consisted either of former peasants or of folk with a lively peasant memory and an instinctive peasant attitude. They hated the factory, not only because it was a hateful place in which they had to work terribly long hours under terribly evil conditions and subject to a rigid and uncongenial discipline, but also because it was new-fangled, and had been the principal means of destroying the accustomed ways and means of life. In its most fundamental aspect, every working-class revolt up to and including Chartism was a peasant movement.

But after 1848, not only was the sorry relic of the peasantry in the countryside too reduced to rebel—it had shot its last bolt in 1831—the factory worker had largely forgotten, at least with his conscious mind, his peasant origin. He had got used to industrialism ; he accepted it as his masters did ; he settled down to make the best of it. The decay of Chartism in the 'forties marks the critical stage in this transition. When the workers forsook Chartism for the new Trade Unionism and the new Co-operation, they turned their backs on the country and became, in feeling, townsmen in a land of towns.

The growth of the new urban working-class movement I shall be tracing in the next section of this study. Here my point is to mark the continuity up to 1848 of the various agitations which this section has described, and to show their connection with the growth of the new industrialism which determined their course. For about the middle of the century comes a turning-point, not merely in the working-class movement, but also in Capitalism itself. Till then, the new industrialism was settling down, and affirming its empire ; thereafter, successfully and, for the time, unassailably established, it was sure of its foundations and could go on to fresh conquests in a somewhat different spirit.

Every writer on the period we call the " Industrial Revolution " has dwelt on the ruthless exploitation of the workers which marked its advance. The abuse of child labour, the long hours of employment, the insanitary state of factories and towns, the low wages and high profits, the rigid discipline, the repressive attitude, based on fear, of master to man, the callousness to industrial suffering at home even of great " humanitarians " like Wilberforce, the savage caricature of Smithian and Ricardian economics which found common acceptance in respectable circles—these have been described in many books and illustrated by evidence from countless Royal Commissions, Parliamentary Debates, and other contemporary sources. Writers may differ in their interpretation of these facts. The facts themselves are not disputed.

Why, I asked almost at the beginning of this book, was the era of the Industrial Revolution marked by this intensity of exploitation ? And why, by the middle of the nineteenth century, do we pass, after a period of transition, into an epoch a good deal less savage in its reading of " economic laws," and less disposed to treat its employees as a species of dangerous wild beasts ? Broadly speaking, I find the answer, not so much in a growth of humanitarian feeling or of civilisation, as in a change in the position of Capitalism itself. Up to nearly the middle of the century, though wealth was accumulating fast and average rates of profit were high, industry suffered from a severe shortage of available capital. Banking was hardly put on secure foundations adapted to the new needs of industry for credit until after the Bank Charter Act of 1844. And, although the joint stock company as a form of organisation was extending its scope throughout the century, it was not securely established, or made into a flexible instrument for the raising of capital for ordinary business, until the principle of limited liability was generally conceded to shareholders by the Acts of 1855 and 1862.

The ordinary employer was thus under the necessity of financing his business either by finding rich partners ready to join in his venture, or by borrowing on his own personal resources and security, or by accumulating out of profits the means wherewith to finance the expansion of his trade. Under these conditions, the " abstinence " of the capitalist, advanced by economists such as Senior as the justification of his reward, was not wholly a myth. The man who had become a big employer might, in course of time, buy a large estate, set up as a squire, and enter the ranks of the aristocracy with a handle to his name ; but the smaller employer often pinched and saved in order to put every possible penny back into his business. And, if he pinched himself, he was not likely to have much compunction about pinching his workpeople a good deal harder, though the reward of their abstinence, as well as of his own, went in the end to swell his wealth.

It may even be said that, until means were devised, in the modern joint stock company, for making the savings of " small " men available for the use of large-scale industry, the very rapid advance of industrialism was only possible by the accumulation of all *surplus* income in the hands of a very limited class. Exploiting almost without competition in many trades the vast markets of a developing world, the capitalist could profitably use in the expansion of his business every penny he could lay hands on. There were, indeed, big fluctuations of trade, due to the unregulated competition with which production was carried on ; but the tendency of trade was to more and more rapid expansion, and it was all manufacturers could do to accumulate enough fresh capital to enable them to keep pace with the growth of demand. Thus, every rise in wages presented itself as a subtraction of so much sorely needed capital from productive use, and its diversion to mere unnecessary consumption by the wage-earning class.

In these circumstances, thrift came to be regarded as the paramount virtue, and the accumulation of wealth as a moral duty. The enforced abstinence of the workers was set side by side with the voluntary abstinence of the capitalists as the twin beacon-light of national prosperity. The humanitarian, prompt to denounce the inhumanity of negro slavery abroad, convinced himself that low wages and factory slavery at home, because they served to promote the rapid accumulation of capital, were the true means to the well-being of the nation and of the operatives themselves. The economists of the Society for the Diffusion of Useful Knowledge composed panegyrics on the blessings brought by machinery with a sublime disregard for the plight of the unemployed hand-loom weaver or the unfortunate child labourer in the factory. Strikes and other movements of unrest seemed treason to the new beneficent power which was causing the trade returns and the national capital to increase by leaps and bounds.

This mood of jubilation was especially prevalent when the interruptions to trade during the Napoleonic wars and the great slump which followed the Peace of 1815 had been successfully left behind. Then Political Economy blossomed like the rose ; then Societies and Institutions arose in all parts of the country to hymn the blessings of the machine age. David Ricardo, the principal exponent of the new economic science, might express his doubts whether machinery had not brought more curses than blessings to the labouring class. This part of his teaching went unheeded by the well-to-do. Complacency became the hall-mark of the economics of the " Manchester School." And against this orthodox Political Economy the economists who took the side of the workers developed their hostile criticisms of the new order of things, and the leaders of working-class opinion learned from Hodgskin, Thompson, and Robert Owen a new gospel of their own.

By the middle of the century these conditions were rapidly passing away. The joint stock company, by mobilising the small investors in the service of large-scale industry, was providing a far simpler means for the accumulation of capital, and one which did not, to the same extent, call for the monopolisation of the whole " surplus " by a small class of employers. It became more readily possible for the *entrepreneurs* to control large masses of capital which they did not own. The supply of industrial capital became more abundant, both because the national income had greatly increased and because more of it could be readily applied to industry by a wider class. There was no longer the same need for the capitalist to " abstain," or for wages to be kept down to the lowest point. Thrift and abstinence were still regarded as eminent virtues ; but they did not to the same extent involve starvation wages. The workman could be urged to save and invest, where before he had only been urged to go without. This is not to say that wages rose at all in proportion to the increase in national wealth. They did not ; but out of the rapidly-growing surplus enough went to the workers as a class to cause an appreciable rise in the standard of living.

Thus, in the case of the cotton industry, real wages, very low on account of high prices during the Napoleonic wars, rose appreciably with falling prices up to 1830, though money wages were appreciably reduced. But between 1830 and 1840 both money wages and real wages fell. Then came a big leap forward in real wages between 1840 and 1850, and after a period of ups and downs a further big advance between 1860 and 1870. An analysis of wages in certain other vital trades brings out the same conclusions, that the factory workers endured the worst sufferings during, and just after, the Napoleonic wars ; that between 1820 and 1830 falling prices caused the standard of living to rise slowly ; that after 1830 came another serious setback ; but that by the middle 'forties the worst period of the Industrial Revolution was over, and the workers, starting at a very low level, began gradually to win a share in the great prosperity of industry under the new conditions, though there was a temporary setback, due to rising prices, in the middle 'fifties.

In the accompanying charts and tables I have done my best to make sense of such wage statistics as are available for the first half of the nineteenth century. In using these figures it is always necessary to bear in mind that there existed no regular compilations of wage-rates or earnings, no machinery for collective bargaining save in a very few trades, and in many no standard rates applicable over all or most firms in a district. For some of the skilled crafts there were rates fairly widely recognised ; but in the factory trades wages varied greatly from firm to firm. Rates for agricultural labour are apt to be misleading until after 1834, as they take no account of the allowances paid in many areas under the Speenhamland system. The estimates here made for the various occupations are based largely on the detailed investigations of Professor Bowley and Mr. G. H. Wood, published in the *Journal of the Royal Statistical Society* half a century ago. They are meant only as very rough approximations, and should be taken only as indicating the broad trends. The money wages have been estimated at approximate intervals of five years from 1800 to 1860, and the figures should not be taken as relating exactly to particular years. I have chosen as good a representative sample as I could find. The first chart deals with the wages of skilled workers in London. The second covers a number of occupations in the cotton industry in the Manchester area. The third shows what information is available about engineers, carpenters, and builders' labourers, also in the Manchester district. The fourth gives the only continuous series available in respect of miners, and is confined to the Scottish coalfield. The fifth selects two counties, one in the North and one in the South, to illustrate the divergent movements of agricultural wages ; and it also gives Professor Bowley's estimate of the average movement of agricultural wages over England as a whole. It will be seen from these charts that, as might have been expected, wages fluctuated most of all in mining, and also considerably in the cotton industry ; they were relatively stable in the skilled crafts, except building.

The sixth chart shows the movement of the cost of living, as estimated, up to 1850, by Professor Silberling, on the basis of price statistics preserved in the Board of Trade. In order to continue this index, which stops at 1850, for another decade I have used Mr. G. H. Wood's index, which begins at that date. I have also shown separately in the seventh chart the annual average price of British wheat, in order to bring out the very heavy fluctuations in the price of bread, which was the principal element in the cost of living of the worse-paid workers.

Finally, in the eighth and ninth charts, I have made an attempt to convert the money wages of a few of the selected groups into real wages by reckoning their purchasing power as measured by the index of the cost of living. The result can be only the broadest approximation ; but it seems to bring out certain essential points. Even if allowance is made for a large margin of error, the trends stand out clearly enough.

The conclusion to be drawn from these figures is plain. Shortly before the middle of the century there began everywhere a substantial advance in the standard of living. At first this was due not to rising wages but to falling prices ; but later, when prices again rose, wages, after a lag, rose more than enough to meet them. The mid-Victorian era was essentially a time of advancing prosperity, and it produced a working-class movement at once far more stably organised than the movement described in the preceding chapters of this volume, and far more disposed to live at peace with the capitalist order of society. Revolts and mass movements gave place to the well-organised but moderate Trade Unions and Co-operative Societies of the new order. The workers were ready to negotiate with their masters on the basis of things as they were, and found their masters gradually becoming more ready to negotiate with them, and to recognise the rights of collective bargaining, because they were no longer afraid that behind the workers' claims was a challenge to the capitalist industrialism on which the new society was based. Conciliation and arbitration became, as we shall see, as typical of the new order as mass movements and revolts, born of despair, had been of the period dealt with in this volume. Of course, these changes did not happen all at once, or at a uniform pace in different industries. They were most noticeable, at first, in the cotton industry, which, as it had been the first to experience the Industrial Revolution in its full force, was also the first to settle down.

It was from very intense suffering that the working class gradually emerged into these smoother waters. It would not, indeed, be true to suggest that all sorts of workers had their lot worsened as a result of the Industrial Revolution. Until the outbreak of the Napoleonic wars, the standard of living among the town craftsmen was slowly improving during the eighteenth century. War prices upset the purchasing power of wages; but thereafter the position of the craftsmen again improved. Builders, printers, workers in the food trades, tailors, skilled mechanics, and similar types of workers were not, for the most part, adversely affected by that growth of machine production which deprived the hand-loom weavers of their former prosperity. The wages of London artisans varied from 12s. to 15s. and more a week in 1760. In 1780, according to Francis Place, they were 18s., and in 1830 they had risen to 36s. This may be an exaggeration; but even if we take Professor Bowley's figure of 28s. to 30s. the rise is still substantial. On the other hand, the wages of the hand-loom weavers suffered a sensational decline. In 1800 the hand-loom weaver made about 19s. a week on the average, or about the same as the skilled artisan in a provincial town. In 1830 the artisan was getting about 23s., whereas the average earnings of the hand-loom weavers had fallen to about 6s. 3d. a week. In a less degree other craftsmen, whose skill was replaced by machinery, went through a parallel experience. From the highest point, reached about 1805, hand-loom weavers' wages fell altogether by from 60 to 80 per cent. Moreover, the once considerable auxiliary earnings of their wives and children by spinning in the home had been previously annihilated by the introduction of factory spinning after 1770. The prosperous hand-loom weavers were reduced to starvation by the growth of machines—a fact which readily explains why they were active in movements of revolt throughout the period we have been describing.

The contrast between the position of the hand-loom weavers and other types of workers is forcibly brought out by the accompanying chart. The average hand-loom weaver, who in 1800 was earning the customary wage of a skilled artisan, fell before 1820 below the standard of the miserably paid agricultural labourer, and declined still further during the following twenty years, until his craft was totally extinguished by the competition of the machine. On the other hand, the mule spinner in the factory, though his earnings varied greatly with the state of trade, and fell below the artisan level for the whole period between 1840 and 1865, asserted his position as a skilled workman, and from 1865 made up more than the ground he had lost.

It is always a most difficult task to measure by any standard the economic conditions of the working class at a period at all remote from our own. Definite wage-rates are usually hard to come by; and, even where these are

known, it is impossible to gather directly from them what the real standard
of living was.   They can, of course, be adjusted to such data as we possess,
showing the change in the level of general prices over the period with which
we are dealing.   But even a corrected figure, purporting to show real wages,
tells us little ; for over long periods there are great changes in the character
of consumption and in the necessary expenses which a working-class family
has to incur.   To take only one obvious instance, the workman of to-day has
usually to spend a considerable sum on travelling to and from his work,
whereas the workman of a century ago, though in most cases he had ceased
to live in his employer's house, or to work in his own cottage, generally lived
near his work.   Moreover, the style, as well as the standard, of living
radically changes from generation to generation, so that no exact comparison
of the purchasing power of wages at widely different times can be made.

Then, again, rates of wages give, at any time, an inadequate basis for
conclusions about the standard of living.   Piecework earnings may diverge
widely from nominal wages ; unemployment and under-employment may
reduce actual earnings far below nominal rates, and, in the days between the
decay of the Gilds and the growth of the Trade Unions, there were in many
trades no standard rates of wages paid generally to all workers of the same
type.

For all these reasons it is necessary to proceed with great caution in
making any comparison between the condition of labour during the Industrial Revolution and either an earlier or a later period.   The predominantly
agricultural civilisation of the earlier eighteenth century had standards and
needs essentially different from those of later times.   It may be that, if we
leave out the period of the Napoleonic wars and the classes of workers whose
skill was specially affected by the new machines, the nominal purchasing
power of wages actually rose during the black days of the Industrial Revolution.   But this does not at all prove that the position of the workers
changed for the better.   Needs multiplied with the growth of towns and
with the aggregation of labour into larger units.   The auxiliary sources of
income on which in the eighteenth century many workmen had relied, both
to augment their normal wages and to help them out in time of unemployment, were largely swept away.   The chance of auxiliary agricultural
earnings was lost by enclosure and urbanisation ; the family's supplementary
industrial earnings vanished with the destruction of the " domestic system " ;
except where the women and children could themselves take up factory
work.   Changes of this character cannot be measured by the recital of
mere figures about wages.

Moreover, the most drastic change caused by machinery had little to do
with wages.   The crying evil of the first half of the nineteenth century was
less the lowness of wages than the horrible factory and housing conditions and
the inhumanely long working day.   The working day not only grew longer,

but was also made, under factory conditions, far more intense. Especially in the case of women and children, there was nothing to check remorseless speeding-up throughout a working day in itself intolerably prolonged. And at the end of it the lodging to which the workers returned was usually a stifling and insanitary den, rushed up with no regard for comfort or sanitation to meet the rapid expansion of population in the factory towns.

The facts on all these points are already well known ; and I have no space to rehearse them here. Even where wages were increased, the accompanying conditions meant a real lowering of the human standard of life, and a real debasing of the human beings who were subject to their tyranny. The peasant, used to a life in the open air, found himself first thrust out of his village by enclosures and farming improvements which reduced the demand for labour, or by the decline of the domestic industry by which he and his family had lived. Then he found himself thrust into a town and a factory, or into a mine—into unfamiliar and terrifying surroundings which made him feel helpless in the hands of a great and hostile power he could not understand. Sometimes, instinctively, he turned Luddite, and smashed the machine that hurt him. At other times he broke into blind revolt, following any leader who held out to him, in language he could understand, a promise of better things. Especially he would follow any leader who, like Cobbett, could speak to him as a fellow-peasant, or, like Owen and O'Connor, in their very different ways, proposed to restore to him the land he had lost and to re-create his independence of the hated machine. Their messages he but half understood, no doubt, but he went on following them until he was tired out, and until new generations had arisen, born to the factory system and accepting it almost as part of the inexorable order of Nature. Then as, for the majority, conditions became gradually a little more tolerable, as wages began to rise, Factory Acts to be passed, employment and prices to be more stable—in short, as the new capitalist conditions became stabilised and the new ruling classes firmly seated in power, the period of revolts came to an end, and the Golden Age of Capitalism began. This section has carried the story of the working-class movement to the threshold of this "Golden Age."

BOOKS

F. M. Eden. *The State of the Poor.*
J. L. and B. Hammond. *The Town Labourer.*
A. L. Bowley. *History of Wages in the Nineteenth Century.*
G. H. Wood. *History of Wages in the Cotton Trade.*
G. D. H. Cole and R. Postgate. *The Common People, 1746–1946.*
G. R. Porter. *The Progress of the Nation* (edition of 1851).

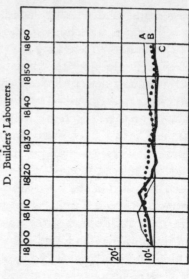

CHART 3.—MANCHESTER CRAFTSMEN.

A. Ironmoulders.
B. Engineers.
C. Carpenters.
D. Builders' Labourers.

CHART 5.—AGRICULTURAL LABOURERS.

A. Cumberland.
B. Sussex.
C. Estimated General Average.

WAGES AND COST OF LIVING, 1800–1860

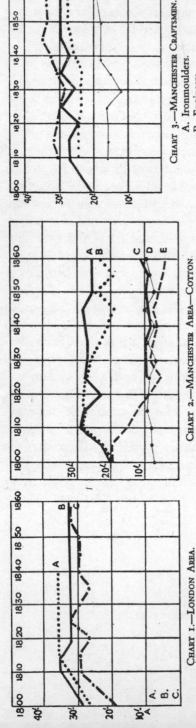

CHART 2.—MANCHESTER AREA—COTTON.

A. Mill Mechanics.
B. Mule-Spinners (Men).
C. Power-loom Weavers (Men and Women).
D. Throstle Spinners (Women).
E. Hand-loom Weavers (mostly Men).

CHART 1.—LONDON AREA.

A. London Artisans (F. Place).
B. London Compositors (Time-work).
C. London Building Craftsmen.

CHART 4.—MINERS, SCOTLAND. Day-wages.

per day

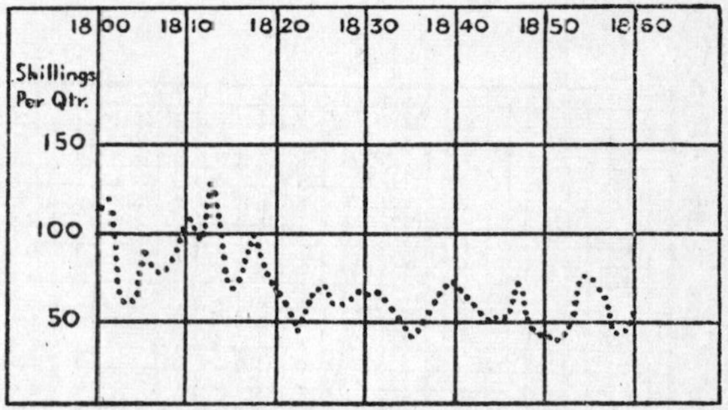

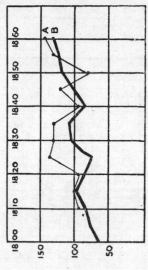

CHART 7.—WHEAT PRICES. Annual Averages.

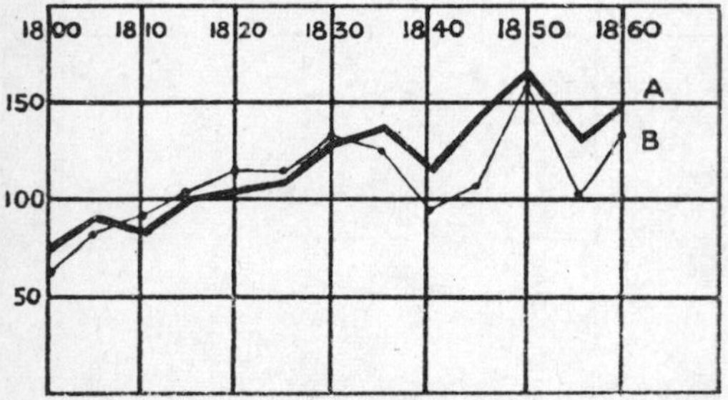

WAGES AND COST OF LIVING,
1800-1860
(continued).

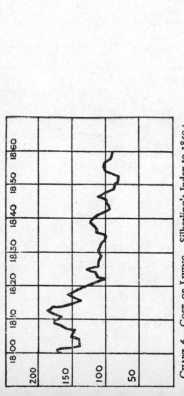

CHART 9.—REAL WAGES. Approximate Purchasing Power,
1815 = 100.

A. Agricultural Labourers, England.
B. Miners, Scotland.

CHART 6.—COST OF LIVING. Silberling's Index to 1850 :
then G. H. Wood's (1790 = 100).

CHART 8.—REAL WAGES. Approximate Purchasing Power,
1815 = 100.

A. London Compositors.
B. Manchester Mule-spinners.

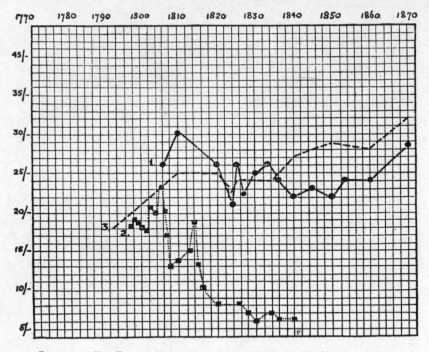

CHART 10.—THE DECLINE OF THE HAND-LOOM WEAVERS. Weekly Wages compared with Wages of Spinners and Carpenters.

1. Manchester Spinners (Bowley).
2. Hand-loom Weavers (Wood).
3. Manchester Carpenters (Bowley).

TABLE 1.—WAGES AND COST OF LIVING, 1800-1860—London

	A. Artisans (F. Place).	B. Compositors (Time Wages).	C. Building Craftsmen.
About 1790–95 .	22s.	30s.	17s.
,, 1800 . .	27s.	30s.	19s. 6d.
,, 1805 . .	30s.	33s.	25s.
,, 1810 . .	33s.	36s.	30s.
,, 1815 .	36s.	—	30s.
,, 1820 . .	36s.	33s.	27s.
,, 1825 . .	36s.	33s.	33s.
,, 1830 . .	36s.	33s.	30s.
,, 1835 . .	36s.	33s.	27s.
,, 1840 . .	—	33s.	30s.
,, 1845 . .	—	33s.	30s.
,, 1850 . .	—	33s.	30s.
,, 1855 . .	—	33s.	33s.
,, 1860 . .	—	33s.	33s.

TABLE 2.—WAGES AND COST OF LIVING, 1790–1860—Manchester

	A. Mill Mechanics.	B. Mule Spinners (Men).	C. Power-loom Weavers (Men and Women).	D. Throstle Spinners (Women).	E. Hand-loom Weavers (mostly Men).	F. Carpenters.	G. Builders' Labourers.	H. Engineers.	I. Ironmoulders.
About 1790 .	18s.	—	—	—	—	18s.	13s. 6d.	—	—
„ 1800 .	21s.	—	—	—	—	—	—	21s.	—
„ 1805 .	24s.	24s.	—	9s.	20s.	—	—	—	—
„ 1810 .	—	30s.	—	9s.	16s.	25s.	15s. 9d.	28s.	31s.
„ 1815 .	29s.	29s.	—	10s.	13s.	—	15s. 9d.	28s.	31s. 6d.
„ 1820 .	24s.	29s.	—	—	9s. 6d.	25s.	15s. 9d.	25s.	31s.
„ 1825 .	29s.	28s.	10s. 6d.	9s.	6s. 6d.	24s.	16s.	30s.	30s.
„ 1830 .	28s.	27s.	10s. 9d.	7s.	9s.	24s.	12s.	26s.	29s.
„ 1835 .	28s.	24s.	11s.	9s. 6d.	—	24s.	15s.	30s.	31s.
„ 1840 .	—	22s.	9s. 6d.	7s. 6d.	7s.	26s.	18s.	28s.	33s.
„ 1845 .	29s.	20s.	10s.	10s.	8s. 6d.	—	—	30s.	35s.
„ 1850 .	26s. 6d.	26s.	10s. 6d.	7s. 6d.	—	28s.	18s.	30s.	34s.
„ 1855 .	—	20s.	10s.	8s. 9d.	—	—	—	—	—
„ 1860 .	26s. 6d.	24s.	12s.	10s.	5s.	28s.	19s. 6d.	30s.	34s.

TABLE 3.—SCOTLAND

	Miners. Day-Wages.
About 1790 . .	2s. 9d.
,, 1800 . .	—
,, 1805 . .	—
,, 1810 . .	5s.
,, 1815 . .	4s. 6d.
,, 1820 . .	3s. 9d.
,, 1825 . .	5s. 3d.
,, 1830 . .	4s. 3d.
,, 1835 . .	4s.
,, 1840 . .	3s. 6d.
,, 1845 . .	3s. 6d.
,, 1850 . .	2s.
,, 1855 . .	4s.
,, 1860 . .	4s.

TABLE 4.—AGRICULTURAL LABOURERS

	A. Sussex.	B. Cumberland.	C. Estimated General Average.
About 1790 . .	9s.	8s.	8s.
,, 1800 . .	12s.	11s.	11s.
,, 1805 . .	13s.	14s. 6d.	11s. 6d.
,, 1810 . .	13s.	15s. 6d.	—
,, 1815 . .	13s.	13s. 6d.	14s. 6d.
,, 1820 . .	13s.	10s. 6d.	11s.
,, 1825 . .	12s.	9s. 6d.	9s. 6d.
,, 1830 . .	12s.	—	11s.
,, 1835 . .	10s.	10s. 6d.	10s. 6d.
,, 1840 . .	12s.	—	10s.
,, 1845 . .	—	—	—
,, 1850 . .	10s. 6d.	13s.	9s. 6d.
,, 1855 . .	—	—	—
,, 1860 . .	11s. 6d.	13s. 6d.	11s. 6d.

TABLE 5.—(1) COST OF LIVING, Silberling to 1850, then Wood, 1790 = 100
(2) WHEAT PRICES, Annual Averages, shillings per quarter

	Cost of Living.	Wheat Prices.		Cost of Living.	Wheat Prices.
1800 . .	170	113s. 10d.	1831 . .	111	66s. 4d.
1801 . .	174	119s. 6d.	1832 . .	109	58s. 8d.
1802 . .	138	69s. 10d.	1833 . .	107	52s. 11d.
1803 . .	140	58s. 10d.	1834 . .	102	46s. 2d.
1804 . .	140	62s. 3d.	1835 . .	99	39s. 4d.
1805 . .	154	89s. 9d.	1836 . .	111	48s. 6d.
1806 . .	148	79s. 1d.	1837 . .	111	55s. 10d.
1807 . .	145	75s. 4d.	1838 . .	118	64s. 7d. .
1808 . .	159	81s. 4d.	1839 . .	123	70s. 8d.
1809 . .	175	97s. 4d.	1840 . .	121	66s. 4d.
1810 . .	176	106s. 5d.	1841 . .	116	64s. 4d.
1811 . .	164	95s. 3d.	1842 . .	106	57s. 3d.
1812 . .	180	126s. 6d.	1843 . .	94	50s. 1d.
1813 . .	187	109s. 9d.	1844 . .	96	51s. 3d.
1814 . .	176	74s. 4d.	1845 . .	97	50s. 10d.
1815 . .	150	65s. 7d.	1846 . .	100	54s. 8d.
1816 . .	135	78s. 6d.	1847 . .	116	69s. 9d.
1817 . .	151	96s. 11d.	1848 . .	97	50s. 6d.
1818 . .	159	86s. 3d.	1849 . .	86	44s. 3d.
1819 . .	143	74s. 6d.	1850 . .	83	40s. 3d.
1820 . .	132	67s. 10d.	1851 . .	80	38s. 6d.
1821 . .	115	56s. 1d.	1852 . .	80	40s. 9d.
1822 . .	100	44s. 7d.	1853 . .	88	53s. 3d.
1823 . .	111	53s. 4d.	1854 . .	101	72s. 5d.
1824 . .	113	63s. 11d.	1855 . .	104	74s. 8d.
1825 . .	128	68s. 6d.	1856 . .	104	69s. 2d.
1826 . .	111	58s. 8d.	1857 . .	99	56s. 4d.
1827 . .	110	58s. 6d.	1858 . .	90	44s. 2d.
1828 . .	108	60s. 5d.	1859 . .	89	43s. 9d.
1829 . .	106	66s. 3d.	1860 . .	92	53s. 3d.
1830 . .	108	64s. 3d.			

TABLE 6.—REAL WAGES,
Approximate Purchasing Power, 1815 = 100

	A. London Compositors.	B. Manchester Spinners.	C. Agricultural Labourers.	D. Scottish Miners.
About 1800 . .	74	64	67	—
,, 1805 . .	89	81	78	—
,, 1810 . .	85	88	—	95
,, 1815 . .	100	100	100	100
,, 1820 . .	104	114	87	95
,, 1825 . .	107	113	77	136
,, 1830 . .	127	130	106	131
,, 1835 . .	135	125	110	133
,, 1840 . .	113	94	86	95
,, 1845 . .	142	107	—	122
,, 1850 . .	166	162	119	80
,, 1855 . .	132	100	—	130
,, 1860 . .	150	135	131	144

PART TWO
1850-1900

CHAPTER I

INTRODUCTORY

1. The Second Phase   2. The " Golden Age "

I. THE SECOND PHASE

THE first part of this study carried the record of the British working-class movement to the year 1848. This seemed a convenient stopping-place because the Chartist failure of that year marked a decisive change in the character of the movement. There was a deep significance in the fact that the " year of revolutions " in Europe produced in this country no more than a feeble and half-hearted demonstration on Kennington Common. Up to that point, the story of the British workers had been one of successive waves of revolt against the rising capitalist order. Against the developing strength of the new employing class one wave after another had been shattered in vain. The Corresponding Societies had echoed the stirring cries of the French Revolution ; the Luddites had broken the hated new machines, only to be broken in their turn. The working-class Radicals had threatened revolution as the alternative to Manhood Suffrage, and had been put off with a Reform Act which seated their masters firmly in power. The great " Trades Union," under Owen's millennial guidance, had vainly tried to strike its way to the Co-operative Commonwealth. And finally the Chartists, reviving the old cry of Manhood Suffrage as the slogan of a movement based on economic distress, had found themselves beaten off the field of propaganda by the Anti-Corn Law League, and reduced to an impotent sect out of tune with the new spirit of the times.

Revolt had failed. Vainly had the workers kicked against the pricks of the new order, which was all the time steadily and swiftly growing in power. Again and again they had tried to organise a separate movement of their own, founded on their own collective strength, and to enforce their will upon the country. There are two outstanding reasons for their failure, each sufficient in itself. In the first place, they could not know what they wanted, or at any rate how to set about the getting of what they wanted. Their movements were, for the most part, reactions of starvation and despair, rather than constructive attempts at economic reorganisation. A few leaders, such as Owen, could see visions of the Socialist future ; a few realists, such as Place, tried to instal reformism and the Liberal-Labour alliance long before their time. But most even of the leaders were either, like O'Connor, devoid of any practicable policy at all, or, like Cobbett, continually harking back to the old days before the coming of the monster, steam, with his insatiable call for human sacrifice.

After all these leaders the procession of misery followed blindly. The wretched slaves of steam caught a glimpse, no doubt, of Owen's vision ; but they were far more deeply stirred when Cobbett, or even O'Connor, seemed to beckon them back to the land from which they had been driven. Helpless in the grip of the new industrialism which they hated the more because they did not understand it, they were ready to throw in their lot with any movement which was at least a movement of revolt. But, gradually, failure made them tired. A new generation arose, born amid the smoke and noise and filth of the spreading factory towns, and the districts devastated by coal-mining and iron-working ; and this new generation accepted wage-labour at machine or furnace, or coal-face as its appointed lot. The call of the fields had grown fainter ; the clanking and puffing of the engines had deadened their ears. They had grown only too prepared to accept the new order as inevitable, and to make the best of it.

It was, indeed, impossible for the working classes of the early nineteenth century to devise a policy at once practical and constructive. They were too weak. In the manufacturing districts the machine was steadily dispensing with the old craftsmen's skill, and enrolling women and children as machine-minders to beat down the wages of the men. In the coalfields and iron-working areas the employers enforced a savage discipline which the law relentlessly enforced. The cheapness of goods which was the gift of the machines made a return to the old order impracticable ; and in the new order children and mothers waged war perforce against fathers to beat down the standard of life. Cobbett and O'Connor were, in fact, radical reactionaries ; and Owen, who saw the true remedy in the co-operative control of the new industrial forces, was compelled to be Utopian because he was calling on the workers to attempt a task which was far beyond their strength.

The second cause of failure is the other side of the same medal. Where the workers were too weak, Capitalism was much too strong. It was not, indeed, in the early part of the century a fully stabilised or established order ; but it was gaining strength all the time. Its leaders were imbued with a tremendous consciousness of power. The machines, which were the workers' masters, were their servants, and the sense of power and achievement which the machines put into their minds gave them irresistible force and courage. They believed in their mission, and regarded the wealth which poured in upon them as the sign of their triumphant achievement. They had used ten bales of cotton where one was used before ; they were covering sea and land with ships, railways, factories, mines, and counting-houses—the tokens of the new plenty. It seemed a small thing to them that men, women and children laboured without rest for a pittance in order to create this wealth, which somehow failed to bring to the many the promised comforts of higher productivity, or that the new factory towns were noisome dens of corruption and disease. Give them a free hand, and the stream of commodities would gush forth in yet greater abundance, until the whole land ran with wealth. Give them a free hand, and all things else would be added unto the people. They resented, as blind folly and wanton obstruction, the revolts of the workers against their misery ; they demanded that Labour, in its own best interest, should be forcibly restrained from combination or independent political activity. The stream of production could be swelled to the full only if capital flowed freely into it. Saving was the cardinal virtue. But higher wages would dry up the flow of saving, and check the increase of wealth. Consumption must be kept down, in order that production might increase without limit.

The topsy-turviness of this view, which strikes us forcibly to-day, could hardly be apparent to most of these early capitalists. The markets of the world were all open to them ; their cheap goods undercut every possible competitor. But, competing fiercely one against another, they were compelled one and all to be forever cheapening their goods yet more. A little on the wage, or a little off the working day, seemed to threaten each individual master with ruin. And, as cheapness was their god, and competition the key to cheapness, every cost must be kept down to the lowest point. The workers, in their own interest, must work long for little, in order that the goods they bought might get ever cheaper.

There was a paradox here ; for many of the persons who promised the workers this increase in wealth in the future, if only they would labour long and for low wages in the present, proclaimed, almost in the same breath, that the Law of Population would always prevent wages from rising above subsistence level, so that the promise of a higher standard of living could, in the nature of things, never be fulfilled. Some, indeed, qualified this view and sought to transfer the responsibility to the workers by asserting that they could, if they would, stop the rise in population by " prudential checks " ; but this view was put forward chiefly by working-class economists, such as Place. The employers for the most part wanted labour to be plentiful, as the means of getting it at a low price.

It is no wonder that men in this mood, and with the sense of achievement behind them, were strong and resolute in pushing the policy which seemed to meet their needs. It is no wonder they were callous about the sufferings of the poor. For their eyes were on the future ; they saw the Golden Age of Capitalism coming, and believed they knew how to reach it by their own strength. They brushed opposition aside. The Reform Act had given them political power ; and from 1832 onwards they used it in masterful fashion.

The early working-class movements failed, then, because they were too weak and because the rising force of Capitalism was too strong. But, if these early struggles seem vain and fruitless, the workers had really no alternative.

Their attempts to organise Trade Unions for collective bargaining met with insuperable hostility from employers who denied them all rights of negotiation. Even after the repeal of the Combination Acts the law of conspiracy and of master and servant still exposed them to constant legal repression. The legal freedom conferred under the Act of 1825 was exceedingly narrow ; and almost all Trade Union activity, unless it was carried on with the full consent of the employers, still involved serious risk of falling foul of the law. The attempt to join forces with the middle-class Radicals had produced the Reform Act of 1832, which left the workers voteless and placed political power firmly in the hands of their masters. The agitations for factory reform met with the most uncompromising opposition from those very Radicals whose political lead the workers were asked to follow. Every means of moderate advance seemed closed to them ; there was nothing for it but a kicking against the pricks which had at least the merit of keeping hope alive in their hearts.

For some time before the middle of the century, this situation was slowly changing. The first sign of the change was the Anti-Corn Law agitation, which steadily drew the workers away from Chartism to the pursuit of a concrete and practicable reform. Here at last was something on which, despite all the more extreme Chartists could say, the interests of workers and employers appeared to be the same. The workers, oppressed by low wages, wanted cheap food and above all a steadying of corn prices which would check violent fluctuations in the standard of living. And the employers wanted free trade in corn, both as a means to the maintenance of low wages, and because corn was the easiest form of payment for British manufactured exports that the foreigner could make. Anti-capitalist agrarians, such as Bronterre O'Brien, denounced the League as a plot for the reducing of wages ; but cheap corn was an appealing cry. The Anti-Corn Law League successfully organised under middle-class leadership the main body of the skilled and better-paid workers. Chartism lost its hold ; and in 1846 Peel gave way, and broke the Conservative Party. The League had made the way plain for a new working-class policy, under which the workers would rest content with picking up the crumbs that fell from the rich man's table, and these crumbs would fall, for the time being, more to the minority of skilled workers than to the less skilled.

Of course, for the capitalists there was far more at stake in the Free Trade agitation than the mere repeal of the Corn Laws. They wanted fully as much the free importation of the raw materials of industry, the unfettered carriage of goods overseas, the final removal of all restrictions on the course and organisation of trade. The repeal of the Navigation Acts in 1849 and 1854, the sweeping away of import duties in 1853 and 1860, the free development of capitalist organisation under the Companies Acts of 1855 and 1862, followed as the logical sequels on the repeal of the Corn Laws in 1846. But it suited the employers of labour best to wage their war first and foremost as a campaign against the Corn Laws ; for on that issue alone could working-class support be ensured, and a great popular movement be built up. The repeal of the Corn Laws was the sign, as Friedrich List might have pointed out, of the capitalist coming-of-age ; and among the gifts made to Capitalism on that auspicious occasion was the surrendered sword of the working-class movement.

This coming-of-age was, indeed, signalised by a change in the character of Capitalism itself. Capitalism had sown, or rather " saved," its wild oats ; and it was, in the 'forties, settling down already to the administration of its inheritance. In the early days, even the successful employer was very often at his wits' end for money. He saw the chance of extending his business, he wanted a constant stream of fresh capital in order to instal the latest new machines. But, unless he could accumulate enough (at his workers' expense) out of the profits of his business, whence was the fresh capital to come ? There was no great investing public ready to take up shares in his enterprise ; for, though gasworks and other public utilities, and later railways, were teaching the middle and upper classes the lesson of joint stock investment, the joint stock form was hardly at all applied as yet to industry proper, and limited liability, the secret of its rapid extension, was still denied by the law, except to " public utility " undertakings. It was under these conditions that the " abstinence " of workers and capitalists alike presented itself as a sovereign duty ; for only by putting every possible penny back into the business could its maintenance and extension be guaranteed.

Before the middle of the century, this situation was changing. The middle class had grown very greatly ; for both the trading and shop-keeping and the professional classes had been increasing by leaps and bounds. The landowning classes, though they still perhaps held their noses, were condescending to invest their money in industry, and to share in the high profits which accrued. In mining they had, of course, held a big stake all along. By 1850, it was getting easier to find money for economic development, and therefore less indispensable to practise " abstinence " to the extent of privation. Many of the big employers had launched out early as country gentlemen with fine estates of their own ; the smaller employers began to follow this lead, to move into comfortable houses, to set up carriages, and in short to become gentlefolk of the solid Victorian kind.

Under these new conditions, there was even the less need to come quite so sharply down on any attempt by the workers to improve their position. Peel's Factory Act was passed in 1844, and the Ten Hours Act in 1847 ; and after the ensuing struggle to get the law enforced, in the course of which the working day was pushed up again to ten hours and a half, the modified law was fairly strictly applied by controlling the hours of factory opening and closing. The worst excesses of overwork at the expense of the women and children in the textile factories were over, though there had been no extension of the Factory Acts beyond the textile trades, and appalling conditions continued for a further period in many unprotected occupations. Wages began slowly to rise, and the intensity of the employers' opposition to working-class combinations gradually diminished. And, so far from being ruined by these changes, the owners of industry found themselves getting richer than ever—trade and production advancing by leaps and bounds, and the profits derived from them growing larger at an unprecedented rate.

There were thus strong inducements on both sides to a change of policy and tactics. The employers could afford to ease off a little the intensity of the exploitation of labour, and to deal less savagely with attempts at working-class combination. And the workers, to whom hitherto Capitalism had seemed to offer nothing but an endless prospect of undiminished misery, began to see gleams of hope in the future. They had long been told that if they would only work with the grain of Capitalism instead of working against it, they would get their share of the good things it had to offer. They began at length to believe, and, instead of fighting against Capitalism, to accept it as an accomplished fact, and to make the best of their lot within it. The New Co-operation of 1844, the New Unionism of 1850, the new Friendly Society Movement recognised and encouraged by the Acts of 1846 and 1855, were all signs of this changed spirit—all attempts to work with and within the capitalist order instead of seeking its overthrow. The lamb had been shorn ; it remained for Capitalism to temper the wind.

The change, of course, did not come all at once. Radicals such as Bright and Cobden, who successfully led a mixed movement of the working and middle classes to the conquest of Free Trade, remained blind to the need for factory reform, and hostile industrially to the Trade Unions the political backing of whose members they were eager to secure. When the skilled workers, from 1850 onwards, began to organise stable Trade Unions based on a moderate and conciliatory programme, the mass of employers in most industries were still unwilling to meet them or to recognise the need for collective bargaining. The old spirit died hard ; but it was dying. The conception of the common interest of employers and employed was slowly coming into its own. The employers in the cotton industry, the pioneers of the new Capitalism, were the first to accept Trade Unionism as a useful agency for collective bargaining about wages and conditions.

The new policy, as we shall see, did not mean that the workers surrendered the right to strike, or to carry on either industrial or political agitation on their own behalf. But the agitations of the 'fifties, 'sixties and 'seventies were unlike those of earlier times in that, with the solitary exception of the " First International," they were all designed to promote limited and specific reforms, and had behind them no general programme or policy hostile to the capitalist order. During these decades the workers fought many hard battles ;

they made great new movements, and built them up on solid foundations or collective loyalty. But they neither created nor inspired any new philosophy or body of social ideas. The philosophy of these leaders was not a capitalist philosophy ; but it postulated the acceptance of Capitalism and did not seek to overpass the limits which that acceptance implied. It was in many respects very like the outlook of the leaders of the American Federation of Labor at the present day.

This limitation of outlook inevitably makes the working-class movements of this second stage of development far harder to describe than those which were outlined in the first part of this study. For those earlier movements were complete in themselves, and represented complete and independent stages in the development of working-class policy and opinion. The newer movements, on the other hand, were incomplete because they were complementary. They represented the reverse of the cloth of which the capitalist side showed the pattern. They had meaning and purpose only in relation to the stage which capitalist development had reached. And, as we shall see later on, they changed their form and colour as soon as Capitalism, under stress of a fresh stage in economic development, was woven into a new pattern of imperialist design.

So far, however, we have to do only with that capitalist golden age which stretches from about the middle of the nineteenth century to the middle 'seventies—the period of Free Trade triumphant, of swiftly expanding markets at home and abroad, of complacent contemplation of a national prosperity which seemed to be boundless and inexhaustible. This was the true Victorian Age, aptly symbolised in the handsomely upholstered comfort of the Victorian middle-class home, with the dark, decent, expressive sumptuousness of its mahogany, with its crowded drawing-rooms and its sentimental ballads, its port wine and its tea—all these the products of a civilisation built on the proud assurance of a middle class that felt itself the maker of all these good things, and not least the maker of its own successful virtue.

To this time belongs too the emergence of the skilled workers from the sheer squalor which beset all save a privileged minority of them in the Industrial Revolution days. If the employer had his plush and mahogany, the skilled artisan began to ape him with his tiny parlour, a symbol too sacred for common use. If the employer had his investments, the skilled artisan was beginning to have his few pounds in the " Co-op." or the penny bank, and his stake in the funds of his Friendly Society or his Trade Union. His virtues were those of his employer, on a smaller scale ; he too felt himself a self-made man, and shared in the complacency of the times. He too hoped that, every day and in every way, he and his country would get richer and richer and richer.

Yet he was far from rich—a mere shade above the line of absolute poverty. And below him there was still a mass of unskilled or unorganised labour too poor to raise its head.   The skilled artisans, however, had too much to do in making the best of things for themselves to be very solicitous about the welter beneath their feet.   There was a chance for them ; but unless they strained every nerve to take it the chance would be lost, and perhaps they would be thrust back among the failures—a sore disgrace as well as a dreadful privation.   So that, whereas in earlier times the main body of the skilled workers, subjected to the common exploitation, had put themselves at the head of the entire working class in the struggle for better things, this rising class of skilled workers was mainly concerned to look after its own narrower interest.   Its charity began at home; and it had little to spare for the bottom dog.   Its Trade Unions, its Friendly Societies, even its successful Co-operative Movement, were carried on under conditions which forbade access to the poorer strata among the workers.   Trade Union contributions were too high ; Friendly Societies demanded an exercise of " thrift" which was beyond the reach of the less skilled operatives ; the Co-operative Society prided itself on supplying only unadulterated goods, which the poor could not afford, and called for cash from men and women who were compelled to buy on credit if they were to live at all.

This restricted scope of the new working-class movements made them much less disposed to unify their forces, or to pursue any common course of action.   During the earlier stages of the Industrial Revolution the workers had been driven together by a common oppression ; under the changing conditions of the Victorian age they were led apart by the severalty of their aims.   Co-operation and Trade Unionism, closely connected and at times almost one in their early stages, became two separate and almost unconnected movements.   Each Trade Union, and even each local Co-operative Society, pursued its own course without feeling much need for any common basis of action.   Political activity for a time almost disappeared ; for after the collapse of Chartism no new movement speedily arose, and after the repeal of the Corn Laws there was no popular agitation under middle-class leadership round which the workers could rally.   In Parliament, Radicalism was dying out.

Gradually, however, as we shall see, the working-class forces began to draw together again.   Co-operators were led to combine, first for the purposes of wholesale trade and production, and then for the pursuit of common propagandist and economic aims.   The movement for the extension of the franchise, temporarily eclipsed after the collapse of Chartism, revived as a purely constitutional and reformist demand, based on the improving status and growing respectability of Labour.   The Trade Unions combined, both to resist dangerous attacks levelled against them and to secure a recognised legal status corresponding to their moderate and constitutional policy.   But all these unifying movements of the 'sixties were quite unlike the earlier agitations, in that there was in them not even the most indirect threat of revolutionary action, and no aim beyond the securing of certain defined and limited reforms.

In the remaining section of this chapter, and in the next, there will be described in more precise terms, first the changing economic conditions of the Golden Age of Free Trade Capitalism, and secondly the new working-class movements which arose as the response to these conditions. We shall have to trace the rise of the new Co-operation from the Rochdale Pioneers of 1844, and of the new Trade Unionism from the "New Model" of the Amalgamated Society of Engineers in 1851, and in bare outline the growth of the great Friendly Societies which were certainly no less influential in forming the character and outlook of the Victorian working and lower middle classes.

In this survey, we shall be studying the real beginnings of modern organisation. Owenism and Chartism speak to us across the years in a dead language; but the direct descendants of the Rochdale Pioneers and of the "New Model" Trade Unions are still with us to-day. These Victorian pioneers built narrow houses; their plans lacked the space and grandeur of the earlier conceptions. But they built on firm foundations—so firm that, even under the vastly changed conditions of our own time, their buildings take a deal of breaking, and their policy still survives, built round and over by the exponents of more up-to-date methods. In their limitation was their strength, and in the source of their strength the cause of their limitation. From the time when they began to build, the British working-class movement has a steady and continuous history.

2. THE "GOLDEN AGE"

The years between 1850 and the middle 'seventies were, taken as a whole, a period of extraordinary and progressive prosperity. To the "Hungry Forties" succeeded the sleek and prosperous 'fifties. The 'sixties, chequered by the terrible Cotton Famine of 1862-3 and the severe financial crisis of 1867, were yet a time of still more rapid advance. And, in the early 'seventies, with trade and production booming as never before, the cup of wealth seemed like to run over. There were few who anticipated the severe depression which, breaking upon the country in the middle 'seventies, lasted, with only a brief intermission, for something like a decade.

In 1850, these set-backs were still far away; and Great Britain was entering upon a rich and pleasant harvest. In the 'thirties and 'forties, to the accompaniment of great hardship and unrest, the seeds of this prosperity had been sown. All over the country, a great network of railways had been built, so that the entire interior had been opened up to swift and easy communication. The mercantile marine had advanced by leaps and bounds; and the application of steam had immensely added to the swiftness and certainty of voyages. The first Industrial Revolution had been primarily a change in the methods of production, heaping up a store of goods which roads, canals and sailing-ships were hard put to it to bear away to profitable markets. The Second Industrial Revolution was primarily a change in the methods of transport, opening up fresh fields of profitable trade to the producer, as well as fruitful chances for investment of the accumulating capital of the rich and middle classes. Steam power had conquered the handicraft producer first ; thereafter it out-horse-powered the horse and defied the winds and waves.

The growth of railways had a hundred decisive social effects. The building of them mobilised men in large masses, and shifted them constantly from place to place. The " mobility of labour " was greatly increased ; a fresh stream of migration from the villages set along the line of the new railroads. A huge iron industry was built up largely for the supply of railway equipment and rolling stock ; a new class of *entrepreneurs* and contractors arose to finance and direct these developments. There were many wildcat schemes, and many insane bursts of speculation. But, whoever gained and lost by the construction, the railways were thenceforth there, and for transport as well as for production British industry was equipped with power and with resources which placed it far ahead of every competitor.

In 1850, though new lines were still a-building fast, the great period of railway construction was over, and that of consolidation was already well advanced. The linking up of the railways into larger groups and systems, and the provision of through running facilities for long distance traffic, were every year making the whole country more nearly a single economic unit and increasing its production and commercial power.

At the same time, the great shipping lines began to be formed. The early 'fifties were a time of extraordinarily rapid development of shipping and shipbuilding ; and the growing demand again reacted favourably on the industries producing metals and machinery. Hitherto, the textile trades had been almost unchallengeably supreme ; and their dominance was hardly to be shaken for some time yet. But already the metal trades were claiming a place beside them. And close upon iron followed coal, fast rising to an independent and important status among industries. It was no accident that in the 'fifties the engineers, and in the 'sixties the miners, occupied the centre of the Trade Union stage.

These great industrial developments called for a larger and steadier stream of capital and credit than earlier methods of organisation had made possible. And these were forthcoming out of the growing resources in the hands of the wealthier classes. The Bank Charter Act of 1844, by regulating the note issue and putting the banking system firmly on its feet, provided an assured basis for credit, and strengthened the position of London as the world's commercial and financial centre. At the same time the legal recognition of the joint stock form of organisation for ordinary business, and the general concession of limited liability to shareholders in 1855, greatly simplified the raising of capital and broadened the basis of industrial and commercial investment. Large-scale industrial ownership ceased to be the prerogative of a small class of *entrepreneurs ;* the entire middle and upper class were drawn into investment, first in the new railway stocks, and before long in all manner of industrial holdings. Even workers whose wages began to provide a small margin above current needs were led into the pursuit of investment. The "Working-class Limiteds" grew up as joint stock companies owned chiefly by manual workers ; while the expanding Co-operative movement provided a non-profit-making investment for a growing mass of working-class savings.

Agriculture, as well as industry, enjoyed a " Golden Age." The prognostications that Free Trade would ruin the farmers and landlords were by no means realised in fact. The price of corn was stabilised rather than reduced, and both rents and farming profits rose. There was, indeed, a certain shifting from the cultivation of wheat crops to stock and dairy farming ; for the growing consumption of meat and milk in the towns opened up a highly profitable demand. This in time reacted on the position of the labourers ; for stock farming needed less labour than arable, and the supply of workers in the villages again became redundant. While, therefore, profits and rents remained high, wages were still very low, and there was a steady migration from the villages to various forms of industrial work or even overseas. The railways, in particular, absorbed a large mass of surplus agricultural labour. When Joseph Arch came to organise the rural workers in the early 'seventies, there was certainly no sign that they had shared in the prosperity of their masters.

Meanwhile, as transport was improved and quite new grain-growing areas in the New World were opened up, corn flowed in freely from abroad to feed the rapidly increasing population, and its price, if not reduced, was certainly stabilised and prevented from rising by the freedom of trade. This in turn steadied wages and conditions of employment ; for corn, as the labourers' principal means of life, was also the most vital raw material of industry. Other raw materials soon shared in the new freedom, and by 1860 Great Britain had gone further still, and, by abolishing the duties on manufactured imports, had become wholly a Free Trade country. Nay, more, Cobden's success in negotiating with France the Commercial Treaty of that year was widely greeted as the beginning of an era of universal Free Trade, in which all other countries would follow the British example. In France, Bastiat loudly echoed as universal truths the Free Trade doctrines of the English classical economists ; in Germany, List's warnings that Free Trade might suit England, because she could, with the aid of machinery, undercut all competitors, but would not suit those who sought to imitate her success, until they had built up their own industries behind a wall of protection, passed for the time almost unheeded.

In the towns, living conditions were becoming rather more tolerable. The Public Health Act of 1848, and the Local Boards of Health established under it, though it had needed the cholera to get them accepted, were real steps forward in the development of sanitary legislation ; and the Clauses Acts of 1847 marked a period of advance in the provision of vital public utilities such as gas and water supply. Textile factory conditions were slowly improving under the Acts of 1844, 1847, 1850 and 1853, and with the Acts of 1850 and 1860 protective legislation began to be applied to the mines also. The whole period from 1847 onwards was one of considerable activity in social and industrial legislation. Public education, it is true, was to be held back until 1870 by the religious controversy ; but the number of schools was steadily growing, and illiteracy was markedly on the decrease. Between 1851 and 1861 State grants for education in England and Wales rose from £150,000 to £813,000, and the illiteracy rate fell for men from 30.7 per cent. to 24.6, and for women from 45.2 to 34.7. In the two following decades, despite the temporary adverse effects of Robert Lowe's code in the 'sixties, the improvement in educational standards was more than maintained.

It must not, however, be supposed that during this prosperous period wages for most types of workers were high. In the 'fifties, the slight advance in wage rates failed to keep pace with the rise in prices, and in the 'sixties hardly more than this leeway was made up. Not till the early 'seventies was there any large general advance in wage rates, measured in purchasing power, and this was enjoyed for but a few years before the coming of the great depression.

Nevertheless, the condition of labour certainly improved. Employment was better and more regular ; for there were many years of prosperity, and few of slump. A larger proportion of workers tended to rise into the skilled grades, and to enjoy the higher wages corresponding to their increased skill. Wage-rates in rapidly developing centres, such as Glasgow, rose sharply towards the rates already in force in the older industrial areas. Working hours were to some extent lessened, and factory conditions improved. There remained a morass of unskilled labour ; but skilled labour was able to raise its head, and largely to imbibe, with increased self-respect, a philosophy of thrift and self-help modelled on that of the masters.

For the upper and middle classes, the growth of prosperity was undoubtedly very great. In the Census of 1851, the professional classes numbered only 2.2 per cent. of the population. In 1871, they had reached 3.9, and in 1881 6.2 per cent. The average yield of a penny income tax more than doubled between 1850 and the end of the 'seventies. House rents and land prices both advanced very rapidly. Apart from the great fortunes which were being made out of industry and commerce, the middle classes were rapidly growing and were steadily consolidating their position. Moreover, to the profitable fields for investment at home was being added an increasing mass of successful investment overseas. British capital was already flowing, in the wake of British goods, into channels of economic opportunity in other parts of the world ; the railways of Europe and America were being built largely with the aid of British capital, with British material, and under British direction.

In 1850, men already looked back to the Industrial Revolution as a distant historical event. They were living in a new epoch, the inheritors of the wealth and the productive power of which the eighteenth century had laid the foundations. The Great Exhibition of 1851 was a triumphant celebration of British prosperity, present and to come. *The Times* described the year as one of "unexampled prosperity," and repeated the phrase as applying equally to 1852. The good trade lasted till 1856, and the slump which accompanied the financial crisis of 1857 lasted only two years. Then followed eight years of good trade ; for even the appalling Cotton Famine of 1862-3, though it caused deep distress in Lancashire, did not suffice to upset the general prosperity of business. The slump of 1866, again due mainly to financial causes, of which the failure of Overend and Gurney was the outstanding example, lasted less than three years, and then gave place to a new prosperous period of six years' duration. Only thereafter, in 1874, came the premonitory signs of the great depression.

With these facts in mind, we can turn to study the growth of the working-class movement during this capitalist " Golden Age." We shall find that its history falls into two periods—a time of consolidation and preparation in the 'fifties and early 'sixties, and a time of intensified industrial and political struggle in the late 'sixties and early 'seventies. These two periods will be the subjects of the two following chapters.

BOOKS

G. D. H. Cole. *British Trade and Industry.*
L. C. Knowles. *Industrial and Commercial Revolutions.*
L. Levi. *History of British Commerce.*
A. L. Bowley. *England's Foreign Trade in the Nineteenth Century.*
L. H. Jenks. *The Migration of British Capital.*
J. H. Clapham. *Economic History of Modern Britain*, Vol. 2.
C. A. Bodelsen. *Studies in .Mid-Victorian Imperialism.*

CHAPTER II

THRIFT AND ABSTINENCE

1. Self-help in the Victorian Era   2. The Co-operative Movement   3. The Friendly Societies

1. SELF-HELP IN THE VICTORIAN ERA

" SELF-HELP " took rank among the principal virtues of the Victorian era. It was a duty, prescribed by moralists and economists, and fully recognised by artisans and tradesmen alike, to put by for a rainy day. An immense literature inculcated the virtue of thrift, and even estimated the chances of happiness in the next life by the test of frugality in this.

As we have seen, there were obvious reasons both for this insistence on thrift, and for the striking success of the appeals made to the middle and working classes to practise it. The Victorian era was the harvest-time for the material gains of the Industrial Revolution. The great social change, which transformed Great Britain from a largely agricultural to a predominantly manufacturing and commercial country, had brought with it new habits and ways of thought. Social relationships had been profoundly altered ; a great new rich class had risen to economic power and political influence. Together with the great employers, merchants and bankers of the commercial era rose a host of lesser men. Small employers and factory managers, professional men and retail shopkeepers, multiplied fast. Social status came to depend more than ever on income ; money became more than ever the key to respect, the hall-mark of an assured place in the social system. Money was not valued merely as a means of enjoyment ; it had an even greater value as the means to social consideration and to a sense of being at peace with both worlds.

These considerations naturally applied in largest measure to the great middle class, which assumed in the Victorian era its characteristic form and internal stratification. But they applied also largely to the working class, or at least to a growing section of the working class. During the earlier stages of the Industrial Revolution the real standard of living of the great majority of the workers was being beaten down. This was the case even where money wages rose faster than prices ; for needs, under the new urban conditions of living, rose faster still. The agricultural labourers were reduced to the extreme of penury ; and many of the artisans belonging to the old-established crafts suffered some degradation through the introduction of new methods and the competition of less skilled labour operating the new machines. The handloom weavers were, of course, the extreme case ; but many other

crafts suffered only in less degree.   Some groups of craftsmen, whose traditional processes were unaffected by the new machines, doubtless profited
from the larger demand for their products ; and some new skilled crafts—
mule spinning and steam-engine making, for example—were actually
created by the new conditions.   These, however, were exceptions.   Great
fortunes were made during the earlier stages of the Industrial Revolution ;
but the main rewards went, not to the ordinary workers, but to the capitalists,
great and small, who were building up the new system.

Fairly early in the Victorian era this situation was already changing.   The
social dislocation caused by enclosures and by the emptying of the villages
into the factory towns was coming to an end ; the new industrialism was
developing fast enough to absorb the vast army of workers seeking employment.   War was no longer draining away national resources in unproductive
expenditure ; and there was abundant wealth in the country to finance rapid
industrial expansion.   With the growth of companies and large partnerships,
and with the development of banking on a securer basis, the area of investment was being broadened out.   Less pinching was needed than in the
earlier days.

Nevertheless, though the acute pressure for more capital for industrial
development was relaxed, and capitalists both became less " abstinent " and
paid rather higher wages, the beneficiaries of the new system did not cease to
preach the virtue of abstinence to their employees.   The workers, moreover,
after the miseries of the Industrial Revolution, saw at length a less desperate
prospect ahead of them.   By rigid saving, those who were better-off among
them could at least hope to put by a pittance for old age and as some security
against unemployment ; and, for those who possessed that " enterprise "
which was the correlative virtue to thrift in the Victorian calendar, there was
the possibility of rising out of the working class into the class of small employers or tradesmen.   In comparison with the hopelessness of the preceding period, the skilled Victorian workman, at any rate after 1848, saw
before him a prospect which made it worth his while to save, and offered
strong inducements to accept the capitalist system as a going concern, and to
try to make the best of it.

This tendency was, moreover, greatly stimulated by the policy of the now
politically dominant capitalist class.   The first great measure of the Reformed
Parliament had been the Poor Law Amendment Act of 1834.   This Act had
swept away the old system of poor relief, under which, over a large part of
the countryside, the subsidising of wages out of the rates had become a
regular practice, and a great part of the working class had come to look
regularly to the Poor Law for relief.   It had also put an end, in the industrial
districts, to outdoor relief for the able-bodied in times of unemployment, and
had offered only the loathed " Bastille " as the alternative to self-support or to
starvation.   The New Poor Law was based definitely on the view that it was

a moral obligation upon the individual to maintain himself, and to provide against the contingencies of life by his own efforts. Its framers meant to attach a strong stigma to pauperism, and to make the conditions of relief unpleasant enough to be thoroughly deterrent to all who were not in the last extremity of destitution. They held, of course, that the enforcement of these principles would, under the favourable conditions of industrial expansion, cause such a rise in wages as to make self-maintenance possible, and that the great distress which the new Poor Law was bound to cause would be only temporary. The distress caused by trade depressions they simply ignored. They pushed through the change with an extraordinary callousness to the distress which it involved, and they pushed it much too far ; but it is undeniable that in the long run the result was broadly in accordance with their expectations.

It is thus easy to see why the opening of the Victorian era coincided with a great growth of organisation designed to further " self-help " among the poorer classes. After the middle 'forties the standard of living was slowly rising for a considerable section of the people ; and the abolition of the old Poor Law had given the maximum inducement to all who could by scraping put aside a small sum for sickness or old age to save lest they should fall into the clutches of the hated " Three Bashaws of Somerset House," or be incarcerated in the new " Bastilles." For these were the names by which the Poor Law Commissioners and the new Union Workhouses soon came to be popularly known.

We find, then, from the second decade of the reign of Queen Victoria, a widespread movement among the working and certain sections of the middle class to create provident organisations of their own. On the one hand, we have the rapid increase of Friendly Societies of all types, of Building Societies, and of other purely provident bodies. On the other, we find the Co-operative Movement at length striking firm roots and, under the Rochdale system begun in 1844, becoming also a powerful stimulant to working-class saving, and a working-class equivalent to the capitalist limited company. We find, moreover, that the House of Commons, now dominated by industrial and commercial interests, was eager to give a helping hand to working-class thrift, and therefore encouraged these developments with a mass of protective legislation.

I have space to deal with these various movements only in the barest outline. All of them have a history going back considerably beyond the Victorian era ; but to all of them the Victorian era brought a great accession of adherents and influence. Let us begin with the Co-operative Movement, in which the new attitude embodied its most significant contribution to working-class organisation.

2. THE CO-OPERATIVE MOVEMENT

The modern Co-operative Movement began in 1844, when the Equitable Pioneers of Rochdale opened their Store in Toad Lane.   Other Societies have disputed with them the first invention of the device of "dividend on purchases," round which the consumers' Co-operative Movement has been built.   It is indeed a well-authenticated fact that this device had been tried not once but many times well before 1844.   But the point does not greatly matter ; for it is clear that Rochdale's success made the way plain for the growth of the movement.   The device was essentially simple.   Previous Societies had either tried to sell at cost price, thus facing a risk of loss and making it difficult to build up a capital fund ; or they had sold at market price, and had applied their profits to the building up of a " community" fund to be applied to the promotion of Owenite "Villages of Co-operation," or to other communal services ; or they had violated the Co-operative principle by paying dividends on invested capital in proportion to their trading success.   In place of any of these methods, the Rochdale Pioneers sold at market price and returned their surplus to the members in proportion, not to their capital holdings in the Society, but to the cost of their purchases.   At the same time, they paid interest on their capital, and encouraged their members to leave their dividends to accumulate as share-capital—a course which made possible the steady and progressive expansion of the business.   The essence of "Rochdale" Co-operation finance was neither the payment of " dividends on purchases " nor the payment of fixed interest on share capital, but the successful combination of the two.

It is a moot point how far these early Co-operators were conscious of the magnitude of what they were doing.   They began, like other early Co-operative groups, as a little body of working-class disciples of Robert Owen, and their first rules were phrased in orthodox Owenite language.   The Rochdale Pioneers set out their aims in these terms :—

The establishment of a store for the sale of provisions, clothing, etc.

The building, purchasing, or erecting a number of houses, in which the members, desiring to assist each other in improving their domestic and social condition, may reside.

The manufacture of such articles as the Society may determine upon, to provide employment for such members who may be without employment, or who may be suffering in consequence of repeated reductions in their wages.

The purchasing, or renting, of an estate or estates of land, which shall be cultivated by members who may be out of employment, or whose labour may be badly remunerated.

And further : That as soon as practicable this Society shall proceed to

arrange the powers of production, distribution, education and government ; or, in other words, to establish a self-supporting home colony of
united interests, or assist other Societies in establishing such colonies.

The language is here the purest Owenism, even to the reference to the
" home colonies " which Owen was at this time energetically advocating
through his latest propagandist organisation, the Home Colonisation
Society. In the minds of the Pioneers, as of other early Co-operators, setting
up shop was only a means to a much greater end, the self-employment of the
members and ultimately the establishment of a complete and self-sufficient
Owenite Community. Rochdale had been for some time a strong Owenite
centre ; a producers' Society for flannel-making had been set up there in the
stirring times of 1830, and in 1838 the faithful had opened an Owenite
" Social Hall." Not of set purpose did the Pioneers break completely away
from the old Owenite tradition.

Besides " dividends on purchases " and limited interest on invested
capital, the Rochdale Pioneers adopted certain other principles which became
the standard practice of true Consumers' Co-operation. They sold only
pure and unadulterated goods, and those only for cash. They refused to sell
intoxicants ; and they insisted on providing education as an integral part of
Co-operative service. Moreover, they insisted on " Open Membership "—
which meant that anyone could join on the same terms as the existing
members, and on " One Member, one Vote," irrespective of the number of
shares held, as essential to the principle of " Democratic Control."

The Pioneers' Store prospered ; and within a few years the need for
expansion faced them. Before long they embarked on production, and then,
as other Societies began to grow up in neighbouring towns, opened a wholesale department. This latter failed for the time ; but it deserves to be
regarded as the forerunner of the Co-operative Wholesale Society. Meanwhile, the right methods of organising productive activity gave the Pioneers
considerable trouble. Instead of founding productive departments under the
control of the members, they created new societies, in which they invested
capital and even accepted investments from the general public. Inevitably,
these societies tended to turn into ordinary joint stock capitalist concerns, and
to lose their contact with the Co-operative Movement. Gradually, productive departments attached to the consumers' Stores came to be preferred ;
but the great development of production under consumers' control did not
come till later, when the growth of Wholesale Co-operation made possible
the establishment of factories directly owned and controlled by the associated
Stores.

In the meantime, there was temporarily a great growth of Co-operation
based on a different principle. In modern times, industrial Co-operation has
taken two sharply contrasted forms. On the one hand, there is consumers'

Co-operation, in which the associated purchasers control the supply and production of the goods which they need, employing labour at a wage, with or without some form of profit-sharing arrangement. On the other hand there is producers' Co-operation, in which a body of associated producers, with or without the backing of their Trade Union, come together to form what is at least designed to be a self-governing workshop, under the control of the workers themselves.

There are sharp differences between these two forms of enterprise. The consumers' Store sells to its own members ; the producers' Society must find a market outside its own membership. The consumers' Store, after the first humble start, gathers its capital from the loans and investments of its members, whereas the producers' Society can seldom acquire the means of production without loans of capital from outside. On the other hand, the consumers' Store as a rule merely employs labour at a wage, whereas the producers' Society at any rate aims at making the workers real partners in the enterprise.

In the pre-Rochdale days of Co-operation, as we saw in the previous section of this study, these distinctions were not fully developed. The Store was regarded merely as a first step towards the self-employment of the members ; the " Union Shop," or producers' Society, sought to link itself to an "'Equitable Labour Exchange " which would enable it to put its trade on a mutual basis, instead of seeking custom in the open market. The distinction between the two types of Society was therefore neither sharp, nor clearly recognised. But the Rochdale method now sharply differentiated the consumers' Society, and, a few years later, the producers' type was no less clearly marked out.

This second differentiation was largely the work of the little group of men known as the Christian Socialists, headed by F. D. Maurice, Charles Kingsley, Edward Vansittart Neale, and J. M. Ludlow. These men, as readers of Kingsley's social novels know, had been deeply impressed by the misery of the workers in the " hungry 'forties," and by the failure of the Church to present any social gospel. The Kingdom of Christ, they proclaimed, must be of this world, not merely of the next—there was a Christian ideal of society, which it was incumbent upon Christians to strive to make real here on earth. Ludlow and his friends were deeply stirred by the atheism and rationalism which they found dominant among Chartists and Owenites, with whose social gospel they largely agreed. They set out to Christianise the Socialists and to socialise the Christians.

For a positive programme the Christian Socialists, with memories of the Owenite movement of 1830-1834 in their minds, turned to the France of 1848. The Charter, Kingsley wrote, " disappointed me bitterly when I read it. . . . The French cry of Organisation of Labour is worth a thousand of it." Under Ludlow's inspiration, the group took up the call of Buchez for Co-operative workshops and of Louis Blanc for the " organisation of labour."

They began founding small Co-operative workshops with the aid of capital mainly supplied by members of the group. They published journals and tracts in furtherance of their propaganda, and sent forth missionaries, of whom the old Owenite, Lloyd Jones, was the chief, to preach the gospel of association. Within a few years they had to accept the fact that they had failed. Their societies, too small, undercapitalised, and torn by internal dissensions, went down one after another. By 1854 the Christian Socialist Movement, as far as it was concerned with founding Productive Associations on Christian principles, was at an end.

The Christian Socialists, however, though they failed in their direct objective, made more than one important contribution to the growth of the Co-operative principle. Apart from their attempts, through the Society for Promoting Working Men's Associations, which they founded in 1849, to create self-governing workshops, they took an active part in the wider activities of the Co-operative Movement, and were good friends to the Societies of the Rochdale type. In Owen's day, there had been regular Co-operative Conferences ; but these had fallen into abeyance after the collapse of 1834. The Christian Socialists were successful in stimulating a revival ; and from the Rochdale Co-operative Conference of 1850 onwards more or less representative meetings were regularly held.

Above all did the Christian Socialists help the Co-operatives to secure the protection of the law. In the early days the lack of legal safeguards for the funds had been a serious difficulty. From 1836 onwards it was possible to secure a limited protection under the " Frugal Investment " clause of the Friendly Societies Act of that year. But Co-operation, as it developed, clearly needed a defined legal status of its own ; and this the Christian Socialists set to work to help the Co-operators to secure. The Industrial and Provident Societies Acts of 1852, 1855 and 1862 at length gave the security that was needed, and endowed the Co-operative Movement with a legal position which has not greatly changed to-day.

Christian Socialism also exerted at least a passing influence on the Trade Unions. The persistence of Owenite ideas was shown when, in 1845, the National Association of United Trades for the Protection of Labour, the new central Trade Union body formed in the industrial revival of that time, created the National Association for the Employment of Labour, with the declared object of promoting Co-operative Societies of producers. The inclusion of a rule enabling the funds to be devoted to Co-operative production in the " new model " constitution of the Amalgamated Engineers in 1851 may be taken either as a survival of the old ideas, or as an instance of Christian Socialist influence. Probably it was in fact due to a mingling of both. But, though a number of Trade Unions adopted such rules, and a few founded actual societies, nothing much came of them. The lasting successes of Co-operation were achieved along " Rochdale " lines.

This, however, was by no means so clear to contemporaries as it now appears in retrospect. The early 'fifties were a season of experiment in all manner of associative enterprise—capitalist as well as working-class. The position of joint stock companies had been partly regularised in 1844, and there was a rush of flotations. As we have seen, even the Rochdale Pioneers, when they launched out into manufacture, experimented at first in various forms of joint stock organisation; and in Lancashire especially, the so-called "Working Class Limiteds"—joint stock companies formed by working-class shareholders—developed in considerable numbers. But these either failed, like the self-governing workshops of the Christian Socialists, or in process of time lost their distinctive character, and evolved into ordinary joint stock concerns.

Meanwhile, the Owenite idea in the older form was far from dead. The Owenite Societies were still vigorously carrying on their propaganda, though this, in the hands of men like Holyoake, was becoming less and less a Socialist, and more and more a secularist agitation. The real successors of the earlier Owenites were rather those bodies of workmen who, between 1847 and 1851, founded and conducted the General Redemption Societies of Leeds, Norwich, Stockport, Bury, and other towns. These Societies aimed, by means of penny contributions, at building up a fund which could be applied to the "redemption of labour" through Co-operative organisation; and, though they either disappeared or developed in time into friendly societies of the ordinary type, they were responsible during their years of activity for setting a number of young Co-operative organisations on their feet. Especially in Yorkshire, the Co-operative Movement owes a good deal to these organisers of the transition from Owenism to consumers' associations of the modern type.

The late 'forties and early 'fifties were thus a season of extraordinary Co-operative growth. After the excitements of these years, the movement settled down to a less sensational course of development. The producers' Societies founded in this period were largely submerged or lost to Co-operation, whereas the consumers' Societies quietly grew, and expanded into new fields. The Industrial and Provident Societies Act of 1862, which for the first time gave full scope for federal development by allowing any Co-operative Society to hold shares in any other such Society, made possible a further great advance, and the North of England Co-operative Wholesale Society, which subsequently dropped "North of England" from its title and became national in scope, was formed the following year.

The history of the movement was already strewn with the wrecks of abortive wholesale organisations. Owen's Labour Exchanges of 1832, the North-West of England United Co-operative Company established a little later at Liverpool, the costly attempt of 1850, under the guidance of a leading, but unorthodox, Christian Socialist, E. Vansittart Neale, to create a

Wholesale Society in London, the Wholesale Department set up by the Rochdale Pioneers, and subsequently abandoned—all these showed the difficulties in the way. But the Act of 1862 made the task a great deal easier, and Abraham Greenwood, William Cooper, and other leading spirits of the Rochdale Society came forward with a plan for repeating on a larger scale the experiment which had proved so successful in the sphere of retail trade. The Societies in the North of England, through the Lancashire and Yorkshire Co-operative Conference Board, had already learned to work together. Why not create, for wholesale trade, a greater society of which they should all be members ?

Thus the Rochdale plan was again followed in the creation of the Co-operative Wholesale Society. Here too, goods were to be sold at their market prices ; dividends were to be paid in proportion to the amounts purchased by the member Societies ; and the recipients of dividend were to be encouraged to leave their money, at interest, in the Society's hands. But the members of the Wholesale were to be the retail Societies. To them dividends were to be paid ; to them as shareholders the Wholesale was to belong. The plan worked. From small beginnings the North of England Wholesale Society grew rapidly. In 1868 the Scottish Co-operators followed the English example, and set up a Wholesale Society of their own. In 1873 the English Society founded its first productive works at Crumpsall and Leicester, and, dropping the prefix " North of England," became simply the C.W.S., and spread its influence over the entire country.

The great trading success of the new Co-operative Movement had, among other effects, that of cutting it off sharply from other forms of working-class organisation. Under Owen's inspiration, Co-operation, Trade Unionism and Socialism had been organised in close connection and for a common end. When Socialism shrank up into secularism, Trade Unionism and Co-operation both went their independent ways. For a time both lost touch with working-class politics, which were indeed almost completely submerged. But, whereas Trade Unionism was drawn back into politics in the 'sixties, to fight both for the extension of the franchise and for amendments of the labour laws that were necessary in order to safeguard its very existence, the Co-operative Movement, having won its legal status and security earlier and with far less difficulty, had no such strong inducement as the Trade Unions had to embark on political action or propaganda. The ideas of Owen were still to some extent cherished, and " the Co-operative Commonwealth " remained a phrase in the Co-operators' mouths. But the merely trading methods of the movement fitted in too well with the dominant Victorian philosophy of thrift and self-help not to sweep all before them. While Trade Unions were still frowned on and repressed, Co-operative Societies were encouraged and patted on the back as agencies of working-class thrift. The private shopkeepers were not yet organised to do battle against them ; and there was hardly a disapproving voice in Parliament when their affairs were discussed. Whigs, Tories and Radicals all voted for legal protection for the Co-operative Societies, even when the Trade Unions were still having to fight an uphill battle for bare recognition. Moreover, the Co-operators, for success in their commercial enterprises, needed just that type of careful and honest artisan who most readily accepted the Victorian gospel. The Co-operators accomplished an immense task of organisation, and greatly increased both the self-respect and the economic strength of the working class. But the cost of their success was to a great extent the sacrifice of the earlier idealism, and an entire separation from the other sections of the movement. All that remained of Owenism was a ritual of phrases and—what was perhaps worth more—some belief in education and a tradition of setting aside a percentage of profits for educational use.

BOOKS

G. D. H. Cole. *A Century of Co-operation.*
B. Potter (Mrs. Webb). *The Co-operative Movement.*
G. J. Holyoake. *History of Co-operation.*
G. J. Holyoake. *History of the Rochdale Pioneers.*
C. E. Raven. *Christian Socialism.*
B. Jones. *Co-operative Production.*
G. Kendall. *Charles Kingsley and his Ideas.*

3. THE FRIENDLY SOCIETIES

Friendly Societies, of a sort, exist at all times among all civilised peoples. They existed in ancient Greece and Rome ; they exist to-day in India and China. The Guilds of the Middle Ages were, in one aspect, friendly societies of a highly developed type. But in nineteenth-century Great Britain, and especially in the Victorian age, Friendly Societies took on a highly specialised form. Side by side with little village slate clubs, informal groupings for mutual credit or insurance, and similar primitive types of society and also with Thrift Societies patronised and controlled by the ruling classes, there grew up to power and influence highly organised democratic Friendly Societies, national in scale or extending over a large area, of which the great "Orders" represent the dominant type. The Oddfellows, the Foresters, the Druids, and several of the other great Orders originated well back in the eighteenth century, though most of them did not assume their present form until well on in the nineteenth. Defoe, in his famous *Essay on Projects*, urged the creation of Friendly Societies early in the eighteenth century, and a little later Huguenot refugees seem to have led the way in forming societies more stable and permanent than the small village clubs and trade friendly societies which had been frequent from about 1700. No form of legal recognition was, however, given until 1793, when the " Rose " Act was passed, mainly for the encouragement of societies under upper-class patronage, and in the hope of checking the growth of bodies of a less " respectable " type. Thereafter, there was a steady stream of legislation. Important Acts extending further legal protection and regulating the working of Friendly Societies were passed in 1819, 1829, 1834, 1846, 1855 and 1875, when a great consolidating Act gave the law practically its present form.

It will be seen that the law began its encouragement to Friendly Societies considerably before the Victorian era. But, until Victorian times, the law was not wholly favourable. After the outbreak of the French Revolution, all forms of popular combination were for a long time regarded with jealous eyes, and from 1799 the Corresponding Societies Act made illegal the creation of societies with branches, and thus placed the great Orders strictly beyond the pale of the law. This prohibition was not rigidly enforced ; but it operated against the growth of the movement on a national scale. Moreover from 1799 to 1824 the Combination Acts were in force, and all forms of Trade Unionism were explicitly forbidden by law. Naturally, many Trade Unions sought to evade the prohibition by disguising themselves as Friendly· Societies ; or perhaps it would be truer to say that many bodies, which were really both Trade Unions and Friendly Societies, sought to cover up the one activity by the other, and thus at the same time to evade prosecution and, in some cases, even to secure legal protection.

The Corresponding Societies Act was still in force at the beginning of the Victorian era ; but it had ceased to be commonly enforced, and, in particular, bodies such as the Oddfellows and Foresters, in which there was a large " petty *bourgeois* " element, were practically exempt from its operation. The Manchester Unity of Oddfellows, which led the way towards the re-organisation of the Orders on modern lines, was started in 1812, and round about the beginning of the Victorian period most of the great Orders began to assume something like their modern form. The Ancient Order of Foresters was reorganised in 1834, and in the same year the Oddfellows underwent a similar process.

Thereafter, growth was rapid, and the Orders tended to embrace a wider section of the people, as the more skilled workers rose above the bare subsistence level. Nor was growth confined to the Orders with their affiliated courts or branches. Every type of Friendly Society multiplied fast, and new types came into existence in order to meet changing needs. The Royal Commission of 1870-1874, on whose Report the Act of 1875 was based, divided Friendly Societies into thirteen distinct types, of which we can here mention only a few of the most important.

The essence of the modern Friendly Society has been that it has enabled the members, by a method of mutual insurance, to provide for themselves certain benefits in case of sickness, death, or other contingencies. Sick and burial benefits have been in practice by far the most important services provided. Clearly the method of insurance could not advance beyond a primitive stage without the aid of the skilled actuary working on data which enabled the proper ratio of benefits to contributions to be calculated with some approach to accuracy. In the eighteenth century, Dr. Price by his vital tables had done a great deal to establish actuarial calculation on a firm basis, though his own tables had to be greatly revised in the light of later experience. For estimating the risk of deaths the societies of the early nineteenth century were in possession of useful data ; but they had to wait long before sickness benefit could be put on a satisfactory basis. The Tables issued in 1850 by Henry Ratcliffe, Corresponding Secretary of the Oddfellows, were a great step forward, and a little later the State took up the matter, and, compelling the Societies to make returns, accumulated a vast mass of data which at length put the science on a firm foundation. Until this was done, it was inevitable that many societies should work on an unsound financial basis. The Government, in regulating Friendly Societies, wavered for some time between its desire to minimise interference and its feeling that, in the interest of the members, unsound finance ought to be suppressed. In 1829 John Tidd Pratt was appointed to examine and certify the rules of all societies desiring registration, and thereafter it was often erroneously supposed that his certificate was a guarantee of financial soundness. But gradually the State gave up the attempt to ensure solvency by compulsion, and resorted instead to the method of enforced publicity and periodical valuation of assets.

Meanwhile, in 1846, the Registry of Friendly Societies was formally constituted, and Tidd Pratt became the first Chief Registrar, many types of society, including Co-operative Societies, Building Societies, and Trade Unions, passing gradually under the supervision of his department. In 1876 he was succeeded by J. M. Ludlow, who had been the principal originator of the Christian Socialist Movement, and in his new post was able to give strong state help and encouragement to Co-operative Societies and to the great Friendly Society Orders. Tidd Pratt, though he was a keen advocate of Friendly Societies, had been an opponent of the national Orders, and had encouraged rather societies of a localised type.

The Royal Commission of 1870, as we have seen, distinguished many separate types of Friendly Society. Besides the great Orders, with their affiliated branches and mainly localised finance, the Commission found in existence many purely local societies in both town and country, a considerable number of County Societies mostly run under patronage rather for the members than by them, dividing societies, deposit societies, collecting societies, and many other kinds.

These various bodies differed greatly in character, though all of them in one form or another provided friendly benefits in return for contributions from their members. In the Orders and in some of the local societies, the element of mutual insurance was combined with a strong element of social activity, so that they existed almost as much for purposes of good fellowship as for the provision of funeral benefits.   At the other extreme, some of the centralised Societies, and particularly the collecting societies specialising in burial benefits and collecting their contributions by house-to-house visitation, were, and are to-day, barely distinguishable from Insurance Companies of the " industrial " type, save in having no body of shareholders, and in being run rather for the benefit of their collectors and directors than of a body of investors.   These societies had no social activity, and only the most per-functory forms of control by their members.   On the other hand, the collecting societies, like certain Insurance Companies, succeeded in reaching a much poorer section of the people than was touched by such Orders as the Oddfellows or the Foresters, but did this at the cost of spending on adminis-tration—that is, on house-to-house canvassing and collection—a very large proportion of the sums contributed by their members.

The Collecting Societies and certain of the other centralised Societies, and also many of the County Societies, never really had any democratic character.   They met a need, and they throve ; but, unlike the Orders and some of the local Societies, they were not created and administered by the members on a really mutual basis.

In some of the other types of Friendly Society are found methods inter-mediate between the true method of mutual insurance and the pure individ-ualism of the Savings Bank.   Such were the deposit societies in which only a part of the contributions was pooled to make a common fund, the rest accumulating as a deposit to the credit of the individual contributor, and the right to a share in the benefits drawn from the common fund depending on the possession of an individual balance.   Other societies were of the " di-viding " type—that is, they were in operation only for a limited period, at the end of which the members, after paying benefits on the mutual basis, divided out the balance, and then started afresh.   This method obviously made it impossible to accumulate funds in order to deal with major con-tingencies.

In short, there were by 1870 societies of very many different types and sorts, assuring most various benefits, and ranging from local slate clubs to great national bodies, and from societies based on good fellowship and social activity to purely business concerns.   But all these various types of society fulfilled, though in many cases they fulfilled most imperfectly, real needs, the nature of which, as well as the reason for their emergence at this time, I have tried already to explain.

Moreover, side by side with Friendly Societies, there grew up many types of organisation serving largely similar purposes.   Savings Banks were suggested by Defoe in 1697, and were founded in various parts of Germany and Switzerland during the eighteenth century.   Bentham again proposed their adoption in 1797, and two years later the first Savings Bank in Great

Britain was started at Wendover. In 1807 Whitbread proposed that the Post Office should establish a Savings Bank ; but this was not done until 1861. Meanwhile, voluntary Savings Banks multiplied fast. In 1817 the first regulating Act was passed, and this was supplemented by many amending measures. The State encouraged the formation of banks by allowing an exceptionally favourable rate of interest on their funds, which had to be deposited with the Commissioners for the National Debt.

Another important thrift organisation of the Victorian era was the Building Society, which, it is hardly necessary to point out, is wrongly named, since it exists in the main, not to build houses, but to advance to its members part of the purchase price of houses built by someone else. Building Societies began to be formed towards the end of the eighteenth century, but did not come under special legal regulation until 1836. At first, they were temporary bodies, lasting only until each of the individual members had received and repaid the advance he needed. But, from 1846 onwards, the modern type of Permanent Building Society began to develop, and at the same time a differentiation began to grow up between investors and borrowers, who had been originally the same people. Thus, the Building Society, like the Co-operative Store, became an important field for the investment of small savings, and a working-class and lower middle-class equivalent to the limited company.

The Building Society, even if its government is to some extent democratic in form, is purely a business concern, usually with no social side. But for a long time the business reputation of Societies of this kind was very bad, though they multiplied none the less. There were many defalcations, and a great many of the societies were for a long time financially unsound. The great " Liberator " crash of 1893 was only the culminating point in a long series of disasters. This at length caused drastic reorganisation. Many Societies were wound up, and the survivors were put on firmer foundations. But, before this, despite the risky finance of many of them, very large sums were invested in a type of body which met an obvious social need.

Of an essentially different type, serving not a financial but a social interest, were the Working Men's Clubs, which sprang up in great numbers from about 1860 onwards. The Club movement owes its inception to a benevolent clergyman, the Rev. Henry Solly, whom we shall meet again as joint editor for a time of the *Beehive*, the most influential working-class newspaper of the 'sixties and 'seventies. Originally intended as temperance rivals to the public-house, the Clubs were gradually brought, by the democratic will of their membership, to supply drink as well as other amenities to the workman. The Working Men's Club and Institute Union, formed in 1862, grew slowly for the first twelve years of its life. In 1873 it was put on a democratic basis, and from 1875, having adopted its modern form, it grew rapidly The

Clubs included some attached to particular political parties ; but the movement as a whole had, and has, no declared political colour. It is purely social, with a very slight admixture of educational activity.

More than any of these organisations, however, the great Co-operative Movement described in the last section made itself felt as a field of investment for working-class savings. This statement, indeed, applied mainly to the distributive societies, in whose case the conditions were the most favourable for the investor. The producers' societies, as we have seen, have at all times to sell their products partly in the open market, and have there to compete directly with capitalist producers, while their members expect better conditions because they are part of a democratic movement. This might not be an insuperable obstacle if the producers' societies were in a position to compete on equal terms. Usually, however, they have not been so ; for they have had by no means the same opportunites for raising capital as the consumers' societies. The working-class investor generally looks for security rather than for a high rate of interest. The consumers' societies, when once they had established their position, were able to offer to the investor both excellent security and the greatly valued right to withdraw capital at short notice in case of need ; but productive societies on a competitive basis necessarily involved both much greater risk and the permanent locking up of the capital invested in them. The workman with money saved preferred to entrust it to the Co-operative Societies of consumers, and the " dividend " also provided these Societies with a means whereby capital accumulated easily ; for often the member was ready to let part of his dividend accumulate as capital instead of drawing it out to meet current expenditure. Thus the consumers' movement soon outstripped that of the producers, and Victorian Co-operation took shape rather as a mutual thrift organisation than as a direct challenge to the capitalist system of wage-labour.

All the movements and organisations which we have been considering in this chapter—Friendly Societies, Savings Banks, Building Societies, Co-operative Societies—together made up a most powerful apparatus for the promotion of thrift and mutual service on a basis of thrift. No one of them developed exclusively as a working-class movement, and none, save the least satisfactory forms of Friendly Society, the slate club and the collecting society, managed to reach to any great extent the lowest strata of the working class. The more democratically conducted Friendly Societies were very largely dominated by what Continental writers call the " petty *bourgeoisie* " ; the Co-operative Movement, on the other hand, though it always included many middle-class persons, still, largely because of the inevitable antagonism between it and the trading interest, remained throughout under predominantly working-class control. The larger Friendly Societies, other than the great " Orders," the Building Societies, and the Savings Banks either were throughout, or speedily became, purely business concerns, having with their members only a cash nexus, and arousing no feelings of loyalty beyond the actual services which they performed. Of all the movements described, the Co-operative Movement alone had in itself the social force that could make it a powerful instrument of economic transformation.

To discuss this wider aspect of Co-operation is, however, beyond the scope of this chapter. We are here concerned with all these movements as they manifested themselves during the Victorian era, at a time when society was settling down after the convulsions of the Industrial Revolution to make the best of Capitalism and to realise its full potentialities. I have tried to show how, during this time, there were powerful social forces influencing the workers to adopt habits of thrift and insurance, and so impelling them to devise both methods of mutual provision against the risks of life and safe places for the investment of their savings. Though Co-operation never lost altogether the idealistic and anti-capitalistic character derived from its early struggles under the influence of Owen, during the Victorian era this aspect of it was thrust into the background, and it developed rather as a mutual type of business organisation adopting many of the features of capitalist business than as a direct and menacing rival to Capitalism. In the same way, the Friendly Societies, without discarding their older character as associations of good fellowship, developed more and more into mutual benefit societies in which this element, once primary, fell to the second place.

Everything thus tended to impress on working-class organisation in the Victorian era the mood and character dominant in Victorianism itself—a mood of acquisitiveness, which measured men by money and reckoned virtues largely in monetary terms. It is of course obvious that in the long run this mood contributed greatly to the accumulation of capital and to the increase of riches and the raising of the standard of life. That it also raised up serious problems to which Capitalism furnished no solution became obvious only at a later stage. As long as fresh markets could easily be found abroad for the goods which a saving people were able to produce in ever-increasing abundance, the process of putting by riches to make more riches passed unchallenged with most men, though a few; Karl Marx among them, prophesied a nemesis to come, when the problem of society would be, not to produce enough, but to devise means of consuming that which it had all the material means of getting produced.

This, however, is looking beyond our period. In the Victorian era, we find a large body of the workers, especially in the more skilled grades and in the more highly organised industries, gradually raising themselves above the starvation level of the preceding period, and acquiring, to a small extent, a "stake in the country." The scope and policy of Victorian Trade Unionism, which are dealt with in the next chapter, illustrate the working of the same forces. The position may be summed up by saying that, in the Victorian era, the possibility of realising a small surplus over the necessary minimum of current expenditure presented itself to a large body of workers, and was at once the cause of a great expansion of mutual activity. Instead of spending his small surplus, the Victorian workman applied it, first to meeting the contingencies of life, in which the State, under the influence of laissez-faire doctrines, refused him its help, and secondly to saving up for old age or for a rainy day by buying his own house through a Building Society, or investing in a Building Society or a Co-operative Store. The Victorian workman learned readily the lesson which his masters were fain to teach him. He was as thrifty as they could desire ; and in many respects his thrift both made him more tolerant than his fathers of the system under which he lived, and led him to assimilate to it his ways of action and thought. The "Lib-Lab" policy of the Victorian working-class leaders is readily understood when it is related to the economic basis of Victorian society.

BOOKS

E. Brabrook. *Provident Societies.*
E. Baernreither. *English Associations of Working Men.*
J. E. Frome Wilkinson. *Mutual Thrift.* ·
J. E. Frome Wilkinson. *The Friendly Society Movement.*
J. H. Clapham. *Economic History of Modern Britain,* Vols. I and II.

CHAPTER III

TRADE UNIONISM RE-MADE

I. TRADE UNIONISM, 1835-1850

THE new method of the Rochdale Pioneers brought about, within a few years, a complete change in the organisation and policy of the Co-operative Movement. No change equally startling or general took place among the Trade Unions, which had to meet a far stiffer opposition from the employing class, and to deal with a far less uniform set of conditions. The problems of Co-operative store-keeping were much the same everywhere ; but what suited the textile operatives as a method of Trade Union organisation would not necessarily suit the builders, nor would what suited the miners be likely to suit the engineers. Trade Unionism everywhere underwent great changes corresponding to the new economic and social conditions ; but the new Unions assumed many different forms, and followed to a large extent different policies.

This fact is apt to be overlooked if attention is unduly concentrated on Unions of one particular type. Thus, the formation in 1851 of the Amalgamated Society of Engineers is generally acclaimed as the introduction of a " New Model " in Trade Union organisation, so as almost to imply that it provided a pattern to which all Unions gradually sought to conform. There is an element of truth in this view, and it is certainly true that the new " Amalgamated Societies " were by far the most characteristic Trade Union products of the Victorian age ; but the new organisations of the miners and cotton operatives are of no less interest, and represent, in some degree, a different attitude and policy based on their different economic circumstances. In this chapter, an attempt will be made to describe these various types of " new Unionism " in both their resemblances and their contrasts.

In the first Part of this study, the growth of Trade Unionism was fully dealt with up to the great collapse of 1834, when the Grand National Consolidated Trades Union broke up under the combined onslaughts of the employers and the Government. Thereafter, only casual mention was made of the subsequent development, as it arose in connection with the Chartist and the later Owenite agitations. It is now, therefore, necessary briefly to pick up the threads, and to describe the fortunes of the Unions from 1834 to their lasting recovery in the eighteen-fifties.

When the great " Trades Union " broke up, the groups which had composed it did not disappear. It had been formed largely on the basis of previously existing local Trade Clubs, and even of embryonic national trade societies. When it was dissolved, many of its units, and most of the new members who had flocked in during the period of excitement, doubtless disappeared ; but many local and some national societies held together. And the same thing happened in the collapse of the other big Unions of 1834—the Spinners, the Potters, the Clothiers, and the Builders.

Thus, there remained in being quite a number of national societies. The Stonemasons and the Carpenters among the building trades lived on, and the former continued as the most stable and powerful Trade Union in the country down to the formation of the Amalgamated Society of Engineers. In the metal trades, which had played little part in the upheavals of 1830-1834, several at least nominally national societies survived. The Steam Engine Makers of Liverpool, the Journeymen Steam Engine Makers of Manchester, the Yorkshire Mechanics, the Old Smiths, and the Friendly Society of Ironfounders all traced their history well back beyond the late troubles, and all survived until some of them lost their identity in the amalgamation of 1851. The Lancashire cotton operatives, the miners on the North-East Coast and in other areas, preserved at least a skeleton organisation. The Potters' Union almost lapsed, but was revived in 1843. The Boilermakers, who had formed their first national society in 1834, managed to maintain it in continuous existence.

By 1841, there were clear signs of a Trade Union revival. Under the leadership of Martin Jude the miners of the North-East Coast and of Yorkshire took the lead in forming the Miners' Association of Great Britain, and began to hold national delegate conferences and to send out organisers to visit every colliery in the country. In the following year broke out in the Northern Counties and in Wales the great strikes of which, for the time, the Chartists assumed the leadership. But trade was bad, and the movement was not strong enough to stand up against the combined force of unemployment and Government repression. The strikers were beaten, and had to return to work on the employers' terms. In 1843 the South Wales Miners suffered a similar defeat, and the collapse of their Union was followed, as in 1834, by an organised terrorist movement known as the " Scotch Cattle." In 1844 the West Yorkshire Miners and the Durham Miners were both engaged in unsuccessful strikes which reduced their Unions to impotence. In 1847 Martin Jude's National Association broke up under the strain, and an attempt in 1850 to re-form it on a national basis was unsuccessful. But large sections of it survived : both on the North-East Coast and in Lancashire, and in parts of Yorkshire the Miners' Unions held together.

To this period of the miners' history belongs their first adoption of a method of Trade Union action which they have ever since largely used.

More than any other body of workers, the miners were faced with continuous legal repression. Their troubles arose largely out of the system of long-term hirings, which bound them to one employer without giving them any guarantee of employment. Jude's Union engaged W. P. Roberts, the well-known Chartist lawyer, at a salary of £1,000 a year, to fight every possible case of repression in the courts. Roberts, who was also closely associated with Feargus O'Connor in his Land Scheme, was extraordinarily successful, and earned himself the name of the " miners' attorney-general." Even after the collapse of the Miners' Union, he was frequently retained for many years later in all manner of Trade Union cases.

While the miners were thus active, the engineering workers, hitherto of little note in the Trade Union world, were rapidly rising to prominence. As early as 1836 the London engineering societies had jointly conducted a successful strike for the ten hours' day ; but it was in Lancashire in the early 'forties that the real forward movement began. In 1844 a joint strike in Lancashire against the employers' attempt to impose a " quittance paper," or leaving certificate system, led to a movement for the better organisation of the trades affected. In the same year the London engineers were again successful, by means of a joint movement, in enforcing a reduction in hours. In 1847 the movement for closer unity was officially taken up by the Journeymen Steam Engine Makers' Society, by far the largest and most important in the industry. William Newton, in London, and in Lancashire William Allan, who became General Secretary in 1848, vigorously pressed the movement, and in 1850 they were successful in getting a number of the leading societies to join forces. The Amalgamated Society of Engineers was formally instituted at the beginning of 1851, and after a few months of hesitation, members and small local societies began to flock in to the new body. Only a few mechanics' societies, of which the Steam Engine Makers' Society of Liverpool was the most important, refused to come in. The Boilermakers and Ironfounders, however, also remained separate, and became the nuclei of large independent societies in other branches of the industry.

The special position and influence of the A.S.E. are described in the following section. Apart from the engineers, other trades were moving in the direction of closer unity. A National Typographical Association, formed in 1845 by the linking up of a number of local societies, broke down two years later in face of internal dissensions. But in 1849 the leading societies outside London drew together again in the loosely knit Provincial Typographical Association, and in London the Society of Compositors, which had long been powerful, assumed something like its present form.

The building trades, without doing much to improve their national organisation, were active in local forward movements. In 1846 they conducted in Lancashire an unsuccessful strike for the nine hours' day, and in 1848 and the following years there were in London and elsewhere a number of small strikes, in most cases successful, for the recognition of the Saturday half-holiday. Richard Harnott, perhaps the most typical and influential Trade Union leader of the time, became General Secretary of the Stonemasons' Society in 1847, and under his guidance the Society gained greatly in power and prestige.

The re-awakening of Trade Union activity is still more clearly shown by the attempt, in 1845, to bring together all the Trade Unions into a single body for common action and mutual defence. On the initiative of the Organised Trades of Sheffield, whose leader was John Drury, a conference of Unions in that year formed the National Association of United Trades for the Protection of Labour, with a name and constitution recalling John Doherty's similar Association of 1830, upon which it was clearly modelled. The continuity with the older ideas was further shown both by the insistence on the use of the combined force of the Association to help the Societies in resisting wage reductions—advances being left to their separate action—and in the revival of the idea of Co-operative production under Trade Union control. As we have seen, an auxiliary body, the National Association of United Trades for the Employment of Labour, was formed to raise funds for the starting of Co-operative workshops. Thomas Slingsby Duncombe, a well-known Radical M.P. sympathetic to Chartism, became President of both bodies, and an energetic propaganda was set on foot.

The event, however, showed that, while the Trade Union revival was real enough, the spirit of the Unions was changing. Relatively few of the larger Unions agreed to join, and the bad trade of 1845 and 1846 caused many strikes and lock-outs, which depleted the Association's funds. Before long the attempt to found Co-operative workshops had to be given up, and the Association for the Employment of Labour was merged in the parent body. But this too declined in power and influence, and underwent a change of policy. Its most important achievement was effected in 1859, when it secured the passage of a short Act legalising peaceful picketing. Thereafter, it accomplished little. Lingering on until 1867, it was known in its later years only as a promoter of conciliation and as an advocate of legislative measures to promote better industrial relations. After the passing of the abortive Conciliation Act of 1867 it was formally wound up, and its place was taken by other bodies.

In its early years, apart from the strain of strikes, the National Association had to stand the hammerings of the law. In 1847, on the unsupported accusation of two convicts, John Drury and three other leaders of Sheffield Trade Unionism were accused of incitement to destroy machinery. They were sentenced to ten years' transportation, and, when the monstrous sentence was quashed on a technical point, a new charge was at once brought forward. The National Association took up the case, and finally, after a year's delay, the prisoners were released. This legal prosecution, though it failed, was one of the factors in hastening the decline of the Association.

The National Association of United Trades stood just at the point of transition between the older Unionism and the new. In one aspect, and probably in the intention of its founders, it was a late attempt to organise a " General Union," primarily for resistance to wage-reductions, but also to some extent on Owenite lines and with a Co-operative or Socialist object. But in another aspect, and in the actual working out, it became an embodiment of the new idea of making the best of Capitalism and of living at peace with the employers. It was not a very successful embodiment of this idea, because neither were most employers ready at this time to be conciliatory, nor most Unions conscious of the need for any central organisation at all. Each Union was busy building up its own strength, and pursuing its own limited objects. " Past experience," wrote the Manchester Stonemasons, " has taught us that we have had general union enough."

BOOKS

S. and B. Webb. *History of Trade Unionism.*
R. W. Postgate. *The Builders' History.*
E. Welbourne. *Miners' Unions of Durham and Northumberland.*
N. Edwards. *History of the South Wales Miners.*
J. B. Jefferys. *The Story of the Engineers.*

2. THE NEW MODELS—THE ENGINEERS AND THE COTTON OPERATIVES

The Amalgamated Society of Engineers is commonly acclaimed as a " New Model " in Trade Union organisation. The " model " was indeed really that of its predecessor, the Journeymen Steam Engine Makers' Society (formed in 1826), whose constitution and methods of organisation it adopted with relatively little change. But the amalgamation and the struggle which followed it made the A.S.E. the leading Union in the country, and attracted to it both observers and imitators. It became the model for a whole series of " Amalgamated " Societies formed during the next twenty years.

The essential basis of the " New Model " was a close combination of trade and friendly activities. The A.S.E. provided for all its members a wide range of benefits, ranging from dispute and unemployment benefit to sickness and superannuation benefit. In order to pay these, it had to exact a high rate of contribution; and the shilling a week which its members had to pay closed it to all but the thriftier and better-paid artisans. It was, and was meant to be, a society of skilled men, bound together by close ties of common craftsmanship, and looking to it not only for trade protection, but equally for mutual insurance. In short, it was a Trade Union and a Friendly Society almost in equal measure.

It was necessary for a body of this sort to adopt a more elaborate and secure financial organisation than mere trade societies had usually possessed. Centralisation of funds was out of the question, since the law provided no adequate safeguards for them; but the system of leaving the funds with the branches while providing for periodical equalisation according to branch membership, combined with the enactment of an elaborate code of rules stating precisely on what terms benefits might be paid, secured the result of central control even without gathering the funds together. In trade matters the control was even tighter; for no strike benefit could be paid out save by direct order of the central executive. The administration of benefits under the rules was left in the hands of the branches; but for industrial purposes the branches in the larger centres were grouped into District Committees, which possessed independent negotiating powers up to, but just short of, the actual calling of a strike.

William Allan and William Newton were the outstanding leaders. Allan, who became General Secretary on the amalgamation, was a cautious Scotsman, and a very competent financial administrator. Newton was of a somewhat different type. He had been a foreman in London till he was dismissed for his Trade Union activities. He then, in 1848, took a public-house at Ratcliff, which became a great centre of working-class activity. He brought London into the amalgamation, and in 1852 stood for Parliament as Chartist candidate for Tower Hamlets. A close friend of Allan's, he seems to have been more disposed to push for an advanced industrial policy. He was, however, never a full-time official of the Society; and it was Allan's caution that mainly impressed itself on the character of the internal admin-istration, and ultimately on the policy that was adopted.

At the outset, the A.S.E. appeared as a militant industrial body. An essential part of the policy embodied in the amalgamation was an attempt to secure an increased control over the conditions of work. Already in 1845 the Journeymen Steam Engine Makers' Society had declared war on the working of systematic overtime, on the employment of labourers on machines, and on "the piece-master system," [1] and piece-work generally. The hope of putting up a more effective struggle against these abuses was one of the main motives behind the amalgamation, and, as soon as the new society was formed, the more active branches began to put forward their claims. The employers at once replied to the threat of the amalgamation by forming a great new organ-isation of their own to fight it; and already in 1851 the two national bodies—the Amalgamated Society of Engineers and the Central Association of Em-ployers of Operative Engineers—were facing each other menacingly.

At this stage the A.S.E. balloted its members on a proposal for the abolition of piece-work and systematic overtime, and secured a huge majority in

[1] I.e., the employment of workmen under sub-contracting charge-hands who received a piece-work payment from the employer and made their own terms with the rest of the " gang."

favour of immediate action. The employers retaliated by announcing that they would meet a strike, even in one establishment, with an immediate general lock-out of all members of the Society. The A.S.E. offered arbitration, which was refused. Thereupon the engineers refused to work overtime, and, in January, 1852, the general lock-out was declared. It extended to London and Lancashire, in which the main strength of both the rival organisations lay.

The struggle lasted for three months. The engineers received considerable financial help from other Unions and from the general public ; but in the end they were forced back to work. The employers at first made plans for the formation of a rival " Trade Union " directly under their own control, and to the end refused to take the men back unless they signed a " document " renouncing membership of the Union. The men, quite rightly, took the view that such a document, signed under duress, could not be binding. They signed, and retained their Union membership. Within a brief space of time, the Society was both numerically and financially stronger than before the struggle.

The engineering struggle created a great public impression. The Christian Socialists, then at the height of their activity, lent the Union powerful support, and joined with Frederic Harrison and the Positivists, later to be staunch allies of the " new " Unionism, in giving publicity to the workers' case. Before the outbreak of the struggle, the newly-formed A.S.E. had been considering plans for launching out upon Co-operative production ; and E. V. Neale and others helped in starting various Co-operative engineering works on a small scale. The larger projects, however, had to be given up when the Society's funds were swept away in the course of the contest. Despite the failure of these schemes, the Engineers had leapt at a single stride to the foremost place in the Trade Union Movement.

Almost at the same time, the cotton operatives were organising their forces afresh. In 1852 and 1853 the Spinners' Union was remodelled, and the first of the modern standard piece-work " price lists " in the industry was adopted. The Blackburn lists of 1853 represent an important stage in the growth of that system of collective bargaining which has ever since dominated the cotton trades. In the same year, however, the cotton workers suffered, in the long-drawn Preston spinners' strike, a notable though not a lasting reverse. The Preston spinners at certain factories struck for an advance in wages, and the employers retaliated with a general lock-out. The movement spread to other towns, where in most cases the workers were successful. But in Preston the employers, aided by contributions from the manufacturers throughout Lancashire, stood firm. Blacklegs were imported, and the strike leaders arrested. At length the men were driven back to work, and the leaders were then released without trial. Yet again the law had intervened to help in the breaking of a strike.

The defeat, however, did not check the development of organisation. During the next few years Unionism rapidly increased, and in 1858 the weavers followed the spinners' example, and formed the North Lancashire Weavers' Amalgamation, the nucleus round which the modern Amalgamated Weavers' Association has grown. This was followed, in 1859, by another serious strike. The Padiham weavers struck in order to secure a standard price list. Again the workers were defeated ; but again defeat failed to check the development of the Unions.

These textile Trade Unions were of a distinctly different type, and followed a distinctly different policy, from such bodies as the Amalgamated Society of Engineers. In structure they were, and have remained to this day, federal. The local associations of each craft, instead of becoming mere branches of a national body, retained their separate existence and funds, only uniting in a central " amalgamation " for industrial purposes. No such uniformity of contributions and benefits as among the engineers was therefore required ; and on local matters and as friendly societies the local associations retained their autonomy. At first, wages were separately negotiated for each town ; but gradually uniform price-lists extending over a wider area were developed, and the practice grew of adjusting wages by making uniform percentage additions or deductions to or from the list prices. Wage negotiations were thus greatly simplified, and, as bargaining on wage issues became centralised, the power of the " amalgamations " grew. Whereas the engineers had a centralised constitution, but local bargaining, the cotton operatives had a localised constitution, but tended more and more to central bargaining.

In a still more important respect, the policy of the cotton operatives differed widely from that of the engineers. As we have seen, the policy of the A.S.E. was directed mainly to the restriction and regulation of the supply of labour and to opposing piece-work and sub-contracting. By limiting overtime and apprenticeship, by the possession of an emigration fund (about this time a very frequent, though ineffective, Trade Union device for restricting the supply of labour), and by insisting that only apprenticed men should be employed on machines, the engineers sought to keep up the value of their skill. By opposing piece-work they sought both to prevent " speeding-up " and to get rid of the " piece-master " system under which one workman was set to exploit his fellows and the solidarity of the workers was destroyed. To the cotton operatives, no such policies suggested themselves as possible or even as desirable. No system of apprenticeship existed, or could have been enforced in the cotton industry. Again, whereas the engineers were mainly time-workers, engaged in a ceaseless struggle against the piece-work system, the cotton operatives were practically all piece-workers, and the piece-work system of payment was far too strongly entrenched for them even to think of altering it. Indeed, in general they favoured it, partly because it enabled men to earn more by operating more machines in trades in which, to a large extent, both men and women were employed.

Under these conditions, the cotton workers were above all concerned to set limits to the length of the working day, and to improve working conditions in the factories. They could use their own organisations to look after wages, provided these things were adequately safeguarded. But the obvious method of reducing hours and improving conditions was by legislation ; for, whereas it was out of the question to get Parliament to pass laws regulating the conditions of adult men, laws which formally applied only to women and children were bound in practice to affect the hours and conditions of adult male workers in the same establishments. From the very beginning of the century the cotton operatives had been continuously agitating for a proper code of factory legislation. They had backed Owen's efforts in 1816; their Short-Time Committees, under Doherty's leadership, had taken a great part in the agitation which led up to the Factory Act of 1833 ; and the same methods had been used again in connection with Peel's Act of 1844, the Ten Hours Act of 1847, and the Sixty Hours Act of 1850. In all these later movements, the workers had acted in close association with Lord Shaftesbury, the Tory leader of the parliamentary movement for factory reform, and had received the support of a progressive minority of the employers in the cotton industry, and, to a much smaller extent, in other textile trades.

The engineers, typical in this respect of a much larger body of skilled craftsmen in many trades, relied almost wholly on their own strength, based on the limited supply of labour, and took little interest in industrial legislation, which they well knew they stood no chance of getting Parliament to enact. On the other hand, the cotton operatives, and the textile workers generally, looked to the law for protection, and were thus led directly into a succession of mainly political agitations.

The outstanding Trade Union development of the eighteen-fifties was the rise of these two types of organisation. On the one hand there arose the " Amalgamated Societies " of the type represented by the A.S.E., with their close combination of industrial and friendly activities, their centralisation of control, and their non-political policy of restrictive regulation of the supply and conditions of labour. On the other, there grew up the " Amalgamations " of the type represented by the Spinners' and Weavers' Associations, with their localised finance and federal structure, their collective bargaining based on standard price lists, and above all their steady pressure for legislative regulation of the hours and conditions of work. These two types were not opposed ; but they tended to look at the industrial problem in different ways, and to concentrate their attention on different aspects. For this reason they tended to work apart, and felt little need for common action. We shall see later how the development among the miners of a third type of organisation affected this attitude, and acted as a unifying force.

BOOKS

S. and B. Webb. *History of Trade Unionism.*
Souvenir History of the Amalgamated Society of Engineers.
S. and B. Webb. *Industrial Democracy.*
J. B. Jefferys. *The Story of the Engineers.*
C. E. Raven. *Christian Socialism.*
Social Science Association. *Report on Trade Societies, 1860.*

3. THE BUILDERS

One effect of the rapid growth of prosperity in Victorian England was a great increase in the scale and importance of the building trades. In the 'fifties and 'sixties, houses, factories, railway stations, public buildings and institutions were all being erected in large numbers. More workers were needed ; and skilled building labour became relatively scarce. It is therefore not surprising to find the building Trade Unions occupying an important place in the Trade Union Movement and displaying considerable industrial activity.

Till the rise of the Engineers, the Stonemasons' Society was, as we have seen, the most powerful single Union in the country. Its central funds were never large, and its branches enjoyed a far greater autonomy that those of the new " Amalgamated Societies." It was, indeed, a Union of the old type, designed as a fighting organisation and not as a friendly society, and preserving the old tradition of local independence. The other building crafts were much less well organised. The Friendly Society of Carpenters and Joiners, the other national organisation which had survived the crash of 1834, was small and ineffective, and the majority of these crafts were organised, if at all, in purely local trade clubs at best loosely knit together by purely local joint committees. The London Order of Bricklayers was formed in 1848, and the Manchester Painters' Alliance in 1855 ; but, though these became the nuclei of national organisations later, they were purely local bodies at least until 1860. The plumbers and probably the carpenters had joined the National Association of United Trades in 1845, and under its auspices an attempt had been made to organise the builders' labourers as in the days of the Owenite movement. But this attempt was abortive, and in the 'fifties the builders were organised mainly in loosely-knit local joint movements based on tiny independent local clubs and on the branches of the few national Unions.

This did not prevent them from displaying great industrial activity. The Stonemasons, under Harnott's leadership, vigorously kept up both wages and the monopoly of their craft. And, from the 'forties onwards, all the building trades were actively engaged in an attempt to reduce the hours of labour and to secure the general adoption of the Saturday half-holiday.   The Lancashire joint movement of 1846 and the London joint movement of 1848 have been mentioned already.

In the 'fifties a new wave of activity began.   In 1853 the London masons inaugurated a shorter hours movement.   In 1856 a big strike of all the Manchester building trades won the Saturday half-holiday.   In the following year the London carpenters, through their joint committee representing the numerous local clubs, demanded the concession of the nine hours' day, which the employers promptly refused.   In both London and Lancashire, moreover, the master builders organised to resist the men's demands, and formed strong associations of their own.   The London men retaliated by putting their movement on a broader basis, and in 1858 formed a Joint Committee of Carpenters, Masons and Bricklayers to press their claims.   This Committee decided in the first instance to petition four selected firms.   One of these firms, Messrs. Trollope, dismissed the leading men who had presented the petition, and their employees thereupon struck.   The masters met the strike with a general lock-out, and refused to negotiate with the Unions on any terms.   Instead, they presented the " document," and announced that they would not take back any man who would not sign a complete renunciation of Trade Union membership.   This was in 1859.

The London building lock-out attracted attention and support from all over the country.   In 1852 the " document" had been presented to the engineers, and the issue had been generally recognised as vital to the whole Trade Union Movement.   Now the building workers were exposed to the same threat, and once more the movement rallied to the support of the section which was attacked.   The Engineers, doubtless mindful of the support they had received seven years before, sent three weekly gifts of £1,000 each to the strike fund.   Everywhere the Unions organised collections, and formed special joint committees to help the builders.   In London a standing Committee of the Unions in other industries was formed to organise the assistance.

The London builders had, moreover, the advantage of an exceptionally popular leader.   George Potter, a member of a small local carpenters' society, was the head of the strike organisation.   And Potter could both speak and write, and knew how to arouse passionate loyalty.   In face of the spirit of the men, and the support accorded to them, the master builders failed to repeat the success which the engineering employers had secured in 1852.   For months the struggle continued ; but at length the masters were compelled to withdraw the " document."   The men, however, were not strong enough to enforce their own claims, and work was resumed on the old conditions.   The demand for the nine hours' day had, indeed, actually been withdrawn some time before the struggle ended, in order that the Unions might concentrate wholly on defeating the masters' challenge to their right to exist and to negotiate.   As in 1834, there was an attempt, during the lock-out, to use the weapon of Co-operative production against the employers, and a group of operatives formed the London Building Company as a sort of Guild.   There had been similar attempts, under Christian Socialist auspices, in the early 'fifties.   But the Company seems to have died out soon after the ending of the dispute.

Potter was unwilling to accept this set-back to the movement for shorter hours.   On the morrow of the dispute he proposed the renewal of the Joint Committee's mandate, and in the following year he got together at Derby a Trade Union Conference which agreed to form an United Kingdom Association for Shortening the Hours of Labour in the Building Trades, and thus endeavoured to give the movement a national basis.   But again the master builders forestalled him by a counter-offensive of their own.   Hitherto the building workers had been in receipt of a weekly wage.   The employers now announced that they proposed to substitute a system of payment by the hour, which would enable the men to fix the working day at whatever length they chose.   This meant, of course, that if the men chose to work only nine hours they would suffer a proportionate reduction in pay.   This move was met by a series of strikes; but gradually the hourly system was introduced, and the movement for shorter hours was for the time defeated. It was not revived till the masons on the North-East Coast struck for the " Nine Hours " in 1867, or generally conceded until after the successful Nine Hours strike of the North-East Coast engineers in 1871.

The building crisis of 1859-60 exerted, however, an important influence on Trade Union organisation, both in the building industry and over a wider field.   As we shall see later, it gave rise to the London Trades Council and greatly stimulated the growth of permanent Trades Councils in the big industrial centres, and also did a good deal to stimulate the sense of unity among the workers in different industries.   In addition, by revealing the chaotic state of organisation in most of the building trades, it set on foot a movement for the creation of effective national Unions on the model either of the Stonemasons or of the Engineers.   The Amalgamated Society of Carpenters and Joiners, formed in 1860, followed closely the latter model. One of the leading promotors, Robert Applegarth, secretary of a local joiners' society at Sheffield, became General Secretary in 1862, and leapt at once to the front rank among Trade Union leaders.   The Plasterers' Society, also formed in 1860, adopted rather the model of the Stonemasons. Gradually, the other building trades followed these examples, and very slowly more effective national organisations were built up.

BOOKS

R. W. Postgate.   *The Builders' History.*
S. and B. Webb.   *History of Trade Unionism.*
G. Howell.   *Labour Legislation, Labour Movements, Labour Leaders.*

4. THE MINERS

Meanwhile, a new movement of organisation was beginning among the miners. We have seen how Martin Jude's Miners' Association of Great Britain had finally broken down by 1848, and his attempt to revive it in 1850 had failed. The Unions did not completely die out, and almost everywhere at least some sort of pit organisation survived. But even on the North-East Coast Unionism became very feeble, and all contact between the separate coalfields was lost.

The first attempt at revival came in 1852, simultaneously on the North-East Coast and in Scotland. In 1855 there were numerous strikes and a further revival of Unionism in Durham and Northumberland, and in 1856 Alexander Macdonald, who had been energetically organising the Scottish miners, turned his attention to the English coalfields, and began his attempt to build up a new national organisation. In 1856 there was a great strike in Scotland, which lasted for fourteen weeks, and involved between 30,000 and 40,000 men. The Scottish Miners' Association was beaten ; but it survived, and Macdonald, as its leader was able to press on with the work of organisation. At length, in 1858, he, managed to get a representative Conference of a number of the northern coalfields together at Ashton—Scotland, Yorkshire, Lancashire and Staffordshire being the chief centres which sent delegates. A resolution was adopted in favour of forming a National Miners' Association, and the miners began to develop their characteristic policy of pressing for legislative protection for their conditions of work. The Coal Mines Regulation Act of 1860, embodying the first ineffective permission to the men to appoint " checkweighers " to check the weight of the coal produced and so ensure the payment of correct piece-work wages, was directly due to Macdonald's organising efforts.

Meanwhile, other coalfields were moving. There was a great strike in South Wales in 1857, ending in the defeat of the men, and another in West Yorkshire the following year, ending in a compromise. In 1860 there were lock-outs in South Staffordshire and South Yorkshire. Meanwhile, despite defeats, everywhere the organisation was getting stronger. Dissatisfaction with the Act of 1860 intensified the unrest, for the colliery owners met the men's attempts to appoint checkweighmen by dismissing their nominees ; and in 1863 Macdonald was able to bring together at Leeds the first really representative Miners' Conference, with delegates from all the important coalfields throughout the country.

At this Conference, the Miners' National Association was definitely formed, with Macdonald as President and Richard Mitchell of Yorkshire as Secretary. But the proceedings were not wholly harmonious. First, a struggle developed between Macdonald and a party which supported a certain John Towers, at that time editor of a journal called The Miner. This dispute seems to have been mainly personal ; but into it entered the conflict between the section which wanted an aggressive industrial policy, and the Macdonaldites, who desired to concentrate chiefly on influencing Parliament and public opinion in favour of further legislation. The majority of the Conference pressed for a legal eight hours day for boys employed in the pits ; but already the Durham men, with William Crawford as their spokesman, were found opposing this on the ground that a longer working day for boys was necessary to keep up the wages of the hewers, as the coal had to be cleared after the hewer had done his work, and the employment of two shifts of boys would tend to lower the hewers' pay.

Macdonald won the day, and the National Association developed chiefly as a political body. In this the state of trade played a part ; for in 1864 and 1865 the coal trade was depressed, and the Unions were seriously weakened. In Northumberland, where Thomas Burt and William Crawford had re-formed the Northumberland Miners' Association in 1863, the Union stood fast ; but in Durham it was broken until Crawford reorganised it in 1869. In Staffordshire the men were beaten in a strike against wage reductions ; and there were bitter complaints against the failure of the National Association to act as an effective co-ordinating body.

At length these quarrels led to a split. In 1869 the Lancashire Miners took the lead in calling a conference of the discontented districts. Macdonald had stood firmly for a completely decentralised control in industrial matters ; the Lancashire men wanted a strong National Union, with central funds and an aggressive centralised industrial policy. The Conference of 1869 launched the Amalgamated Association of Miners as a rival to the National Miners' Association.

Thenceforth for some time the miners were divided. Macdonald held Scotland and the East ; the Amalgamated captured the West. Northumberland and Durham, Yorkshire, the East Midlands and Scotland, with a few strong *enclaves* elsewhere, constituted the National ; the Amalgamated held South and most of North Wales, Lancashire, the West Midlands, Cumberland, and the South-Western Counties. In 1873 the National had about 125,000 members, and the Amalgamated about 100,000. " They took to the left," said Macdonald in 1873, " and we held on our way to the right."

The chief centres of activity for the Amalgamated Miners' Association were Lancashire and South Wales. In 1871 there was a twelve weeks' strike in South Wales for an advance in wages, following a reduction enforced by the owners. Supported by the Amalgamated Association, the men were victorious. But in 1873 the owners again demanded a reduction, and locked the men out. The result was inconclusive, the terms of settlement varying from pit to pit. Again, in 1875, when trade and prices were falling off, the owners enforced a reduction, and the men struck. By this time the

Amalgamated had exhausted its resources. The strike was beaten, and the men were compelled to accept a sliding scale system for the regulation of wages. An attempt was made to form a new Union, affiliated to Macdonald's National Association, out of the wreck ; but save in Monmouthshire this gained few adherents. Unionism was nearly crushed out over the greater part of the South Wales coalfield, and the sliding scale system, to be described hereafter, took its place.

The collapse of the Amalgamated Miners' Association was due partly to this exhausting series of disputes in South Wales, and partly to another cause. In 1874 there was a miners' strike in Lancashire, and Cornish blacklegs were imported, under signed contracts, to break it. The leaders of the Amalgamated addressed the blacklegs, and induced them to return home. For this they were charged with conspiracy to induce breach of contract. Thomas Halliday, the General Secretary of the Amalgamated, offered to give an undertaking not to " seduce " men under contract ; but the owners demanded an undertaking that he would not try to make men who were working leave work, whether they were under contract or not. This being refused, the case was held over, or in other words the threat of sentence was held over the leaders' heads as a means of breaking the strike. For five years the Amalgamated had pursued a vigorous fighting policy. But under pressure of the employers, of the law, and of the increasing depression of trade, it broke down. About 1875 it ceased to exist.

In the meantime, the National Association had been pressing on with its policy of political agitation. At length, in 1872, it secured the passing of the Coal and Metalliferous Mines Acts, which form the basis of modern mining legislation. Industrially, it was far less militant than the Amalgamated, encouraging the district associations to pursue a pacific policy of conciliation. This policy was adopted with success in Durham and Northumberland. In 1871 the Northumberland coalowners recognised the Miners' Association, and a regular process of joint negotiation began. In the following year the Durham owners followed suit, and the Durham Joint Committee was established. In 1874 there were unofficial strikes in Durham, against wage reductions enforced on plea of bad trade. But, whereas in South Wales the Union fought the reductions, in Durham the Union accepted them. Three years later Durham also adopted the sliding scale for the regulation of wages.

The clearest idea of Macdonald's policy as leader of the miners can be gleaned from his presidential addresses at successive national conferences. He placed his chief faith in legislative action, and he was a strong advocate of working-class representation in Parliament. Industrially, he believed in conciliation, but was hostile to the sliding scale, which was favoured by the Northumberland and Durham leaders. He was a strong supporter of Co-operative production, and it was partly under his influence that, in the late 'sixties and early 'seventies, the miners in a number of districts embarked on a policy of Co-operative enterprise, buying up collieries, often with the aid of funds supplied by the consumers' Co-operative Societies and by their members. These Co-operative mines mostly failed within a few years, in face of the falling coal prices which accompanied the depression of the later 'seventies. For example, in 1873, the North-East Coast miners launched a Co-operative Mining Company, which failed four years later in the course of the slump. Macdonald, apart from his work for the miners, took an active part in the general work of the Trade Union Movement. He was on the Parliamentary Committee of the Trades Union Congress from 1871 to 1874, and in 1874 was returned at Stafford as one of the two first Labour Members of Parliament.

The National Miners' Association, or National Union of Miners, as it was later called, suffered a severe set back in the depression of the later 'seventies. After Macdonald's death in 1881, it ceased to be of any importance, and passed wholly into the hands of the Durham and Northumberland leaders, the other districts rapidly falling away. But, while it lasted, it undoubtedly performed a very valuable work, forcing to the front the lamentable conditions under which the miners had to work, and preparing the way for the modern code of mining legislation. Industrially, it was never so important as its short-lived rival ; but by its political agitation it accomplished a more lasting work.

The miners, during the 'sixties, came, as we have seen, to form an important third group within the Trade Union Movement. On the whole, they were allied in policy more closely to the textile workers than to the new " Amalgamated Societies " of the engineers and the carpenters, because they too demanded legislative protection—a practicable policy in view of the exceptionally hazardous conditions under which they worked. There had been a fearful increase of mining accidents, due largely to speeding up in face of the rapidly increasing demand for coal ; and even those who in general strongly opposed State intervention were in many instances prepared to admit the miners' case as exceptional. There were, however, cross-currents among the miners' Unions. Northumberland and Durham followed a policy more like that of Applegarth and Allan, and perhaps for this reason formed the most stable Unions. The Amalgamated Miners' Association, with its militant industrial policy, resembled neither of the two dominant groups. The " National " depended so much on Macdonald's personality that it ceased to count when his influence was removed. On the whole, the miners were still very isolated, and were exposed to a more primitive hostility to collective bargaining on their employers' part than the workers in other industries. For a few years, they built up the two largest and most imposing Trade Union bodies that had ever existed. But the effort wore them out. Save on the North-East Coast, they relapsed into a disorganisation from which they recovered only with the coming, in the 'eighties, of the new forces that created the Miners' Federation of Great Britain.

BOOKS

S. and B. Webb. *History of Trade Unionism.*

R. Fynes. *Miners' Unions of Northumberland and Durham.*

G. D. H. Cole. Article in *International Review of Social History, 1937.*

E. Welbourne. *Miners' Unions of Durham and Northumberland.*

N. Edwards. *History of the South Wales Miners.*

George Howell Papers in the Bishopsgate Institute, London.

CHAPTER IV

POLITICAL MOVEMENTS

1. The London Trades Council and the "Junta"   2. Working-class Politics in the 'Sixties
3. The International Working Men's Association

I. THE LONDON TRADES COUNCIL AND THE "JUNTA"

WE have seen how, during the builders' struggle of 1859, the workers in other industries were roused to great activity in organising help for the strikers.   In all the big towns temporary joint committees of all trades were set up, and these both gathered money and rallied working-class opinion. There was nothing new in this.   Again and again in the past history of the movement similar committees had been established, either to deal with a big strike or to organise resistance to some actual or proposed legal oppression, or to demand some particular reform.   Often they had maintained their existence continuously over long periods, and become virtually permanent bodies.   In London, Manchester and a few other centres, such joint bodies, or Trades Councils as we should call them nowadays, can be traced almost continuously during the period of unrest between 1816 and 1834, and on many separate occasions subsequently they were called into existence to deal with some special problem.

It is impossible to say in which centre the first lasting and permanent Trades Council was created.   Liverpool, where the Trades Guardian Association dates back to 1848, has often been accorded the honour ; but probably other towns have just as good a claim.   The Aberdeen Council, for example, has been said to date from 1846, and Glasgow, Sheffield, Manchester and London have all long records of practically continuous organisation.

Be that as it may, the building dispute had undoubtedly a great influence both in creating new Councils and in giving to those which already existed a more permanent form.   In this connection the influence of London was of outstanding importance.   During the building dispute the other trades held regular meetings, and when the struggle ended it was decided to give the emergency organisation a definitely permanent character.   Accordingly, in 1860, the London Trades Council was formed.   It consisted of an executive of fifteen members, to be elected at an Annual Delegate Conference of the trades of London.   Its objects were defined as follows : " That the duties of the Council shall be to watch over the general interests of labour, political and social, both in and out of Parliament ; to use their influence in supporting any measure likely to benefit Trade Unions ;   also to publish (if necessary) an Annual Trades Union Directory."

The objects proposed for the new body were thus clearly meant to be political as well as industrial, and from the first the Council was actively engaged in various forms of political agitation on behalf of Trade Unions. But it had also a very important industrial function, no less clearly defined by its constitution. "Council to have power to investigate cases of appeal made to them by trades in distress. If, after strict investigation, they are found worthy of support, they shall recommend them to trades for assistance."

It is probable that the form of this organisation was largely copied from the Glasgow Trades Council, which, under the skilful leadership of the old Owenite, Alexander Campbell, had assumed much the same form and policy in 1857, and was, by 1861, already proposing the creation of a General Federation of all the Trade Unions in Scotland. But, even if Glasgow anticipated London, it was London's adoption of the new form of organisation that was of decisive importance. For in London were the head offices of the growing Amalgamated Societies of Engineers and Carpenters, and it was mainly under the influence of their leading officials that the new Council throve. Its first secretary was George Howell, a bricklayer and close associate of Applegarth and Allan, and later an M.P. and an important contributor to the history of Trade Unionism; and in 1862 he was succeeded by George Odger, by trade a shoemaker, and the leading orator of the working-class Radicalism of the time.

Mr. and Mrs. Webb have given to the group of men who now began, from London, to dominate the Trade Union Movement, the name of the "Junta." Allan of the Engineers, Applegarth of the Carpenters, Daniel Guile of the Ironfounders, Edwin Coulson of the Bricklayers, and George Odger of the London Trades Council—these men and their immediate associates were at the head of the leading working-class organisations in London, and, acting together, occupied an extraordinarily strong strategic position. Macdonald and Campbell in Scotland, John Kane of the Ironworkers and William Crawford in Durham, Thomas Halliday in Manchester, were no less important leaders; but they were scattered, whereas the Junta was together, and right at the centre of political gravity.

The London Trades Council became for some years the instrument through which the Junta exercised its leadership. Almost every Trade Union which became involved in any considerable strike had to appeal to it for help; for the credentials issued by the London Trades Council came to be the key to success in securing financial aid from other Unions. The Council became in effect not a mere joint committee of the London trades, but a central Cabinet for the Trade Union Movement as a whole. Of its political activities we shall have to speak later; here we are concerned with it solely as a controlling industrial authority.

This position of dominance was not won without opposition. The provincial leaders were inclined to resent it ; and in London, George Potter, whom we have met already as the builders' leader in 1859, was soon in open opposition to the policy of the Junta. For the leaders of the Amalgamated Societies were strongly in favour of a moderate policy of conciliation, and frowned severely on strikes which they considered as inopportune or provocative. In 1865 matters came to a head when the Junta opposed, while Potter supported, the strike of the Staffordshire ironworkers. The London Trades Council denounced Potter as a " strike-monger."

George Potter, on his side, was by no means a person to be neglected. For, apart from his great personal popularity, he was editor and controlled the policy of the one really effective working-class newspaper, *The Beehive*, which he had started in 1861 as the organ of militant Trade Unionism. From 1865 Potter and the Junta, and above all Potter and Applegarth, were permanently at loggerheads, and Potter was trying to appeal from the London ascendency of the Junta to the wider Trade Union Movement in the provincial centres.

In order to do this effectively, he needed to have some London organisation behind him. For this purpose, he joined forces in 1866 with Robert Hartwell, a printer and an old Chartist, and with other London Trade Union leaders, in creating the London Working Men's Association, a primarily political body, which became for a time a lesser rival to the Trades Council, and set to work to get similar political bodies established in other areas. Under its auspices, as we shall see, Potter successfully called the famous Trades Union Conference of 1867, the immediate precursor of the Trades Union Congress.

BOOKS

S. and B. Webb. *History of Trade Unionism.*
C. Richards. *History of Trades Councils.*
G. Howell. *Labour Legislation, Labour Movements, Labour Leaders.*

2. WORKING-CLASS POLITICS IN THE 'SIXTIES

The group of leaders whose ascendency has just been described was active in the political as well as in the industrial sphere. In the slow death of Chartism after 1848 little had survived of independent working-class political action. But in its latter days the Chartist Movement had taken on a markedly international character, and a tradition of sympathy with revolutionary agitations on the Continent survived its eclipse as a national movement. In 1854 Ernest Jones had formed the International Welcome and Protest Committee, which organised welcomes to revolutionary refugees and protests against the repressions practised all over Europe by the triumphant counter-revolution. Through a series of changes of name this body survived

until 1860, when it finally expired as the International Association.   But a
part of the work was speedily taken over by other bodies.   In the 'sixties,
under Odger's leadership, the London Trades Council took an active part in
organising welcomes and protests.   Garibaldi became an idol of the London
workers, Kossuth was enthusiastically received, deep sympathy was expressed
for the Polish revolt.   And, in the American Civil War, when opinion in
Great Britain was sharply divided, the Trades Council unhesitatingly took
the side of the North.   In all these demonstrations, however, the workers
went no further than the majority of middle-class Radicals were prepared
to go.   There was no " Socialist " intention behind their internationalism
until the coming of the International Working Men's Association.   And of
that more will be said in the next section.

Chartism, apart from its international activity, was virtually dead by 1856.
But within a few years fresh political movements began to arise.   Again the
demand was for Manhood Suffrage and the Ballot ; but this time the movement was purely constitutional, and had behind it none of that half-blind
revolutionary impulse which had been the real driving force of working-
class Chartism.   The new leaders wanted votes for the workers ; but they
did not want a revolution, and they were prepared to work to the fullest
extent with any middle-class Liberals who were willing to endorse their
programme.

As early as 1857 new organisations began to spring up.   In that year was
established the Northern Reform Union, with its headquarters at Newcastle,
and John Kane, the Ironworkers' Secretary, as one of its moving spirits.
Within the next few years a great many similar associations arose.   In London,
where a National Reform Association was already in existence, a North
London Political Union was formed in 1859, with Benjamin Lucraft, a well-
known Trade Union leader, as its secretary.   A Midland Counties Reform
Association was active in 1860, and in the same year a National Conference
held at the Guildhall in London proposed the formation of a National
Reform League on the model of the Anti-Corn Law League.   Reform
meetings were held all over the country.   Old Chartists, such as Ernest
Jones, G. W. M. Reynolds, and W. P. Roberts, Trade Union leaders, such as
Kane, Lucraft and Howell, joined with middle-class Radicals such as Bright
and Edmund Beales in addressing them.   So far, the movement was
on a basis of co-operation between the workers and the parliamentary
Radicals.

Before long, however, the Trade Unionists began to move independently.
In 1862 Applegarth and his friends of the Junta and the London Trades
Council created the Trade Union Political Union, with a programme of
Ballot and Universal Suffrage.   In the following year this body took the
name of the Manhood Suffrage and Vote by Ballot Association, and early in
1865 it broadened its basis, and became the National Reform League, with

Edmund Beales, the Radical barrister, as its President and George Howell as Secretary. Though it thus opened its ranks to middle-class supporters, it continued to be essentially a working-class body, based mainly on Trade Union affiliations throughout the country. Odger was, with Beales, its principal orator.

At the same time, mainly in the North of England, a second national organisation grew up. In 1861 the Leeds Working Men's Parliamentary Reform Association convened a conference of the Reform societies of Lancashire and Yorkshire, "to consider the position of the Liberal Party" in relation to Reform. This was followed by a national conference held in London in 1862, and attended by the leading Radical Members of Parliament. A resolution was carried in favour of Universal Suffrage ; but the Conference also called for the co-operation of classes in working for Reform, and urged Reformers to concentrate for the present on household suffrage, the ballot, redistribution of seats, and triennial Parliaments, instead of pressing at once for the whole working-class programme.

A further conference was to have been held in 1863 ; but the cotton famine, then at its height, caused a postponement. In 1864 the Conference met, and formed the National Reform Union. Reform Societies and Trade Unions were invited to affiliate, and a considerable number joined.

These three bodies—the League, the Union, and the Northern Reform Union—shared between them the work of agitation for Reform. The League was mainly working-class, and was almost completely dominated by the Trade Unionists. The Union had many working-class adherents, but was mainly dominated by the middle-class Radicals. The Northern body stood somewhere between these two, with the Radical, Joseph Cowen, as its chief leader, but with the miners and ironworkers playing an active part. In 1866 the League had seventy branches—nineteen in London and fifty-one in the Provinces, including most of the principal centres. In the same year the Union had one hundred and thirty branches, mainly in the Midlands and in Lancashire and Yorkshire. The League was centred on London, the Union on Manchester.

The parliamentary history of the Reform Movement of the 'sixties has been often told. After the Act of 1832 the general attitude of the Whig party was that "finality" had been reached in the extension of the franchise. Not only the Chartist demands, but moderate plans for further Reform were brushed aside. Despite Lord John Russell's conversion to moderate Reform, the Whigs continued to coldshoulder the question right up to Palmerston's death in 1865. When at length that formidable obstacle was removed, it became clear that, in face of the growing agitation in the country, the Whig ministry would have to take the matter up. Russell introduced his moderate Reform Bill in 1866, only to be defeated by the secession of a section of his party—the "Adullamites," headed by Robert Lowe. The Whigs fell, and the Tories under Derby and Disraeli assumed power. But the question had still to be tackled ; for the feeling in the country was too strong to be ignored. Disraeli introduced his famous Reform Bill of 1867, with its proposals for "fancy franchises" for University graduates and other specially qualified groups. But in the House of Commons one amendment after another was carried by the Radicals, and the Bill emerged, shorn of its fancy provisions, as the Reform Act of 1867. Disraeli had "caught the Whigs bathing and stolen their clothes." The Tories had carried the Second Reform Act. The miners in the villages and the agricultural workers were left voteless (until 1884) ; but the workers who were householders in the towns had at length won their way to the franchise, though there was a prolonged localised struggle before many of them were allowed to appear on the register. In the North, a Miners' Franchise Union played a leading part in getting votes for those who lived in houses owned by their employers, and did not pay rates.

Best remembered of the incidents in the campaign which led up to the victory of 1867 is the prohibited Hyde Park meeting of 1866, when the Reform League's projected demonstration in the Park was forbidden by the Commissioner of Police, acting on the instructions of the Home Secretary. Despite the prohibition, the League went on with the demonstration, and a vast crowd, headed by Beales, Howell, Applegarth, and other leaders, reached the Park only to find the gates closed against them. Outside the railings the huge multitude surged, demanding admission. By intention, or by the mere pressure of numbers against them, the park railings were broken down, and the crowd swept into the Park, where a hundred impromptu meetings were held despite the police. Meanwhile, the official leaders had led off a section of their followers to Trafalgar Square, where they addressed a great meeting of protest against the Government's action.

Whether the Park railings were broken by accident or by design, the Hyde Park demonstration scared the governing classes, and was a big factor in winning the vote for the urban workers.

On the passing of the Reform Act, the leaders of the Reform League held that its work was done, and decided to dissolve it, giving place to bodies of whose fortunes we shall speak later, designed to promote working-class representation in Parliament. But the National Reform Union lived on, to become an auxiliary of the Liberal Party in building up local Liberal and Radical Working-men's Associations with a wide membership. The new associations gradually ousted the self-appointed Whig caucuses which had hitherto controlled the nominations in most areas ; and at a later stage many Liberal-Labour Trade Unionists were associated both with these bodies and with the National Reform Union. In 1875 both George Howell, then Secretary of the Trades Union Congress, and George Potter, fallen by this time from his position as leader of the militants, were members of the Executive Council of the N.R.U.

BOOKS

G. D. H. Cole.   *British Working-class Politics, 1832–1914.*
F. E. Gillespie.   *Labour and Politics in England, 1854–1867.*
George Howell Papers in the Bishopsgate Institute.

3. THE INTERNATIONAL WORKING MEN'S ASSOCIATION

The British Trade Union leaders, while they were conducting their struggle for Parliamentary Reform, were also playing some part in a working-class movement of a very different character.   In 1864 a conference held in London formed the International Working Men's Association, of which Karl Marx, then a refugee living in London, soon assumed the leadership. For some years we are presented with the paradoxical sight of men such as Applegarth and Odger engaged at the same time in fomenting revolutionary working-class movements on the Continent of Europe and in conducting, largely in alliance with middle-class Liberals, a strictly constitutional struggle for franchise reform in their own country, where they stood, moreover, in Trade Union affairs, for a policy of conciliation and were strongly hostile to the " strike-mongering " of Potter and his friends.

In order to understand this seeming paradox, it is necessary to recall what was said earlier of the internationalist record of the British working class. London had long, and especially since 1848, been the home of Socialist and nationalist political refugees.   Thence Mazzini organised his Italians; thence Marx inspired the growing Socialist movement of Europe.   The Continent appeared to Liberals a place of counter-revolutionary triumph, in which Liberal principles were at a heavy discount.   To the British workers, it appeared, too, as a place in which Trade Unions were severely repressed, and the rights of combination denied.   Even men who were strict constitutionalists under British conditions might well feel that the policy of many of the continental Governments admitted of no answer except in terms of underground conspiracy leading towards revolution.

In the minds of the British working-class leaders, of whatever complexion, no clear line was drawn between continental nationalism and the class movements of the continental workers.   The Chartists, and after them the London Trades Council, demonstrated actively in support of Italian and Polish nationalism.   Mazzini was a close friend of many of the working-class leaders, and Polish exiles played an active part in many British Radical movements. The Socialists were still but a small section, and were but little regarded. The " Communist Manifesto ", drafted by Marx and Engels and issued by the Communist League in 1848, had clearly proclaimed the Socialist doctrine of the class-struggle ; but it had been forgotten, save by a few, in the subsequent reaction. The first volume of Marx's "Capital" did not appear until 1867. Marx himself was known rather as a learned German political exile than as the leader of any clearly-marked Socialist movement.

Indeed, even on the Continent, Socialism was only just beginning to reshape itself as an independent force. The French movement was divided between the followers of Proudhon, whose doctrines were much more closely akin to Anarchism and to certain forms of Co-operation than to Socialism, and the small revolutionary group led by Blanqui, which had taken over the insurrectionary traditions of Babeuf and of the "Conspiracy of the Equals." In Germany, Lassalle's General Workmen's Union was formed only in 1863, and the Marxist propaganda of Bebel and Wilhelm Liebknecht only began at about the same time. The international Anarchist movement led by Bakunin had scarcely emerged. Italy was still almost wholly under the influence of Mazzini. Everywhere little Socialist groups were growing up ; but only in the 'sixties did they emerge into prominence.

In founding the International Working Men's Association, therefore, the British leaders, at any rate, meant no more than a gesture of sympathy with continental movements of the oppressed. The meeting which formed the "First International" was conceived by Odger and other London Trade Union leaders. It arose, in part, out of contacts which had been established with the French workers at the Paris and London International Exhibitions— for at about this time the Government of Napoleon III began to adopt a less repressive policy towards Trade Unions and other working-class movements. The I.W.M.A. included, besides the British elements, continental refugees of all complexions from Mazzinians to Marxists. The first, provisional, committee was made up of most diverse elements. Rival drafts for the rules and inaugural address were drawn up by a follower of Mazzini and by an Owenite, only to be brushed aside in favour of a third draft prepared by Marx himself, which, though its phraseology made many concessions to current ideas regarded by its author with contempt, put the movement definitely on a purely working-class basis. Marx's draft defined the object of the Association as the conquest of political power by the workers, regarded as the only means of improving the conditions of labour. But it also urged the workers to master the mysteries of international politics and to vindicate the simple laws of morality and justice in international affairs. "To fight for such a foreign policy forms a part of the general struggle for the emancipation of the working classes. Workers of all countries, unite ! "

The British leaders who subscribed to these doctrines probably saw in them little more than expressions of international friendship of the workers. Certainly they had no conception of what the First International was to become, or of what Marx meant it to become, and they valued it partly as an agency which could be used to prevent the importation of foreign blacklegs to break British strikes—a measure more than once attempted by the British employers during the Trade Union unrest of the years after 1867. The service rendered by the International in this respect helped to hold Trade Union support ; but from the first it was, in their eyes, only a side-show. They were primarily engaged first in the struggle for the Reform Act and then in the great contest for legal emancipation of the Trade Unions which will be described in the next chapter. From the outset Marx dominated the International, and it travelled the road he had marked out for it.

The International Working Men's Association was governed by a General Council nominally representing the different countries, but actually composed of British working-class leaders and of foreign refugees resident in London, who were treated, with the most slender credentials, as representatives of their several countries. Applegarth, Odger, Henry Broadhurst, Howell, Lucraft, and W. R. Cremer were among the British Trade Union leaders who were associated with it. J. G. Eccarius, a nationalised German and a follower of Marx, was its Secretary. Marx, left to do largely as he pleased, concentrated his attention mainly on building up the organisation abroad. From Germany, France, Italy, Russia and many other countries he had no difficulty in gathering adherents to the new body, which rapidly became a power throughout Europe. But very soon dissensions began to develop. The Germans who accepted the I.W.M.A. were mostly strict Marxists—for the followers of Lassalle held aloof; but from Italy and Russia and Spain came a large Anarchist contingent, strongly opposed to the working-class parliamentary action advocated by the Marxian Socialists. The original French adherents were mainly followers of Proudhon. In Germany, the International was at variance with Lassalle ; in France, the followers of Proudhon fought with the Blanquists. The Mazzinians in Italy had dropped out when Marx obtained control ; and within the International the strongest single influence against Marx was that of the Russian, Michael Bakunin. But these dissensions, though serious almost from the outset in the Conferences of the International, did not at first prevent the spread of its influence or much affect the policy of the General Council, which Marx continued to control.

The general history of the First International falls outside the scope of this book, which has to deal only with its influence in Great Britain. The other countries had, at any rate in theory, each its own National Federal Council of the International, representing the various affiliated bodies. Great Britain, as the seat of international government, had no Federal Council of its own, but only its preponderant representation on the General Council of the International as a whole. At a fairly early stage, the formation of a British Federal Council was mooted ; but Marx, who saw that such a body would slip wholly out of his control and into the hands of the moderate British Trade Union leaders, successfully obstructed this development until 1871.

There are amusing passages in Marx's correspondence in which he describes his successful manipulation of the British leaders.

Though the British working-class leaders were associated with the International, no powerful British Section ever arose. A number of Trade Unions—among them the Bricklayers and the Bootmakers—joined, together with some miscellaneous working-class societies. The London Trades Council refused to join. And from 1867 onwards, as the revolutionary character of the continental sections became more clear, the British Trade Union leaders gradually fell away.

There was another reason for this withdrawal. All over the Continent, the growth of the International had caused widespread alarm, and it was being fiercely denounced in the continental press. The British newspapers re-echoed these denunciations, and applied them to the British Trade Union leaders, who were at that time chiefly engaged in seeking to prove their respectability before the Royal Commission on Trade Unions, in order to secure an assured legal status. These attacks caused the leaders to scrutinise the affairs of the International more closely, and to take greater account of the tactical disadvantages of association with it. Most of them withdrew. Marx said that they had " offered up the principle of Trade Unionism on the altar of middle-class legitimisation."

Applegarth, who, if he knew how to appear on due occasion a moderate of the moderates, appears really to have held more advanced political views than most of his colleagues, did not resign at this stage, despite the attacks directed by name against him in *The Times* and elsewhere. He had, indeed, taken a more active part in the International than any other of the British leaders. But at length he too fell away, when the ill-starred Paris Commune, generally denounced as the work of the International, brought the issue of revolution finally and decisively to the front. Marx, in the name of the General Council, issued his famous manifesto in support of the Commune, best known under the title, " The Civil War in France ". This was too strong meat for most of the remaining Trade Union members of the Council.

The Trade Union leaders having withdrawn, the British section, now composed of less manageable elements, became restive, and Marx was com-pelled to yield and to allow a British Federal Council to be set up side by side with the General Council. This body, of which Maltman Barry was Chair-man, and John Hales, Secretary, attempted in 1872 to form a new British working-class party, wholly independent of other parties, for political action and agitation. But there was no widespread support, for by this time the Trade Unions had, in the Labour Representation League, a moderate political organ of their own. Moreover, the leaders of the British Federal Council could not agree among themselves, and after an internal split the movement speedily broke down.

In the same year the International itself virtually came to an end. Every year the quarrel between the followers of Bakunin and Marx had become more bitter. Then the defeat of the Paris Commune, encouraging reaction throughout Europe, had administered a further shattering blow. At the Congress of 1872 mutual recriminations reached their height. After a stormy debate, the Bakuninists were expelled from the International. But Marx, apparently despairing of success in Europe, moved the transference of the International's headquarters to New York. There, four years later, the great First International was quietly dissolved. But it left behind it the nucleus of a Socialist movement all over Europe. The German Social Democratic Party had been formed in 1869, and in 1875, uniting with the Lassallians on the basis of the Gotha Programme, which Marx denounced as a betrayal of revolutionary Socialism, took shape as the mass party of the German workers, and survived despite Bismarck's Anti-Socialist Law of 1878. In France, the Marxist *Parti Ouvrier* was formed in 1876, and in the same year the Marxian Socialist Labour Party was founded in the United States. Except in England, modern Social Democracy was beginning to take shape. But in the country where the First International had been born a decade was to pass between the collapse of the International and the coming of the Social Democratic Federation.

BOOKS

R. W. Postgate. *The Workers' International.*
K. Marx. *The Civil War in France.*
M. Beer. *History of British Socialism,* Vol. II.
G. M. Stekloff. *History of the First International.*
L. Lorwin. *Labour and Internationalism.*

CHAPTER V

THE LABOUR LAWS, 1864-1871

1. Master and Servant—Trade Union Conferences
2. The Sheffield Outrages and the Royal Commission on Trade Unions
3. The Labour Laws of 1871

1. MASTER AND SERVANT—TRADE UNION CONFERENCES

WHILE the political movements described in the last chapter were developing, the Trade Unions were also drawing together industrially, and were conducting a combined agitation for the improvement.of the laws affecting the workers. The first phase of this struggle opened in 1864, when the Unions began their concerted campaign for the amendment of the Master and Servant Acts. The second, and far more critical, phase began in 1867, when the public outcry which followed the " Sheffield outrages " and the decision of the courts in the famous case of *Hornby* v. *Close* threatened the Unions with fresh legal repression. The third phase extended from the passing of the Trade Union Act and the Criminal Law Amendment Act in 1871 to the further drastic amendment of the " Labour Laws " in the workers' interest in 1875. During these critical eleven years the public status of Trade Unionism was profoundly changed, the Trades Union Congress was founded, and the Trade Union Movement assumed something like its modern form.

The new development began in 1864, with the decision of the Glasgow Trades Council, under the leadership of Alexander Campbell, to set on foot a national campaign for the amendment of the Master and Servant Acts. The need was very great. We have seen already how in the mining industry the employers used these Acts against the workers, and how the Unions, in the 'forties, attempted to meet them by employing W. P. Roberts as their " attorney-general " to fight every case. But the grievance was not confined to the miners. A whole series of Acts, from the Statute of Artificers of 1563 down to the Master and Servant Act of 1824, subjected the workers to severe penalties for breach of contract, for leaving work unfinished, and for similar crimes against their employers. For such offences, the worker was liable to imprisonment on the verdict of a single justice, who might be himself an interested employer. He was liable to summary arrest on the order of such a justice, and though, under an Act of 1848, he might in England be summoned instead of being arrested by warrant, this Act did not apply to Scotland, where arrest by warrant was still the only procedure. An employer could give evidence against a worker in his own cause ; but a worker could not give evidence against his employer, or in his own defence. Imprisonment was the only penalty in the workman's case ; for breach of contract by a

" servant" was regarded as a criminal offence.   But an employer who broke his contract with a workman could only be ordered to pay the amount due, or at the most be sued for damages.   The law was thus grossly unfair, and was based on the conception of compulsory servile labour.   It had come down from a time when the inequality of masters and servants had been taken for granted ; and this attitude was firmly embedded in the common law as well as expressed in numerous statutes.   In Scotland matters were worse than in England, where in most cases the procedure was by summons instead of warrant, and a good number of prosecutions were dropped when the work-man had made due submission to his " betters."

This helps to explain why the initiative was taken by the Glasgow Trades Council.   But another cause was certainly Alexander Macdonald's close connection with the Council ; for the weight of the law fell far more hardly upon the miners.   There was, however, in all trades amply enough to be put right ; and when the Glasgow Trades Council convened a national Trade Union Conference in London to deal with the matter, most of the big Unions eagerly took the question up, and all the best-known leaders, including Campbell, Applegarth, Macdonald, and George Potter, attended the meeting, which deserves to be regarded as in effect the first of the modern series of Trades Union Congresses.   A Committee was appointed to carry on the agitation ; and, under its influence, local Trades Councils were formed in a number of fresh centres to help.   J. M. Cobbett, one of William Cobbett's sons and M.P. for Oldham—his father's old seat—agreed to introduce a Bill into Parliament on the Unions' behalf.

Success was not secured until 1867, when at length the Master and Servant Act became law.   The power of proceeding by warrant was abolished in normal cases, and summary arrest was thus prevented.   Power was, however, left to the magistrates to order arrest before trial where they had reason to suppose that the accused might abscond ; and this power could be—and was —abused, especially in the mining areas.   In future, hearings were to be in open court, and not in a justice's private house, and a single justice was no longer able to act.   Workmen were allowed to give evidence on their own behalf.   Power of imprisonment was retained, but was confined to cases of serious injury to persons or property.   In normal cases fines or payment of damages took its place.   The Act of 1867 was by no means satisfactory, since it left breach of contract still in certain cases a criminal offence and arrest before trial still a possibility.   But it was a great success to have won even so much.

The Trade Union Conference of 1864 prepared the way for further developments.   There was urgent need for some co-ordinating authority in the Trade Union world.   The National Association of United Trades for the Protection of Labour, founded in 1845, was indeed still nominally in existence; but it had shrunk to a few thousand members, and no important Union was connected with it.   In its latter days it had occupied itself solely in pressing for the establishment of Boards of Conciliation, and its Secretary, Thomas Winter, had again and again tried to get Parliament to take up this question. At length, in 1867, the Association got a mainly abortive Conciliation Act passed into law.   This Act, which proposed to constitute local Courts of Conciliation, on the basis of a wide suffrage, for friendly adjustment of trade disputes, was from the first almost a dead letter.   But the effort of promoting it was too much for the National Association, which expired in the year of its passage.

We have seen how, in the absence of any other central agency, the London Trades Council for a time usurped the function of co-ordinating Trade Union action.   This, however, did not suit either the rising Trades Councils of the other big towns, or the big Unions, such as the Miners, whose membership was mainly in the North.   Nor could the London Trades Council effectively bring the Unions together, or organise mutual help in strikes.   Moreover, it was very much under the influence of the Junta, and its authority was not well received by those who objected to the Junta's strictly conciliatory methods.

In the early 'sixties, the need for some more representative agency for organising mutual help was felt to be very great.   Confronted with the rise of new powerful Unions, the employers in one industry after another, and especially in the coal mines, resorted to the wholesale use of the lock-out.   A Yorkshire miner complained in 1866 that he had been locked out for two years out of the past six.   In these circumstances the Sheffield Trades Council, prompted by the Yorkshire Miners, convened in 1866 a second national Trade Union Conference to consider methods of organised Trade Union defence against the weapon of the lock-out.   Two hundred thousand Trade Unionists were represented, and the Conference decided to form a permanent body, the United Kingdom Alliance of Organised Trades, to provide a central fund for the support of trades in which lock-outs occurred. This was very like a revival of the United Trades' Associations of 1831 and 1845, except that the new body did not directly embark on plans of Co-operative production.   Some of its affiliated groups, however, did embark on such schemes, which, as we have seen, were particularly common at this period among the Miners.

Nearly all the big Unions were represented at the Sheffield Conference, at which the representatives of the " Amalgamated Societies " strongly denounced a militant strike policy, and urged the importance of conciliation. But of the 200,000 represented, only Societies representing 60,000 affiliated to the Alliance, and by the end of 1867 the paying membership had fallen to less than 25,000.   The Alliance held further Conferences, and remained in existence until 1870, when it was finally wound up.   But it was from the first a failure.

The principal reason for its collapse was lack of funds. The rich Amalgamated Societies did not join it, and the bodies which did—the Miners of South Yorkshire and Nottinghamshire, the Amalgamated Tailors, the Boilermakers, the Cotton Spinners, the Ironworkers, and a few others—had troubles enough on their hands. There was, moreover, the greatest difficulty in defining a " lock-out," as distinguished from a strike, and this led to internal dissensions. The rules laid down that the Alliance was to be used only for resisting wage-reductions or other attacks on existing conditions ; but it was often not easy to draw the line. Wages and conditions were then much less uniform from firm to firm, even in a single district, than they became later ; and the claim to a particular wage or term of employment might be simply a defence of an existing practice in one establishment, and in others a claim for an advance. The Alliance was governed by an Executive drawn from the Sheffield area, with William Dronfield, the veteran leader of Sheffield Trade Unionism, as its Secretary, and by a " Judicial Committee," drawn from the nine districts into which the organisation was divided, which dealt with applications for help. But, with the speedy exhaustion of the funds, this mechanism ceased to work and, in practice, the Alliance was governed by Dronfield and the Sheffield Executive. It never acquired a truly representative character in relation to the country as a whole.

A second reason for the failure of the Alliance was the sudden shifting of Trade Union attention, in 1867, the first year of its formal existence, from industrial action to parliamentary agitation. For in 1866 occurred the Sheffield outrages, and in 1867 the case of *Hornby* v. *Close*. And over these two issues the battle was at once fairly joined between the Trade Unions and the forces of legal and political repression.

BOOKS

S. and B. Webb. *History of Trade Unionism.*
G. Howell. *Labour Legislation, Labour Movements, Labour Leaders.*
G. Howell. *The Conflicts of Capital and Labour.*
A. Macdonald. *The Law of Masters and Workmen (1867).*
W. A. Holdsworth. *The Law of Master and Servant (1867).*
R. Y. Hedges and A. Winterbottom. *Legal History of Trade Unionism.*

2. THE SHEFFIELD OUTRAGES AND THE ROYAL COMMISSION ON TRADE UNIONS

The " Sheffield Outrages " were a series of acts of violence directed chiefly against blacklegs. The Sheffield cutlery trades were organised in a large number of very small societies, each confined to a single narrow craft, and aiming at a rigid exclusion of non-society men. It had long been the way of these tradesmen, if a non-unionist was given employment or if a unionist broke the rules of his society, to make things hot for him by the process known as "rattening." His tools were abstracted, or, in more serious cases, sand or even, occasionally, it appears, a can of gunpowder was inserted in the machine on which he was working. In some cases vengeance was carried into the blackleg's home, and at any rate in one instance a can of gunpowder was thrown down a blackleg's chimney. Such outrages had occurred from time to time for many years before 1866 ; but in 1865 and 1866 they became numerous, and in October, 1866, the house of a man named Fearneyhough was blown up, and the crime was charged to agents of the Saw Grinders' Union. Some similar, though less extreme, acts of violence occurred among the brickmakers in the Manchester district. At once there was a great outcry, in which the employers, then actively pushing their campaign of lock-outs against the Trade Unions, eagerly joined. Penal legislation for the suppression of the Trade Unions was demanded ; Trade Unionism in general was denounced as a criminal conspiracy against the public.

The first proposal, put forward by the Sheffield Town Council, was for an enquiry into the outrages alone. This did not at all suit the Unions ; and the London Trades Council at once replied with a demand for an enquiry into the whole subject of Trade Unionism. This demand was successful ; and, early in 1867, the Government passed the Trade Union Commission Act, setting up a Royal Commission " to enquire and report on the organisation and rules of trades' and other associations, with power to investigate any recent acts of intimidation, outrage, or wrong alleged to have been promoted, encouraged, or connived at by such Trade Unions or other associations." But, even with the extended scope of the enquiry, the outlook for the Unions seemed black enough, especially when William Broadhead and other members of the Sheffield Grinders' Union confessed to a series of crimes paid for out of Union funds. Everywhere the Unions and Trades Councils passed strong resolutions condemning the crimes, and calling for the most stringent enquiry. But middle-class opinion inevitably hardened against Trade Unionism, and the demand for repressive legislation was re-doubled. It would probably have gone hard with the Unions had it not been too late to draw back from the step of extending the franchise to the urban workers, which made the Trade Unionists for the first time a political power.

Just when the agitation against the Unions was at its height came the decision of the Court of Queen's Bench in the case of *Hornby* v. *Close*. The formation of the " Amalgamated Societies," with their high contributions and benefits, had made the adequate protection of Trade Union funds against defaulting officials a matter of vital importance. In 1855, when the Friendly Societies Act was before Parliament, the Metropolitan Trades Committee, a forerunner of the London Trades Council, succeeded in getting a clause inserted for this purpose. The clause laid down that any association established for a purpose not illegal might, on depositing its rules with the Registrar of Friendly Societies, have the advantage of getting disputes among its members dealt with summarily by the magistrates.   Under this section of the Act the leading Societies concerned, including the Engineers, Carpenters and Joiners, Ironfounders and Boilermakers, had deposited their rules, and had proceeded, where necessary, against defaulting officers.

In 1867 the Court of Queen's Bench decided, in a case brought by the Boilermakers' Society against its Bradford secretary, that a Trade Union could not come within the scope of the Friendly Societies Acts, and was, moreover, so far " in restraint of trade " as to be of its nature illegal at common law, though no longer " criminal " in itself, in view of the legalisation of combinations by statute in 1824-5.   This meant that, although no one could be indicted under the common law merely for forming or joining a Trade Union, the common law taint of illegality was held to persist, despite the statute, to the extent of preventing the law courts from giving any countenance or protection to Trade Unions or to their funds.   The immediate result of the decision was not only to deprive Trade Unions of the legal protection for their funds which they had in fact enjoyed for more than twenty years, but practically to outlaw Trade Unionism altogether, so that no man knew where the next blow would fall.

At once the Trade Unions proceeded to take action, but not, unfortunately, at first united action.   The Amalgamated Societies, chiefly anxious to protect their own funds and to dissociate themselves from the Sheffield outrages, determined, instead of organising the whole movement for a campaign to secure redress, to act independently on their own behalf.   Robert Applegarth took the lead in this, and in January 1867 the Junta set up a new body, called the " Conference of Amalgamated Trades," and consisting entirely of their own friends.   This body at once attempted to take into its hands the entire conduct of the Trade Union case, including not only the legal position but also the whole work of the Royal Commission.

Their first task was to influence the composition of the Commission itself, which the Government proposed to appoint entirely from persons supposed to be impartial.   One friend of the Unions, the Christian Socialist Thomas Hughes, was given a seat ; but the Conference pressed strongly for further representation.   A working-class Commissioner was suggested ; but such a thing was then unheard of.   Finally, the Government agreed to appoint Frederic Harrison, the Positivist, a lawyer and long a staunch supporter of the Amalgamated Societies and of the moderate Trade Unionism which they represented.   Permission was further obtained for representative Trade Unionists to be present during the examination of witnesses ; and the Conference of Amalgamated Trades selected Applegarth for this task.

This assumption of authority by the Junta did not pass without challenge. George Potter, after his quarrel with the London Trades Council in 1865, over their failure to support the Staffordshire Puddlers' strike, had founded the

London Working Men's Association, with the old Chartist, Robert Hartwell, as Secretary. With the political activities of this body we shall have to deal later ; but at this stage it became the instrument for organising the Trade Unions which the Junta had excluded from their counsels. In March 1867 Potter and Hartwell called a national Trade Union Conference to deal with the situation created by the case of *Hornby* v. *Close* and by the appointment of the Royal Commission. There was a big attendance, 200,000 Trade Unionists being represented directly, and another 400,000, it is said, indirectly by the local Trades Councils. These figures, even allowing for exaggeration, make it by far the most representative Trade Union gathering that had ever been held despite the absence of the Amalgamated Societies. Alexander Macdonald, John Kane, Thomas Connolly of the Stonemasons, and John Allen of the Boilermakers, were among the prominent leaders in attendance.

This Conference proceeded to appoint a rival committee to watch the progress of the Commission, and take steps for safeguarding the legal position of the Unions. The Committee at once passed a resolution deploring the action of the Conference of Amalgamated Trades and the refusal of the London Trades Council, on " objections wholly and solely party and personal," to take part in calling the Conference. Indeed, it is clear that the object of the Junta was to keep the conduct of the Trade Union case to themselves, because they feared that the attitude of the more militant Unions would prejudice their own claims. In opposition to this, the March Conference Committee elected Connolly, its Chairman, to attend the sittings of the Royal Commission, and to present the Trade Union case.

The dice, however, were loaded on the side of the Junta. The friendly members of the Royal Commission were their friends, and early in the proceedings they allowed Connolly to be excluded without protest for a speech to which objection was taken. Thereafter the conduct of the case fell into Applegarth's hands, in collaboration with Hughes and Harrison. Everything was done to divert attention from the more militant Unions to the moderate and " friendly " activities of the Amalgamated Societies, and to dissociate these, not only from outrages of the Sheffield type, but from all forms of militant Trade Union action. The work of the Unions as friendly societies was strongly stressed ; courts of conciliation were advocated as the alternative to strikes and lock-outs. In every way, Trade Unionism was made to appear almost unbelievably respectable, as indeed, so far as the Amalgamated Societies were concerned, it really was trying to be.

That Applegarth, Harrison and Hughes conducted their case with extraordinary skill is evident. When the reports of the outrages at Sheffield and other places appeared, attention was successfully drawn away from them, and it was shown that only a very few small Unions were in any way implicated in such practices. From a wholesale attack on Trade Unions, the

Royal Commission began to turn into a justification of them, where they were really as respectable as Applegarth and his friends made out.

While the Commission was still sitting, the Unions secured some relief from their difficulties. Russell Gurney's Larceny and Embezzlement Act of 1868 was so worded as to allow Trade Unions to use it to prosecute dishonest officials, and in 1869 a temporary Act—the Trade Union (Protection of Funds) Act—made possible civil proceedings for the recovery of money from defaulting officials pending the Royal Commission's Report.

The success of the Trade Union tactics was seen when the Royal Commission made its Final Report. Even the majority recommended the legalisation of Trade Unions, provided they were not formed to do acts involving breach of contract, or to refuse to work with any particular person. Under certain conditions, the majority also proposed that protection should be given to Trade Union funds. But they held that this protection should be confined to Unions whose rules were free from restrictive clauses, such as the prohibition of piece-work or contract work, the limitation of apprentices, or any limitations on the use of machinery. These last provisions would, of course, have hit directly at the Amalgamated Societies, which, though they had tried to keep the fact in the background, based their policy largely on restrictions of these kinds.

The minority, composed of Harrison, Hughes and the Earl of Lichfield, brought forward a separate report of their own, of which the gist was the proposal that all special legal discriminations against workers or their combinations should be repealed. No act, they urged, should be unlawful when committed by a workman unless it would be unlawful if committed by someone else ; and no act done in combination should be criminal unless it would be so if done by a single person.

It remained to be seen what action the Government would take. The Conference of Amalgamated Trades at once began to press for legislation on the lines of the Minority Report, and Frederic Harrison drafted for them a comprehensive Bill based on its recommendations, and embodying a complete scheme for the legalisation of Trade Unions and of strikes, and for the protection of Trade Union funds.

Meanwhile, in 1868, the Manchester Trades Council had convened a further national Trade Union Conference to consider the position. At this meeting, there were acrimonious disputes between those who supported the proposals of the Junta, and those who held that it was better for the Trade Unions to maintain a fighting attitude outside the law. But, on this issue, many who had opposed the Junta's arbitrary assumption of power felt with them, and a resolution of confidence in the policy of the Conference of Amalgamated Trades was carried on the motion of John Kane, the Ironworkers' Secretary, by this time a strong advocate of moderation, and two years later the sponsor of the sliding scale under the Iron Conciliation Board of 1869.

The Manchester meeting of 1868 is generally regarded as the beginning of the Trades Union Congress. The Junta, indeed, still held aloof, and the Amalgamated Societies were but thinly represented at it. But Kane's success began their conversion, and in 1869 Odger and Howell attended the Congress held at Birmingham, and managed to get the Junta's full programme accepted. The Conference of Amalgamated Trades, however, continued in existence as a separate body, and it was not until 1871 that the Junta finally accepted the Trades Union Congress as the central authority for the Trade Union Movement. As we shall see later, by that time the weaknesses of the Junta's strategy had become more evident, and even they saw the need of getting the entire Trade Union Movement united for the second critical phase of the struggle.

BOOKS

S. and B. Webb. *History of Trade Unionism.*
G. Howell. *Labour Legislation, Labour Movements, Labour Leaders.*
Royal Commission on Trade Unions (1867). *Reports and Evidence.*
R. Y. Hedges and A. Winterbottom. *Legal History of Trade Unionism.*

3. THE LABOUR LAWS OF 1871

The General Election of 1868 was the first at which large numbers of workmen were able to vote. A number of Labour candidates appeared in the field; but it was of more effect that everywhere Trade Unions and Trades Councils pestered the candidates with questions about their attitude on the problem of Trade Union rights. A considerable number of candidates, with the new electorate in mind, gave favourable answers, and returned pledged to support the Trade Union case. The Liberal Government, however, was hostile, and had no desire to introduce any legislation at all. In these circumstances, the Unions kept up a vigorous agitation, holding meetings throughout the country, and ceaselessly lobbying the Members in the House of Commons.

For some time the Government refused to make any concession, urging that Trade Union funds were already sufficiently protected. This was a reference to the Larceny and Embezzlement Act of 1868, known as Gurney's Act, which had enabled members of a co-partnership to prosecute their defaulting officials. Gurney's Act had no specific reference to Trade Unions ; but actually Trade Unions were successful in taking action under it. It did not, however, give the protection the Unions wanted ; for, though it enabled defaulters to be convicted, it did not make possible civil proceedings for the recovery of the missing money. The Unions, therefore, continued to press the Government, which at length agreed to pass a purely temporary measure to safeguard the Unions until permanent legislation was carried through. The Trade Union (Protection of Funds) Act accordingly became law in 1869.   But still the Government was in no hurry to give the Unions the legal status which they desired.

Throughout 1870 the pressure was maintained ; and at length, in 1871, the Government produced its Bill.   It was then that the defects of the Junta's policy became plain.   In one respect, the Bill gave the Unions all they wanted. No Union was to be outside the law merely because it was in restraint of trade.   All Unions whose rules did not infringe the criminal law were to be allowed to register, and to secure the protection which registration con-ferred.   And, in addition, the Unions were to be free from external inter-ference in their internal affairs, and were not to sue or be sued in a court of law in respect of such affairs.

But with this concession of the points chiefly pressed by the Junta, the Government coupled severe penal clauses against all forms of "molestation," "obstruction," or "intimidation," and against picketing of premises in pursuance of a trade dispute.   The Government, in fact, took the Junta at its word.   If the Trade Unions were really no more than friendly societies and bodies for promoting industrial conciliation, they could have no reason for objecting to the repression of these objectionable practices.   In fact, the Government quite logically set out to legalise the Trade Unions on condition of their acting up to the pious professions of Applegarth and his friends.   It professed, indeed, to be merely re-stating and codifying the existing law ; and this may have been literally true.   But the practical effect was to revive, and give fresh sanction to, old common law and statutory penalties which were becoming, or had become, obsolete.

This, of course, did not suit the Unions.   Indeed, it did not suit even the Amalgamated Societies, which had to fight on occasion, and had no wish to fight with both hands tied behind their backs.   It became necessary to mobilise the whole force of the Unions to fight the new danger, and the Conference of Amalgamated Trades, seeing that the situation had passed beyond its control, surrendered its attempt to act as the sole manipulator of the parliamentary wires.

Hitherto, as we have seen, the Junta had looked with some suspicion on the new Trades Union Congress.   Odger and Howell did indeed attend the Birmingham Congress of 1869 ; but Odger refused to serve on the Parlia-mentary Committee which was then first appointed.   Moreover, though the Congress decided to meet in London the following year, the London Trades Council took no steps to convene it, and actually no Congress was held in 1870.   But now the Junta made up their minds to appeal to the wider movement.   They decided to dissolve the Conference of Amalgamated Trades, and allowed the London Trades Council to convene the Trades Union Congress which it had failed to call the year before.   From this point the leaders of the Amalgamated Societies took their place on the Trades Union Congress Parliamentary Committee, which they at once began to dominate. George Howell, their faithful follower, became Secretary, and held the post till 1875. The Parliamentary Committee became the recognised " Cabinet " of the Trade Union Movement.

The Government, despite strong pressure from the Trade Unions and their friends, stood firm, and refused to withdraw the penal provisions of the Trade Union Bill. Its spokesman, indeed, disclaimed all intention of altering the law, even though the Bill proposed to repeal the Act of 1859 which, passed on the initiative of the National Association of United Trades for the Protection of Labour, had legalised peaceful picketing. But, even if this disclaimer had been sincere, it would have been cold comfort for the Trade Unions, which had been constantly in conflict with the penal provisions of the law as it stood.

At length, a concession was secured. The Government, without modifying its proposals, agreed to divide its Bill into two, and, leaving in the Trade Union Bill the provisions dealing with the status of the Unions, to include the penal proposals in a separate Bill, which was called the Criminal Law Amendment Bill. This, of course, enabled the friends of the Unions to vote for the one Bill and against the other, and so to avoid endangering the proposals which the Trade Unions wanted to see passed. But it also enabled the Unions, if both Bills were passed, to agitate for the repeal of the one without jeopardising the continuance of the other, or re-opening the general question of the status of Trade Unionism under the law.

Despite the opposition of the Unions to the Criminal Law Amendment Bill, both Bills became law in 1871. Trade Unions had acquired a legal status, thanks to the Junta's efforts. But they had also suffered a dangerous stiffening up against them of the criminal law.

How dangerous this was speedily became apparent. At once criminal prosecutions under the new Act began. Men were convicted and imprisoned for all manner of trivial offences. In a case arising out of the Nine Hours Movement of the London engineers, a man was sentenced to imprisonment because he had urged workers not to enter into fresh contracts with their employers. This was stigmatised as " coercion," punishable under the Act of 1871. This particular sentence was never carried out ; for on appeal the prosecutor failed to appear. But hard upon this case came, at the end of 1872, the trial and conviction of the London gas-stokers.

The industrial significance of the Gas-stokers' movement of 1872 is discussed in a later section. Here we are concerned only with its legal aspect. In the summer of 1872 the gas-stokers at the Beckton Gasworks formed a Trade Union, and demanded a rise in wages and a reduction in working hours, which were in many cases as many as eighty a week. The movement spread to other gas-works, and in the majority a reduction in hours was secured. But the employers retaliated by victimising the leaders of the movement. This the men resented. The Union decided in the Beckton case, where a leader named Dilley had been dismissed, to support him without a strike ; but at Fulham, when the men expostulated against the dismissals there, the management locked them out. This led to a general strike, which involved breach of contract by some of the strikers. At once criminal prosecutions began. The Gas Light and Coke Company took out summonses in five hundred cases under the Master and Servant Act ; and at once twenty-four men were sent to six weeks' hard labour, and one, the chairman of the Beckton men, to three months. But the company was not even content with this. It selected six of the leaders and prosecuted them for conspiracy under the Criminal Law Amendment Act of 1871. They were sentenced to twelve months' imprisonment.

These vindictive sentences, for no crime other than concerted strike action—for the breach of contract had been dealt with by the earlier suit—roused the whole Trade Union world to a sense of its peril. A Gas-stokers' Defence Committee had already been formed, and this both demanded the reversal of the sentences, and called for the repeal of the Act under which they had been given. At length, after four months, the Government released the prisoners, remitting the remainder of their sentences ; but it still firmly refused to take any action for the amendment of the law. Gladstone, questioned in Parliament, denied that there was any need for further legislation ; and the Government rigidly maintained this attitude up to the very end of its term of office. It appeared that the Trade Union agitation had failed, and that the effect of the great campaign for legal status had been to render all strike action, if not unlawful in itself, at all events pretty certain to bring both strikers and strike leaders into conflict with the law.

BOOKS

S. and B. Webb. *History of Trade Unionism.*
G. Howell. *Handy Book of the Labour Laws.*
G. Howell. *Labour Legislation, Labour Movements, Labour Leaders.*
H. H. Slesser. *The Law Relating to Trade Unions.*
R. Y. Hedges and A. Winterbottom. *Legal History of Trade Unionism.*

CHAPTER VI

THE LABOUR LAWS (*continued*)
TRADE UNIONISM IN THE 'SEVENTIES

1. Labour Representation to 1874 3. The Nine Hours Movement—Joseph Arch
2. The Labour Laws of 1875   4. The Factory Acts—The Plimsoll Line

I. LABOUR REPRESENTATION TO 1874

THE Reform Act of 1867 and the critical situation of the Trade Unions in relation to the law turned the attention of the working-class leaders to parliamentary action.   There had, indeed, been working-class political action at a much earlier stage.   In 1830, Henry Hunt was elected for Preston, a constituency with a big working-class electorate in the days of the unreformed Parliament.   In 1832 William Cobbett was returned for Oldham ; and he held the seat till his death in 1835.   Chartist supporters, such as John Fielden and Thomas Attwood, who had won seats in 1832, were in the Reformed Parliament to back up the successive petitions.   But Attwood retired in 1840, and Fielden was beaten in 1847, just after he had successfully piloted the Ten Hours Act through the House of Commons.   Feargus O'Connor won Nottingham as a Chartist in 1847 ; and both earlier and later many Chartists presented themselves as candidates, sometimes going to the poll, but more often retiring after getting in their share of propaganda.   William Newton, of the Amalgamated Society of Engineers, stood for Tower Hamlets in 1852, probably the first Trade Unionist to go to the poll ; and Ernest Jones after many previous contests, stood for Nottingham as a Chartist as late as 1859.

Thereafter came a pause.   Chartism died out, and the new Reform societies contented themselves with agitation for an extended franchise, shorter Parliaments, and the ballot, and did not put forward candidates of their own. Apparently the first body to attempt the organisation of the workers as a political force after the fall of Chartism was the London Working Men's Association, which, as we have seen, was founded by George Potter and Robert Hartwell, the old Chartist, in 1866, partly as a rival to the London Trades Council.

It was in 1867, the year of the Reform Act, that the London Working Men's Association launched its movement for working-class representation in Parliament.   The great legal struggle of the Trade Unions was just beginning ; and from the first the L.W.M.A. appealed directly to the organised working-class movement.   It did not confine its activity to London.   It issued a manifesto to trade organisations throughout the country, urging the creation of a Working Men's Parliamentary Election Fund, and calling upon Trade Unions, Trades Councils, and Co-operative Societies to take steps to organise in their own areas for the purpose of securing the return of working men to Parliament. The signatories to the manifesto were all Trade Unionists, and included, besides Potter and Hartwell, Henry Broadhurst of the Stonemasons, afterwards Secretary of the Trades Union Congress, and Joseph Leicester, of the Glass-makers' Society. In 1868 we find George Potter's paper, *The Beehive*, as the organ of the new movement, suggesting the general imposition of a Trade Union political levy.

The appeal of the L.W.M.A. seems to have produced little response. The Junta, then at the height of their quarrel with Potter, stood aloof, and a proposed National Convention of Trade Union Delegates to put the movement on a proper basis was never held. The General Election of 1868 came before there had been time to develop any proper organisation. Three Trade Union candidates—Howell for Aylesbury, W.R. Cremer for Warwick, and William Newton for Tower Hamlets, as well as E. O. Greening, the Co-operator, for Halifax—did go to the poll under the auspices of various local bodies ; but no candidate fought directly under the auspices of the L.W.M.A. Hartwell, indeed, was put up first for Lambeth and then for Stoke-on-Trent, but had to retire for lack of funds—a sure sign of the movement's weakness. Odger, who put up for Chelsea, was persuaded to retire.

The appearance of Cremer and Howell as candidates shows, however, that the Junta was not opposed to working-class candidatures, and in the following year, seeing the need for working-class pressure in order to get their Trade Union Bill considered, they themselves took steps to organise the movement. At about the same time it appears that George Potter, hitherto their most formidable opponent, came to terms with them, or made his surrender to them. At the beginning of 1870 *The Beehive*, his influential iournal, was taken over by a company in which the Junta and their friends held the control, and Potter, retained as editor, had to submit to the association in the post of the Rev. Henry Solly, who in 1862, had founded the Working Men's Club and Institute Union. Already, at the Trades Union Congress of 1869, which, as we saw, endorsed the Junta's policy in connection with the Royal Commission, we find George Odger moving, and Potter seconding, a successful resolution in favour of Labour representation in Parliament. In the same year, at a critical stage in the Trade Union struggle, we find Odger at Stafford and Potter at Nottingham retiring in order not to split the Liberal vote. But this, as we shall see, was by no means inconsistent with the new attitude of the working-class leaders towards working-class representation.

The decision of the Junta to take up parliamentary action assumed shape in a new organisation. In 1869 the Labour Representation League was formed, practically as a successor to the National Reform League. Its objects were to secure the return of working men to Parliament, to promote the registration of working-class voters throughout the country "without reference to their opinions or party bias," and to recommend to the support of working-class electors candidates whose attitude on labour questions commended them to the movement. The League was based on individual membership, with a subscription of 1s. a year from working men and 10s. from those who had been working men but had "passed into other occupations." The President was R. M. Latham, a barrister ; William Allan of the Engineers was Treasurer ; and Lloyd Jones, the old Owenite, was Secretary. The Executive included Applegarth, Coulson, Cremer, Guile, Howell, Odger and Shipton of the Junta group, as well as William Newton of the Engineers, Connolly of the Stonemasons, Holyoake, and George Potter. Charles Bradlaugh was nominated, but withdrew because he objected to the absence of any statement of political principles from the declarations of the League.

It will be seen that the L.R.L. was so far mainly a London movement, and did not include the Northern leaders. Its early candidatures were all in the South of England. In 1870 Odger fought in a three-cornered by-election at Southwark. The Liberal withdrew in favour of Odger towards the close of the poll, but too late to prevent a Conservative victory. Later in the same year Odger was nominated for Bristol, but withdrew in the Liberal's favour. Howell did the same thing at Norwich in 1871.

In these early by-elections, the League's object was to secure the adoption of its candidate by the Liberal Party in the constituency. The working-class candidates desired to run as Liberals, and, if elected, to sit as members of the Liberal Party. Many Liberals, including John Stuart Mill, had expressed the desire to see some working men in Parliament to put the working-class point of view, and the League's ambitions did not go beyond this. Indeed, one of its principal aims was, not so much the return of working men, as the influencing of Liberals to support working-class claims in the House for fear of the new working-class vote. Many of them did not even go so far as Mill, when he wrote to Odger that "the working men's policy is to insist on their own representatives and, in default of success, to permit Tories to be sent into the House until the Whig majority is seriously reduced when, of course, the Whigs will be happy to compromise and allow a few working-men representatives in the House."

Gradually, however, the persistent refusal of the Government to repeal or amend the Criminal Law Amendment Act drove the Trade Union leaders to this point, and at the General Election of 1874 the working-class vote was undoubtedly responsible to some extent for the defeat of the Liberal Government and the return of the Conservatives to power. On this occasion, when the Labour Representation League first tested its strength, not only did a number of working-class candidates go to the poll against Liberals, but a substantial part of the working-class vote was cast for Tories against the more reactionary of the Liberal candidates. In about half a dozen constituencies, moreover, the Conservatives nominated either no candidate, or only one for two seats, thus leaving the Labour man a free run against the second Liberal.

In all, besides Charles Bradlaugh, who unsuccessfully fought Nottingham, at least twelve working-class candidates went to the poll at this election, including Odger, Potter, Howell, Burt, Macdonald, Broadhurst, Cremer, Halliday and Pickard of the Amalgamated Miners, Lucraft and John Kane. Both Miners' Unions were active in the fight, the National, after an address from Lloyd Jones, having thrown in its lot with the movement for Labour representation in the previous year. Of the twelve candidates, two were successful—both miners. Thomas Burt was elected for Morpeth and Alexander Macdonald for Stafford—in both cases without Liberal opposition. These two became the first Labour Members; but both were returned by a combined Liberal-Labour vote, and ranked as Liberals in the House of Commons. At the election of 1880, one more member, Henry Broadhurst, the Secretary of the L.R.L., was added; and he too sat as a Liberal. Thereafter, the Labour Representation League perished.

Before 1874, the L.R.L. had tried its hand at local elections. It created a special body, the Working Men's School Board Central Committee—to fight the elections for the new School Boards set up under the Education Act of 1870, and secured Benjamin Lucraft's election for Finsbury. This was the small beginning of the movement for working-class representation in the sphere of Local Government. But no considerable development followed till after the reform of Local Government in 1888.

Meanwhile, at the Trades Union Congress, the question of Labour representation was a matter of annual debate. With little opposition, resolutions in its favour were carried year after year. At the Congress of 1873 the Parliamentary Committee was instructed, where it was asked to act by the local trade associations, to take steps to help in running Trade Union candidates; but no steps appear to have been taken, though in that year the Federation of Associated Employers of Labour had been formed, chiefly on the initiative of the Engineering and Shipbuilding Employers' Association, for the express purpose of combating the political pretensions of the Unions and of preventing the repeal of the Criminal Law Amendment Act. Thereafter, the annual pious resolutions were resumed; but there was no further development until the 'eighties.

The movement for working-class representation described in this section had clearly neither the intention nor the desire to form a separate working-class party. This aim was, indeed, probably in the minds of some of the leaders of the London Working Men's Association in 1867, and may have been the principal cause of their failure.   But as soon as the movement was taken over by the Junta and their friends, any such idea was dropped.   In the first instance, the Junta was chiefly using the movement for the purpose of increasing the pressure for amendment of the Labour Laws ; and, when it had served this immediate purpose, it became for them merely an auxiliary of the left wing of the Liberal Party, which, under the influence of Charles Dilke and of Joseph Chamberlain, was then moving fast in a Radical direction. With the outlook of this new Radical Liberalism the Trade Union leaders, for the most part, fully sympathised.   For a while, the Trade Unionists had fallen out with the leaders of the Liberal Party over the Labour Laws.   But, when that question had been satisfactorily settled by the Conservatives in the manner shortly to be described, they were ready to enter the Liberal fold, and the movement for Labour representation ceased, for a time, to play an independent part in working-class development.   The true " Lib-Lab " era began in 1875.

BOOKS

G. D. H. Cole.   *British Working-class Politics, 1832–1914.*
A. W. Humphrey.   *History of Labour Representation.*
H. Broadhurst.   *Autobiography.*

2. THE LABOUR LAWS OF 1875

In 1874 the Liberal Government fell, and the Conservatives came to power.   For the Trade Unions, the great question was how this change would affect their demand for the repeal of the Criminal Law Amendment Act. The Liberals had refused all amendment, and many of the working-class voters had turned against them.   But were the Conservatives likely to be more favourable to the Trade Union claims ?   It was true that the Conservatives had passed the Reform Act of 1867, and had given a substantial section of the workers the vote.   But the workers had requited them by voting Liberal in 1868.   What would Disraeli do now ?   The Trade Union leaders had their doubts, and meant to apply all the pressure they could command.

The Government's first step was the appointment of a Royal Commission to enquire into the entire operation of the Labour Laws.   At once the Trade Unionists raised a howl of protest ; for this seemed to re-open the whole question, and to put the Trade Union Act of 1871 in jeopardy.   Thomas Burt, after consultation with Howell and Frederic Harrison, refused to sit on the Commission.   The Parliamentary Committee of the Trades Union Congress passed a resolution of protest against its formation, and called for immediate legislation.   Nevertheless, Alexander Macdonald and Thomas Hughes were at length persuaded to accept seats ; but, though Macdonald was the Chairman of the Parliamentary Committee of the Trades Union

Congress, that body persisted in recommending the whole Trade Union Movement to boycott the Commission. In these circumstances the Commissioners set to work.

Before long the Trade Unions had further cause for alarm. The Government brought forward a comprehensive Bill amending the law relating to Friendly Societies. It was found that the draft proposed to repeal the Trade Union Act of 1871, and to bring Trade Unions under the new Act. At once there was a storm of protest, and finally the proposal was dropped, only minor technical amendments of the Trade Union Act being included in the Friendly Societies Act of 1875. Meanwhile, the Royal Commission was taking evidence; but only a very few Trade Unionists, including George Shipton, the Painters' Secretary, defied the wish of the Parliamentary Committee of Congress, and appeared to give evidence. The report, published early in 1875, and signed by all the members (including Hughes) except Macdonald, who presented a minority report, was thoroughly unsatisfactory to the Unions. Only minor amendments to the Criminal Law Amendment Act and a slight modification of the law of conspiracy were proposed. The repeal of the penal clauses of the Master and Servant Act was, indeed, also proposed; but otherwise the Act was left as it stood. Macdonald, in his report, stood for the full Trade Union claims, including the complete repeal of the Criminal Law Amendment Act and full equality of employers and workmen before the law.

Trade Union feeling was, by this time, thoroughly aroused, and a great agitation began. This apparently caused the Government to change its mind; for when, in June 1875, they produced their Bills, it was seen that the Trade Union claims had been substantially met. The Bills were two, in addition to the Friendly Societies Bill.

The Master and Servant Act of 1867 was replaced by the Employers and Workmen Act, 1875—a change of name which signified also a vital change of substance. Imprisonment for breach of contract was abolished, save in the special cases of certain vital public services or of danger to life or to valuable property. The contract of employment was made, like other contracts, a purely civil engagement, into which employer and worker entered as legally equal parties.

The Criminal Law Amendment Act of 1871 was completely repealed, and was replaced by a new measure, the Conspiracy and Protection of Property Act, 1875. By this Act, peaceful picketing was once more legalised, and it was laid down that no act should be punishable if done in combination unless it would be criminal if done by an individual acting alone. The dangerous phrases about " molestation," " obstruction," and " coercion," were swept away, and cases of intimidation or violence were left to be dealt with by the general body of law. In other words, the Trade Unions secured a charter which appeared, until the Taff Vale decision of 1901, to give them adequate legal status and immunity in the conduct of industrial disputes. The Trade Union (Amendment) Act of 1876, which made only minor administrative amendments in the Act of 1871 (though its defining clause afterwards acquired a sinister significance in the Osborne Judgment of 1909), completes the tale of the Labour Laws of the 'seventies.

This astonishingly complete victory was yielded by a Conservative Government, busily engaged in wooing the new working-class electorate. But the working-class electors were not grateful. Having got their emancipation from the Conservatives, they became more tied to the Liberal apron-strings than ever.

BOOKS

See Chapter V, section 3.

3. THE NINE HOURS MOVEMENT—JOSEPH ARCH

The period between 1867 and 1875, during which the Trade Unions were pursuing their long struggle for legal recognition of their rights, and making their first considerable experiment in collective political action, was also a time of acute and widespread industrial unrest. Between 1867 and 1874 numbers were flocking into the Unions, and new Unions were constantly being formed. We have already watched this growth in the case of the miners, whose organisations reached their greatest development during these years. We have now to survey it, not in relation to one particular industry, but as it affected the movement as a whole.

After the financial crisis of 1866 came two years of bad trade, during which the Unions were chiefly struggling to resist reductions in wages. To this time belongs the great lock-out of 1867 in the Clyde shipyards. In the previous year the employers had formed a powerful organisation of their own—the Clyde Shipbuilders' and Engineers' Association—to fight the Unions. In 1867 they locked the men out, and presented the " document " demanding renunciation of Trade Union membership, and after a six months' struggle the Unions were beaten. This was in the first year's life of the United Kingdom Alliance of Organised Trades, to whose work reference has been made already ; and the Clyde lock-out was the severest strain on its undeveloped resources.

But in 1869 the situation changed, and a great revival of trade began. From 1870 to 1873 ensued a period of great prosperity, followed by a gradual falling off from 1874 onwards. In these years of booming trade the great development of Trade Unionism took place.

It began, in 1869 and 1870, with a revival in the building trades. In these years there were many local building strikes, and in London the Nine Hours Movement was revived, though without immediate result. In most of the provincial centres, these strikes were successful both in increasing wages and in reducing hours of labour ; and they certainly played an important part in stimulating activity in other industries. The success of the builders seems to have been a direct cause of the great Nine Hours Movement of the engineers in 1871.

The form of this successful strike movement among the engineering workers is as notable as its result. It owed less than nothing to the central leadership of the Amalgamated Society of Engineers, which, under William Allan's canny guidance, had become far too cautious to embark upon any big forward movement. Allan was far more intent on conserving his Union's funds and on developing its activities as a friendly society than on fighting for either higher wages or shorter hours. The movement began under purely local auspices, with a strike at Sunderland early in 1871, in which the men demanded, and after four weeks' stoppage won, the nine hours' day.

The employers on the North-East Coast, anticipating an extension of the struggle, at once organised in readiness for it. The men, on their side, were for the most part not organised at all, the Engineers, the Boilermakers, and the other Unions concerned having only a fraction even of the skilled workers in their ranks. But at once an organisation was improvised, the local Union leaders creating the Nine Hours League as a temporary body in which Unionists and non-Unionists alike were enrolled. John Burnett, a young and active local member of the A.S.E., became President of the new body, and the recognised leader of the strike. As in previous great conflicts, appeals were made to the whole working-class movement to help with contributions to the funds, and for five months the League successfully kept up the struggle. The employers, on their side, levied themselves throughout the country for the support of the firms which were held up. Attempts were made to introduce blacklegs from abroad ; but these were for the most part successfully countered by the efforts of the International Working Men's Association, which sent Cohn, its Danish Corresponding Secretary in London, to the Continent to stop the blacklegs from coming. Finally, the employers were compelled to give way, and the fifty-four hours' week was generally recognised throughout the engineering shops and shipyards in the North-East.

The effect of this victory was speedily seen. Throughout the country, engineers and builders, as well as many workers in other trades, put forward demands for shorter hours. The Durham coalowners agreed to recognise the Durham Miners' Association, and to abolish the yearly bond. The South Wales Miners struck, and won a victory. Almost alone in failure were the Oldham Spinners, who struck in vain for the Saturday half-holiday. But their failure was due largely to the absence of a concerted movement throughout the cotton districts. Throughout 1872 and 1873 the strikes continued, especially in the engineering trades. In 1872 the Clyde engineers retrieved their failure of 1867 by winning the fifty-one hours' week. In London, many of the building workers struck in 1872 for the nine hours' day and for a rise in wages, and the employers replied with a general lock-out. The movement was in the hands of an Amalgamated Building Trades Committee ; but the Stonemasons finally made a separate settlement on the basis of a compromise, and the other trades, accusing them of betraying the cause, were compelled to resume work. It was in connection with this dispute that Patrick Kenney, afterwards a renegade from the Labour Movement, formed his General Amalgamated Labourers' Union, which collapsed in the subsequent depression, and that George Shipton succeeded in getting a number of the Painters' Societies to join forces in an Amalgamated Society on the approved lines. London had only a partial success ; but in many areas the fifty-four hours' week was conceded without a strike.

The Nine Hours Movement had a further effect. It seemed to show that victories could be won without the expensive and difficult organisation of " Amalgamated Societies." It opened up the hopes of victory to others besides the skilled craftsmen, and set the less skilled workers thinking of the possible benefits to themselves of Trade Union organisation. The Gasstokers' Union of 1872, which has been described already, was only one of a large number of new Unions of less skilled workers which sprang into existence during these stimulating years. The railway workers, hitherto practically unorganised, formed the Amalgamated Society of Railway Servants in 1872, with financial aid from Michael Bass, the Liberal brewer M.P. Mrs. Emma Paterson began to organise Unions for the women workers, and formed in 1874 the Women's Protective and Provident League, which later became the Women's Trade Union League. And, most notable of all, came the uprising of the agricultural workers who, since their complete suppression in the 'thirties, had seemed incapable of any considerable movement of organisation.

There had, indeed, been one or two scattered agricultural strikes in the 'sixties ; but these had been easily crushed. Suddenly, in 1871, the labourers began to stir. An agricultural workers' Union was formed in Herefordshire in that year, and soon enrolled 30,000 members. But the great impetus came from Warwickshire, where in 1872 Joseph Arch, himself a labourer and a Methodist preacher, organised the Warwickshire Labourers' Union, in the course of a successful local strike for higher wages and a shorter workingday. The movement spread with extraordinary rapidity south, east and west. Within a few months the Warwickshire Union became the National Agricultural Labourers' Union, and, a few months later, the membership rose to 100,000. In addition, many local Unions sprang up, and, refusing to merge themselves in the " National," formed a loosely-knit Federal Union of Agricultural and General Labourers, with a further membership of about 50,000. Kent, too, had a powerful Union of its own, and this subsequently spread to Sussex.

Wherever branches of any of these Unions were organised, demands for higher wages and reduced hours at once followed. In some cases—indeed, wherever they dared—the farmers met the agitation by victimising the leaders, and the country gentlefolk and the parsons took a strong line against the Unions. But the labourers were for the moment strong enough, and strongly enough supported, to bring about an almost general rise in wages and a widespread reduction in working hours. The industrial Trade Unions, and many middle-class sympathisers, gave them valuable help in money and organising effort. It seemed as if the countryside was rising at last.

Before long, however, the farmers and the gentry recovered from the effects of their first surprise. Victimisation became more widespread. At Chipping Norton, in Oxfordshire, two clergymen magistrates sent sixteen labourers' wives to prison for the crime of intimidating blacklegs during a dispute. Then, in 1874, the lock-out was extensively employed to break the power of the Unions. Some of the Suffolk labourers demanded a rise of wages from 13s. to 14s. for a week of fifty-four hours. The farmers replied with a general lock-out throughout the county, and this rapidly spread to other areas, till the whole of the Eastern Counties and most of the Midlands were involved. The Unions were unable to stand up against this onslaught, and thousands of men were forced to renounce their membership in order to get work.

This was the first great set-back. It was followed by the great depression in British agriculture—the long-deferred consequence of the repeal of the Corn Laws thirty years before. As the general industrial depression developed in the late 'seventies, there came a heavy fall in prices, and foreign corn began to stream in at prices with which the British farmer could not compete. Wholesale conversion of land from arable to pasture greatly reduced the demand for agricultural labour ; and the efforts of the Unions to meet the situation by aiding members to emigrate were ridiculously inadequate to offset the shortage of demand. Trade Union membership among the labourers rapidly dwindled. Many of the Unions disappeared altogether. By 1881 Arch's National Union had shrunk to a membership of 15,000. Such other Unions as survived at all abandoned their protective activities, and became practically Friendly Societies of no industrial importance. Only in Norfolk did the National Union retain any vitality. There it was still strong enough to help Joseph Arch to win his way to Parliament in 1885, when the agricultural workers had at length been given the vote by the Reform Act of 1884.

While it lasted, however, the labourers' movement was a portent. For a few years there seemed to be growing up a Trade Union Movement wide enough to embrace the entire working class of town and country alike. The narrowness and sectionalism of the " Amalgamated Societies " seemed in process of eclipse by a larger ideal of working-class unity. Old ideas,

prevalent in the great movement of the 'thirties, began to revive. The
workers dreamed again of the control of industry, and began again to experiment in self-governing workshops and factories under Trade Union control.
The Yorkshire and Durham Miners' Associations both acquired collieries ;
the North-East Coast engineers started the Ouseburn Engineering Works ;
the Hosiery Workers' Union acquired a factory of its own. One Trade
Union after another embarked on schemes of Co-operative production.
Lloyd Jones, the old Owenite and Co-operative organiser, now Secretary of
the Labour Representation League, was especially active in advocating these
developments ; and even the cautious Alexander Macdonald, probably influenced by his Owenite friend, Campbell of the Glasgow Trades Council,
urged them upon the miners.

This temporary revival of Co-operative production was accompanied by
a great expansion of the consumers' Co-operative Movement. We have
seen how the Scottish Co-operative Wholesale Society began business in
1868, and in 1873 the North of England Co-operative Wholesale Society
became simply the C.W.S., began to cover the entire country, and opened its
first productive works for the manufacture of biscuits and boots. Thereafter
its development was rapid, and fresh productive enterprises were soon added.
Meanwhile, the consumers' movement as a whole was moving towards more
effective national organisation. In 1869 the Central Co-operative Conference
Board was established and the modern series of fully representative Annual
Co-operative Congresses began. A few years later the Board became the
Co-operative Union, the recognised central body for the movement as a
whole, to which practically all the Societies, including the Wholesales and the
Producers' societies, became affiliated. The control of the movement, however, remained wholly decentralised, each local Society retaining its full
independence. The Industrial and Provident Societies Act of 1876 gave
increased legal powers, and brought banking, at which the C.W.S. had
already made a tentative beginning in 1872, fully within the competence
of the movement.

Consumers' Co-operation pursued its successful career, little affected by
the ups and downs of trade. But the great Trade Union revival of the early
'seventies did not last. All its schemes, hopes and organisations perished in
the great depression. From 1875 onwards trade grew steadily worse. The
Co-operative mines and factories had to close down ; the new Unions lost
their members, and had in many cases to dissolve ; to the period of hope and
confidence succeeded apathy and despair. The great miners' organisations
broke down, and almost disappeared. Only the Amalgamated Societies and
the " Amalgamations " of the textile workers were able to stand up against
the troubles of the late 'seventies ; and they withstood the storm only by an
almost entire abandonment of industrial activity. But the story of this
collapse, and of the subsequent revival, belongs to a later chapter. Here we

need only note that, but for the depression of the later 'seventies, the great movement which, ten years later, was to create the " New Unionism " and express itself in the Dock Strike of 1889, would have proceeded without a break from the uprising described in this chapter. Between 1867 and 1875 the " bottom dog " made his voice heard ; the great depression of the late 'seventies firmly silenced him for a decade. But then he rose again.

BOOKS

S. and B. Webb. *History of Trade Unionism.*
Souvenir History of the Amalgamated Society of Engineers.
J. B. Jefferys. *The Story of the Engineers.*
J. Arch. *Autobiography.*
W. Hasbach. *History of the Agricultural Labourer.*
F. E. Green. *History of the Agricultural Labourer.*
E. R. Selley. *Village Trade Unions.*
B. Jones. *Co-operative Production.*
G. D. H. Cole. *A Century of Co-operation.*
P. Redfern. *History of the Co-operative Wholesale Society.*

4. THE FACTORY ACTS—THE PLIMSOLL LINE

While the agricultural workers were endeavouring to improve their position by organisation, the miners and textile operatives were agitating for further protection from the law. In 1872, as we have seen, the miners secured the passing of the Coal and Metalliferous Mines Acts. In Lancashire the failure of the Oldham Spinners' strike caused the Spinners' and Weavers' Unions to come together in a new " Short Time " movement. In 1872 they formed the Factory Acts Reform Association, and Short Time Committees were once more set up throughout the textile districts. The Factory Acts, which up to 1867 had extended only to textiles and to a few scheduled " dangerous trades ", were applied to all factory trades by the Act of that year, and workshops (i.e. broadly speaking, small establishments not using power) were also for the first time brought generally under regulation ; but the permitted hours were left as in the Act of 1850, at sixty a week, and the regulations were less strict for the non-textile establishments now first brought under regulation than for the factories previously subject to control. The aim of the textile Unions was now to secure by law a maximum working week of fifty-four hours—that is, a working day of nine and a half hours, with a half-holiday on Saturday. In response to this pressure, Commissions were sent by the Government to investigate conditions in the textile districts ; and their reports, issued in 1873, endorsed the demand for the fifty-four hour week. In the same year A. J. Mundella, acting as usual in close association with the moderate Trade Union leaders, introduced the Factory (Health of Women) Bill into the House of Commons. At once a storm arose. Many Liberals opposed the Bill on *laissez faire* principles ; and this contributed to the defeat of the Liberal Government at the Election of 1874. The Tories, on their return to power, passed an Act which, after a year's grace, raised the minimum age of textile factory employment to ten ; but they refused to concede the fifty-four hours week. A week of fifty-seven hours was, however, secured.

On this, the agitation was redoubled, and in 1876 the Government was induced to set up a Commission to go into the Factory Acts as a whole. Before this body a quarrel, already foreshadowed in the opposition to the Act of 1874, developed a good deal further. The Trade Unions, as usual, put forward their demand for shorter hours for all workers in the industries concerned in the form of a demand for legislative protection for women and children. They knew well enough that, if women and children had their working day shortened by law, the men would share in the benefit, because most of the factories could not be kept open for men alone. But they had now for the first time to deal with the developing Feminist Movement, whose leaders objected to any special regulation of women's conditions as prejudicing their chances of employment, and as manœuvres of the men to drive the women out of industry. The new women's Trade Unions, under Mrs. Paterson's guidance, opposed the claims of the Factory Acts Reform Association, and many *laissez-faire* Liberals, headed by Professor Fawcett, whose wife was a leader in the women's movement, were eager to snatch at this excuse for opposition.

The result was that, while the Act of 1878 achieved an important consolidation of the law, and greatly improved its administration, no further reduction of working hours was secured, and the textile workers were driven back upon their own resources. In the same year came the great cotton strike, which brought the workers' forward movement to an end. Depression of trade had set in by 1877, and the employers had begun to enforce local reductions in wages, which led to more than one strike. But in 1878 trade became much worse, and the employers in all districts demanded a wage reduction of ten per cent. The Unions replied that the trouble was due to over-production, and demanded that output should be restricted by running the mills only four days a week. This the employers rejected as interference with the freedom of industry and with their management of their own businesses. The result was a great ten weeks' stoppage, accompanied by some disorders, in the course of which the house of the employers' chairman was sacked and burnt down. Finally, the men were driven back to work on the employers' terms. Their defeat brought the shorter hours movement to an end for the time.

At the same time as the cotton operatives launched their movement for factory reform, Samuel Plimsoll, Radical M.P. for Derby, began his agitation on behalf of the seamen. In 1871, Plimsoll approached the Trades Union Congress for help in his campaign for a new Merchant Shipping Act, and at the Congress of 1873 he distributed copies of his book, *Our Seamen*, and definitely inaugurated his agitation. *Our Seamen* was a description, eloquent and heavily documented, of the scandalous conditions under which the men of the mercantile marine had to work, of the unnecessary hardships and hazards to which they were exposed, of " coffin ships " and murdering shipowners. Names and instances were freely given, and abundant opportunity for libel actions was intentionally afforded.

The Trade Unions took up the Plimsoll agitation with great energy. The Liverpool Trades Council played a leading part, but Unions of all sorts helped. The Yorkshire Miners levied their members a shilling each, and sent over £1,000 to help the campaign. The Engineers and the Amalgamated Miners each sent a similar sum. A Plimsoll and Seamen's Fund Committee was formed, with leading Trade Unionists upon it, and George Howell became its secretary. Lord Shaftesbury was chairman. Meetings were held all over the country in support of Samuel Plimsoll's Bill.

Very soon the Government began to give way, despite the strong opposition of shipowners on both sides of the House. In 1873 a temporary Act was passed, under which over four hundred vessels were detained as unseaworthy during the first year. The Plimsoll agitation played its part in the Election of 1874, and in the following year the new Conservative Government introduced a Bill, which became law a session later as the Merchant Shipping Act of 1876.

These two agitations give some idea of the social ferment of the early 'seventies, by far the most active period for social legislation of the entire nineteenth century. Within seven years, besides the Mines Acts of 1872, the Factory Act of 1875 and the Merchant Shipping Act of 1876, there were passed the Education Acts of 1870 and 1876, which first set up a general system of elementary education throughout the country. The Judicature Act of 1873 reformed the legal system. The Public Health Acts of 1872 and 1875 effectively inaugurated the modern era in Local Government, outside the corporate towns, and greatly improved sanitary services in these towns as well as elsewhere. The Cross Housing Act of 1876, following up the beginning made in the Torrens Act of 1868, gave the first clear recognition of the public responsibility for housing conditions in the towns. In addition, the Civil Service was reformed in 1870, and was put on its modern basis of open examination ; and, in 1873, the growth of the demand for adult education was signalised by the beginning of the University Extension Movement. There was also a rapid growth of state-aided classes under the Science and Art Department. The Building Societies Act of 1874, the Friendly Societies Act of 1875, and the Industrial and Provident Societies Act of 1876 gave to Friendly and Co-operative Societies the same sort of legal charters as the Labour Laws of 1871 to 1875 conferred upon the Trade Unions. Never had there been such activity in legislation—not even in the years immediately following the Reform Act of 1832. And the most active period was in the first three years under the Conservative Government of 1874.

These social developments were destined to suffer an abrupt check. The movement for social reform shared the fate of the expanding Trade Union Movement. The depression of the late 'seventies suddenly cut it short. To that great reverse and to its causes we must now turn our attention.

BOOKS

G. D. H. Cole and R. Postgate. *The Common People, 1746–1946.*
B. E. Hutchins and E. Harrison. *History of Factory Legislation.*
S. Plimsoll. *Our Seamen.*
G. Howell. *Labour Legislation, Labour Movements, Labour Leaders.*
G. Slater. *The Growth of Modern England.*
F. Smith. *A History of English Elementary Education, 1760–1902.*

CHAPTER VII

THE GREAT DEPRESSION

I. THE COMING OF IMPERIALISM

In the late 'seventies the long period of trade prosperity came to an end. British exports, which had amounted to £256,000,000 in 1872, fell gradually to £192,000,000 in 1879. Unemployment, measured by Trade Union returns, rose from 1 per cent. to nearly 12. 1878 was a bad year ; 1879 was infinitely worse. Then came a partial recovery. 1880 was bad, but improving ; 1881 and 1882 were fairly good. In 1882 exports rose again to £241,000,000, and unemployment fell below 3 per cent. But there followed a new and more prolonged slump, which lasted till 1888. The worst years were 1885 and 1886, when exports fell to £213,000,000, and unemployment rose to 10 per cent. Then at last came the boom of 1889 and 1890, followed by the relatively stable conditions of the following decade.

The great depression, as we have seen, swept away the movement for social reform, and brought the rapid advance of the Trade Unions abruptly to an end. The great Unions of agricultural workers shrunk almost to nothing. Macdonald's National Miners' Union broke up. The cotton operatives, the builders and the engineers were all defeated in great strikes against heavy reductions in wages. The Trade Union Co-operative factories went bankrupt ; even the consumers' Co-operative Movement suffered a check. Moreover, the Trade Unions which survived were placed rigidly on the defensive, and confined their activities as far as possible to the administration of friendly benefits and to the promotion of schemes of conciliation. Sliding Scales, under which wages were made to depend on the selling price of the product, became prevalent at a time when prices were continuously and sharply falling. For those who had steady employment the fall in prices, which was greatest in basic foodstuffs and materials, brought higher purchasing power in spite of falling wages. But there was much intermittent employment, as well as heavy long-term unemployment in the main industries ; and Trade Union bargaining power was effectively undermined.

What were the causes of this great depression ? Above all, it was the logical outcome of the previous period of prosperity. For a generation, Great Britain had abundantly prospered by supplying the world with products of which she had, by virtue of her mastery of technique, her machine equipment, her coal, her command of the iron trades, the skill of her operatives, and her abundant supply of surplus capital available for investment, a virtual monopoly. She could produce more cheaply than any rival, and yet make a larger profit. The advance in the workers' standard of life between 1850 and 1875 represented but a small share in the wealth which had flowed into Great Britain from every quarter of the globe in a rich and increasing stream.

By the middle 'seventies the situation was rapidly changing. Rival producers were beginning to threaten seriously the dominance of British industry. The United States began increasingly to supply its own needs behind a tariff wall which effectively kept out many classes of British goods. For wheat, and growingly for meat as well, Great Britain looked more and more to the United States ; but, while British imports from America grew, British exports ceased to grow. Germany, too, was becoming a powerful rival, especially in the metal industries, and was also changing over to a protective system which damaged the British export trades. Most of Britain's best customers were beginning in some measure to produce for themselves with the aid of the new techniques of which Britain had been the pioneer.

There were, moreover, internal causes for the depression. The great period of intensive railway building, which had provided a profitable outlet for British capital in every part of the world, was drawing to an end ; and the substitution of mild steel for iron, by lengthening the life of rails and other equipment, was diminishing the need for renewals. In the shipping industry, the opening of the Suez Canal, the increase in the speed and carrying capacity of vessels, and the substitution of steel for iron in shipbuilding, created an oversupply of tonnage, and caused intensive competition for cargoes. Above all, a series of great inventions in the metal trades—the Bessemer process of 1856, the Siemens process of 1866, and the discoveries of Gilchrist and Thomas in the 'seventies—had revolutionised the processes of iron and steel manufacture.

These inventions compelled Great Britain, the possessor of by far the largest and best equipped iron industry in the world, to reconstruct her entire methods of production, and to scrap a huge capital which had been sunk in the old processes. They involved also a big importation of iron ore, and an eclipse of British iron mining ; for some of the best British iron deposits were already getting used up and most British iron ores, containing phosphorus, were unsuitable for the new methods of manufacture devised by Bessemer and Siemens. The great depression was greatest of all in the constructional trades, which were hit at once by the growth of foreign competition based from the first on the new methods, by the decline in demand owing to the slackening of railway construction and the use of steel, and by the need for almost complete capital re-equipment of the British works.

At the same time, while other countries were building up tariffs against

Great Britain, the Free Trade system was for the first time beginning to oper-
ate effectively in relation to British imports. The real effects of repealing the
Corn Laws were not seen until the interior of North America had been
opened up, and improved facilities for transport by land and sea brought
cheap food to our ports. Prices indeed fell, and before long counteracted in
large measure the effect of lower wages for the town workers. But British
agriculture was hard hit, and the depopulation of the countryside, begun in
the generation between 1850 and 1880, was immensely speeded up in the
following decade.

Great Britain, in fact, had lost her world monopoly. She remained by
far the wealthiest country in the world ; for the large capital export of the
past generation continued to bring in a heavy annual tribute of interest from
overseas. Capital continued to accumulate ; for much of this interest was
reinvested abroad, and the richer classes continued to apply their surplus
incomes largely to foreign investment. But this could no longer be relied
upon to create the same steady stream of orders as before ; for even where
Great Britain continued to supply the capital, it no longer followed as a
matter of course that she would receive the resulting orders for goods.

The 'eighties echoed with complaints at the prostration of trade, and
lamentations at the passing of Great Britain's world monopoly. The Reports
of the Royal Commission on the Depression of Trade, appointed in 1886, are
full of them. With the great depression the illusion of an endless, effortless,
automatic progress in wealth and trade—so dear to the Victorians—was
shattered, and the air began to be thick with prophecies of ruin and incite-
ments to action. A great change came over British commercial and economic policy. The doctrine of commercial *laissez-faire*, which had been
practically unchallenged for a generation, was now energetically challenged.
Tariff Reform began to be heard of as an economic heresy claiming adherents
among business men.

Nowhere was the change in policy more evident than in the British
attitude towards the Empire. In the " golden age " the popular attitude was
that of bored expectancy of dissolution. Men such as Bright and Cobden
were only waiting for the Colonies to drop off like ripe fruit from the tree.
Colonial self-government was regarded as a preliminary to entire independence. The non-self-governing parts of the Empire were treated, for the
most part, as a troublesome responsibility. India, indeed, was always to
some extent an exception to this rule ; for the Indian market was of great
importance ; but, generally, this was the prevailing attitude, and even the
Indian Empire's economic value was doubted by high authorities. All the
world seemed an open market for British wares. Why should Great
Britain give herself the trouble of governing it ?

In the 'seventies, and especially as the depression grew, this attitude
changed. In the 'eighties an opposite attitude became clearly dominant.

The Colonies came to be regarded as potentially great markets for British exports, but as markets needing conscious and scientific development ; and importance began to be attached to them as sources of valuable minerals and of other raw materials for working up in Great Britain.   The idea spread of peopling Canada and Australia with the unemployed surplus population of Great Britain, and thus of both relieving the congestion at home and settling abroad fresh customers for British trade.   The Colonial Conference at the Jubilee of 1887 gave clear expression to the new attitude.

Economic Imperialism, however, did not develop in Great Britain alone, or apply only to lands already within the Empire.   Germany and France, followed later by other countries, began to build up overseas Empires of their own in rivalry to Great Britain.   From 1880 a new partition of the un-exploited places of the world began.   Africa was rapidly shared out between the European Powers ; and the Far East became a sphere of new economic rivalries.   Each country sought, not only for markets in which to sell goods, but also for concessions for railway building and for the exploitation of natural resources and of cheap native labour, for sources of valuable raw materials of industry, for every kind of new sphere of influence and of imperial power.

It was in this new world of intense economic rivalries that British Labour entered on a fresh phase of development, and that modern Socialism began to grow.   Till the great depression came, the British workers had shared in the illusions of their masters.   They too had thought that every year, with only a small set-back here and there, Britain was destined to grow richer and richer. They had believed that more and more crumbs would fall to them, almost automatically, from the rich man's table.   They had therefore, on the whole, tried to work with the grain of Capitalism rather than against it.   Only the unwillingness of the employers to work with them had prevented the growth of a general spirit of harmony between Capital and Labour.   But when they saw the monopoly of their masters threatened, and began to experience in falling wages and unemployment the results of the set-back to British industry, a section of them became growingly inclined to question the basis of the entire system.   The nearly-forgotten doctrines of Karl Marx were revived, and found followers.   Socialism, a British export in the eighteen thirties, was re-imported from Europe by Henry Mayers Hyndman and the other leaders of the Social Democratic Federation.

Naturally, however, the established leaders of the British Labour move-ment were too old to change their views.   In the 'eighties and 'nineties a great war was waged between the New Unionism and the Old, which was itself the New Unionism of 1850 grown decadent, and in politics between the " Lib-Labs " and the Socialists, who headed the advocates of purely inde-pendent working-class political action.   Neither side completely won the day—out of their conflict emerged a new working-class movement which followed neither Broadhurst and his friends of the Parliamentary Committee of the Trades Union Congress nor Hyndman nor even the more moderate Socialism of Keir Hardie and the Independent Labour Party. The New Unionism and the old blended and intermingled ; and out of the political struggle rose the Labour Representation Committee, hovering uncertainly on the fringe of Socialism, but casting many a longing glance back at the old Liberal love with which it was still disposed to maintain a clandestine liaison.

The following sections deal with this conflict and with its immediate results. But for the moment we must pause, on the threshold of the new, to watch the slow decline of movements that had spent their force.

BOOKS

G. D. H. Cole. *British Trade and Industry*.
L. C. Knowles. *Industrial and Commercial Revolutions*.
L. C. Knowles. *Economic Development of the British Overseas Empire*.
Goldwin Smith. *The Empire*.
C. W. Dilke. *Greater Britain*.
C. A. Bodelsen. *Studies in Mid-Victorian Imperialism*.
C. M. Waters. *Economic History of Great Britain and the Colonies from 1875*.
A. Viallate. *Economic Imperialism*.

2. CONCILIATION AND ARBITRATION—THE "LIB-LABS"

We have seen how, in the great struggle of the Trade Unions for legal recognition, the leaders of the Amalgamated Societies successfully established their ascendancy over the entire movement. Applegarth, indeed, retired from the Secretaryship of the Carpenters and Joiners in 1871, as the result of a quarrel, and Allan, of the Engineers, died in 1874. But the men who succeeded to the leadership, Burnett, of the Engineers, J. D. Prior, of the Carpenters, and Henry Broadhurst, of the Stonemasons, carried on the tradition of the Junta. Throughout, they stood for a policy of conciliation, deplored the use of the strike save as a final and rare resort, and aimed at building up Joint Boards for friendly negotiation with the associated employers.

Until 1871, the advocates of conciliation had faced an uphill task. A few formal Conciliation Boards had, indeed, been started in the early 'sixties—the Nottingham Hosiery Board by A. J. Mundella in 1864, and the Wolverhampton Building Trades Joint Committee by Sir Rupert Kettle four years later. But most employers were at this stage far more intent on smashing Trade Unions than on negotiating with them. The vindictiveness of the anti-Trade Union campaign which followed the Sheffield outrages shows the strength of the prevalent feeling.

After 1871 this feeling underwent a rapid change. The law had given the Trade Unions a definite status, and Applegarth and his friends had demonstrated before the Royal Commission that many Trade Unions were, after all, very mild and inoffensive bodies, which it might be better to recognise than to fight. The Conciliation Act of 1867, for which the National Association of United Trades had worked so long, had been abortive, both because the employers were not ready for it and because it was framed on the wrong lines. But a few years later conciliation was spreading rapidly in many trades.

Among the pioneers of the new system were the ironworkers. The North of England Manufactured Iron Board was established at Darlington in 1869, and soon adopted the method of regulating wages by means of a sliding scale based on the selling price of the product. From Durham the system spread rapidly to other districts, until practically the whole iron and steel industry was governed by a system of conciliation boards and sliding scales. We have seen how, by 1871, the coalowners in both Northumberland and Durham had recognised the Miners' Associations, and had entered into formal arrangements for regular negotiation. By 1875 Yorkshire had done the same, and Alexander Macdonald was rejoicing over " the glorious state of things " and the " perfect confidence " felt by the miners in the new machinery. To have secured recognition from the employers seemed a glorious victory. Conciliation and Arbitration appeared as the realisation of the Union leaders' dreams.

The result of recognition was a rapid spread of the sliding scale to the coal industry despite Macdonald's opposition to it. Between 1874 and 1880 sliding scales were adopted in South Staffordshire, South Wales, Somerset, Cannock Chase, Durham, Cumberland, Northumberland, West Yorkshire and North Wales. It should be noted, however, that this system, of which the miners in the North-East were the pioneers, being opposed by Macdonald, did not extend to Scotland (save in Lanarkshire from 1887 to 1889), while in South Wales it was first imposed by the owners as the outcome of the men's defeat in the strike of 1875, and even in Durham it was at first accompanied by great friction. It was established there in 1877 ; but in 1879 the men struck against the reductions imposed, and in 1884 terminated the scale, and were only with difficulty persuaded to renew it. Gradually, however, most of the coalfields passed under the sliding scale system, which, after the collapse of Macdonald's National Union in 1879, ruled practically unchallenged till the coming of the new Miners' Federation a decade later.

The sliding scale system could not readily be applied to the great majority of industries. But the growth of conciliation extended over a much wider field. The Arbitration Act of 1872, promoted by the Parliamentary Committee of the Trades Union Congress, and providing for voluntary arbitration by consent of both parties, remained a dead letter ; but trade after trade designed its own machinery. The cotton operatives, after the great strikes of 1877 and 1878, settled down to make the best of the bad times by perfecting their methods of negotiation ; joint committees were created in the engineering trades, after a great outburst of strikes and lock-outs in 1879 ; the boot and shoe operatives set up a Conciliation Board. In London, the

Chamber of Commerce established a General Conciliation Board to promote the friendly settlement of disputes in any trade ; and this example was followed in other centres. Strikes became rare ; Trade Unionism appeared to be justifying Applegarth's politic disclaimers of its disturbing intentions. The great excitement of the years between 1867 and 1875 had completely passed away.

There was, moreover, a check to legislative as well as to industrial progress. The 'eighties were not fertile in social or industrial legislation. The Employers' Liability Act of 1880 did, by abrogating the doctrine of "common employment," take the first step towards a proper system of workmen's compensation ; but it remained necessary for the workman to prove " negligence " on the part of the employer or of his agents—a point not met till the Workmen's Compensation Act of 1897, and then only within a restricted group of occupations. The Coal Mines Act of 1887 did at last put on a satisfactory footing the miners' right to appoint checkweighmen at every colliery, and the Truck Act of the same year, passed mainly through the insistence of Charles Bradlaugh, did some good. But these were the only important Acts dealing with industrial conditions. The textile workers formed a new Northern Counties Factory Reform Association in 1886 ; but this achieved no important result till the Factory Act of 1891. The most important social legislation of the 'eighties, apart from the Reform Act of 1884, which at last enfranchised the miners and agricultural labourers, and from the Re-distribution Act of the following year, related to Local Government. The Municipal Corporations Act of 1882, and the Local Government (County Councils) Act of 1888, carried through the reform of local organisation which was completed by the Local Government (Parish Councils) Act of 1894.

Politically, the Trade Union Movement committed itself more and more to the Liberal creed. Many Trade Union leaders, resting their faith on their Conciliation Boards and Sliding Scales, joined with employers in renouncing State intervention in industry, and in opposing legal regulation of the hours of labour. The Miners' Associations in Northumberland and Durham dropped the demand for a guaranteed minimum wage. Just when the employing classes were abandoning *laissez-faire* economics, the conversion to them of the older Trade Union leaders seemed to be proceeding apace.

In the House of Commons the General Election of 1880 brought only one recruit, Henry Broadhurst, to the working-class ranks. After this, however, there was some revival of activity. In 1881 the Trades Union Congress instructed the Parliamentary Committee to take steps to help working-class candidates. But nothing at all was done at the centre ; and when at the next Congress George Shipton moved for the creation of a parliamentary fund, his resolution was heavily defeated. He returned to the attack in 1884 and 1885 with the same result, despite the new opportunities created by the Reform

Acts of those years. The most Congress would do in 1885 was to urge the Trade Unions, on the motion of John Wilson, the Durham Miners' leader, who had just been elected to Parliament as a "Lib-Lab," to organise politically for themselves. But in 1886, the year of the next General Election, T. R. Threlfall had better success, and Congress created a special Labour Electoral Committee, side by side with the Parliamentary Committee.

In the election of 1885, the number of working-class representatives rose to eleven, not counting two representatives of the Highland crofters, or Charles Bradlaugh, who was re-elected at Northampton as a Radical. Alexander Macdonald had died in 1881 and his seat had been lost ; but the miners accounted for six of the eleven : Thomas Burt, John Wilson, William Abraham, William Crawford, Charles Fenwick and Ben Pickard. The others were Henry Broadhurst, William Randal Cremer, George Howell, Joseph Leicester and Joseph Arch, the agricultural labourers' leader, who won his seat in Norfolk. But in the General Election held the following year Arch, Leicester and Wilson lost their seats, and only two new members—the cab-driver, James Rowlands, and the Scottish "Socialist laird," Robert Bontine Cunninghame Graham, who won his seat as a Radical—were elected. In this year the Labour Electoral Committee separated from the Trades Union Congress, and became an independent body, under the name of the Labour Electoral Association. The Labour Representation League had painlessly expired about 1881.

It must not be supposed that this handful of working-class members acted, or regarded themselves, as a separate party. They all sat and voted as Liberals of one sort or another ; and Broadhurst accepted office as Under-Secretary to the Home Office in the Liberal Government. On specifically Labour questions they acted to some extent as a group ; but on all general matters they followed the Liberal Government, and ranked as part of its majority.

The aim of the Labour Electoral Association was not to create a Labour Party, but to promote the return of working men to Parliament. In 1888, it decided that all its candidates must be working men, or of working-class origin. Though it formed branches in a number of centres, and claimed, in 1888, an affiliated membership of 600,000, its practice was to secure the adoption of its candidates by local Liberal and Radical Associations, so that they not only sat, but stood, as Liberals. As local agencies it mainly used the Trades Councils, at this time in many cases still dominated by Liberal Trade Unionists. It opposed three-cornered fights, and refused to support independent Labour candidates against Liberals. It lasted on until 1895, and spent its last years in a struggle against the rising force of Independent Labour. But already in the late 'eighties many of the local bodies nominally associated with it were beginning to break away, and to insist on taking their own line in both parliamentary and municipal elections.

In the period between the decline of the International Working Men's Association and the rise of Socialism in the 'eighties, such Radical working-class propaganda as survived centred mainly round Land Reform.   Until his death in 1864, Bronterre O'Brien had continued to preach a sort of agrarian Socialism in *Reynolds' Newspaper*, and after his death his mantle fell on others. The Land and Labour League, founded in 1867 and led by James Harvey, was regarded by Marx as a promising organisation, and entered into friendly relations with the British Federal Council of the " International."   But the more advanced Liberals were also Land Reformers.   In 1870 John Stuart Mill founded the Land Tenure Reform Association, in which Radicals such as Dilke and Thorold Rogers were associated with Trade Unionists such as Cremer, Lucraft and Odger, and several other British members of the " International."   A little later, in Scotland, the Scottish Land Restoration League carried on a lively campaign among the crofters.   Other Land Reform organisations sprang up and prepared the way for the influence of Henry George, whose *Progress and Poverty*, published in America in 1879, soon began to sell largely in Great Britain.   In 1882 Alfred Russel Wallace published his *Land Nationalisation*.   But by that time British Socialism was beginning anew.

BOOKS

G. D. H. Cole.   *British Working-class Politics, 1832–1914.*
S. and B. Webb.   *History of Trade Unionism.*
S. and B. Webb.   *Industrial Democracy.*
A. W. Humphrey.   *History of Labour Representation.*
H. Broadhurst.   *Autobiography.*
G. Howell.   *Labour Legislation, Labour Movements, Labour Leaders.*
T. Johnston.   *History of the Working Classes in Scotland.*

CHAPTER VIII

SOCIALISM AND THE DOCK STRIKE

1. THE RETURN OF SOCIALISM

By 1880 the continental Socialist Movement was beginning to take its modern shape, and to recover from the repression which had followed the Paris Commune of 1871. In Germany the followers of Marx and Lassalle had united in 1875 to form the unified German Social Democratic Party on the basis of the Gotha Programme. In France, Jules Guesde had organised the Parti Ouvrier in 1876. Both these Parties, as well as the rising movements of other countries, were Marxian in theory, and stood for Socialist parliamentary action and the public ownership of the means of production, which now for the first time appeared as the distinctive Socialist doctrine.

It was natural that in Great Britain, when in face of trade depression Trade Unionism was losing strength and the benefits of Liberal-Labour political action were beginning to be questioned, the idea should arise of forming a new working-class party to act on independent lines. The political attitude of the British workers found expression at this time chiefly through the Radical working-men's clubs, which were becoming restive as Liberalism decayed and had less to offer them. These clubs were Radical, but in no sense Socialist. They stood, however, for an advanced programme of land reform, on the lines advocated by the Land Tenure Reform Association and the other bodies mentioned in the last chapter.

In 1879 Henry George published in America his *Progress and Poverty*, advocating the Single Tax on land as the cure for all the ills of society. The book was at once introduced into Great Britain, and was widely read. The land campaigns of the 'seventies had prepared the way for it ; and its influence was very great. But in Great Britain the main inference drawn from Henry George's arguments was that the land should pass, by nationalisation, into public ownership.

It was at this stage that Henry Mayers Hyndman, a well-known Radical writer and a man of some wealth, conceived the idea of creating an independent working-class political movement in Great Britain. His idea was, or so he put it, something like a revival of the Chartist agitation. Hyndman had read Marx, and he appealed to Marx, still resident in London, for advice. Marx, he says, was doubtful of the practicability of the scheme ; but it appears that Marx was doubtful of Hyndman as well as of the plan itself.

In any case, Hyndman determined to take the plunge, and to try to build up an organisation first of all on the basis of the London Radical Working Men's Clubs. In 1881, as a result of his efforts, the Democratic Federation was formed, and in the same year he published *England for All*, a short book in which he expounded his policy, basing his fundamental doctrines directly on Marx's *Capital*.

The Democratic Federation, however, was not at the outset in any sense a Socialist or Marxian body. Its demands were for the most part those of the Chartists and of earlier generations of Reformers from the days of Major Cartwright. It stood for Universal Suffrage, Equal Electoral Divisions, Payment of Members, Abolition of the House of Lords, Prevention of Bribery and Corruption, and Triennial (instead of Annual) Parliaments. Its only other claims were for Self-government for Ireland and the Colonies and Dependencies, and for Nationalisation of the Land. In fact, Hyndman, Socialist as he himself had become, set out to create, not a Socialist Party, but an independent working-class agitation for Reform on the old Chartist lines.

For a time the tide seemed to be flowing in favour of his plan. In 1882 Henry George came to the United Kingdom, and set out on a lecture tour in Ireland, accompanied by J. L. Joynes, a master at Eton and one of the pioneers of the new Socialist Movement. The Government arrested them both and removed them from Ireland. George, on his release, lectured in England, and had the wider influence because of the Government's action. In the same year the Trades Union Congress, against the will of the platform, carried a resolution in favour of the Nationalisation of the Land.

The Radical Clubs, however, refused to be captured by the Democratic Federation, and the vote of the Trades Union Congress was reversed, in a fuller meeting, the following year. It became clear that, in face of the strength of Liberal-Labour doctrines in the Clubs and Trade Unions, there was no prospect of a big independent organisation based on either. The Democratic Federation had attracted few who were not Socialists, and in 1883 it changed front, and became definitely a Socialist body, with a more distinctly Socialist programme. It now declared for nationalisation of banking and railways as well as of land, for State-aided schemes of working-class housing, for universal free education and school feeding, for the legal eight hours' day, for the public provision of work for the unemployed in Co-operative groups and workshops, for progressively graduated taxation, and for the speedy redemption of the National Debt. In the following year, it started *Justice*, the first modern Socialist periodical in Great Britain, and adopted the name of " Social Democratic Federation." It also found in William Morris, poet and craftsman and the leader of a movement in the arts based largely on the teachings of John Ruskin, a powerful new recruit, who brought both money and energy to the Socialist cause.

Scarcely, however, had this reorganisation been carried through when violent dissensions arose inside the Social Democratic Federation. It had been joined by men of very different views on questions of policy—from orthodox Social Democrats who believed in parliamentary action to Anarchists who would have none of it, and from keen Trade Unionists who wanted to reform the Unions from within to pure politicians who regarded the Unions as mere impediments to the conversion of the workers to Socialism. In particular, it absorbed a most indigestible morsel in Joseph Lane's Labour Emancipation League, which was definitely anarchist in doctrine, and had a considerable following in the East End of London. All sections were agreed in attacking the Trade Unions as they were ; and in 1884 the S.D.F. issued a manifesto violently denouncing them for their compromising policy and their indifference to the plight of the unskilled workers and the " bottom dogs." But the Socialists were not agreed about the attitude which the workers ought to adopt towards the Trade Unions. A third, and equally serious, cause of dissension was personal. Hyndman was both exclusively political in his outlook and extremely autocratic in his methods. Soon, within the S.D.F., relations were severely strained.

By the end of 1884 these dissensions had led to a positive split. Under the leadership of William Morris and Belfort Bax, the malcontents, including the Labour Emancipation League, broke off, and founded a rival body—the Socialist League. The chief occasion of the split seems to have arisen over Hyndman's autocratic conduct of the Federation's affairs ; but behind this lay a dispute about the question of immediate parliamentary action. Hyndman and his followers had made up their minds that the S.D.F. must take the field at once as a political party, and begin to fight parliamentary elections. Morris and his followers, who included the Anarchists, were opposed to this either because they were against parliamentary action altogether, or because they thought electioneering premature until by Socialist propaganda the electorate had been much more fully educated in the new ideas. The seceders had the support of Friedrich Engels, the leader of Marxist thought after Marx's death in 1883.

The Socialist League was never a large body. But under Morris and Belfort Bax it had for a time a considerable educational influence, especially on the Clyde and in Yorkshire. In 1885 it started the *Commonweal*, which Morris edited until 1889, contributing to it *News from Nowhere* and many of his best Socialist writings. For it he wrote, in collaboration with Belfort Bax, *Socialism, Its Growth and Outcome*, expounding the Marxian theory of history and the struggle of classes. The Socialist League opposed parliamentary action, and laid stress on the necessity of building up the new Society on the basis of a Trade Unionism purged of reformism and converted to Socialist ideas. It borrowed, like Syndicalism later, from Anarchist ideas of social organisation, and anticipated much of Guild Socialist doctrine.

But gradually the Anarchist element in it got the upper hand. In 1889 Morris was deprived of the editorship of the *Commonweal;* and in the following year he resigned from the League. Thereafter the Socialist League fell to pieces, and only a remnant of Morris's own followers held together in the little Hammersmith Socialist Society until their leader's death in 1896.

While the Social Democratic Federation was being torn asunder by the conflict between the followers of Hyndman and Morris, a Socialist body of a very different kind was being born in an obscurity from which it gradually emerged into a position of considerable influence. This was the Fabian Society, founded in 1884 by a small group of " intellectuals " who, joined at an early stage by Bernard Shaw and Sidney Webb, set out to formulate a Socialist doctrine widely different both from Marxism and from the Anarchism which had been the principal rival of Marxism in the disputations of the S.D.F. The Fabians built their Socialist economics and their Socialist political theory not on Marx but on John Stuart Mill and Jevons. They argued that the Utilitarian principle of " the greatest happiness of the greatest number " could best be promoted, not by *laissez-faire,* but by State intervention and State control and ownership of the means of production, distribution and exchange. To this end, they sought, not, like Marx, to destroy the State and establish a proletarian dictatorship, but to use the instrument of the franchise, newly widened in 1884, to capture Parliament and thus convert the State into an instrument of public welfare. The influence of the Fabians was small at first ; but presently they began to pour out a stream of tracts applying their doctrines to particular problems and expounding their " new Utilitarian " philosophy. The publication of *Fabian Essays* in 1889, and their work in Local Government, and especially in the London County Council established that year, brought them into prominence ; and the high quality of their writings gave them an influence extending far beyond their membership.

Meanwhile, the Social Democratic Federation went on its way under the leadership of Hyndman and H. H. Champion. In 1885, after the Reform Act, came a General Election. The S.D.F., helped in two cases by the money of Conservatives who hoped to split the Liberal vote, put up three candidates. At Nottingham, John Burns, without the aid of " Tory gold," got 598 votes. The other two candidates, at Kennington and Hampstead, polled 32 and 27. The fiasco was complete, and seemed likely to deal the S.D.F. a crushing blow.

The trade slump saved it. There had been a revival of industry from 1881 to 1883 ; but from 1884 to 1886 trade got progressively worse. Unemployment rose from just over 2 per cent. in 1882 to over 10 per cent. in 1886. The S.D.F. retrieved its position by putting itself at the head of a growing agitation among the unemployed. In 1886 and 1887 the new

Socialism first began to be an influence beyond a narrow circle in London, and to produce an impression on the Trade Union Movement. The changed situation speedily influenced its attitude. In 1884 it had regarded the Trade Unions merely as reactionary craft organisations which diverted the workers' minds from Socialism. In 1887 it urged all its members to join Unions and to work from the inside for their conversion to a Socialist attitude. From the beginning of the unemployed agitation to the great Dock Strike of 1889, the S.D.F., which had been a purely political body, assumed the leadership of a growing industrial agitation. In order to follow this startling development, we must now survey the new forces which, in the 'eighties, were arising in the Trade Union world to challenge the supremacy of the old leaders. For, while Socialism was developing as a political creed, the Unions were also undergoing a process of transformation from within which corresponded to the changed economic situation.

BOOKS

G. D. H. Cole. *British Working-class Politics, 1832-1914.*
M. Beer. *History of British Socialism*, Vol. II.
T. Kirkup and E. R. Pease. *History of Socialism.*
S. Webb. *Socialism in England.*
J. W. Mackail. *Life of William Morris.*
H. M. Hyndman. *Record of an Adventurous Life.*
G. B. Shaw. *Early History of the Fabian Society.*
G. B. Shaw (ed.). *Fabian Essays.*
Margaret Cole. *Beatrice Webb.*
E. R. Pease. *History of the Fabian Society.*
J. B. Glasier. *William Morris and the Early Days of the Socialist Movement.*
J. Clayton. *The Rise and Decline of Socialism in England.*

2. THE TRADE UNION REVIVAL

We have seen how, in the early 'seventies, there was a great rush into the Trade Unions of workers who had been unorganised until then. The Miners' Unions had become a power in the 'sixties ; but both the National Union and the Amalgamated Association of Miners reached their high-water mark in the early 'seventies. Then Joseph Arch organised the agricultural labourers ; then the railwaymen formed their Amalgamated Society ; then the Gas-stokers created their Union which went down in the prosecutions of 1872. We have seen, also, how this " New Unionism " of the 'seventies died out in the trade depression which reached its height in 1879. The Amalgamated Society of Railway Servants shrank up into a friendly society of small membership and influence ; the agricultural Unions mostly disappeared. The Amalgamated Miners' Association died out ; and the National Union hardly survived outside Northumberland and Durham, though it continued to act as the convening body for periodical National Conferences of delegates from the various coalfields. Separate Unions in the main coalfields survived ; but they were greatly weakened, and in South Wales in particular only a shadow of organisation was left.

In the depression, as we have noted already, the miners in most of the coalfields passed under the operation of the " sliding scale." But early in the 'eighties the revolt against this system set in. The falling price level made it work peculiarly to the miners' disadvantage, and everywhere wages had dropped more heavily than in other trades. This fact led to a campaign amongst the younger miners against the sliding scale system, and in favour of the establishment of a minimum, not regulated by the price of coal, below which wages should not be allowed to fall. In 1881 the Yorkshire miners, hitherto divided into two separate associations, amalgamated to form the Yorkshire Miners' Association, and ended the sliding scale system.

During the next few years, there was great activity in the coalfields. In 1882 the Lancashire Miners, almost unorganised since the fall of the " Amalgamated," united to form the Lancashire and Cheshire Miners' Federation. In the West of Scotland, Keir Hardie became active in the Ayrshire Miners' Union, of which he became the first secretary on its reorganisation. In 1885 the Mid and West Lothian Miners' Association was re-formed ; and in 1886 the various Unions in Scotland joined together in the Scottish Miners' Federation. The Midland Miners' Federation was formed in 1885. In South Wales and in the North East there were serious troubles over the sliding scale. The Durham Miners terminated the scale in 1884, and were with difficulty persuaded by their leaders to renew it. In South Wales, where, except in Monmouthshire, only a shadowy Sliding Scale Association kept the various districts together, the formation of a new Federation of the district bodies was proposed at the Sliding Scale Conference of 1886, and in the following year the men voted to end the scale, and were with difficulty talked into renewing it. In the same year the Northumberland Miners struck unsuccessfully against a reduction in wages.

At length, in 1888, a new move was made. The districts which were against the sliding scale and in favour of a minimum wage decided at a National Conference to form a new Federation of their own, and to throw off their shadowy allegiance to the old National Union, now wholly dominated by the Northumberland and Durham leaders. No district governed by a sliding scale was to be allowed to enter the new body. Thus the Miners' Federation of Great Britain was born. It began with only 36,000 members, but rose rapidly to over 200,000 in 1893. Durham and Northumberland, with a few small districts, remained outside. Not until 1908 did the two great districts of the North East throw in their lot with the new Federation.

The battle against the sliding scale, however, was in most districts speedily won. Durham ended it in 1889, and soon South Wales, where it survived till 1903, was the only important district still regulated by this system. The delegates of the new Miners' Federation became a power at the Trades Union Congress, and lent valuable aid in its transformation under the influence of the new ideas.

In other industries, also, new Unions were arising. In 1881 the woollen industry, hitherto almost unorganised, apart from a few small skilled crafts, ever since the overthrow of the great Clothiers' Union in 1834, created the General Union of Textile Workers, in which the spinners, weavers, and less skilled workers began to enrol in considerable numbers. In 1884 the remaining local Weavers' Associations joined the North East Lancashire Weavers' Amalgamation, and formed the Amalgamated Weavers' Association. The Card and Blowing Room Operatives' Amalgamation followed in 1886, and in the following year nearly all the Unions in the cotton trades drew together in the United Textile Factory Workers' Association, a body formed less for industrial purposes than for the promotion of factory reform by political means. In the same year, John Hodge formed in Scotland the Steel Smelters' Union, and began his long and ultimately successful fight against the " contract " system in the iron and steel trades, in which it had been the practice for a small minority of highly skilled leading hands to exploit the main body of the workers by employing them at day wages, while they themselves appropriated the piecework balances accruing under their contracts with the employers. A similar system, known in some coalfields as the " butty " system, was widely used in coal-mining, and its destruction was one of the main objects of the new Miners' Federation of Great Britain. In the same year, 1887, Ben Tillett, a docker in the Port of London, formed the Tea Operatives' and General Labourers' Union, and began the great struggle of the transport workers, while in the North, Havelock Wilson began building up the National Sailors' and Firemen's Union.

In yet other respects 1887 was a fateful year. Then both the unemployed troubles and the struggle between old and new at the Trades Union Congress reached a critical phase. The struggle at Congress had really begun with the Land Nationalisation resolution carried in 1882. But, as we have seen, this decision was reversed in the following year, and until 1887 similar resolutions were regularly defeated. In 1883, however, Adam Weiler, an old Socialist and former follower of Marx in the " International," successfully carried, against the platform, a resolution in favour of the legal eight hours' day. But, even so, nothing was done by the Parliamentary Committee, still dominated by the old school, to make this effective.

The first really organised attack of the " new " Unionists came in 1887, the first Congress attended by Keir Hardie. The Parliamentary Committee, under pressure from Congress, had sent delegates to the International Labour Congresses of 1883 and 1886 ; but when the latter Congress instructed them to convene its successor in London, they referred the proposal to the 1887 Trades Union Congress, and played for its rejection. On this point the old school leaders met their first signal defeat. A second followed when the Congress again voted for the Nationalisation of the Land.

In the meantime, the Social Democrats had placed themselves at the head of the unemployed agitation. Protectionism, under the name of " Fair Trade," was in these years the theme of an active campaign, which extended to the sending of subsidised delegates, nominally representing small Trade Unions, to the Trades Union Congress. In January 1886, the Fair Traders arranged for a demonstration in Trafalgar Square. The Social Democrats at once organised a counter-demonstration of the unemployed for the same time and place. The police shifted the unemployed procession away from the Square towards Hyde Park. As it passed along Pall Mall, there were jeers from the windows of some of the fashionable clubs, and the demonstrators replied by smashing the windows. Hyndman, John Burns, H. H. Champion and J. E. Williams, all leading figures in the Social Democratic Federation, were then arrested, and brought to trial. Burns delivered a fiery speech in court, winning for himself his nickname "The Man with the Red Flag," and Hyndman practised diplomacy. All four were acquitted by the jury. This incident gave a great impetus to the agitation. Immediately after the procession a large relief fund was raised for the unemployed, and the prestige of the Social Democrats was greatly increased.

In 1887 trade, though still bad, was improving, and the unemployed agitation began to ebb. But by this time the Social Democrats had other strings to their bow. A great Radical demonstration on the Irish question had been arranged for Trafalgar Square ; but the use of the Square was forbidden by the Government. The demonstrators resolved to defy the prohibition, and publicly announced that they proposed to hold the meeting. The Government packed the Square with soldiers and police, through whose ranks columns of demonstrators fought in vain to make a passage. Many were injured, and John Burns and Cunninghame Graham were arrested and sentenced to six weeks' imprisonment. The day of the meeting came to be known as " Bloody Sunday." But other meetings followed, and at one, in 1888, a workman named Linnell was killed by the police. The Socialists arranged a great funeral procession, and William Morris wrote his death-chant for the occasion :—

> " Not one, not one, nor thousands must they slay,
> But one and all if they would dusk the day."

During these years the propaganda of the Socialists first reached the ears of the ordinary workman. There was a rain of pamphlets and leaflets, and the Socialist press attained to a respectable circulation. *Justice* and the *Commonweal* were reinforced by other papers. In 1887 Keir Hardie founded *The Miner*, which grew into the *Labour Leader* two years later. In 1888

Champion started *The Labour Elector*, as the organ of the movement for independent Labour representation in Parliament. Annie Besant edited
another new journal, *The Link*, devoted chiefly to the struggle for free speech
and for the rights of public meeting and procession. It gave great publicity
to the proceedings of Charles Bradlaugh's Law and Labour League, which
joined with the Socialists in the contest with the police and the Government.
Bradlaugh was no Socialist ; but he was a doughty Radical and Republican,
as well as a " notorious infidel and blasphemer." He had at this time a
great popular following, and Annie Besant for a time worked closely with
him. In all these papers the old Trade Union leaders, and the " Lib-Labs "
in Parliament, were fiercely attacked. In 1888, moreover, the movement for
Labour representation took a new direction. Keir Hardie stood as Independent Labour candidate in a three-cornered by-election at Mid-Lanark. The
" Lib-Lab " leaders of the Labour Electoral Association first tried to persuade
him to withdraw, and then opposed him, and he got only 712 votes. But
the results were far-reaching. At the beginning of 1889 the Scottish Labour
Party came into being as a direct outcome of the contest. A new movement
for Labour representation was beginning outside and apart from the Social
Democratic Federation. Its foundations had been laid earlier in the 'eighties
by the Scottish Land Restoration League, which had succeeded in getting two
representatives of the Highland crofters returned to Parliament in 1885.
Cunninghame Graham, who had won his seat as a Radical at the same
election, also gave support to the new Scottish Party.

A discussion of the significance of this new development will arise when
we have carried somewhat further the story of the " New Unionism " which
was behind it. We have seen how Trade Unionism, under the control of the
older leaders, had surrendered to *laissez-faire* ideas, just at the time when
these ideas were wearing out in face of the changing conditions of trade and
industry. The leaders, with a few exceptions, were as vehement as the
employers against State regulation of wages and conditions, and believed in
settling all issues by methods of conciliation which rested on the assumption
that the real interests of Capital and Labour were the same. The Socialists,
reacting against this view, were at first disposed to dismiss the Trade Unions
as useless, or even to regard them as bulwarks of Capitalism and as means of
keeping the workers divided into craft groups and so concealing the real
unity of their class interests. This was the basis of the S.D.F.'s attack on
Trade Unions in 1884. Later, under the influence of Tom Mann and other
leaders of the younger Trade Unionists, the S.D.F. officially changed its tune,
and advised all its members to join their Unions and to work for their transformation from within. But most of the Socialist leaders were still inclined
to envisage the class struggle as purely a political affair ; and the S.D.F., as an
organisation, was never quite at home in its dealings even with the new
Unions which were springing up.

There were several reasons for this.   One was the domineering personality and exclusively political outlook of Hyndman, and his ascendancy in the
S.D.F.   A second was the use of a pedantic Marxian phraseology which was
so much Greek, not only to the main body of the workers, but even to most
of the new Trade Union leaders.   The rigidly dogmatic Marxism of the
S.D.F. was indeed a long way off Marx's own attitude, and earned the strong
disapproval of his surviving partner, Engels.   A third reason, certainly not
less important, for the Socialists' lack of success, was that the S.D.F. paid the
penalty of being the pioneer.   It had been for some years a tiny circle of
theoretical Socialists, endeavouring to preach the new gospel to an uninterested world.   Inevitably, it had on its hands ample time and opportunity
for exploring its own theoretical position.   But such a situation gives the
maximum of chance, both for the development of dissensions on points of
theory, and for the working out, on the basis of these dissensions, of a
rigid theoretical orthodoxy which it is treason to question.   In this sense,
and for these reasons, the S.D.F. by 1888 had become highly doctrinaire,
and had proportionately lost its efficiency and appeal as a propagandist
body.

The " New " Unionists were hardly less political in outlook than the
S.D.F., and, as far as their immediate programme was concerned, were
advocating many of the same reforms.   But their tendency, even if they were
Socialists and members of the S.D.F., was to concentrate attention on these
reforms, and to give their whole agitation a severely practical turn.   In the
years of which we have been speaking, the first planks in their platform were
the compulsory eight hours' day and the living wage.   In the unemployed
agitation they put forward the eight hours' day as the cure for unemployment
—Tom Mann published his pamphlet expounding this view in 1886.   In the
Trades Union Congress they fought the old leaders on the question of an
Eight Hours Bill.   In their Union branches they stressed above all this and
the need for a legal minimum wage.   When Nationalisation figured at all in
their propaganda, it occupied a far less prominent position than these
reforms.

But if the remedies proposed by the " New " Unionists were legislative,
they could clearly hold out no hope of immediate legislation.   And the
mass of the workers to whom they made their appeal wanted something
immediate.   Inevitably, the outcome of their propaganda, as soon as
trade became good enough to offer a hope of success, was an outbreak of
strikes.

By 1888 unemployment had fallen from over 10 per cent. to 5 per cent.,
and trade was rapidly improving.   A small, but significant, strike in May of
this year was the advance warning of the coming upheaval.   In *The Link*,
Mrs. Besant exposed the appalling conditions of the London match-girls.
The article reached the girls, and nearly 700 of them struck work.   Mrs.

Besant and her friends gathered funds to help them, and after a fortnight the employers gave way. The first blow had been delivered, but few realised in 1888 how great a struggle was soon to come.

BOOKS

G. D. H. Cole. *British Working-class Politics, 1832-1914.*
S. and B. Webb. *History of Trade Unionism.*
G. Howell. *Trade Unionism, New and Old.*
W. J. Davis. *History of the Trades Union Congress.*
T. Mann. *Memoirs.*
J. Clayton. *Rise and Decline of Socialism.*
H. B. Bonner. *Life of Charles Bradlaugh.*
T. Besterman. *Life of Annie Besant.*
H. M. Hyndman. *The Record of an Adventurous Life.*
J. W. Mackail. *Life of William Morris.*
A. Vallance. *William Morris.*

3. THE LONDON DOCK STRIKE

In the annals of the working-class movement, 1889 is remembered chiefly as the year of the great Dock Strike in London. It is really much more than that—a year in which the gathering storm of industrial unrest suddenly burst, and the New Unionism became a recognised power in Great Britain.

Trade was very good, better than it had been since the early 'seventies. The great depression seemed to be quite over, and the lost markets to have been made good. Practically every industry except agriculture was prosperous. Unemployment had fallen to little more than two per cent., and remained at that level through both 1889 and 1890. The opportunity was therefore extraordinarily favourable for a forward industrial movement.

As in 1872, but with better success, the London gasworkers took the lead. Early in 1889 they began again to organise, and in May the Gasworkers' and General Labourers' Union was formed, with Will Thorne at its head. At this time the gasworkers worked a twelve-hours shift : they now demanded the immediate concession of the eight hours day. In August the demand was formally presented, and to the general surprise the gas companies gave way. The Gasworkers' Union had won the eight hours' day without striking a blow.

A few months later came a set-back. There were three big gas companies in London. At two of these no trouble arose ; but the third, under Sir George Livesey, made up its mind to fight the Union. At the end of 1889 it again enforced the twelve-hours shift, and refused to employ Trade Unionists, instituting at the same time a scheme of profit-sharing. In this case the men were beaten ; but elsewhere the eight-hours day was retained, and in some cases a higher wage was secured as well.

In August, the set-back of December was not foreseen, and the Gas-workers' success had its immediate reactions throughout the country. Especially it affected the position at the London docks, where a small strike had broken out at the West India Dock just at the moment of the Gasworkers' victory. Swiftly the movement spread, until practically all Dockside was at a standstill. Everywhere the men demanded a wage of sixpence an hour, special payment for overtime, the abolition of sub-contracting and piecework, and that four hours (or a half shift) should be the minimum period of employment. Ten thousand men came out on strike.

The vast majority of the dockers were at this time outside any Union. The Stevedores (the skilled men who load ships) had two Unions, and were fairly well organised. The only dock labourers' Union seems to have been the little Tea-porters' and General Labourers' Union, founded by Ben Tillett two years before. But during the dispute the strikers streamed rapidly into the Unions, and " Trade Unionism for All " became the war-cry of the " New Unionists."

The dockers' struggle lasted for a month, and received wider publicity throughout the world than had been given to any previous dispute. Nearly £50,000 was raised by public subscription for the strikers, and this enabled reasonable strike allowances to be paid. The dock employers, for all their efforts, were unable to secure an adequate supply of blacklegs ; for the feeling of solidarity had spread from trade to trade, and the striking dockers, with public sympathy behind them, had sometimes a short way with interlopers. The employers felt even middle-class opinion to be against them. The first results of Charles Booth's great survey of the *Life and Labour of the People of London* had opportunely just been made public, and no one could defend the appalling conditions under which the casually employed dockers lived and worked. Finally, Cardinal Manning and Sydney Buxton were accepted as mediators, and practically the whole of the dockers' demands were conceded. The " docker's tanner " became an accomplished fact.

The dock strike gave the Socialists an even better opportunity for propaganda than the unemployed agitation of three years before. They led the struggle. Ben Tillett was aided by Tom Mann and John Burns, who, both engineers by trade and members of the A.S.E., became the chief organisers of the dock workers. Burns, indeed, was the real leader of the strike—at any rate in the eyes of the public. He had a flair for publicity ; but he also used his prominence to good effect. Burns took the greatest care to keep on good terms with the police, and to check disorder—which might easily have wrecked the strikers' chances. His famous white straw hat, in which he went everywhere, was meant not only to put him in the public eye, but also to get the strikers to recognise and to take notice of him when he intervened to prevent trouble.

The resounding successes of the gasworkers and dockers in London at once produced their effects all over the country. The Sailors' and Firemen's Union enrolled many thousands of members. While the Tea-porters' Union was being transformed into the Dock, Wharf, Riverside, and General Workers' Union, with Tillett as secretary, James Sexton was creating the National Union of Dock Labourers at Liverpool, and this Society soon spread to Scotland and Ireland. On the North-East Coast the Tyneside and National Labour Union, which later became the National Amalgamated Union of Labour, enrolled both dockers and general workers and even spread into the mining districts. The Gasworkers' Union became a national body, and organised not only gasworkers, but also general labourers of every kind. The National Agricultural Labourers' Union revived, and a new body, the Eastern Counties Labour Federation, enrolled 17,000 members, including both farm and general workers. The General Railway Workers' Union arose as a more militant rival to the old-fashioned and inactive Amalgamated Society of Railway Servants.

These new Unions differed markedly in policy and organisation from the older Amalgamated Societies. It had been a firm principle of the " Old " Unionists—once, in their day, the " New "—that Trade Unionism could thrive only on the basis of a firm conjunction of trade and friendly activities. They aimed at holding their members in times of bad trade by means of friendly benefits. The member who had paid money into his society in expectation of superannuation benefit in his old age had a plain interest in keeping up his contributions, even at a considerable sacrifice and even when his Union could do little for him industrially. The Old Unionists held that Unions formed on any other basis might thrive temporarily in times of trade prosperity and industrial unrest, but that they would necessarily perish in the subsequent depression.

There was evident force in this argument ; but it wholly ignored the disadvantages of the type of organisation in which the " Old " Unionists believed. Societies of this type were compelled to have high rates of contribution, and to be very careful of their funds. The latter obligation led them to discourage even justifiable strikes and forward movements, and to place all their reliance on conciliation and arbitration ; the former had an even more serious drawback in that it practically restricted their membership to those who could afford high contributions—that is, to a limited group of relatively well paid and highly skilled workers.

It is true that this type of Unionism was not at any time universal. In the cotton trades, while the Spinners' Unions were of this kind, the Weavers' and Cardroom Operatives' Unions, having to cater largely for women's labour, could not force up rates of contribution at all high. And among the miners, while in Northumberland and Durham and in one or two other districts the Miners' Associations became largely assimilated to the " Amalgamated

Societies " of the skilled craftsmen, lower contributions and a more inclusive policy were more the rule, and became the recognised basis of the new Unions founded in the 'eighties, and of the Miners' Federation of Great Britain.

These two industries stood, however, somewhat apart from the rest, and the Amalgamated Societies of Engineers, Carpenters and other types of skilled workers appeared far more typical of the " Old " Unionism which the " New " Unionists were out to challenge. In most cases, the " New " Unions dispensed with friendly benefits altogether, and concentrated on the possession of funds for use in strikes and lock-outs and in the expenses of organising and administration. Their leaders denounced friendly benefits as leading to stagnation and reaction in industrial policy. They set out to build up Unions which would be able to appeal to the entire working class, and to follow a fighting policy based on class solidarity and directed, by implication at any rate, against the capitalist system itself. In short, the " New " Unions were in intention Socialist, in the sense that the leaders, while they concentrated on immediate " bread and butter " issues, had as their further objective a definitely Socialist policy of class organisation and action.

The industrial unrest of 1889 reacted on the " Old " Unions in addition to creating the " New." In 1889 the skilled workers' Societies in the engine shops and shipyards at last drew together, under the influence of Robert Knight, the leader of the Boilermakers, in the Engineering and Shipbuilding Trades Federation. The membership of the " Old " Unions went up by leaps and bounds. The Bricklayers and the Railway Servants more than doubled their membership ; the Boot and Shoe Operatives rose from 12,000 in 1888 to over 30,000 in 1891. The Engineers, the Carpenters—in short, every Union—experienced an inrush of new members. There are no exact figures of total Trade Union membership before 1892 ; but it is safe to say that before 1888 there were not more than three-quarters of a million Trade Unionists in Great Britain. By 1892 the total had risen to over a million and a half.

From the less skilled manual workers the wave of organisation spread to the " black-coated proletariat." The National Union of Clerks was formed in 1890, and in the following year came the Shop Assistants' Union and the Manchester Society which developed into the Amalgamated Union of Co-operative Employees. These did not gain many members ; but their beginning was none the less significant of the spreading of the new ideas.

The idea of solidarity, prominent in the upheaval of 1889, led to a great extension in the number of Trades Councils, through which the local re-presentatives of the " Old " and " New " Unions were brought together. Of the Trades Councils still alive in 1910, 11 were formed in 1889, 19 in 1890, and 21 in 1891. The remainder of the 'nineties added another 53. Thus, as a result of the " New " Unionism, Trades Councils, previously found as a rule only in the larger centres, spread over practically the whole of the industrial districts, and provided an opportunity for Socialist propaganda, and for the regular interchange of information and ideas between trade and trade.

Wages rose sharply during this great boom in Trade Union activity. With or without strikes, the workers in nearly every trade secured advances. Wages rose least among the skilled craftsmen enrolled in the old-fashioned Unions ; but even they added greatly to their membership and secured a share in the general improvement. The largest gains of all went to the miners ; the wages of coal-hewers actually rose by more than a third between 1888, when the Miners' Federation was formed, and 1891. Practically all the " new " Unions of less skilled workers gained substantial advances for their members. On the average, wages in all trades rose at least 10 per cent. in these three years, whereas prices rose less than 4 per cent.

The effect of these successes was speedily shown at the Trades Union Congress. In 1889, indeed, the " New " Unionists suffered a defeat. Making the mistake of attacking the persons rather than the policy of the old leaders, they delivered a frontal onslaught on Henry Broadhurst, then Secretary of the Congress, accusing him of personal corruption. This attack aroused intense antagonism on the part of the delegates, and the Socialists were overwhelmingly beaten. By the following year they had learnt wisdom, and, eschewing personal attacks, put forward a long series of resolutions embodying their policy. The demand for a legal eight hours' day, long the test issue between the parties, was at last endorsed, and nearly all the Socialist resolutions were carried. The " New " Unionism had captured the Trades Union Congress, and Henry Broadhurst resigned his position as Secretary.

This victory was, of course, due to the conversion of many of the older Unions. The delegates of the Engineers and the Carpenters all voted, under instructions, in favour of the legal eight hours' day. The Socialists had not only founded the " New " Unions, but were also rapidly permeating the old.

The object of the Socialist leaders of the " New " Unions was not, however, to be secured merely by the passing of their resolutions at the Trades Union Congress. Their policy was one of State action, and almost all their main demands were demands for legislation. In these circumstances, they aimed above all at the creation of a powerful working-class political party, ready to pursue an independent policy based on Socialist ideas. The political movement which gave rise to the Independent Labour Party and to the Labour Party came naturally out of the industrial movement which created the " New " Unionism. Out of the Socialist propaganda of the 'eighties

had come the " New " Unions ; now out of the " New " Unions came a
new political movement.

BOOKS

S. and B. Webb. *History of Trade Unionism.*
G. Howell. *Trade Unionism, New and Old.*
T. Mann. *Memoirs.*
B. Tillett. *History of the Dockers' Union.*
J. Burgess. *John Burns.*
H. H. Champion. *The Great Dock Strike.*
H. Llewellyn Smith and Vaughan Nash. *The Dockers' Strike.*
G. D. H. Cole. *Keir Hardie* (Fabian Tract).
G. D. H. Cole. *John Burns* (Fabian Tract).
G. D. H. Cole. *British Working-class Politics, 1832–1914.*

CHAPTER IX

INDEPENDENT LABOUR

1. The Independent Labour Party   2. Trade Unionism in the 'Nineties
3. The Labour Representation Committee

I. THE INDEPENDENT LABOUR PARTY

WE have seen how, in 1888, Keir Hardie stood as third candidate for Mid-Lanark, and how in the following year the Scottish Labour Party arose out of the contest. After 1889, there was a rapid growth of similar organisations in all parts of the country. In 1891 the London Trades Council formed a London Labour Representation Committee, and in the provinces the Bradford Labour Union, the Colne Valley Labour Union, the Salford Labour Electoral Association, and many other bodies were created to work for independent Labour representation in Parliament and on local bodies. Many of the branches of the "Lib-Lab" Labour Electoral Association changed sides and rallied to the cause of independent labour representation. In 1890 Joseph Burgess started the *Workman's Times*, which became, with its local editions, an influential organ of the new opinions. It ceased to appear in 1894, when Keir Hardie's *Labour Leader* became a weekly, and took its place. Robert Blatchford, a propagandist writer of real genius with a warm-hearted sympathy for the "bottom-dog," founded the *Clarion* in 1891, and speedily made it the most widely read of all Labour journals, with a public extending far beyond Socialist circles. His book, *Merrie England*, marking the summit of his political influence, came out in 1894. *Fabian Essays* had been published in 1889, and through these years the Fabians, led by Bernard Shaw and Sidney Webb[1], poured out a steady stream of useful and informative tracts. The Socialists had at last an efficient press, and a good supply of propagandist literature.

The General Election of 1892 brought them their first parliamentary successes. On the wave of the new movement Keir Hardie was elected for West Ham, John Burns for Battersea, and J. Havelock Wilson, the leader of the then militant Sailors' and Firemen's Union, for Middlesbrough. Of these only Wilson won in a three-cornered fight. Joseph Leicester, who was in the field as a "Lib-Lab" against Hardie, withdrew before the poll, and Burns had only a Conservative against him. Twelve "Lib-Labs," mostly miners, but including also Joseph Arch and George Howell, were also returned in 1892.

---

[1] Beatrice Webb did not join the Fabian Society until 1893.

The political successes of the "Independents" greatly encouraged the Socialists, and led directly to the formation of a national organisation. At the 1892 Trades Union Congress a resolution for refusing Trade Union support to all non-Socialist candidates was only defeated by twenty-five votes. The advocates of independent Labour representation held, during Congress week, a meeting of their own with Keir Hardie as chairman, and decided to call a national conference for the purpose of forming a new party on national lines.

In January 1893 the Conference met at Bradford with Hardie again in the chair, and formed the Independent Labour Party, rejecting by a large majority the alternative name of Socialist Labour Party. One hundred and twenty-four delegates attended, representing mainly local bodies from all parts of the country. The Social Democratic Federation and the Fabian Society both sent delegates, but, for opposite reasons, refused to merge their identity in the new organisation. The S.D.F. regarded the I.L.P. as too compromising, whereas the Fabian delegate, Bernard Shaw, insisted that the Fabian Society could be most useful if it continued as a separate body its work of Socialist research, education and "permeation" of all who were open to its influence. The local Fabian Societies which had sprung up in many areas for the most part went over to the I.L.P., and were in no way discouraged from doing so by the parent Society. Practically all the local electoral bodies, including the Scottish Labour Party, came in. The I.L.P. began its existence with a large and widely diffused membership in numerous local bodies. At the very outset, its structure was meant to be federal ; but within a year the local bodies had either left or become branches of the new Party.

The object of the Independent Labour Party was defined in what were regarded as distinctively Socialist terms—" to secure the collective ownership all the means of production, distribution and exchange." Its programme, drawn up at the Conference, embodied a large number of immediate reforms, mostly to be achieved by legislation. These included the legal eight hours' day, the abolition of overtime, piece-work, and child labour, State provision out of taxes on unearned increment for the sick, the disabled, the aged, the widows and the orphans, the provision of properly paid work for the unemployed, the extension of the franchise, and the reform of taxation—a programme obviously designed for execution by an independent working-class political party, but at the same time clearly reformist and opposed to the revolutionary policy urged by the Social Democratic Federation.

Between the permeative tactics of the Fabians, who in the absence of a really effective Labour Party in Parliament believed mainly in influencing the older parties to adopt Socialist measures piecemeal, and the Marxian revolutionism of the S.D.F., Keir Hardie and his colleagues aimed at keeping a middle course. Unlike the Fabians, they were firmly opposed to any kind of collaboration with the Liberals—even with the Radical Liberals who supported Joseph Chamberlain's " Unauthorised Programme " of 1885. But they were no less hostile to the S.D.F., which, they alleged, scared away Trade Unionists by its talk of revolution, and uttered an unintelligible Marxian jargon devoid of propagandist appeal. Their aim was, while plainly affirming their ultimate Socialist aim, to concentrate their propaganda, as they had done in the " new " Unionist agitation, mainly on immediate reforms, in the hope of thus leading the main body of the working class gradually towards Socialism. Hence their rejection of the word " Socialist " from the title of their organisation ; hence their preference for the title " Independent Labour," which had already shown its appealing power, and more correctly expressed their immediate policy.

Even before the formation of the I.L.P., the " New " Unionists had been turning their attention to local as well as to national government. The Local Government Act of 1888 had enlarged the opportunities for such action, and in London and in the mining areas Labour candidates were put up for the new County Councils. John Burns was elected to the London County Council in 1889. In these developments the influence of the Fabians counted for a great deal ; for they, under Sidney Webb's influence, were keen advocates of " Municipal Socialism," and their pamphlets provided ammunition for Labour candidates at the local elections. The new I.L.P. eagerly took up this policy, which had much effect in training its members, by service on local bodies, for subsequent parliamentary activity.

The " New " Unionists had now a national party of their own—at least in embryo. They did not, however, cease to attempt the capture of the Trades Union Congress, or to urge the Trade Unions themselves to form an independent working-class party. At the Congress of 1893 they secured substantial successes. The delegates voted in favour of the establishment of a special fund for the support of independent working-class candidates, and also decided to support only candidates who subscribed to the Socialist slogan of " collective ownership and control of the means of production, distribution and exchange." Congress, however, still refused to go to the length of establishing an independent working-class party, and Hardie's amendment to secure this was defeated by twenty-three votes.

There is an apparent contradiction in the attitude of the new leaders who, having set up a political party of their own, were still endeavouring to persuade the Trades Union Congress to set up another. But the contradiction is only apparent. Throughout, the aim of Keir Hardie and his friends was to establish a political party under Socialist leadership and guidance, but definitely based on the mass organisation of the Trade Union movement. They were well aware that, without the active participation of the Trade Unions, they could not hope either to create or to finance a really powerful working-class party ; and they had set up the I.L.P. rather as the forerunner of an effective Labour Party than as itself the party they desired to see. Throughout the following years Hardie was never weary of affirming his belief in the policy of the " Labour Alliance," by which he meant the linking up of the Socialist I.L.P. with the organised economic power of the Trade Union movement.

This policy, of course, involved too much of compromise and of keeping Socialism in the background, to satisfy Hyndman and his followers of the S.D.F. They wanted a party definitely Marxian, and based on the model of the German Social Democratic Party. Also, they felt that, having done the pioneer work for Socialism in Great Britain, they were being brushed aside by the " New " Unionists for whose advent they were largely responsible. They were, however, helpless ; for Hardie's opportunist Socialism made a far stronger appeal than their Marxism to the younger Trade Unionists, because it offered an immediate and easily intelligible programme of reform directly grounded on Trade Union needs and claims.

One very important factor making for the I.L.P.'s success in its early days was the support given to it by Robert Blatchford and the very wide appeal of his journal, *The Clarion*, and of his book, *Merrie England*. Round Blatchford as leader and friend gathered a host of local groups and a number of organisations which did extremely effective propagandist work for Socialism. " Clarion " Vans toured the country with itinerant speakers ; " Clarion " Cycling Clubs, " Clarion " Dramatic Societies, " Clarion " Scouts, provided a social element which drew many thousands into the fellowship of Socialism. Blatchford and his faithful colleague, Alexander M. Thompson, gathered round them a team of writers who knew how to write for the common people as no one on the Labour side had written for them since the days of Cobbett. It is at any rate arguable that Blatchford won more converts to Socialism than anyone else—even than Keir Hardie.

The I.L.P., with this invaluable help, made rapid headway, while the S.D.F. stagnated. No further progress, indeed, was made at the Trades Union Congress of 1894, and no steps were taken by the Parliamentary Committee to give effect to the resolution for the establishment of a parliamentary fund. But Hardie was doing excellent propagandist work in the House of Commons, especially in connection with the Hull dockers' strike of 1893 and the national mining strike of the same year. The membership of the I.L.P. was growing rapidly, and many new branches were being formed. In 1895 the membership stood at 6,000, and included most of the younger active Trade Union leaders and the keenest local Labour workers in many districts. Weaknesses were to reveal themselves later ; but for the time the I.L.P. seemed to be undoubtedly on the road to success.

Set-backs were soon to come. In 1894 the new party fought several by-elections without success, and at the General Election of 1895 it put twenty-eight candidates in the field. Keir Hardie was among them ; but John Burns and Havelock Wilson had both remained outside the new body, and had by this time passed into definite hostility.   They both held their seats ; but Hardie, in a straight fight against a Conservative, lost his, and not a single I.L.P. member was returned.   The " Lib-Labs " lost three seats, and " Independent Labour " ceased for the time to be represented in the House of Commons.   Hyndman stood for Burnley, and the S.D.F. put up several other candidates ; but none came near being returned.

In the meantime, the Trades Union Congress had been reforming itself. The Socialist victory of 1893 had led to the charge that the Congress was being perverted to political uses, and in 1894 the Parliamentary Committee was instructed to revise the standing orders.   It used this power to make drastic changes.   In 1895 the Trades Councils, in which the " New " Unionist and Socialist element predominated, were expelled from Congress, though they had been its founders, on the plea that their presence involved " dual representation," their affiliated branches being represented also through the national Unions to which they belonged.   At the same time the personnel of the delegates was restricted to Trade Union officials or men actually working at their trades—a change which excluded not only John Burns, then actually Chairman of the Parliamentary Committee, but also both Henry Broadhurst and Keir Hardie, the leaders of the rival groups of " Old " and " New " Unionists.   The " card vote," under which decisions are taken, not by the delegates voting as individuals, but in accordance with the number of members represented by each delegate, was also introduced.   These changes went far to undo the Socialist victory of 1893, and postponed for a few years more the decisive entry of the Trade Union movement into independent political action.   James Mawdsley, the Conservative leader of the Cotton Spinners, is said to have been the prime mover in this change, which was carried through mainly by an appeal to working men to exclude political adventurers from their ranks—a manœuvre repeated in later years in the unsuccessful appeal during the first World War for a new Trade Union Labour Party free from the influence of Socialist " intellectuals."

The success of the Socialists at Congress was, however, only postponed, They were still able to get representatives elected as Trade Union delegates, and by 1899 their majority was again secure.   In 1897, and again in 1898, a proposal to ask the Unions whether they would agree to a political levy was defeated.   A number of Unions were, and had long been, paying the election expenses of their own members and supporting them while they sat in Parliament.   Some of the Miners' Unions had done this ever since 1874, and other Unions had followed their example.   But the proposal for a general levy to be paid into a common fund for Labour representation raised a different set of issues, and even in 1899 the Socialists were not strong enough to carry such a scheme.

Instead, and as the easier way of proceeding, the resolution carried by the Congress of 1899 instructed the Parliamentary Committee to call, apart from the Congress, a special Conference of representatives from " Co-operative, Socialist, Trade Union, and other working-class organisations " in order to " devise ways and means for the securing of an increased number of Labour Members in the next Parliament." No mention was made of a levy, and it was by no means clear that any form of permanent organisation was proposed.

Out of this equivocal resolution arose the Labour Party.

BOOKS

G. D. H. Cole. *British Working-class Politics, 1832-1914.*
G. D. H. Cole. *Keir Hardie.* (Fabian Tract).
W. Stewart. *Life of Keir Hardie.*
D. Lowe. *From Pit to Parliament.*
A. W. Humphrey. *History of Labour Representation.*
W. J. Davis. *History of the Trades Union Congress.*

2. TRADE UNIONISM IN THE 'NINETIES

While the " New " Unionists were busy forming the Independent Labour Party, and urging the Trades Union Congress to adopt a Socialist policy, the " New " Unionism itself was menaced by a change in the economic situation. By the end of 1891 the trade boom was at an end. Unemployment rose from 2 per cent. in 1890 to over 6 per cent. in 1892, and to over 7 per cent. in 1893. The membership represented at the Trades Union Congress fell from 1,593,000 in 1890 to 721,000 in 1893. The " New " Unions lost members almost as fast as they had made them during the boom. Once more the old leaders prophesied the speedy disappearance of the new forces which threatened their supremacy. Once more they proclaimed that only high contributions and friendly benefits, which the " New " Unionists denounced, could hold the workers together in any stable combination proof against the fluctuations of trade.

The old leaders were wrong. The " New " Unions were seriously reduced in membership ; but they did not disappear. After 1893 trade began to mend, and the years from 1896 to 1900 brought a fresh trade boom. In 1899, during the South African War, the unemployment rate again fell to 2 per cent., and by the end of the century the " New " Unions had regained most of the members they had lost. In 1900 the Trades Union Congress had 1,250,000 affiliated members, and the total number of Trade Unionists had risen again to 1,972,000—probably about the same total as ten years before. No figures of total membership are available before 1892, when the Board of Trade gave the number as 1,501,000 ; but this was probably a decline from the level of a year before.

The 'nineties were, for the Trade Unions, a time of trouble followed

by partial recovery. In 1891, alarmed by the growth of the " New " Union-
ism, the Conservative Government appointed a Royal Commission on
Labour, to discuss the entire question of industrial relations. Seven Trade
Unionists were given seats upon it ; but six of them belonged to the old
school, and Tom Mann was the only representative of the " New " Unionism.
The Commission did not issue its final Report until 1894 ; but from 1892 it
poured forth a stream of memoranda on all phases of the labour question.
In the event, it accomplished nothing ; but for a time it seemed as if it might
lead to a serious attack on the legal position gained by the Trade Unions in
1871 and 1875. A section of the Commissioners desired to introduce a
system under which collective agreements would become enforceable at
law, and Trade Union funds would be liable for any breach of such agreements by their members. In the end, however, this plan secured the support
of only a minority of the Commission, who put it forward in a separate
memorandum. The Majority Report was, on the whole, innocuous and
non-committal. A Labour Minority Report was presented ; but three of
the Trade Unionists on the Commission refused to sign this, and acted with
the Majority.

Meanwhile, a series of big industrial conflicts had been in progress. In
1893, when trade and employment were at their worst, the employers in many
industries demanded substantial reductions in wages. In that year took
place a general stoppage of the Lancashire cotton spinners, and a strike of
miners which extended over most of the English coalfields—the first great
conflict in which the Miners' Federation as a whole was concerned.

The Lancashire cotton strike lasted twenty weeks, and ended in a compromise on the whole favourable to the workers, who got off with a comparatively small reduction in wages. The most important feature of the
settlement was the famous Brooklands Agreement, which set up machinery
for the adjustment of future disputes without stoppage of work. From 1893
onwards this agreement governed conditions in the spinning mills, and no
important strike or lock-out took place.

A second important dispute of 1893 was the Hull dock strike—a struggle
forced on by the Shipping Federation in an attempt to break the power of the
Sailors' and Firemen's Union, and ending in a settlement unfavourable to the
workers. Keir Hardie's work in concentrating attention through Parliament
on this struggle has been mentioned above.

By far the greatest conflict of the year, however, was the miners' strike,
in which 400,000 men were involved. Miners' wages, which had risen very
fast during the boom, were being rapidly cut down as prices fell with the
slump. The Miners' Federation, which had rejected the sliding scale,
demanded that there should be a minimum below which wages should not
fall whatever the course of trade or of prices might be. For more than four
months the main English coalfields (but not those of Scotland, South Wales

or the North-East Coast) were paralysed by the strike, at the end of which the miners, though they had to submit to considerable reductions, gained the practical recognition of minimum wage rates for the coalfields affected. The settlement was followed by the establishment of the English Coal Conciliation Board for the " Federated Area " (Lancashire, Yorkshire, the Midlands and North Wales) which continued to govern wage-rates in these coalfields until after 1914.

There were many other miners' strikes in these years. In 1892 the Durham miners struck against a proposed reduction, but finally, through Bishop Westcott's mediation, accepted a reduction of smaller amount. In 1893 there was a separate strike of the hauliers in South Wales. Despite the adverse trade conditions, the men claimed an advance, and were naturally defeated. In 1894 the Scottish miners struck unsuccessfully against a wage reduction ; but a reorganised Scottish Miners' Federation emerged from the struggle. In 1898 the miners in the West of Scotland successfully struck for an advance. In South Wales, where the sliding scale system remained longest in force, and the miners, badly organised, were still outside the Miners' Federation of Great Britain, there was constant bickering between the " New " and the old Unionists. At length, in 1898, the miners struck for an advance in wages, and for a revision of the scale by which they were governed. The struggle lasted for six months, during which the men hung out grimly with practically no resources. The I.L.P. raised what funds it could to help them, and conducted a great organising campaign throughout the area, gaining members and founding branches in all the principal centres. At length, despite these efforts, the men were defeated and driven back to work. But they were sick both of the sliding scale and of their isolation from the main body of the miners in other coalfields. The sequel to the strike was the reformation of the South Wales Miners' Federation, and its affiliation to the M.F.G.B. By the end of the century, the M.F.G.B. covered all the coalfields except Durham and Northumberland, which still held aloof until 1908. The National Miners' Union, the surviving fragment of Macdonald's organisation, was, however, wound up in 1898, when its last group in Monmouthshire disappeared, and the Durham Miners withdrew, leaving Northumberland as the sole remaining district.

An indication of the prevalence of mining strikes and lock-outs during this period can be got from the fact that between 1893 and 1900 the number of miners involved in trade disputes considerably exceeded the total of all other workers so involved. Moreover, the mining stoppages lasted, on the average, a good deal longer than those in other industries. There was no national mining dispute between 1893 and 1912 ; but no year passed without at least one important stoppage in one or other of the coalfields.

The railwaymen, as we saw, were roused to activity by the unrest of 1889, when the General Railway Workers' Union was founded as a rival to the old-fashioned Amalgamated Society of Railway Servants. The railway workers were still very weakly organised, and the companies still refused all manner of recognition to the Unions and denounced combination as subversive of the quasi-military discipline which they maintained to be necessary for railway work. Railway wages were very low, and hours were appallingly long ; and it was to the second grievance that the Unions first directed their attention. In 1890 the A.S.R.S., stimulated by the formation of a rival Union, awoke from its slumber, and launched a new programme, chiefly directed to the reduction of hours. At the end of the same year the separate Scottish Society of Railway Servants took a more drastic step, and declared a strike for shorter hours. This was savagely defeated, and the remnants of the Scottish Society were merged in the A.S.R.S. But the stoppage, the first of any importance in the railway service, helped the agitation which the A.S.R.S. was conducting ; and in 1891 Parliament was induced to appoint a Select Committee to consider the position. This enquiry led to an Act of 1893, under which the Board of Trade was given very restricted powers to deal with cases of excessive overwork. But these powers were not used, and the Unions were still too weak to make a stand.

The railway companies, with the exception of the North-Eastern Railway, which had recognised Trade Unionism in 1890, continued their repressive policy. In 1896 the London and North-Western Railway, under Sir George Findlay's leadership, began a systematic policy of dismissing all active Trade Unionists. This, however, led to a public outcry, and the Unions were able to secure the re-instatement of the victimised men. Indeed, Sir George Findlay's action had quite the opposite effect to that which he desired. The A.S.R.S. launched its first " All-Grades Programme " in 1897, and actually doubled its membership during the year. All the companies were approached with demands for shorter hours, higher wages, and payment for overtime. But the employers resolutely refused to negotiate, and the Unions were not strong enough to call a strike. The All-Grades Movement was abortive, and nothing further was done nationally till the new All-Grades Movement of 1906. The Railway Clerks' Association was founded in 1897, and aroused even more hostility on the part of the companies than the Unions of manual workers ; but it did not become important until the new century.

Apart from the miners, the body of workers who engaged in the greatest conflict with their employers during the 'nineties were the engineers. The Amalgamated Society of Engineers had provided many of the leaders of the " New " Unionism of 1889, and, craft Union as it was, had been considerably affected by the new ideas. It remained, in the 'nineties, by far the largest Union, apart from the federal miners' organisation, and very much the richest and most stably organised. In 1897 it had over 90,000 members, a reserve fund of over £300,000, and an annual income of over £500,000. Its weaknesses were its failure to include the less skilled workers in the industry, who were more and more being used to man the new simplified machines, the existence of a number of smaller rival Unions of skilled workers, such as patternmakers, toolmakers, brass finishers and moulders, and a slowness in adapting its craft policy to meet changing economic conditions. It had, moreover, against it a newly reorganised Engineering Employers' Federation, whose leaders had made up their minds to stand no nonsense.

During the 'nineties, causes of friction accumulated steadily. Engineering practice was being rapidly revolutionised by the introduction of new machines, and in nearly every factory the skilled craftsmen were fighting a rearguard action against supersession by less skilled and less highly-paid workers. These conditions led to a succession of workshop disputes, in which the A.S.E. members demanded the removal of " labourers " from machines claimed as the monopoly of skilled men, and more generally put forward a claim for a share in the " control of industry." Early in 1897 these quarrels came to a head, and the Employers' Federation threatened a national lock-out unless the men who had struck in certain establishments returned at once to work. Temporarily, the dispute was smoothed over by the mediation of some of the other Unions. The men went back to work, and the lock-out notices were withdrawn. But a conference failed to settle the points at issue, and at this stage the London engineers declared a local strike for the forty-eight hours' week. The employers met this move by a partial lock-out ; and the Unions retaliated by a general strike at all works where the lock-out notices had been posted. Eventually nearly 50,000 workers were directly involved.

The general stoppage began in July, and lasted on into the following year. The engineers received substantial help from other Unions, after their own available funds had been exhausted ; but in the end they were driven back to work. The demand for the forty-eight hours' week was withdrawn, and the Unions had to promise to abstain from " interference with the management," and to agree that the employers should have the right to employ any man they chose on any type of work, or to introduce anywhere any system of payment previously operative in any establishment. Only after three ballots were the men persuaded to accept these hard terms—so hard that they were, in practice, impossible to enforce, and, after a period for recovery, local bickering over the old issues was resumed much as before. By 1900 the membership of the A.S.E. had recovered almost to the numbers in the Union before the dispute.

Of strikes in other industries during the 'nineties, the most important were the boot and shoe operatives' strike of 1895, which resulted in the establishment of a system of arbitration for the settlement of future disputes, the two unsuccessful strikes of the Dundee jute workers in 1895 and 1899, and the successful strike of the potters in 1900. On the whole, apart from the miners and engineers, the decade was one of relative industrial tranquillity. After the great unrest of 1889-90, the Unions paused to take breath, and the energies of the new leaders were mainly absorbed in the growing political movement.

Trade Unionism, however, after the set-back of 1893, resumed its growth, and by 1900 there were nearly two million workers enrolled in Unions. There was also, side by side with the movement towards political consolidation, a movement for the closer unity of the various societies for industrial purposes. *The Clarion* took an active part in this movement, urging strongly the linking up of all Unions into a central federation for mutual defence. The engineering struggle of 1897 made the need seem manifest, and in 1898 the Trades Union Congress was induced, largely by the efforts of Robert Knight, the secretary of the Boilermakers' Society, to take the necessary steps for setting up a new body. The Congress, as in the case of the Labour Representation Committee a year later, did not itself assume the new functions, or enrol all its affiliated societies in the new federation. It only called a Conference, and this Conference set up a General Federation of Trade Unions, which societies were free to join or not to join as they thought fit.

In its inception, the G.F.T.U. aroused great hopes. Many people looked to it as a great co-ordinating authority for the Trade Union movement as a whole—a sort of "One Big Union" destined to achieve great things. But in fact the new Federation was not so organised as either to supersede the Trades Union Congress, or to take any part in directing the policy of the Trade Union movement. It developed as a purely financial federation for mutual insurance against strikes and lock-outs. Each Union joining it paid contributions at a regular rate into a central fund, and was entitled to receive from the fund subventions at a regular rate in aid of its own expenditure on dispute pay in any strike or lock-out in which it might become involved. There was no power given to the G.F.T.U. either itself to call strikes, or to co-ordinate the policy of the Unions connected with it. Its business became merely that of an insurance society—to receive premiums, and to pay out benefits.

At the outset, forty-four Societies, with a total membership of 343,000, joined the G.F.T.U. The main strength came from the metal and textile workers and from the less important trades. The miners held aloof, perhaps fortunately for the Federation, which a big miners' strike might speedily have made insolvent. So did many other Unions, which could not afford the contributions demanded. At first, the G.F.T.U. was subjected to no severe strain; for its early years were a period of relative industrial peace. The troubles which attended its later history fall outside the scope of this chapter.

Thus, by 1900, the Trade Union world had settled down. The "New"

Unions had taken their place beside the old as an integral and permanent part of the movement. Indeed, the difference between " old " and " new," without disappearing entirely, had been considerably blurred. The fighting enthusiasm of the " New " Unions had waned in the slump of 1893, when they had been hard put to it to hold together at all. Some of them had even abandoned their dislike of friendly benefits, and had started voluntary friendly activities for such members as chose to pay additional contributions for this purpose. Only the poverty of the less skilled workers prevented considerable further developments of this sort.

On the other hand, the old Unions had been influenced by the " New." Some of them had opened their ranks to less skilled workers, and all had to some extent accepted the policy of the " New " Unionists in pressing for industrial legislation, and had largely given up their old acceptance of *laissez-faire* principles. " Lib-Labism," though it was still strong, was definitely declining, and even the older Unions were more and more coming to be led by men who accepted the newer views. There were no longer two clearly defined sections in the Trade Union movement, waging mutual war. Sectional jealousies and quarrels, of course, remained ; but on the whole an intermediate type of Trade Unionism, betwixt the two extremes of 1889, was being developed. The process of political consolidation, which called the Labour Party into being, served further to obliterate the old differences of type.

The growth of Trade Unionism was necessarily subject in some degree to the fluctuations of trade and employment. Its tendency was upward ; but it always lost in a slump some of the members it gained during a boom in trade. The sister movement of consumers' Co-operation, on the other hand, pursued a steady upward course, comparatively unaffected by industrial fluctuations. During the 'nineties, there were few Co-operative events of importance. An improved Industrial and Provident Societies Act was passed in 1893 ; and, under the influence of Horace Plunkett, there were important fresh developments of the movement in Ireland, marked by the formation of the Irish Agricultural Organisation Society in 1894, and the Irish Agricultural Wholesale Society in 1898. Agricultural Co-operation spread rapidly in all parts of Ireland—including Ulster ; and the new Co-operative Creameries controlled by the farmers were a great business success and resulted in a rapid improvement in the quality of Irish butter, which had been losing ground seriously in face of Danish competition. Unfortunately, disputes soon arose between the developing Irish movement and the English Co-operative Wholesale Society, which had set up its own creameries in Ireland. These quarrels helped to prevent a parallel growth of the Irish consumers' Co-operative Movement, except in a few centres ; and the Irish agricultural movement was left to develop without close links with British Co-operation. A British Agricultural Organisation

Society was set up in 1900, but made no progress at all comparable with that of the Irish body. The remaining event of importance in Co-operative history was the formation in 1895 of the International Co-operative Alliance, linking up the growing Co-operative Movements of a large number of countries.

The chief features of Co-operative development in the 'nineties, however, were the steady and rapid growth of membership and trade and the development, under the inspiring leadership of Margaret Llewelyn Davies, of the Women's Co-operative Guild, originally established in 1883. The Women's Guild, and its sister organisation in Scotland, came to exert very great educational influence, and contributed much, not only to the better understanding of Co-operative principles, but also to equipping working-class women to take a larger part in the life of the political Labour movement and in public affairs generally. Meanwhile, the Co-operative Movement as a whole expanded fast. In 1880 the number of British Co-operators, in Societies of all types, was about 600,000. By 1890 they numbered nearly a million, and by 1900 well over a million and three quarters. The growth in capital and trade was still greater. Share capital rose from £6,226,000 in 1880 to £10,367,000 in 1890, and £23,256,000 in 1900. Sales rose from £23,000,000 in 1880 to £36,000,000 in 1890, and £77,000,000 in 1900. There was a great increase in Co-operative production by the consumers' movement, and the Co-operative Wholesale Societies greatly expanded their output of goods. Producers' Co-operation went through a revival in the 'nineties, under the influence of Thomas Blandford, who reorganised the Co-operative Productive Federation, originally set up in 1882, and helped to set the more enterprising Producers' Societies firmly on their feet. Despite his efforts, the movement remained small, and represented at the end of the century only a tiny fraction of total Co-operative activity.

BOOKS

S. and B. Webb. *History of Trade Unionism.*
Board of Trade. *Reports of Labour Department.*
A.S.E. *Report on the Engineering Strike and Lock-Out of 1897.*
J. B. Jefferys. *The Story of the Engineers.*
G. Howell. *Trade Unionism, New and Old.*
G. D. H. Cole. *A Century of Co-operation.*
M. Llewelyn Davies. *The Woman with the Basket.*

3. THE LABOUR REPRESENTATION COMMITTEE

We have seen how the Trades Union Congress of 1899 was induced to take the step which led to the formation of the Labour Party. After the passing of the Congress resolution, a committee representing the Trades Union Congress, the I.L.P., the S.D.F., and the Fabian Society was appointed to make the arrangements for the proposed special Conference. This met in

February, 1900, when 129 delegates attended, representing about half a million Trade Unionists (or considerably less than half the number affiliated to the Trades Union Congress), and about 70,000 members enrolled in the various Socialist societies and miscellaneous bodies.

The provisional Committee had drawn up, in advance of the Conference, a draft plan of organisation for the new body, making it an independent federation of Trade Unions, Trades Councils, and Co-operative and Socialist societies. It was to be organised quite apart from the Trades Union Congress. Bernard Shaw, Keir Hardie, and Ramsay MacDonald were among the draftsmen of this constitution, which gave the Labour Party its distinctive form as an alliance of Trade Unionism and Socialism in the political field. Keir Hardie's plan of the " Labour Alliance " had come to birth.

At the Conference, the first trouble arose over the types of candidates to be supported. Was the new body to promote the election only of candidates who were themselves members of the working class, or was it to be open to all who accepted a distinctly working-class policy? The former notion was in line with the old " Lib-Lab " conception of Labour representation, which had aimed not at the creation of a new party, but at the return to Parliament of members of the working class. The " New " Unionists and Socialists all united to attack the proposal that only working-class candidates should be supported ; and it was overwhelmingly defeated.

Next came the question of objects. The S.D.F. delegates moved a resolution calling for the creation of " a distinct party—separate from the capitalist parties, based upon the recognition of the class war, and having for its ultimate object the socialisation of the means of production, distribution and exchange." This was far too strong meat for most of the delegates, and a counter-proposal was at once made from the opposite extreme. Alexander Wilkie, the Secretary of the Shipwrights' Association, moved that a simple platform of a few agreed working-class proposals should be drawn up, and that candidates should be asked only to subscribe to these. This would have been fatal to the formation of a distinct party or group, and was far too weak for the great majority, and in the end a compromise proposal of Keir Hardie's was unanimously accepted. It urged the establishment in Parliament of a distinct Labour Group (not Party), with its own Whips ; but it also pledged the group " to co-operate with any party which, for the time being, may be engaged in promoting legislation in the direct interest of Labour "—or " in opposing measures having an opposite tendency." The I.L.P. representatives, in order to carry the Trade Union delegates with them, thus both stopped short of creating a definite new party and left the door open for a continuance of some sort of collaboration with the Liberal Party.

After some dispute, the name " Labour Representation Committee " was adopted. The new body did not take the name " Labour Party " until 1906.

James Ramsay MacDonald was elected Secretary, and was largely responsible for steering the new body through the difficulties of its early years.

These began soon. Within a few months of the formation of the L.R.C. came the " Khaki Election " of 1900, held in the midst of the South African War. The L.R.C. had no money, for there was no political levy paid to it by the Unions until after the Conference of 1903. The fifteen candidates who were placed in the field were for the most part the nominees of the three affiliated Socialist bodies. The conditions were highly unfavourable, and only two seats were secured. Keir Hardie was elected for Merthyr—an aftermath of the help given by the I.L.P. in the Welsh miners' strike of 1898 ; and Richard Bell, the railwaymen's secretary, won a seat at Derby. The " Lib-Labs " fared ill, and their numbers in the new Parliament were reduced to eight.

The launching of the Labour Representation Committee brought to a head the long struggle of the Socialists to create an independent working-class party. The new body had, indeed, a long road to travel before it emerged as a national party in any full sense. But the Conference of 1900 gave to it the distinctive form which it has since retained, by basing it upon a federal alliance between the Trade Unions and the Socialist Societies. The Co-operators were invited to join, but refused at that stage to give up their policy of political neutrality. The most powerful Trade Union group—the Miners' Federation—remained outside till the eve of the General Election of 1910. But the form of the organisation was laid down, and thereafter it grew steadily.

Any account of its growth must be reserved for a later part of this survey. Only in the light of later experience can it be judged whether Hardie's policy of the " Labour Alliance " was right or wrong. But this at least can be said at this stage. The Socialist Societies in 1900 could neither have formed a party of any real account without the support of the Trade Unions, nor have persuaded the Trade Unions to join a body more explicitly and pronouncedly Socialist than the L.R.C. The new body was based on compromise ; but the compromise had its roots in the situation with which its founders had to cope. It seemed to them—and it was—a great achievement to have so far weaned the Trade Unions from *laissez-faire* and from their subordination to the Liberal Party. The dangers inherent in this success were not equally apparent. They did not emerge clearly until after the formation of the Liberal Government of 1906.

BOOKS

G. D. H. Cole. *British Working-class Politics, 1832–1914.*
A. W. Humphrey. *History of Labour Representation.*
S. and B. Webb. *History of Trade Unionism.*
Labour Representation Committee. *Reports.*
H. Tracey (ed.). *The Book of the Labour Party.*

CHAPTER X

THE CONDITION OF THE WORKERS IN THE SECOND HALF OF THE NINETEENTH CENTURY

I ENDED the first part of this history with a brief comment on the condition of the workers during the first half of the nineteenth century. It now remains to see how that position was changed during the period with which this second part has dealt. Something has been said already of the vast technical changes which revolutionised industry in the second half of the century almost as drastically as the coming of power-driven machinery had revolutionised it in the first, and of the effects of these later changes on working-class organisation and policy. We have now to look at these changes from a rather different angle, and to enquire how they affected working-class ways and standards of life.

Clearly, they led to no such sensational and obvious changes as the Industrial Revolution immediately produced in men's ways of living. There was no uprooting of a whole social order on the scale of that which followed the rise of the modern factory system. The destruction of the peasantry had been thoroughly accomplished well before 1850 ; and the agricultural labourers had little, though the farmers had much, to lose by the decline of agriculture which set in with the great depression of the later 'seventies. Despite the immense growth of the mining industry, the proportion of the British population living in villages continued to decline, and the proportion of town-dwellers to increase. But for the agricultural labourers of 1880, driven to the towns in search of work, there was no such wholesale change in the way of life as for the labourers of the early nineteenth century.

The technical changes in industry were not, indeed, less important or far-reaching than those of earlier times. The new methods of steel manufacture, the vast growth of the railway systems, the extraordinarily rapid expansion of the mining and engineering industries, were constantly revolutionising the methods of production, rendering old kinds of skilled labour obsolete and creating new skills, replacing craftsmanship by the cunning of the machine-tool, and raising up semi-skilled machine-minders to aid or supersede the skilled tradesmen. The grades and classes of labour were constantly shifting under stress of these changes, which led to drastic readjustments in wage-rates and in Trade Union rules and organisation. The proportion of workers employed in different callings was steadily changing. Cotton and wool were yielding their leadership of the industrial world, among both employers and workers, to metals and mines. The large part played by coal miners and engineers in the history of Victorian Labour is no accident, but a product of changing economic conditions.

Nevertheless, from the standpoint of the workers, the changes of the second half of the century appear far less drastic than those of the earlier period. For, apart from the steady movement of agricultural workers into the mining industry, the shifting was mainly from one factory process to another. The factory had become the recognised and accepted centre of English life ; and the vast mass of the workers knew no other way of living. The number of " blackcoated " workers was also rising fast, but not nearly so fast as it was to rise in the new century.

Within the limits of the factory system, there is no doubt that, on the whole, working-class conditions were getting better. The factory code was being stiffened up, both by legislation and by better inspection and administration and as a consequence of increased Trade Union strength ; and the methods of the Factory Acts were being gradually applied to fresh industries, including the mines. The hours of labour, still very long, were being slowly reduced, especially at first for children and women. Factories were becoming rather less vile and insanitary ; and very slowly sanitary and housing conditions in the towns were being improved. It is, however, a notable fact that overcrowding remained an unsolved problem. In 1801 the average number of persons to a " house " was 5·67 ; in 1901 it had only fallen to 5·2. The crude death-rate in England and Wales had been reduced from 22·7 per thousand in 1851-5 to 16 per thousand in 1901-5, and the birth-rate from 34 to 28. The infant mortality rate, on the other hand, had actually risen from 14·6 per cent. in 1850 to 15·4 per cent. in 1900.

There had been a great decrease in crime, due in part to the diminished ferocity of the criminal law ; and the number of paupers had fallen from over a million in 1850 to under 800,000 in 1900, despite the increase in population. An almost universal system of public elementary education had been built up. In 1851 the State spent only £150,000 on this service. In 1901, it was already spending nearly £11 millions, in addition to the sums expended out of local rates. The services of local government in the sphere of public health were practically created during the second half of the century. The conception that it was the State's business to take at least some precautions to safeguard the health of its citizens found expression in a re-modelled system of local government to which large powers were entrusted.

These changes undoubtedly made life more tolerable for the ordinary man, and gave him something to hope for in a world that to the generations immediately before him had seemed to offer no hope at all. We have seen how, given this small ground for hope, the upper strata of the Victorian working class clutched at the chance, and strove by thrift and conciliatory behaviour to make the best of things. We have watched the rise of the

Friendly Societies and of the Co-operative Movement, and have seen how Victorian Trade Unionism and Victorian working-class politics took their colour from the changes in the economic basis of the workers' life.

Of course, it was not for the workers alone that better times came with the settling down of industrialism in the second half of the century. A huge new middle class came into being ; the professions, the managerial grades in industry, the middlemen of every sort increased enormously in numbers. Employers and financiers made fortunes undreamed of by the greatest magnates of the Industrial Revolution. In 1851 the professional classes were 2·2 per cent. of total population, and the commercial classes 4·3 per cent. By 1881 the corresponding figures were 6·2 and 7·8. In 1840 under 2,000 persons died leaving more than £500 ; by 1877 the number had risen to 4,478, and there were more than 1,100 persons with incomes of over £10,000 a year. There can be no doubt that, up to 1880 at least, profits were rising considerably faster than wages.

Wages, however, were rising, both in money and in purchasing power. In the absence of reliable statistics, it is not easy to present any comprehensive view of the change in the wages of the whole industrial population, and it is necessary to fall back on estimates which are admittedly based on somewhat inadequate data. But, though the precise figures are doubtful, the general tendency admits of no dispute. There were set-backs ; but between 1850 and 1900 the average real wage, measured in purchasing power, rose at least by seventy, and perhaps by as much as eighty per cent.

In two of the diagrams which illustrate this chapter, I have set out this general movement of real and money wages in graphic form. The first diagram, based mainly on Mr. G. H. Wood's figures and on their arrangement by Lord Layton, shows the annual changes in money wages, retail prices, and real wages, in as far as any of these can be correctly ascertained. The annual percentages of unemployed workers recorded by the Trade Unions making returns are also shown, in order that the reader may be able to estimate the effect of trade fluctuations on wage rates. But no account has been taken, in calculating real wages, of time lost through unemployment. The diagram represents, not actual earnings, but, primarily, weekly *rates* of wages.

The second diagram reproduces Professor Bowley's rough estimate, by five-year averages, of the general movement of money wages and real wages. This makes the increase in both larger than any other estimate I know of. But the tendency remains the same, and, save at one or two special points, the same upward and downward movements are recorded as in other estimates. In the following observations, however, the annual figures recorded in the first diagram are taken as a basis.

It will be seen that money wages rose very sharply at certain definite periods—from 1852 to 1855, from 1863 to 1866, from 1869 to 1873, from

1888 to 1890, and from 1898 to 1900. A glance at the curve of unemployment will show that each of these periods coincides roughly with a period of exceptionally good trade. A study of the curve of prices, however, modifies the first conclusion that might be drawn from these facts. Between 1852 and 1855 prices rose considerably faster than wages, and real wage-rates considerably declined. Between 1863 and 1866, on the other hand, prices declined for most of the time, so that there was a real appreciation in the purchasing power of wages. Between 1869 and 1873 prices were at first stationary, and then rose, but not enough to offset the rise in wages. Between 1888 and 1890 prices rose far less than wages, and the same is true of 1898-1900. Real wages rose sharply at three points— between 1861 and 1864, between 1868 and 1876, and, apart from two brief set-backs in the early and late 'nineties, through the whole period from 1882 to 1900. But, whereas the two earlier advances were mainly due to the rise in money wages, the long rise after 1882 was due still more to the fall in prices.

It will be noticed at once that the great advances in money wages coincide for the most part with periods of exceptional Trade Union activity. The early 'fifties saw the rise of the " New Model " Trade Unionism ; the early 'sixties, the great development of mining Trade Unionism under Alexander Macdonald and the great growth and activity of Unionism in the building and textile trades ; the late 'sixties and early 'seventies, the great struggle of the Unions with the law, the Nine Hours movement of the Engineers, further big developments among the miners, and the first rise of Unions among the less skilled workers ; the years from 1888 to 1890, the birth of the Miners' Federation, the Gasworkers' and Dockers' Unions, and a host of other active pioneers of the " New " Unionism. The closing years of the century were not, indeed, marked by great industrial activity ; but they saw the formation of the General Federation of Trade Unions and of the Labour Representation Committee.

This coincidence of time does not, of course, settle the question of cause and effect. If Union activity helped to bring about these advances in wages, it is no less true that the favourable opportunities presented by periods of good trade helped to call forth this activity. It is impossible to disentangle cause and effect. Unions cannot raise wages unless the economic conditions are in their favour ; but even favourable economic conditions may not bring better wages where Unionism is lethargic or non-existent. The trade revival of the early 'eighties produced no advances in money wages, and the cause, at least in part, was Trade Union lethargy.

The whole period of fifty years dealt with in this section really falls into two periods of rapid economic advance, separated by a period of acute depression. From 1850 to the middle 'seventies British Capitalism passed through what has been called its " Golden Age." By the end of this period money wages had risen by more than one half over the level of 1850, and real wages by at least one third. Then came the period of the great depression, extending, with only a brief interval of good trade in the early 'eighties, from the late 'seventies to the late 'eighties. Over this period money wages fell in nearly all trades; but owing to the rapid fall in prices no decline in real wages, apart from loss of earnings through unemployment or under-employment, was experienced. Then followed the great revival of 1889, bringing big advances in both money and real wages. The slump of the early 'nineties caused some reduction in both; but then the upward move-ment was sharply resumed. Between the late 'eighties and the end of the century both real and money wages rose by at least 20 per cent. In all, as we have seen, the rise in real wages during the latter half of the century was, on the average of all trades for which particulars are available, certainly not less than 70 per cent.

This rise was by no means equally distributed among the different groups of workers. The heaviest increases seem to have been secured by the cotton operatives, whose wages were approximately doubled during the half century. These, of course, had been among the most desperately exploited of the wage-workers during the first part of the century. According to Mr. Wood, the average earnings of all classes of cotton operatives in 1850 were about 9s. 4d. a week. By 1880 they had risen to 14s. 10d., and by 1900 to 18s. 3d. The workers in the woollen and worsted industry, on the other hand, were better paid in 1850, but got only about 40 per cent. more in 1900 than in 1850. Carpenters' money wages actually advanced by less than 25 per cent. between 1850 and 1900.

In mining and iron and steel work, wages rose rather more than the aver-age, and in the building trades considerably more. In engineering, the rise was about the average; but there was a considerable up-grading of unskilled workers to semi-skilled work. On the whole, the constructional trades, on account of their great expansion, tended to improve their relative postition. But they were also subject to abnormally heavy fluctuations in wages, owing to their exceptional liability to booms and slumps. This is most marked of all in the mining industry. In the middle 'seventies mining wages rose to 90 per cent. of the 1900 level. Five years later they had fallen to 70 per cent. This extreme fluctuation, of course, largely explains the prevalence of mining strikes and lock-outs.

The third diagram accompanying this chapter shows, in so far as particu-lars are available, the growth of the Trade Union and Co-operative Move-ments. There are no figures of total Trade Union membership before 1892, when the Board of Trade first issued a general return. But from 1866 onwards we have the numbers represented at the annual Trades Union Con-gresses. These do not at any point show the full strength of the movement; for there were always Unions not affiliated to Congress, or affiliated on less than their full numbers. For the later period, the relation between the two sets of figures can be seen by comparing them on the chart. For the first few years the Congress figures bear little relation to total Trade Union membership ; for it was only by gradual stages that the Congress established its position. The first figures of any real significance are those of 1869.

The Co-operative figures are drawn throughout from official sources, and show the membership of Co-operative Societies of all types registered under the Industrial and Provident Societies Acts. The point of interest is to observe their steady growth in comparison with the ups and downs of Trade Union membership. Co-operative Societies are, of course, affected in some degree by the fluctuations of trade. But these do not influence their membership to anything like the same extent as that of the Trade Unions ; and they affect the volume and value of trade much more than the membership. Trade Union membership goes forward in a series of violent jerks ; Co-operative membership is relatively slow and steady in its advance. But the tendency of both movements is upward, and, on the whole, at a not markedly different rate.

Over the second half of the nineteenth century there was at least as considerable a growth of organisation among employers. Employers' Associations sprang up to cope with the rising Trade Unions, and, especially towards the end of the century, there was a marked growth of trusts and combines formed for the purpose of regulating prices and output. The attitude and organisation of the employing class were no less responsive than those of the workers to changes in economic conditions. *Laissez-faire* was abandoned as a principle by capitalists as much as by workers.

The growth of relatively stable Trade Unions and of a stable Co-operative Movement is but one of the signs of a marked change in the habits and outlook of the British workers during the latter party of the century. Though by 1900 the Trade Unions were gradually discarding their "Lib-Lab" policy and Socialism had become a real and powerful force among them, much that they had learned in the Victorian era remained with them as a lasting acquisition. General elementary education, of course, had made a huge difference to manners, habits, and social outlook. The rise in wages had made possible ways of living which had been beyond the reach of the workers during the bad times of the Industrial Revolution. The improvement in sanitary conditions had profoundly altered, save for the unfortunate slum-dwellers, the conditions of urban life. The appeals which had roused the workers in the 'thirties and 'forties would have made no impression on their successors in the latter part of the century. Though there were still, even in 1900, many thousands of hopelessly exploited " bottom dogs," such as Charles Booth's famous survey had brought to common knowledge ten years before its close, these were not typical of the organised or organisable working class. In the great industries, the workers had ceased to be a ragged and starveling mob, easily roused, either by a Feargus O'Connor or a James Rayner Stephens, or by some one of the many " Messiahs " who sprang up in the early years of the century. They had acquired a status, and in many cases a little " stake in the country," if only to the extent of a few pounds in the " Co-op." or a house in process of being bought through a Building Society.

No longer were mass uprisings, huge sudden revolts bred of despair and spreading like wildfire none knew how, likely or even possible. Strikes had become, for the most part, orderly movements, prepared for in advance and conducted by organised bodies and under duly constituted leadership. The orators of the Social Democratic Federation had thundered revolution in vain ; the evolutionary Socialism of the I.L.P. made a far greater appeal. But even this did not rouse the mass ; the I.L.P. set itself to win over the individuals one by one. Socialist propaganda had become far less an appeal to emotions and instincts, and far more an appeal to reason. O'Connor had been hot as hell ; Sidney Webb was always as cool as a cucumber.

This is not said by way of approval or censure, but merely as a true account of what had happened. There were working-class leaders in the first part of the nineteenth century as clever, as well-read, and as educated as any since. But the average level of culture immensely changed. In the early days, there was a small minority that read Owen and Richard Carlile, and a far wider minority that appreciated Cobbett. In the latter part of the century Darwin and Spencer and Huxley were making their mark on working-class thought to an extent that would have been impossible before the advent of popular education.

In certain respects, the wide differences of education hampered the working-class propagandists. In the early part of the century, the workers were left to provide their own newspapers because it was not worth anyone else's while to provide for them. The work of Lord Brougham and of Charles Knight, who founded the *Penny Magazine* and produced a great stream of cheap educational manuals for working-class readers, was the beginning of the change. The Mechanics' Institutes in the 'twenties, and the Society for the Diffusion of Useful Knowledge in the 'thirties, set themselves to teach the workers what it was good for them to know. But all these were subsidised and propagandist, and not commercial ventures.

The coming of popular education altered the whole situation. It became worth while, commercially, to provide reading matter for the poor as well as for the rich. The result was seen in a flood of cheap novels, cheap magazines, cheap newspapers. The commerical classes vied with the working-class propagandists in catering for the workers' reading. John Cassell and many others catered for the reading masses and made money by doing so, with no need of subsidies from the well-to-do. With ample resources behind them, they made it far harder for the Socialists to maintain a press of their own, or to get the workers' ear.   Such papers as *Reynolds' Newspaper*, which began as a Chartist organ, had to be commercialised in order to survive.   Propagandist papers had a hard struggle, and failures were many.   *The Beehive* was often at the point of death.   After the rise of Socialism in the 1880's, *Justice* and the *Labour Leader* did not pay.   Only *The Clarion*, through Robert Blatchford's special genius as a popular writer, established itself as a commercial success.   And even Blatchford could have made much more money than he did if he had been content to go on writing for Hulton's newspapers instead of setting up a propagandist paper of his own.

To a great extent, in habits and way of life, the upper strata of the workers became assimilated to the lesser middle class.   To be a Trade Union leader became a respectable calling.   Even the " New " Unionism of 1889, which started up as a revolt against the respectability of the " Lib-Labs," became respectable in its turn.   It could not be otherwise.   By the end of the century, Socialism itself had become respectable.   And all this had happened precisely because the working-class standard of living had risen to a point which made respectability possible without heroic effort.

In this part of my book, the story has been brought down to 1900.   At the next stage of the survey it will be seen that, with the turn of the century, the long-continued rise in the working-class standard of living suffered a sharp check, and real wages began to fall.   The new Imperialism which had been rising, step by step, with the development of the coal and metal industries, began to show more clearly its consequences in international rivalries, in the race of armaments, and in intensified economic competition.   But with these developments we are not yet concerned.   During the Victorian era, it is beyond doubt that working-class standards were very greatly improved, and that the main body of the workers successfully emerged from the sheer disaster which had overtaken them during the Industrial Revolution.   Hope replaced despair ; criticism superseded revolt.   Hyndman sought to revive the Chartist agitation ; but the Socialism of the 'nineties was a very different thing from the Chartism of the 'thirties, and made an essentially different appeal.

BOOKS

A. L. Bowley.   *Wages and Income since 1860.*
A. L. Bowley.   *Wages in the United Kingdom in the Nineteenth Century.*
A. L. Bowley.   *National Progress in Wealth and Trade.*
W. T. Layton.   *Introduction to the Study of Prices.*
G. R. Porter and F. W. Hirst.   *The Progress of the Nation.*
G. H. Wood.   *History of Wages in the Cotton Trade.*
S. Webb.   *Labour in the Longest Reign.*
G. D. H. Cole.   *British Trade and Industry.*
G. D. H. Cole and R. Postgate.   *The Common People, 1746-1946.*

TABLE 7.—WAGES, PRICES AND UNEMPLOYMENT, 1850–1900

Date.	Per cent. of 1850.			Employment per cent. (i.e., Unemployment reversed).
	Retail Prices.	Money Wages.	Real Wages.	
1850 . . .	100	100	100	96
1851 . . .	97	100	102	96
1852 . . .	97	100	102	94
1853 . . .	106	110	105	98
1854 . . .	122	114	96	97
1855 . . .	126	116	95	95
1856 . . .	126	116	96	95
1857 . . .	119	112	96	94
1858 . . .	109	110	102	88
1859 . . .	107	112	104	96
1860 . . .	111	114	103	98
1861 . . .	114	114	100	95
1862 . . .	111	116	105	92
1863 . . .	107	117	109	94
1864 . . .	106	124	117	97
1865 . . .	107	126	117	98
1886 . . .	114	132	116	97
1867 . . .	121	131	109	93
1868 . . .	119	130	110	92
1869 . . .	113	130	115	93
1870 . . .	113	133	118	96
1871 . . .	113	138	121	98
1872 . . .	120	146	122	99
1873 . . .	122	155	128	99
1874 . . .	117	156	133	98
1875 . . .	113	154	135	98
1876 . . .	110	152	137	96
1877 . . .	113	151	133	95
1878 . . .	110	148	132	93
1879 . . .	103	146	137	89
1880 . . .	107	147	134	94
1881 . . .	105	147	136	96
1882 . . .	106	147	135	98
1883 . . .	102	149	139	97
1884 . . .	100	150	144	92
1885 . . .	96	149	148	91
1886 . . .	92	148	151	90
1887 . . .	89	149	155	92
1888 . . .	89	151	157	95
1889 . . .	91	156	159	98
1890 . . .	91	163	166	98
1891 . . .	92	163	164	96
1892 . . .	92	162	163	94
1893 . . .	89	162	167	92
1894 . . .	87	162	170	93
1895 . . .	84	162	174	94
1896 . . .	83	163	176	97
1897 . . .	86	166	176	97
1898 . . .	87	167	174	97
1899 . . .	86	172	180	98
1900 . . .	89	179	183	97

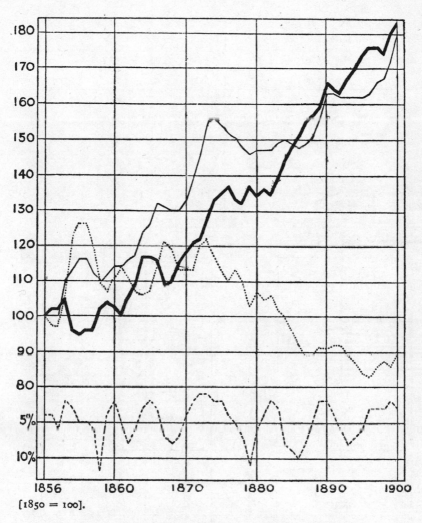

[1850 = 100].

CHART 11.—WAGES, PRICES AND UNEMPLOYMENT, 1850–1900.
—— Real wages.   —— Money wages.   ...... Retail prices.
- - - - Percentage of trade unionists unemployed (reversed).

TABLE 8.—NOMINAL AND REAL WAGES, 1850-1900
Professor Bowley's Estimate

Date.			Nominal Wages.	Real Wages.
1850–1854	.	.	55	50
1855–1859	.	.	60	50
1860–1864	.	.	62	50
1865–1869	.	.	67	55
1870–1874	.	.	75	60
1875–1879	.	.	80	65
1880–1884	.	.	77	65
1885–1889	.	.	79	75
1890–1894	.	.	87	85
1895–1899	.	.	92	95
1900–1904	.	.	100	100

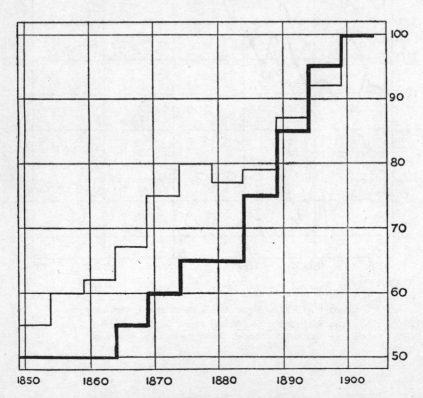

CHART 12.—NOMINAL AND REAL WAGES, 1850-1900. Professor Bowley's Estimate.
——— Real wages.   ——— Money wages.
[Average of 1900-1904 = 100.]

TABLE 9.—MEMBERSHIP OF TRADE UNIONS AND CO-OPERATIVE SOCIETIES

Membership in Thousands.

		Trades Union Congress.		All Co-operative Societies.
	All Trade Unions.	Unions only.	Total.	
1866	—	110	199	·
1867	—	155	193	·
1868	—	50	114	·
1869	—	250	—	·
1870	—	—	—	·
1871	—	289	—	·
1872	—	270	—	·
1873	—	509	735	388
1874	—	594	695	453
1875	—	414	531	480
1876	—	455	577	508
1877	—	565	695	529
1878	—	486	622	561
1879	—	412	522	573
1880	—	381	476	604
1881	—	—	—	596
1882	—	404	507	654
1883	—	467	561	681
1884	—	488	598	848
1885	—	500	631	802
1886	—	515	638	834
1887	—	561	696	895
1888	—	568	727	942
1889	—	687	863	1,012
1890	—	1,593	1,927	1,054
1891	—	1,094	1,354	1,126
1892	1,501	1,155	1,651	1,221
1893	1,479	721	871	1,266
1894	1,439	1,015	1,081	1,285
1895	1,407	1,000	—	1,394
1896	1,493	1,076	—	1,437
1897	1,669	1,093	—	1,521
1898	1,702	1,184	—	1,597
1899	1,861	1,200	—	1,685
1900	1,972	1,250	—	1,778

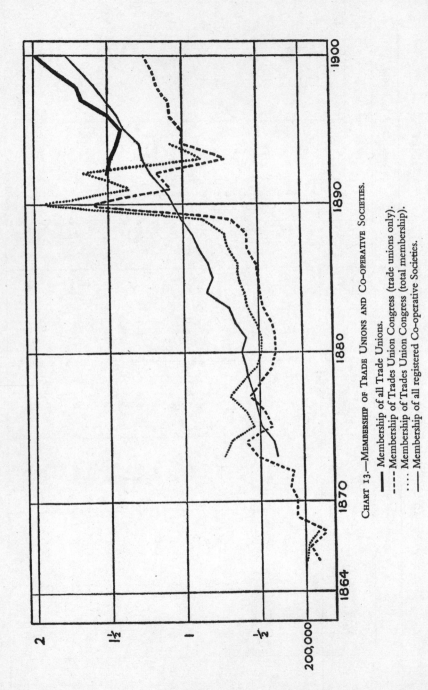

CHART 13.—MEMBERSHIP OF TRADE UNIONS AND CO-OPERATIVE SOCIETIES.

——— Membership of all Trade Unions.
- - - - Membership of Trades Union Congress (trade unions only).
- - - - Membership of Trades Union Congress (total membership).
· · · · Membership of Trades Union Congress (total membership).
——— Membership of all registered Co-operative Societies.

PART THREE
1900-1947

CHAPTER I

THE NEW CENTURY

THE second part of this study brought the history of the British workers to the beginning of the present century. In the latter half of the nineteenth century the working-class movement passed through two great phases of development. The main body of the more skilled workers, after 1850, abandoning revolutionary aspirations and mass movements born of despair, turned to the narrower task of building up an effective organisation for the protection of their interests within, and without fundamental challenge to, the capitalist order. Trade Unions and Co-operative Societies alike assumed a more stable form, and adopted methods and policies based on making the best of the world as they found it. Along these lines they achieved great, though narrowly limited, success. The Amalgamated Societies of the skilled craftsmen, the " Amalgamations " of cotton spinners and weavers, the less stable but always active and powerful Unions of the miners, remain as lasting monuments of this phase of growth. The local Co-operative Stores scattered through every industrial area and the great English and Scottish Co-operative Wholesale Societies are no less successful and typical products of this stage of working-class development.

We saw, however, how the limitations of this success had begun, in the last quarter of the nineteenth century, to be more and more widely realised. The Trade Unions which were the backbone of Trade Unionism in the struggles of the 'seventies represented, and could with their methods and policy represent, only a fraction of the whole working class. The Co-operative Movement appealed powerfully to the thrifty artisans, but made, as a rule, little appeal to the unskilled or casual labourers, who could afford neither to save nor to buy goods of unadulterated quality, nor even regularly to pay cash for what they bought. The less skilled workers found themselves of little account in the calculations of the working-class leaders, and even, in some cases, in actual hostility to them. The organised skilled workers some-times exploited the less skilled workers under the aegis of craft Unionism, and were often unsympathetic to the claims of a class of men whom they regarded as incapable of organisation or of self-help. The unskilled workers had to find new ways of fighting their own battles ; and neither the Trade Unions nor the Co-operative Societies, as they were before 1889, seemed to offer them much help.

These limitations of the older methods of organisation had become very plain during the great depression which set in towards the end of the 'seventies.

The attempts at self-organisation among the less skilled workers died away ; the agricultural workers, the gas-stokers, and the engineering labourers all failed to maintain the movements which they had launched in the booming years of the early 'seventies. The great Amalgamated Societies and the textile workers were forced back into a rigidly defensive attitude ; the miners' movement only saved itself from entire collapse by the acceptance of the sliding scale system. In the early 'eighties, it seemed as if the working-class movement had reached the limits of its expansion, and would need all its wits to prevent a serious decline in numbers and influence. Even the Co-operative Societies, although less seriously affected by adverse economic conditions, were able to make only a slow advance.

Then, as we saw, the last twenty years of the nineteenth century brought a whole series of new movements to birth. The memorable Dock Strike of 1889 was only the outstanding event in a great process of change. Amid the sceptical comments of the older leaders, the unskilled workers began again to organise. The dockers and gasworkers founded Unions which spread far beyond the occupations in which they first arose. The miners formed a new and powerful Federation, based explicitly on the repudiation of the sliding scale. In one calling after another, new Unions were formed ; the effective strength of Trade Unionism grew by leaps and bounds. The Co-operative Movement made rapid, though less sensational, advances. And, last but not least, the idea of independent working-class political action, which had died away in the great depression, vigorously revived and took shape in a series of movements which captured the imaginations of the active young men and women of the Trade Unions and the Co-operative Societies.

At the outset, these new movements were marked by an insistence and an immediacy which constituted half their challenge. In face of the great and recurrent trade depressions through which Great Britain had been passing, the early Socialists felt sure of the essential instability of the capitalist system. The great days of Capitalism, they believed, were over; the system was de-clining and would speedily and inevitably pass away. The nemesis pro-claimed by Marx was at hand; and the mantle of the capitalists would soon fall upon the broad shoulders of the working class. They believed that the prosperity of the Victorian age had been deceptive and transitory. Great Britain had prospered awhile because by a mixture of luck and cunning she had become the workshop of the world. For a generation and more, she had dumped her goods and her capital in every market ; but now her customers were taking their revenge. The export of capital had served to create power-ful rivals to the British producers. Other States were becoming better and better able to supply their own needs for manufactured goods ; and soon they would become eager rivals in the remaining markets of the world. Already Great Britain was living partly on tribute from overseas ; soon her lop-sided industrial system would tumble down as its props—the markets of the foreigner—were one by one withdrawn. Private enterprise would be utterly unable to hold its own in the pitched battle of economic forces ; and to the Socialists would fall the task of reconstructing the industrial order on a new foundation.

So men spoke and thought in the unemployed troubles of the eighteen-eighties—anticipating what lay much further ahead than they believed. The boom of 1889 seemed to them but a temporary halt upon the road to ruin ; and the slump of the early 'nineties followed hard upon it. But thereafter, —to confute their prophecies—came an amazing recovery. The last years of the nineteenth century and the first thirteen years of the twentieth, despite the continued alternation of relatively good and bad times, were on the whole a period of astonishingly rapid advance. In 1890 exports of British goods were valued at £263,000,000. In 1900 they were valued at £291,000,000, in 1910 at £430,000,000, and in 1913 at £525,000,000. In 1890 British exports had been worth £7 per head of population ; in 1913 they were worth £11 10s. In 1890 British shipowners had five million tons of steamships ; in 1913 they had over eleven million tons. Imports, no doubt, had risen as well—from £420,000,000 in 1890 to £768,000,000 in 1913 ; but in face of the rapidly mounting exports it was very difficult to talk convincingly about the impending downfall of British Capitalism.

If the eighteen-eighties were the season of the great depression, the opening years of the new century were assuredly that of the great recovery. The prophets of evil had been cheated again ; and the great Victorians turned once more in their graves and lay quiet, reassured that progress was a reality after all. And yet nothing that was fundamental appeared to have changed ; Great Britain was prosperous in spite of the conditions which, a little while before, had seemed to threaten her with imminent ruin. Germany and the United States had not ceased to develop their own power of industrial production ; increasingly they were making for themselves what previously they had bought from Great Britain. Nay, more—Germany, if not America, not content with supplying her own markets with goods competitive with British products, was becoming a powerful rival in almost every market and in almost every branch of export trade. Tariff walls had not been lowered, but had been raised even higher to Great Britain's apparent disadvantage. The old British monopoly was gone. In nearly every commodity, some other nation was disputing fiercely Great Britain's command of the markets of the world.

And yet, by any ordinary standard of measurement, Great Britain was more prosperous than ever before. Tariff Reformers, playing with percentages, could no doubt show that British trade and production had failed to advance nearly as rapidly as those of Germany and America. The Free Traders were on solid ground when they replied to these percentages with

actual amounts. In volume and value of trade and of manufacturing production Great Britain, despite the loss of her monopoly, still led the
world.

How had this miracle happened, and how had the pessimists of the great
depression been proved so signally in the wrong ? One country's gain, it
appeared, was not necessarily another's loss. The more Germany made for
herself and the more she exported to markets which had been Great Britain's
prerogative, the better customer of Great Britain she became. Not quite the
same could be said of the United States ; but British trade with other parts of
the American continent was more than enough compensation for the slackening of the United States demand. The Indian market had expanded beyond
all belief ; Australia and South Africa were taking more and more British
goods ; and new and promising markets, as well as sources of vital raw
materials, were being opened up in tropical Africa and elsewhere. The world
was a bigger place, economically, than the Victorians had ever discovered.
British exporters were finding out that new markets could be developed to
take the places of the old.

Even the Tariff Reformers, though they continued to use the argument
that the country was going to the dogs, now based their case rather on the
gigantic possibilities of an Imperial *Zollverein* than on the need for a protective
dyke to keep out the floods of economic ruin. The deserted tanneries of
Bermondsey might serve the purpose of a by-election candidate or of a
Daily Mail leader ; but the real case for Protectionism was based on hopes
rather than on fears. Free Trade statisticians, such as Professor Bowley, had
little difficulty in beating the Tariff Reform pessimists clean off the field ; the
optimistic Imperialists gave them more trouble. For the demonstration that
Great Britain had not been ruined was no answer to the reformers who
professed to know how to make her a great deal richer still.

> Wider still and wider
> Shall thy bounds be set.
> God, that made thee mighty,
> Make thee mightier yet !

None the less, all was not well. For there was one class—and that by far
the greatest—that could not be shown to have shared in the great prosperity
which the Free Traders so easily demonstrated to exist. It was easy enough
for Professor Bowley to show that real wages had risen even during the long
depression of the later nineteenth century ; it was by no means so easy to
show that they were still rising in the early years of the twentieth century.
During the long period of falling prices from the later 'seventies to the later
'nineties, real wages had undoubtedly risen, but had done so mainly because
of a rapidly falling cost of living. Prices, however, both wholesale and
retail, had touched bottom about 1896, when the great downward movement of the latter decades of the nineteenth century came finally to an end.

Thereafter, the cost of living began definitely to rise.   Between 1896 and 1907 wholesale prices, according to the Board of Trade index, rose by 20 per cent., and retail food prices in London by 14 per cent.   Money wages, according to the same authority, also rose by 14 per cent., but practically the whole of this advance took place before the end of 1900, and from 1900 to 1906 money wages actually fell, while retail prices rose.   The set-back to working-class standards of life was, indeed, slight, and both price and wage movements may seem insignificant in comparison with those of later years.   But the long continued advance in standards of life, which had continued through the era of falling prices, came decisively to an end, and the workers, who had been used to a slowly rising standard, found themselves faced with a real, though still slight, decline in their purchasing power.

This was the flaw in the Free Trade argument, as it was seen from the working-class point of view.   It did not, indeed, as appeared in 1906, cause the workers to accept the protectionist alternative ; but it did, to a growing extent, set them looking for an alternative of their own.   Modern British Socialism may have been a child of the depressed 'eighties ; it certainly throve on the revival which followed.

Moreover, to those who looked beneath the surface, the situation was not so reassuring as the trade statistics made it appear.   The British producer was, indeed, competing successfully with his newer rivals, and was to some extent increasing his trade because of the growth of theirs.   But, because of competition, he was trading on a narrower margin, and was less willing to incur higher wage costs which might hamper him in his competition with the foreigner.   In the period of falling prices, the workers had done well as long as they could keep money wages relatively stable ; but now they needed wage advances to compensate them for rising prices—and advances were not easy to get.

Nor was an analysis of the trade returns so comforting as a study of the mere totals of British exports.   Great Britain had found Germany an increasingly good customer ; but the Germans were buying from Great Britain fewer manufactured goods and much more coal.   British exports of machinery had, indeed, nearly doubled in value between 1900 and 1913, and British exports of cotton goods and yarns had grown in hardly less proportion.   But of the latter advance a good deal was due to a great rise in cotton prices, and the quantity exported had increased much less than the value.   British exports of coal had risen enormously in both quantity and value ; but the coal trade was highly unstable from year to year, and those who looked ahead were wondering what was to happen when Germany and other countries had been given time for an adequate development of their own fuel resources. Great Britain, as far as its prosperity could be measured by the trade returns, was doing excellently in 1910 and more than excellently in 1913.

But there were reasons for disquiet about the future. And the workers could hardly be expected to rest satisfied with a prosperity in which, even after the belated wage advances of 1911-13, they enjoyed practically no share.

The statistics of the Liberal economists provided, for the workers, neither food nor lodging. And the workers wanted a fuller ration of both. Therefore, despite the " national prosperity," there swept over the country, in the years immediately before the Great War, the biggest movement of unrest since the days of the Chartists. There was an " epidemic " of strikes in nearly every trade ; and fresh winds of economic doctrine blew into Great Britain from overseas, sweeping away the comfortable acceptances and complacencies which had survived both the great depression and the onslaughts of the Socialist pioneers.

This unrest, though it found its most significant expression in the world of Labour, was by no means purely economic. It flamed up, no less, in the passionate excesses of the militant Suffragists, and in a ready questioning of established doctrines and prejudices of every sort. George Bernard Shaw, the idol-breaker of the 'nineties, became a prophet to more than a narrow circle ; H. G. Wells, in his novels and social tracts, was the leading populariser of a new type of semi-scientific scepticism groping after new constructive ideals ; G. K. Chesterton, breaking with the Liberal *Daily News*, brandished a flaming sword side by side with Will Dyson in the lively, irresponsible, exuberant pages of the pre-1914 *Daily Herald*. There came a sense of great things stirring in the world, and of old things crumbling before their onset.

And then, after repeated martial alarums and excursions, came the Great War, threatening with its fierce atavisms to sweep all these new things away. The race of men ran mad, tearing down a civilisation whose foundations had been, without it, none too sure. Four years of horror, and a staggering forth into a changed world.

But this is to anticipate. What concerns us here is that pre-historic age before 1914—the age of the Pankhursts and of Jim Larkin, of Suffragism and Syndicalism, of H. G. Wells's best novels and of Will Dyson's cartoons. An exciting age, an age of new tidings, an age whose influences we can see still at work among us to-day. But an age vastly different from ours, alike in its mental attitudes and in the economic situation which it had to face !

Briefly, in the earlier chapters of this part, these developments will be studied from the special standpoint of the British working-class movement. Out of the deceptive quiet of the first years of the new century we shall see growing the great unrest. We shall see Trade Union membership more than doubled in a few years ; strikes unprecedented in number and animated by an essentially new spirit ; a new assertion by the bottom dog of his claim to be considered as good as other men, and of no less account—the outward signs of a great inward change in the make-up of Society. But first we must survey the calm before the storm, that orderly return of Victorian progressivism that gave so little hint of the strains and stresses that were speedily to follow its apparent triumph.

BOOKS

A. L. Bowley. *National Progress in Wealth and Trade.*
C. M. Waters. *The Economic Development of Great Britain and the Colonies.*
G. D. H. Cole. *The World of Labour.*
H. G. Wells. *Tono Bungay, Mankind in the Making,* etc.
G Dangerfield. *The Strange Death of Liberal England.*

CHAPTER II

THE RISE OF THE LABOUR PARTY

1. The New Socialism—The Fabians and the Independent Labour Party   2. The Taff Vale Case
3. The Growth of the Labour Representation Committee

I. THE NEW SOCIALISM—THE FABIANS AND THE INDEPENDENT LABOUR PARTY

IN the closing sections of the second part of this study, the growth of the new political movements which led up to the Labour Party was briefly surveyed. The new Marxian Socialism of H. M. Hyndman and the Social Democratic Federation, the idealistic revolutionism of William Morris and the Socialist League, the intellectualised and Utilitarian Socialism of the early Fabians, the mobilisation of the " New Unionists " under the Socialist banner by Keir Hardie and the Independent Labour Party, all went to the making of the new working-class political movement.   We saw, especially, how the I.L.P. first supplanted the Marxian Social Democratic Federation in the effective leadership of British Socialism, and then set to work to bring the Trade Unions into active collaboration for the establishment of an independent working-class political party.   We saw the I.L.P.'s efforts crowned with success, and, in 1900, the Labour Representation Committee launched on its career.   Keir Hardie had realised his dream of the " Labour Alliance."   The Trade Unions had not, in so many words, accepted Socialism, but they had been detached from their old allegiance to Liberalism and successfully persuaded to throw in their electoral lot with the Socialist Movement.   The great Miners' Federation, indeed, still stood aloof, and the district Miners' Associations maintained their Liberal connections.   But elsewhere the Socialist victory appeared to be decisive.

The Socialism which triumphed in the formation of the Labour Representation Committee was, however, a Socialism *sui generis*—a peculiarly British product.   Continental Socialism was almost everywhere, apart from certain Anarchist tinges, Marxist in its ideas and outlook.   It was based definitely on the doctrine of the class struggle, and accepted the Marxian economic and historical analysis as the essential basis of its teaching.   The Democratic Federation, pioneer of modern Socialism in Great Britain, had set out on its career with a minimum of doctrinal equipment, and had owed at the outset almost as much to Henry George as to Karl Marx.   But very soon it had adopted the entire Marxian gospel and, under Hyndman's leadership, had constituted itself the expositor of Marxism to the British workers.   Thus, for a few years, British Socialism had taken a turn which united it closely to the Socialism of the Continent; for the Socialist League was, on the surface at any rate, as Marxist as its larger rival, and, where it diverged from Marxism, was associated with continental Anarchism.

This situation, however, did not last long. The Marxists of the S.D.F. and the Socialist League had a big share in creating the " New Unionism " of the 'eighties, especially through the part which they played in the unemployed troubles of 1886-7. But having helped to create, they could not control. Neither the New Unionism of the miners, dockers, and gasworkers nor the widespread sympathy which flowed out towards its efforts for a raising of the " bottom dog " was fundamentally Marxist. The movement among the masses, in as far as it was Socialist at all, created a Socialism almost without doctrines ; and the new Socialism of the intellectuals began far more as an ethical and Utilitarian than as a class-war movement. It owed more to Mill than to Marx, and though it sought a radical reconstruction of the social system, was strongly disinclined to accept the class-struggle as the instrument of change.

Two bodies are peculiarly typical of this British kind of Socialism, and these two bodies exerted a powerful influence not only on the general move-ment of opinion, but also on each other. The Independent Labour Party, led and personified from the first by Keir Hardie, sought above all to make Socialism a broad, human movement on behalf of the bottom dog. It was not Social Democratic in the Marxian sense ; it was rather humanitarian Radicalism adopting a Socialist policy as the means to a more equal distribu-tion of wealth and happiness. It gathered up into its ranks a great mass of ethical as well as of economic discontent and aspiration—Trade Unionists sick of the narrow exclusiveness of the older craft Unions, middle-class sympathisers whose generous impulses led them to throw in their lot with the poor and needy, intellectuals who realised the bankruptcy of the older parties in face of the growing need for a collective control over the immensely complicated forces of the economic system, and seekers after a new way of life to whom the great depression had laid bare the illusions of Victorian progress. A sufficiently heterogeneous mass out of which to make an effective and coherent party, and clearly a mass likely to be welded together more by opportunity than by doctrine.

If the I.L.P. expressed the soul of the new ferment, the Fabian Society aspired to be its brain—and the Fabians had a clear social philosophy, though it was far removed from that of Karl Marx. First founded in 1883 as a " Fellowship of the New Life "—a tiny group of intellectual idealists brought together by the " wandering scholar," Thomas Davidson—the Fabian Society soon broke sharply away from its origins, and developed into a small intellectual group intent on working out the mechanics of the new society its members felt to be growing up around them. They became

Socialists less by spiritual conversion than by a process of intellectual conviction. It seemed to them obvious that the gross inequalities of wealth and opportunity ought to be put right by better social organisation, and they set themselves deliberately to think out the means of change. Moreover, being for the most part middle-class people in a settled way of life, they were not in a hurry. They could think in centuries or at least in decades, whereas the weltering mass of New Unionists was compelled by its economic position to think in terms of immediate remedies and alleviations. Their name, "Fabian"—from Fabius Maximus, the "Delayer," the great Roman general—expressed their conviction that they could afford to wait.

The Fabian Society was a very small body, which owed its influence to the intellectual quality of its membership. Mr. and Mrs. Sidney Webb, Bernard Shaw, Mrs. Annie Besant, Prof. Graham Wallas, and its other leaders, were persons of really outstanding ability, whose collaboration, continued over a series of years, was singularly fruitful. *Fabian Essays*, edited by Bernard Shaw and published for the Society in 1889, is the most important single publication in the history of British Socialism. It, and the long series of *Fabian Tracts*, had a tremendous influence on the development of British Socialist thought and policy. Above all, they profoundly affected the growth and policy of the Labour Party.

Hardie and the I.L.P. created a genuine and influential popular movement, which was bound together by a strong sentiment of humanity and justice, and knew perfectly well what it wanted in terms of immediate social reforms, but lacked a clear or constructive long-term policy; the Fabians were a group of highly intelligent leaders, in possession of a definite social philosophy but lacking a rank and file. These two groups helped and mutually formed each other. If there had been no I.L.P., the Fabians might easily have become a band of influential theorists wholly unconnected with the working-class movement, or at least no more connected with it than Jeremy Bentham was with the followers of Cobbett and "Orator" Hunt. The existence of the I.L.P. helped them to proceed from theorising to the formulation of a practical and constructive programme which they set out to persuade the I.L.P. to accept. For a long time, indeed, they did not throw themselves wholeheartedly into the working-class movement. They were sceptical about the early attempts to form a Labour Party independent of Conservatives and Liberals alike, and some of their leaders were disposed to prefer a policy of permeating the existing parties with Socialist ideas. But the I.L.P. was, above all other bodies, the most natural and the easiest for them to permeate; and to it a large and growing part of their efforts was directed. There were no such obstacles in the way of permeating it as prevented the Fabians from bothering their heads much about the Social Democratic Federation.

For the Fabian Society was from the first, and remained, essentially non-Marxist in its habit of thought. It built its economics from the top of an orthodox ladder, of which the rungs were Ricardo, Mill and Jevons. It rejected with scorn the Marxian theory of value, to which the economic knowledge of the earlier British Marxists was apt to be confined ; and it was profoundly uninterested in the class-struggle as an expression of the Materialist Conception of History. It thought, indeed, in terms of social evolution, as Marx did; but its evolutionism came from Darwin, Spencer and Huxley, and not from Hegel and Marx, and was thought of as a gradual and continuous process, and not as involving catastrophic change. In effect, it rooted itself firmly in established British ways of thought, and visualised Socialism as arising rather by a natural and gradual development of British institutions and tendencies than by any process of revolutionary upheaval. It set itself not to smash the capitalist State, but to turn it, in accordance with the needs of the times, into the " Welfare State." Its policy was rather to use and to adapt than to destroy things as they were.

This Fabian Socialism, clear-cut and closely reasoned, largely provided the I.L.P. leaders with just what they had lacked—a carefully worked-out programme applicable to their immediate situation and yet wide and far-reaching enough in its Socialist objectives to make an idealistic appeal. It was the Fabian Society that chiefly taught them, instead of awaiting the complete nationalisation of all the means of production, distribution and exchange, to think in terms of piecemeal nationalisation, and especially of the " gas and water " Socialism of municipal enterprise. It was the Fabian Society that chiefly set them off to capture municipal government with the aim of using it as an instrument for the achievement of some measure of constructive Socialism. The Fabians, it is true, did not need to teach the New Unionists to look to the State as an instrument of social reform. That lesson, through long decades of factory agitation, had been learnt already. But they did give form and precision to the demand for the legal eight-hours day and the legal minimum wage, which became the corner-stones of immediate I.L.P. policy. Moreover, it presented the policy of public ownership and control of industry as a logical development of the State intervention already embodied in Factory and Mines Acts, in Education and Housing Acts, and of the further measures of intervention which figured in the immediate programme of the I.L.P. and of the younger Trade Union leaders. The I.L.P. would doubtless in time have hammered out a complete policy for itself even without the help of the Fabians. But this does not lessen the decisive influence which, largely through the I.L.P., Fabianism exerted on the development of British Socialism.

Neither of the Fabians nor of the I.L.P. can the influence be at all measured by numbers. In 1889, when *Fabian Essays* were published, the Fabian Society had only 150 members. Even in 1900 it had only about 850. These figures do not include the local Fabian Societies, which grew rapidly after 1889, but dwindled again after the formation of the I.L.P., and were, indeed, largely merged in it. The I.L.P. in 1900 still numbered only a few thousands. But, while the Fabians included in their ranks most of the men and women who were actively thinking out the new Socialist policy, the I.L.P. included in the main just those who were best placed for securing its adoption—the younger leaders in the Trade Unions, the active promoters of every phase of working-class activity, the men and women who, mostly without aspiring to creative leadership, were ready to put in hard work and to make great personal sacrifices for the cause in which they believed.

This explains how this handful was able, in less than ten years, to bring the Trade Union Movement round to the acceptance of independent working-class representation in Parliament, and of the "Socialist-Trade Union Alliance" as the means of achieving it. It was not easily done ; and success, when it came, was not at once complete. But the doing of it at all was a very great achievement ; and in the successful formation of the Labour Representation Committee Keir Hardie and his colleagues felt a not unnatural elation.

What had they done ? They had made a new Socialism, violent sometimes in its expression, because there were strong ethical impulses behind it, but essentially moderate and evolutionary in its conception of social change ; British to the backbone in its policy and methods of expression, however internationalist and pacifist in its outlook ; simple enough to be easily and widely understood, and so undefined in its doctrinal basis as to make recruits readily among persons of quite different types. There were weaknesses in these very sources of immediate strength. But it is certain that on no other basis could British Socialism have grown so rapidly or won so soon the alliance of the Trade Unions.

Keir Hardie was, indeed, a most typical embodiment of the I.L.P. attitude. No less than Blatchford and the rest of the " Clarion " group, he could be moved by cruelty or injustice to fierce anger and to violence of expression. But his anger was always ethical, and his entire attitude made Socialism a moral crusade for human decency and good fellowship. One of his best-known pamphlets was called *Can a Man be a Christian on a Pound a Week ?* ; and its title was characteristic of him. Blatchford, meanwhile, vigorously attacked the Churches for their apathy in face of misery and for their failure to provide a Christian social gospel. In *God and my Neighbour*, in *Not Guilty : a Plea for the Bottom Dog*, and in his stream of articles in the Press, Blatchford gave the British people, with its strong nonconformist religious tradition, an ethical version of Socialism which made it a substitute for the orthodox doctrines in which they were losing faith. John Trevor, with his Labour Church movement, provided opportunities for collective expression of an ethical religion of Socialism. All these forces worked together to strengthen the I.L.P.'s influence and to weaken that of the S.D.F., whose leaders were scornful of such moralisings, and were by no means willing to temper the wind of scientific Socialism to the shorn Christian.

Armed with this new Socialism, the I.L.P. set to work to bring the Trade Unions round, if not to a declared faith in Socialism, at least to the formation of an independent working-class political party. Year after year they hammered away at the Trades Union Congress, learning by their early mistakes to put less weight on personal attacks upon the older leaders, and· more on the promotion of Socialist resolutions upon questions of policy. This grew the easier for them as, with the help of the Fabians, their own practical policy became clarified. Above all, they pressed steadily for the creation of the new party, till at last, in 1899, they secured the passage of the resolution under which the Labour Representation Committee was formed in the following year.

As we saw in the second part of this book, this did not mean at once the creation of a definite Labour Party. Independence of other parties was indeed proclaimed ; but this was not to exclude arrangements or coalitions. The " out-and-out " Socialist basis demanded by the Social Democratic Federation was rejected equally with the proposal of the " Old Unionists " to limit the platform of the new body to purely industrial questions, so as to leave each member free in general politics to follow his own line. There was no explicit declaration of Socialist faith—even of the ethical Socialist faith of Keir Hardie—and the L.R.C. began life not as a clearly defined party, but merely as a group. Last, but not least, there was still no general levy on the members even of the Trade Unions which became affiliated to the L.R.C. Hardie and his friends had drawn the Trade Unions officially into politics on at least a semi-independent basis. But the Miners and some other big Unions remained aloof; and the new body could not feel at all sure of the continued or whole-hearted allegiance even of its nominal constituents.

Circumstances, however, favoured the new movement, and enabled it to gain rapidly in strength and prestige. And the men who had made it were quick to seize opportunities when they arose. James Ramsay MacDonald, a relatively unknown man before 1900, became the first secretary of the L.R.C., and steered it with unwearying adroitness through its early troubles. But above all it was helped by the new embroilment of the Trade Unions with the law. The Taff Vale Case created the Labour Party, and brought Keir Hardie's work within a few years to a point which without it would have been far harder to reach. But equally, unless Hardie and his friends had first created the L.R.C., the development of the Labour Movement after Taff Vale might have taken quite a different turn. It took the Taff Vale Case ot " make " the Labour Party ; but its foundations were laid, with the help of the Fabians, by the "New Unionists" and the I.L.P.

BOOKS

G. D. H. Cole. *British Working-class Politics, 1832–1914.*
E. R. Pease. *History of the Fabian Society.*
G. B. Shaw. *Early History of the Fabian Society.*
H. W. Laidler. *History of Socialist Thought.*
M. Beer. *History of British Socialism.*
W. Stewart. *Life of J. Keir Hardie.*
G. D. H. Cole. *Keir Hardie* (Fabian Tract).
H. M. Hyndman. *The Record of an Adventurous Life.*
A. M. Thompson. *Here I Lie.*
A. Neil Lyons. *Robert Blatchford.*
P. Snowden. *Autobiography.*
G. Elton. *Life of James Ramsay MacDonald.*

2. THE TAFF VALE CASE

The Taff Vale Case, which cost the Amalgamated Society of Railway Servants £50,000 and "made" the Labour Party, arose out of a local dispute. In 1900, without authority from their Society, the railwaymen employed by the Taff Vale Railway Company in South Wales came out on strike. At this time, except in the North-East, railway Trade Unionism was still wholly unrecognised by the railway companies, which maintained that a *quasi*-military discipline, inconsistent with Trade Union organisation, was essential for the proper conduct of the service. The only important railway strike before 1900, that of the Scottish railwaymen in 1890, had ended in the complete defeat of the Scottish Railway Servants' Union and its absorption into the English Society. The railway "all grades" movement of 1897 had not been pushed to the length of a strike. The Taff Vale's General Manager, Mr. Beasley, was therefore acting in accordance with the traditional railway attitude in making up his mind to fight the strike with every weapon within his reach.

His first effort was to secure enough "blacklegs" to maintain a service in spite of the stoppage. This brought the Amalgamated Society of Railway Servants officially upon the scene. Although the Society had not authorised the strike, it now granted strike pay to the men who were out, and sent its General Secretary to South Wales, where he played a part in dissuading the company's blacklegs from going to work. There was also, on the part of the strikers, a certain amount of tumultuous picketing, and some acts of violence were done ; but it was never alleged that the Trade Unions in any way instigated or authorised these acts. The Taff Vale Company, however, apart from prosecutions brought against individual strikers, decided to proceed against the Amalgamated Society of Railway Servants itself. Two actions were begun. An injunction was sought to restrain the Society and its officers from committing acts calculated to damage the company in its business, or, in other words, from trying to stop the blacklegs from working during the strike. And, secondly, the Society itself was sued for damages caused by the actions of its officers and members. Both actions were successful. The injunction was granted, and the company got £23,000 in damages from the Society, the decision being upheld, after a succession of appeals, by the House of Lords.

In order to explain the sensation caused by this judgment, it is necessary to cast our minds back to the Trade Union legislation of the 'seventies. It had been generally accepted, until the Taff Vale Case, that no such actions as were now successfully brought against the Railway Servants could be sustained in any court. Indeed, it is on record that Mr. Beasley actually brought his actions in face of the advice of the Taff Vale Company's lawyers. The reasons for this belief were twofold. In the first place, despite proposals to the contrary, the Acts of 1871-76 had definitely withheld from the Trade Unions the rights and responsibilities of " incorporation." These Acts had removed the criminal taint previously attaching in some measure, despite the legislation of 1824 and 1825, to combinations of employers and workmen, had given Trade Unions in certain respects a defined legal status, including the right in property cases to sue and be sued in the courts, and had legalised not only the existence of Trade Unions, but a number of activities essential to their effective conduct. They had, at the same time, explicitly barred the direct enforcement in the courts either of any internal contracts made by the members of Trade Unions—about rights to benefits, for example—or of any collective agreement between a Trade Union of workers and an employers' association. It had been generally supposed, though it now appeared that the belief had no legal ground, that the denial of " incorporation " and the provisions of Section 4 of the Trade Union Act of 1871 definitely excluded the sueing of a Trade Union in its registered name or in any collective way for any wrong not explicitly mentioned in the statutes. The Trade Union Acts were believed, by implication though not in so many words, to bar any such actions as the Taff Vale Railway Company had now successfully brought.

It is, indeed, almost certain that this was the intention of those who framed and passed the Acts of 1871-76. But the development of legal practice in the last quarter of the nineteenth century had materially altered the situation. The lawyers, much troubled to square with their principles the growth of large numbers of powerful unincorporated associations doing important acts and owning substantial property, gave during this period a rapidly extending sphere of operation to what is known as a " representative action," by means of which an unincorporated association can sue or be sued in the name of one or more of its officers or members on behalf of the membership as a whole. According to the earlier legal theory, the law had recognised only on the one hand individuals and on the other corporations—collective persons definitely endowed by statute or charter with the legal attribute of corporate personality. Municipal Corporations, and the great Guilds and Livery Companies, Colleges and other privileged institutions acting under royal charter, and such special creations as the Bank of England and the East India Company, were leading examples of this type of collective legal personality. To these were added, during the nineteenth century, various new types, including joint stock companies incorporated under the Companies Acts and a large number of public utility companies, including the railway companies, incorporated under special statutes. The corporation proper loomed larger and larger in English law as the century advanced.

But there was at the same time an immense growth of unincorporated associations of the most diverse types, and it became more and more difficult for the lawyers to follow the practice of treating all these merely as crowds of individuals or as de facto " partnerships," whose collective existence, as distinct from that of the individuals belonging to them, the courts would not recognise at all. Hence the growth of the " representative action," which enabled the existence of such bodies to be recognised where the lawyers thought fit. This growth was entirely apart from any cases affecting Trade Unions as such. Nor was the point specifically raised in the Taff Vale Case, in which the Union was sued, not in a " representative action," but in its registered name.

There can, however, be little doubt that the changed attitude of the courts to unincorporated associations in general influenced the judges' decision. It would clearly have been of no advantage to the Trade Union to be immune from an action brought against it by name, if it had been liable to precisely the same damages as a result of a " representative action." But for the growth of "representative actions" it is very doubtful if the judges would have held that a Trade Union could sue or be sued at all, save in the quite minor cases specified in the Act of 1871. But, as the " representative action " opened the way to bringing the Trade Union effectively into court, the judges had little difficulty in reaching the conclusion that it could sue or be sued by name as well. In granting to it the rights accorded by the Acts of 1871–76 Parliament, they held, had given to it, not indeed incorporation, but enough of a corporate character to enable it to sue or be sued in this way. Its appearance by name in the courts had been explicitly recognised in certain cases; and, if in these, why not in others ?

It is probable, then, that the judges, though their decision caused almost universal surprise, were correct in their interpretation of the law. This, however, did not make the matter any the less serious for the Trade Unions. For the judgment struck at the essential basis of all strike activity, and threatened not only the Trade Union funds available for strike payments, but also those destined for the payment of friendly benefits of every kind. Every strike caused damage to someone, or, at least, if it did not, it would usually stand no possible chance of success. And now no one could tell what limits the courts would set to the civil liability of Trade Unions for damages caused by strikes conducted by their orders or with their countenance—or even by their members or local branches without official consent.

The question, it must be emphasised, was one of civil, and not of criminal, liability. It had been well understood before the Taff Vale Case that individual Trade Unionists or officials were liable to prosecution for criminal acts committed in the course of a trade dispute, such as acts of violence in connection with picketing. Indeed, the interpretations placed by the courts on the picketing clause of the Conspiracy and Protection of Property Act of 1875 had already given the Unions substantial grievances, for which they were seeking redress, before the Taff Vale troubles began. During the Taff Vale strike, undoubtedly certain acts of violence in connection with picketing did occur, though these were not countenanced by the Union ; but the Taff Vale judgment itself was grounded, not on these isolated acts of violence, but on the civil damage caused to the railway company by the strike itself and by the attempts of the Union and the strikers even peacefully to deter blacklegs from accepting employment. It was not alleged that these acts were in any way criminal ; but on them was successfully based a civil action for damages against the Union itself, as well as an injunction calling on the Union to refrain from repeating them.

If these non-criminal acts constituted, as the courts now held, a civil wrong, for which the Unions could be assessed in damages, what could a Trade Union safely do ? What ordinary incidents of a trade dispute might not be construed as wrongful interference with the employer's trade or business ? Might not all picketing, lawful for the individual picket, expose the Union to a civil action for damages ? Might not every attempt to bring pressure to bear on the employer by organised action be similarly regarded by the courts ? The Trade Unions were well aware that the judges had no love for them or for their methods. The law would certainly not be strained in their favour ; and it might very well be strained against them.

Of course, it would have to be shown, before the Union could be made liable, that it had been in some way responsible for the wrong done. It would have to be demonstrated, to the satisfaction of the court, that the persons who actually committed the wrong had acted as the Union's agents. But this was cold comfort. Apart from the fact that the Unions themselves desired to do many of the things which the courts had declared to be wrongs, and could scarcely conduct a dispute at all without doing them, would not the courts be inclined to hold the Unions responsible for all the actions of their members in relation to the Union's affairs, or at the very least for all the actions of all their branch officers and representatives ? But all these actions, taken by many thousands of individuals up and down the country, the Unions could not possibly hope to control.

The Taff Vale judgment therefore struck at the roots of all effective strike action under Trade Union auspices. As long as it remained the law of the land, no strike would be safe except a purely unofficial movement conducted without any organisation at all behind it. The entire right to strike, conceded in 1824 and, as it was believed, triumphantly reaffirmed in the legislation of 1871-76, was not merely jeopardised, but virtually abrogated, by this one decision of the courts.

It was obvious that the Trade Union Movement must bestir itself in order to get the effects of the judgment reversed by fresh legislation. And it was natural that the Unions should turn, apart from the direct pressure which they could exercise on the older parties, to the newly created Labour Representation Committee to help them in their trouble.

BOOKS

R. Y. Hedges and A. Winterbottom. *Legal History of Trade Unionism.*
Report of Royal Commission on Trade Disputes, 1906.
W. M. Geldart. *The Present Law of Trade Disputes and Trade Unions, 1914.*
H. H. Slesser. *Trade Union Law.*
S. and B. Webb. *History of Trade Unionism.*
G. A. Alcock. *History of the Amalgamated Society of Railway Servants.*
W. M. Bailey. *Trade Unions and the State.*

3. THE GROWTH OF THE LABOUR REPRESENTATION COMMITTEE

The Labour Representation Committee began its work under very difficult conditions. Within a few months of its formation it was in the thick of a General Election—the " khaki " election of 1900. The Boer War was in progress, and, in the country as a whole, war sentiment was strong. The Socialist bodies, the I.L.P. and the S.D.F., had taken up a strong anti-war attitude ; and a substantial section of the Liberals, headed by John Morley and Lloyd George, had adopted a similar position. The L.R.C. was naturally unprepared with any long list of candidates, and had practically no money. Its whole income for the year 1900-01 amounted only to £243. It was therefore in no position to finance candidatures, but only to give endorsement to those financed by the separate bodies of which it was made up. In these circumstances, it was thought highly satisfactory that fifteen L.R.C. candidates went to the poll.

The War being the dominant issue in the election, the question at once arose of common action between the Liberal and Labour anti-war candidates. No official decision was taken on this issue ; but the *Labour Leader*, the official organ of the I.L.P., supported collaboration, and this, left to the discretion of local bodies, was largely practised. Consequently, there were only five three-cornered fights out of the fifteen, and the L.R.C.'s two successes were both scored with some Liberal support. Richard Bell, the railwaymen's secretary, was elected at Derby without Liberal opposition, and Keir Hardie won the double constituency of Merthyr in informal alliance with D. A. Thomas, afterwards Lord Rhondda, the great coalowner, who was a strong opponent of the War. The third candidate, whom Hardie defeated by a large majority, was a "Liberal Imperialist" and a supporter of the War.

These were the only L.R.C. successes, though John Burns, who counted by this time as a "Lib-Lab," was again returned for Battersea, and Broadhurst, Burt, Cremer, Fenwick, Pickard and John Wilson were elected under Liberal-Trade Union auspices. All these last, except Broadhurst (a mason) and Cremer (a carpenter), were miners. But though the L.R.C. won but two seats, its candidates polled well, with a total of 62,000 votes and an average poll of 35 per cent. of the votes cast in the fifteen constituencies fought. There were in addition a number of "straight" Socialist candidates; but none of these was elected. Actually, the number of working-class representatives in the House of Commons was reduced by five; for several of the older "Lib-Labs" were beaten. But this was a cause of no regret to the supporters of the L.R.C.

The interest of the first six years of the new party's life is to be found rather outside than within the House of Commons. In face of the parliamentary situation, it was impossible for Hardie and his one colleague, even if they had seen eye to eye, to do more than skirmish. Richard Bell did indeed score an immediate success by blocking a Bill promoted by the Great Eastern Railway, and so helped to defeat a project under which a compulsory scheme of contributory pensions without any control by the employees was to have been set up; and Hardie indefatigably made propaganda speeches and impressed his abilities on the House and the country alike. But both before and after Joseph Chamberlain's severance from his colleagues on the question of Tariff Reform the parliamentary situation was unfavourable to the pushing forward of distinctively working-class claims. The Education Act of 1902, which laid the foundations of public secondary education, the Factory Act of 1901, which was mainly a consolidating measure, and the Unemployed Workmen Act of 1905, the first faint recognition of a public duty towards the unemployed, were the chief social measures of the 1900 Parliament.

It was outside the House of Commons that the Labour Representation Committee grew to be an important body; and the growth hardly began until the Trade Union Movement had been effectually roused by the Taff Vale decision. At first prospects looked bad. In 1901, the Miners' Federation decided to launch a common political fund for the promotion of miners' candidatures throughout the coalfields; but this was done wholly apart from the L.R.C., and the miners' candidates were left free to run as Liberals, or in any other affiliation they might choose. In the same year the Social Democratic Federation decided to secede from the L.R.C. Its delegates had taken part in forming the new body ; but the S.D.F. Conference now seceded because their resolution in favour of basing its policy on the " class-war " had been rejected. Moreover, when at the L.R.C. Conference of 1901 the Fabians proposed the institution of a compulsory levy of the affiliated societies, this plan was rejected as premature, though it was obviously essential to the success of the movement. The membership of the affiliated societies was only 376,000 in 1900-01 and 469,000 in 1901-02, out of a total Trade Union membership of about two millions. The income rose only from £243 to £343 in the latter year.

In 1902, however, thanks largely to the Taff Vale decision, the tide began to turn. During that year a number of Trade Unions started political funds of their own, and, encouraged by this development, the L.R.C. Conference instructed its executive to prepare a scheme for a general levy in readiness for the next year. Moreover, in 1902 the L.R.C. scored its first by-election success, D. J. Shackleton being returned unopposed for Clitheroe under its auspices as the nominee of the cotton operatives. The cotton Trade Unions, which had hitherto held aloof—James Mawdsley, the general secretary of the cotton spinners, had even stood as a Conservative in 1899—began to come in. For 1902-03 the affiliated membership nearly doubled, rising to 861,000. The L.R.C.'s income rose to £800.

1903 brought further successes. Will Crooks, under Fabian auspices, won Woolwich with some Liberal support, and at Barnard Castle, Arthur Henderson, of the Ironfounders' Society, previously a Liberal, was the first L.R.C. candidate to succeed in a three-cornered fight, against both Liberals and Conservatives. The Newcastle Conference adopted the proposal for a levy, though this was fixed on a voluntary basis and at the rate of only one penny per member per year—a suggestion by Arthur Henderson to ask for a shilling a member being decisively rejected. At the same time, the policy and constitution of the L.R.C. were thoroughly overhauled. Henderson and Crooks, among others, had supported Liberal candidates, though not from the Liberal platform, at by-elections where there was no Labour candidate. These events led to a stiffening of attitude. Candidates and executive members were definitely instructed that they must not identify themselves with any other party, and it was decided to exact from successful candidates a pledge either to abide by the decisions of the parliamentary group or to resign their seats. This latter resolution, carried in face of executive opposition, was rescinded the following year ; but the prohibition of connection with other parties was maintained. On the other hand, an attempt from the Socialist side to secure for candidates the right to describe themselves as " Labour and Socialist," instead of plain " Labour," was rejected at the Newcastle Conference of 1903.

At the Trades Union Congress the same year an unsuccessful attack was launched upon the now prosperous policy of the " Labour Alliance." A proposal was put forward seeking to confine membership of the L.R.C. to active Trade Unionists only, which would have excluded both Keir Hardie and Ramsay MacDonald, as neither of these was either working at a trade or a full-time Trade Union official. This was an amendment to a resolution calling on the Trade Unions to support the L.R.C. ; but the amendment was rejected, and the resolution approved, by a large majority.

Up to this point the L.R.C.'s status in relation to the Trades Union Congress had been somewhat anomalous. Created by the Congress, it was no part of Congress, but a wholly separate body with a different membership. Nevertheless, Congress was still vaguely supposed until 1904 to preserve some sort of undefined jurisdiction over it. At the 1904 Trades Union Congress, however, resolutions dealing with the status and policy of the L.R.C. were ruled out of order, on the ground that it was an " outside organisation " over which Congress could claim no authority. This settled the question. Thenceforth, though the two bodies often worked in conjunction, their entire independence of each other was fully recognised.

This emancipation of the L.R.C. was partly due to accidental circumstances. Richard Bell, one of the two L.R.C. candidates returned in 1900, had been for some time at variance with his colleagues on a number of points. The crisis came in 1904, over a by-election at Norwich. The L.R.C. candidate was defeated ; and Bell wired congratulations to his successful Liberal opponent. On this and other matters resolutions were to have been moved at the Trades Union Congress censuring Bell's attitude ; but Bell, who was himself Chairman of the Congress, ruled them out of order. This left the problem of dealing with him to the L.R.C., and Bell, in accordance with the Newcastle decision, ceased to rank as a Labour representative.

Apart from this incident, the chief events of 1904 were the placing of the parliamentary levy on a compulsory basis—which raised the income of the L.R.C. to over £12,000 in 1905-06—and the withdrawal of the rule that L.R.C. Members of Parliament must either obey party discipline or resign. In the following year, a final attempt to exclude the Socialist societies and put the L.R.C. on a purely Trade Union basis was defeated. When at last, at the end of 1905, the Conservative Government resigned, the L.R.C. entered the new General Election as a Labour Party in all but name.

BOOKS

G. D. H. Cole. *British Working-class Politics, 1832–1914.*
A. W. Humphrey. *History of Labour Representation.*
L.R.C. Annual Reports.
Independent Labour Party Annual Reports.
W. Stewart. *Life of J. Keir Hardie.*
M. A. Hamilton. *Arthur Henderson.*

CHAPTER III

1906 AND AFTER

1. The 1906 Election—The Trade Disputes Act   2. Labour and the New Liberalism of 1906
3. Internal Labour Politics—The Osborne Judgment

1. THE 1906 ELECTION—THE TRADE DISPUTES ACT

THE General Election of 1906 brought the Liberals back to power with an overwhelming majority, large enough to make them independent of both Nationalist and Labour support.   It also created the Labour Party as an effective parliamentary force.   In 1900 the Labour Representation Committee had secured the return of two members ; in 1906 its representatives numbered twenty-nine, *plus* one Trade Union member, J. W. Taylor, who joined it immediately after the election.   The miners' group, still outside the L.R.C., but disposed to act with it on many questions, rose from five to fourteen, and there were about a dozen "Lib-Labs" of varying complexions in addition.   Thus the increase was not in L.R.C. representation alone, but in working-class representation generally.   The sensational victory, however, was that of the L.R.C., which came back to the new Parliament a compact and powerful force which the older parties were at length compelled to take into account.   Its new position was signalised in the same year by a change of name.   The Labour Representation Committee became, in name as well as in fact, the Labour Party.

This astonishing advance was, doubtless, due primarily to the working-class resentment caused by the Taff Vale decision and the determination to get the law relating to trade disputes satisfactorily amended.   But the victory certainly could not have been won without a great deal of Liberal collabora-tion.   Only five of the twenty-nine successful candidates of the L.R.C. had Liberal opponents, and in nearly all the unsuccessful three-cornered contests the Liberal was ahead of the Labour candidate.   Nine seats were won in two-member constituencies in which there were only one Liberal and one Labour candidate.   Almost everywhere, except in Scotland, there was in effect an informal alliance between Labour and the Liberals.   The Scottish Liberals, however, rejected this policy ; and the Scottish Workers' Repre-sentation Committee, formed by the Scottish Trades Union Congress independently of the L.R.C., had everywhere to face Liberal opposition, and did not win a single seat.   The L.R.C., however, did win two seats in Scot-land, both against Liberal opposition.   The Labour successes were, in fact, largely a part of the great Liberal victory of 1906.   But, while this must be conceded, it must also be remembered that the Liberals would not have made way for so many Labour candidates unless they had regarded Labour help as important enough to be worth buying at a high price.

The Liberal victory was, of course, among the most astonishingly complete reverses of fortune in British political history. The Conservatives had been continuously in office for more than ten years ; and, although they were expected to suffer a set-back, nothing like the great Liberal sweep was expected. The Conservative Government, however, had been not only incompetent and weakly led, but also torn asunder by the great Tariff Reform controversy which followed Chamberlain's resignation in 1903. They had declared against Free Trade, but hesitantly ; and many of them fought halfheartedly and without a programme. The Liberals, on the other hand, like Disraeli after 1867, were prepared to bid high for working-class support and were able to combine this appeal with the old appeals to Nonconformity and Free Trade. The " Chinese Labour " issue played some part in the election ; but the outstanding issues were Free Trade, Social Reform, and Trade Union rights.

The Labour politicians, for their part, were in most cases fully prepared for informal collaboration with the Liberals. Though the leading Trade Unions, except the Miners, had been persuaded to set up a separate party, many of their leaders, as well as of the " rank and file," remained essentially Liberals ; for the Labour Party had neither made nor required any explicit declaration of Socialist faith. The Fabian Society, though it was affiliated to the Labour Party, still included a good many Liberals in its ranks, and some of these actually stood as Liberal candidates in the 1906 election. Moreover, the Labour leaders wanted social and industrial reforms which had been long held up by Conservative predominance, and wanted above all the drastic reversal of the effects of the Taff Vale judgment ; and it was plain that none of these things could be secured except by Liberal help. The Labour Party was firm in maintaining its formal independence ; but, this conceded, it was ready for a substantial measure of common action.

The Liberals, on their side, were alarmed in the midst of their triumph—perhaps unduly alarmed—at the Labour Party's sensational growth. Shortly after the election they made an attempt to organise a Liberal-Labour League based on the " Lib-Lab " Members of Parliament. But this project was abortive, presumably because the miners refused their co-operation, and instead the miners and the other " Lib-Labs " formed a separate Trade Union group in the House, and worked in close conjunction with the Labour Party over the Trade Disputes Bill. After 1907 this Trade Union group gradually died away. When, in 1909, the Miners' Federation at length officially entered the Labour Party, the remaining " Lib-Labs," joined by a few miners who refused to come over to the Labour side, were to all intents and purposes completely absorbed into the main body of Liberalism.

" Lib-Lab," as a distinct group label, had practically ceased to exist before the General Election of 1910.

The first task of the new Labour Party was to get the effects of the Taff Vale decision removed by fresh legislation. In 1903, the Conservative Government had appointed a Royal Commission to consider what action should be taken in face of the decision ; but this body consisted mainly of lawyers, and no Trade Unionist was given a seat, though Sidney Webb, who had qualified as a barrister, was among the members. The Trade Unions refused to give evidence before it. By accident or design, the Commission's Report was delayed until after the General Election of 1906, so that it fell to the incoming Liberal Government to deal with the situation.

The Report, when it at length appeared, fell far short of the Trade Unions' demands. It proposed to limit the liability of Trade Union funds to actions arising out of proceedings definitely authorised, or at least not definitely repudiated, by the Trade Union executive concerned ; but, subject to this restriction, the liability of the Unions was to remain unaltered. Individuals were indeed to be protected against actions for damages based solely on the fact of their interference, in contemplation or furtherance of a trade dispute, with someone else's business, employment, or " right to dispose of his capital or labour as he wills." Acts which an individual might commit without fear of legal proceedings were not to become actionable merely because they were done in combination. And finally, in connection with picketing, " peaceful persuasion " was to be explicitly legalised, as it had been as long ago as 1859, only to be prohibited again in 1871, and not restored by the legislation of 1875.

Some of these provisions were fairly satisfactory to the Trade Unions. But the main thing they wanted was complete security for their funds ; and this the Commission was very far from conceding. When, therefore, the Liberal Government introduced a Bill following fairly closely the lines of the Commission's Report, the entire Trade Union Movement was speedily up in arms. The Labour Party, with almost unanimous Trade Union support, pressed strongly for its own alternative Bill, in which it was laid down simply that "an action shall not be brought against a Trade Union . . . for the recovery of damage sustained by any person or persons by reason of the action of a member or members of such Trade Unions."

As soon as the Government produced its Bill, it appeared that the Trade Unions had done at the General Election a good deal of effective work besides promoting the return of their own candidates. A very large number of Liberal Members, it was found, had pledged themselves to the complete reversal of the effects of the Taff Vale decision. Not a few Conservatives, hard driven by Trade Union pressure in the constituencies, had done the same. The Government was unwilling to incur the unpopularity of resisting the Trade Union claims. It hastily dropped overboard both the

Royal Commission's Report and its own scheme, and capitulated almost entirely to the Trade Unions. There was no effective opposition, and when the Trade Disputes Act became law, it included the famous " section 4," which gave the Unions practically all they wanted : " An action against a trade union, whether of workmen or masters, or against any members or officials thereof on behalf of themselves and all other members of the trade union, in respect of any tortious act[1] alleged to have been committed by or on behalf of the trade union, shall not be entertained by any court."

The remaining clauses of the Act of 1906 did not depart so widely from the terms of the original Government Bill. Their scope was slightly widened, so as to give the Unions fuller satisfaction ; but no vital changes were made in the original draft, which was itself a sufficiently vital change from the law as it stood. The Unions were granted freedom, in contemplation or furtherance of a trade dispute, but not otherwise, to interfere with other people's trade or business, or with their right to dispose of their capital or labour at will. The law relating to peaceful picketing was redrafted almost in the terms which the Unions desired, and the principle was laid down finally that in civil, as well as in criminal, matters relating to trade disputes, men could not become amenable to the law merely by reason of acting in combination. But these sections passed almost unnoticed in the hurricane of argument which speedily burst round " section 4."

This section, it was widely urged, especially by lawyers, who were almost solidly hostile, placed the Trade Unions in a privileged position above the law. The Unions' immunity was not even, in this section, explicitly limited to acts done " in contemplation or furtherance of a trade dispute." Trade Union funds were simply and comprehensively protected from all risk of civil proceedings either by way of direct action against a Union or by way of " representative action " against certain of its members. Henceforth, it appeared, a Trade Union was free to commit, with very few exceptions, whatever civil wrongs it might choose, without exposing itself or its officers to any risk of an action at law.

The question was, of course, only one of civil liability. If the officers or members of a Trade Union committed any criminal act, either on behalf of the Unions or otherwise, " section 4 " gave them no protection. But the fear of the Unions was of civil actions directed to the spoliation of their funds ; and this fear the section seemed completely to remove. Later events did, indeed, suggest that the courts might hold its scope to be narrower than appeared by ruling that it applied, by implication, only to acts done in connection with trade disputes, or only to actions done by the Trade Union in a distinctively " trade union " capacity, and that the Act might possibly be held not to apply at all to certain types of dispute, such as the General Strike of 1926. Indeed, in 1926 high legal authorities took directly opposite views

---

[1] A tort is, in effect, any civil wrong (as distinct from a criminal act) other than a breach of contract.

about its meaning ; and the Act of 1927, as we shall see, created a new category of "illegal" strikes that were to be excluded from protection under the Act of 1906. But these possible limitations were not thought of at the time ; and the section appeared to confer an exceedingly wide immunity.

The Trade Unions, in fact, in their mood of 1906, were ready to accept nothing short of what they believed to be complete escape from the nightmare which had haunted them since the Taff Vale decision ; and the extreme difficulty of drafting any less comprehensive alternative which would give them a reasonable measure of protection served to strengthen their hands. They secured a concession which was admittedly anomalous, because no one could devise an alternative method of meeting even their more obvious grievances.

The difficulty, indeed, arose from the anomalous position which Trade Unionism as a whole occupies in the modern capitalist State. The strike and the lock-out are, on the face of the matter, ridiculous things. It would be absurd, in any reasonably ordered society, for men to settle their differences by such means. But society, organised as it is, has been unable to find any third alternative, and has had to choose between the slavery of forced employment by a master and the effective recognition of the right to strike. If this right is recognised, the rights necessary in order to make it operative must be recognised as well. Every strike, or nearly every strike, is aimed at coercing someone to do what he does not want to do by inflicting some damage upon him, or possibly upon a third party. If such damage is to be actionable, clearly in effect the right to strike is taken away. Nor is this all. If the right to strike is to be effective, the Trade Unions must be free to exist, to build up funds, and to organise for strike action. This involves freedom to proselytise the non-unionist, and to conduct peaceful picketing. It further involves freedom to induce breach of contract ; for otherwise the employer will tie down his " blacklegs " by contracts which will make it unlawful for the Unions to proselytise them or to persuade them to abstain from working. It would be very difficult to draft a clause which effectively conceded these rights and yet fell much short of " section 4."

The alternative, often considered from 1871 onwards and as often rejected, of making the Trade Unions definitely corporate bodies, is not really an alternative at all. For, whether they are corporate bodies or not, the problems just mentioned have still to be faced. Without the immunity conferred by " section 4," or something closely resembling it, they would be unable to build up any stable funds ; and this would not only stop their activities as benefit societies, but also, in effect, negative the right to strike.

There is a further point in justification of the obduracy of the Unions in resisting any compromise on this question of liability of their funds. No one who studies the history of the Trade Unions' legal experiences can doubt that the judges have, again and again, been actuated by a strong anti-Trade Union bias. Any compromise would therefore have been likely to be interpreted in the courts in such a way as to concede as little as possible to the Trade Unions. The only effective way of tying the judges' hands was to get a simple and inclusive declaration from which legal subtleties would offer no way of escape. This the Unions sought to do ; but the observations of Mr. Justice Astbury's judgment in 1926, to which reference is made hereafter, serve to show that not even the most far-reaching clause is proof against unexpected judicial interpretation.

In 1906, however, both the " General Strike " and the Trade Union Act of 1927 were still very far off. In the eyes of all, the Trade Unions appeared to have won a complete and unequivocal victory and to have more than wiped out the effects of the Taff Vale decision. This result brought great credit to the Labour Party. In 1907 its affiliated membership rose to over a million, and its income exceeded £15,000. Two years later the accession of the Miners' Federation brought the " Lib-Lab " period of Trade Unionism finally to an end, and made it nearly as representative of the Trade Union Movement as the Trades Union Congress itself. The separate Scottish Labour Party was also disbanded in 1909. The Trade Disputes Act was won largely by electoral pressure on Liberal candidates, combined with the impressive demonstration of the Labour victories in the General Election. But the Labour Party reaped the benefit of the success. At the end of 1906 its prestige was very great, and high hopes were widely entertained of its future.

BOOKS

R. Y. Hedges and A. Winterbottom. *Legal History of Trade Unionism.*
W. M. Geldart. *The Present Law of Trade Disputes and Trade Unions, 1914.*
H. H. Slesser. *Trade Union Law.*
W. M. Bailey. *Trade Unions and the State.*
R. H. Gretton. *A Modern History of the English People.*

2. LABOUR AND THE NEW LIBERALISM OF 1906

By 1905, ten years of opposition had deeply changed the policy of the Liberal Party. Side by side with old Gladstonians, such as John Morley, were new Liberal Imperialists, such as Asquith and Sir Edward Grey, on the one hand, and new Radicals, such as Lloyd George, on the other. The Prime Minister, Campbell-Bannerman, had, on the whole, Radical sympathies ; and the Liberal Party was prepared, as we have seen, to bid high in order to retain its hold on the working-class electorate. The Liberals had not given up hope of attaching the Trade Unions once more firmly to the Liberal cause, or even of making the Labour Party itself a semi-dependent wing of the Liberal Movement.

Inevitably, the first affair to be settled was that of the right to strike.

We have seen how this was dealt with by an almost complete yielding to Labour on the main issue in dispute. This concession naturally increased the inclination of the Labour Party to work in with the Government; and during the early years of the new Parliament there were few occasions on which the two parties were decisively at variance. If the Labour Party occupied seats on the Opposition side of the House, this was rather because the huge Liberal majority left no room on the Government side than because Labour felt itself to be definitely in opposition. Indeed, after the first General Election of 1910, when the Liberal majority had been heavily reduced, the Labour Party moved across to new seats below the gangway on the Government side.

The years from 1906 to 1909 were rich in measures of social reform. In 1906, though the Government's chief measure, an Education Bill dealing mainly with the religious question in the schools, had to be withdrawn owing to a dispute with the House of Lords, a number of important measures were passed. The Merchant Shipping Acts were amended; the Education (Provision of Meals) Act—a Labour Party measure, sponsored particularly by F. W. Jowett, the Bradford I.L.P. leader—allowed feeding of school children by the Education Authorities in cases of distress ; the Workmen's Compensation Act granted compensation rights to all manual and many non-manual workers, and extended the system to certain specified industrial diseases, as well as accidents ; and, lastly, under pressure from the Labour Party, £200,000 was voted in aid of relief works for the unemployed under the Unemployed Workmen Act of 1905.

1907 was less productive, yielding only the Education Act which established school medical inspection ; but in 1908 came the granting of Old Age Pensions and the Coal Mines (Eight Hours) Act, for which the Miners' Federation had been struggling ever since its inception in 1888. In 1909—the year of Lloyd George's famous " Penal Budget "—came the largely abortive Housing and Town Planning Act, the Trade Boards Act, the fruit of the long agitation against sweated labour and for a legal minimum wage, the Labour Exchanges Act, forerunner of the system of unemployment insurance, and a remodelling of the Fair Wages Clause in response to Labour pressure.

The year 1910 was fully occupied by the controversy with the House of Lords over the Finance Bill. Two General Elections were fought on this issue, and it was not until the Parliament Act had been passed in 1911 that the Government was able to resume its social programme. Then came the Coal Mines Regulation Act and Lloyd George's National Insurance Act, incorporating in one measure the two essentially different schemes of Health and Unemployment Insurance—the latter confined to a small group of industries specially liable to fluctuation. In the same year the Shops Act granted the long-sought half-holiday, and Payment of Members was introduced. By this time, however, the Government had largely exhausted its impetus towards social legislation. Apart from the Coal Mines (Minimum Wage) Act, the direct outcome of the miners' national strike, 1912 produced no important social measure. 1913 brought only a slight extension of the Trade Boards Act to a number of new trades, and a small measure amending the Industrial and Provident Societies Acts at the request of the Co-operative Movement; and the first half of 1914 was almost barren.

Though the Liberal impulse had thus died away after 1911, the social legislation passed during the Liberal Government's first six years of office represented a substantial achievement. This legislation falls roughly into two periods. Up to and including 1909 the Government was engaged in promoting social measures which the Labour Movement desired to strengthen, but not to alter. There was difference about the pace, but not on the whole about the direction, of reform. After 1909, on the other hand, Liberal social legislation took a course which sharply divided the Labour Movement on questions of principle. The Coal Mines (Eight Hours) Act, the Workmen's Compensation Act, the Trade Boards Act, and Old Age Pensions had received practically solid Labour support, although the Labour Party would fain have made many improvements in the actual measures passed. The National Insurance Act, on the other hand, though it received a large amount of Trade Union support, was on the whole opposed by the Socialists on grounds of principle, and was denounced by many Radicals as " Bismarckian State Socialism " and as a step towards the establishment of the " Servile State."

This difference is important. The Labour Movement was practically united in demanding State action for the protection of working-class conditions and for the uplifting of the bottom dogs. It pressed steadily for the universal application of the legal minimum wage, for the State regulation of hours and conditions of labour through Mines, Factories and Shops Acts, for a satisfactory system of workmen's compensation, and for an improvement and extension of public education, including school meals and medical treatment as well as inspection. But, apart from plans for nationalisation, which were not regarded as immediately practicable, the Labour Party's primary measure was the Right to Work Bill, which it reintroduced session after session under different names and in different forms. The basic principle of the Bill, prominent in all Socialist agitations since the unemployed troubles of the 'eighties—and indeed long before then—was the duty of the State to find either satisfactory work or, in default of work, adequate maintenance for all its citizens. Keir Hardie had been, from his first election to Parliament in 1892, above all the spokesman of the unemployed; and the Right to Work Bill carried on his tradition, and summed up the Labour Party's conception of the State as a co-operative undertaking with a responsibility for securing to all its members the conditions of a good life.

The Liberals, though in sanctioning such measures as the Trade Boards Act they had moved very far from their old individualist tradition, would have nothing to do with the Right to Work Bill, which they denounced as sheer Socialism. The State, in their view, had no such duty as the Labour Party suggested. It might step in to save the bottom dog from sufferings dangerous to society as a whole, or even on purely humanitarian grounds. But each man's life was his own responsibility and not the State's ; and the " Right to Work " seemed to the Liberals a flat denial of all the doctrines of self-help and incentive to labour which had made capitalist Great Britain what it was.

It became more and more evident, however, that in one way or another the Liberals would have to face up to the problem of the unemployed. Good trade in 1906 and 1907 postponed the urgency of the question ; but in 1908 and 1909 unemployment rose to nearly 8 per cent., and it became manifest that something must be done if Liberalism were not quite to lose its grip on the working-class electors. The troubles over the Budget of 1909 and over the Parliament Act caused action to be deferred until 1911 ; but then came the National Insurance Act, for which the way had been in part prepared by the Labour Exchanges Act of 1909.

Only Part II of the Insurance Act—which consisted of two quite distinct measures—dealt with unemployment, by setting up for certain trades a system of insurance based on contributions from the workman, the employer, and the State. Part I—the larger part of the Act—set up a system of National Health Insurance, providing medical and certain supplementary benefits for the great majority of employed persons, but not for their dependants, on the same contributory principle. In the case of both sickness and unemployment, the worker was to be given a small measure of security ; but the Liberal way of tackling both problems was on the lines of compulsory self-help. The duty of the State was not to provide for the worker, but, as far as practicable, to compel him to help in providing for himself. The benefits proposed neither were, nor were meant to be, sufficient for decent maintenance ; and in both schemes the proportion of the cost to be contributed by the State was left deliberately small, the main financial contribution coming from the compulsory levies on employers and workers.

In the Trade Unions, an increasing number of workmen had been making thrifty provision for both sickness and unemployment solely by their own contributions, without any aid from either the employer or the State. But only the Unions of relatively well-paid and skilled workers had been able to do much along these lines. Many of the better-paid workers had been making additional provision for sickness and incapacity through Friendly Societies ; but these too catered in practice mainly for the better-off. The less skilled workers, who needed the provision most of all, could not afford to pay contributions which would enable their Unions to provide such allowances. Their Unions usually paid little beyond dispute and, perhaps, funeral benefit.

To the Trade Unions generally both parts of the National Insurance Act made a considerable appeal. The Unions which already paid benefits saw a prospect of further relief for their members, and of some diminution of their own financial obligations ; while the less skilled workers' Unions saw the inviting prospect of both sickness and unemployment benefits which Trade Union action unaided would never be able to provide. There were many points in the Bill to which the Trade Union leaders took strong objection. But the great majority of them were anxious that the Bill should be passed even unamended rather than not at all.

The Socialists, on the other hand, were disposed in most cases, for various reasons, to denounce the Bill. They were strongly opposed to the contributory principle, which they regarded as a denial of the Socialist doctrine that the provision of work or maintenance and also the care of the people's health were direct obligations falling on the community as a whole. Moreover, the Fabians regarded Lloyd George's Bill as a Liberal attempt to queer the pitch for the elaborate scheme for the prevention and relief of unemployment which Mrs. Sidney Webb and George Lansbury had recently put forward in the Minority Report of the Poor Law Commission (1909)— a refined and clarified version of the Socialist doctrine of the right to work. Again, many Socialists and Radicals objected profoundly to the method by which the employer was empowered to deduct contributions from wages, as placing a stigma of inferiority upon the worker and preparing the way for a new plan of financing social measures directly at the expense of the poor. Finally, Hilaire Belloc found many supporters for his fulminations against a type of public assistance designed only for the poor, and calculated to emphasise their " servile " condition in relation to their masters.

These differences caused the Labour Party to cut a somewhat sorry figure while the Insurance Bill was before Parliament. The majority of the Trade Union leaders supported it, and moved amendments only on particular points. But a small Socialist minority, including Philip Snowden and George Lansbury, felt so strongly against the Bill as to oppose it without regard to any party discipline. This placed the party in a considerable difficulty, and helped to undermine its prestige and influence in the country.

The Insurance Act can be accepted as the point at which Socialist and Liberal ideas of social reform clearly diverged. But, as we have seen, the majority of the Labour Party, though they would have greatly preferred a non-contributory measure, in effect supported Lloyd George in Parliament. The very limited extent to which the Labour Party could really be regarded as Socialist began to be plain. As long as the Liberals were either passing social measures on which both Radicals and Socialists were agreed or conducting a battle with the House of Lords there was little to force this question to the front.   The Insurance Bill did bring it clearly to light, and compelled all sections of the working-class movement to take stock of their position. There were other things besides the Insurance Bill over which differences hitherto concealed began to take on a threatening appearance.   Above all, a change was coming over the industrial situation, and new forces were beginning to stir in the minds of the younger Trade Unionists and " intellectuals."   The close alliance of Liberals and Labour which was established in 1906 had become formally closer in the fight over the Lloyd George Budget and the Parliament Bill.   It was, from the Liberal standpoint, far more essential after the big fall in the Liberal majority as a result of the elections of 1910—for from January 1910 onwards the Government depended for its majority on Labour and Irish Nationalist votes.   But what had hitherto been generally acceptable, save to a handful of the more extreme Socialists, was now far more widely criticised.   The critics were no longer content with a nominally independent party ; they began to demand a real independence, based on the systematic pursuit of a directly Socialist policy.

BOOKS

G. D. H. Cole.   *British Working-class Politics, 1832–1914.*
R. C. K. Ensor.   *England, 1870–1914.*
R. H. Gretton.   *Modern History of the English People.*
Labour Party Annual Reports.
J. R. MacDonald.   *Socialism and Democracy.*
H. Belloc.   *The Servile State.*
Fabian Society.   Various pamphlets on the Insurance Act.
P. Snowden.   *Autobiography.*

3. INTERNAL LABOUR POLITICS—THE OSBORNE JUDGMENT

Some departure from strict chronological order was made in the last section, in order to allow of a clear description of the unfolding of Liberal social policy.   The point of cleavage between Socialism and Liberalism regarded as social policies was there placed between 1909 and 1911 ; but it was seen that even in 1911 this could not be identified with a cleavage between Liberalism and Labour.   It is rather the point at which others besides a small group of convinced Socialists became conscious of a fundamental difference between the two policies, and criticism of the Labour Party's attitude became widespread in the working-class movement.   Long before that there had been rumblings of Socialist discontent, and others besides the Social Democratic Federation had become dissatisfied with the fruits of the " Labour Alliance."

These discontents, however, hardly made themselves felt until the Trade Disputes Act had been finally passed.   It was rather from the Trade Union side that the first attack on the " Labour Alliance " came, when in 1907 a renewed proposal to confine membership of the Labour Party to Trade Unionists was only defeated by a narrow majority. But in the same year the onslaught came from the other side, and a movement for an independent Socialist Party was set on foot. The first sign of this movement's advance was the unexpected election to Parliament for Colne Valley of Victor Grayson, a young fire-eater of considerable oratorical power, as an Independent Socialist pledged to subordinate all other issues in Parliament to the relief of the unemployed. The "Grayson protest" of 1908 aroused widespread attention. He was out of order, and was suspended by vote of the House, the majority of the Labour Party, which did not recognise him as belonging to it, refusing him support. Grayson thereupon toured the country, raising support for an independent Socialist Party. The result was the formation, in 1909, of the Manchester Socialist Representation Committee, followed by similar movements in other towns. The dispute waxed hot inside the Socialist societies, and both the I.L.P. and the Fabian Society passed through internal crises arising out of it. At length, in 1911, a Socialist Unity Conference, consisting of the Social Democratic Federation, Blatchford's *Clarion* groups, and a number of dissident branches of the I.L.P. and other bodies, formed the British Socialist Party, in open opposition to the Labour Party. The B.S.P., however, attracted few fresh supporters, and in practice differed little in attitude and policy from the old S.D.F., which was merged in it. Discontent was by this time widespread in the Socialist bodies; but relatively few were prepared to take the drastic step of severing connection with the Labour Party altogether. Most Socialists, including the great majority of the I.L.P., continued to believe in the "Labour Alliance" as the means of gradually converting the Trade Unions to Socialism.

Before this movement of revolt had got past its initial stage, the law had dealt the Trade Unions a new blow almost as serious as the Taff Vale decision. In December, 1909, it was finally decided in the House of Lords that a Trade Union had no right to spend money on financing the Labour Party, or indeed on any form at all of political activity. Again the brunt of the attack fell on the Amalgamated Society of Railway Servants, in an action brought by W. V. Osborne, one of its branch secretaries, who sought to restrain it from a form of expenditure which, he maintained, was *ultra vires*. This decision, whatever its legal basis, clearly threatened the very existence of the Labour Party ; for both the party machine and its candidates were necessarily financed mainly out of Trade Union funds. The case had originally come before the High Court in 1908, and the judge had dismissed Osborne's case. Then Osborne had appealed, and in turn the Appeal Court and the House of Lords had given judgment in his favour. Other cases soon followed ; and one Union after another was restrained by legal injunction from contributing to the Labour Party's funds.

The Osborne Judgment, as much as the Taff Vale case before it, took the

Unions by surprise.   There had been, before Osborne was heard of, objectors to the political use of Trade Union money ; but they had been few, and the cases had been quietly settled.   Trade Unions had been using their funds for political agitation at least since the early 'sixties, and for promoting Trade Union candidatures at least since the Reform Act of 1867.   Two famous lawyers—Lord Loreburn and Sir Edward Clarke—had both been consulted by the Unions, and had expressed the view that such action was entirely within the law. But the word of the House of Lords was final ; and Trade Unionists had either to give up the Labour Party or to get the effects of the judgment undone.

The judgment itself was none too easy to understand ; for the various judges had given a large number of different reasons for their decision. There were at least two major points involved.   Was all political action by a Trade Union illegal, on the ground that it was *ultra vires*—beyond the Union's powers conferred by law ?   Or was it merely action through the Labour Party that was illegal, because the Labour Members were bound by a "pledge" to act in accordance with party instructions, and any such " pledge " was contrary to public policy ?   The House of Lords decided, by a majority, that all Trade Union political action was illegal. The second question, therefore, did not necessarily arise ; but one of the Law Lords grounded his judgment upon it, and the remarks of others seemed to indicate that Osborne might have won his case on this ground had not the wider issue taken precedence.

The second question, not striking at the roots of Labour policy, was the easier to deal with.   From 1903 onwards, in order to establish a common discipline, the Labour Party had exacted from its candidates a " pledge " of loyalty to the constitution and decisions of the party.   The existence of this pledge was widely used as an argument against the party, on the plea that a Member of Parliament should be free to represent his constituents, and could not be free if he agreed to act on the decisions of any outside body, or to accept payment from such a body for his services in the House of Commons. In order to meet these criticisms, the Labour Party in 1911 abolished the pledge, and in the same year, on the introduction of Payment of Members, discontinued the allowances which it had previously paid to candidates elected under its auspices—though it still continued of course, directly or through its affiliated bodies, to contribute towards the election expenses of candidates and sitting members.

The Osborne Judgment as a whole could not be so lightly disposed of. The main ground given by the Law Lords for their decision was that no reference was made to political activity in the defining clause of the Trade Union Act of 1876, and that such activity could not be regarded as a necessary subsidiary to the purposes there mentioned.   In other words, the defining clause of the Act of 1876, which had amended the definition laid down in the Act of 1871, was regarded as enumerating all the activities, except purely subsidiary ones, that a Trade Union could lawfully pursue, and all other forms of activity were, by inference at least, declared to be *ultra vires*.

This view was clearly based on treating the Trade Unions as virtually, if not actually, corporate bodies, owing their entire existence and powers to statute law. In the Taff Vale Case, the judges had already taken a long step towards the proclamation of this doctrine ; and now, despite the definite refusal of the legislators of 1871, 1876 and 1906 to give the Trade Unions a corporate standing, the doctrine that they must be treated as corporations or *quasi*-corporations was definitely laid down by some of the judges. It is difficult to see any justification for this view ; for clearly Trade Unions existed, and performed all manner of functions, before and apart from the powers conferred upon them by the Trade Union Acts. But there is no use in inquiring too closely whether the House of Lords as a court of law is right or wrong ; for, when it has pronounced a judgment, that judgment is the law—until the law is altered by statute.

The Labour Party, then, unless it could get the judgment reversed by fresh legislation, was faced with an almost complete disappearance of its sources of income. One by one, its big affiliated Trade Unions were restrained by legal injunction from contributing to its support. At once an agitation was set on foot to demand a complete reversal of the decision, and the Government was approached with a view to the passage of an amending Bill. The Liberals, however, were in no hurry ; for it suited them by no means ill that the Labour Party should suffer from financial embarrassments. Moreover, they could plead preoccupation with the struggle over the Budget, and the need for reducing the pretensions of the House of Lords before attending to any other matter. In 1910 the Labour Party had to fight two successive General Elections under the shadow of the Osborne Judgment. Fortunately for it, this was before there had been time for its central funds seriously to feel the effect. But the number of Labour candidates in the field in 1910 was less than it would otherwise have been ; for several Unions had to withdraw their nominees for lack of money.

The General Elections of 1910 were fought virtually by a Liberal-Labour Alliance. In the election of January, not a single member was returned against official Liberal opposition,[1] and in only twenty-six contests out of seventy-eight had the Labour candidate a Liberal against him. The party, reinforced by the miners' representatives, who had joined in 1909, won three seats and lost eight—a net loss of five. It returned to the House of Commons forty strong. In December, 1910, the number of seats contested fell perforce to fifty-eight, and in only eleven of these were Labour and Liberal in opposition. No seat was won in a three-cornered contest, but in one case, in

[1] Keir Hardie, at Merthyr, had an unofficial Liberal opponent.

West Fife, a Labour candidate won against a Liberal with no Conservative in the field.   The net result was a gain of two seats to the party.

As soon as the elections were over the Labour Party, which had done its best under difficulties to keep the issue to the front during the campaign, again demanded the introduction of a Bill to reverse the effects of the Osborne Judgment.   But the Liberals, while they promised a Bill, would not agree to a complete reversal ; and for the time the negotiations broke down. Not until 1913 did the Labour Party and the Trade Unions finally accept the compromise embodied in the Trade Union Act of that year.

Under this Act not only was political action allowed, but it was declared that a Union might engage in any lawful activity of any sort duly authorised by its rules.   On the exercise of political activities, however, certain definite restrictions were imposed.   No Trade Union could engage in such activities unless it first took a ballot and secured a favourable majority of those voting. Special political rules had then to be drawn up, in a form approved by the Chief Registrar of Friendly Societies.   All payments for political purposes, as defined in the Act, had to be made out of a distinct political fund ; and, finally, any member who objected to contributing to the fund had, on signing an approved form, to be exempted from all payment towards it without forfeiting any of his rights as a member of the Union, save in relation to the management of this special fund.

This was the compromise, accepted under protest by the Trade Unions, which remained in force until the passage of the Trade Unions and Trade Disputes Act of 1927, and was re-instated on the repeal of that Act in 1946. It was regarded as unsatisfactory, not so much because objection was taken in fact to the exemption of political recusants as because the Unions resented the imposition upon them of special restrictions which were not applied to other bodies.   They claimed that they had a moral right to take political action as freely as any other society, and that the Act pursued the old policy of the law in placing them under special and onerous disabilities.   They complied, however, with the Act ; and as in most Unions the number of registered objectors was relatively small—though it varied widely from case to case—the funds of the Labour Party were not in the long run seriously restricted by the conditions which the Act imposed.   They were in practice limited very much more by the failure of many Trade Unions to collect political contributions from members who had registered no formal objection to paying.   Nevertheless, the episode served both to strengthen in the minds of Trade Unionists their rooted distrust of the law in its dealings with organised Labour and to create a coolness between Labour and Liberalism which was not without its effects on later political developments.

While this struggle was in progress the Labour Party was by no means entirely happy in its internal affairs.   After the elections of 1910 the Liberals in the House of Commons were actually out-numbered a little by the

Conservatives, so that the Government depended for its majority on Labour and Irish Nationalist support. It might be thought that this would have strengthened Labour's hands ; but actually it had the opposite effect. The probable result of defeating the Liberal Government would have been a return of the Conservatives to office after serious Labour losses at the polls. For the party which forced yet another election would certainly be unpopular, the electoral understanding with the Liberals would have been broken, and, owing to the Osborne Judgment, the Labour Party had no money. The return of the Conservatives to power would have meant not only the defeat of Irish Home Rule, to which Labour was fully committed, but also the abandonment of all hope of a speedy upsetting of the Osborne Judgment. The Liberals were, of course, well aware of this ; they knew that the leaders of the Labour Party did not dare to bring about their defeat. Consequently, they refused to give way over the Trade Union Bill as they had given way in 1906, and were less disposed to make concessions in social legislation than they had been when they had had a clear majority over all parties combined. In 1906, they had been scared by the spectacular advent of the new Party : by 1911 they thought they had taken its measure.

This situation seriously weakened the standing of the Labour Party with its own supporters. The party seemed to be making no headway with the Trade Union Bill and, in fact, to be achieving almost nothing at all. Moreover, its position of dependence on the Liberals led to some awkward incidents. Despite the decision of the Miners' Federation to join the Labour Party, a number of the mining Members of Parliament proved recalcitrant. At least three of the old " Lib-Lab " contingent, including Thomas Burt, who had first been returned in 1874, definitely refused to come over, and had to be left undisturbed in their seats. Several others, although they stood as Labour candidates in 1910, afterwards fell out with the party over questions of discipline and, refusing to sever their connections with Liberalism, dropped out of the Labour ranks. As late as 1914 Barnet Kenyon, a nominee of the Derbyshire Miners and an official Labour candidate, persisted in accepting the endorsement of the Liberal Association as well, and had to be formally repudiated by the party. There were troubles too about electoral arrangements between Liberal and Labour. When a vacancy arose at Leicester, a double constituency represented by Ramsay MacDonald and a Liberal, the local Labour Party wanted to fight the seat ; but the existence of a private arrangement between the two parties to share the representation was disclosed, and led to considerable internal controversy. Events such as these stimulated the movement towards a break from the " Labour Alliance " and the promotion of an independent Socialist Party. But, while these movements more and more deeply stirred the Socialist Societies, the bulk of the Trade Unionists were little affected by them. There was never much serious prospect of the dissolution of the party alliance of Socialism and the Trade Unions.

There was, indeed, from the purely opportunist standpoint, a strong case for the policy which Ramsay MacDonald and his colleagues pursued. They had no prospect of becoming a Government, and their easiest course was to keep the Liberals in power at any rate till Home Rule had been achieved, the new Trade Union Bill passed, and time allowed for Labour to build up at least the nucleus of a fighting fund. From the purely parliamentary standpoint, these arguments seemed convincing. The case against them was that, in pursuing this policy, the Labour Party inevitably lost caste in the country, and ceased to stand in the public mind for any independent policy or principle. This was at least a powerful contributory cause of the shifting of working-class activity from politics to industrial action, and of the great " epidemic " of strikes which spread over the country during the years immediately preceding the Great War.

BOOKS

G. D. H. Cole.　British Working-class Politics, 1832–1914.
Labour Party Annual Reports.
W. V. Osborne.　My Case.
W. M. Geldart.　The Osborne Judgment and After.
M. Beer.　History of British Socialism.
S. and B. Webb.　History of Trade Unionism.
R. Y. Hedges and A. Winterbottom.　Legal History of Trade Unionism.
W. M. Bailey.　Trade Unions and the State.

THE GREAT UNREST

1. THE SEEDS OF UNREST

IN the Trade Union world, the opening years of the twentieth century were a period of " industrial tranquillity." Real wages were going down, and yet there were few strikes or lock-outs. This seems at first sight surprising, for under normal conditions it might have been expected that the workers would have put up a fight. Mining wages, for example, having soared in the boom year 1900, fell by nearly 20 per cent. between then and 1905. This was a far bigger fluctuation than occurred in any other important industry. Yet even the miners, after an abortive strike in Lanarkshire in 1901 and an un-official stoppage of pit-boys in the " Federated " English coalfields in 1902, accepted the position, and engaged in no further big strike until 1909. Nearly eleven million days a year had been lost by strikes and lock-outs between 1893 and 1898 ; between 1899 and 1907 the average was well under three million days.

This quiescence is explained mainly by three causes. The first, and by far the most important, was the Taff Vale decision, which, though it could not prevent strikes altogether, did deter the Trade Unions from attempting any big forward movement as long as it remained in force. The Trade Union leaders had no wish to jeopardise their accumulated funds, which were badly needed for other purposes, by exposing themselves to actions for damages on the lines of the Taff Vale case. For the time they preferred to hold their hands, in the hope that amending legislation would not be long deferred.

Secondly, the active spirits in the Trade Unions, who would otherwise have been most forward in urging strike action, were during these years mostly busy building up the Labour Representation Committee. Their minds were more on politics than on industry; and they were disposed to put high hopes in the new party which they had expended so much energy in bringing to birth.

Thirdly, trade conditions, while they were not so bad as to exclude the possibility of forward movements, were until about 1910 on the whole unfavourable to any sustained advance.

After the passing of the Trade Disputes Act Trade Union activity gradu-ally increased. In 1906 there were strikes among the linen and jute workers in Dundee and Belfast, among the Clyde boilermakers, and on a small scale among the engineers in many districts. These were mostly unsuccessful; but in the same year the South Wales Miners' Federation began, by a series of stoppages at particular pits, a successful drive against non-unionism. This policy continued through subsequent years, and spread gradually to other coalfields. In 1907 there were fewer strikes, but Trade Union activity increased. The Engineers negotiated, without a stoppage, a new and improved national agreement, and a local engineers' strike at Erith secured the abolition of the premium bonus system, which the employers were at that time making widespread efforts to introduce. There were numerous disputes in the cotton trade, leading to a threat of a general lock-out on the spinning side of the industry; but this was averted at the last moment by a compromise. There were, however, important local stoppages of the Blackburn weavers against bad materials and of the Oldham ring-spinners for higher wages.

The really important dispute of 1907 occurred on the railways. In 1897 the Amalgamated Society of Railway Servants had launched its first " All-Grades Programme." The companies had refused either to recognise the Union or to negotiate in any way; and the railwaymen, who did not at that time feel strong enough to take drastic measures, had postponed further action. The forward movement would probably have been resumed early in the new century; but the Taff Vale affair, in which the A.S.R.S. had been directly involved, then made any extensive strike highly dangerous. Consequently, it was not until the Trade Disputes Act of 1906 had cleared the way that the railway workers launched their second All-Grades Programme. This was presented to the railway companies in January, 1907; but the companies persisted in their refusal to recognise Trade Unionism in any form, and would have no dealings with the Society. For six months the A.S.R.S. conducted a campaign of propaganda throughout the country; and then, in July, it again approached the railway companies, only to meet with an absolute refusal to negotiate. A strike ballot was taken in September, and an overwhelming majority was secured. This led Lloyd George, as President of the Board of Trade, to intervene, and under his auspices the railway companies were persuaded to agree to the establishment of a system of conciliation and arbitration. This was accepted by the A.S.R.S. and the other railway Trade Unions, and the dispute thus ended without any stoppage of work, Lloyd George gaining considerable reputation through his success in effecting a settlement.

The Railway Conciliation Scheme of 1907 was, nevertheless, a most unsatisfactory affair. The railway companies still persisted in their refusal to recognise Trade Unionism in any way; and the new Conciliation Boards for the railway service were elected by votes of the railway workers without the Unions having any recognised part in their choice. Only actual employees of the various companies could sit upon the Boards ; and the officials of the Trade Unions were thus altogether excluded, even from acting as officers of the Boards or presenting cases before them. Only strong pressure from the Government induced the companies (except the North Eastern Company, which already recognised Trade Unionism) to agree even to this form of collective bargaining. Moreover, the Conciliation Scheme was so devised as to interpose long delays in the way of getting grievances remedied, and to divide the workers on each railway from those on other railways, as well as into a number of distinct groups of grades. It was certain from the first that the scheme of 1907 could not last. Having gained the first step towards recognition, the railway Trade Unions were certain to take the next opportunity of asking for more.

That opportunity, however, did not at once arise. The Boards were elected in 1908, and at once began the consideration of a huge mass of accumulated grievances. But by this time trade was seriously declining. 1908 and 1909 were bad years, in which the average level of unemployment was nearly 8 per cent. Wages, which had risen in 1907, fell again ; and the time was clearly inopportune for big forward movements. The important disputes of 1908 nearly all arose in opposition to attempted reductions in wages. The woodworkers in the North-East Coast shipyards were beaten by the use of the national lock-out, and the engineers in the same area yielded to the threat of one. In the cotton industry, the spinners agreed to reduced wages without a strike, and the cardroom operatives after a national stoppage.

In 1909 the position was quieter in most trades ; but there was a big outbreak of strikes among the miners. In the previous year, the Coal Mines (Eight Hours) Act had become law. The reduction in hours involved re-adjustments of wage rates and piecework prices, and over these considerable friction arose, and there were big strikes in Yorkshire, South Wales, and other areas. At the same time, the Conciliation Boards in most of the coalfields awarded substantial reductions in wages on account of the fall in the price of coal, which, despite the abolition of the sliding scale system, remained still the chief factor governing miners' wages.

1910 began with a further crop of mining strikes. In consequence of the Eight Hours Act, the coalowners in Northumberland and Durham introduced large changes in the method of working, including, in many collieries, a three-shift system. This was intensely unpopular with the miners ; and, although their county Associations had agreed, under pressure, to accept the changes, unofficial strikes broke out over large areas in both counties. Receiving no support from their own Unions, the strikers gradually drifted back to work ; and by April the stoppage was over. But it left behind bitter memories, and the new system of working remained, because of the disturbance of home life which it inevitably created, extremely distasteful to the rank and file of the miners.

The mining troubles had scarcely ended when a serious dispute in the cotton industry began. On the instructions of the Cardroom Amalgamation, a grinder named George Howe refused to carry out certain orders of the firm which employed him. He was thereupon discharged, and all the workers at the mill then struck, demanding his reinstatement, which the firm refused. The dispute dragged on through the summer, and in October the cotton employers, following a practice which later became common, declared a general lock-out in order to force the men to give way. This action led the Government to intervene, and a settlement was quickly made, the employers agreeing to re-employ the discharged man at another mill, and the points originally in dispute being held over for subsequent adjustment.

The national lock-out was also used as a weapon by the shipyard employers during 1910. During the summer a number of local disputes occurred among the boilermakers of the Clyde and Tyne. The employers alleged that, in these cases, the workers had failed to observe the terms of the shipyard agreement of 1909 ; and in September they declared a national lock-out of all members of the Boilermakers' Society in the federated ship-yards. After abortive negotiations between the parties, the Government intervened in this dispute also, and in December an amended agreement, embodying new provisions for the settlement of differences, was accepted by both parties, and the dispute ended.

This catalogue of mainly unsuccessful strikes may seem to have little purpose. But it is an essential preliminary to the story of the next few years. High hopes had been roused by the Liberal and Labour political victories of 1906 ; but after four years of Liberal government and Labour action in Parliament the workers found themselves, economically, worse off than before. The slight rise in wages during 1906 and 1907 was almost wiped out in 1908 and 1909, and in the meantime there had been a fairly sharp rise in the cost of living. Trade Unionism, after a quick growth in the two former years, was standing still. The workers who struck against reductions in wages were compelled to give way, and found little or no help in the change of Government. It was manifest that, as soon as trade improved, a big forward movement was bound to begin.

BOOKS

Board of Trade. *Annual Reports on Strikes and Lock-outs.*
G. D. H. Cole and R. P. Arnot. *Trade Unionism on the Railways.*
G. A. Alcock. *History of the Amalgamated Society of Railway Servants.*
J. Watney and J. A. Little. *Industrial Warfare.*

2. SYNDICALISM—INDUSTRIAL UNIONISM—GUILD SOCIALISM

The few years immediately preceding the Great War were the occasion of a general ferment of industrial unrest. Strikes not merely increased greatly in number and extent, but also changed their essential character. Trade Unionism woke out of its long quiescence, and became class-conscious, militant, aggressive. Unofficial and spontaneous movements were common ; the old leaders seemed to be losing their grip. Conciliation and arbitration in trade disputes, and reformism in politics, were alike severely criticised. A new idea sprang up, and won wide acceptance, of using Trade Unionism not merely as a means of defending wages and conditions, but as an offensive weapon in a war upon capitalist society. Names and ideas were imported from abroad to convey the new meanings which were struggling for coherent expression. Syndicalism and Industrial Unionism, and later Guild Socialism, became the gospels of the day among the younger Trade Unionists and Socialists. While the Labour Party in Parliament was shaping its course in close alliance with the Liberalism of Lloyd George, Labour in the country appeared to be worshipping new gods, and bent on the creation of a new Society by " direct action."

This dramatic change in the Labour attitude coincided with similar changes elsewhere. A large section among the advocates of Women's Suffrage grew weary of the continuing failure of constitutional agitation to yield any practical result, and, under the energetic leadership of Emmeline Pankhurst and her daughters, launched the Militant Suffrage movement of the Women's Social and Political Union. The violent tactics of the " Militants " had undoubtedly some effect in undermining the prevalent respect for " law and order " ; and the Labour Left Wing, sympathising with the women's agitation, learnt something from it—not least a hatred and contempt for the Liberal statesman, Asquith, and for the more reactionary elements in the Liberal Party of which he became the leader. There was, in effect, under the double stress of the Feminist Crusade and of the Labour revolt, a general weakening of the traditional respect for constitutional behaviour, and a growth of philosophies of action based on the notion of " Creative Revolution."

All this was, of course, an intellectualisation of what was really happening. The underlying movement was a mass movement of sheer reaction against the failure of either orthodox Trade Unionism or moderate parliamentarism to secure any improvement in working-class standards of life. The theorists, working-class and middle-class alike, who sought to give this movement form and direction and to interpret its vague strivings into a new social gospel, never really captured the great mass of the working class. They might lead it in this or that particular struggle, and might help to stir up troubles that would not have occurred without their impulsion. But the mass, as ever, was thinking not of Utopia and not even of the class war, but mainly of the immediate issues involved in each separate dispute. If a new temper was abroad, and the moderate leaders found their control of the movement seriously threatened, this did not imply a wholesale conversion of the British working class to revolutionary doctrines.

The change was, nevertheless, startling enough. Never since the fall of Owenism in 1834 had Trade Unionism been at all widely regarded in England as a positive instrument for the creation of a Socialist Society. William Morris and his followers of the Socialist League had come near to this idea in the late 'eighties ; but they had never formulated it clearly, and by other Socialists Trade Unionism had either been denounced as a reactionary division of the workers into narrow " craft " sections or regarded mainly as an instrument to be used for the building up of a working-class political party. The former had been the attitude of the Social Democratic Federation in its early years ; the latter was characteristic of Keir Hardie and the Independent Labour Party movement. Throughout, in the eyes of orthodox Trade Union leaders, the movement had been no more than a means of maintaining and improving the conditions of employment within the capitalist system.

On all these conceptions of Trade Unionism the new movements declared war. To the moderate Trade Unionist they replied by citing the failure of orthodox collective bargaining to secure, in recent years, any real improvement in working-class conditions. To the Labour Party politician, they pointed out the equal failure of political action to yield either better wages or any vital modification of the capitalist system. And to the remaining upholders of the old S.D.F. attitude they replied that Trade Unionism, though it might have been often reactionary in fact, need not be so if the militants would but set out to inspire in it a different tone and temper. " Direct Action " became the new gospel. No one would or could help the workers unless they helped themselves, by taking into their own hands the task of organising a mass attack upon the capitalist system and upon all its works.

Elsewhere I have sought to analyse in detail the ferment of doctrine that went to the making and interpretation of this new movement among the workers.[1] It drew its inspiration from many sources. In France the Trade Unions, weak in numbers but rich in intellectual leadership, had long been pursuing, largely under semi-anarchist inspiration, a militant policy of guerrilla warfare against the employers and the State. Travelling light, unburdened by friendly benefits such as the older British Unions were accustomed to provide, the French *syndicats* lost little by a defeat, and were able easily to re-form and launch their attacks in a new place. Lacking the

[1] In *The World of Labour.*

British stability, they were far more mobile and adaptable. And they had against them a capitalism far less developed and organised than the British system.

Under their Anarchist inspirers, the Trade Unions of France had denounced working-class parliamentary action as useless, and had repudiated all dealings with the Socialist Party. Instead, they had preached a doctrine of " Direct Action," which the theorists of the movement elevated into a " social myth." There were to be strikes and strikes, wearing down the resistance of the employers and of the capitalist State, until the great day when the General Strike of all the workers would end the capitalist system and usher in the new workers' Society. In this Society there would be no government and no coercion. Power would pass to the workers, organised in their natural industrial and social groups. The Trade Unions would become the administrative agents of the new social order. Moreover, the new Society would be essentially localised—based on the local fellowship of the workers in a particular place. Only so could the workers act directly, without placing their reliance on the sham of representative democracy. Similarly, Trade Union policy in the present must be based on local action. The Trades Council must count for more than the national Trade Union ; the spontaneity of the movement, and its direct dependence on the rank and file, must be the essential basis of all effective working-class action.

With this Syndicalism from France was curiously blended another stream of doctrine, flowing from the United States. In France, the small employer still predominated ; the American workers were concerned with the gigantic mass-production factory and the trust. In America, accordingly, revolutionary Trade Unionism had taken to some extent a different turn. Active chiefly among the low-paid immigrant workers, and in strong hostility to the moderate policy of the main body of American Trade Unionists, the Industrial Workers of the World had from 1905 been preaching the doctrine of mass organisation in " One Big Union " based on the direct antagonism of the working and employing classes. Centralisation was the watchword of this movement as much as localism was of the French ; but both alike stressed the necessity of Direct Action as the means to social revolution. The workers must not look to the politicians to do things for them, or to build the Socialist State. They must do things for themselves both in fighting the employers under Capitalism and in building up the new workers' Society to take its place. For them, as for the French, the ideal in prospect was a Workers' Republic, based on the industrial organisation of the working class. But for the one strong centralisation, and for the other guerrilla warfare on a local basis, was the instrument to be employed.

The would-be interpreters and leaders of the Labour unrest in Great Britain seized on these two bodies of doctrine, and set out to make, with their aid, an interpretation suited to British conditions. There emerged a variety of movements, which for a time made up by their ceaseless activity for their lack of coherence and direction. In 1910 Tom Mann, who had been a leader in the great Dock Strike of 1889, returned from Australia and South Africa with vigour unimpaired to become a leader of the new movement. The Industrial Workers of the World had exerted a good deal of influence in Australia, especially upon the miners and transport workers, and Mann came back both well acquainted with their doctrines and with a rooted detestation of the systems of wage regulation and compulsory arbitration in force in the Australian States. Finding Syndicalism widely preached, he incorporated the two doctrines into one, and combined with them his old advocacy of the shorter working day as the first objective of working-class policy. In a series of monthly pamphlets, published during 1911 under the title of *The Industrial Syndicalist*, and in countless speeches up and down the country, he put the force of his eloquence and personality behind the movement for a new fighting Trade Unionism on a class basis. His influence counted for a great deal in the great wave of unrest which swept over the country in 1911.

As soon as the new ideas began to gain acceptance, it became manifest that the Trade Unions, with their existing structure, were quite unsuited for acting upon them. In almost every industry except the mines, the main body of the workers was split up among a number of sectional and often over-lapping Unions organised on a basis of "craft," with the less skilled sections either not organised at all, or organised in " general labour " Unions which competed one with another over a wide range of industries. In the cotton, printing and building industries, for example, each craft or group of crafts had its separate Union ; in the engineering and shipbuilding, as well as in the building, trades, the skilled and unskilled workers were organised apart, and were often on bad terms with each other ; in the transport trades there jostled one another a large number of independent societies organised on almost every conceivable basis.

It seemed, to the advocates of the new ideas, a bounden duty to begin with some attempt at straightening out this tangle. The first step was the formation, in 1910, of the National Transport Workers' Federation, linking together all the heterogeneous mass of Trade Unions in the sea-going, waterside and road transport trades. Powerful movements for promoting amalgamation on industrial lines were launched in the railway, building, printing, engineering and other industries. The " Amalgamation Move-ment," with connected organisations for the various industries, became the chief outward and visible sign of the growing acceptance of the new militant policy by the younger men in the Trade Unions. " Amalgamation " be-came almost a synonym for the militant New Unionism of the Syndicalists and Industrial Unionists. " Reform " and " Forward " Movements were launched by the miners in various coalfields ; and in South Wales, where the extremist elements were strongest, a new policy was preached in *The Miners' Next Step*.

Published in 1912, this famous pamphlet attacked not only the orthodox conceptions of Trade Union policy but also the policy of nationalisation as preached by the orthodox propagandists of British Socialism. For its authors, the State, as well as the employer, was the enemy ; and the means to change was an intensified form of revolutionary industrial action, based on a strong, highly centralised organisation of the workers. By strike upon strike, Capitalism was to be made unprofitable, until the miners were able to take their industry into their own hands, and to conduct it under a complete system of working-class control. " The Mines for the Miners," said the South Wales revolutionaries ; and cries such as " The Railways for the Railwaymen " echoed their policy elsewhere. The place of *The Industrial Syndicalist* was taken in 1912 by a new journal, *The Syndicalist*, edited by Guy Bowman, whose ideas owed more to French than to American influence ; and there appeared also *The Syndicalist Railwayman*, *The South Wales Worker*, *Solidarity*, and a host of other journals expressing, with varying emphasis, the new ideas.

Meanwhile, in the *New Age*, a small body of intellectuals, ably headed by A. R. Orage and S. G. Hobson, was developing the new doctrines along another line. The *New Age* had long been an acute critic of orthodox Labour policies. It had supported Victor Grayson in the troubles of 1908, and had preached, at all events from that date, a doctrine which made economic rather than political action the key to social change. Gradually, this doctrine emerged as Guild Socialism. It began as a plea by a medievalist craftsman, Arthur J. Penty, for a restoration of the gild system in industry. But after 1911, in the hands of S. G. Hobson and Orage, it became a plea for the capture of control in industry by National Guilds essentially different from those of the Middle Ages. The medieval gilds had been regulating bodies made up of independent masters, each in business on his own account. The proposed National Guilds were to be great corporations for the actual control and management of the various industries ; and, according to the *New Age* plan, they were to be based on, and developed out of, the Trade Unions, which were to be widened to include all the workers " by hand and brain." The workers, it was urged, should organise not merely for defence but for the winning of control ; the protective Trade Unions should turn into great workers' corporations which should demand and secure from a reorganised State the whole responsibility for the conduct of industrial affairs.

Obviously, this doctrine owed much to French Syndicalism and something to American Industrial Unionism. It took these doctrines, and made of them a new doctrine more directly applicable to British conditions. If it had few direct adherents, their skill and activity made them influential far beyond their numbers in the formation of working-class policy.

These various movements, it should be observed, went on side by side. All of them remained largely formless and unorganised, and all depended for their influence on the existence among the British workers of a great mass of unrest which was not caused, though it may have been accentuated, by their propaganda. They did not create the unrest ; they were only its would-be interpreters and leaders.

The rise of these doctrines, and the unrest itself, profoundly stirred the entire world of Labour. Among the older leaders, both of the Trade Unions and of the Socialist Societies, they aroused deep hostility. Ramsay MacDonald wrote a whole book against Syndicalism; Philip Snowden, in *The Living Wage*, set out to demonstrate the futility of the strike weapon as an instrument of social change. The Trade Union leaders, roundly denounced by the " Amalgamationists," retorted with allegations of mischief-making and treason to the Trade Union Movement. The pursuance of a virtual Liberal-Labour alliance in Parliament coincided with a strike epidemic which the orthodox Trade Union leaders found themselves largely unable to control.

Meanwhile, Trade Union membership was increasing by leaps and bounds. From 1907 to 1909 the Trade Unions had about two and a half million members. By the end of 1911 their membership passed three, and by the end of 1913 four, millions. Almost every Union shared in the increase. Greatest among the less skilled types of workers, it was hardly less marked among the engineers and cotton operatives than among the railwaymen, transport workers and general labourers.

Soon, an old dream was realised ; and Labour ventured into daily journalism. *The Daily Herald*, beginning in 1911 as a strike sheet of the London printers, became, under George Lansbury as editor, the organ of all the new movements and tendencies, hitting out light-heartedly at Trade Union leaders and politicians alike, and opening its columns equally to all schools of Amalgamationists, Syndicalists, Industrial Unionists, and Guild Socialists. Living from hand to mouth, and often threatened with death through failure to pay for the next day's paper—let alone the printers' wages —it miraculously survived as the rallying point for militants of all schools right through the period of unrest which came to an end with the outbreak of the Great War. Meanwhile, in 1912, the more moderate elements had launched a newspaper of their own. *The Daily Citizen*, under the official control of the leaders of the Labour Movement, competed with the *Herald* for working-class support, and waged, during its two years of life from 1912 to 1914, truceless war on the new doctrines and on their exponents.

These were stirring times. The great unrest made the Labour problem beyond dispute the question of the day. The ordinary newspapers were filled with news of strikes and threats to strike. Denunciations of the new extremism were everywhere. But the ferment of ideas attracted into the working-class movement a rapidly growing body of men and women from all classes and occupations. - The Socialist Societies, as well as the Trade Unions, increased rapidly in membership and activity.

The excitement was at its height from the latter part of 1911 to the end of 1913. Thereafter came, as we shall see, a lull. There were signs of a renewal of intense Trade Union activity about the middle of 1914 ; but at that point the outbreak of war sharply cut the movement short. What would have happened if there had been no war in 1914 the historian need not profess to know. Largely, this would have depended on the course of trade. 1911 and 1912 were both, from this standpoint, good years ; and 1913 was, for most industries, a year of unexampled prosperity. 1914 showed some slight falling off, and it may be that, in August, a trade slump was on the way. At all events, in that month the outbreak of war changed the entire situation. The great unrest did not die ; but it took, perforce, new forms and directions. The story of the years from 1910 to 1914 is a story without an ending ; but in the events of that period can be seen the foreshadowing of much that has happened since the Great War. From this brief survey of the general character of the period we must now turn to a consideration of certain of its outstanding events.

BOOKS

G. D. H. Cole.   The World of Labour.
S. and B. Webb.   The History of Trade Unionism.
S. G. Hobson and A. R. Orage.   National Guilds.
T. Mann.   The Industrial Syndicalist.
T. Mann.   From Single Tax to Syndicalism.
G. Lansbury.   The Miracle of Fleet Street.
Files of The Daily Herald to 1914.
G. Dangerfield.   The Strange Death of Liberal England.
R. Strachey.   The Cause.
E. Sylvia Pankhurst.   The Suffragette Movement.

CHAPTER V

TRADE UNIONISM IN ACTION

1. 1911—The Seamen's and Dockers' Strikes   2. The Railwaymen
3. The Miners   4. Larkinism and the Struggle in Dublin
5. The Industrial Council—The Triple Alliance

1. 1911—THE SEAMEN'S AND DOCKERS' STRIKES

THE great unrest, which had been developing for some time below the surface, burst out in a flood of strikes in the early summer of 1911. Apart from the Cambrian Combine struggle in the South Wales coalfield, the early months of the year were comparatively free from disputes, the most important being a strike of the London printers for shorter hours. This ended, on the whole, inconclusively, but it was the means of bringing to birth *The Daily Herald* as the first Labour daily newspaper and a vital rallying-point for all the new movements of unrest.

The strike wave, however, began with the seamen. In the summer of 1910 the National Sailors' and Firemen's Union put forward a national programme, demanding the formation of a National Conciliation Board, the granting of a national wage scale and a minimum wage, reform of manning scales and methods of engagement of seamen, and a number of other concessions. The Shipping Federation, which, like the railway companies, had always refused to recognise Trade Unionism in any form, would not even discuss these demands, on the plea that any recognition of seamen's combinations would be subversive of discipline. The Union spent the ensuing months in an active propagandist campaign at all the ports, and then, in June, 1911, declared a national strike. Within a few days the principal ports throughout the country were largely held up by the stoppage. The shipowners, who had always met attempts at strike action by a systematic resort to blackleg labour, attempted to carry on by this means. But this only served to widen the area of dispute, and within a few days there had been sympathetic strikes of dock-workers at Goole, Hull and other centres.

In order to understand the events which followed, it is necessary to glance briefly at the state of Trade Union organisation among the transport workers at this time. Tom Mann, after his return to England in 1910, had launched, as we have seen, a campaign in favour of Syndicalism and "Direct Action." The seamen were then busy with their national programme, and Tom Mann, in conjunction with James Havelock Wilson, undertook the work of organisation. But Mann's views were not limited to a seamen's movement alone. Through Ben Tillett, secretary of the Dockers' Union and his old colleague in the Dock Strike of 1889, he set to work to organise a National Transport Workers' Federation, which was formed late in 1910, and included all types of transport workers except the railwaymen.   Under the auspices of this body, an active movement of organisation in all the ports went on side by side with the national agitation of the seamen.   As there was at the same time acute discontent on the railways over the working of the Conciliation Scheme of 1907, every section of the transport industries was in a mood for trouble when the national seamen's stoppage gave the signal.

The completeness of the seamen's response to the strike call seems to have taken the shipowners entirely by surprise.   The Shipping Federation found itself powerless to supply blacklegs in face of a comprehensive national movement.   Within a few days, at one port after another, the shipowners began to meet the Union officials and to grant substantial concessions, especially in respect of wages, in order to secure a return to work.   It became plain that the seamen, thanks to the unexpectedness of their attack and to the manifest readiness of other waterside trades to support their claims, were winning a great victory all along the line.

This, however, did not dispose of the trouble ;   for in one port after another the waterside trades were coming out, either in sympathy with the seamen or with demands of their own.   Even where the strikes were originally sympathetic, the strikers had no lack of grievances, and refused to return to work unless these were put right.   There was, however, no national dockers' or carters' programme similar to that of the seamen.   The workers in each port, and often each section in each port, formulated their separate demands, or even remained on strike without any clear or definite claims.

The first big dockers' strike, as we have seen, was at Hull.   This began on June 20th, and was settled, by Government intervention, on July 3rd.   But before this, on June 27th, the Manchester dockers had come out, followed a few days later by the carters, including those working for the railways.   The Liverpool dockers had just been granted an advance in wages without a strike ;   but on June 28th they too struck, in consequence of a dispute over working conditions.   At Liverpool work was resumed on July 3rd, on the understanding that negotiations were to be resumed, and an agreement on the disputed points was signed a month later.   In Manchester, Government intervention was again needed ;   but there too a settlement was reached on July 9th.   Although the seamen were still out at some ports, and there were still a number of small dock strikes in progress, the critical phase of the dispute seemed by this time to be over.

In mid-July, however, the waterside workers came out at Cardiff, where the seamen were still on strike.   And this affair was scarcely settled when the troubles began in London.

The London dockers, early in the year, had formulated a programme of demands, which later received the endorsement of the Transport Workers'

Federation. Under threat of a strike, the Port of London Authority and certain other big groups of employers in the port at length agreed to negotiate, and on July 27th a provisional agreement (known as the " Devonport " Agreement) was reached. This, however, did not cover all sections, and when it was placed before mass meetings of the men strong hostility to the terms of settlement made itself felt. A few days later the coal-porters went on strike, followed immediately by the dockers who were not covered by the " Devonport " Agreement. This grievance was referred to arbitration ; but in the meantime lightermen, carters, stevedores, and other sections of the waterside workers were pouring out, the non-unionists, who were numerous, joining their fellows till the stoppage was practically complete. In these circumstances, the Transport Workers' Federation decided to make the dispute general throughout the port, and decreed that no section should return to work until an agreement had been reached on behalf of all. Again the Government intervened, and under its auspices a long series of sectional negotiations took place. By August 11th agreement had been generally reached, and the Transport Workers' Federation ordered a return to work. But, owing to a series of disputes about the interpretation of the agreements, the resumption was not complete until the end of the month.

The London dispute, like those in other parts of the country, ended in a signal triumph for the Transport Workers' Federation. Recognition of the Trade Unions, hitherto refused by the majority of the employers, was definitely won ; and the general rate of wages for dockers was raised from 6d. and 7d. to 8d. per hour, with advances for the higher-paid workers as well. Conditions of labour were also substantially improved. The transport workers, who had been standing still ever since the granting of the " Docker's Tanner " in the great Dock Strike of 1889, had won a success which resounded through the whole country.

This, however, was by no means the end of the transport strikes. After the brief stoppage at the end of June, Liverpool had remained at work. But there was widespread unrest, and Tom Mann, who was leading the movement there, had succeeded in establishing a close working arrangement among the various trades. At the beginning of August the trouble flared up. Angered at the delays and evasions of the railway Conciliation Boards, the railwaymen employed in the goods traffic department of the Lancashire and Yorkshire Railway came out on strike. Two days later they were followed by the dockers, and in the next few days carters, tramwaymen, and many other workers joined in the struggle. The port employers at Liverpool replied with a general lock-out, and the Strike Committee thereupon declared a general cessation of all forms of transport in the Liverpool area, the railwaymen coming out with the rest.

How this purely local and unofficial stoppage among the railwaymen developed into the national railway strike of 1911 we shall see later. For the moment we are concerned only with the fortunes of the local struggle. For some time in August, Liverpool was almost in a state of civil war. The military were called in ; there were serious riots and conflicts between soldiers and police and the strikers ; the Government sent a special Commission to enquire into the food supply and the general condition of affairs in the city. Gradually, with the aid of this Commission, settlements were reached for most of the strikers. But trouble arose over the refusal of the City Corporation, backed by the shipowners, to reinstate the tramwaymen who had struck ; and the other trades would not go back until this question was settled. Tom Mann and the Strike Committee threatened to call for a national sympathetic strike ; and at length, under Government pressure, the Corporation gave way. The strike ended on August 28th.

This turmoil of sudden strikes throughout the country, conducted by workers for the most part poorly organised and regarded as incapable of effective action, took all England by surprise. It recalled the great days of 1889 ; but the new movement was altogether more widespread and on a larger scale. The Government, hampered by the simultaneous occurrence of a serious crisis in foreign affairs, was divided between its desire to avoid trouble at home and its feeling that it ought to take a strong line against manifestations of disorder. The shipowners, after giving way under the influence of the first surprise attack, speedily repented of their concessions, and did their best in the later troubles to stand out against any yielding to the strikers. In London great meetings on Tower Hill, addressed by Ben Tillett and others, and in Liverpool the eloquence of Tom Mann and his followers, gave the new gospel of industrial action a huge popular audience. The movements of ideas described in the preceding chapter, noticed hitherto only by small minorities, became suddenly widespread in their influence. In a few months, the temper of British Trade Unionism radically changed ; and the easy victories of 1911 seemed to justify all the promises of the new leaders of the masses. But the shipowners were not alone in vowing vengeance : before the troubles of 1911 were over the port employers, in London at any rate, were busily preparing for the " next time."

There was speedily a renewal of trouble. In January, 1912, the Glasgow dockers struck for a wage advance. The strike ended in a compromise ; but after the resumption of work there were further disputes, leading to a lock-out in which the men were worsted. In February, there was an inconclusive stoppage at Manchester on the non-unionist question. In July, there were dockers' strikes at Liverpool and Birkenhead against the new Clearing House scheme designed to reduce the amount of casual labour. The Liverpool men went back almost at once ; but it was a month before the Birkenhead dockers gave way.

By this time London was again in turmoil. Ever since the settlements of 1911 the employers had been doing their best to undo the effects of the men's victory. They hated the Transport Workers' Federation, and desired, if they could not dispense with Union recognition altogether, at any rate to deal with the separate Unions, and not with a united body. This led to constant friction both over the interpretation of the agreements of 1911 and over the recognition of the " Federation Card " issued by the N.T.W.F. through its affiliated Societies. The employers said they would recognise the cards of the separate Unions, but not that of the Federation. The men retorted that they insisted on freedom to organise as they thought best.

The trouble came to a head in May over the question of working with non-unionists. This led to a strike of the lightermen, and to an unofficial sympathetic stoppage of a number of dockers. The port employers refusing to employ only Federation members, the N.T.W.F. hastily called a general strike of all workers at the port, not only on this issue, but also on the numerous grievances over the working of the settlements of 1911. The Government thereupon stepped in, and ordered an enquiry into the causes of the dispute. This resulted in a recommendation that, in accordance with the terms of the 1911 settlement, the points of difference should be referred to the Board of Trade, which accordingly called a conference of the parties. The men accepted ; but the employers, led by Lord Devonport, who was determined to smash once and for all the new militancy of the Trade Unions, refused to attend. The Government thereupon proposed the formation of a joint body representing all the port employers, with a view to a settlement embracing all sections. The employers at first replied evasively, and announced that they could give no promise to reinstate the men on strike. Later they refused to form any joint body, and announced that in no circumstances would they agree to recognise the Federation Card, or even to discuss such recognition. The Government withdrew its scheme, and suggested a series of sectional agreements covering the various trades in the port, with monetary guarantees against breach of agreement. The men, eager for a settlement, accepted the principle of monetary guarantees, but pressed for recognition of the Federation. The employers rejected the entire proposal out of hand.

By this time it had become evident that the London dispute was a life-and-death struggle between the New Unionism on the one hand and Lord Devonport, the chairman of the Port of London Authority, on the other. Lord Devonport meant to smash the Federation. In these circumstances the Federation, feeling its whole existence at stake, issued on June 10th the call for a national sympathetic strike of transport workers in all the ports.

The call to strike at once revealed the real weakness of the Federation. The transport workers had won their victories in 1911 by local action, and their movement was still essentially local in feeling. The Federation as a body had little strength outside London ; and the various Trade Unions which had organised the other big ports were not ready to risk their existence in order to support the Londoners, who were largely organised in separate Unions of their own. About 20,000 transport workers in the provinces responded to the strike call ; but the great majority remained at work. The seamen, who had been angered earlier in the year by the refusal of sympathetic support to a movement of their own, refused their backing. The provincial strikers, conscious of failure, were compelled after a few days to go back to work.

Meanwhile, in London the port employers were using every effort to man the port with blacklegs, and were refusing to have any dealings with the strikers except on the basis of an unconditional return to work. By the end of June it had become clear that the strike was broken, and on July 27th the Strike Committee ordered a general resumption. There was some delay in obeying this order, and many conflicts between strikers and blacklegs occurred. But the men were beaten, and they knew it. By the second week of August the dispute was wholly at an end.

Thus Lord Devonport and his fellow-employers had their revenge for the discomfiture of 1911, and the real weakness of the spontaneous movement which had sprung up at that time stood revealed. The New Unionism had received a serious check, and the leaders had been compelled to realise that only detailed organising work and closer Trade Union unity could make safe the gains won by a surprise attack. After the defeat of 1912 the Transport Workers' Federation settled down to an attempt to consolidate its strength. There was no really big strike movement among its members between 1912 and 1914. The biggest—a successful strike of the Hull dockers for higher wages in July, 1913—was a purely local affair.

BOOKS

Board of Trade. *Annual Reports on Strikes and Lock-outs.*
B. Tillett. *History of the Transport Workers' Strike.*
G. R. Askwith. *Industrial Problems and Disputes.*
J. Watney and J. A. Little. *Industrial Warfare.*
T. Mann. *Memoirs.*

2. THE RAILWAYMEN

Ever since the settlement of 1907 unrest on the railways had continued to grow. The Conciliation Scheme by means of which Lloyd George had secured a patched-up settlement in that year satisfied nobody. The principle of recognition, for which the Unions were above all contending, had not been conceded ; and on the Conciliation Boards the workers' representatives, with no Trade Union officials to put their case, were at a serious disadvantage. The machinery of the Boards, moreover, had been intentionally made slow and cumbrous ; and the men alleged that the railway companies systematically obstructed its working. Every case had to go first before a

Sectional Board and then, on appeal, before the Central Board for the railway concerned. If the Central Board failed to agree, the dispute had to be referred to arbitration. Each railway company stood entirely apart from the others ; there was, as the Unions were still not recognised by the companies, no means of raising general issues affecting all railways alike. And, finally, the scope of the Boards was restricted to questions of wages and hours ; and no form of collective bargaining was recognised by the companies on any other issue.

It had been agreed in 1907 that the Conciliation Scheme should remain in force for a minimum period of six years. There was, therefore, no means of securing any change without breach of agreement. This explains why, despite the strong feeling among the men, the Unions had taken no official action, and it was left for an unofficial and unauthorised stoppage to raise the question in a practical form. The strike at Liverpool was speedily followed by similar strikes at Manchester and in many other places ; and within a few days it became obvious that the railway Trade Unions would have either officially to recognise the movement or to lose all influence over their members. Hastily the executives of the four railway Trade Unions met in conference, and on August 15th announced an immediate national strike unless the railway companies agreed to meet them and negotiate. This the companies still refused to do. The Government thereupon intervened with an offer, if the men would return to work, to set up a Royal Commission to consider the question of amending the Conciliation Scheme ; but, as the companies still refused a meeting, the Unions rejected this offer, and on August 17th declared a national strike.

The stoppage was not complete ; but it effectively held up a large part of the main line traffic, about 145,000 railwaymen ceasing work at the Union's call. The Government continued its efforts to promote a settlement, and, under its auspices, the companies at last, on August 19th, empowered representatives to meet the spokesmen of the Unions. At this meeting, on the same day, a settlement was reached.

Under the terms of settlement a Royal Commission was to be appointed and the major questions at issue were deferred pending its report. Meanwhile, work was to be resumed, and all the strikers were to be reinstated without penalties for any breach of contract which might have been committed. All grievances affecting men covered by the Conciliation Scheme were to be referred for settlement under it, and the grievances of workers outside the Scheme, which applied only to the traffic grades, were to receive consideration. But no form of Trade Union recognition was conceded ; the companies undertook to meet only their own employees, and not the representatives of the Unions.

In accordance with this agreement, work was generally resumed, though there was a temporary hitch on the North Eastern Railway, which had a conciliation scheme of its own, and was not a party to the settlement of 1907. This matter, however, was adjusted, and the Royal Commission began its work. Two months of quiet followed ; but when, on October 18th, the Commission produced its Report, the trouble began afresh. On November 2nd the Trade Unions rejected the Report and, through the Government, demanded an immediate meeting with the companies for discussion of its terms. The companies flatly refused to meet the men, and the Government took their part. The Unions thereupon decided to ballot their members on the question of renewing the strike. The Labour Party moved in the House of Commons a resolution condemning the companies for their refusal to agree to a meeting for discussion of the Report ; and an amended resolution, calling for a meeting " to discuss the best means of giving effect to the Report," was carried and forwarded to the companies, which thereupon agreed to attend a meeting held under Government auspices. After difficult negotiations, the meeting arrived at a settlement on December 11th, modifying the terms of the Report in certain directions desired by the Trade Unions. The strike threat was then definitely removed.

The new Conciliation Scheme of 1911, though it was in certain respects better than the old, was still far from meeting the Trade Unions' demands. The Sectional Boards for particular grades were retained, as under the old scheme, with two vitally important changes. The Central Boards were abolished, and instead each Sectional Board was provided with an independent chairman, who was given the full powers of an arbitrator if the two sides disagreed. Moreover, though all recognition of Trade Unions as such was still refused, the workers' representatives on each Sectional Board were allowed, if they so desired, to choose a secretary from any source they thought fit. This in effect enabled the Trade Union officials to come in as secretaries to the Boards, and in nearly all cases this was done when the scheme was put into operation. The scope of the Boards was widened so as to include conditions of labour as well as wages and hours ; but questions of " discipline and management " were still excluded—a provision out of which endless troubles subsequently arose. Moreover, in the absence of Trade Union recognition the workers were still compelled to deal with any question they wished to raise by the deeply resented method of deputation to the management. There were the seeds of further trouble in the amended Conciliation Scheme of 1911, almost as much as in the scheme of four years before.

For the time, however, the question was settled ; and the strike of 1911 made a huge difference to the status of the railwaymen in relation to their employers. The companies, though they persisted in their refusal to recognise the Trade Unions, had, in fact, been compelled to negotiate with them ; and their attitude had been explicitly condemned by the House of Commons. Moreover, the railwaymen had successfully asserted their right to strike—a right which the companies had always vehemently repudiated as destructive of all discipline—and had, after a national strike, secured complete reinstatement without penalties and a substantial victory on the points at issue. It is not surprising that they were encouraged by their success, or that railway Trade Unionism leapt suddenly from a position of backwardness and comparative insignificance to the front rank of the Trade Union world.

In the year or two following the national railway strike of 1911 the railwaymen as a whole were decidedly " uppish." In 1910, all the railway Trade Unions together, including the Railway Clerks' Association, which was not directly involved in the strike of 1911, had only 116,000 members. The total had risen to 184,000 by the end of the following year, and by 1914 to 337,000, which made the railwaymen, after the miners and the cotton operatives, the largest group in the Trade Union world. And these new Trade Unionists were keen to use their power. There was no repetition until 1919 of the national strike ; but in the sustained industrial conflicts of 1912 and 1913 the railwaymen again and again played a part.

This arose largely through the growth of the idea of " sympathetic " action. The sympathetic strike had been a powerful factor in the success of the strikes of 1911, and thereafter it was preached by the adherents of the " New Unionism " as a weapon to be freely used in industrial conflicts. The railwaymen were constantly receiving requests from workers on strike to refuse to carry " tainted " goods, i.e. goods consigned to or from a works at which a dispute was in progress. The systematic adoption of such a policy would clearly have involved them in practically every trade dispute ; and the Union leaders accordingly took a strong line against it. But, in the prevailing excitement, spontaneous strikes and refusals to handle " tainted " goods were of fairly frequent occurrence, and continued right through the period of unrest.

In addition there occurred in 1912 one important stoppage among the railwaymen on a grievance of their own. A certain Driver Knox, employed by the North Eastern Railway, was convicted on a charge of drunkenness, and was thereupon reduced in rank by the company. His fellow-workers, alleging a miscarriage of justice and further that in any case the offence had been committed off duty, struck work to the number of over six thousand. The Government intervened, and ordered a special Home Office enquiry into the case. As a result of this, Driver Knox was reinstated ; but the Unions agreed that the strikers should be fined a week's pay in lieu of proceedings for their breach of contract in leaving work without notice. In this strike, most of the press was vehemently hostile to the men, and the affair was denounced as a strike for " the right to get drunk." On the other side the strike was no less strongly defended, on the ground that the company's action was an attempt to interfere with the private lives of its employees outside their hours of duty. The episode is interesting chiefly as a highly typical occurrence of these eventful years, when feeling ran high on both sides, and purely local or individual disputes were apt to become matters of high principle in the minds of Trade Unionists and employers alike.

One great result of the successful railway movement of 1911 had been a keen desire for closer unity on the part of those who had fought together in the struggle. There were at this time five railway Trade Unions, apart from the numerous engineering and other societies which had members in the railway shops. Throughout the dispute the four Unions of manual workers had acted closely together ; and the Amalgamation Movement, strong in most industries at this time, found ready support among the railwaymen. By far the largest railway Union was the Amalgamated Society of Railway Servants, and this was now made the basis of a wider combination. The General Railway Workers' Union, founded as a militant body in the troubles of 1889, and the United Signalmen and Pointsmen's Society agreed to join forces with the A.S.R.S. ; and at the beginning of 1913 the National Union of Railwaymen came into existence as an amalgamation of these three. The important sectional Associated Society of Locomotive Engineers and Firemen, however, refused to merge its identity in the new body, holding that its members' special interests would not be adequately protected in a general Union. The disputes between these two Unions were a fertile source of trouble later on.

The formation of the National Union of Railwaymen was widely acclaimed as the first triumph of the New Unionism—a " new model " as influential for the twentieth century as the Amalgamated Society of Engineers had been for the Victorian age. The Amalgamationists, as we have seen, stood for the principle of " union by industry " in place of the sectional Unionism of the older crafts. Many of them, indeed, desired " One Big Union," to include all workers in every craft and industry, on the principles proclaimed by the American Industrial Workers of the World. But even this group realised that the only practicable approach to its ideal was by amalgamations on industrial lines. To all the forward groups, the N.U.R., at the time of its foundation, appeared a great victory for the new militant Trade Unionism of which Tom Mann and *The Daily Herald* were the leading prophets.

Troubles were not slow in following. The N.U.R., in accordance with the policy that had called it into being, set out from the first to organise railway workers of every craft and grade. This brought it into conflict, not only with the Locomotive Engineers and, less seriously, with the Railway Clerks' Association, but also with the numerous craft Unions which had members in the railway locomotive and carriage shops. In this sphere above all, the struggle raged between the New Unionism and the Old, and repeated conferences brought no solution of the difficulty. The N.U.R. would not surrender its right to organise all railway workers ; and the craft Unions would not surrender their right to organise craftsmen employed on the railways.   The problem remained unsettled—a constant source of trouble and weakness in a vital section of the railway world.   It remains unsettled to this day.

Meanwhile, the new Conciliation Scheme of 1911 was giving hardly less dissatisfaction than the old.   All through 1913 the railwaymen were getting ready a new national programme for presentation at the earliest opportunity. In November, 1913, the first date on which notice could be given to end the scheme, the necessary year's notice was handed in ; and in the early months of 1914 the new programme, providing for full recognition of Trade Unionism, for an all-grades wage advance of 5s. a week, and for numerous other concessions, was made public.   Various rank-and-file bodies of railwaymen promulgated, and began agitating for, a considerably more drastic programme of their own.   During the summer the first moves and counter-moves were being made, and negotiations for a new agreement had been set on foot. Before War broke out in August, 1914, there seemed every probability that the winter would bring with it a national railway strike far more general than that of 1911.   For the companies still refused to recognise Trade Unionism as the agency through which collective bargaining should be carried on ; and on this point, as well as on a substantial wage advance, the railwaymen were determined to insist.   Despite the movements of 1907 and 1911, they remained in 1914 by far the worst-paid body of workers in any great industry except agriculture.   Conscious that at length they were strongly organised, they were in no mood to suffer a continuance of the old servitude.

BOOKS

G. D. H. Cole.   *The World of Labour.*
G. D. H. Cole and R. P. Arnot.   *Trade Unionism on the Railways.*
Board of Trade.   *Report on Strikes and Lock-outs, 1911.*
R. Kenney.   *Men and Rails.*
G. A. Alcock.   *History of the Amalgamated Society of Railway Servants.*

3. THE MINERS

Each year from 1907 onwards there had been growing trouble in the mining industry.   Mention has been made already of the successful campaign of the South Wales Miners' Federation against non-unionism, and of the troubles in South Wales, Yorkshire, Durham and Northumberland over the readjustments consequent upon the Eight Hours Act of 1908.   In addition to these major disputes, there occurred each year a growing number of small strikes at particular pits, arising in each case out of special grievances ; and in September, 1910, there began a minor dispute of this order which rapidly took a serious turn.   At one of the pits belonging to the Cambrian Combine, the most powerful colliery concern in South Wales, trouble arose over a new list of piece-work prices.   No agreement could be reached, and the men

struck, alleging that the firm was trying indirectly to cut wages and was refusing to give proper regard to the vexed problem of the " abnormal place,"
i.e., to the working place in which, by reason of the special difficulty of coal-
getting, the hewer could not, at piece-work prices, earn a reasonable wage.
For a short time the strike was confined to the pit at which the trouble first
arose ; but very soon the workers at other pits owned by the Combine
came out in sympathy with the original strikers. The chairmen of the two
sides of the South Wales Coal Conciliation Board met, and agreed upon a
provisional price-list, which was to be given a period of trial ; but this was
rejected by the men, and the stoppage spread to further pits, until about
10,000 men were out on strike. The Government intervened, and obtained
an assurance from the owners that they were not seeking to cut wages, and
that consideration would be given to the men working in " abnormal
places " ; but revision of the price-list was refused. The strike therefore
continued ; and the South Wales Miners appealed to the Miners' Federation of
Great Britain for financial aid. The M.F.G.B. gave its help after a vain
attempt to bring about a settlement. At this point the stoppage had already
lasted for more than four months.

A month or so later renewed attempts were made to reopen negotiations ;
but the owners refused a meeting, and a ballot of the men showed an overwhelming majority against giving way. The M.F.G.B. again intervened, and
after negotiating directly with the owners, reached a provisional agreement
under which the rejected price-list was to be given a year's trial. This the
strikers refused ; and the M.F.G.B. thereupon withdrew its financial help.
Not until the strike had lasted almost a full year were the men at last starved
into acceptance of the employers' terms.

The Cambrian Combine dispute was one of a number of troubles that led
to the miners' national strike of 1912. The " abnormal place " question was
a constant source of friction, not only in South Wales, but in many other coalfields. Largely as a remedy for this grievance, the Miners' Federation of
Great Britain, which since the accession of the North-East Coast miners in
1909 had included the great majority of the colliery workers throughout the
country, decided to demand from the coalowners the national concession
of an individual minimum wage. The actual rates demanded differed from
coalfield to coalfield, but the claim was that in each area a certain minimum
should be guaranteed to every miner.

On this issue the Miners' Federation attempted to open negotiations
nationally with the Mining Association, as representing the district associations of colliery owners. The Mining Association, however, would only
agree to recommend that local negotiations should take place in the various
districts. To this the miners ultimately agreed, affirming at the same time
their intention to take national action unless a settlement was reached in every
area. Accordingly local negotiations were opened. In the English Federated

Area, embracing the collieries in Yorkshire, Lancashire, the Midlands, and North Wales, the owners agreed to accept the principle of the minimum wage ; but in Scotland, South Wales, Northumberland, Durham, and other areas a deadlock was reached. After further attempts at negotiation in these areas the Miners' Federation determined to take a strike ballot, and a large majority of the members voted in favour of a national stoppage. Strike notices were accordingly handed in throughout the coalfields, and the miners announced that nothing short of the granting of a schedule of rates drawn up by them for each district would prevent a national stoppage of work. Negotiations were resumed on a national basis, but again broke down ; and even in the " Federated Area," in which the district negotiations had been continued, a deadlock was reached on the question of the actual rates to be paid.

At this stage the Government took a hand in the dispute, and the Prime Minister, H. H. Asquith, invited both parties to meet him. After a series of meetings Asquith decided to draw up his own proposals for the settlement of the dispute, and to submit them to the disputants. On behalf of the Government, he endorsed in general the miners' claim to a minimum wage, but laid down that this must be settled on a local basis, either by agreement or, failing agreement, by Government arbitration.

The Asquith plan divided the owners. Those of the Federated Area, Durham, and Cumberland agreed to accept it ; but it was rejected by the owners in Scotland, South Wales and certain other districts. The Miners' Federation replied by reiterating its demands and by stating its willingness to continue district negotiations with the owners with a view to their acceptance. The fundamental difficulty, on the miners' side, arose from their insistence that, even if the minimum wage were to be settled locally by arbitration, it should be laid down in advance that it should nowhere (save in one or two small areas) be less than 5s. per shift for an adult miner. Upon the final rejection of its proposals the Government broke off its negotiations with the parties. Enoch Edwards, the politically moderate but tough and unyielding President of the Miners' Federation, had replied to every overture with a reiteration of the miners' chosen formula.

At the end of February, 1912, the national strike began. A few days later the Government again intervened, and the three-cornered conversations were resumed. The miners, however, stood firm in their insistence that the actual wages they demanded should be accepted by the owners ; and finally Asquith determined to introduce into Parliament a Bill incorporating his own proposals. The Labour Party, on behalf of the miners, attempted to include the 5s. minimum in the Bill, and opposed the measure. It was, however, carried, and became law as the Coal Mines Minimum Wage Act at the end of March, 1912. Upon this the coalowners agreed to accept the plan. The Miners' Federation took a ballot of its members, which showed a small majority in favour of continuing the strike. The majority was, however, considered insufficient, and on April 6th the Federation ordered a resumption of work. Minimum Wage Boards, with independent chairmen, were subsequently established in all the coalfields, and the trouble died down. The Act, however, was only to remain in force for a period of three years, and was thereafter annually renewed in the Expiring Laws Continuance Act. It was in many respects unsatisfactory. In effect, the Wage Boards were given no independent power to fix wages. All they could do was to prescribe as a minimum for each individual miner a wage based on the standard wage fixed on by collective bargaining between the district owners' and miners' associations. Thus, if the owners were able to enforce a reduction, with or without a strike, the legal minimum wage had also to be reduced. In general, what the Act did was not to regulate wages, but only to safeguard the position of miners working in " abnormal places " or prevented by other causes from earning the current district wage.

The miners' strike of 1912 was by far the largest strike that had ever occurred in Great Britian. It involved altogether over a million workers, of whom 850,000 were directly parties to the dispute, whereas all the strikes of 1911 put together had directly involved only 830,000 workers. It was also the first miners' dispute in which all the coalfields were simultaneously included. The great dispute of 1893 had extended only to the Federated Area, and all other disputes had been confined to one or at most two neighbouring coalfields. Behind it was undoubtedly, besides the desire to enforce the universal adoption of the minimum wage, the will to secure fuller recognition for the Miners' Federation of Great Britain as the representative negotiating body for the industry as a whole. This is shown incidentally by the evidence submitted on behalf of the Federation in 1912 before the Government's Enquiry into Industrial Agreements, then proceeding under the auspices of the newly formed joint Industrial Council, to which reference is made in a later section.

For negotiating purposes the miners were, in 1912, divided into a number of district groups. Separate Conciliation Boards, which fixed wage-rates, existed for the Federated Area, Northumberland, Durham, South Wales and Scotland ; and there were also separate local arrangements for a few smaller districts. The miners, without demanding a uniform wage level throughout the coalfields, did desire a national system of wage negotiation. This was strongly repudiated by the coalowners, who refused to give any power of wage settlement to their own national association. Thus the seeds of many later troubles had been sown even before the national upheaval of 1912.

For the time the Coal Mines Minimum Wage Act settled the procedure to be adopted. The minimum wages to be fixed under the Act were, however, distinct from the standard wages fixed for the main bodies of miners by the various Conciliation Boards. When the national struggle was over, the

Miners' Federation began an attempt to achieve its object of national negotiation by another method. An effort was made to get all the agreements fixed
by district negotiation so arranged as to come to an end at the same date. This,
which would have made national action possible on the general wage question,
by no means suited the owners ; and it was found impossible to effect it.
Later in 1912, for example, the miners of the Federated Area secured a wage
advance only by agreeing that the existing Conciliation Board system should
continue until August, 1915.

1912 and 1913 were years of abounding prosperity in the mining industry.
The selling price of coal rose fast, and wages rose with it. Local strikes
were numerous, particularly on the non-unionist question, and usually ended
in victory for the strikers ; but they were neither extensive nor in most cases
prolonged. The most important was a strike of 50,000 miners in South
Wales, who refused to continue working with non-unionists ; and in this
case, as in others like it, the strikers got their way. The non-unionists joined
the South Wales Miners' Federation. Already, however, difficulties were
arising out of the double system of wage-fixation established in 1912. The
Conciliation Boards and the Minimum Wage Boards were wholly distinct
and independent bodies, and did not in all cases cover the same areas. Trouble
soon arose out of this arrangement. Did an advance under the Minimum
Wage Act cancel a Conciliation Board advance, or should the two be added
together in order to arrive at the amount payable ? This question led to a
general stoppage of the South Yorkshire coalfield early in 1914, and the
compromise by which this affair was brought to an end failed to settle the
question, so that a similar dispute took place in West Yorkshire twelve months
later, and actually laid the coalfield idle early in 1915, when quarrels in most
industries were in abeyance owing to the War. In this case, partly owing to
the war conditions, the miners won their point.

The most important dispute of 1914, however, arose in the Scottish coalfield. After the great prosperity of 1913, coal prices had begun to fall, and
the Scottish coalowners demanded a substantial reduction in wages. The
Scottish miners met the claim by announcing that they proposed in future to
work only four days a week. The owners, they said, had often restricted
output in order to maintain prices when it served their turn. Why should
not the miners, since their wages depended mainly on the price of coal, take a
leaf out of the owners' book, and, with the same object, refuse to work more
than four days a week ? The Miners' Federation of Great Britain, asked to
endorse this new policy and to promise the Scottish miners financial support,
rejected the request ; the Scottish miners nevertheless announced their
intention of resisting the wage reduction. Thus matters stood when, in
August, 1914, the declaration of war changed the whole situation, and caused
the adjournment of the dispute *sine die*.

The course of the miners' movement from 1910 to 1914 has been traced in some detail, not only for its intrinsic importance at the time, but also because it throws a clear light on the still more important developments of later years.   There is no doubt that during this period the Miners' Federation was passing through an extraordinarily rapid process of change.   At the opening of the century the miners were almost everywhere led by men of exceedingly moderate outlook.   Many of their leaders were " Lib-Lab " Members of Parliament ; and we have seen that up to 1909 the Miners' Federation refused to identify itself with the Labour Party.   But, slowly at first and then with growing swiftness, there came a change in the temper of the men.   The South Wales miners, who had been the last to cling to the old sliding scale system, became after 1906 the leaders of the new militant movement.   The Scottish miners also adopted an aggressive policy, and Miners' Forward Movements were launched in Durham and elsewhere during the troubles over the introduction of the eight hours day.   With the spread of Syndicalism and Industrial Unionism, the miners in some of the coalfields, already organised largely on industrial lines, became ready converts to the new doctrines.   The Federated Area, indeed, and especially the Midland districts, remained true to the old policies, and were little touched by the new ideas ; but in the South Wales coalfield more and more extreme counsels prevailed. The miners there launched, about 1911, an Unofficial Reform Movement, urging a rigid centralisation of Union control with a view to a stronger fighting policy. Their attitude found expression in the famous *Miners' Next Step*, published just before the strike of 1912, to which allusion has been made already.   Under the auspices of the Central Labour College, which had been founded in 1909 by a secession of students and teachers from the moderate Ruskin College, Oxford, Marxian classes were organised throughout the coalfield, and an intensive propaganda went on in favour of the new ideas. This is by no means to say that these views were dominant in the Miners' Federation as a whole.   The rejection in 1914 of the Scottish miners' policy showed plainly that they were not.   But they gained a considerable and increasing hold.   When, in August, 1914, the outbreak of war for a time put a stop to aggressive industrial movements, it was to the miners and the railwaymen that men were looking with hope or apprehension as the main fighting forces of the New Unionism of pre-war years.

BOOKS

Board of Trade.   *Report on Strikes and Lock-outs, 1912.*
Miners' Federation of Great Britain.   *Reports, 1912.*
H. S. Jevons.   *The British Coal Trade.*
F. Evans.   *Labour Strife in the South Wales Coalfield.*
G. D. H. Cole.   *Labour in the Coal-mining Industry.*

4. LARKINISM AND THE STRUGGLE IN DUBLIN

Meanwhile, in other trades, the unrest continued to spread.   In February, 1912, the jute and flax workers of Dundee struck for higher wages, and advances were secured in the spinning and preparing sections.   In April the West London tailors came out, both for high wages and for the redress of a complicated list of special grievances.   The East London tailors followed in May, and in the end secured concessions which the original strikers were unable to gain.   Between July and September there were widespread and mostly unsuccessful strikes of engineering apprentices for higher wages— sure signs of the prevalence of unrest.   Apart from these major movements, there were very many small strikes.   Even if the miners are excluded, there were over 350,000 workers involved in trade disputes, or many more than the total in any year of the new century except 1910 and 1911.

Moreover, a good many wage advances took place in 1912 without any stoppage of work.   This was the case, for example, in both the engineering and the shipbuilding industries.   Requests for a reduction of hours were, however, refused ; and it was after this refusal that the engineering and shipyard workers came together in that shorter hours campaign which, interrupted by the War, succeeded only in 1919 in securing the forty-seven hours week.

1913 opened stormily.   On New Year's Day the London taxi-drivers launched a successful strike.   Ten days later the Yorkshire dyers were out. In the course of January the Cotton Spinners' Amalgamation gave notice to terminate the vaunted Brooklands Agreement, under which the affairs of the spinning trade had been regulated for twenty years past.   In March the Amalgamated Society of Engineers withdrew from the Engineering Agreement of 1907.   The continued rise in prices and the boom in trade were leading even the more moderate craft Unions to free their hands for the adoption of a more militant policy.   At the same time, the movement towards Trade Union organisation among the less skilled workers spread rapidly from transport to agriculture and manufacture.   From April to July the tube workers and others in the minor metal trades of the Midlands were out on strike to the number of 50,000 or more in a demand for higher wages, the strike ending in a substantial victory.   In June there occurred in Lancashire the first considerable strike of agricultural workers since the days of Arch, and the Saturday half-holiday was won.   Municipal employees in Leeds struck, and secured wage advances, in the same month.   In August the London printers conducted a successful strike for higher wages.

So far 1913 had been a year of steady and considerable successes.   But in August there began, in Dublin, a struggle which for the rest of the year drew the entire attention of the Trade Union world, and confronted the New Unionism in its most militant form with a challenge even more menacing than the challenge of Lord Devonport. In England, sectional strikes continued ; but in the eyes of all observers the great Dublin struggle dwarfed everything besides.

Before the critical Dublin dispute of 1913 the fortunes of Irish Labour were little followed in Great Britain. There had been, indeed, a big transport workers' strike in Belfast in 1907 ; and its leader had been James Larkin, then an Irish official of the British National Union of Dock Labourers, the Liverpool-centred rival of the London Dockers' Union. Thereafter had come rumours of a growing prevalence of strikes across the Irish Channel ; but, in face of the general unrest in Great Britain itself, not much attention was given to the doings in Ireland. In fact, however, the New Unionism, in a more extreme form than it ever assumed in Great Britain, had taken definite shape in Ireland some time before the great British outbreaks of 1911.

For this development two men—James Connolly and James Larkin— were mainly responsible. Connolly had begun the propaganda of militant Socialism in Ireland with the foundation of the Irish Socialist Republican Party in 1896. From 1903 to 1910 he was absent in the United States, closely associated there with the Industrial Workers of the World as well as with the Irish Republican movement, and continuing to influence his own countrymen through his writings, in which the doctrine of fighting Industrial Unionism was strongly emphasised.

Meanwhile, in 1908, Larkin had broken away from the British Dock Labourers' Union, and had founded the Irish Transport Workers' Union as a militant body. When Connolly returned to Ireland in 1910, he found Larkin already at the head of a strong Union deeply imbued with Industrial Unionist doctrines. Thereafter the two men worked together, with Larkin as the popular leader, in a great Trade Union crusade. Their aim was no less than to make the Irish Transport Union, as far as in them lay, the " One Big Union " dreamed of by Connolly and preached by the I.W.W. They enrolled not merely transport workers, but unorganised workers of every type, leaving alone only those groups which were already organised in powerful separate societies. And they sought to use the big Union which they made as a single and united instrument for the waging of constant war on the employers.

Their methods were the sudden and the sympathetic strike. They did not call great stoppages preceded by long negotiations which gave the employers ample time to prepare. They preferred to call out suddenly the workers at a single establishment, and then, as seemed most helpful, to bring out other workers in sympathy with the original strikers. If, for example, an employer tried to carry on with blackleg labour, they would stop the carmen or the shops in which his goods were sold. Or they would call out the workers in other establishments in which the employer whom they were fighting was known to have an interest.

For some time this policy was pursued with success.   Wages and conditions in Ireland were appallingly bad; and there is no doubt that "Larkinism" made them better.   In Belfast the power of the Transport Union was limited, because there the majority of the organised workers belonged to British Unions, and the religious trouble stood always in the way of unity.   But in Dublin Larkinism had become by 1913 a great and redoubtable power.

The effect of Larkin's success was to unite the employers against the Transport Union.   In particular, W. M. Murphy, leading proprietor of the Dublin tramways, of the *Irish Independent* and other newspapers, and of various business enterprises in Dublin, as well as a well-known Nationalist politician, took the lead on the capitalist side.   In the middle of 1913, matters came to a head.   After certain sectional disputes, in which Larkin had pursued his usual methods, W. M. Murphy declared war on the Transport Union, and began dismissing all its members from the various enterprises of which he was in control.   This provoked retaliatory strike action on a large scale ; and the main body of the Dublin employers thereupon followed Murphy's lead.   James Larkin replied with a general strike of the services covered by the Transport Union, and the members of numerous other Trade Unions came out, or were locked out, in sympathy.   Many of the masters meanwhile sought to obtain from all their employees a signed "document" repudiating membership of the Transport Union or of any body connected with it, and, in some cases, also renouncing the sudden and the sympathetic strike.

The Dublin struggle thus became a symbolic contest.   From the standpoint of the workers generally, Murphy and his fellow-employers were attacking the right to combine ; from the standpoint of Murphy, Larkinism stood for a method and policy which made the continuance of Capitalism impossible.   Each, accordingly, was quite determined to extirpate the other ; and all the repeated attempts of various mediators to settle the dispute broke against this rock of immovable antagonism.

The Dublin dispute could not, in these circumstances, long remain confined to Dublin, or even to Ireland.   Not only had the British Unions many Dublin members, who soon became involved in the struggle ; it was also inevitable that Larkin and his followers should, in pursuance of their usual policy, soon call on the British Unions for help.   Supplies were reaching and leaving Dublin in spite of the dispute ; but Larkin wanted British Trade Unionists—seamen, dockers, railwaymen, and others—to refuse absolutely to handle these "tainted goods."   The British Trade Union leaders, on the other hand, had no love for the sympathetic strike, which was causing them plenty of trouble in their own country ; they had certainly no desire to invoke it in Great Britain in support of Larkinism.

They were, however, in a difficulty, just because the intransigeance of Murphy and of the Dublin employers generally had made the dispute centre round the elementary rights of Trade Union combination. They hated Larkinism ; but they were not prepared to let employers dictate to Trade Unionists what form of organisation they should adopt. They could not, therefore, turn an entirely deaf ear to Larkin's appeals.

In August, 1913, Larkin and several other strike leaders had been arrested on a charge of sedition. Released upon bail, Larkin left for England to raise funds for the strike and to stir up sympathetic support. Under his influence, there were strikes of railwaymen and transport workers in various places, following on the dismissal or suspension of men who refused to handle tainted goods. The British Unions, unwilling to become involved, quickly settled these disputes and prevented them from spreading, much to the anger of Larkin, who was by this time loudly denouncing the British leaders for cowardice and treachery, and calling in vain on the British workers for a sympathetic general strike.

Meanwhile, the British Trades Union Congress, on receipt of an appeal from the Dublin Trades Council, which included many branches of British Unions, had sent a deputation to Ireland in the hope of settling the dispute. The delegates, out of sympathy with Larkinism though they were, reported that, in face of the anti-Union attitude of the Dublin Employers' Federation, there was no hope of agreement. Nor did the Government, which late in September sent a special Commission of Enquiry to Dublin, meet with better fortune. The Commissioners, after condemning on the one hand Larkinism and on the other the " document " issued by the employers, proposed, according to the favourite recipe of those years, a system of compulsory conciliation. The men agreed to discuss this ; but the employers would have none of it, and the Commission thereupon retired from the field.

At the end of October Larkin was tried and sent to prison for seven months. But this created so huge a wave of resentment in Great Britain as well as in Ireland that the Government, fearing widespread strike action, hastily released him a fortnight later. He at once resumed his propaganda in favour of a sympathetic strike. The British Unions met this move by calling a special Conference, and by sending a second delegation to Dublin in the hope of negotiating a settlement. Discussions were resumed, but broke down because the employers would give no guarantee that all the strikers would be reinstated, or the blacklegs, who had been introduced in large numbers, dismissed. The special Trade Union Conference met, and sent a third delegation to Dublin ; but once more negotiations broke down over the question of reinstatement.

During all this time there had been an active effort in Great Britain to raise funds for the support of the men involved in the dispute. The Trades Union Congress, through the Co-operative Wholesale Society, sent shiploads of food to the starving Dublin workers, and the *Daily Herald* and other agencies collected large sums on their behalf. A movement to find homes in

England for the children of the strikers broke down in face of denunciations by Irish priests of the placing of Catholic children in Protestant homes.

By the end of 1913 it was clear that there could be but one end to the dispute ; and in the course of January, 1914, under the influence of sheer starvation, men began to drift back to work on the employers' terms. The latter, in most cases, silently dropped the " document," and exacted no pledges about membership of the Transport Union. But in many instances pledges to abandon the sympathetic strike were required. At last, at the end of January, the dispute collapsed, and during February the rest of the men gradually resumed work. On the face of things, the employers had won ; but, as appeared later, they had not smashed the Transport Workers' Union, which during the War immensely increased its strength, and became for a time almost the " One Big Union " of Ireland. James Connolly later referred to the struggle as " a drawn battle " ; and this fairly summarises the result.

In Great Britain, though the Trade Union leaders succeeded in preventing any widespread sympathetic action, the Dublin dispute exerted an enormous influence on men's minds. Larkinism, though it went much further than any British Trade Union group was prepared to go, came to stand for the New Unionism ; and Larkin's denunciations of the British leaders were echoed hardly less ferociously by the *Daily Herald* in its leading articles and in Will Dyson's trenchant cartoons. All the " left wing " rallied behind Larkinism ; and when the dispute at length collapsed, it had done a good deal, in Great Britain, to knit together the working-class elements which were striving for a militant policy. It had, on the other hand, solidified the older Trade Union leaders in opposition to the new tactics. In 1914, on the eve of the Great War, the left and right wings of British Trade Unionism confronted each other fiercely over the grave of the Dublin struggle.

BOOKS

W. P. Ryan. *The Irish Labour Movement.*
D. Ryan. *James Connolly.*
C. Wright. *Disturbed Dublin.*
J. Connolly. *The Re-conquest of Ireland.*
Board of Trade. *Annual Report on Strikes and Lock-outs, 1913.*
G. R. Askwith. *Industrial Negotiations and Disputes.*

5. THE INDUSTRIAL COUNCIL — THE TRIPLE ALLIANCE

The story of the big strikes of the pre-war years has been told in some detail because in these eventful times each great movement had its own significance. In their cumulative effect, these strikes stood for a profound change not only in Trade Union policy, but still more in the whole mind and temper of the British working class. Whatever the immediate issues might be, there was a new spirit behind them—a kicking against the pricks of

Capitalism, an insistence on the human rights of the worker as a person who was set on " counting " as an individual and refused to be " druv," a capacity for spontaneous mass action which seemed, after the long-sustained orderliness of the Victorian era, something wholly new.

It was, above all, this aspect of the unrest that alarmed the employers, the Government, and, scarcely less, some of the older Trade Union leaders.   Consequently, from its very beginning, there was a feverish search for cures for the prevailing industrial trouble—cures, of course, which would leave the capitalist system intact.   Much was heard of the virtues of conciliation and arbitration, of the systems in force in Canada, Australasia, and other countries, of the need for more goodwill as the basis of satisfactory industrial relations. Even profit sharing, as is usual at such times, enjoyed its little boom.

Again and again, as we have seen, the Government and its agents directly intervened in order to settle the recurrent industrial crises.   But it was recognised by the Liberals that such direct intervention had its political dangers and inconveniences, and that it would be both nicer and safer if employers and workers could be induced to settle their differences peaceably among themselves.   Out of these fears arose, in 1911, the Industrial Council —a joint consultative body of well-known employers and moderate Trade Union leaders, designed to act as a conciliatory influence.   This body proved wholly impotent to settle disputes ; but it conducted in 1912 an exhaustive enquiry into industrial agreements, in which much valuable material bearing on the pre-war history of Labour is embedded.   Its chairman was a Government official, Sir George Askwith (later Lord Askwith), who was in constant request as a conciliator during the troubles.

The plan chiefly discussed before the Commission, on Sir George Askwith's initiative, was some form of compulsory conciliation before a strike could take place.   This plan was based on the Canadian Industrial Disputes Investigation Act of 1907, generally known as the " Lemieux Act."   Under this Act, which applied only to certain services, no stoppage of work could lawfully take place until a dispute had been considered by a special court of enquiry, and a report had been issued embodying recommendations.   These recommendations had no binding force, and after the report had been published both parties were free to take what action they chose.   But it was hoped that the moral force behind the report would be enough, in most cases, to prevent a stoppage of work.

Such a plan for Great Britain was widely canvassed ; but the Industrial Council could not be brought definitely to recommend it.   They went only so far as to propose that voluntary agreements should be given the force of law, provided that they embodied conditions allowing no stoppage of work without previous enquiry by some impartial tribunal.   So timid a proposal was almost nothing ; and the Council's Report attracted very little attention. Indeed, the Government, having found that it was of no use as a conciliator for the prevention of strikes, had virtually dropped it before the Report appeared. It was quietly allowed to lapse in the year following its creation.

While the Government was thus striving to dam up industrial unrest by schemes of conciliation and arbitration, the great Trade Unions, on their side, were also seriously considering their position. The strikes of transport workers and railwaymen in 1911 had thrown many miners out of employment because the coal could not be got away from the pithead ; and in 1912 the miners' strike had thrown out thousands of railwaymen and waterside workers. Separate action by the three groups seemed, in these circumstances, deplorably wasteful ; and, after the formation of the National Union of Railwaymen in 1913, plans for common action were widely discussed. The outcome of these discussions was the formation of the Triple Industrial Alliance of Miners, Railwaymen and Transport Workers by the three great bodies which represented the majority of the workers in these industries. The Miners' Federation took the official initiative, and in 1914 the Alliance was created, though its terms were not definitely ratified until a year later. The idea behind it was not, as is widely supposed, that of the sympathetic strike. It was not intended that, when any of the three industries became involved in a dispute, the other two should give it sympathetic support. This was, as we shall see, how it tended to work out in practice ; but it was not the plan on which the Alliance was based.

The miners, as we saw, were trying after 1912 to arrange for the simultaneous termination of their agreements in all districts, in order to enable them to act effectively as a national body. The idea of the Triple Alliance was to extend this to all the three industries. Miners, railwaymen and transport workers were all so to arrange their agreements that they would all end at the same time. Each body would then put forward its own demands simultaneously with the others, and each would agree not to accept any settlement unless the others settled too. Then either the employers would give way before the massed power of the three groups, and no strike would be needed, or, if a strike did occur, all three industries would be stopped at once, but each group would be striking for its own programme as well as in support of the others.

If, however, there was difficulty in arranging for simultaneous termination of agreements in one industry, the difficulty was obviously far greater when three industries were concerned. The employers clearly would not wish to facilitate a vast strike of all three groups, and there would be strong pressure for the acceptance of agreements ending at different times. In fact, the Triple Alliance never realised this fundamental principle of joint action. But to this point we shall come back later on.

The formation of the Alliance was hailed as a great victory for Trade Union solidarity. The Syndicalists, and others who had been advocating the General Strike, were greatly encouraged by the threat of the three great basic services to act together. Almost the General Strike seemed to have secured official endorsement. But the new instrument was not to be used as yet. Before the preliminary stages of its formation had been completed, the outbreak of war interrupted the movement. Despite war conditions, it was officially ratified by the three bodies in 1915 ; but no chance of testing it in practice arose until the War was at an end. It is none the less worthy of notice that the threat of something approaching a General Strike—a perpetual theme of post-war Trade Union diplomacy—had been definitely made before the War, as the direct outcome of the great industrial movements which this chapter has described.

BOOKS

Industrial Council. *Report and Minutes of Evidence of Inquiry into Industrial Agreements.*
G. R. Askwith. *Industrial Problems and Disputes.*
G. R. Carter. *The Triple Industrial Alliance.*
G. D. H. Cole. *Labour in the Coal-mining Industry.*

CHAPTER VI

LABOUR IN WAR-TIME

1. LABOUR AND THE WAR

THE full seriousness of the war threat of July, 1914, was not at first generally realised in the working-class movement. There had been too many war scares in the preceding years for it to be readily believed that this was the real thing. The continental workers were no doubt more alive to the seriousness of the situation ; in Great Britain, up to the very moment of the invasion of Belgium, there were many who believed that the trouble would pass away.

What was the duty of the working class in face of the threat, and later of the reality, of war ? The question had been widely discussed in international Labour and Socialist gatherings. In 1907 the International Socialist Congress, to which the British Labour Party as well as the I.L.P. and other Socialist societies belonged, had laid this duty down in a unanimous resolution. Before war broke out, every effort must be made to prevent it, and every Socialist or Labour Party must put out all its powers in order to dissuade its own country from taking part. If this failed, and war broke out, the Socialists were to do two things. They were to " intervene to bring it promptly to an end," and they were to " use the political and economic crisis created by the war to rouse the populace from its slumbers, and to hasten the fall of capitalist society."

In the years after 1907, there was a good deal of discussion about the means of carrying this policy into effect. The French Trade Unions pressed the International Federation of Trade Unions, which had been formed in 1901, to declare for an international general strike as a means of preventing war ; but the I.F.T.U., holding itself to be a purely industrial body, referred the question to the International Socialist Congress. When it was brought up there, it was decided to refer it to the various countries for discussion ; and the British Labour Party sent out a questionnaire on the subject, to which hardly any of its affiliated bodies took the trouble to reply. On the question of method, the position remained in 1914 wholly indefinite.

If, however, the resolution of 1907 meant anything at all, it implied a militant anti-war policy, both before and after the outbreak. In August, 1914, the Socialist and Labour Parties did everywhere demonstrate against war, and against their own States becoming involved in war, up to the point at which they actually became involved. But at that point the Labour and

Socialist opposition nearly everywhere crumbled.   In Germany, France and
Great Britain alike, the majority of the working-class leaders gave support to
their own Governments.   In Great Britain, the Labour Party and the Trades
Union Congress, after taking part in peace demonstrations up to August 4th.
1914, speedily rallied to the national cause, leaving the I.L.P. and a majority
of the British Socialist Party to form a small minority in opposition.   Even
Ramsay MacDonald, who resigned the chairmanship of the Parliamentary
Labour Party because of his hostility to the War, soon after expressed the view
that " victory must be ours."   The Labour Party, which began by urging
the working-class movement to concentrate on measures for the relief of
distress, was soon involved, jointly with the other political parties, in a recruiting campaign.   The Trades Union Congress issued a strongly worded
appeal for soldiers.   Among the strongest supporters of the war were
Robert Blatchford, who had for years been denouncing Germany's aggressive
designs, and H. M. Hyndman, the veteran leader of the B.S.P., who, with
many of his old followers, later seceded to form a National Socialist Party,
which presently resumed the old name of " Social Democratic Federation."

Undoubtedly at this stage, and throughout the earlier part of the War, the
overwhelming mass of working-class, as of other, opinion in Great Britain,
was strongly " pro-war," just as it was in France, or Germany, or even
Austria-Hungary.   Everywhere in Western Europe, the declared Socialist
policy of opposition had dramatically collapsed ; and the small minorities
which opposed the War were for the time driven almost to silence.   As the
logical sequel to the predominant attitude, a truce to internal disagreements
was rapidly declared.   In the course of August the political parties declared a
by-election truce, and the Trade Unions, without awaiting any definite
understanding with the employers, proclaimed an industrial truce.   Immediately after the outbreak of war, the trade disputes then in progress, including
a big building strike in London, in which the employers had resorted to the
" document," were called off.

Meanwhile, the dislocation caused by the outbreak of war had led to a
sharp leap in prices and to the closing down of many factories.   It seemed at
this stage as if prolonged and widespread unemployment would be the lot of
the workers.   The Labour bodies formed a War Emergency Workers'
National Committee, which demanded measures for the prevention of
profiteering, the control of prices, and the relief of distress.   But within a few
months the situation dramatically changed.   Prices fell after the first rapid
rise, and there was an interval before they began their long and steep advance.
Work was resumed in many factories which had closed down, and there
came from the industries engaged in producing war supplies a growing and
insatiable demand for more labour.   It was not long before it had become
clear that, in face of the Army's growing need for men and materials, a shortage rather than a surplus of labour would be the fundamental problem.

Soon prices again began to rise, and the workers found difficulty in existing on the wages of 1914. The industrial truce seemed to preclude strike action ; but it became clear that something must be done. The railwaymen, the first to move, negotiated with the companies, which had been virtually taken over by the State, the first " war bonus." But this was not extended to other trades ; and towards the end of February, 1915, the whole country was startled by the outbreak of a great unofficial strike of engineering workers on the Clyde. This was a serious matter ; for the Army was perilously short of munitions, and the Clyde was one of the greatest armament-producing areas. The Government at once called on the men to resume work, and the Trade Unions officially seconded their efforts. But the Central Withdrawal of Labour Control Committee, the unofficial body of rank-and-file delegates in charge of the movement, waited some days after the expiry of the Government's ultimatum before ordering a return. The dispute was then referred to Government arbitration, and ended by the granting of a somewhat larger advance than the employers had offered to concede.

Just before the Clyde strike the Government had appointed a Committee on Production in Engineering and Shipbuilding Establishments, to enquire into the whole position in the munitions industries. After the strike, this body assumed a new importance. It not only acted as arbitrator in the dispute, but came forward with a complete plan for the organisation of labour in the munitions industries and for the settlement of all disputes in them by arbitration for the period of the War. The problem of labour shortage was by this time becoming acute, and the employers were insisting that Trade Union rules must be abrogated in order to give them full freedom to reorganise the workshops in view of war needs, and to employ unskilled workers in jobs ordinarily reserved for skilled men.

The Committee on Production, in March, 1915, proposed that the Trade Unions should accept both compulsory arbitration and the abrogation of Trade Union restrictions, on condition that the Government should pledge itself to the restoration of the *status quo* at the end of the War. At the Treasury Conferences of March, 1915, most of the Unions accepted these terms. The Miners' Federation, however, refused to be bound by them, and the Amalgamated Society of Engineers exacted from the Government a guarantee to limit employers' profits in the industries concerned.

The Treasury Agreements had at first no legal force behind them ; but in July, Lloyd George, at the head of a newly-established Ministry of Munitions, secured the passage of the Munitions of War Act, 1915, which made compulsory arbitration, as well as the suspension of Trade Union customs and the limitation of profits in the munitions trades, legally binding. The Act applied primarily to engineering and shipbuilding ; but power was taken to apply compulsory arbitration to any industry supplying vital war needs.

The Act was soon tested in practice. There had already been some trouble in the mining industry. In January, 1915, a serious dispute in Yorkshire had been settled only by conceding the men's claims. In March, the Miners' Federation had unsuccessfully demanded a national wage advance, in order to meet the rising cost of living. Instead, only local advances of inadequate amount had been secured, with the result that unrest was widespread. In July came a general stoppage of the South Wales coalfield.

The old agreement in South Wales had expired in the middle of 1915, and negotiations for a new one had hopelessly broken down. The Government put forward proposals for a settlement, which the men rejected, and after some further negotiations the Government " proclaimed " the South Wales coalfield under the Munitions Act, or, in other words, used its legal authority to forbid a strike and to refer the dispute to compulsory arbitration. This action had no effect on the miners, who struck solidly in defiance of the law, knowing very well that, in face of the shortage of skilled labour, it would not at all suit the Government to attempt to use its power of sending 200,000 men to gaol. Indeed, in face of the strike, Lloyd George and his colleagues promptly gave way. The strikers got most of what they wanted, and returned to work unpunished. A month later a further dispute arose over the interpretation of the settlement. The Government gave a decision against the men, but in face of a renewed strike threat hastily reversed this decision. The South Wales Miners' Federation had certainly lost no time in driving a coach and four through Lloyd George's measure of compulsory arbitration.

Nevertheless, throughout the War, strikes were relatively few and small. After the troubles of 1915 wage-rates, while they did not advance so fast as prices, moved steadily upward in nearly all trades. Employment was plentiful, and overtime was largely worked. In the war trades high piece-work earnings were common, though not universal. Apart from isolated disputes, the machinery of arbitration under the Munitions Acts worked well enough to prevent serious troubles on the wages question. The important strikes of the war period, after those of 1915, arose rather on other issues. They were, moreover, mostly unofficial ; for the Trade Unions were bound by the Munitions Acts and by the industrial truce. Of these unofficial stoppages we shall have something to say in the next section.

It must be remembered that, practically throughout the War, Labour was officially represented in the Government. In June, 1915, the Liberal Government gave place to a Coalition, in which Arthur Henderson and two other Labour Party representatives were included. When Lloyd George drove Asquith from power in December, 1916, the Labour Party agreed to form a part of the new Coalition, and Arthur Henderson entered the War Cabinet. When Henderson resigned, after his return from Russia, in June, 1917, G. N. Barnes took his place, still as an official representative of Labour.

Although for the last eighteen months of the War the relations between the Government and the Labour Party were becoming more and more strained, as the demand for peace gained strength in the Labour ranks, it was not until after the Armistice that the Labour Party finally withdrew from the Coalition.

At any rate up to the end of 1916, although the dissentient elements were gradually gaining force, the bulk of British Labour opinion was favourable to the prosecution of the War. Then three things worked together to modify this attitude. The first of these was the rejected German "peace offer" of December, 1916. The second was the Russian Revolution of 1917, and the launching of a peace movement by the Russian workers. The controversy over the proposal to attend an International Labour Peace Conference at Stockholm in the summer of 1917 marks a turning-point. It was then that Arthur Henderson withdrew from the War Cabinet, and a representative Labour Conference voted by a small majority in favour of attending the Stockholm meeting. The Bolshevik Revolution of November, 1917, while it sharply divided the British workers, who had unanimously welcomed the downfall of Czardom, helped to introduce into the policy of the "Left Wing" a new note of militant revolutionism which had been almost absent from the earlier movements of war-time unrest. And the negotiations at Brest-Litovsk and the signing of peace between Russia and Germany in March, 1918, undoubtedly heightened the feeling of war-weariness in Great Britain, and gave a new impetus to the movement for peace in Germany as well as in the Allied countries. Brest-Litovsk was, indeed, as became plainer later on, the real beginning of the German internal collapse.

In official Labour circles, the growing desire for peace took shape in an attempt at independent formulation of "War Aims," with a view to the finding of a possible basis for a negotiated peace. The Inter-Allied Labour Conferences and the Labour Party's War Aims Conference gave the movement a definite basis, and were not without their influence on the German workers, who perhaps overestimated the power of the workers in the Allied countries to affect the terms of settlement. To the end, the real anti-war movement remained unofficial. One section of it was led by the Independent Labour Party, which adhered throughout the War to a pacifist attitude. Other sections, especially influential in the workshops, and above all on the Clyde and in South Wales, took a more militant line, preaching the class-war in opposition to the war of nations, and, at any rate after the Russian Revolutions, taking on a definitely revolutionary tone. The unofficial Leeds Conference of June, 1917, which called for the formation of British Workers' and Soldiers' Councils on the Russian model, set the movement definitely on foot, though many of those who took part in it had really no revolutionary intention. It should be remembered that this Conference took place before the Bolshevik Revolution, and before the idea of Soviet

revolution had acquired the full meaning which it took on when the
" dictatorship of the proletariat " had been proclaimed.

The third factor making for a change in the working-class attitude to the
War was Conscription. The way for this had been prepared by gradual
stages—the National Registration Act of July, 1915, and the " voluntary "
recruiting scheme conducted under Lord Derby, with Labour participation,
in the autumn of the same year. With the New Year it was announced that
voluntary methods had failed, and in January, 1916, the first Military Service
Bill, for single men only, was introduced. A Labour Conference decided to
oppose it, on the ground that it was too soon to proclaim the failure of the
voluntary system, but not to offer resistance to it when it had become an Act.
Thereafter, by successive Acts and administrative changes, the bonds of Conscription were steadily tightened. Married men were taken, the age was
raised, exemptions granted on exceptional grounds were reviewed with
growing stringency. On every possible job women and older or unfit men
were substituted for men serviceable to the fighting forces.

The enforcement of Conscription inevitably placed a huge power over
the workers' lives in the hands of the Government. In the vast majority of
cases, it was the Government that decided whether men should join the forces,
or be retained in industrial life. This was done mainly by negotiation with the
Trade Unions, which were called upon to agree to the release of more and
more men for the Army, and therewith to a steadily increasing amount of
" dilution of labour " by the substitution for their members of women and
of less skilled workers returned from the forces as unfit, or drawn from other
trades. Thus to a growing reluctance among the remaining workers to
join the Army was added an increasing amount of friction over the terms of
" substitution " ; and these factors combined with a growing war-weariness
and a developing suspicion of the purity of the aims with which the War was
being carried on to create a stronger and stronger unofficial movement of
unrest. The longer the War lasted, the stricter the control and rationing of
the nation's " man-power " grew ; and every intensification of recruiting
and civil discipline at home swelled the ranks of the anti-war opposition,
which had been even from the outset much larger than any working-class
opposition ever became during the second World War.

It is, therefore, not surprising either that the Labour participation in the
Coalition Government showed signs of dissolution during the later stages of
the War, or that the number and magnitude of strikes tended to increase.
In 1916, the only important stoppage was the Parkhead strike at Glasgow,
mentioned in the next section. But in 1917 there were engineering strikes
in March at Barrow-in-Furness and on the Tyne, and in November at
Coventry, besides the widespread " May strikes " on grievances arising out
of the extension of " dilution " and the workshop discipline imposed under
the Munitions Acts. The great German " offensive " of 1918 caused a

temporary lull in disputes ; but in the latter half of 1918 strike followed strike in rapid succession. The Coventry engineers struck again in July, in protest against an " embargo " on the changing of employer by skilled munition workers ; in August, there was a strike of transport workers in favour of equal pay for women engaged on men's work, as well as a successful sudden strike of the London police ; and in September, a stoppage of the cotton spinners, followed by an extensive unofficial strike on the railways. All these movements were signs, in part, of the increasing severity of war-time conditions, but even more of growing anti-war feeling among the workers.

Nearly all these strikes were called and conducted by unofficial leaders, acting against the will of the official leaders of the Trade Unions. The " industrial truce " tied official Trade Unionism down, and to some extent this fact cost it its force and authority among the rank and file. The Unions as such could do little to remedy the men's grievances, or even to voice their point of view, and this gave the self-constituted unofficial leaders their chance. To the nature and policy of this unofficial leadership the next section of the chapter will be devoted.

BOOKS

H. N. Brailsford. *The War of Steel and Gold.*
A. W. Humphrey. *International Socialism and the War.*
W. E. Walling. *The Socialists and the War.*
G. D. H. Cole. *Labour in Wartime* (1915).
G. D. H. Cole. *Trade Unionism and Munitions.*
G. D. H. Cole. *Labour in the Coal-mining Industry.*
The Labour Year Books, 1916 and *1919.*
W. A. Orton. *Labour in Transition.*

2. THE SHOP STEWARDS' MOVEMENT

" Shop Steward " is an old name in Trade Union affairs ; but during the Great War the old name came to stand for a new thing. The shop steward, as he existed before 1914, was a minor Trade Union delegate appointed, in a particular shop or factory, to perform certain routine functions such as the periodical inspection of Trade Union contribution cards, and to report generally to the Union branch or district concerning the condition of affairs in his shop. Sometimes he had rather wider functions, especially at certain great factories, such as Woolwich Arsenal, and in certain of the minor metal trades. But usually his powers were very restricted, and his main duty was merely that of report. He was above all the Union's recruiting sergeant in the workshop.

Shop stewards did not exist in nearly all industries, or in nearly all factories in industries where the system was common. They flourished chiefly in the engineering and shipbuilding trades ; and these were, of course, the trades most directly affected by the demand for munitions of war and by the

consequent " dilution " of skilled labour.   As long as the War lasted, conditions in the engineering shops were in constant change.   Almost every
day new problems had to be faced, as methods of production were altered,
new machines introduced, and unskilled and women workers set to jobs
previously done by skilled men.   All these changes called for delicate and
detailed workshop adjustments ; and the workers in the shops imperatively
needed someone to represent them in dealings with the management over
these constantly recurrent issues.

The shop stewards stepped naturally into the breach, and assumed a
wholly new importance in the life of the workshop and in the organised
relations of employers and employed.   The Trade Union and its officers, while
they dealt with the broad principles of dilution and similar matters, were
much too remote to handle the detailed troubles of each particular shop.
The shop steward was on the spot ; and the duty fell upon him.   The result
was a rapid increase in the number of shop stewards.   The system spread right
through the munitions trades, and was imitated in other industries, such as
boot and shoe manufacture.   Moreover, there arose side by side with the old
type of shop steward, who was directly responsible to the Trade Union from
which he held his appointment, a new type, neither representing nor officially
responsible to any Trade Union at all—a nominee of a group of workers in
the shop, often irrespective of their connection with any particular Trade
Union.   This occurred especially where the workers in a shop or factory
were divided between several rival Trade Unions.

The Trade Unions, as we have seen, were prevented during the War from
leading any militant movement, first by their voluntary declaration of an
industrial truce, and later by the penal provisions of the Munitions Acts.
But, under the conditions of rapid workshop change, constant differences
and disputes were bound to arise ; and in these the shop stewards, as less
official and responsible persons, usually took the lead.   The Munitions Acts
included, besides the provisions mentioned in the last section, disciplinary
clauses under which men could be punished for bad time-keeping and
similar offences, and also a system of " Leaving Certificates," which,
until their abolition in 1917, seriously restricted the mobility of labour.
Finally, with the introduction and the progressively severe enforcement
of Conscription, many grievances arose over the order in which men
were to be taken from the workshops to fill up gaps in the fighting
ranks.

On all these grievances the shop stewards' system was built up as a guerrilla
movement designed to replace the official Trade Union conduct of affairs.
As a movement, it arose first in connection with the unofficial Clyde strike of
February, 1915, mentioned above.   The Strike Committee which conducted
that affair was a body of delegates from the various workshops throughout
the Clyde area ; and, when the dispute was over, this body decided to hold

together on a permanent basis, under the name of the Clyde Workers' Committee. It was speedily imitated in other areas, and Workers' Committees, usually including official and unofficial shop stewards alike, were set up in most important engineering centres. Finally, these bodies linked up into a loose central organisation, generally known as the National Workers' Committee Movement. Both national and local Committees constantly fell foul of the official Trade Union Executives, which accused them of usurping their authority. The Government and the employers, save at a few moments of exceptional stress, refused to recognise the unofficial movement, and insisted on dealing with the regularly constituted Trade Union leaders. Prominent shop stewards were deported from the Clyde in 1916, and in other cases were arrested and imprisoned. But the movement held its position, above all, because in the war-time circumstances of industry it supplied a new need which the Trade Unions were not otherwise in a position to meet.

The origin of the wider " Workers' Committee " movement on the Clyde was no accident. Just as South Wales was the storm-centre of the coalfields, the Clyde was the storm-centre of the metal industries. American Industrial Unionist influence had been exceptionally strong there ; and the idea of " One Big Union" built up on a basis of all-grades workshop organisation had been steadily preached before the War. The narrow craft structure of engineering Trade Unionism made even an approach to this ideal unattainable through the existing Trade Unions ; but the rise of the shop stewards gave the Industrial Unionists just the basis of organisation that they wanted. They did not, indeed, urge the workers to break away from the craft Unions ; but in the shop steward system and in the Workers' Committee they found an alternative form of leadership which men would follow in disregard of official Trade Union instructions.

All the important engineering strikes of the war years were in effect organised and run not by the Trade Unions but by the shop stewards. The " Parkhead " strike of March, 1916, which led to the deportation of the strike leaders, arose out of a dispute as to the privileges to be accorded to the elected chief steward, or " convener ", in the Parkhead Forge, at Glasgow. The wages strikes at Barrow and on the Tyne, in March, 1917, were under shop steward leadership. Finally, the great " May strikes " of 1917, the one instance of a war-time strike movement extending over the greater part of the country—arose mainly out of troubles over the dilution of labour, and were nationally organised by the Workers' Committee Movement.

In the early stages, the Shop Stewards' Movement was purely industrial in character. It was concerned with wages, dilution, the administration of discipline in the workshops under the Munitions Acts, and similar grievances. But, especially from 1917, it began to assume a more political character. From the first, it was led mainly by left-wing Socialists, usually hostile to the

War on Socialist grounds. As rank-and-file opinion began to turn against the War and as the stiffer administration both of workshop discipline and of Conscription created growing resentment, the leaders increasingly took a political line. The Russian Revolutions further accentuated this tendency. The Shop Stewards' Movement began to cry loudly for international peace. and at least to hint at social revolution.

As long as the War lasted, though an individual here and there might be sent to gaol for his activities, the movement as a whole was in an impregnable position. The shortage of skilled labour and the need for munitions were such that the Government could not afford to provoke strikes, or to delay settling them when they occurred. But no sooner was the War over than these conditions were radically changed. The munitions industries, hugely swollen in personnel, were drastically cut down ; and in most cases employers found excellent chances of getting rid of inconveniently militant shop stewards. Many found themselves dismissed, on the plea of redundancy of labour, and others kept their mouths shut for fear of losing their jobs. Within a few months of the Armistice it was clear that the unofficial Shop Stewards' Movement was dying. What was left of it—a small body of leaders without a rank and file—mostly passed over a little later into the new Communist Party of Great Britain.

Nevertheless, the movement produced a permanent impression on Trade Union structure. In 1918 and 1919 the engineering Trade Unions negotiated with the Engineering Employers' Federation national agreements, providing for the recognition of shop stewards and of workshop committees as bodies of first instance in industrial negotiations. They also revised their rules so as to admit official shop stewards to a place on the Trade Union District Committees. The main body of the ordinary shop stewards, under these conditions, deserted the unofficial leaders and returned to the official Trade Union fold. The shop steward system, greatly as it declined after 1918, remained more widespread and more fully recognised by both employers and Trade Unions than it had been before the first World War. But it was no longer an " all trades " movement, standing for the solidarity of all the workers irrespective of craft or grade. It ceased for the time being to constitute a challenge either to official Trade Unionism or to the capitalist control of industry, and became merely a useful supplementary piece of Trade Union machinery. We shall see later what became of it in the second World War.

The shop steward system, as such, was obviously suitable only to industries organised on a factory or workshop basis. Analogous movements, however, sprang up during the first World War in a number of other industries. The miners, already organised mainly on a pit basis, had little need of it ; but in Lanarkshire and in some other areas local organisations partly based upon it arose. In the National Union of Railwaymen an elaborate system of semi-official District Councils, already in existence before 1914, developed on unofficial lines during the War years, and was responsible for a steady stream of left-wing propaganda, and for one or two strikes, including an important unofficial stoppage in South Wales and elsewhere in September, 1918. Transport workers and builders, among other groups, developed somewhat similar methods of rank-and-file organisation in particular areas.

It was mainly in and through these various unofficial bodies that the propaganda of workers' control in industry was carried on during the War. Syndicalism, as a name for a distinct movement, disappeared; but Industrial Unionism continued to grow, and Guild Socialism, known in 1914 only to a comparatively narrow intellectual circle, gained from 1915 onwards large bodies of disciples, especially in the various workshop movements to which its doctrines of workers' control made a special appeal. The rank-and-file movements of the War years were, indeed, essentially the continuation of those which had developed during the great unrest of the preceding years. They changed their form, and adapted their methods and propaganda to the changed conditions. But the driving force remained the same—an increasing anti-capitalist feeling expressing itself largely in a somewhat vaguely but insistently expressed desire for a real share in the control of industry.

In the war-time movements, this desire found expression with many variations of vehemence and emphasis. The Clyde and South Wales extremists had no more use for Guild Socialism than for the orthodox Collectivism of the Labour Party and the I.L.P. But, although they were the most vocal leaders, they were only a small fraction of the shop stewards' movement as a whole. Guild Socialism and kindred doctrines appealed strongly to those who were less intent on the political aspect of the movement than on its application to workshop affairs. As the workshop movement became more political towards the end of the War, some of its supporters dropped away, and it undoubtedly became less effective as an industrial force affecting workshop conditions. It was, nevertheless, for the few years of its effective existence, a very remarkable demonstration of working-class capacity for rapid self-organisation, and a significant expression, in a practical form, of that desire for workers' control which had been a prominent feature of pre-war left-wing agitations.

BOOKS

G. D. H. Cole. *Workshop Organisation.*
G. D. H. Cole. *Trade Unionism and Munitions.*
W. A. Orton. *Labour in Transition.*
J. T. Murphy. *The Workers' Committee.*
Labour Party. *Report on the Clyde Deputations.*

3. STATE CONTROL

Under war conditions, not only the millions of men drafted into the forces of the Crown, but also a large part of the industrial " army," became to all intents and purposes employees of the State. The railwayman, the miner, the munition worker, or the seaman, might remain nominally the employee of some private firm ; but increasingly, as the War advanced, the use to be made of his labour and the terms and conditions of his employment were determined by his virtual employer, the Government. The State, in view of military requirements, became the greatest customer of a wide range of industries ; and, even where this was not the case, the need for the most careful use of every man and of every productive agent in the nation compelled the Government to intervene in order to regulate, with increasing closeness, the working of the economic system. Moreover, the sharp rise in prices created social discontents which forced the Government to exert a growing control over the sale as well as the production of goods, lest it should have to meet the rising prices by means of a swollen wages bill which the taxpayer would have to pay. Without control, runaway inflation would have been unavoidable : even as things were, State control was developed too little and too late, and a considerable inflation did occur. The State's position as virtual employer and as arbiter of trade disputes gave it the duty of regulating wages ; but this power was clearly bound to be ineffective unless prices were regulated as well.

The comprehensive system of State control which existed in the later years of the War was a very gradual development. The railways, and some ships, were indeed taken over by the State immediately upon the outbreak of war, because so much control was obviously necessary for the mere transport of troops and of military supplies. Beyond that point control was not at once advanced. For some time the War Office endeavoured to get its supplies by the system of contracts used in time of peace, and it was deemed no business of the Government to undertake the organisation of supplies on behalf of the civil population. This policy, however, speedily broke down, and early in 1915 the nation awoke to the fact that there was a serious shortage of munitions. This led to a big campaign of organisation. At first local Armaments Committees, consisting of employers' and workers' representatives, were set up to organise higher production in various areas. But these were soon discarded and their place was taken by the bureaucratic Ministry of Munitions, under which the important firms producing munitions of war were brought as " controlled establishments." The War Office Contracts Department in the meantime was organising the supply of khaki cloth and of other textiles, as well as the supply of foodstuffs, etc., for the armed forces. More and more shipping tonnage was requisitioned, and one by one other commodities were brought under some sort of control, or, without direct control, were effectively supervised under the drastic provisions of the Defence of the Realm Acts.

It was not, however, till the coming of the Lloyd George Government at the end of 1916 that State control of industry became at all complete or systematic. The scarcity of shipping space was by that time acute, and imports had to be rigidly rationed. Labour was scarce, and little could be spared for services not regarded as essential. Moreover, the sharp rise in prices, which by the end of 1916 were about 90 per cent. above the pre-war level, had created a situation which called for some attempt at drastic control.

The new Government set energetically to work. Owing to Labour troubles, the South Wales coalfield had already been taken over under the Defence of the Realm Act in November, 1916, and in February, 1917, the whole of the coalfields were brought under direct State control. A Ministry of Shipping was set up, and practically all British tonnage was brought under the State. In April the wool industry was regulated by a " costings " system which considerably checked the rise in prices, and in August a Wool Control Board, on which the employers, the Trade Unions, and the Government were equally represented, was set up with large powers for the organisation of the industry. A Cotton Control Board had already been established in June, with less extensive powers. A Wheat Commission and a Food Controller had been appointed in 1916 by the Asquith Government ; but in the middle of 1917, under Lord Rhondda as Minister, the Food Ministry was drastically reorganised, and was given greatly extended powers, a " costings " system based on the experience of the War Office Contracts Department being introduced for a large number of commodities.

The agricultural industry was also brought under a special system of regulation. Early in the War a Food Production Department was created under the Board of Agriculture with the object of increasing the supply of home-grown food and of decreasing Great Britain's dependence on imported foodstuffs. Under the direction of County Agricultural Committees, land was put compulsorily to the plough, and in 1917, by the Corn Production Act, a guarantee of certain high minimum prices for cereals was given to the farmers in order to encourage them to produce as much as possible. At the same time a minimum wage was granted to the agricultural labourers, an Agricultural Wages Board, acting on the advice of County Committees representing farmers and labourers, with appointed members, being set up, with power to fix the actual rates to be paid. One of the effects of this Act was an extraordinarily rapid spread of Trade Unionism among the agricultural workers, among whom a campaign of organisation had been proceeding during the years immediately before 1914.

All the war-time systems of control were made effective largely because the Government, through its control of shipping space and its arrangements for collective purchase of foreign supplies of sugar, wheat, meat, oils and fats, wool and many other commodities, had practically complete control of the raw materials of most industries, and was able by giving or withholding supplies to determine precisely what should or should not be produced. Furthermore, as the greatest customer by far, it was in a position to check the costs of manufacture and to fix prices for supplies not only to itself, but also to Allied Governments and to the civilian consumers. In practically all cases, both rationing and price-fixing were carried out by the Government Departments in very close consultation and agreement with the employers concerned, and Advisory Committees or Control Boards, on which employers, and in some cases workers also, were represented, were set up for one industry after another. These developments furnished a powerful stimulus to organisation among employers, and undoubtedly did a very great deal to foster the growth of those trusts and combines which became a prominent feature of the British industrial system after the War.

War prices were generally fixed on a basis generous enough to allow the employer of average efficiency a high margin of profit. But in face of the acute shortage of supplies, they were undoubtedly much lower than they would have been in the absence of State control. First in the munitions trades, and then generally by means of the Excess Profits Duty, the State sought to take away in taxation a part of the huge profits which employers were able to obtain because of the general shortage of supplies. But this taxation largely failed to achieve any result except a further rise in prices. In spite of it, war profits were immense, and huge fortunes were easily made. When all prices were rising rapidly, it was difficult to be incompetent enough not to make a big profit in almost any line of business connected with war supplies or essential civilian services.

The workers, from the very outbreak of war, had pressed strongly for the effective State control of industry and of prices. We have seen that in August, 1914, the principal Labour bodies came together to form the War Emergency Workers' National Committee, which throughout the War busied itself with these aspects of the problem. The changes effected by the Government in 1917, under the heavy pressure of the shortage of man-power and of the " intensified " German submarine campaign, were to a great extent on the lines which the Labour movement had been urging steadily ever since August, 1914.

Among the earliest sources of trouble, and among the earliest prices to be brought under control, was the rent of houses. In 1915 there was a serious " Rent Strike " of Glasgow tenants, and similar movements occurred later both on the Clyde and in other areas. These led to an increasingly drastic limitation by statute of the rents which landlords were permitted to charge. The pit-head price of coal, but not the retail price, was also limited by statute in 1915 ; but control of prices in general was unfortunately, owing to the *laissez-faire* prejudices of the Asquith Government, deferred until it was absolutely forced upon their successors by the inflationary rise in the cost of living.

By 1918 State control of industry had become an almost all-embracing system. The Labour movement, though it was dissatisfied with many of the actual features of the system in force, was naturally disposed to regard its rapid development as a demonstration of the inadequacy of " private enterprise " to cope with the national emergency and of the necessity of State control—regarded as a half-way house to Socialism—as a remedy. As the end of the War drew near the Labour bodies pressed strongly for the permanent retention of many of the features of the war-time system. This, however, would by no means have suited the book of the employers or of the other parties. Immediately after the Armistice the vast majority of the " controls " were either entirely removed or greatly relaxed. It was not possible to dispense at once with control of either mines or railways ; and in the case of shipping and of some other services control could be relaxed only by gradual stages. But as much as it was in any way practicable to give up was surrendered at once, with the consequence of an immediate leap in profits during the short-lived post-war boom, and of at any rate an accentuation of the dramatic collapse which followed.

BOOKS

Labour Year Book, 1919.
E. M. H. Lloyd. *Experiments in State Control.*
E. M. H. Lloyd. *Stabilisation.*
C. Delisle Burns. *Government and Industry.*
L. G. Chiozza Money. *The Triumph of Nationalisation.*
A. Salter. *Allied Shipping Control.*
G. D. H. Cole. *Labour in the Coal-mining Industry.*
W. H. Beveridge. *British Food Control.*

4. RECONSTRUCTION

At an early stage during the progress of the War men's minds began to turn to what was to come after it, in relation not only to the terms of the international settlement, but also to the internal future of Great Britain. The War had caused a huge disturbance in the national life ; and it was said on all hands that " things could never be the same again." At first, indeed, men spoke largely in terms of a restoration of pre-war conditions. Industries were taken over " for the duration of the War," with an implied pledge to hand them back to their previous controllers ; the Trade Unions agreed to a suspension of their workshop regulations on the explicit condition, legally sanctioned in the Munitions Acts, that these should be restored intact " at the end of the War." Advances in wages were given largely as " war bonuses," to last only for the " duration."

But gradually men awoke to the fact that a literal return to the conditions of 1914 would be, in many cases, sheerly impossible. The development of industry was profoundly affected by war needs. Some industries were hugely expanded, and some were almost shut down. New machines and processes were widely introduced. The places of men absent on war service were filled by other men and women, who in four years acquired a technique which made them permanent competitors. The number of women in industry proper greatly increased—largely as the correlative of a sharp fall in the number of domestic servants. The State entered into elaborate financial arrangements with the various groups of producers, such as it was clearly impossible to cancel suddenly at the end of the War.

Even more important than these purely industrial changes were the social changes which the War brought about. Not only in the factories, but everywhere, women stepped into responsible positions previously reserved for men. In the working-class movement, for example, they came to play a quite new part in both Trade Union and political affairs. Many women became branch secretaries of Trade Unions, or secretaries of I.L.P. branches and of other political bodies. The old isolation of the rural workers was largely broken down by war service, and by the extensive migration of labour. Every class was appealed to again and again in the name of the nation to " do its bit " ; and it was not easy to rebut the argument that sacrifices should be compensated by the concession of rights. The conscription of men was met in Labour circles with a demand for the conscription of wealth—a quite unsuccessful claim, in that fortunes were being made very much faster than Excess Profits taxation could take them away. Indeed, such taxation was for the most part promptly transferred to the consumers by means of higher prices, creating a new demand for more effective steps towards real equality of sacrifice and of status and rights.

Something had to be done, or promised, in order to meet these claims. In 1916 the Asquith Government set up a Reconstruction Committee, which developed later into the Ministry of Reconstruction. Under its auspices, one " post-war " problem after another was brought under review. A separate committee, under Lord Balfour of Burleigh, surveyed in advance the post-war condition of industry and trade. Long before the War ended there were showers of reports laying down what should be done to meet the anticipated conditions.

From the standpoint of the working-class movement, the most important of these plans for post-war reconstruction were those dealing directly with the suffrage, with education, and with industrial relations. Before the end of 1918 substantial changes had been provided for in all these spheres. The Representation of the People Act, 1918, granted what amounted to manhood suffrage and enfranchised women over thirty years of age—a tribute both to the real driving force of the pre-war suffrage movement and to the new position which women had assumed during the War in nearly every sphere of public life. The " Fisher " Education Act of 1918 abolished all exemptions from school attendance under fourteen, thus sweeping away the half-time system in the textile trades, extended the public provision for higher education, and proposed a system of compulsory " continuation schools," which was in fact shelved during the post-war depression without ever becoming operative.

Industrial relations, however, were clearly the crux of the social problem. These were referred to a Committee on the Relations of Employers and Employed, under the chairmanship of Mr. J. H. Whitley, a well-known Liberal Member of Parliament ; and this body in the summer of 1917 issued its first and most famous Report. Essentially, the aim of the " Whitley " Committee seems to have been that of meeting the claim of the workers for a share in the " control of industry " as far as this could be met without any interference with the rights of property or with the capitalist system. The Committee took the half-revolutionary and essentially anti-capitalist notion of " workers' control "—then very much in the public eye through the activities of shop stewards and Guild Socialists—and sought to make of it an essentially non-revolutionary idea of co-operation between Capital and Labour. As a means to this end, they proposed the establishment, in all well-organised industries, of standing Joint Industrial Councils, representing the Trade Unions and employers' associations, and with similar District Councils and Works Committees acting under their authority. The main business of these Councils was conceived as being not the fixing of wage-rates or the determination of other matters customarily dealt with by pre-war collective bargaining but the co-operation of employers and employed in promoting industrial efficiency and the creation of a harmonious understanding between the rival groups. " Whitley " Councils were proposed only for well-organised industries. For others the Committee suggested a comprehensive extension of the Trade Boards Act, so as to provide for collective bargaining and for a legal minimum wage in all the worse-paid and less organised trades.

The failure of the great Whitley scheme, apart from its proposals for Trade Boards, is now a matter of history. Such great industries as mining, cotton, engineering and shipbuilding, and iron and steel rejected the plan altogether. It was tried in building, and broke down owing to the secession of the employers as soon as the building trades operatives attempted to put it to serious use. In the industries—many of them relatively small—in which Councils were set up, the great majority became mere agencies for collective bargaining about wages and labour conditions, almost indistinguishable from the Conciliation Boards and similar bodies which had existed before the War. The Whitley scheme did result in an extension of national collective bargaining to new industries ; but it did nothing to change the fundamental relations of employers and employed.

A significant element in this failure was the omission of practically all the Councils even to set up the workshop machinery recommended by the Whitley Committee. If "joint control" was workable at all, its best chance was obviously in the workshops, because there arose the questions in which the ordinary workers felt the most direct interest and with which they were best equipped to deal. But the Trade Unions feared that workshop bodies might fall under unofficial control, so as to subvert the influence of the national Unions ; and employers had mostly no intention of granting any real control, and therefore would have nothing to do with machinery for joint consultation in the sphere in which it was likely to be most real and effective. The Whitley scheme did no harm ; but it did very little good either. Its results were ludicrously small in relation to the aspirations of its promoters.

Indeed, by far its most important results were, first, the extension of effective methods of collective bargaining throughout the State and municipal services, and, secondly, the Trade Boards Act of 1918. The State, while commending Whitley Councils to others, at first entirely refused to adopt them for its own employees. It was, however, compelled to take its own medicine, with undoubtedly beneficial results. Moreover, the Trade Boards Act of 1918 did extend the experiment of 1909 to a wide range of new trades, and did bring several million workers under the protection of the legal minimum wage. Under the Act of 1909, Trade Boards had been confined to trades in which " sweating " was common : under the Act of 1918, they could be set up wherever adequate machinery was wanting for the adjustment of conditions of collective bargaining between employers' and workers' organisations. Until the Government, in 1921-22, refused to create any more Trade Boards and, under excuse of the trade slump, unsuccessfully tried to destroy the powers of those already in being, this part of the Whitley scheme made excellent progress, and contributed to a real improvement in the position of the worst-paid classes of workers.

Reconstruction was also practised, to some extent, in the working-class movement. The big amalgamation campaign among the Trade Unions, which had been in progress before the War, was unfortunately held up owing to the difficulty of securing the majorities necessary by law. Until 1917 no two Trade Unions could amalgamate without securing a favourable vote of at least two-thirds of the total membership of each Union concerned. With so many members absent on service, and many more working in districts far from their homes, the Trade Unions could not get even the modified majorities required by the Trade Union (Amalgamation) Act of 1917, which was passed on the initiative of the Labour section of the Coalition. Trade Union reconstruction was therefore held up, and, apart from the final ratification of the Triple Alliance in 1915, the only important consolidation was that which resulted, in 1917, in the formation of the Iron and Steel Trades Confederation, created by an ingenious method which avoided the necessity of a ballot vote under the law. Many groups, including engineers and transport and general workers, discussed amalgamation ; and the building operatives succeeded in strengthening their loose federal Council into a closer National Federation ; but for the most part the Trade Unions, though they greatly increased their membership, did little or nothing towards the improvement of their organisation.

The important new step in working–class organisation was taken in politics. The Labour Party up to 1918 was a loose federation of Trade Unions, Socialist Societies, and a number of miscellaneous local bodies such as Trades Councils. The Socialist Societies, and especially the Independent Labour Party, acted virtually as an individual members' section of the wider party, and any sympathiser who wished to join did so by becoming a member of the Fabian Society, of the British Socialist Party (which rejoined the Labour Party in 1916), or of the I.L.P. The Fabian Society, however, was very small, and both the I.L.P. and the B.S.P. had taken up an anti-war attitude which had temporarily weakened their position with the Trade Unions. In these circumstances, and with a view to a widened post-war appeal, the Labour Party in 1918 revised its constitution so as to admit individual members to its local Labour Parties, which were rapidly extended throughout the country, each with its contingent of individual members as well as its affiliated Trade Union branches and Socialist or other working-class groups. Thus re-organised, mainly by Arthur Henderson, the Labour Party set up the definite claim to be regarded as the party of the " workers by hand and brain." A pamphlet, *Labour and the New Social Order*, embodying this claim and setting out the party's policy and programme, in terms much more Socialist (of the Fabian, gradualist type) than any of its pre-1914 pronouncements, was drafted by Sidney Webb and adopted, after discussion, by the Party Conference early in 1918. It attracted widespread attention, and members from all social classes came flocking in.

Meanwhile, the employers, unhampered by the difficulties which prevented Trade Union consolidation, were vastly improving their own industrial organisation. Before 1914 there was no effective federation of employers' associations corresponding to the Trades Union Congress, and in many of the smaller industries the employers were weakly organised or even not organised at all. We have seen how the war-time growth of State control stimulated the formation of bodies of traders and manufacturers which afterwards turned into permanent combines. Similarly, State regulation of wages and labour conditions caused a rapid growth of employers' associations for dealing with the workers. These two developments combined to cause the foundation in July, 1916, of the Federation of

British Industries, a militant new combination of British industrial interests which rapidly swallowed up the older, ineffective Employers' Parliamentary Association. Thenceforth the labour policy of the employing bodies was much more closely co-ordinated than ever before ; and although the F.B.I. subsequently handed over dealings with labour questions to another body formed in 1919, the National Confederation of Employers' Organisations, it was in July, 1916, that the new co-ordination of employing interests really began. The F.B.I. undertook the work of impressing the employers' point of view on Parliament and on the Government ; the Confederation presently assumed the task of formulating a common policy on labour matters, and of meeting the Trade Unions with a united front.

When the Armistice was signed, there were, then, on both sides great new forces waiting to be unloosed. Nothing less than the social and economic structure of post-war Britain was in the balance. And, Whitleyism having already in effect failed, the rival organisations of employers and employed confronted each other menacingly in a new world of unknown possibilities.

BOOKS

Reports of the Whitley Committee on Relations between Employers and Employed.
W. A. Orton. Labour in Transition.
D. Sells. The British Trade Boards Acts.
Labour Research Department. The Federation of British Industries.
Labour Research Department. The Workers' Register of Capital and Labour.
Labour Party Reports, 1918 and 1919.
H. Tracey (ed.). The Book of the Labour Party.
G. D. H. Cole. A History of the Labour Party from 1914.

CHAPTER VII

POST-WAR BRITAIN

THE Great War of 1914-18 changed the economic configuration of the world. In every country the abnormal forms of war-time demand altered the character of industrial production. Some industries were greatly stimulated ; others languished. In the belligerent countries, effort was concentrated mainly on two things—the production of munitions of war, and the increase of agricultural output. The submarine campaign and the blockade compelled the belligerent countries to aim at cutting down their demand for imports, and the preoccupation of the world's great workshops with war production compelled neutral States to become more self-sufficient, and forced the pace of industrial development in the Far East—especially in Japan. The destruction of shipping led to a feverish campaign of shipbuilding.

Consequently, when the War ended, and the nations sought, over the greater part of the world, to resume normal economic intercourse, pre-war conditions of normality had largely ceased to apply. Industrial production had developed greatly in neutral countries and, especially, in the comparatively undisturbed East. The vanquished countries, prostrate and devoid of purchasing power, were largely out of the market. Russia, devastated by war and revolution, and surrounded by a ring of hostile Powers eager for the fall of her Socialist rulers, was neither a market nor a source of supply for foodstuffs or materials. The new States set up by the Peace Treaties, animated by an intense national consciousness, began the building up of high tariff walls behind which each hoped to become rich by industrial production and to go on selling its raw products abroad without taking the manufactures of its customers in exchange. Finally, the United States, a late entrant into actual hostilities, had enormously developed its manufacturing power during the years when the Allied nations asked only for supplies and more supplies, without counting the price that they must pay.

These underlying material facts were complicated by others less permanent, but hardly less disturbing in their effects. Everywhere, under the influence of financial inflation, the world's price system had run mad. National currencies were worth anything or nothing, and the foreign exchanges fluctuated wildly under the influence of political, as well as of economic, movements of every sort and description. This was the speculator's chance, and his intervention made them fluctuate more wildly still. The printing presses of the great States worked overtime in catching up with the ever-increasing need for currency to meet the rising prices ; and every fresh note they printed helped prices to rise still more. Moreover, a fantastic muddle of international indebtedness made the confusion worse. Great Britain's Allies had borrowed from Great Britain, and Great Britain in turn had borrowed from the United States. Germany was to pay everybody, according to the promises lavishly held out in 1918. But from what source was prostrate Germany to pay, especially to creditors who refused to receive German goods that might compete with their own products ? The long, tragic farce of reparations was beginning.

Under these uncertain conditions, capital played general post. Free money, available for short or for long term investment, flitted from market to market in accordance with almost daily changes in the situation. For, in the new world of after-war days, there was no fixity, based on reasonably stable exchange rates, in what money would buy. Its purchasing power differed enormously from market to market, and from moment to moment. And the owners of free money sent it chasing after fortune round the money markets of the world, thereby greatly increasing the general instability of the economic conditions.

The statesmen went mad. In sharp contrast to the spirit of President Wilson's "Fourteen Points," they produced a treaty of peace much more foolish than it was vindictive. They encouraged impossible expectations of " squeezing " Germany. They bit off colonial Empires that they could not possibly chew. And they chopped up Europe with a mincing machine into economically impossible areas. Everywhere barriers were raised in the way of free international intercourse ; everywhere responsible statesmen firmly shut their eyes to the most obvious economic facts.

The causes of this insanity were clear enough, even at the time, to the few who kept their heads. For four years, statesmen had been used to a reckless flinging about of money, as a means of command over economic resources. Nothing mattered, as long as the War was won. A million, ten millions, a hundred millions, a thousand millions, were nothing in the ascending scales of war-time megalomania and in the descending scales of monetary values. While civil servants in the various " State controls " plodded away with their costings systems, statesmen were having the time of their lives round a roulette-table as big as the world.

Great Britain, the country most dependent of all on imports and exports, stood to lose most by the world's lapse from economic commonsense, as well as by the inevitable economic changes of the years of war. For half a century, Great Britain had been gradually ceasing to hold her former position as the one great workshop of the world—a position in its essence temporary, and due to a series of lucky coincidences. In the pre-war world, it had seemed to be demonstrable that the loss of this old monopoly was doing Great Britain no harm ; for the countries that became rivals as exporters remained also the best customers for a wide range of products. Great Britain had been able, after the serious depressions of the eighteen eighties and nineties, to adapt herself to the changing conditions ; and the growth of German and American productive capacity had lost its sting in face of the huge enlargement of the world market as a whole. But adaptation was necessarily a matter of time ; and the condition of trade after the War demanded, not merely a sudden and unprecedentedly drastic adaptation of methods, but also a wholesale reversal of the lines of development which had been encouraged by the abnormal demands of the war period.

Thus, the metal industries had expanded vastly ; but so they had in almost every country in the world. In relation to productive capacity for other goods, the world's capacity to produce certain kinds of machinery was grotesquely expanded. The cotton industry, on the other hand—still easily the first of British export trades—had been largely shut down, and had made, save in one or two quite special branches, absolutely no technical advance. But in America and the East the production of cotton goods had enormously increased, and technique had been greatly improved. The coal mines had been exploited for immediate production, regardless of later developments. New shafts had not been sunk, and in the existing pits the most easily accessible coal had been taken out. Quite apart from wage-rates, the human cost of getting coal was bound for some time to be a good deal higher than it had been under pre-war conditions. The railways had suffered abnormal wear and tear and could not be expected for some time to regain their full efficiency.

These are but a few selected instances of a general malady. British industry, readjusted in order to meet war needs, was a tragic misfit in the post-war world. Doubtless this was true of other countries besides Great Britain. But this was cold comfort ; for, so far from profiting by her neighbours' troubles, Great Britain lost by them still more. Her dislocation raised her costs of production ; theirs decreased their ability to buy. World trade shrank greatly in total volume. Only the East, with its terribly low labour costs, and the United States, with its vast internal resources and its almost inexhaustible domestic market, could raise themselves above the general calamity.

And yet, by all accounts, there was a trade boom after the War, and Great Britain shared in it. In 1919 the returning soldiers were, for the most part, rapidly absorbed into industry. In both 1919 and 1920, it was almost more difficult than during the War for any business man with the rudiments of a brain to avoid making a fortune. Prices soared far beyond the highest levels of the War years ; capital values became fantastic ; and, despite rapidly rising wages, the margins between costs and selling prices were greater than ever before. How did this boom square with the black account that has just been given of Great Britain's economic position in the post-1918 world?

The boom of 1919-20 was a boom, not of production, but of prices. British exports were valued at £1,334,500,000 in 1920, as against £525,000,000 in 1913—itself a record year. But the quantity of goods exported in 1920 was only about 70 per cent. of the quantity exported in 1913. Great Britain prospered because British industries were able to sell reduced exports at enormous prices—not because they were doing more to meet the world's needs.

Such a state of affairs could not last. The wily speculator knew this, and made his pile by unloading on the foolishly optimistic investors huge blocks of grossly over-valued capital assets. Producing plants changed hands at ridiculous values, based on the capitalisation of unreal expectations of continued profits at the 1920 level. Bonus shares were issued on a wholly fictitious valuation of capital assets. The unwary put their money into new enterprises, or into expansions of old ones, that had no chance of yielding for long a satisfactory return. For, though there were goods that the world had to have at any price in order to repair the worst damages of the War, as soon as these had been supplied the demand was bound to break. Great Britain's customers simply could not pay the prices charged by the British exporters. In due course, the slump came, first in the coal trade, which had profiteered most exorbitantly of all at Europe's expense, and then generally.

Two points here seem to need further explanation. First, if the boom was of prices and not of production, why was there not more unemployment even while it lasted? The answer is that, while industry was readjusting itself after its war-time dislocation, output per worker was abnormally low. This was due partly to relaxation after the long strain, partly to labour troubles, and partly to the need for large mechanical readjustments which absorbed labour on processes not directly productive, and temporarily prevented industry from working with full efficiency. Secondly, why could not Great Britain's customers pay high prices, and recoup themselves by charging just as highly for their own products? In this case, the answer is that one great effect of the War had been to increase agricultural production in many countries. Imports from distant markets had been restricted by shortage of ships; as shipping became available in abundance, the inflow of agricultural products was resumed on a grand scale, but, in face of the even more rapid release of tonnage previously used on war service, a heavy fall in shipping freights brought down the European prices of foodstuffs from the New World. The agricultural producers of the Old World thus found their purchasing power diminished, and could not raise their prices so as to enable them to buy the higher priced manufactured products of Great Britain.

Wholesale prices, reflecting world conditions, were already falling in the latter half of 1920. Retail prices, which, through their influence on wages, largely governed British manufacturing costs, were slow to follow. For every class resisted fiercely the idea that the prosperity of 1919-1920 had been illusory. Capitalists were determined to go on earning, through high prices, high dividends on grossly inflated capital : workers were determined not to take lower money wages on a mere promise that, if they did, retail prices would fall. The Bank of England and the Joint Stock Banks stepped in, and sought by rapid deflation of currency and restriction of credit to enforce both lower prices and lower wages, as necessary conditions for a return to the gold standard at the pre-war parity of exchange. Then followed the great industrial struggle of 1921, in which the defeat of the miners symbolised the defeat of the whole working class on the wage issue, but at the same time the stubbornness of the struggle warned employers in other industries against attempting to push victory too far. The forty-eight-hour week was retained despite the slump ; and wages, except in the main exporting trades, certainly did not fall as fast as the cost of living.

The prices of British manufactures, however, still obstinately refused to fall to the level at which elastic demand would, it was hoped, bring trade up to the required volume. This was mainly due to the immense capital burdens with which industry had been weighed down during the boom. These now stood in the way of improvements in industrial technique ; for prudent investors would not throw good money after bad, and investors had perhaps learnt from the slump to be more prudent than enterprising. Excess of caution replaced the mad optimism of the preceding years. Consequently, when the first effects of the slump were over, British industry as a whole, instead of gradually improving its efficiency, continued to stagnate, and appeals in the political part of the newspapers to " Buy British Goods " were effectively offset by advice, in the financial columns, to " Buy Foreign Investments."

Meanwhile, the fall of profits and wages lowered purchasing power in the home market. Unemployment had become widespread, and differed from pre-war unemployment in character as well as in amount. A large class of chronically unemployed workers came into existence. The proportion of skilled men fell, and the number of tradeless casuals increased. The quality of the British industrial population deteriorated ; and this was exceptionally serious because Great Britain depended for her position in world markets largely on the high quality of her workmanship.

It became, indeed, more and more evident that the troubles of British industry were due, not to any temporarily adverse phase of the " trade cycle," but to a deep-seated disease. Readjustments far more drastic than those with which the Great Depression of the eighteen eighties was met were clearly required ; but no one appeared to possess the power, or the will and the power together, to make the necessary changes. A few great capitalists, such as Sir Alfred Mond (later Lord Melchett), the inspiring genius of Imperial Chemical Industries, set to work to revolutionise particular trades by the creation of huge combines equipped with up-to-date technical resources ; and a few industries—notably the electrical, the motor, and the new artificial silk trades—prospered with the aid of new techniques meeting a rapidly expanding demand for their particular services. Coal enjoyed a temporary boom in 1923, owing to the purely political cause of M. Poincaré's madness over the occupation of the Ruhr. But for the most part the great British industries—cotton, coal, iron and steel, shipbuilding, and many branches of engineering—stagnated helplessly.

Socialists, for a while, drew comfort from prophesying the impending collapse of capitalist Society, and the advent of the Socialist Commonwealth. But Capitalism did not die ; it only rotted. And the forces which weakened it still more seriously weakened the workers for any frontal assault upon it. Politically, Labour made great headway, but returned, after the first excitement of 1919, to its pre-war moderation in an endeavour to attract the section of the electorate previously attached to the Liberal Party, which was left in a state of disintegration by the war-time split between the followers of Asquith and of Lloyd George ; industrially, the Trade Unions were flattened out by the slump, and could fight only a purely defensive battle. Moreover, as Labour politicians began to see office as an early possibility, the difficulties of Socialism came home to them in a new way. Socialism was doubtless the cure for all troubles ; but it was not an easy cure, nor would Socialism enable Great Britain to resume her old position in the markets of the world. She would have to find for herself a new position ; and that would involve a drastic reshaping of her economic system which could hardly be pleasant in the transition, however triumphantly effective the ultimate result might be.

The struggle over the coal mines became, as we shall see in subsequent chapters, the symbolic issue between Capitalism and Socialism in the industrial field. But behind it loomed always the land question. Great Britain, in the nineteenth century, had bidden her agriculture go to the devil its own way. Sure of her ability to buy all the food she needed with her coal and manufactures, she had let agriculture decay in order to get cheap living and so lower the costs of manufacturing production. Had she, in the long run, been right, or was nemesis now overtaking her, with the crumbling of her export trade ? Every man who thought at all had to think about this issue. Every political party toyed with it ; but none could make up its mind to face it fairly and squarely. Behind the hesitant Conservative revival of Tariff Reform, the land question loomed—counting in reality far more than the ostensible arguments about Imperial Preference and Safeguarding of

Industries. Labour and Liberals launched land policies which, both in their terms and in their propagandist use, revealed nothing more clearly than the dubieties behind them. Was Great Britain to send an increased part of her population " back to the land," or was she not ? Was she even to make a serious effort to increase agricultural output by mechanisation, without necessarily employing more labour on the farms ? Nobody knew ; and almost everybody said the more for not knowing what to say.

For clearly the issue raised was fundamental. It involved, not merely an abandonment of Free Trade and an acceptance of British inability to pay for unlimited imports of food with exported manufactures, but the assumption that it was the business of the State to shape a systematic economic policy for the whole nation—to create conditions within which economic laws were to work instead of yielding blindly to the play of economic forces under private enterprise. This was the essential conflict between Socialism and Capitalism in the sphere of manufacturing and commercial policy. But Socialists were almost as ready as capitalists to run away from it.

Under these conditions of stagnation and doubt, it was impossible for Great Britain to make any assured advance. Capitalism could not rebuild its shaken edifice ; and the workers could not get more out of a pint pot with a hole in its bottom. Capital and Labour went on fighting their industrial and political battles ; but there were scanty fruits of victory for either side. Meanwhile, in the United States, up to 1929, triumphant Capitalism continued to advance. The United States enjoyed a prosperity which enabled its industrial rulers to avoid any Labour challenge because they could grant a steady advance in the standard of life. Modern America reproduced the social appearances of Victorian England, but with the difference that American prosperity, based more largely on the vast home market, had less to fear from the impact of external forces making for change.

Lacking a faith in their own powers, British capitalists turned in their trouble to the new land of plenty. America became in their eyes the pattern capitalist State, as Great Britain had been in the Victorian Age. The virtues of the American capitalist and the American working man were dinned into British ears. But both capitalists and workers in Great Britain were slow to act. British Capitalism was too tangled up in its own distresses and complications to make a move ; and British Labour, after a half-hearted attempt to run a revolution in the spirit of a friendly game of cribbage, relapsed into an apathetic wait for the highly uncertain results of the next General Election. It had roused its opponents ; but it had not roused itself. The " General Strike " of 1926 was followed by an outburst of reactionary legislation ; and exhausted British Labour was unable, for the time, to offer any effective opposition.

The great doubt remained.   Britain's pre-war position in the world had gone.   She must make for herself a new one, or sink in population and in standard of life.   Would she make good ?   And, if she did, would there arise a new Capitalism headed by the leaders of great monopolistic combines, or would the Labour Movement after all throw up the policy, the leadership, and the will-power needed to give it the making of the new world ?   1919 was full of hope ;   1926—the year of the General Strike—saw dark clouds across the future's face.[1]

[1] I have deliberately left this chapter practically as I wrote it in 1927, when the first edition of this section appeared.   Readers will inevitably draw for themselves comparisons between the economic situation of Great Britain after 1918 and the much more serious situation which existed after 1945.   I have left unaltered what I wrote twenty years ago because I wish to emphasise the point that the underlying conditions, however greatly they may have been intensified by the second World War, were not fundamentally different in the two periods.   (February, 1948).   G.D.H.C.

CHAPTER VIII

LABOUR AFTER THE FIRST WORLD WAR

1. Introductory   2. The Labour Offensive
3. The Post-war Slump   4. The Guild Movement
5. The First Labour Government

1. INTRODUCTORY

THE history of the working-class movement between the two World Wars falls into six periods. First came a period of sharply rising prices and wages, of great apparent prosperity, and of rapid increase in Trade Union, Co-operative, and Labour Party membership. During the greater part of this period the working classes were engaged in an " offensive " against Capitalism, and the Government and the employers were pursuing, on the whole, a stone-walling policy of defence. Then came a rapid change in the situation. Trade slumped, financial deflation was carried to drastic lengths in the endeavour to restore the " gold standard " at the old parity, prices fell heavily, and wages came tumbling down. The offensive passed from the workers to the employers, and the Trade Unions, losing rapidly in membership, could do no more than fight a largely unsuccessful rearguard action. The slump did not, however, check Labour's political advance, and may have stimulated it ; and towards the end of this period, in 1924, the Labour Party found itself for a brief period in office as a Government, but dependent on Liberal support, as it fell far short of a majority in the House of Commons, in which it was not even the largest party. After this brief interlude, Conservatism came back to power, and a third period began. Despite the depression of trade, the workers again turned their minds to industrial action, not, as in 1919, as a means of offence, but as a defensive measure in face of renewed attacks on wages and conditions. This third period reached its culmination in the " General Strike " of 1926, and had its aftermath in the Trade Union Act of 1927.

Upon the industrial defeat of 1926 followed the election victory of 1929, which enabled the Labour Party, though still in a minority in the House of Commons, to form the second MacDonald Government. The two years this venture lasted were those of the transition from the process of post-war recovery and supposed stabilisation to the greatest depression in the history of world Capitalism. The first sign of what was happening was the American stock market crisis of 1929 ; but the consequences of this were not seriously felt in Europe until the early months of 1931, when the withdrawal of American capital and custom set on foot a severe financial crisis which spread from one country to another—from Austria to Germany, and from Germany to Great Britain.   This crisis finished the MacDonald Government, which had already shown, even in 1930, its incapacity to handle the problems of unemployment and of the international balance of payments.   MacDonald, Snowden, Thomas and a few other leaders abandoned their own party, and MacDonald reappeared as Prime Minister in a "National" Government based mainly on Conservative support.   At the General Election of 1931 the Labour Party, shorn of its best-known leaders and bewildered by a calamity which most of its members did not understand, was ignominiously defeated.   Thus ended the fourth period of Labour's history between the wars.

The fifth period began with two years of widespread unemployment under a Government pledged to a policy of "national economy," largely at the expense of those who were out of work.   These years were, however, much less disastrous in Great Britain than either on the European continent or in the United States.   The British Labour Movement, though defeated, remained unbroken, and wage-reductions were kept within bounds ; and British consumers benefited from the very sharp fall in the prices of imported foodstuffs and materials.   Production and employment fell much more catastrophically in the United States, where the crisis led to the far-reaching measures known as President Roosevelt's "New Deal."   In Germany, the prostration of the Weimar Republic enabled the Nazis to seize power, and such democracy as had existed in the States of South-Eastern Europe was speedily overwhelmed.

A sixth period began as slow recovery set in from 1934.   But the crisis had transformed the political as well as the economic face of the world ; and from this point onwards the centre of political interest shifted more and more to international affairs.   The Labour Party, torn between its strong pacifism and its hatred of the Nazis, who were destroying the European working-class movements, took some time to readjust itself to the changed conditions. At the General Election of 1935 it won back some of its lost seats, but not nearly so many as it had hoped.   The Conservatives remained firmly seated in power, but, under Neville Chamberlain's leadership, most unwilling to face the danger of conflict with Nazi Germany, with which, indeed, not a few of them sympathised as a bulwark against Communism, and in the hope that Hitler would turn his war-machine against the Soviet Union rather than against the Western Powers.   The Labour Movement, in face of this attitude, shed its pacifism and became the champion of the democratic forces in Europe, urging rearmament against the Nazis, aid to the Spanish Republic against General Franco's rebellion, and, in 1938, aid to Czechoslovakia at the time of the Munich crisis.   In the meantime, the Labour Party was actively working out its domestic policy of social reform and public ownership of essential industries, and was rapidly regaining popular support and recovering from the disaster of 1931.

13*

Through all these six periods, the problem of the coal trade was the most pressing of all domestic issues. In the first period, the Miners' Federation appeared as the leader of the Labour offensive, with its demand for national ownership and workers' control. The second period opened with the great coal lock-out of 1921, and the defeat of the miners in that struggle symbolised the general defeat of the working-class forces. In the third period, again, the miners held the centre of the stage. It was in their defence that the oft-threatened " General Strike " was at length proclaimed ; and their defeat made possible the Conservative reaction of 1927.

The entire period, up to 1926, differed sharply from the period of labour unrest which preceded the War. Then, the advance movements were for the most part spontaneous and unofficial and the official leaders were mostly in opposition. In the after-war unrest, on the other hand, except for the troubles in the first months of 1919, official Trade Unionism was throughout directly involved, and the successive struggles were conducted by, and with the full sanction of, the great Trade Union bodies. The strikes of 1910-1914, except the national mining dispute, were a sort of guerrilla warfare. Those of 1919-1926 were confrontations of great disciplined forces on both sides.

It is true that, at all times after 1919 as before, there were unofficial movements striving to " ginger up " the official leaders, and that after 1920 these movements found, to some extent, an unofficial leadership of their own in the new Communist Party and in its various auxiliaries, such as the National Minority Movement in the Trade Unions and the National Unemployed Workers' Committee. But the Communists, despite their ceaseless activity, never commanded wide support, except in a few very depressed areas, though disappointment and disillusion following upon the defeat of the General Strike in 1926 drove a number of the younger workers into their ranks. Even then they could get no real hold on any important Trade Union and their political influence remained very small. British Communism, in comparison with Communism in almost any Continental country, remained through the period under review the creed of a tiny minority, energetic enough to take advantage of recurring opportunities for exploiting discontent and disappointment with the official Labour leadership, but never able to command any mass following. For some time the Communist Party itself was little more than the old British Socialist Party with the addition of the rump of the " left wing " shop stewards ; and not until the great depression of 1931 and the succeeding years did it begin to build up a policy at all applicable to British conditions. Thereafter, the international situation helped it ; for it could endeavour to organise a " United Front " against Fascism, could point to Conservative endeavours to persuade the Nazis to attack the Soviet Union, and could enlist wide sympathy for its demands for effective action to help the Spanish Republicans against the aid which German and Italian Fascists were giving to Franco.

Although the Communist Party failed to attract more than a small following, the influence of the Russian Revolution was deep and widespread. Despite the repudiation of Communism by the great mass of the organised working-class movement, there was the keenest sympathy with the Russians in their often desperate struggle to maintain their Socialist Republic in face of an aggressively and unscrupulously hostile world of capitalist States. This was seen plainly in the Russo-Polish crisis of 1920, and seen again as often as the question of Anglo-Russian relations was raised. The "Red Letter" in the General Election of 1924 doubtless scared off a number of timid voters ; but it had no effect on the great mass of the organised workers. Its real result was rather to bring apathetic Conservatives to the poll than to diminish the Labour vote.

Indeed, it was scarcely possible, whatever view men might take of Communist doctrines and policy, for them not to feel differently about Socialism with a vast Socialist Republic actually in existence. In 1914, Socialism still seemed a distant ideal ; after 1917, it presented itself to men's minds as a real and immediate possibility. The capitalist system had lost its inevitability ; the sense of a possible alternative sank deeply into the minds of the active workers in the Labour Movement.

It sank no less deeply into the minds of employers and men of property in general. The uncertain prospects of Capitalism rallied all these elements to its defence. Labour pursued in the 1920's a more vigorous offensive, and was met with a counter-offensive more vigorous still. To some on both sides, the clash which came in 1926 and brought the country within measurable distance of civil war had seemed for some time inevitable. When the moment came, however, it was the workers who drew back. The inherent constitutionalism of the main body of the Labour Movement never asserted itself more plainly than in the great "unconstitutional" movement known as the "General Strike." On the other hand, the readiness of the defenders of law and order to force the issue when the crisis came, rather than meet the Trade Union leaders' evident will to come to terms, showed a very different temper. The pacific General Council and the bellicose Mr. Winston Churchill, the mild *British Worker* and the furious *British Gazette*, presented a contrast no less instructive than ironic. It became plain that, if civil war did threaten, at any rate the threat did not come from the organised working-class movement.

During the war years, the position of the Labour Movement in the social system had radically changed. Politically, Labour had been before the War a third party, representing a special interest, contesting only a small number of seats, in selected industrial areas, and with no early hope of challenging the supremacy of the two great historic parties. In 1918 Liberalism was in dissolution, and the Labour Party, under its new constitution, was making a bid for recognition as its successor. A Labour Government was not yet an early possibility, but it was no longer inconceivably remote.   Becoming, in view of Liberal divisions, the official Opposition, Labour had to be recognised as a possible Government.   Its programme clearly contemplated this, for it had been re-drafted to cover the entire field of national and international affairs.   It remained, indeed, a party based mainly on the Trade Unions ; but it had necessarily changed its relation to them.   No longer was it largely a group of representatives of particular Trade Unions, as it had been even in 1914.   From 1918, it was a national party standing for a common policy opposed to that of the Government in power.

The new Labour Party constitution and attitude also made a great change in its relations to local affairs.   The newly established Local Labour Parties throughout the country set energetically to work to capture seats on municipal bodies.   Local politics, which the headquarters of the Labour Party had hitherto largely ignored, became an important part of its activity, with the effect of speedily creating against it, in many areas, local coalitions of the capitalist parties for the retention of municipal power.   These local coalitions proved in practice far easier to maintain than the post-war coalition of Tories and Liberals in national politics ; for the issues were clearer locally and more apt to take on a class form.   Throughout the period described in the rest of this book, Labour was fighting, in municipal politics, a ding-dong battle which exercised a big influence on its national fortunes.

Gradually in the 1920's, especially in the mining areas and in the poorer parts of London, Labour won majorities on a number of local authorities, and on some of these attempted to put an advanced policy into force. Especially it raised the wages of municipal employees, and, in the case of Boards of Guardians, raised poor relief and used it, in some measure, as a means of relieving those destitute in strikes and lock-outs.   This brought down upon it the heavy displeasure of anti-Labour Governments, which retaliated with laws and administrative measures, reinforced by decisions in the courts, circumscribing the powers of local bodies and bringing them under stricter central supervision and control.   The imprisonment of the Poplar Councillors in 1921 and the supersession of the Guardians at West Ham and Chester-le-Street in 1926 by commissioners directly appointed by the Minister of Health were the outstanding examples of this extension of the central power—forecasts of more widespread and drastic measures that might follow an extensive conquest by Labour of local political power unless the Labour Movement could establish its control in national politics too.

The changes in the structure and working of the Labour Party were paralleled by changes in the Trade Union movement.   During the War, as we have seen, the Government, through a complicated series of arbitration tribunals as well as through its direct control of mines and railways, became virtually the regulator of wage-rates.   This system led to a widespread substitution of national for local bargaining.   Wage changes were fixed nationally for whole industries instead of separately for and in each locality. This led to greater centralisation in Trade Union affairs, and also caused the Trade Unions to draw more closely together in large industrial groups. When compulsory arbitration was abolished at the end of 1918, these methods persisted ; and the Trade Unions, freed from their war-time difficulties, set on foot an active movement for amalgamation. The leading societies of skilled engineers joined to form the Amalgamated Engineering Union, which in the main continued up to 1939 the traditions and methods of the Amalgamated Society of Engineers. As the result of a series of sectional fusions, nearly all the societies of vehicle and waterside workers came to-gether in the Transport and General Workers' Union, which practically superseded the looser federation of pre-war days, and became in addition, after its absorption of the Workers' Union in 1929, a huge " general labour " Union with a membership scattered through a host of industries. The old-established Friendly Society of Ironfounders was merged, with other bodies, in the National Union of Foundry Workers ; the bricklayers and masons joined forces in the Amalgamated Union of Building Trade Workers ; and the old Gasworkers' Union became the nucleus of the National Union of General and Municipal Workers, embodying a large number of societies of less skilled and miscellaneous workers. In this last fusion was included the National Federation of Women Workers, which had risen to considerable importance during the period of extensive employment of women during the War. Finally, the Amalgamated Union of Co-operative Employees, absorbing the Warehouse and General Workers' Union and changing its name to " National Union of Distributive and Allied Workers," became the larger rival of the Shop Assistants' Union in enrolling the rapidly increasing members of distributive employees.

Trade Union membership had risen from 4,000,000 to 6,500,000 between 1914 and the end of 1918. Thereafter, during the post-war boom, it rose even more rapidly, reaching 8,300,000 at the end of 1920. This growth affected all societies and all sections of the movement. It was, however, especially marked among the less skilled workers and in non-manual occupa-tions. While the number of the older Unions was being rapidly reduced by amalgamation, new societies were constantly springing up in 1919 and 1920 among previously unorganised groups. Such non-manual workers' Unions as existed before increased their membership at a quite extraordinary pace. Railway clerks, bank clerks, insurance clerks, civil servants, draughtsmen, shop assistants, actors, musicians, local government employees, commercial travellers, teachers, and many other groups either formed Unions or greatly increased their Trade Union strength. Trade Unionism, as well as the Labour Party, rapidly reorganised itself as a movement of the workers " by hand and brain." For a time these new bodies pursued a highly successful activity ; then the slump hit them, as it hit the manual workers, but with greater force, because they had less stability and a less practical faith in Trade Union methods than the members of the older societies. The groups which had experience of organisation before the War—railway clerks, postal workers, teachers, and civil servants among them—stood fast ; but some of the others had a hard struggle for existence in the difficult years after 1920.

Even in face of the prolonged slump, however, Trade Unionism remained both a bigger and a broader movement than it had been in pre-war days. Membership had sunk in 1926, just before the General Strike, from 8,300,000 to about 5,250,000 ; but this was still well ahead of the numbers reached in 1914, even after the extraordinarily rapid growth of the years of unrest just before the first World War. It must be remembered that as recently as 1910 there had been only about 2,500,000 Trade Unionists in the whole country.

In smaller measure, the Co-operative Movement shared in the great post-war increase of membership. Co-operative retail trade rose from £85,000,000 in 1913 to £246,000,000 in 1920, falling to £166,000,000 in 1923 with the slump in prices and prosperity. Membership of distributive societies, which had reached 2,878,000 in 1913, rose to 4,531,000 in 1921, and was scarcely affected by the slump, mounting to well over five millions by 1926. As always, Co-operation advanced more slowly than Trade Unionism in the good times, but made up for this by its stability of membership in face of adverse conditions.

The War had a big influence on the Co-operative Movement in another way. War-time control hit the Co-operatives hard, and checked their expansion because they could not get increased supplies of goods from the State to match the rise in membership and in demand. They were, moreover, made subject to war-time profits taxation in ways which were strongly resented. These grievances combined with the change in general working-class feeling to force the Co-operative Movement into a sharp break with one of its strongest traditions, that of abstention from politics. In 1917 the Co-operative Congress formed the Co-operative Party, separate from the Labour Party mainly for tactical reasons, but working in close conjunction with it. The new party did not grow very fast, and ten years after its foundation only about half the Co-operative Societies in the country were associated with it, a number of others having joined the Local Labour Parties in their areas and many still refusing to take any political action at all. The decision of the Co-operative Movement, however, added a new element to working-class politics, and Co-operative Members of Parliament took part as Ministers in the Labour Governments of 1924 and of 1929.

This brief survey of trends, mainly in the 1920's, is intended only as an introduction to the narrative of post-war events which follows in the next sections. This narrative could, however, hardly be understood without some reference both to the changed structure and to the changed attitude of the working-class movement in the years after 1918. In the year or two following the War, all settled things seemed to have been uprooted. No one knew what shape the new society was to take ; and inevitably the new and almost unknown power of the working-class movement figured prominently in men's thoughts. It seemed, no doubt, to the outside observer, much more conscious and formed than it seemed to its own members. These had, indeed, had their faith in the old things rudely shaken ; but they had scarcely begun to build up a faith in the new things or in their own power. They floundered, therefore, amid the difficulties and intricacies of the new world, shaping their policy rather to the immediate occasion than to any clear vision of the future. It could not well have been otherwise. Labour had scarcely begun devising a policy to deal with one set of conditions when it was confronted with quite different conditions urgently calling for decisive action. If it did not always act wisely, who did in these years act so wisely that he can afford to cast a stone ?

BOOKS

The Workers' Register of Labour and Capital, 1923.
G. D. H. Cole. *Chaos and Order in Industry.*
W. A. Orton. *Labour in Transition.*
A. Hutt. *Post-war History of the British Working Class.*

2. THE LABOUR OFFENSIVE

The Armistice of November, 1918, was almost immediately followed by a General Election. The Labour Party, which had at once left the Coalition along with the Asquithian Liberals, appeared before the electors for the first time as a national party, with independent candidates throughout the country, and with an untried and greatly enlarged electorate to woo. It put up 361 candidates, and returned only 61 ; but even so the complete defeat of the Independent Liberals gave it the status of His Majesty's Opposition. The smallness of the Labour gains is readily explained by the atmosphere in which the election was fought. The Coalition came out of the War with the prestige of victory, and its partisans had no scruple in raising the popular cries of " Hang the Kaiser ! " and " Make Germany pay ! " Against these conditions the Opposition was almost powerless ; and with a few exceptions, only " safe " Labour men got home. A " Coalition Labour " group, based mainly on the wartime " jingo " British Workers' National League, but including a few Labour Ministers who refused to leave the Coalition, came back to the House of Commons 14 strong. Ramsay MacDonald, Philip Snowden, and Arthur Henderson were among the leaders who lost their seats. In the new Parliament, Lloyd George was for the time omnipotent ; for the weakness of his dependence on mainly Conservative support had not yet made itself evident.

Meanwhile, the cessation of hostilities had immediately brought to the front all those industrial problems which had been either set aside or dealt with on a purely temporary basis during the War. The Trade Unions began at once to consider what programmes of immediate demands they should put forward, and to press for the fulfilment of promises made to them during the war years. In some cases there was delay in bringing the Trade Union machinery into action, but during the month or two following the Armistice almost every Union came forward with a more or less ambitious programme of demands.

While the Unions were preparing their case and getting their machinery into order, emergency steps had to be taken to deal with the double process of demobilisation. The returning soldiers had to be drafted back into industry, and the pace of demobilisation was, to some extent, accommodated to the ability of industry to absorb them. At the same time, and even more suddenly, the vast armies of civilian munition workers had to be disbanded and guided back into occupations ministering to the requirements of peace-time production. For both these classes provision had to be made until they could find work ; and a special system of Out-of-Work Donation was instituted in November, 1918, for both ex-soldiers and civilians.

It was also clearly necessary to make some provision for the regulation of wages during the period of transition from war to peace, and on November 21st the Wages (Temporary Regulation) Act passed into law. The effect of this Act was to stabilise, as enforceable minimum rates, the wages in force for each occupation at the time of its passing, with provision for the variation of these rates by an Interim Court of Arbitration, which was, in fact, the war-time Committee on Production under a new name. Compulsory arbitration was at the same time abolished, and the Court of Arbitration could fix only *minimum* rates and could not, in law at least, prevent the Trade Unions from asking or getting more. The Wages Act was originally passed for six months only, but it was renewed for a further six months in May, 1919, and certain of its provisions were continued for a further period under the Industrial Courts Act of 1919.

The first phase of the post-war industrial struggle centred mainly round the question of hours of labour. The railwaymen had secured during the War a Government promise, and the date for the introduction of the forty-eight hours week and the eight hours day was fixed for February 1st. The engineering and shipbuilding trades, in which the normal working week varied from fifty-four to fifty hours, resumed their pre-war demand for a shortening of working time, and obtained the forty-seven hours week in February, 1919. The cotton operatives secured by negotiation the forty-eight hours week ; and the eight hours shift was generally introduced into the iron and steel industry. In almost every trade, the Trade Unions made, in one form or another, the demand for the eight hours day or for the forty-eight hour week, and during the earlier months of 1919 these demands were granted in the majority of organised industries.

The question of hours, however, led to the first really serious industrial crisis of the post-war period.   On the Clyde and in Belfast local joint movements, extending over a number of industries, were launched in January, 1919. On the Clyde there was a general demand for the forty hours week, and in Belfast for the forty-four hours week.   In both these centres general strikes were declared, with the support of the district Trade Union organisations, but without the backing of the national Trade Unions.   Both movements ended in failure, accompanied, on the Clyde especially, by a large display of military force by the Government.   The rest of the country did not follow the Clyde and Belfast examples, and, isolated from the general movement, the local strikes gradually broke down, and work was resumed under the terms of the agreements concluded nationally.   Thus, the forty-eight hours week became the maximum in most organised occupations, and a few trades secured a working week shorter than this ; but the movement for a general eight hours day (involving a maximum working week of forty-four hours) was defeated.

Meanwhile, a still more serious crisis was developing in the mining industry.   On January 14th, 1919, the Miners' Federation of Great Britian met in conference and formulated a definite programme, including both increased wages and shorter hours and the public ownership and democratic control of the mining industry.   The demand for nationalisation was old : the Miners had drafted a Nationalisation Bill in 1912.   But the demand for workers' control was new, and was largely the outcome of Guild Socialist influence. Negotiations, in which the other parties to the Triple Alliance lent their support to the miners, coupled with the threat of strike action, continued up to February 27th, when the miners agreed to postpone their strike notices in return for the setting up of a Royal Commission on the Coal Industry, but only after they had successfully insisted on their claim to nominate or approve the choice of half the members, excluding the Chairman.

In the midst of this threatening situation the Government called together a National Industrial Conference, which was meant to include all important organised groups of both employers and Trade Unionists.   This Conference met on February 27th.   On the employers' side, there were one or two groups which refused to be associated with the Conference, but its representative character was much more seriously interfered with on the Labour side by the refusal of four powerful groups, the Miners, Railwaymen and Transport Workers, forming the Triple Industrial Alliance, and the Amalgamated Society of Engineers, to take any part in its work.   The Conference appointed a Provisional Joint Committee, equally representing the two parties, and this Committee at the beginning of April presented to a second National Conference a unanimous report recommending (1) the passing of a general forty-eight hours law, (2) the establishment of a minimum wage Commission, and (3) the setting up of a permanent National Industrial Council, equally representing employers' and workers' organisations. This third proposal was made by the second Conference contingent on the carrying into effect by the Government of the remaining recommendations. The Government did indeed draft Bills dealing with the minimum wage and the forty-eight hours week, but it insisted on so many exceptions to the latter that the Labour side of the Provisional Committee refused to accept the draft. Thereafter negotiations dragged on until the middle of 1921, but the Government, with the silent, but indubitable, support of the National Confederation of Employers' Organisations, persisted in its refusal to accept the Committee's report ; and finally the Labour side of the Committee, by belated resignation, brought the whole useless affair to an end.

There can be no doubt, however, that the protracted negotiations in which this body became engaged were an important factor in checkmating the post-war unrest of 1919. The entry of Labour into the Industrial Conference and the Coal Commission—the latter acclaimed at the time as a great Labour triumph—was the determining factor in tiding over the critical industrial situation of the first half of 1919. At the Industrial Conference the Labour representatives were able to secure the promise of considerable concessions, but this promise was not honoured when the time came for fulfilment, because the immediate danger which extorted it was no longer present. Similarly, before the Coal Commission, the Labour representatives were able to give a convincing exposure of the capitalist working of the coal industry, and to secure, because of the support of the Chairman, Mr. Justice Sankey, a majority in favour of public ownership and of some measure of democratic control ; but these recommendations, which the Government had pledged itself to honour, in Mr. Bonar Law's words, " in the spirit and in the letter," were also disregarded when the time of most urgent danger to Capitalism had gone by. Views will differ about the results of a persistence in the militant spirit which seemed to be gaining the upper hand at the beginning of 1919, but there can be no doubt that the Industrial Conference and the Coal Commission together gave the Government time to pass the point of most urgent danger without the development of a general militant policy on the part of Labour.

The " Sankey " Coal Commission began its work on March 3rd, pledged to present an Interim Report by March 20th. During this first stage of its inquiry, the miners' strike notices were suspended and not withdrawn, and there was still considered to be imminent danger of a national stoppage. The Interim Report, duly issued, conceded a wage advance of two shillings a shift, and, what was even more important, a reduction of the hours of labour for underground workers from eight to seven per shift. It also expressed the opinion that, even on the evidence already submitted, the existing system of ownership and working in the industry stood condemned, and that some system of public ownership or of unification with joint control ought to take its place.

This Report, accepted by the Miners' Conference, put an end to the crisis for the time being, and the Coal Commission resumed its labours, with the object of devising a scheme for the future regulation of the industry. The acceptance of the first Sankey Report, rather than the establishment of the Coal Commission, marks the definite halting of the immediate Labour offensive.

Meanwhile, demobilisation was proceeding rapidly. This was obviously a dangerous process for the Government, which had to consider both the risks of trouble among the Forces if demobilisation were slow and the danger of placing huge bodies of men on the labour market before industry had readjusted itself for their reception. At times, serious trouble seemed to be threatening in certain camps, and discipline had to be greatly relaxed in order to keep the men quiet. If, at the same time, there had been a big Labour upheaval, the chances of trouble among the soldiers, and even of revolutionary disturbances, would obviously have been very much increased. The averting of the immediate Labour troubles, however, enabled the Government to carry demobilisation through without serious difficulty, and the great majority of the nearly 4,000,000 soldiers and sailors demobilised during 1919 were reabsorbed into industry within a short time. The number in receipt of ex-service donation benefit in November, 1919—a year after the signing of the Armistice—was 353,000. The donation benefit, of course, acted as a further powerful factor in preventing militant unrest.

The industrial atmosphere, however, continued to be threatening. In June the cotton workers struck on a question of wages, and in Juy the Yorkshire miners came out, in the course of a dispute arising out of lhe readjustments consequent on the March settlement. Troops, and navatl ratings for pumping work, were hurried to the coalfield, and every attempt was made to overawe the miners, who finally returned to work after a compromise settlement, applying to all the coalfields, had been reached between the Government and the Miners' Federation. In July came also the unsuccessful strike of the Police Union, which had won a lightning strike in London the year before, actually during the war, but now failed to hold its own against the Government Bill prohibiting Trade Unionism in the police forces.

The Yorkshire miners' strike followed immediately upon the Final Report of the Coal Industry Commission. The Commission reported unanimously in favour of the public ownership of the coal itself—that is, of the nationalisation of mineral rights and royalties—but it disagreed over the future ownership and operation of the mines. By a majority of one, it pronounced in favour of the nationalisation of the mining industry, with some participation in control by the workers. Sir John Sankey's Report, urging these changes, was supported with reservations by the six Labour representatives. Of the six employer representatives five, including the three colliery owners, advocated the retention of the existing system with few changes save the institution of arrangements largely based on the Whitley Reports. One member of the Commission, Sir Arthur Duckham, put forward a scheme for district unification of the mines under private ownership, but with some workers' representatives on the directorates, and subject to some measure of Government control. The miners, at their National Conference in July, expressed their willingness to give the Sankey proposals a trial, though they fell short of the Miners' Federation's own plan. They called upon the Government at once to redeem its pledges by carrying the Sankey proposals into effect. This the Government refused to do, and in August Lloyd George outlined, as the Government policy, a scheme of unification based on Sir Arthur Duckham's Minority Report, and popularly known as "Duckham and water." This was repudiated by owners and miners alike, and no more was heard of it. The miners then appealed to the Trades Union Congress, which, in September, passed a resolution calling upon the Government to nationalise the mines, and threatening, in the event of its failure to do so, to take steps to compel it to act on the Sankey Report in accordance with the pledge which it had given to accept the Commission's findings.

At this point attention was sharply diverted from the mining industry by the threat of serious trouble on the railways. Throughout the year the railway Unions had been negotiating with the Government for a new wage agreement, based on a re-classification and standardisation of the hundreds of distinct grades into which the employees of the various companies had been divided hitherto. In September a crisis was reached, the Government, in the so-called "definitive offer" of Sir Eric Geddes, insisting on very large reductions as the cost of living fell. On September 26th a national railway strike was declared, and the railway service was almost completely held up until the settlement of October 5th. Emergency arrangements were made on a huge scale for road transport of food and other necessaries, a roll of volunteer blacklegs was instituted, and a great display of military force was made. Lloyd George and other Ministers denounced the strike as an "Anarchist conspiracy," but, as a result of the full publicity secured for the railwaymen's case through an organisation improvised by the Labour Research Department,[1] public opinion was brought decidedly round to the side of the

[1] The Labour Research Department, originally a section of the Fabian Society, had broken away in 1917 and had developed into a federal body supported by a large number of Trade Unions, Trades Councils, Labour Parties, and Co-operative Societies. In 1919 it was closely associated with the Trades Union Congress and with the Labour Party, which were only beginning to create their own research organisations. The L.R.D. was subsequently discarded by these two bodies, when they had built up their own organisations. It then passed largely under Communist influence, but continued, on account of its excellent research and information services, to receive considerable support from Trade Unions and other working-class bodies. This is still the position in 1948.

workers. A contributing factor was the attitude of the printing workers, who threatened to refuse to produce the newspapers unless the case were fairly stated. Both the Government and the N.U.R., which was supported throughout by the Locomotive Engineers' Society, spent large sums on publicity ; but the workers, with a far smaller expenditure, had by far the better of the contest.

The railway strike profoundly stirred opinion throughout the Labour world. That it did not spread to other industries was largely due to the attitude of the railwaymen's leaders. No appeal was made by the N.U.R. to the Triple Alliance, and the function of mobilising general Labour opinion was assumed by a specially constituted Mediation Committee appointed at a conference called by the Transport Workers' Federation. This Committee, while threatening strike action in the last resort, used all its efforts to secure a settlement, and it was largely through its instrumentality that the N.U.R. and the Government were brought together and that an agreement, on the whole favourable to the workers, was reached on October 5th. Negotiations then continued on the new basis reached, and the full agreement was signed early in 1920.

The railway strike seemed for a moment to have brought back the acute Labour unrest of the early part of the year, but after its settlement feeling again died down, and the remainder of the year was marked by no great strike or strike threat. Of numerous small disputes, indicative of the general unrest, the most significant was the strike of shop assistants at the Army and Navy Stores in December, 1919. The strikers won their demands for better pay, and gave a powerful impetus to Trade Union action among non-manual workers. On the other hand, the ironfounders, who struck in September for an advance in wages, were defeated and returned to work in January, 1920, with nothing gained.

Among the other most important events of the autumn were the big " snap " victories of Labour at the November local elections throughout the country, resulting, especially in London, in the temporary conquest of power by Labour on a number of local councils. These elections showed a big change of political opinion since the General Election of 1918. But the polls were very small ; and many of the most sensational gains were subsequently reversed.

Meanwhile, on October 29th, 1919, the First International Labour Conference under the auspices of the League of Nations met at Washington. Under the Treaty of Peace had been set up, side by side with the new League of Nations, an International Labour Organisation, on which Trade Unions and employers' associations, as well as Governments, were represented. The I.L.O. was empowered to draft Conventions to be recommended to each country for incorporation in its legal code regulating labour conditions. The most important Convention drafted by the Washington Conference dealt with hours of labour. It recommended, subject to a few exceptions, the universal enforcement in developed industrial countries of a maximum working week of forty-eight hours, and aimed at giving legal sanction everywhere, subject to less stringent provisions for backward countries, to the changes already secured in the more advanced countries. The British Government, however, by refusing to ratify this Convention, provided other countries with an excuse for adopting the same attitude, and rendered it largely inoperative.

In November, 1919, the Wages (Temporary Regulation) Act was due to expire. It was not renewed, but certain of its clauses were continued in force in a modified form up to September, 1920, by the Industrial Courts Act, the existing rates of wages in each trade becoming a stabilised minimum up to the latter date. The Industrial Courts Act also placed the Interim Court of Arbitration, under the new name of the Industrial Court, on a permanent footing as a voluntary Government Court of Arbitration without compulsory powers. Provision was further made for the establishment of a Court of Inquiry, with powers to take evidence, to deal with any particular dispute. It was under this clause that the Dockers' Inquiry of 1920 was set up. The Trade Unions agreed to this measure, after all traces of compulsory arbitration had been eliminated from the original draft. Disputes could be sent to the Industrial Court for arbitration only with the consent of both parties ; but the Minister of Labour was empowered to set up a Court of Inquiry without the consent of either of the parties.

Meanwhile, the Trade Unions had been considering what action should be taken in view of the Government's refusal to nationalise the coal mines. After the September Trades Union Congress further efforts were made, both by the miners and by the Labour movement as a whole, to persuade the Government to agree to nationalisation on the lines of the Sankey Report. These were unsuccessful, and, on the demand of the Miners' Federation, a Special Trades Union Congress was summoned in December, 1919, to consider the situation. This Congress decided to institute an educational " Mines for the Nation " Campaign, for the purpose of securing further support from public opinion. It was already clear that not merely the colliery owners, but the whole body of employers, headed by the Federation of British Industries, would offer the most strenuous opposition to any form of public ownership and democratic control. The idea of Congress, which was very reluctant to resort to strike action in support of the miners' claim, was to evoke as a backing for its demands a body of opinion too powerful to be resisted.

The attempt failed, both because the mere opinion of Labour had little influence on the Government and still more because it proved to be impossible to focus even working-class attention on this problem. When the adjourned Special Congress met in March, 1920, to consider its policy, the situation had appreciably worsened. The Coal Commission was no longer fresh in men's minds, and the mining industry was no longer the effective centre of interest. Congress took a vote between two courses—a general strike in support of the demands for public ownership of the mines and political action (not further defined). The miners pressed for direct action, but Congress, by a large majority, decided in favour of political action, which in effect meant the indefinite postponement of the nationalisation issue.

While the general Labour Movement was thus suffering a serious set-back —the more serious because the mining question had come to be regarded as the test issue between Labour and the Government—in a more limited sphere the workers were winning a notable success. Under the Industrial Courts Act the dockers secured, through the Transport Workers' Federation, a special Court of Inquiry to deal with their claims for higher wages and decasualisation of labour. The Court had as its President Lord Shaw, and consisted of employers' and workers' representatives in equal numbers. The dockers, led by Mr. Ernest Bevin, used their opportunity to the full, exposing both the high profits made by the port employers and the bad conditions and insecurity of the docker's life. The result was a report which recommended the concession of a national minimum wage of sixteen shillings a day, subject to certain exceptions in the smaller ports. The parties were also recommended to work out and apply a comprehensive system of maintenance for the unemployed, combined with the decasualisation of dock labour.

The dockers thus secured a big victory on the wages issue ; but the other recommendations were never carried into effect. The Transport Workers' Federation did indeed prepare and submit to the port employers a scheme for the provision of "industrial maintenance." But meanwhile had come the trade slump, the growth of unemployment, and the beginning of the great capitalist counter-offensive of 1921.

The months immediately following the Dockers' Inquiry were a period of comparative quiescence—the lull before the storm. About the middle of the year wholesale prices, which had hitherto been rising sharply, began to fall—a clear forecast of the coming slump. Retail prices, however, did not show their first decline until almost the end of the year, and the imminence of bad times was still largely unrealised among the workers. Wages were to some extent protected under the regulative clauses of the Industrial Courts Act until the end of September, 1920, and could in any case hardly have been reduced in face of still rising retail prices.

Into this ominous stillness of the industrial atmosphere came suddenly at the end of July the threat of open war of Great Britain upon Russia. Intervention in Russia by British troops had, of course, been proceeding steadily, in support of one " White " General after another, almost since the November Revolution of 1917 ; but now came the threat of military action by Great-

Britain on a large scale in support of Poland in the Russo-Polish war then in progress. This threat gave rise at once to a great national movement of protest, in which Labour took the lead. The Labour organisations rapidly formed a Council of Action, which came into existence on August 9th, 1920. A National Labour Conference both authorised the formation of this emergency body and gave powers for the calling of a general strike against the war, and for the raising from all Trade Unions of a general levy to finance the movement. Spontaneously, local Councils of Action, based on the Trades Councils and local Labour Parties, were formed throughout the country. Excitement rose high ; and the main body of public, and even of Press opinion, took for once the side of Labour. It speedily became clear to the Government that war against the Soviet Union was out of the question and that persistence would give rise to a revolutionary situation. The Government gave way. There was no war.

But, in face of this partial success, the Council of Action, and the whole movement to which it had given rise, speedily melted away. It had been instructed to secure the effective reopening of trade with Russia and full recognition of the Russian Soviet Government, as well as to stop the war. But, its primary purpose accomplished, the impetus behind it was gone. The Council of Action was not dissolved ; it simply ceased to exist. It was the last national rallying of the Labour forces before the slump.

In the second week of September, 1920, the annual Trades Union Congress at Portsmouth at length took steps for the further consolidation of Trade Union forces. A scheme of " Trade Union Co-ordination," drawn up by a representative Labour Committee acting under Congress auspices, had already been approved in principle. A fully worked-out scheme was now adopted by the Congress, to come into force in September, 1921. The railway dispute of 1919 had forced into notice the inadequacy of the existing central machinery of Trade Unionism, and the new scheme was designed to prevent a repetition of the situation which then arose. The old Parliamentary Committee of the Trades Union Congress, which had been mainly a body for lobbying Ministers and had lacked any real co-ordinating authority over the affiliated Trade Unions, was scrapped and was replaced by a new General Council, more fully representative of each important section of workers and with far wider industrial powers and duties. The nature of the change is more fully explained in the next chapter.

While these events were in progress a further crisis was developing in the mining industry. In July, 1920, the miners had put forward a demand for increased wages and also for a reduction in coal prices, claiming that the financial position of the industry was such as to allow of both demands being met. The Government unequivocally rejected the double claim, and a strike ballot showed a large majority for a stoppage. Strike notices were handed in, to expire on September 25th, and the miners approached their partners in the Triple Alliance with a view to enlisting their aid. Resumed negotiations with the Government ended in a further deadlock. The next few days were spent in fruitless discussions by the Triple Alliance, which, unwilling to declare a stoppage, attempted in vain to promote a compromise. On September 24th it had become clear that there was no prospect of a Triple Alliance strike, and the miners accordingly suspended their own strike notices for a week, and resumed negotiations with the Government and the colliery owners. By this time the question of coal prices, for lack of public support for the miners' attempt to enforce a reduction in the consumers' interests, had been dropped, and the dispute had come to be purely about wages. New wage proposals were worked out, and the strike was again postponed in order that a ballot might be taken. The result was their overwhelming rejection, and a national mining strike began on October 16th, 1920. It lasted until November 3rd, when a settlement was made on revised terms, a further ballot having resulted in rejection by too narrow a majority for the Miners' Executive to think it wise to sanction a continuance of the struggle. Under the terms accepted a wage advance was granted, but this advance was to be related to and dependent upon output (the so-called *datum line*). The scheme was to last only until the end of March, 1921, by which time the owners and miners were called upon to work out a more permanent settlement between themselves. The strike thus ended inconclusively, with the real issues only postponed to a season when, as it proved, the miners found themselves in a disastrously disadvantageous situation.

The mining dispute of 1920 was important both in itself and as showing the radical defects of the Triple Alliance, which had not been tested either in the railway dispute of the previous year or on any other occasion. The plan on which the Alliance had been formed was that of simultaneous action by all three sections, each putting forward and fighting on its own programme, with the assurance of support from the others. This plan, in fact, was never tried. In 1920 the railwaymen and transport workers found themselves called upon to strike on an issue which directly affected only the miners, and it speedily became clear that their Unions were very reluctant to sanction such a course. It is true that the railwaymen, almost on the eve of the settlement, did vote in favour of strike action in the miners' support. But the decision, afterwards cancelled with the miners' assent, was taken too late, when the harm had already been done by the apparent collapse of the Alliance's strike threat before the stoppage had actually begun. It was widely held, after the dispute of 1920, that the Triple Alliance had been proved to be useless, and there was even considerable doubt of its continuance.

The dispute of 1920 was notable also because it gave rise to an Act of Parliament designed to clothe the Government with extraordinarily wide powers in dealing with any great industrial dispute. The Emergency Powers

Act of 1920 enabled the Government, on threat of any action calculated to
" deprive the community, or any substantial portion of the community, of
the means of life," " by interfering with the supply and distribution of food,
water, fuel or light, or with the means of locomotion," to declare a " state of
emergency."   The Government was empowered, by Order in Council, to
take any steps necessary for the preservation of the peace, for securing and
regulating the supply of food and other necessaries, for maintaining transport,
and for any other purpose vital to " public safety."   All such regulations
were to be laid before Parliament and needed its confirmation.   The proclamation could remain in force only for a month, but could be renewed.
At the instance of the Labour Party, the Bill was so amended as, at least in
name, to preserve the right to strike and to exclude " industrial conscription " ; but, despite the disappearance of the Triple Alliance's strike threat,
the Government insisted on passing it into law.   It was put into force, and
was effectively used, during the great mining disputes of 1921 and 1926.

BOOKS

Labour Research Department.   *Memorandum on the National Railway Strike.*
W. A. Orton.   *Labour in Transition.*
G. D. H. Cole.   *Labour in the Coal-mining Industry.*
A. Hutt.   *Post-war History of the British Working-class.*
Reports of the Coal Industry Commission, 1919.
Reports of the National Industrial Conference, 1919.
The People's Year Book.   (Annual Issues.)

3. THE POST-WAR SLUMP

With the winter months of 1920 came the beginning of a serious industrial depression.   The new Unemployment Insurance Act, applying con-
pulsory insurance to practically all grades of workers, was brought into
operation in November, and by the end of December there were already
691,000 unemployed, or 5·8 per cent. of the number insured.   The numbers
out of work rose very sharply during the early months of 1921, reaching
1,355,000, or 11·3 per cent., at the end of March and 2,171,288, or 17·8 per
cent., exclusive of workers involved in disputes, at the end of June, when the
national lock-out in the mining industry was just ending.   Wages, for the
most part, either rose or remained stationary up to the end of 1920, and the
movement for wage reductions set in seriously with the new year.   Already,
however, in November, 1920, the shipyard joiners were forced into a strike
against a proposed reduction in wages.   They remained out until August,
1921, when a compromise was at last arranged.

During December, 1920, and January and February, 1921, three National
Labour Conferences were held to deal with the question of unemployment.
A national Labour policy of " Work or Maintenance " was drawn up and
presented to the Government ; but the sole concession was a slight increase

in the rates of unemployment benefit, and even this was cancelled, on the ground of the depletion of the unemployment fund, later in the year.

Meanwhile, the miners and owners had been meeting for the purpose of drawing up an agreement for the future regulation of wages and conditions after the expiry of the temporary settlement on March 31st. These negotiations were sharply interrupted by the Government's announcement that it proposed to introduce a Bill providing for the termination of State control of the mines on March 31st, instead of August 31st, the date laid down in the Coal Mines Act of 1920. The rapid fall in export prices and the growth of depression at home had upset the financial basis of the industry, and decontrol on March 31st left no time for any new settlement to be worked out. The Government's announcement was made public only on February 15th ; but it is clear that the owners knew of its intention a considerable time earlier, and came to an agreement safeguarding their own financial position behind the backs of the miners. On the announcement of decontrol, they at once announced drastic reductions in wages, and, while the Decontrol Bill was still before Parliament, lock-out notices were posted throughout the coalfields. The Bill, in face of strong Labour opposition, became an Act on March 24th, and on March 31st the national lock-out in the mining industry began.

It was clear before this that the miners were in sharp opposition to both the owners and the Government with regard to the future regulation of the industry. The miners were intent on preserving the national system of wage regulation which they had secured under State control : the owners were determined to return to a district wage basis. The national basis desired by the miners clearly involved in some measure the treatment of the whole industry as a single financial unit. The miners proposed the establishment of a National Pool, drawing upon the surpluses of one coalfield in order to maintain wages in another at a level to be fixed by a National Wages Board.

The mining lock-out lasted from March 31st to the end of June, when it ended in the defeat of the miners, and the enforced acceptance both of the district basis for wages and of an agreement under which earnings fell rapidly to a point ranging from 20 to 40 per cent. above the 1914 level. The dispute fell sharply into two parts. During the first fortnight, it seemed likely to develop into a general struggle, involving the railwaymen and transport workers, and probably other trades : after April 15th this prospect vanished and it became a war of attrition against the miners alone.

Immediately upon the beginning of the dispute, the miners appealed for aid to their partners in the Triple Alliance. After full discussion, and after repeated attempts to bring about a settlement, the Alliance declared for a strike of all sections on April 12th. This was on April 8th, and, on this day the Government proclaimed a " State of Emergency " under the Emergency

Powers Act. Even more extensive military preparations than in 1919 or in 1920 had been made : the parks were again requisitioned and were filled with troops and supply depots ; the reservists were called to the colours and a special Defence Force was enrolled. Every attempt was made to overawe the Triple Alliance with a display of force. Meanwhile a tentative reopening of negotiations took place. The Government had sought to insist, as a condition of negotiations, that the safety men, who had received notices and had stopped with the rest, should resume work. This was refused, but the Miners' Federation issued orders that the men who were engaged on pumping and similar operations should not be molested, and thereupon the Govern-. ment again met the miners. In view of this the Triple Alliance, on the 12th, agreed to postpone its strike action to the 15th. But on the 14th negotiations again broke down, the Government siding with the owners against the national basis of settlement demanded by the miners. An informal meeting of M.P.'s thereupon endeavoured to mediate, and to these, on the evening of the 14th, Frank Hodges, the secretary of the Miners' Federation, made what was understood to be an offer to enter into a temporary wage settlement, waiving for the time the miners' main demands. On the following morning this proposal was rejected by a small majority by the Miners' Executive. The Triple Alliance thereupon met, and decided, in face of the miners' repudiation of the Hodges proposal, to call off the strike of the other sections. The day on which this decision was taken has come to be known in the Labour movement as " Black Friday."

The ignominious collapse of the Triple Alliance in April, 1921, has some-times been regarded as a mere betrayal of the miners by their Allies. In fact, this view of the situation is unjust. The trouble, aggravated by person-alities on both sides, really arose out of the ambiguous nature of the Alliance itself. As we have seen, the original idea behind it was that the three sections should fight as one, but each on its own programme. No provision was made for " sympathetic " action, in the shape of a united strike in support of one section only. When, therefore, a situation arose in which precisely this claim had to be faced, the Alliance had no satisfactory means of dealing with it. The miners claimed that their allies ought to strike when they were bidden ; but the railwaymen and transport workers replied by claiming that, if the miners wanted their support, they must also take their advice. In other words, J. H. Thomas and his colleagues claimed the right to settle the dispute as they thought fit, and to command the miners' acceptance of their decision. The miners would have none of this, and called on the Alliance for un-conditional support. Clearly, the case ought to have been definitely pro-vided for in advance ; as it was not, a clash, very similar to the clash between the miners and the General Council in 1926, was almost inevitable.

Nevertheless, the Triple Alliance's collapse was widely felt among the workers as a mean desertion of the miners in their trouble. And this feeling was accentuated when the fact of defeat could no longer be burked.

The withdrawal of the Triple Alliance left the miners to struggle alone. At last, at the end of June, when their resources were completely exhausted and further credits could not be obtained, the Executive agreed to terms, and, despite an adverse majority on a ballot vote, ordered a return to work. A temporary government subsidy was used to ease the fall in wages during the following months, but when the period during which it was available ended, wages fell rapidly to the minimum provided for in the agreement—20 per cent. above a standard rate, which was in most districts little above the rate paid in July, 1914. For certain of the lower-paid grades, it became absolutely necessary to fix a subsistence wage at a slightly higher level.

The miners thus suffered overwhelming defeat, followed by a heavy decline in Trade Union membership. The coal lock-out, indeed, struck a heavy blow at the whole Labour movement, and was the real beginning of a general offensive by the employers against the wages and conditions secured since the War. The demands for wage reductions now spread rapidly from industry to industry, and a general fall in wage-rates began. Already the shipyard workers, faced with serious unemployment, had accepted reductions. The engineers attempted to resist, but in July were compelled to agree to similar terms. Building trade wages were reduced in May, and the seamen's at the same time ; the ships' cooks and stewards, who attempted to resist by means of a strike, were defeated in face of the surrender of the other sections. In June the wages question led to a general lock-out in the cotton industry, and this was ended by the acceptance of substantial reductions. In one industry after another wages came tumbling down.

The passing of the high hopes and ambitions of the " reconstruction " period was further marked, on July 19th, 1921, by the dissolution of the National Industrial Conference. The Trade Union side, which had held on until then in the hope of securing the passage of the Forty-eight Hours Bill and the implementation of the other proposals agreed with the employers in 1919, resigned in protest at the Government's refusal to carry its earlier promises into effect.

On August 14th 1921, Government control of the railways came to an end, and on August 19th the Railways Act, reorganising the railway service into four big main-line companies on a basis of private ownership, came into force. Railway decontrol was accomplished without any industrial dispute, on the basis of terms agreed upon between the companies and the Trade Unions. As part of the bargain a plan for workers' representation on the railway directorates, put forward by the Government in the summer of 1920, was dropped ; but the Wages Boards, created in connection with the National Agreement which followed the dispute of 1919, became statutory bodies, and Consultative Councils, based on the Whitley scheme, were established for each railway. The same Act established a Railway Rates Tribunal to oversee charges, and embodied provisions about the " standard revenue " which the companies were to be allowed to earn on their reconstructed capital—provisions which were to lead to much trouble later on.

Meanwhile the pressure of unemployment was being more and more severely felt as the depression was prolonged. The number out of work fell after the mining lock-out, but then, with the coming of winter, rose again to 1,934,000 by the end of December. By the end of 1921 the Trade Unions alone had spent at least £7,000,000 in unemployment benefit, and in many cases their funds were nearing exhaustion.

The depression fell with exceptional severity on certain industries and districts, and, as the scheme of Unemployment Insurance failed either to cover the whole of the workers or to provide benefits adequate in duration or amount, ever-growing numbers of the unemployed were driven to the Poor Law for relief. As the distress continued, the Boards of Guardians in the poorer districts found increasing difficulty in meeting the claims upon them. This was specially the case in London, where Poor Law administration was divided among a large number of separate Boards. There was great difference in the wealth of the various areas, and some of them, such as Poplar, found the claims made upon them more than could be endured. The Poplar Borough Council, unable to bear the strain upon its resources, at length refused to pay the sums required from it by the London County Council and other authorities in respect of services administered by them. This action was taken as a protest, and in order to force the Government to come to the aid of the poorer areas. On September 1st, 1921, on account of this refusal to pay, the majority of the Poplar Councillors, headed by George Lansbury, were committed to prison for contempt of Court. The struggle continued for six weeks longer, but at the end of this time the Government rushed through Parliament a temporary Act placing the cost of outdoor relief more largely on the Metropolitan Common Poor Fund, and thus distributing the burden between the richer and poorer districts in the metropolis. The militant policy of the Poplar Labour Councillors thus resulted in an important success, but, the conditions of Local Government in London differing largely from those in other parts of the country, the victory was mainly local, and the Boards of Guardians in other depressed areas continued to stagger under a burden too heavy to allow the payment of reasonable maintenance. Even in London the Ministry of Health was able in most districts to prevent the Guardians from paying relief beyond an inadequate maximum scale fixed by the Government.

In the midst of the Poplar dispute, the Government struck yet another formidable blow at the workers. The Agriculture Act of 1920 had provided for the continuance of the Agricultural Wages Board set up during the war, and had thus given the labourers the assurance of a legal minimum wage. In the late summer of 1921 the Government suddenly reversed its policy, and rushed through Parliament the Corn Production Acts (Repeal) Act, under which both the guaranteed prices given to the farmers and the minimum wage accorded to the labourers were swept away. The reason advanced was one of economy. Agricultural prices were falling fast, and the guarantees given to the farmers looked like costing a great deal of money. The Government contended that guaranteed prices and the minimum wage were parts of a single bargain with the farmers, and that, if the one went, so must the other. Labour protests were unavailing ; the huge anti-Labour majority in Parliament voted the Agriculture Act of 1920, and with it the Wages Board, out of existence. Agricultural wages fell rapidly throughout the country, and the rates paid under the Board were in many cases almost halved by successive cuts. Twenty-five shillings a week became the normal labourers' wage in many counties. Under the impact of this blow, Trade Unionism in the rural districts melted away much faster than it had grown after the Act of 1917.

The autumn of 1921 also saw the beginning of what was destined to be by far the greatest industrial dispute of the following year—the rupture between the Amalgamated Engineering Union and the Engineering Employers' Federation on the questions of overtime and workshop management. In January, 1922, the engineers rejected an agreement demanded by the employers, and recommended, owing to the adverse trade conditions, by their own Executive. This agreement would have placed the working of overtime practically at the sole discretion of the employer, whereas the workers contended that, save in emergency, overtime should be worked only by mutual consent. The employers thereupon accused the A.E.U. of interfering with the management of their businesses, and delivered an ultimatum that it should not merely accept the overtime terms, but also sign a definite undertaking against interference with the " managerial functions " of the employers—a demand which recalled the issues that had been fought over in the great engineering stoppage of a quarter of a century before. The employers' demand was refused, and, on March 11th, the Engineering Employers' Federation locked out all members of the A.E.U. and also delivered to all the other Unions in the industry—numbering no fewer than forty-seven—an ultimatum in similar terms. The other Unions also rejected the ultimatum, and lock-out notices were given to their members too. Negotiations were thereupon reopened, and on April 4th the other Unions agreed to accept certain terms as a basis for reopening discussions, whereas the A.E.U. rejected the proposed basis, which gave the employers practically all they wanted. The lock-out of the other Unions was thereupon suspended, but the resumed negotiations broke down and lock-out notices were shortly afterwards reissued, and the stoppage extended to the entire industry. On April 27th the dispute was referred to a Court of Inquiry under the Industrial

Courts Act, which reported on May 10th, mainly in favour of the employers, but had no power to bring the dispute to an end. There was no real change in the position during the rest of May, except that the employers made an unsuccessful attempt to break the Unions by reopening the shops to men willing to accept their terms. At length, on June 2nd, all the Unions except the A.E.U. and two others accepted slightly modified terms. The other two Unions shortly followed suit, and at last, on June 13th, the A.E.U. also had to accept defeat, its very large resources having been completely exhausted by the struggle.

While the engineering dispute was in progress, wage reductions were being enforced in a number of other industries. Nor were the onslaughts confined to the organised trades. For a long while there had been fierce attacks by employers upon the Trade Boards Acts, which had been extended to a large number of additional trades between 1918 and 1920. These attacks had resulted, in September, 1921, in the appointment of the Cave Committee, to investigate the whole working of the Acts. This Committee reported in April, 1922. It recommended the continuance of the Trade Boards, and disposed of the more serious charges against them, but proposed drastic restrictions in their scope. The opposition, happily, proved to be so strong that the Government introduced no legislation modifying the Acts. Trade Boards, however, followed the action of employers in other trades by rapidly reducing wage-rates.

Throughout the years 1922 and 1923 wages continued, on the whole, to fall. There was, however, during the latter year a considerable increase of unrest. In February there was a big builders' strike in the Eastern Counties, caused by an attempt to reduce wages and to increase working hours ; and in March a national stoppage on the same issues was averted at the last moment by a reference to arbitration. In the same month occurred a strike and lock-out of the agricultural workers in Norfolk, where, as in most of the agricultural districts, wages had fallen almost to starvation point in consequence of the slump. This struggle ended in a compromise. In April, 1923, J. Havelock Wilson's National Sailors' and Firemen's Union accepted a drastic cut in wages, which was followed by unofficial strikes of seamen at many of the ports. The Union, however, helped the shipowners with " loyal " labour, and the strikers were defeated. In May, a dispute about overtime conditions led to a national lock-out of the boilermakers, which lasted until November, when the workers at length accepted defeat. Meanwhile, in July, there were widespread unofficial strikes of dockers throughout the country. The strikes were for higher wages ; but the men were at length persuaded to return on the old terms on the Transport Workers' Union's promise to launch a national wage movement. At the same time, the Miners' Federation opened negotiations for an improved agreement to replace the enforced settlement of 1921.

Meanwhile, political Labour had by no means shared in the effects of the Trade Union slump. The Labour Party went into the General Election of 1922 with only 75 members, and came back with 142. And when, a year later, towards the end of 1923, Baldwin suddenly dissolved Parliament and again appealed to the country on the Tariff Reform issue, the Conservatives lost 90 seats, and the Labour Party gained 48, returning to the new House 191 strong. The Conservatives were still the strongest party, but were in a minority of 89 against Liberals and Labour combined. The Liberals, after some hesitation, decided to help in turning out the Government, and in putting the Labour Party into office. Accordingly, on January 22nd, 1924, the first Labour Government was formed, with James Ramsay MacDonald as Prime Minister.

BOOKS

G. D. H. Cole. *Labour in the Coal Mining Industry.*
Cave Report on the Trade Boards Acts.
Labour Research Department. *The Workers' Register of Labour and Capital, 1923.*
G. Lansbury. *My Life.*
S. and B. Webb. *History of the English Poor Law.*
J. B. Jefferys. *The Story of the Engineers.*

4. THE GUILD MOVEMENT

It was during the dispiriting period described in the preceding section that the practical Guild movement among the Trade Unions ran its troublous course. Guild Socialist propaganda, as we have seen, progressed rapidly during the years of war. The National Guilds League, formed in 1915, campaigned with energy. It influenced the shop stewards, profoundly modified the old State Socialist attitude of the Independent Labour Party, and largely helped to form the new constructive demands of the Miners' Federation for public ownership and workers' control. Always small, it had in its ranks able writers and speakers who were able to exert an influence quite disproportionate to their numbers. Whitleyism was largely framed as a counterblast to its ideas ; and its effect on Socialist and Trade Union policy was for the time being deep and widespread.

Until the end of 1920 Guild Socialism remained purely a propagandist movement. But for some time an attempt to apply some of its ideas in practice had been under discussion. The first move came from the building industry, where employers and operatives had formed during the War a " Builders' Parliament," subsequently reconstructed as an Industrial Council under the Whitley scheme. A committee of this " Parliament " produced, in 1919-20, a drastic plan for the reorganisation of the industry, signed by a number of employers as well as by leading Trade Unionists. Under this plan, the employers were to become virtually salaried servants, and the

14

industry, hiring its capital at interest, was to be conducted in partnership by its managers and operatives. Attached as an appendix to the report was a complete plan for a National Building Guild.

It was hardly to be expected that such a scheme would carry the main body of the employers with it. In fact, it did not ; but it set the operatives thinking about the question of Guild organisation, and at the end of 1920, under the leadership of S. G. Hobson, a well-known Guild Socialist, the Manchester building Trade Unions launched a Building Guild wholly under Trade Union control. Almost at the same time an ex-employer and Guild Socialist, Malcolm Sparkes, persuaded the London operatives to launch the London Guild of Builders.

The movement spread with extraordinary rapidity, until the whole country was covered with a network of Building Guilds, which in 1921 mostly joined to form a single body, the National Building Guild. What made possible this astonishing growth was mainly the acute need for houses and the steps taken by the Government in order to meet it. Under the Housing Acts passed just after the War, it was possible for building contractors to work with little capital, securing payment for the work done as it proceeded. The new Guilds succeeded in getting the consent of the Ministry of Health to their employment by local authorities as contractors, under an agreed model scheme, which satisfied the Guild principles of workers' control and production at cost without profit. The Co-operative Wholesale Society and the Co-operative Insurance Society gave some help with finance, and work to a value of over £2,000,000 was taken in hand. The Guilds' workmanship was agreed to be in most cases excellent, and their costs were on the average well below those of private contractors. They attracted the best operatives, and carried on the work, under Trade Union auspices, with real and effective workers' control. There seemed to be no reason why the Building Guilds should not extend to cover the entire industry. In a number of other trades —clothing, furnishing, pianoforte-making, engineering etc.—small Guilds on the model of the Building Guilds were set up, and flourished for awhile.

Then, in 1922, the whole movement began to crumble away. The Government drastically revised its methods of housing finance ; and the new terms made it impossible for the Guilds to continue at work without large capital resources which they had no means of securing. They might, perhaps, have saved themselves at this stage by a drastic curtailment of their activities. But their members wanted to carry on, without realising the financial difficulties in the way—the more so, because, despite the acute shortage of houses, the slump had by this time led to widespread unemployment even in the building trades. One effect of this was that men crowded to get jobs with the Guilds, and a number of the Guild contracts soon came to be seriously overmanned. Living from hand to mouth on unstable credit, and buying dear from this cause, the National Building Guild plunged to disaster, dragging down with it the local Guilds, some of which were in excellent condition and would have been able to stand on their own feet had they not been involved in the general calamity. At the end of 1922 a receiver was appointed to wind up the National Building Guild's affairs. The local Guilds made some efforts at reconstruction ; but faith had been utterly shaken, and they could get neither contracts nor credit. Gradually, the entire movement melted away, and its collapse was followed by that of most of the Guilds which had arisen on a smaller scale in other industries.

The Guild Movement of 1920-1922 inevitably recalls the great Owenite Builders' Guild of 1834, which ended similarly in disaster. It was, indeed, an almost impossible task that, in both cases, the building operatives had set themselves to carry through. They had no capital, and they would not attempt to get capital on ordinary capitalist terms, because their principles excluded production for profit. When they built cheaply, as they often did, they handed the saving on the contract price back as a present to the local authority or to any other body which had employed them. They could thus build up no capital out of profits. And, as they made no profits, they could stand no losses. The Trade Unions, however sympathetic, could not afford to finance them adequately ; for they were compelled to keep their funds liquid for the payment of benefits and the financing of trade disputes. In these circumstances, the Guilds attempted to dispense with capital under an economic system which makes capital indispensable. If the Government's housing scheme had not been altered, they might have won through by getting their capital from it in the form of payment down by instalments for work done. This, in fact, is how they were financed in the earlier stages, with the aid of short-term credit from the C.W.S. Bank to cover the period of waiting. But as soon as the Government reversed its financial policy, and was no longer prepared to make payments on the instalment plan, the failure of the Building Guilds, unless they had been prepared to cut down their activities at once and to continue only on a very modest scale, was practically inevitable.

The collapse of the Building Guilds brought down with it the organised Guild Socialist Movement as a whole. A small section of the Guild Socialists had at an earlier stage joined the Communist Party, and another had followed after Major C. H. Douglas, a currency reformer who believed himself to have an infallible method of putting everything right by a plan of " Social Credit." The National Guilds League, after the rise of the Building Guilds, merged itself in a new body, the National Guild Council, on which the Trades Union Congress and a number of Trade Unions, as well as the working Guilds, were represented. This body died away after 1922. Guild Socialism thus perished as a movement ; but it left its permanent impression on the doctrines and policies of Trade Unions and Socialist bodies alike. Its special contribution was made in this way ; after the disappearance of the shop stewards' committees and the failure of the working Guilds, there was no longer an adequate basis for its existence as a separately organised movement.

BOOKS

S. G. Hobson and A. R. Orage. *National Guilds.*
G. D. H. Cole. *Guild Socialism Re-stated.*
G. D. H. Cole. *A Century of Co-operation.*
C. L. Goodrich. *The Frontier of Control.*
N. Carpenter. *Guild Socialism.*
The Guild Socialist. The Building Guildsman. Reports and pamphlets of the various Guild bodies.
Report of the National Federation of Building Trades Operatives on the Affairs of the National Building Guild.

5. THE FIRST LABOUR GOVERNMENT

The Labour Government of 1924 assumed office under very difficult conditions. It did not even have behind it the largest party in Parliament, and it held its position purely upon Liberal sufferance. Any attempt to apply a Socialist policy would have meant immediate defeat, followed either by a new election, or by a Liberal-Conservative Coalition. The pursuance of a policy which would command Liberal support was likely, on the other hand, to be productive of very scanty results and to provoke strong criticism among its own followers. It elected, however, to follow the latter policy, and to content itself with such small measures as it could carry through with Liberal backing. Before its fall in October, the Labour Government passed, besides Philip Snowden's " Free Trade " Budget, four measures of importance— John Wheatley's Housing Act, Noel Buxton's measure restoring the legal minimum wage in agriculture, an Act raising Old Age Pensions, and an amendment of the Unemployment Insurance system which extended benefit rights to the long-term unemployed, and thus took many thousands out of the hands of the Poor Law authorities. In addition, it reversed the policy of drastic economies in education and in other social services which had been inaugurated by its predecessors in consequence of the slump, and, after granting formal recognition to the Soviet Union, negotiated, but did not survive to ratify, a formal Russian Treaty. It also helped to carry through the " Dawes Plan " for the stabilisation of German finances under Allied control, and attempted, without much success, to persuade the nations of Europe to pursue a more co-operative and pacific policy. As an earnest of its good intentions, it restricted naval construction, and suspended work upon the new Singapore naval base. But its term of office was too short for the Labour attitude on foreign policy to exert any really considerable effects.

Considering the difficulties in its way, the Labour Government of 1924 achieved a good deal. Indeed, if we assume the rightness of the policy of taking and trying to retain office at all under the conditions which then existed, it could not well have done more. For, apart from out-and-out opposition, it had to face the impossibility of " managing " a House of Commons in which its supporters were in a serious minority. The conditions offered the maximum of opportunity for obstruction ; and they were exploited to the full in order to delay any business which the Labour Government's opponents wished to hold up. Ramsay MacDonald and his colleagues may have been right or wrong in the general policy which they followed. Whatever they did was bound to appear wrong at the time to a large number of their followers, and to look wrong, or at best insignificant, in historic retrospect. Moreover, the Labour Government got less than due credit for what it achieved because, in the end, it collapsed in a very stupid and undignified way. Philip Snowden's Budget was, indeed, no more than a competent exercise in orthodox Free Trade economics ; it was essentially a Liberal measure. But the Wheatley Housing Act, by far the most important measure of the session, deserves to rank as the initiation of a new policy in social reform, and was very much the best of all the Housing Acts passed between the two Wars. It did provide houses for letting at reasonable rents, and it was accompanied by a treaty with the building industry which, if its terms had been honoured, would have avoided many subsequent difficulties. Though the Government disappointed its supporters, that was largely because they were disposed to judge it by the standard of its own policy, which it could not implement without a majority behind it, and also because of the unfortunate blunders which marred its last days of office. In the difficult parliamentary situation, the Government's position was complicated by a recurrence of industrial troubles. The very existence of a Labour Government, coupled with a distinct, though not very great, improvement in the trade situation, was enough to cause a considerable extension of industrial disputes. A big strike on the railways was actually in progress when the Government was formed. The National Railway Wages Board set up under the Railways Act of 1921 had decreed considerable adverse changes in railway wages and conditions, particularly at the expense of the locomotive grades. These changes were accepted by the National Union of Railwaymen ; but the rival Union, the Associated Society of Locomotive Engineers and Firemen, struck against them, gaining small concessions, but on the whole failing in face of the maintenance of services by N.U.R. members. In February came a national dock strike, the aftermath of the troubles of 1923 ; and this time the men were successful in securing advances in wages. Strikes of tramwaymen and busmen followed in March, and were also successful ; but an unofficial stoppage on the London Underground railways in June ended in defeat. Meanwhile, in April, came yet another national lock-out in the shipyards, arising out of a local wage dispute at Southampton, and leading to the reference of the dispute to arbitration.

In May, a threatened national dispute in the coal mines ended without a stoppage, the miners securing an agreement which raised their wages considerably above the minimum levels fixed in 1921. The new settlement, however, was to last only for a year, and was the direct precursor of the troubles of 1925-1926. In July came a big builders' strike, met by the employers with a national lock-out, and ending in a compromise on both hours and wages. Also, there were throughout the year a great many minor disputes. The number of strikes rose from 628 in 1923 to 710 in 1924, and of strikers from 405,000 to 613,000. In addition, a large number of workers started negotiations for improved conditions, with indifferent success. Except in the mines, which had been restored to temporary prosperity by the French occupation of the Ruhr, the wage changes of the year were mostly small.

In October, the Government gave an opportunity to the Liberals, who had been growing more and more restive, to trip it up. It first started, and then as suddenly dropped, a prosecution of J. R. Campbell, the Communist editor, for certain articles in his paper, *The Workers' Weekly*. In itself, the incident was trivial ; but it coincided with the negotiations over the Russian Treaty, against which most of the newspapers, and many of the Liberals in Parliament, were up in arms. The Campbell case, woefully mismanaged by the Cabinet, furnished a most convenient chance for turning the Government out of office. Defeated in the House of Commons, Ramsay MacDonald dissolved Parliament on October 9th.

In the General Election which followed, one thing—the famous " Red Letter "—overshadowed all others. In the midst of the election the Foreign Office suddenly despatched to the Soviet Government a strong note of protest against its subversive propaganda in Great Britain, producing as evidence a letter of instructions alleged to have been sent by Zinoviev, on behalf of the Communist International, to the British Communist Party. This note came as a bombshell, especially as MacDonald was himself Foreign Secretary and was presumably responsible for it. Labour speakers, till then actively defending the Russian Treaty, found themselves apparently repudiated by their leader, and knew not what to say. The Communists stated that the " Red Letter " was a forgery, and this came later to be widely believed, at any rate in Labour circles. But for the time being, MacDonald remained mysterious and equivocal, and the " Red Letter " served both to bewilder his supporters and to rally hundreds of thousands of slack or doubtful voters to the Conservative cause. After the election, a Labour Cabinet Committee reported that there was nothing to show whether the letter was genuine or not. But by then all was over except the shouting. Labour lost 42 seats and the Liberals actually lost 119 out of 158, and were reduced to a position of parliamentary insignificance. The Conservatives gained 152 seats, and returned to Parliament with a huge clear majority over both the other parties combined.

Immediately after the election Ramsay MacDonald resigned, and Stanley Baldwin resumed office.

The Labour Government thus ended in inglorious fiasco, as the result of a series of muddles, the making of which is still wholly beyond understanding. Their followers were already restive before these events, and naturally they added to the vehemence of criticism. It seems probable that, in deciding to attempt to govern with Liberal support, MacDonald, whether he was wise or unwise, correctly interpreted the wish of the majority of his supporters. But the most active, though by no means the most numerous, section of the Labour Party consisted of the Socialists organised in the I.L.P., MacDonald was himself the old leader of the I.L.P., and his Government was largely drawn from its ranks. But the I.L.P. as a body, finding that the Government could not, or would not, pursue a definitely Socialist policy, became growingly critical, and came, especially after 1924, to form a sort of organised "left-wing" opposition within the Labour Party's ranks. From the episode of Labour in office, in 1924, certainly dates the emergence of a new type of "left-wing" Socialism, hostile to Communism on the one hand and to moderate Labour on the other, and grouping itself partly in the I.L.P. and partly round the one really individual figure in the British left-wing Socialist movement of the time—George Lansbury. "Socialism in Our Time" became, after 1924, the slogan of these two groups, whose activity—and especially that of *Lansbury's Labour Weekly*—helped to prepare the way for the industrial militancy of 1926.

To the British people, Labour's first brief term of office brought neither the ruin that had been freely prophesied nor the benefits for which its supporters had hoped. Its chief result was, both by encouragement and by reaction, to clear the ground for the events of the next two years.

BOOKS

G. D. H. Cole. *History of the Labour Party from 1914.*
The Labour Year Book, 1925.
Labour Party Annual Reports and Pamphlets.
J. McNeill Weir. *The Tragedy of Ramsay MacDonald.*
P. Snowden. *Autobiography.*
H. R. Tiltman. *Life of Ramsay MacDonald.*
M. A. Hamilton. *Arthur Henderson.*

CHAPTER IX

THE "GENERAL STRIKE" AND AFTER

1. The Rise of the General Council
2. The Coal Question
3. The " General Strike "
4. Aftermath—The Trade Unions Act

1. THE RISE OF THE GENERAL COUNCIL

THE organisation of the Trades Union Congress remained, at the end of the War, almost what it had been at the time of its formation half a century before. Congress itself met annually for a week, and wrestled with an enormous agenda of resolutions sent in by the affiliated Societies. The sole executive was the Parliamentary Committee, originally formed largely to carry through the Trade Union reforms of the eighteen-seventies, and still retaining many traces of its origin. Apart from the expulsion of the Trades Councils in 1895, there had been no important changes in Congress structure.

Its position in the working-class movement, however, had radically altered. As the name of the Parliamentary Committee implied, Congress in its early days was regarded mainly as a means of bringing pressure to bear on Parliament in connection with industrial legislation. It was not regarded, and did not regard itself, as a Trade Union legislature appointing an executive responsible for the co-ordination of the industrial work of the movement. Thus, when closer industrial unity was felt to be necessary in 1898, Congress did not itself undertake the task, but set up an independent body, the General Federation of Trade Unions—which, for reasons given earlier, wholly failed to achieve what was hoped of it.

The formation of the Labour Representation Committee—also by a decision of Congress—created a new situation. After 1900, and still more after 1906, the Trade Unions looked to the new and purely political body, rather than to Congress, to deal with matters needing parliamentary action. The Parliamentary Committee of Congress continued to go an annual round of deputations to Ministers ; but these became more and more formal and less and less important. Gradually losing its old functions, and failing to find new ones, the Parliamentary Committee counted for less and less. It played, except for a brief period during the Dublin struggle, hardly any part in the great industrial movements of 1910-1914.

In 1918, though the Parliamentary Committee had been drawn largely into war-time activities as the most representative industrial body in the movement, nothing had been done to re-define its position, or to confer upon it any industrial powers. When the national railway strike broke out in 1919, and revealed an evident need for some central co-ordinating body for the movement as a whole, the Trade Unions did not use the Parliamentary Committee, or the Parliamentary Committee claim to be used, for this purpose. They created a new *ad hoc* Mediation Committee, representing the Trade Unions which desired to help the railwaymen in their struggle.

An effect of the railway strike, which had threatened to become a generalised struggle between Labour and the Government, was to arouse in the working-class movement a keen sense of the need for effective central co-ordination. There were in existence at the time five bodies which might conceivably have been made the basis for this co-ordination. But the failure of the General Federation of Trade Unions, with less than one-fifth of the total number of Trade Unionists in its ranks, to become more than a strike insurance society for a limited group of Unions was by this time generally accepted. Up to 1916, indeed, the G.F.T.U. had been recognised as a co-ordinating body, and had been given status as an equal member, with Congress and the Labour Party, of the Labour Joint Board. But in that year, after a quarrel with the Miners' Federation, the G.F.T.U. was expelled from the Joint Board, and lost its representative status—a decision further confirmed when the International Federation of Trade Unions was re-formed in 1919. Congress then took the place previously held by the G.F.T.U. as the the British section of the International.

The second possible claimant was the Triple Alliance, which it had been often proposed to widen so as to include other industries. But the industrial basis of the Alliance, and the obvious difficulty of providing for simultaneous termination of trade agreements over a wider field, practically ruled the Alliance out of court.

The third claimant was an *ad hoc* federation of the Trade Unions which formed the workers' side of the National Industrial Conference of 1919. Just as the employers' side of the Conference did actually develop into the National Confederation of Employers' Organisations, so the Trade Union side had thoughts of becoming a central body co-ordinating the industrial work of the Trade Unions. But the abstention of the Unions forming the Triple Alliance and of the Engineers prevented the development of this project.

There remained the *ad hoc* Mediation Committee formed during the railway strike, and the Trades Union Congress with its Parliamentary Committee. In the result these two bodies joined with the Trade Union side of the National Industrial Conference in drawing up a scheme for the reorganisation of the Trades Union Congress as an effective confederation of Trade Unions.

Their plan, provisionally approved in 1919, was ratified in 1920, and came into force in the autumn of 1921—too late to be used in the great mining dispute of that year. It abolished the Parliamentary Committee, and replaced it by a Trades Union Congress General Council, representative of each of the great industrial groups in very rough proportion to their importance. Special seats were also reserved for women, and it was provided that, though nominations were to be made by the Unions in each group, the Council should be elected by vote of the whole Congress. At the same time, the Congress Standing Orders were radically altered, so as to give the General Council a clear mandate for the co-ordination of Trade Union action in great industrial disputes affecting the movement as a whole. The functions were clearly defined ; but the powers were not. The big Trade Unions were ready to agree to the creation of a co-ordinating body ; but they were not willing to give it definite powers of action at the expense of their own autonomy.

Before the change had come actually into effect, circumstances arose, which called for a trial of the new authority. The threat of a general strike and the improvisation under Congress of a Council of Action, over the Russo-Polish crisis of 1920, fore-shadowed the new lines of development. In 1921, owing to the existence of the Triple Alliance, Congress was not seriously called on to act in the mining dispute. But after " Black Friday " the Triple Alliance was defunct ; and it was clear that in any future crisis the movement would look to the new General Council to take the lead.

During the next few years the General Council gradually increased its authority. Alone or in conjunction with the Labour Party, through the Joint Labour Council which had replaced the Joint Board, it attempted mediation in a number of disputes, and it also came more and more to be looked to as the arbiter in inter-union differences. Its powers, however, were still not clearly defined ; for, though the granting to it of fuller authority was repeatedly discussed, the Unions were still jealous of their autonomy and reluctant to make a definite surrender of any part of it. Until 1925, the General Council was not called upon to act in any matter which raised acutely the question of its authority. Indeed, it seemed as if it might not be called upon at all ; for in 1925, under the leadership of Ernest Bevin and of the Transport Workers' Union, an attempt was made to revive the defunct Triple Alliance on a broadened basis and in a new form. The refusal of the National Union of Railwaymen to co-operate in the proposed " Industrial Alliance," except on terms which the other Unions would not accept, delayed the realisation of this project ; and the mining crisis of 1925 came upon the Labour world while it was still in embryo. In these circumstances, it was to the General Council that the miners turned for help in their trouble, with results which culminated in the " General Strike " of 1926.

BOOKS

The Trades Union Congress.   The General Council (pamphlet issued by the General Council).
Trades Union Congress Annual Reports.
W. M. Citrine.   *The Trade Union Movement in Great Britain.*
W. Mellor.   *Direct Action.*
G. D. H. Cole.   *Organised Labour (1924).*
G. D. H. Cole.   *British Trade Unionism To-day (1939).*

2. THE COAL QUESTION

The coal question has been described earlier in this book as the symbolic issue of the post-war labour struggle.   The successive troubles in the coal industry were in essence struggles between Capitalism and Socialism as rival social policies and attitudes.   This happened, both because in 1919 the Miners' Federation was incomparably the strongest Trade Union in Great Britain, and because the coal industry was buffeted about above all others by the ups and downs of post-war economic fluctuations.   It should be added that miners and mineowners alike were stubborn folk, tenacious and unadaptable, and therefore out of their element in a world of rapid change needing above all the constant application of new methods and new ideas.

After the disastrous struggle of 1921, the coal industry settled down to bad times.   Wages, under the dictated terms of the 1921 agreements, sank very low ; but the beaten miners were in no position to offer effective resistance.   Then, in 1923, the occupation of the Ruhr brought a purely temporary prosperity.   Coal exports rose higher than in the record year, 1913 ; and miners' wages rose in sympathy as high as the unfavourable terms of 1921 would allow.   Under the influence of the revival, the Miners' Federation set out to negotiate an improved agreement.   This the coalowners at first refused ; but finally, as we have seen, a new agreement was signed in 1924, providing for a substantially higher minimum wage.   There can be little doubt that the principal reason for the coalowners' acceptance of this was the fact that a Labour Government was in power, and, if they had not given way, would probably have framed a new Miners' Minimum Wage Act, raising the wages by law.   The owners, therefore, signed ; but the operation of the new agreement was limited to a single year.

Long before its expiry in the summer of 1925, both the Labour Government's tenure of office and the temporary prosperity of the coal trade were over.   The owners, with criminal stupidity, had done nothing to improve the efficiency of the industry in preparation for the bad times.   The return to the gold standard, at the 1914 parity, had set on foot a general process of deflation and had particularly affected coal exports.   Exports and export prices were falling fast ; and the colliery owners, in order to save themselves from the consequences of their own incompetence, were demanding, not only a return to the wage conditions of 1921-1924, but also the repeal of the Seven Hours Act of 1919, and the resumption of the eight hours shift. Negotiations reached a complete deadlock ; and it became clear that a national coal stoppage was imminent.

In deciding firmly to resist the owners' claims, the miners were well aware that the economic conditions were against them. The owners, in face of depression and falling prices, would not greatly mind a stoppage, whereas the miners had not yet fully recovered from the defeat of 1921. In these circumstances, the Miners' Federation appealed to the General Council for help. Arguing that the colliery owners' attack was only the first move in a general onslaught on wages and working hours, they urged the whole of the Trade Union movement to make common cause with them in resisting the demands, and insisting on a solution of the coal industry's recurrent troubles.

The Trade Unions were, indeed, at this time widely threatened with fresh attacks on their standards and conditions. The slight upward movement of 1924 had proved to be purely transitory, and trade generally was again on the down grade. Employers were everywhere arguing that labour costs were too high, and were pressing for lower wages as a means of reducing them. Instead of improved efficiency of management, low wages were preached, as usual, as the cure for all troubles. Moreover, among the workers, what counted most of all was an acute sense of shame for the events of 1921. Then, it was felt, the other Unions had left the miners shamefully in the lurch, and " Black Friday " was largely blamed for the working-class tribulations of subsequent years. It was felt to be impossible to leave the miners to fight their battle alone, or to urge acceptance of the owners' drastic terms. In July, 1925, the Trades Union Congress pledged its full support to the Miners' Federation, to the length, if need were, of a general sympathetic strike.

This threat was at once effective in causing the Government to intervene. Baldwin proposed a temporary subsidy to the colliery owners in order to allow the existing wages and conditions to be maintained. This subsidy was to continue while a new Royal Commission investigated the immediate issues in dispute and the position of the coal industry as a whole, and prepared a scheme for dealing with both. Though there was trouble over the refusal to allow any Labour representative to sit on the Commission, the offer was finally accepted, and all threats of stoppage were withdrawn pending the report.

Thus, for the fourth time since 1918, a tribunal of investigation set to work to study the problem of the coal mines. The Sankey Royal Commission of 1919 had definitely recommended, by a majority, nationalisation with some measure of workers' control ; but its advice had been rejected by the Lloyd George Government. The Buckmaster Inquiry of 1924 and the Macmillan Inquiry of 1925, both under the Industrial Courts Act, dealt only with wages and hours, and did not touch the root problems of the industry. But now the Samuel Commission, composed of two well-known Liberals, Herbert Samuel and W. H. Beveridge, and two big employers, was instructed to go into the whole question afresh.

It was obvious from its composition that the new Commission would not recommend either nationalisation of the mines, or even any drastic interference with their private control. It did, in fact, propose nationalisation of royalties (already urged by the Sankey Commission), organisation of research, and encouragement of colliery amalgamations designed to improve efficiency, to be effected by compulsory powers if after some years voluntary methods definitely failed. As a means of dealing with the immediate situation, it suggested wage reductions considerably smaller than the owners claimed. Increases in working hours it rejected, unless the miners preferred them to the wage reductions otherwise proposed. The coal subsidy, which had been admittedly fixed on the most idiotic basis imaginable, so as to put large sums into the pockets of prosperous owners who did not need them, was to be definitely discontinued.

The Commissioners' Report, issued early in 1926, pleased neither party. The miners repeated their slogan, " Not a penny off the pay, not a second on the day," and called on the Trade Union Movement as a whole for support. The owners reiterated their demand for heavier reductions in wages and for longer hours. The Government, despite the again-and-again-proved necessity of drastic reorganisation, and the manifest incompetence of the coalowners, undertook to adopt the Report only on condition that it was accepted by both parties to the dispute—a condition which it knew would not be fulfilled. After a series of futile negotiations a complete deadlock was reached. The miners renewed their appeal to the Trades Union Congress for support, and the General Council found that it must either repeat its strike threat, or ignominiously climb down. A general conference of Trade Union Executives was called, and voted with practical unanimity in favour of strike action. Eleventh-hour negotiations with the Government were broken off brusquely by the Government itself; and on April 30th, 1926, the miners were locked out. On May 4th the sympathetic " General Strike " began. Already it had been made abundantly clear that the Government and the colliery owners were hand in glove.

BOOKS

Report of Coal Industry Commission, 1926.
R. P. Arnot. The General Strike.
A. Hutt. Post-war History of the British Working Class.
R. Postgate, J. F. Horrabin and E. C. Wilkinson. A Workers' History of the Great Strike.
G. D. H. Cole and R. Postgate. The Common People, 1746–1946.

3. THE "GENERAL STRIKE"

Up to the very last moment, there was a lively hope among the Trade Union leaders that the trouble would be averted. In order to avoid any appearance of " provocative " action, they made practically no preparations for the strike, whereas the Government, with no such scruples, was fully prepared at almost every point. The Unions, indeed, were deceived by the apparent effectiveness of their mere threat to strike in the previous year. They thought that Baldwin had capitulated, when, in fact, as the subsequent events clearly showed, his Government had only been gaining time. They thought, if not that the walls of Jericho would fall instantly at the blast of their trumpet, at any rate that Baldwin, that constant preacher of " goodwill," would meet them half-way. Their hopefulness seems to have lasted through the final negotiations, up to the very moment when, on the flimsy pretext that the *Daily Mail* machine men had refused to print a leading article hostile to the strike, the Cabinet banged the door of the conference room in their faces. Then they returned in a bewildered condition to the headquarters of the Trades Union Congress in Eccleston Square, to carry into effect a threat which frightened those who made it, and one they were by no means in readiness to implement.

The Trade Unions had declared war ; but their leaders had not meant to be taken at their word. The Government took them at their word. The shilly-shallying Baldwin was swept aside and the Tory militants, headed by Winston Churchill, took charge of the situation.

Strictly speaking, the " General Strike " was not a general strike at all. The General Council called out only the " first line " of the Labour forces— the railwaymen and transport workers, the iron and steel workers, the builders, and the printers. The rest were held in reserve. The aim was to stop transport and certain other key groups, and to shut down the Press, which had been for the most part vehement in its denunciations of the strike as a declaration of war against the community. Few doubted after the event that the stopping of the Press had been a mistake. It gave to Churchill the chance for his hate-breathing, inflammatory *British Gazette*, and to the Government, through its command of broadcasting, almost complete control of the dissemination of news. It enabled Churchill, for example, almost wholly to destroy the effect of an appeal for peace issued by the Archbishop of Canterbury. It left the strikers largely without news ; for there were great difficulties in the circulation of the *British Worker*, the temporary paper which replaced the *Daily Herald*. And this, in any case, hardly reached the outside public at all. Above all, it was the one feature of the strike that really made the middle classes believe Churchill's ravings about " revolution." The absence of the morning newspaper was, for the middle-class householder, the symbol of working-class revolt. It is, however, easier to see such errors after the event.

The response to the strike call was practically universal. The manual workers in the trades involved came out solidly, and remained, with only insignificant breakaways, solid to the end. A very high proportion of the non-manual workers came out with them, and remained hardly less solid. There can be no doubt that the completeness of the stoppage astonished, not only the Government, but scarcely less the strike leaders themselves. Everywhere, local Councils of Action were formed to take charge of the situation ; and, despite the lack of preparation, effective strike machinery was everywhere improvised with extraordinary skill and rapidity.

The Government, for its part, adopted throughout a highly provocative line, in strong contrast to the counsels of peace, moderation and order constantly issued by the strike leaders. It armed special constables in thousands, called out troops and reservists, and issued what was practically an incitement to violence in the form of a promise of full support to these auxiliaries in any act they might commit in repressing the strike. It arrested and imprisoned hundreds of strikers under the Emergency Powers Act, which was at once brought into use. And the tone of its pronouncements, alike in the *British Gazette* and elsewhere, was as provocative as it could have been. Meanwhile, with the aid of a host of volunteers, it organised emergency services for the transport of food and other commodities. The power of the motor-lorry in supplying for a short period the place of the railway was plainly demonstrated ; and the possibility of running road services with chance volunteers, as the railways could not be run save to a very small extent, showed clearly the impossibility under the altered technical conditions of making even the most extensive strike an effective instrument of national blockade. Doubtless, if the struggle had been protracted the emergency services would have begun to break down. But no " general strike " is ever likely to last long ; and for the purpose in view the Government's methods were certainly efficient enough.

From the first the strikers' only real chance of success lay in frightening the Government into surrender or persuading it into compromise. The temper of the Government throughout the dispute excluded the latter solution, which the strike leaders would, of course, have welcomed. The struggle therefore became one of *morale*—it was a question of waiting to see which side would crumple up first. But, with Winston Churchill in command and thoroughly enjoying the " scrap," the Government was not likely to crumple up. Baldwin might have done so ; but he had been flung into a corner until he was needed to pronounce the final benediction. All things considered, the strikers had from the first little real chance of winning. Their only chance lay in the emergence of a peace movement so strong as to overthrow Churchill's command of the situation. But this could hardly develop in face of the shutting down of the ordinary means of publicity.

The rank and file of the strikers, however, had little understanding of the situation at headquarters. They had struck, and they were standing firm, and they did not see why they should not win. They had even, for the most part, little understanding of the class-war spirit that had been stirred up against them. Most of them were striking out of loyalty to the movement, and in order to support the miners on what seemed to them a purely industrial issue. There were revolutionaries among them, no doubt ; but these were a tiny minority, and even they steered clear of talking revolution to the main body of the strikers. The rest did not understand the savage rally of the men of property round the sacred ark of the capitalist covenant that their uprising had provoked. They did not see why Churchill was shouting about revolution when they only wanted him to give the miners a " square deal."

The strike leaders, meanwhile, were in a vastly complicated state of panic. They were afraid of their own followers—afraid at one and the same moment that they would drift back to work and that they would get out of hand and imitate Churchill by giving the strike a revolutionary turn. They were afraid of the Government and afraid of themselves, afraid to lead and afraid to admit failure.

Their position was admittedly difficult. They had called the strike (which they had at most only half meant to call at all) in a last-moment hurry and without reaching any clear understanding with the miners as to its objects, or as to their respective shares in its control. It was all very well to talk of a " square deal " ; but what sort of deal was square, and how much squareness could be secured in face of the coal industry's economic plight, the blockheadedness of the colliery owners, and the Government's refusal to take reorganisation in hand ? The need for a precise definition of objects became evident. The General Council wanted to work for a compromise on the lines of the Coal Commission's Report ; but Herbert Smith and A. J. Cook, the miners' leaders, met every suggestion with a fresh incantation of their formula, " Not a penny off the pay, Not a second on the day." Relations between the miners' leaders and their allies soon became strained.

At this point Sir Herbert Samuel, the Liberal Chairman of the late Coal Commission, made his unofficial incursion into the dispute. Ostensibly on his own authority, and without consulting the Government or anyone else, he produced the " Samuel Memorandum," embodying proposals for a compromise rather better than those in the Commission's Report. The General Council, apparently believing that these terms had the Government behind them (Sir Herbert Samuel is known to have consulted Baldwin about them), agreed to recommend them to the miners. But the miners' leaders would have none of them. A definite breach followed, and without further consultation with the miners or the rank and file, and without any understanding from the Government either as to the acceptance of the Samuel terms or as to reinstatement, the General Council, on May 12th, called off the strike, and, through the various Trade Union executives, ordered an immediate return to work, incidentally cancelling the order just previously issued calling upon the "second line," the engineers, ship-builders and certain other trades, to join the stoppage.

The unexplained order to resume work everywhere bewildered the strikers, who had no idea of what had happened. The Government organs and the small newspapers which had gradually reappeared with the aid of blackleg labour announced the utter collapse of the strike and the uncondi-tional surrender of the General Council. When copies of the *British Worker* arrived, they put quite a different face upon the matter. From the *British Worker* it appeared that the strike had been honourably settled on the basis of the Samuel Memorandum. The General Council were trying to cover up defeat in order to get the men to resume work. Their effort very nearly failed. The railwaymen went back to work, but found many of their number refused reinstatement, and instantly came out again on strike. Only a hasty settlement between the railway Unions and the companies pre-vented something like a general resumption of the stoppage. For the strikers did not feel beaten, and as soon as they realised that their leaders had secured no terms there was widespread resentment and disgust. For some days, however, the position remained too uncertain for anyone to be sure just how matters stood. It was but gradually realised that the collapse of the "General Strike" had left the miners still locked out, to make the best terms they could, or to struggle on alone.

In retrospect, both the declaration of the "General Strike" and its ignominious collapse look inevitable. The General Strike "myth" had haunted the working-class movement ever since the days of Syndicalism and labour unrest before 1914. It had revived powerfully in 1919, and had been behind the successive attempts at the consolidation of Trade Union forces. It was by no means, in the minds of the workers, an essentially revolutionary idea. On the contrary, the basis of its appeal was a simple feeling that all the workers were subject to the same dangers, and that all must stand together in meeting them. It was as a weapon of defence, and not of aggression, that the General Strike idea won most of its adherents. The employers, it was said, had their National Confederation and their Federation of British Indus-tries. They did not need a general stoppage to enforce their will, because they were the people who controlled industry as things were, and could give their orders to their employees without needing to lock anybody out. But the employers did hang together, and did pursue a common anti-Labour policy. The workers too must act together. When one industry was attacked, the rest must rally to its support. This would probably cause the other side to give way, or at least to accept a compromise. If it would not, then, and not till then, in the very last resort, the workers must fall back upon their last constitutional weapon—the General Strike.

To the Government, however, and to the main body of the upper and middle classes as well, the " General Strike " appeared in a different guise—as a challenge to the duly constituted authority of the State. Even Churchill can hardly be supposed to have believed that the strikers, or the members of the General Council, were attempting to overthrow the State, or that he and Sir William Joynson-Hicks had heroically saved the country from bloody revolution. But it was easy for them to work up their feelings so as to induce this illusion temporarily in the middle-class mind, and even in their own. And what they did believe was that the time had come to deal with the long-continued " uppishness " of Labour, and to teach the working classes a salutary lesson. The chance as they saw it was so good that compromise would have been a disaster, and the use of the *Daily Mail* incident for breaking off negotiations was an act of national duty as well as a very " cute " move.

From the standpoint of the workers the " General Strike " can hardly avoid looking rather foolish. Those who organised it embarked upon it without any understanding of its inevitable consequences. They are bound to look, in the eyes of history, as inept as the German Nationalists of 1848. The Government, for its part, must look, if not foolish, wantonly reactionary and perfidious in the extreme. The only people who came creditably out of the affair were the ordinary strikers ; for it is beyond question that the local Labour bodies, left for the most part without any central leadership, performed a remarkable work of improvisation during the ten days for which they had the control of affairs largely in their hands. The local Councils of Action gave a fine display not only of working-class solidarity but also of competence and capacity to control. The Trade Union rank and file had no cause to feel ashamed, and the local leaders had least of all ; but, naturally, they got the worst of it. For the return to work was followed by an orgy of victimisation.

BOOKS

G. D. H. Cole and R. Postgate. *The Common People, 1746-1946.*
H. H. Fyfe. *Behind the Scenes of the Great Strike.*
R. Postgate, J. F. Horrabin and E. C. Wilkinson. *A Workers' History of the Great Strike.*
R. P. Arnot. *The General Strike.*
G. Glasgow. *General Strikes and Road Transport.*

4. AFTERMATH—THE TRADE UNIONS ACT

The miners kept up their resistance for more than six months after the collapse of the " General Strike." Throughout this time it was obvious to every observer that they were bound to be defeated ; but they held out grimly and obstinately even after they themselves had lost hope. The Government, after the collapse, soon turned more and more openly against them. It repealed the Seven Hours Act of 1919, and so opened the way for the colliery owners to increase hours as well as reduce wages. It caused pickets to be arrested, and refused to allow the Proclamation under the Emergency

Powers Act to lapse. It waged war, through its Minister of Health, Neville Chamberlain, on those Boards of Guardians which sought to use public money for relieving the distresses of the men on strike. It repudiated not only the Samuel Memorandum but even the Samuel Report, refusing either to nationalise coal royalties or to apply any effective measures of compulsion to the colliery owners in any part of their business.

Meanwhile, the workers throughout the country raised funds in the miners' support until the whole movement was drained dry. Still more substantial support came from the Soviet Trade Unions ; but the strain was too great to be indefinitely borne.

In the end, the men were literally starved into surrender. There were sporadic returns to work first in the Midland counties, and then elsewhere. At length, in November, the Miners' Federation was compelled to accept terms even worse than those of 1921, involving both terribly low wages and the extension of working hours. Many of the owners made savage use of their victory, victimising active Trade Unionists and taking every chance of destroying old working customs and of making the men smart under the consciousness of servitude. They were getting their own back, they freely said. And, worst of all, the condition of the industry grew more and more desperate, in face of falling prices and intensified competition ; and nothing, or next to nothing, was done to set it again on its feet.

The Conservative Party, having tasted reaction, wanted more. It felt that the Trade Unions were down, and it could not bear to miss the chance of stamping on their faces. Accordingly, the " General Strike " of 1926 was followed by the Trade Disputes and Trade Unions Act of 1927.

During the " General Strike " there had been a considerable controversy over the question whether the movement was lawful or unlawful. The Liberal, Sir John Simon, who took a violent part against the workers, pronounced it illegal, and attempted to frighten the workers with the fear of legal penalties. A certain Mr. Justice Astbury, best known as a judge whose previous decisions on Trade Union law had been admittedly unfortunate, took the same side, and in deciding a case during the strike plunged into a long and irrelevant series of *dicta* denouncing it as illegal. Many lawyers held, on the other hand, that there was nothing illegal about it. It was, of course, true that, in striking, many workers had broken contracts of employment and were liable for civil damages on that account. But this was a purely civil and not a criminal matter, and had nothing to do with the legality or illegality of the strike itself. In the Trade Union Act of 1927, ostensibly in order to clear up these doubts, the Government, with the aid of its huge parliamentary majority, pronounced illegal, not only the General Strike, but all sympathetic strikes which were held by the courts to be designed to coerce the Government either directly or by inflicting hardship on the community. The Act also drastically altered the law of picketing, so as to put the Trade

Union picket back almost into the unenviable position he had occupied before the Act of 1859. It banned all regular State employees from belonging to any association or federation not consisting wholly of State employees, inaugurated a new and highly dangerous procedure of legal injunction, on the Government's motion, against "illegal" strikes, made it possible, in connection with such strikes, for Trade Union funds to be attacked as in the Taff Vale case, and destroyed the Trade Union Act of 1913 by substituting "contracting in" for "contracting out" in the clauses enabling Trade Unions to spend money on political action. After the passing of the new Act, no Trade Union could collect any money for its political fund except from members who had actually signed a form expressing their desire to contribute for this purpose.

This extraordinarily drastic measure was, in addition, so ill drafted that, pending the decision of actual cases in the courts, no Trade Union could tell what would be its precise effects. As a Bill it was fought line by line by the Labour Party in the House of Commons; but the huge Conservative majority carried it through without any substantial changes. They were still engaged in teaching the workers a lesson. Meanwhile, by-elections went steadily and heavily against the Government; and there seemed to be every chance that the Act would not long survive the next General Election.

The Trade Union world of 1927 was, however, weak and dispirited after its defeat; and the Labour Party, though still gaining political adherents, shared in the general depression. The Independent Labour Party tried to keep matters alive with its slogan of "Socialism in our Time"; but, despite its efforts, the movement languished. The Communists undoubtedly made adherents fast in 1926 and 1927 among miners and among others who were disgruntled and inclined to despair of all moderate courses. On the other side, a few mining Trade Unionists of some standing split away, and endeavoured to form "non-political" Trade Unions in alliance with the employers, especially in the Midland coalfields. Liberalism, too, began again to bid for working-class support with a policy of social and industrial peace, profit-sharing, public works to mitigate unemployment, and a hotchpotch of similar "remedies" for unrest. Thus attacked from both sides, the working-class movement held sullenly on its way, disillusioned and weary, but showing scant inclination to be torn from its old loyalties. The active minds in the movement were groping for a new policy; but it was evident that years must pass before the effects of 1924 and 1926—of political and industrial set-back—could wear off, and Labour could be ready to resume its gradual, but broken, advance.

BOOKS

A. Henderson. *Trade Union Law.*
C. Asquith. *Trade Union Law for Laymen.*
R. Y. Hedges and A. Winterbottom. *Legal History of Trade Unionism.*

CHAPTER X

THE SECOND LABOUR GOVERNMENT AND THE WORLD DEPRESSION

1. THE MOND-TURNER NEGOTIATIONS

THE General Strike of 1926 was, in its essence, not a revolutionary upheaval, but an act of instinctive resistance. The Trade Unions rallied to the support of the miners, partly out of instinctive class-loyalty, but also partly because they saw the attack on mining wages and conditions as the first step in a general capitalist offensive. The singularly misguided and disastrous return to the gold standard in 1925 on the basis of the pre-war gold and dollar value of the pound had seriously damaged British export trade, and had led to a demand that all wages should be reduced in order to bring down British costs of production to a competitive level. The Trade Unions were determined to resist this attempt to reduce their members' standard of living ; and the struggle came first in the mining industry, because its export trade was hardest hit by the return to gold, and because in it wages formed by far the largest element in the cost of production. But the Trade Unions showed in 1926 that, although their members were prepared to strike in support of the miners and possessed a very high degree of instinctive solidarity, they were not ready—and still less were their leaders ready—for anything in the nature of a revolution, or even for such an assumption of authority by unconstitutional means as could have possibly enabled the strike to succeed. In these circumstances, if the Government and the capitalist classes seriously resisted the strike, there was only one possible ending. But, even so, it is arguable that it was preferable from the workers' standpoint to strike and to be defeated than to give way without a struggle. For, though the Trade Unions emerged from the General Strike with their forces seriously weakened, they had given a clear enough indication of their will to resist to make employers cautious about further attempts to cut wages or to worsen conditions on the scale necessary to offset the effects of the return to the gold standard. It can hardly be doubted that, if in 1926 the Trade Unions had given way without a struggle, wages would have been reduced in the following years far more drastically that they were in fact reduced, or that Trade Unionism would have been in a much weaker position at the onset of the great depression than it actually was. In all probability the forty-eight hour week, the chief positive economic gain of the previous decade, would have been lost.

The General Strike, ignominiously as it ended, was therefore worth while from the standpoint of the working class. Nevertheless, its failure seriously weakened the Trade Union movement. The great majority of Unions suffered a fall in membership, and the Unions which had taken part directly in the struggle had to face a depletion of funds which was bound to take years to make good. The miners, naturally, suffered most of all. The victorious coal-owners not only pressed home their advantage by drastic wage-reductions as well as by the increase of working hours, but also refused to recognise the Mineworkers' Federation in any form and compelled the miners to deal with them separately, district by district. In some of the coalfields reaction went further still, and an attempt was made to break up the miners' solidarity by starting " non-political " Unions subsidised by the employers and bound down by agreements which prevented their members from making common cause with their fellow-workers in other areas. Of these " non-political " Unions, only the Nottinghamshire Miners' Industrial Union survived for any considerable period, and the threat of a national mining strike was needed, in 1937, to re-establish the recognition of the Nottinghamshire Miners' Association, and to put a stop to the victimisation of Union members by the Nottinghamshire colliery owners. The threatened strike was averted by an agreement to unite the rival associations into a single body, which became affiliated to the M.F.G.B. and gradually reassumed its old position in relation to Union affairs. The other coalfield in which a serious attempt was made to set up a rival Union was South Wales ; but the South Wales Miners' " non-political " Union never acquired much strength except in a few pits, and was liquidated pit by pit as the miners recovered from their defeat of 1926. All the same, it took the miners ten years after that defeat to rebuild their shattered industrial strength to the point of being able to re-establish unity by threatening another national stoppage.

The mineworkers came off worst in the reaction which followed the General Strike. But the Trade Union movement as a whole suffered severely enough. Total Trade Union membership fell from five and a half millions before the General Strike to well under five millions in 1927, when the numbers affiliated to the Trades Union Congress were less than four million. Nor was the fall in funds less severe. At the beginning of 1926 the accumulated funds belonging to Trade Unions amounted to over £12,500,000 ; a year later they had been reduced to less than £8,500,000. But these figures quite fail to measure the real change in Trade Union finances ; for the accumulated funds were held largely on account of friendly benefits, and the sums available for fighting industrial disputes had been almost completely swept away. Indeed, many Unions had borrowed large sums from their friendly funds in order to finance the General Strike ; and these borrowings had to be paid back before they could be again in a satisfactory position for financing even local strikes.

Nor was this the worst. The morale of the movement had been seriously weakened by the defeat. There was danger that the remaining members might continue to drop away, and that the Unions might be helpless to protect their wages and conditions if the employers seized the opportunity for launching a general offensive. The Trade Union leaders, in 1927 and 1928, wanted above all else a quiet period for recovery and rehabilitation. They were in a mood to seize any chance that promised, on tolerable terms, some sort of industrial truce with the employing class.

If all employers had been like the colliery owners, no truce would have been offered. But in fact a good many sections of the capitalist forces took a different view. The great American boom, which was then developing fast, offered a prospect of good profits in Great Britain ; for it meant brisk American orders not only for Great Britain but also for the raw material producing countries to which British exports were largely sold. British employers in general did not want a further period of industrial dislocation, even if they were in a position to win. Many of them, seeing further ahead and realising the probable political repercussions as well as the direct economic consequences of an " all-out " conflict with Labour, preferred to come to terms with the Trade Unions on the basis of preserving the *status quo* ; for, with profits rising fast, the keeping of things as they were offered very large advantages from the capitalist standpoint.

There was, accordingly, no general employers' offensive against the Trade Unions. Instead, Sir Alfred Mond, the leader of the great chemical combine, was allowed to gather round him a group of employers who preferred an attempt to come to terms with Labour and to approach the Trade Unions with a proposal that a pact should be negotiated between the two parties in industry. The Mond proposal was that employers and workmen should come together, not merely for the prevention of disputes, but in order to launch a joint policy for the furtherance of industrial prosperity. Industry, united at last, was to tell the Government what economic policies it should pursue ; and in return for lying down in amity with the lion, the Trade Union lamb was to be given concessions in the form of better provision for unemployment, the recognition of collective bargaining over a wider field, and the concession of a limited right to participate with the employers in the discussion of economic policy.

The " Mond-Turner " conversations—so called after Sir Alfred Mond, afterwards Lord Melchett, who headed the employers' group, and Ben (afterwards Sir Ben) Turner, the leader of the woollen operatives, who was Chairman of the Trades Union Congress General Council at the time—were officially engaged in by the Trades Union Congress General Council, as representing the entire Trade Union movement. But on the employers' side they were " unofficial " ; and the Federation of British Industries and the National Confederation of Employers' Organisations were in no way committed to them, beyond allowing them to proceed. In fact these two bodies did in the event refuse to endorse the proposals of the " Mond-Turner Conference " for a National Industrial Council representing employers and workers, with wide terms of reference covering the broader issues of economic policy. The most the central employers' organisations would accept was the establishment of occasional consultative machinery, which could be called together for the discussion of any issue both sides were prepared to lay before it. In practice, this meant nothing, and the joint machinery set up as the outcome of the Mond-Turner Conferences was never really operated until something rather like it came into existence under very different conditions during the second World War.

Nevertheless the Mond-Turner conversations served their purpose. They gave the Trade Unions a breathing space after the events of 1926, and they allowed the employers to reap the harvest of the 1928-1929 boom without interference from Labour. Only when the world slump had set in and employers, faced with a floundering Labour Government, preferred to act alone, were the Mond-Turner proposals liquidated, without any fulfilment of the hopes of economic betterment which had been dangled before the Trade Unions in 1928.

The Conferences, while they lasted, aroused acute controversy in the Labour world. To some Trade Unionists, notably to A. J. Cook, the Miners' Secretary, the projected pact between Capital and Labour seemed a betrayal of the workers' cause. But most of the Trade Union leaders wanted, above all else, a breathing space ; and the Mond-Turner negotiations and proposals received overwhelming endorsement at the Trades Union Congress —much less on account of any hopes aroused by them than because they appeared to offer the prospect of an interval of industrial peace.

Meanwhile, on the whole, British industry was moderately prosperous, according to inter-war standards, except in the depressed areas, despite the handicap imposed on British exporters by the unwarrantably high level at which the pound sterling had been stabilised on the restoration of the gold standard in 1925. The consequent over-valuation of sterling required from the Bank of England a steady deflationary pressure, designed to reduce incomes and prices in Great Britain. But this pressure, although it checked industrial expansion, was not enough to prevent British industry from sharing to some extent in the temporary prosperity generated mainly by the American boom and stimulated in many countries by the belief that the troubles due to the war had been for the most part overcome and that the prospects of steady progress in world production and trade were becoming much brighter. The coal trade and certain other industries dependent upon keenly competitive exports remained depressed ; and unemployment persistently refused to fall below the million mark. But this unemployment was largely concentrated in a limited number of industries and areas, and over most of the country employment was fairly good, while profits rose fast in the majority of industries, and there was active investment both at home and abroad.

The Baldwin Government, during these years of comparative prosperity, managed to make itself increasingly unpopular. In particular, it administered the Unemployment Insurance Acts in such a way as to arouse widespread discontent among the workers. The principal grievance was concerned with the provision which allowed an unemployed person to be deprived of benefit on the ground that he was " not genuinely seeking work." Moreover, it was widely felt that the continuance of unemployment at a high level in face of high profits and evident world prosperity was intolerable, and that the Government ought to take effective action in order to get the unemployed back to work. Nor was there absent a sense that the workers might regain by political action what they had lost in their industrial defeat.

In these circumstances, the General Election of 1929 resulted in a remarkable Labour victory. Both Labour and the Liberals, under Mr. Lloyd George's leadership, fought the election largely on the issue of unemployment, promising that, if they were returned to power, active measures would at once be taken for getting the unemployed back to useful work. Labour in addition promised to abolish the unpopular " not genuinely seeking work " clause in the Insurance Act, to repeal the Trade Disputes Act of 1927, and to give the miners a square deal. Both " progressive " parties pledged themselves to an active policy of housing and slum clearance, and to a monetary expansion which would reverse, if necessary by measures of public control, the deflationary policy followed by the Bank of England since the restoration of the gold standard.

Probably what counted most in bringing about the " progressive " election victory of 1929 was the widespread belief that the Conservative Government, by its failure to act, was depriving the British people of its share in world prosperity. The electoral pendulum swung against the Government, and the Labour Party came back to Westminster still some distance short of a clear majority, but with many more seats than even its optimistic supporters had dared to hope. In the new Parliament Labour had 287 seats, and the Liberals, pledged to many of the same immediate measures, had 59, out of a total of 615. Ramsay MacDonald, as the leader of the predominant party, was called upon to form the second Labour Government.

This Government, it is important to bear in mind, took office at a time of rapidly advancing capitalist prosperity. America was in a condition of high activity—which was, indeed, already turning into a sensational business boom—and the propagandists of American Capitalism were loudly proclaiming that, in the United States, everyone would go on getting richer and richer, and slumps would never be heard of any more.   Moreover, Germany had carried through after 1924 a truly remarkable feat of industrial and economic reconstruction ; and all over Europe, as well as elsewhere, production had been advancing fast as the industrial apparatus recovered from the dislocation and destruction of war.   The economic difficulties from which Great Britain was still suffering seemed to arise mainly from causes peculiar to Great Britain itself ; and it looked as if, in a world fast advancing in wealth and prosperity, they would prove readily amenable to courageous national treatment.   It seemed reasonable, in these conditions, to set about a policy of progressive social amelioration, to be financed largely by higher taxation of the richer classes, on the assumption that there would be a substantial social surplus available without any undue squeezing of the capitalist orange.   The new Labour Government began in this spirit by amending the Unemployment Insurance Acts so as to abolish the " not genuinely seeking work " dis-qualification for benefit, and by announcing a programme of re-housing and other public works designed to provide employment for a large section of the workless population.   It also declared its determination to raise the school-leaving age, to repeal the obnoxious Trade Disputes Act of 1927, and to undertake promptly the reorganisation under public auspices of the coal industry and of other services and industries which were noticeably suffering from inefficient management and unco-ordinated control.

BOOKS

G. D. H. Cole.   *History of the Labour Party from 1914.*
G. D. H. Cole and R. Postgate.   *The Common People, 1746–1946.*
A. Hutt.   *Post-war History of the British Working Classes.*
Trades Union Congress Reports, 1927 and subsequent years.
G. D. H. Cole.   *British Trade Unionism To-day (1937).*
P. Snowden.   *Autobiography.*

2. THE SECOND LABOUR GOVERNMENT

Courage was the quality most needed in tackling both the comparatively easy problems which confronted the second Labour Government when it took office and the very much harder problems which developed during its two years' tenure.   Courage was, however, least of all qualities the character-istic of Ramsay MacDonald's second Government.   The Cabinet's policy was to remain in office as long as possible with Liberal support, to concentrate upon secondary measures which the Liberals could be persuaded to accept, and to avoid anything likely to upset the even tenor of capitalist recovery as it was assumed to exist when the Government was laying its plans.   But, even on these assumptions, the Labour Government was slow in getting to business.   Before the apparent prosperity had come to an end, it had encountered serious difficulties.   The Liberals would not agree to the unconditional repeal of the Trade Disputes Act of 1927 ; and even where agreement could be reached with the Liberals, Labour measures had to run the gauntlet of a predominantly Conservative House of Lords. The Government was compelled to withdraw its Trade Disputes Bill, and also its Education Bill raising the school-leaving age to 15 ; and a number of other measures became law only after severe mutilation at the hands of the Upper Chamber. Perhaps these obstacles could have been surmounted if the Government had shown, from the beginning, a bolder front ; but, under Ramsay MacDonald's leadership, the Labour Party was timid in facing its difficulties, and was always readier to compromise than to fight. Only in international affairs did it show, with Arthur Henderson as Foreign Secretary, any sign of real capacity in facing major problems. In particular, it failed to take any effective steps towards getting the unemployed back to work ; for J. H. Thomas, who was put in charge of co-ordinating this aspect of its policy, soon found much too powerful to be resisted the arguments of the Treasury and of the Civil Service in general against doing anything on a scale large enough to be capable of producing any noticeable effect.

Moreover, the Government, under the guidance of Philip Snowden at the Exchequer, was determined to preserve the gold standard, and to act in strict accordance with the tenets of financial orthodoxy, which in his mind necessarily involved a deflationary financial policy inconsistent not only with wage advances but also with any scheme of public expenditure on a scale sufficient appreciably to reduce unemployment. Philip Snowden's strong personality induced his colleagues to acquiesce in this policy, and in this mood the Government was not even prepared to go as far as the more advanced of its Liberal supporters, prompted by J. M. Keynes, would have allowed it to go in promoting a programme of economic reconstruction and development. It would take no major step to get the unemployed back to work ; and it would apply no coercion to colliery owners, or to cotton employers, or to iron and steel manufacturers, to set their disorderly houses to rights. It preferred doles to development ; and, above all, it expended its energies in endless backstairs negotiations designed to make possible the evasion of dangerous controversial issues.

So much had become manifest in the early months of Labour's second tenure of office, even before the entire position of affairs was changed by the coming of the world slump. The Labour Government was, no doubt, unfortunate in having to face, in its first year of office, a situation which was bound to be difficult and disastrous whatever was done. But this extenuation cannot rescue it from the charge of plainly demonstrated incapacity. In face of the slump it continued to wobble helplessly to and fro, though the need for courage had become far greater than ever. The number of the unemployed mounted up ; industry plunged into deeper depression and worse chaos ; and the power of the Trade Unions was progressively undermined.

But while one or two Ministers—notably Arthur Henderson at the Foreign Office and Dr. Addison at the Ministry of Agriculture—did what they could, the Cabinet as a whole remained visibly without the shadow of a constructive, or even of a defensive, policy. By far the strongest personality in the Cabinet was the Chancellor of the Exchequer, Philip Snowden; and he, in his declining years, appeared to retain his faith in only three things—Free Trade, the Gold Standard, and his own unquestionable rightness about everything. But the Gold Standard was putting a heavier and heavier strain on the British economic system, and was aggravating the growing depression in industry; while the combination of Free Trade with it was allowing every country to dump upon the British market the exports which could no longer be sold elsewhere, and was thus piling up the British bill for imports, in face of sharply declining exports. Thus the strain on the balance of payments was getting more and more severe, and the way was being prepared for the British financial crisis of 1931.

Under Philip Snowden's policy of negations the second Labour Government staggered on, finding more and more difficulty in financing its policy of doles out of the dwindling revenue of the period of depression. It was driven to "economise," as the burden grew heavier of maintaining the unemployed whom it would do nothing to set to work. It tried half-heartedly to "economise" at the expense of the unemployed; but it was too divided to be more than half-hearted in anything. Consequently it steadily lost ground in the country, and had gone far, even before the financial crisis of the summer of 1931, towards digging its own grave. This is not to say that it did nothing good or useful. Some of its departmental measures were excellent. But governments are judged by their skill and courage in facing the major issues of their time; and by this test the second Labour Government was found lamentably wanting.

The coming of depression abroad made the British situation immensely more difficult. As long as the American boom lasted, Great Britain, under any financial policy, was bound to share in it to some extent. But when the United States began plunging headlong towards the deepest economic crisis in history, British trade and industry were bound to feel severely the effects of the overvalued pound. It is even surprising that, in face of the American collapse, British economic activity did not collapse sooner. Temporarily, no doubt, it was sustained by filling up the void in Europe which had been left by the American retreat. Through 1930 the situation got steadily, but not sensationally, worse. Only in 1931 did the full consequences of the collapse begin to become plain, with the crisis in German and Austrian banking, and the growth everywhere of the demand for "liquidity" which brought industrial investment almost to nothing, and provoked, in face of the inevitable lack of capitalist "confidence" in a Labour Government, however moderate, an inescapable run on the pound.

The MacDonald Government was slow to realise what was happening. Pressed by its own supporters to adopt more far-reaching measures of social reform, such as it had promised in 1929, and pressed on the other hand by bankers and capitalists to retrench in view of world economic difficulties in order to " save the pound," it elected to do nothing, as the easiest way of striking a balance between its critics. But, in the circumstances of 1931, to do nothing was the worst possible policy. As world prices tumbled and one country after another resorted to measures of high protection in the hope of saving its own industries from destruction, the maintenance of the Gold Standard at the existing parity became more and more plainly inconsistent with any policy except domestic deflation. Great Britain, under the Free Trade system, became a worse and worse market in which to buy, and a better and better market in which to sell. The goods excluded from other markets came pouring into Great Britain, and British exports fell off sharply. Only the most drastic scaling down of wages and other incomes could in these conditions have made it possible to keep the Gold Standard in being at an unaltered parity ; but it was plainly impossible for a Labour Government to follow such a policy, though it did in fact go as far as it dared in checking public expenditure and in adopting, under the so-called " Anomalies Act," modified measures of retrenchment at the expense of the intermittently employed, and especially of married women claimants to benefit.

For many months before the financial crisis which finally drove the Labour Government from office the trend of events was sufficiently plain. The Government's sole chance of saving itself would have been to abandon the Gold Standard, or at all events to alter the rate of exchange by drastic devaluation and thus to regain its power to pursue an active policy of employment and social reform. But the capitalist interests, ready as they were to accept such a policy at the hands of a " National " Government when the crisis had actually made it inevitable, would have raised a howl of protest if it had been applied by a Labour Government in time to prevent the crisis from occurring at all. Nor could the Labour Government make up its mind to face the necessity of devaluation. Philip Snowden continued to be fanatically opposed to any tampering with the Gold Standard ; and most of the Ministers, with little understanding of financial matters, were disposed to take his word for what was right. Consequently, throughout 1931 the Government was drifting helplessly towards the rocks.

The more its difficulties increased on account of the international situation, the more intractable its critics became. The Liberals joined in the clamour for " national economy," and induced Ramsay MacDonald to appoint the " May " Economy Committee, whose alarmist report of an impending budget deficit gave the signal for a flight from the pound. The House of Lords mutilated the Government's Bills with a growing sense of power. And, on the other side, its supporters became more and more restive as it grew plainer how far MacDonald was prepared to go towards meeting the demands of his capitalist critics.

In this atmosphere of increasing tension Sir Oswald Mosley, then reputedly on the left of the Labour Party, broke away early in 1931 and formed his abortive " New Party," with a programme in which the demand for a more active policy of public works and financial reflation took the most prominent place.   Very few Labour supporters followed Sir Oswald Mosley in his secession, even though his movement had not at this stage revealed its real Fascist character, and seemed to be a breakaway to the left of the official party.   But disillusionment was spreading rapidly among the Labour voters, and there was a growing sense of the Government's incompetence to handle the crisis.   The plain fact was that, if the crisis was to be dealt with along capitalist lines, a frankly capitalist Government was likely to deal with it a good deal more effectively than a Government unprepared or unable to apply Socialist remedies but hampered by nominal allegiance to Socialism, and therefore unable to command the confidence of the capitalist and financial interests.

As the year 1931 advanced, the crisis became steadily more severe. Exports fell off faster and faster, whereas imports increased, as foreign producers scrambled to dispose of their products in the principal free market that remained.   The May Economy Committee's Report, widely understood in Great Britain to be grossly exaggerated, had a great effect abroad in undermining confidence in the British currency.   These two forces combined to bring about a flow of gold out of the Bank of England's reserves.   Meanwhile, the growth of unemployment put a new strain on the national finances, and entirely submerged the Labour Party's half-hearted attempts at the provision of work.   The " Anomalies " Act was widely regarded as merely the first step towards the capitulation of the Cabinet to the demand for " economies " at the expense of the unemployed.   It became known that further economies were being actually devised, and that the financiers were pressing the Government to resort to domestic retrenchment as the only means of saving the pound.

Under stress of these growing difficulties the Labour Cabinet drifted, in effect, without any policy at all.   It was clear that the adverse balance of payments, in view of the reactions which it provoked, could not go on long without positively driving Great Britain off the Gold Standard.   There were some who urged that the balance could be restored by the imposition of a tariff and the use of the proceeds by way of subsidies to the export trades, and that by this method the pound could still be saved.   But Philip Snowden believed fanatically in Free Trade as well as in the Gold Standard ; and until the chance had passed he flatly refused to abandon either.   Soon it became plain that no tariff could possibly save the pound ; for the trickle of gold out of Great Britain was becoming a torrent as more and more of the financiers joined in the scramble to get their liquid resources out of the threatened area.

But still Snowden held on tenaciously, and in face of his determination the weak and divided Labour Cabinet, most of whose members had very little idea of what was happening, continued simply to drift.

It is easy to see in retrospect that this fatal weakness was due to an utter lack of agreement on first principles. There were in the Government Socialists who were prepared to face the difficulties and dangers of a constructive Socialist policy, and to risk the immediate fall of the Ministry as a consequence of their action. There were others in whose minds instinctive loyalty to the working-class movement held a dominant place, but who could not master the difficulties of financial policy, or see their way clearly enough to offer good counsel in the growing emergency. But there were others—and they held the leading positions in the Cabinet and in the eyes of the public—who had in reality ceased to be Socialists at all, save in a purely Utopian sense, and were determined that the capitalist system must be kept working at all costs, and the country be governed in accordance with capitalist principles, subject only to such small injections of socialistic reform as Capitalism could stand without risk of weakening its stability.

It is now clear that for some time before the actual collapse the Labour Prime Minister had half seen it coming and had begun to dream of a " national " coalition under his own leadership with a mission to " save the country " from financial disaster. But most of his colleagues had no inkling of this, and when they were pressed to agree to a drastic means test for the unemployed, to wage-reductions, and to other forms of retrenchment in order " to save the pound," their instinctive loyalty to working-class interests held them back, and made them refuse, in however bewildered a fashion, to accept the logical consequences of the policy which had been followed in their name. Thereupon, MacDonald broke up his own Government, seceded with Philip Snowden, J. H. Thomas, and a handful of followers to the reactionary side, and reappeared at the head of a " National " Government, professing to represent all parties and all good men.

The first act of MacDonald's " National " Government was to abandon the Gold Standard which it had promised to preserve. This was done even though Philip Snowden remained at the Exchequer ; for Snowden, now that he had flung over Socialism, appeared to be ready to fling over with it all the cherished convictions of a lifetime, and to acquiesce not merely in the fall of the pound, but also in a series of protectionist measures which the Conservatives promptly exacted as the price of accepting the new coalition. This done, MacDonald and his Conservative and Liberal supporters immediately appealed to the electorate for a " Doctor's Mandate " to deal with the crisis in any way that they thought fit ; and the rump of the Labour Party found itself involved in a General Election against the combined Conservative and Liberal machines, and with its own most prominent leaders taking part against it in the name of " National " solidarity.

READ THIS ↓

What did the Labour Government of 1929-1931 actually achieve? Its legislative record, considering that it had no majority in the House of Commons and had to face a good deal of obstruction by the overwhelmingly Conservative House of Lords, would have been fair, if it had been dealing with an ordinary situation. But it was not, and it never succeeded in adapting itself to the sharp change which came over the economic position of Great Britain between its assumption of office and its fall. Thus, it began by improving very considerably the conditions for the receipt of unemployment benefit, by sweeping away the rules which had allowed the preceding Government to disqualify many thousands on the ground that they were not genuinely seeking work; and then it was forced into passing measures for disqualifying other applicants under pressure of the demand for "national economy." It started little "public works" schemes that might have looked respectable if unemployment had not increased so fast as to render them merely insignificant. It passed a Coal Mines Act which reduced the length of the miners' shift from eight hours to seven and a half, and set up a scheme for the regulation of coal output and marketing that might have worked tolerably well if the world depression had not speedily converted it into a plan for restricting output and for maintaining prices. It passed an important Housing and Town Planning Act which led to considerable achievements in slum-clearance—but had this effect only after its fall from office. It made a beginning with the regulation of Road Transport under the Transport Act of 1930; and it put on the statute book a Land Utilisation Act for land settlement and an Agricultural Marketing Act which laid the foundations for a new policy of development of food production and marketing on a more rational basis. It also extended the scope of the contributory old age pensions introduced by the Conservatives in 1925, and carried through a number of other secondary social reforms.

In addition to these internal measures, the Labour Government passed a Colonial Development Act which was the beginning of a new economic attitude towards the colonies. But its most important achievements were in the field of international policy. It signed both the Optional Clause of the Covenant of the League of Nations, providing for the reference of all international disputes of a justiciable character to the Hague Court, and the General Act, which bound Great Britain to refer non-justiciable disputes to international arbitration. It was also largely responsible, through Arthur Henderson and William Graham, for the institution of an International Disarmament Conference and of an attempt to secure a Tariff Truce—both of which came to shipwreck in face of the world depression and of the rise of Fascism in Europe. It also gave to India the first definite promise of self-government (though not of full independence) and made an endeavour to settle the Indian problem at the abortive Round Table Conference. The excellence of Arthur Henderson's work as Foreign

Secretary won general praise ; and so, for the time and with much less cause, did Philip Snowden's activities in furtherance of yet another " settlement " of the question of German Reparations—the so-called " Young Plan." But this settlement, like most of the Government's international work, was speedily swept away by the European crisis of the ensuing years.

BOOKS

G. D. H. Cole.   *History of the Labour Party from 1914.*
G. D. H. Cole and R. Postgate.   *The Common People, 1746–1946.*
A. Hutt.   *Post-war History of the British Working Class.*
M. A. Hamilton.   *Arthur Henderson.*
J. McNeil Weir.   *The Tragedy of Ramsay MacDonald.*
P. Snowden.   *Autobiography.*
A. Fenner Brockway.   *Socialism over Sixty Years : Jowett of Bradford.*
Labour Party Reports, 1929–1931.
G. D. H. Cole and E. Bevin.   *The Crisis* (in Cole, *Economic Tracts for the Times*).
G. D. H. Cole.   *The Intelligent Man's Guide Through World Chaos.*

3. THE GENERAL ELECTION OF 1931 AND THE ECONOMIC CRISIS

The result of the General Election of 1931 was a foregone conclusion. Although the great majority of the Labour Cabinet, despite their previous acquiescence in MacDonald's policy, broke with him when the final test came and remained faithful to the Labour Party, even the faithful were in no position to give their followers any effective lead.   Nevertheless, despite a big defection among the marginal electors, the great majority of organised Labour voters in the constituencies also refused to be diverted from their allegiance.   In many quarters, the refusal to follow MacDonald was much more instinctive than rational.   Even the most moderate Labour men revolted by instinct against cutting down unemployment benefits and public wages and salaries, and still more against doing any of these things in alliance with the Conservative Party.   But, despite the faithfulness of the great majority of organised Labour voters, there were not many constituencies in which the Labour Party's bewildered following remained strong enough to return a Labour M.P.   If it had not been for the mining areas, and for a few other districts such as the East End of London, Labour representation in Parliament would have been almost completely swept away. As it was, the Labour Party, which had held 287 seats in the Parliament elected in 1929, sank to 52 in the new Parliament of 1931—a mere handful, which included, with the exception of George Lansbury, not a single member of the outgoing Labour Cabinet.   Even in the industrial areas, which were supposed to be Labour strongholds, " National " candidates were for the most part returned.   The Labour Party held the votes of convinced Socialists and of the majority of active Trade Unionists ; but it lost an enormous proportion of those lukewarm supporters who, under ordinary circumstances, would almost by instinct have voted Labour. The entire floating vote was cast for the " National " candidates, and the new " National " Government, formed on the morrow of the election, promptly interpreted its " Doctor's Mandate " as giving it a right to introduce a thorough-going policy of tariff reform, even though the case for an emergency tariff had practically disappeared with the abandonment of the Gold Standard. In all essentials the new "National" Government was simply Conservative, though it retained for the time being the official support of the Liberal Party as well as of the in-significant " National Labour " group which had followed MacDonald. Presently, in 1932, the Samuelite Liberals seceded, for they could not quite swallow the new protectionism insisted on by the Tories, who were in complete command of the political situation. On the other hand, the Simonite Liberals, Tories in all but name, and the " National Labour " rag-tag and bobtail remained within the Government, relying for a place in the sun on the continuance of the Tory necessity for camouflaging Conservatism as " National Coalition."

In the General Election of 1931 the Labour Party was at a hopeless dis-advantage, not only because it had been deserted by its best-known leaders, but even more because those who remained within its ranks had very little notion what to say. After all, they had to acknowledge their share in the policy which appeared to have got Great Britain into so terrible a mess, and as most of them had no clear understanding of what had really been happening, and very little idea of any alternative policy, they were greatly at a loss when they were called upon to explain to the electors either their attitude to the past, or their intentions for the future. On the Labour side the election of 1931 was essentially a " soldiers' battle." Each man said what he thought about the crisis, and there was little agreement between one man and another. The leaders were largely engaged in trying to explain away the Labour Government's failure, and in denouncing the treason of Ramsay MacDonald and his associates ; while the " rank-and-file " orators spent most of their time in abusing the financiers and in denouncing the fall of the Labour Government as the outcome of a sinister " bankers' conspiracy " stirred up by Montagu Norman, the presiding genius of the Bank of England, in collusion with the City of London and the leading financiers of the United States.

With the large body of " floating voters " these denunciations and self-exculpations cut no electoral ice. Except to convinced Socialists or to voters swayed powerfully by a sense of working-class solidarity, it seemed plain that the Labour Government had got things into a very bad mess and that there was no reason for supposing that the Labour leadership, deprived of the services of MacDonald, Thomas and Snowden—who, with Arthur Henderson, were the leaders most in the public eye—would be at all likely to do better if it were given a further chance. On the " National " side, propaganda was directed almost exclusively to making the electors afraid—to arousing in them the fear that, if they voted Labour, their savings would be swept away in the general collapse of financial confidence, their employment lost, or at best their wages drastically curtailed with the breakdown of industry, even their homes snatched from them by a predatory Government ready to adopt any method of confiscation in order to save itself from disaster. Philip Snowden especially distinguished himself by the virulence of his attacks on his former colleagues and by the unscrupulousness with which he appealed to the fears of the voters. It was no wonder that the election was ignominiously lost ; for not even the best leadership in the world could under the circumstances have saved Labour from defeat, and in 1931 Labour went into the fight virtually without any leadership at all.

In 1932, while the Conservatives were triumphantly bringing in their general tariff on imports and imposing on the unemployed the Means Test which had so consistently been urged on the Labour Government before its fall, Labour supporters throughout the country were taking stock of the situation and trying to measure the real extent and significance of Labour's defeat. There were, at this stage, two rival currents of opinion within the Party. One group, including most of the remaining leaders, continued to believe that the policy followed by the late Labour Government had been, in general, right, and that the Party had fallen a victim to sheer misfortune, occasioned partly by the world-slump and partly by the ·" treason " of Ramsay MacDonald. Most of the leaders who remained faithful to the Labour Party in 1931 had been parties to the policy of MacDonald and Snowden—or rather to the want of policy—that had led up to the political crisis. These leaders now wished the Party to carry on with its existing policy, making it more precise and working out in more impressive detail plans in readiness for the advent of the next Labour Government. They were prepared, in deference to the strong feeling which existed among its supporters, to admit that the late Labour Government had not done in all respects all that it might have done, and that an incoming Government would need to proceed at a somewhat less leisurely pace with the work of social reform and socialisation. Rightly they took credit for the excellent work which Arthur Henderson had done in foreign affairs ; in home affairs they were inclined to blame the deficiency of the Government's achievements on its lack of a clear majority in the House of Commons, on the mutilation of its measures in the House of Lords, and on the dilatory tactics of its former leader. But the new policy which they proposed was in essence identical with the old. The only real difference was to be that, the next time, Labour would really *do* the things which it promised.

As against this view, another section urged strongly that the Labour Party needed a radically different policy. The experience of the years 1929-1931 was held to have demonstrated the failure of " gradualism," and to have shown conclusively that the Party would remain impotent to carry through even moderate measures of social reform until it had stormed the strongholds of Capitalism and thus taken the key-points of finance and industry into its hands.

For the time being, the controversy between these two schools of thought came to centre largely round the question of the joint stock banks. Those who took the second view argued strongly that it would be impossible for an incoming Labour Government to stand up against the obstruction of the financial interests unless the joint stock banks, as well as the Bank of England, were immediately socialised, so that they could be used as instruments of a Socialist economic policy. As against this view, the gradualists argued that any announcement of the Party's intention to socialise the joint stock banks would seriously prejudice its chances of securing power, and that, if it went to the country with such a policy and won the election, the first effect would be to cause a financial panic which would wreck its chances of pursuing any ordered programme of social reform and would in all probability provoke immediately a major economic crisis.

In 1932 this question was fought out at the Labour Party's Annual Conference at Leicester, and the victory went temporarily to those who advocated the more radical policy. This was largely because many of the big Trade Unions, notably the miners and railwaymen, were bitterly resentful of the part which the financiers had played in destroying the Labour Government. But, despite the voting, most of the Labour Party leaders were not convinced, and effective power in the Party remained in the hands of men who continued to believe in the more gradualist policy.

Meantime, there had been a second split in the ranks of the Labour Party—or a third, if Sir Oswald Mosley's secession early in 1931 be counted as the first. For some time before the fall of Ramsay MacDonald's Government in 1931 the Independent Labour Party, headed by James Maxton, had been exceedingly critical of the Government's actions, especially of its treatment of the unemployed. In the General Election of 1931 the I.L.P. candidates fought virtually as an independent Party, and early in 1932, after abortive negotiations with the Labour Party leaders, the I.L.P. formally disaffiliated from the Labour Party. This secession in its turn provoked a split in the ranks of the I.L.P. itself; and the section which desired to remain inside the Labour Party, headed by E. F. Wise and Patrick Dollan, joined forces with the Society for Socialist Inquiry and Propaganda—founded a few years previously by a group including Ernest Bevin, Sir Stafford Cripps and the present writer as a planning and propagandist body designed to work out the constructive policy which the Labour Government seemed so sadly to lack. These two groups (but without Ernest Bevin) formed the Socialist League as an affiliated organisation representing definitely Socialist opinion within the Labour Party.

During the next two years economic depression remained severe, and it became perfectly plain that there existed in the depressed areas a large mass of able-bodied workers for whom there was no prospect at all of re-employment at their old trades. The Labour Party in the House of Commons was constantly pressing the Government to take some action for the restoration of the depressed areas, and from time to time it was reinforced by members of the other parties, including Conservatives who had captured seats in districts where unemployment was severe. At the same time the unemployed themselves were beginning to reorganise, largely under the leadership of members of the Communist Party, in the National Unemployed Workers' Movement, with Wal Hannington of the Amalgamated Engineering Union as its principal organiser, and there were hunger marches and unemployed demonstrations, organised chiefly by the N.U.W.M. and frowned upon by the official Trade Union and Labour leadership on the ground that they were conducted under Communist influence. The administration of the Means Test introduced by the National Government caused widespread dissatisfaction and resentment ; and there were numerous local protest movements and deputations and demonstrations directed to the local relief authorities. These sometimes led to violence, when they were broken up by the police.

Meanwhile the Government was engaged in preparing for a reorganisation of the system of unemployment relief. Acting on the advice of the Unemployment Insurance Commission, which had been set up by the Labour Government, the National Government proceeded in 1934 to confine benefit under the unemployment insurance system within limits designed to secure the actuarial soundness of the Unemployment Fund. This involved restricting benefits to a limited period of weeks, depending on the number of qualifying contributions previously paid by the recipient. It therefore excluded from the unemployment insurance system a number of workers who had previously been in receipt of what were called " transitional benefits" which had been administered since 1932 subject to a Means Test. In order to deal with these cases there was set up in 1934 an Unemployment Assistance Board, to be financed entirely from national funds and to act independently of day-to-day Parliamentary control. This Board proceeded to announce a new scale of payments under the Means Test which was to come into force near the beginning of 1935.

The new scales proposed by the U.A.B. would have involved severe curtailment in many cases of the incomes paid to the unemployed—especially in the mining areas. In other areas in which the Means Test had been more stringently administered these payments would have been to some extent increased ; but there arose, above all in the mining centres, so great a storm of protest against the U.A.B. scales that the Government was compelled to withdraw the scheme, and to substitute for it a transitional scheme under which workers eligible for unemployment assistance were to receive for the time being either payments according to the new scales or their own old transitional rates of benefit, whichever were the higher. This concession sufficed for the moment to damp down the unrest, and when after a long delay the Unemployment Assistance Board ultimately produced a revised scale of benefits it was found that the hardships involved in the Means Test had been appreciably relaxed, although the vicious principle of reckoning family earnings as a unit in calculating the need for relief had not been given up.

Some mention must be made of certain other events of this period in order to estimate the changing situation of the British Labour Movement. In 1934 the London Labour Party was successful, at a time when Labour was making only slow progress elsewhere, in capturing a clear majority on the London County Council; and after three years of Labour rule this majority was held and increased at the L.C.C. election of 1937. To a large extent Labour's victory in London was due to the discontent which had been engendered by a long period of Conservative rule at County Hall, and had been aggravated by the slow progress made with housing and slum-clearance, and by inhumane operation of public assistance in the London area. In the three years between 1934 and 1937 the London Labour Party, under Herbert Morrison's leadership, was able to make great progress with housing and with the development of hospital services and the improvement of educational facilities, and the Labour L.C.C. also fundamentally reorganised the system of public assistance in London, on lines which appear to have provoked singularly little criticism. Undoubtedly this success, achieved by a moderate Socialist policy in the London area, encouraged the Labour Party nationally in its swing to the right, for the national leaders were disposed to argue that the experience of London showed both that moderation was the key to victory and that a moderate policy could demonstrate its soundness by its practical results. In fact, however, the conditions for local and national political action were widely different; for Labour on the L.C.C. did not have to face the type of capitalist and financial opposition which had wrecked the Labour Government of 1931. Labour's success in the municipal administration of London, which was confirmed by the Party's return to power in the election of 1937, was of great value as a demonstration of efficiency, but it provided no real clue to the problems of national Labour policy.

While these events were proceeding at home the entire situation of the Labour Movement was being profoundly altered by occurrences abroad. Up to 1932 there seemed to be some hope of European appeasement, for under pressure of the crisis the fantastic demands of the Allies for reparations were in practice being given up, and though the Disarmament Conference was making no appreciable progress and the negotiations for a Tariff Truce had definitely broken down, hope was still entertained that in the end at least some measure of disarmament would be agreed upon—to the accompaniment of some attempt to remove German grievances and to bring about a revival of international trade by means of lower tariffs and closer international economic co-operation.

By 1932 the world slump had swept these hopes away. In that year the successful Japanese aggression in Manchuria seriously undermined the prestige of the League of Nations and made it plain that the Great Powers within the League were not prepared to take seriously their obligation to come to the assistance of a nation which was the victim of wanton attack. Meanwhile, in Germany, the deepening of the economic crisis, and the failure of successive democratic Governments to take any effective measures for dealing with it, brought nearer and nearer the victory of the Nazi Storm-Troopers, which was finally consummated in 1933. Thereafter, there existed in Europe two Great Powers which openly proclaimed their allegiance to the gospel of force and their determination to build up for themselves empires by conquest even in open defiance of international obligations into which they had solemnly entered. Until Germany went Fascist, Italy was not strong enough to embark on any major adventures. But the Nazi victory in Germany, combined with Japan's demonstration of the League's impotence in the Far East, speedily encouraged Mussolini to lay his plans for the war of aggression upon Abyssinia which was finally launched in 1935.

BOOKS

G. D. H. Cole. *History of the Labour Party from 1914.*
Labour Party Reports, 1932 and subsequent years.
G. D. H. Cole. *The Intelligent Man's Guide through World Chaos.*
G. D. H. and M. Cole. *The Condition of Britain* (1937).
P. Snowden. *Autobiography.*
A. Fenner Brockway. *Socialism over Sixty Years : Jowett of Bradford.*
A. Hutt. *Post-war History of the British Working Class.*
W. Hannington. *Unemployed Struggles.*
W. Hannington. *The Lean Years.*
R. Sinclair. *Metropolitan Man.*
H. Dalton. *Practical Socialism for Britain.*

4. TRADE UNIONISM IN THE WORLD DEPRESSION

Meanwhile, what of the Trade Union Movement? The difficulties which beset the Trade Unions before the struggle of 1926 by no means grew less during the following years. They were indeed greatly increased by the world slump. They were not, however, mainly the product of the slump, nor would they have disappeared automatically even if world trade had entered upon a new period of prosperity and if Great Britain had shared to the full in the benefits of economic recovery. They would, of course, have grown less under these conditions, and the Trade Unions would have been able again to win victories and to face the prospect of strikes or lock-outs without dismay. But there were forces inimical to Trade Unionism and calling for substantial adaptation in its structure and policy even before the world slump. Although the slump added to the menace of these forces, they would have persisted even if economic conditions after 1929 had gone on improving instead of getting dramatically worse.

As things were, Trade Union membership continued to fall until 1933, for even when the effects of the General Strike had worn off the world depression paralysed Trade Union activity and caused many lukewarm members to drop out of the Unions. Nor was the movement successful, during the years of depression, in organising the workers in the new industries, located chiefly in the South of England, which were expanding even in face of the general economic slump. But by about 1935 the Trade Union tide began to turn. In that year the Trades Union Congress was able to record a small increase in membership ; and in the following year membership rose more sharply and in many areas a beginning was made with the organisation of workers in the newer industries and in the distributive trades, which had been rapidly increasing their working personnel. At the same time activity in the older industries began to revive, and by the early months of 1937 there were all the symptoms of developing labour unrest. This was partly due to the steady upward tendency of prices, which was the inevitable outcome of the high protective policy adopted by the National Government and of the support given by the Government to producers' combines designed to maintain prices at a level adequately " remunerative " from the standpoint of the profit-makers. But the unrest was due even more to a sense that the depression was not merely over, but had passed into what was in reality a boom, despite the persistence of unemployment at a high level in the depressed areas. The workers were beginning to feel that, unless they took action immediately to secure improved wages and shorter working hours, their opportunity would very likely be gone ; for already economists were beginning to speak of the imminence of a new recession, as soon as the intensive building and equipment of new factories for purposes of re-armament had passed its peak.

Actually, there was a recession after the relatively high industrial activity of 1937, and even increased re-armament activity in 1938-1939 did not quite restore conditions to the level reached in 1937. Thanks, however, to these activities, the recession was much less severe than it would otherwise have been, and the recovery of Trade Unionism continued at a slow pace up to the outbreak of war in 1939. Right through these years the Trade Union movement retained its essentially pacific policy. Strikes and lock-outs were few, and for the most part small, and the Trade Union leaders gave them little encouragement. The strikes which did occur were in a number of cases unofficial, and in some cases they involved a breach of agreements entered into by the Trade Union officials with the employers. The Trade Union leaders accused the Communists of stirring up these strikes with an

entire disregard for the necessary conditions of orderly collective bargaining :
how, it was argued, could Trade Unionists who were not prepared to honour
agreements made on their behalf expect employers not to retaliate in kind ?
Under these conditions the wave of strikes positively intensified anti-Communist feeling among the Trade Union leaders, and made them more determined than ever to set their faces firmly against any proposal for a " United
Front." Troubles of this sort came to a head in the London Omnibus Strike
of 1937, when the Transport and General Workers' Union, under Ernest
Bevin's leadership, after giving the Central Bus Committee of the Union full
power to conduct the dispute, recalled this power and ordered the men back
to work, and subsequently signed an agreement on their behalf without
consulting them. This settlement included minor concessions to the busmen,
but did not meet their major demand for the forty-hour working week.
In addition, the Transport Workers' Executive suspended the Central Bus
Committee and the local Bus Committees of the Union from office, on the
plea that they had fallen under the influence of " unofficial " (i.e. Communist)
bodies, and set on foot an enquiry into the activities of the unofficial movements among the omnibus workers. The battle between official Trade
Unionism and the " Left Wing " was thus definitely joined, with consequences which were bound to extend far beyond the immediate matters in
dispute. It was not, however, possible, in the circumstances of 1937, to
check the growth of labour unrest, whatever Trade Union leaders might say.
Profits were obviously rising fast, and wages lagging behind ; and then, if
ever, the chance existed of bringing about that reduction in normal working
hours which seemed to be the next economic objective for the working-
class movement.

BOOKS

G. D. H. Cole. British Trade Unionism To-day (1939).
N. Barou. British Trade Unions (1947).
A. Hutt. Post-war History of the British Working Class.
Trades Union Congress Reports, 1931 and subsequent years.

5. FASCISM AND WAR PREPARATION

While the Fascist menace was growing in Europe the swing of opinion
in Great Britain was undoubtedly in the direction of a policy of peace and
reconciliation. This was abundantly shown by the remarkable results of the
Peace Ballot, organised by the League of Nations Union in the early months
of 1935. In this ballot the League of Nations Union was able to secure a vote
of over 11,500,000 persons, of whom over 11,000,000 voted in favour of
continued British membership of the League of Nations, and nearly 10,500,000
in favour of all-round disarmament and the abolition of the private manufacture of arms. At the same time over 10,000,000 persons voted for the use

of economic sanctions against any nation guilty of aggression, over 9,500,000 in favour of the total abolition of military aircraft, and over 6,750,000 in favour of military sanctions against an aggressor. The much smaller majority in favour of military sanctions was significant of the fact that the true implications of the Nazi menace in Europe had not yet been generally appreciated.

As the immediate sequel to the Peace Ballot, Great Britain, in common with other countries, was compelled to take up an attitude towards the wanton aggression of Italy in Abyssinia. Under strong pressure from public opinion the Government reluctantly embarked upon a half-hearted policy of economic sanctions, in the hope that Mussolini might be induced to accept some sort of compromise. But sanctions were never pushed to the point of interfering seriously with Italy's conduct of the war ; for no attempt was made to cut off supplies of essential materials such as oil, or to stop war supplies for the Italian Armies by closing the Suez Canal. The Government, in effect, was not prepared to take, against the aggressor, any action which involved even the smallest risk of war. In these circumstances the policy of economic sanctions was of course bound to fail ; and it is plain that from the first the British Government was fully prepared to acquiesce in an Italian conquest of a large part of Abyssinia, provided only that British interests were safeguarded and the British Government was enabled to save its face. In the event, the Government's pusillanimity did not allow it to do either of these things. Italy conquered Abyssinia in defiance of the League ; and Fascist aggression received a fatal encouragement, the results of which were speedily made plain in the help given by Germany and Italy to the Fascist rebels in Spain.

In the midst of the Abyssinian crisis a General Election was held in Great Britain—under circumstances highly favourable to the Conservative Party. MacDonald, though he remained in the Cabinet, was superseded as Prime Minister by Stanley Baldwin in June 1935 ; for the Conservatives, having consolidated their position with MacDonald's aid, were no longer prepared to serve under a non-Conservative leader. In the General Election of November, 1935, the Labour Party naturally recovered some of the ground which it had lost in the crisis of 1931. It returned to Parliament with 154 seats, as against 60 in the old Parliament at the time of the dissolution. But the " National " Government, with 433 seats, as against 517 in the old Parliament, still retained an enormous majority. It is true that these figures greatly exaggerate the disparity in the actual voting ; but, even so, the Government parties, with 11,800,000 votes, had a clear majority of over 1,750,000 against all the Opposition parties combined, and a majority of 3,500,000 against Labour alone. Labour failed, in fact, to get back at all nearly to the position which it had reached in 1929 ; and a large number of predominantly working-class industrial constituencies again returned

" National " candidates. It was not easy to wipe out the stigma of inferiority which had been set upon the Labour Party by the ignominious collapse of 1931.

Before the General Election death and resignation had deprived the Labour Party of the two best-known among its remaining leaders. Arthur Henderson died in October, 1935, after devoting his last years to an unavailing struggle to keep the cause of disarmament alive in face of the rising menace of European war. George Lansbury, who had led the Party since 1931, resigned the leadership in the same month on account of his disagreement with his colleagues on the questions of war and re-armament—for in the new crisis he followed a completely pacifist attitude. Clement Attlee succeeded him as leader, but the Party found great difficulty in clearing its own mind upon the urgent international issues which it was called upon to face. It wanted on the one hand to stand for peace and disarmament, and on the other not to leave European democracy defenceless in face of the aggressiveness of the Fascist Powers. The result was a compromise capable of being differently interpreted by various spokesmen of the Party ; but in practice Labour, both in and out of Parliament, gave qualified support to the campaign for intensified re-armament launched by the National Government on the morrow of the General Election of 1935.

At the election itself there was a good deal of confusion. The Government candidates appeared in the constituencies as staunch supporters of the League, demanding that the nation should be given the means of implementing to the full its commitments under the League Covenant, and of applying effective pressure to Italy and to any future aggressor. But as soon as the election was over these pretences were cast aside, and the Government set out upon a policy of half-hearted re-armament based, not on any system of pooled security with other democratic countries, but rather on an attempt at isolation of the British Empire with a view to armed neutrality in the European conflict. At the election Baldwin had promised that there would be no extensive re-armament—only a filling up of such gaps as existed in the national defences. But the election victory was complete enough for these pledges, which had indeed never been seriously meant, to be promptly set aside. Italy was allowed to complete the conquest of Abyssinia without further molestation, and when in 1936 the Fascist Powers openly fomented armed rebellion in Spain, Great Britain speedily made it plain to France that the French Government of M. Léon Blum and the *Front Populaire* could expect no help if it allowed itself to become embroiled with Germany and Italy by going to the help of the Spanish Republican Government.

Before this, the growing menace of European Fascism had forced the Soviet Union into the League of Nations and had induced France to enter into a Pact of mutual assistance with the Soviet Union. The changed international situation involved, in effect, a profound revision of Communist tactics throughout Europe. Prior to the Nazi victory in Germany and to the threat to European peace which followed upon its consolidation, the Communist Parties in the various countries, including Great Britain, had based their strategy chiefly on an attempt to stir up revolutionary feeling among the workers and to detach them as far as possible from their "reactionary" leaders. In Great Britain the Communist Party had throughout expressed its desire for "unity" of working-class forces, and had from time to time sought admission to the Labour Party as an affiliated body. But it had combined this propaganda of unity with unsparing denunciation of the orthodox Labour leaders and had endeavoured to build up wherever it could rank-and-file movements inside the Trade Unions and among the unemployed in opposition to the official elements.

With the adhesion of the Soviet Union to the League of Nations and the conclusion of the Franco-Soviet Pact, the immediate strategy of the Communist Party underwent a change ; for the Communists both in Russia and elsewhere had ample cause to fear the Fascist menace, and the Soviet Union was intensely desirous of being left at peace to pursue the colossal tasks of Socialist construction upon which it was engaged. In the circumstances of the years following the Fascist victory in Germany it came more and more to seem to the Communists that the primary task for the time being was not the stirring up of Socialist revolution in the countries of Western Europe, but rather the defence of peace and of democratic or partly democratic institutions, wherever they existed, against Fascist aggression. This change of attitude gave a new meaning to the Communist slogan of the "United Front."

The Trade Union and Labour Party leaders, on the other hand, were no more prepared to accept the Communists under the new conditions than they had been before. Between 1932 and 1935 the Labour Party had been moving back steadily towards the position which it had occupied before the crisis of 1931. Its leaders had become convinced that their chance of winning a majority of the electorate depended on their offering to the country an essentially moderate policy which would not involve any risk of economic dislocation or allow their opponents to play effectively upon the electors' fears. With this end in view, they were determined to dissociate themselves from the Communists, and this determination was reinforced by the strongly anti-Communist attitude of the Trade Union leaders, who resented Communist attempts to stir up rank-and-file agitation inside the Trade Unions and to provoke strikes which the leaders maintained were bound to upset the orderly processes of collective bargaining. The figures of strikes, however, sufficed to show that this policy produced no very considerable effects. A rise in strike activity during the year 1937 was due much more to improved economic conditions than to any specific Communist agitation, and after 1937 the figures of strikes again fell off sharply[1]. Nevertheless, the Labour Party continued to pursue a policy of vendetta against the Communists, and against any Local Labour Parties which ventured to give practical support to the policy of the United Front.

These troubles came to a head in 1937, with the launching of a joint campaign for "working-class unity" by the Communist Party, the Independent Labour Party and the Socialist League, on the basis of an appeal for immediate working-class action against the Means Test, for improved wages and shorter working hours, and against the National Government's policy of re-armament. The Labour Party Executive at once threatened with expulsion from the Party all who participated in this "Unity Campaign," and when the Socialist League refused to call off the campaign it was formally disaffiliated. Thereupon the Socialist League decided, pending the result of an appeal against the Executive to the Labour Party Conference, to dissolve ; but its leading members announced their intention of persisting as individuals with the Unity Campaign in open defiance of the Executive's prohibition. A little later, however, it was decided to suspend joint meetings for the time being, pending an appeal to the Labour Party Conference, while continuing to agitate for unity from separate platforms. This was done in order to meet the Labour Party Executive's threat to expel members who ventured to appear on the same platform with Communist speakers.

From 1937 onwards the Spanish question came more and more to occupy the key place in the controversy which centred round the issues of the "United Front" or the "Popular Front." These two phrases were used with a variety of meanings ; but in general the "United Front" came to be the slogan of the Communists and of a section of the Labour "Left Wing," and to mean unity of the working classes in the fight against Fascism and Capitalism. "Popular Front," on the other hand, was the phrase favoured by those who, while they favoured working-class unity, wished to create against the Government and against Fascism a combination of forces wide enough to include the more progressive Liberals and even such "progressive Conservatives" as were prepared to join in condemnation of the Chamberlain Government's policy. Both these groups demanded more active help for the Spanish Republican Government, and a repudiation of the policy of "non-intervention," which was in practice allowing the German and Italian Fascists to intervene as much as they pleased.

At one point, the policy of the "Popular Front" secured the endorsement of the Co-operative Party ; but this attitude was repudiated by the Co-operative Congress, with which the final authority remained. The Labour Party Executive kept up a steady opposition to both the "United" and the "Popular Front" agitations, treating both as Communist devices to enter into the control of the Labour Movement by a back door. As the defeat

---

[1] For the actual figures, see Table 13 on p. 484.

of the Spanish Republican Government came to be realised as inevitable, and as the inadequacy of the help that could be rendered by the supply of medical aid and by the small and ill-equipped International Brigade that fought in Spain in face of all the obstacles was fully seen, there was bitter disappointment among British Socialists, and the attitude of the official leadership was widely criticised. But the crisis was fast spreading out to become worldwide; and the "Munich surrender" of 1938 presently re-united the membership of the Labour Party in hostility to the Government's policy, but did not bring about any change in the leaders' hostility to collaboration with the Communist Party. The dissolution of the Socialist League and the expulsion of Sir Stafford Cripps and of other advocates of the unity movement had left the opposition forces inside the Labour Party scattered and leaderless; and after "Munich" the "United" and "Popular Front" agitations died away as the official Labour Movement took up a more definite anti-Fascist and anti-Government line.

BOOKS

G. D. H. Cole. *History of the Labour Party from 1914.*
G. D. H. Cole and R. Postgate. *The Common People, 1746–1946.*
G. D. H. Cole. *The People's Front.*
G. D. H. Cole. *A Plan for Democratic Britain (1939).*
H. Pollitt. *Serving my Time.*
A. Fenner Brockway. *Socialism over Sixty Years: Jowett of Bradford.*
C. R. Attlee. *The Labour Party in Perspective (1937).*
Labour Party Annual Reports, 1935 and subsequent years.

CHAPTER XI

THE SECOND WORLD WAR AND AFTER

1. The Second World War 2. Trade Unionism in the Second World War
3. The Labour Party in War-time and After

I. THE SECOND WORLD WAR

BRITISH Labour, in general, had been slow in making up its mind to the necessity of fighting Fascism ; but, when its mind had been made up, there was no shaking it. At the outset, on the outbreak of war in 1939, there occurred what would have been, under less tragic circumstances, a curious comedy. For years past, the Communists had been demanding a United Front of the working classes primarily for resistance to Fascism ; and they had been foremost in urging active intervention on the Republican side in the Spanish Civil War, as well as in pressing for a practical policy of collective security under the League of Nations. Yet, when war actually came, the Communist Party suddenly changed front and, obeying the signal from Moscow, began to denounce the War as an "imperialist war," and to demand that it be brought immediately to an end. They even, following the lead given from Moscow, went out of their way to accuse the Western Powers of "aggression" against the Nazis, and to do something (they could not do much) to impede the British war effort. This change of front was not accomplished without loss of "face." Harry Pollitt, then Secretary of the Communist Party of Great Britain, who had been rash (and honest) enough to continue saying when war broke out what he had been saying for years previously, was displaced from his position, and was compelled to recant. Meanwhile, those Labour leaders who had been most hostile to working-class unity before the War became loudest in their denunciations of the Fascist enemy—some of them the more happily, because they could couple these denunciations with anathemas against the Soviet Union for concluding the Soviet-German Pact of August, 1939.

This is not the place for any full discussion of the reasons for the Soviet Union's action. Undoubtedly, the Pact was signed, on the Soviet side, in the belief that the British Government under Neville Chamberlain was unwilling to enter into any effective arrangement for collective security against Nazi aggression and was even eager to induce Hitler to turn his forces against the Soviet Union and to come to terms which would give him a free hand to do this. Over and above this, the leaders of the Soviet Union wanted to gain time, and no doubt expected that the War in the West would be protracted and evenly enough balanced to wear out both sets of antagonists,

so as to leave the Soviet Union in a much stronger relative position. Whatever their motives, and whatever justification they may have found in the
British and French Government's policies in and after the Munich crisis of
1938, the effect of the British Communist Party's sudden change of front in
1939 was greatly to weaken its influence upon the British working class—an
influence which had previously been increasing as a consequence of its attitude
during the Spanish struggle and at the time of the Munich surrender. Communist influence both in the political movement and in the Trade Unions sank
low in 1939 and 1940 ; and the main body of the British workers not only
gave solid support to the war effort, but also rallied behind the leaders of the
Labour Party in a demand that it should be more energetically pursued.

Besides the Communists, some other groups, including what was left
of the Independent Labour Party, also took up an anti-war line, refusing to
support a war waged under capitalist auspices, and demanding a purely
" Workers' Government " ; and there remained a small body of out-and-out
pacifists attached to the Labour Party. But none of these groups commanded
any wide following. There was never, during the second World War, any
anti-war movement nearly equal in size or influence to that which existed
even in 1914—much less to that which developed during the later stages of the
first World War. The overwhelming majority of the British working class
was in no doubt at all about the sheer necessity of final victory over the
Nazis as a very condition of democratic survival.

Nevertheless, as long as the Chamberlain Government remained in power,
no more than half-hearted collaboration in the war effort was even possible,
because the Government itself was only half-hearted in prosecuting the War
and was not prepared to accept the conditions for securing whole-hearted
Labour support. Only with the advent of the Churchill-Labour Coalition
in May, 1940, did the war effort become truly national ; and upon the change
of Government followed almost at once the disasters in Western Europe,
the collapse of France, the evacuation of the British forces from Dunkirk, and
the imminent danger of invasion. The full measure of British unpreparedness became apparent ; and the British working classes followed up
the achievement of the evacuation with an effort of war production
in the factories that abundantly proved their whole-heartedness in the
struggle.

Then followed the greater part of a year during which Hitler was digesting
and extending his conquests in Western and Central Europe without either
attempting the invasion of Great Britain or turning his forces against the
Soviet Union. This was the period of intense air attacks on Great Britain,
of the beginnings of American aid to Great Britain (Lease-Lend), of the fall
of Yugoslavia and of Greece, and, in January, 1941, of the renewal of the
Soviet-German Pact. Then, in June, 1941, came the Nazi invasion of the
Soviet Union, which immediately converted the Communists all over the

world into enthusiastic supporters of the war effort against Germany and of the Resistance Movements in the countries under Nazi occupation. In Great Britain, the Communist Party set to work at once to re-build, especially in the Trade Unions, the influence which it had forfeited in 1939 ; and in this it was, in consideration of its record, remarkably successful—not indeed in making any large number of converts to Communism, but in securing the election of many of its members to positions as shop stewards and as workers' representatives on the Joint Production Committees and similar bodies which were being set up in many of the war factories. In working along these lines, and in endeavouring to stir up a demand for a " Second Front " in the West, in order to relieve the pressure on the Soviet Union, the Communists displayed an energy which soon recovered for them an influence far beyond their number, though politically they made no successful impact on the solid front presented by the Labour Party leadership.

In December, 1941, came the Japanese attack on the American Navy at Pearl Harbour, and the entry of the United States into the European War, which was from that point a World War in the full sense. The effect was to turn Great Britain more than ever into an arsenal for the production of war supplies, and presently into an armed camp for American as well as British forces preparing for the invasion of Europe. An almost wholly united British working class gave itself unsparingly to the war effort, less intense than that of the hectic months after Dunkirk only because the pace then set could by no possibility have been sustained for long. The effort became much better organised, and the Labour Ministers, especially Ernest Bevin at the Ministry of Labour and National Service, Clement Attlee, as Deputy Prime Minister, and Herbert Morrison, first as Minister of Supply and later as Minister of Home Security, rapidly acquired the stature of recognised national leaders. With America in the War, it became possible to divert a greater proportion of man-power into the forces and into the making of munitions, and to draw a larger fraction of civilian supplies from the United States. Compulsory service was extended to women in December, 1941, in conjunction with the raising of the age for compulsory military service for men to 51 ; and " direction of labour " was more and more stringently applied in order to secure the needed workers for the war factories and for other essential services, such as agriculture and mining. Ever-increasing use had to be made of women's labour ; and a stringent process of " concentration " had to be applied to all industries that could be scaled down without damage to the war effort. Exports were ruthlessly sacrificed in face of the shortage of man-power and materials, though it was realised that the effect would be to leave the British economy in an exceedingly dangerous situation when the War ended. The War had to be won at all costs ; and it was already evident that, economically, the costs were bound to be very high. Vast debts were being incurred, not only to the United States, but also to other countries, some, such as India and Canada, within the Empire, but others, such as the Argentine, outside.

Thus it came about that, in 1944, at the height of the war effort, no fewer than 10,250,000 persons, out of a total man-power of 22,000,000, were either in the armed forces or in civil defence or in the industries making munitions of war and military stores—not counting the many more who were engaged in war transport or public utility services, or in the civil service, or making clothing or food or other necessaries for the armed forces. This had been rendered possible by an increase of more than 2,000,000 in the labour force, through increased employment of women and the postponement of retirements by elderly people ; but there had been a fall of nearly 4,000,000 in the total numbers at work in all industries and services except the making of munitions. This fall had been met partly by a decrease of 16 per cent in consumption per head of population, partly by an almost complete cessation of house-building, partly by large-scale disinvestment—i.e. failure to replace obsolete plant, with inevitable repercussions on post-war productive capacity—and partly by borrowing from overseas imports for which there was no current means of paying. It was officially estimated that in 1944 total expenditure, excluding what was secured under Lease-Lend arrangements, amounted to ten per cent. more than total national income, and that this total of 110 could be divided into 53 for war expenditure and 57 for consumption.

So great a diversion of activity to the war effort was bound to involve a tremendous strain, and to make a large call on the endurance and responsiveness of the working population—the more so because the strain had to be borne under conditions of great discomfort due to the black-out, to the need for long and difficult journeys to and from work, to the breaking-up of homes, and, for considerable periods, to intensive air attack. To all these trials the men and women in the industries and services at home stood up with steadfast courage and tenacity ; and, bad as the conditions of work often were and despite the inevitable friction attending the great and constant changes in workshop practices, the number of labour disputes remained astonishingly low. This can be seen by comparing the number of days lost by strikes and lock-outs in the first and second World Wars.

NUMBER OF WORKING DAYS LOST BY LABOUR DISPUTES
(thousands)

1915	2,969	1940	940
1916	2,367	1941	1,080
1917	5,865	1942	1,530
1918	5,892	1943	1,810
		1944	3,710

Only in 1944, largely on account of an accumulation of grievances in the coal-mining industry, did the loss in working days rise above 2,000,000, which, for a working force of at least 16,000,000, would represent an average loss of one-eighth of one day for each person.

BOOKS

G. D. H. Cole.   *History of the Labour Party from 1914.*
N. Barou.   *The British Trade Unions.*
National Income and Expenditure of the United Kingdom, 1938-1945.   (White Paper.)
Statistics Relating to the War Effort of the United Kingdom, 1944.   (White Paper.)
Ministry of Labour Gazette (monthly).
The Times.   British War Production, 1939-1945.

2. TRADE UNIONISM IN THE SECOND WORLD WAR

The Trade Unions entered the second World War with an aggregate membership of rather over 6,000,000, of whom about 4,750,000 were affiliated to the Trades Union Congress. Those outside the Congress included the Post Office and Civil Service Unions, which had been forbidden to retain their affiliation by the Trade Union Act of 1927, the Local Government Officers' and Teachers' Associations, a number of Scottish Unions connected with the Scottish Trades Union Congress, some purely local societies, and a few professional associations officially classified as Trade Unions. The Trades Union Congress in effect represented the overwhelming mass of the organised workers. By the end of 1944 total Trade Union membership had risen to more than 8,000,000, and of these over 6,500,000 —roughly the same groups as in 1939 being outside—belonged to the T.U.C. Total membership had actually exceeded 8,100,000 in 1943, but was already beginning to fall a little before the end of 1944 owing to the increased numbers in the armed forces.

Even at 8,000,000 the Trade Unions included only about half the total man-power outside the forces, including employers, farmers and professionals of every sort as well as wage-earners. Their strength was, however, immensely greater in the essential industries, and the relative numbers in different Trade Unions were naturally much affected by the great war-time changes in occupational distribution. The number of women Trade Unionists nearly doubled between 1938 and 1944, from 925,000 to 1,805,000 ; but even so women remained very much less fully organised than male workers. The greatest increases in membership occurred in the Amalgamated Engineering Union, which set out for the first time to organise women as well as men, and in the two big " general " Unions—the Transport and General Workers and the General and Municipal Workers. By 1946 the Transport and General Workers' Union, with 975,000 members, was much the largest Union : next came the A.E.U., with 704,000, and then the National

Union of General and Municipal Workers, with 605,000. The National Union of Mineworkers, consolidated into a single Union in place of the old Federation, followed, with 533,000. The National Union of Railwaymen had 410,000, and the National Union of Distributive and Allied Workers 275,000. Moreover, the N.U.D.A.W. was in process of amalgamating with the Shop Assistants' Union (101,000), to form the National Union of Shop, Distributive and Allied Workers. Six other Unions—the Amalgamated Society of Woodworkers, the Electrical Trades Union, the National Union of Tailors and Garment Workers, the National Union of Public Employees, the Civil Service Clerical Association, and the Union of Post Office Workers, exceeded 100,000 members; and eleven others exceeded 50,000. These twenty-four, soon to be twenty-three, Trade Unions had a combined membership of well over 5,000,000.

It is a noteworthy fact that not a single Union of textile workers was among those with more than 100,000 members, and only two exceeded 50,000. The once-powerful Weavers' Amalgamation, which a quarter of a century earlier had over 200,000 members, had shrunk to 73,000. As against this, there had been sharp increases among civil servants and public employees generally and, on a smaller scale, among many groups of non-manual workers. But the greatest rise in all had occurred among the highly miscellaneous groups enrolled in the two vast general Unions. Some part of this growth was doubtless temporary, and was destined to disappear with the final liquidation of the war industries. But the growth itself had been very noticeable for a long time before 1939, and was significant of the shift from the old basic industries to a widely diversified range of new manufacturing trades.

The second World War, like the first, involved very great changes in labour organisation, the suspension of Trade Union rules and customs on a large scale, the introduction of women into countless jobs normally done by men, and the utmost practicable dilution of that highly scarce factor of production—skilled labour. As in 1915, these changes were made under general agreements concluded with the Trade Unions, and under promise that suspended rules and practices should be restored, if restoration were desired, when the War was over. But the entire process of dilution and substitution of labour was carried through with very much less friction than on the previous occasion, because, at any rate from the crisis of 1940, the Trade Unionists in the workshops, as well as their leaders, were eager to help on any changes that they believed would contribute towards winning the War. Moreover, the technical changes of the years between 1914 and 1939 had already done a good deal towards breaking down the old craft systems, and women's labour in the engineering and kindred industries was no longer the novelty that it had been. From the establishment of the Coalition

Government in 1940 the Trade Unions and employers' associations were brought into close consultation at every stage ; and, what was perhaps even more effective, large numbers of local Trade Union leaders and officials were brought into the service of the Government under the auspices of the Ministry of Labour and of the other departments concerned with war production.

Under the new conditions, the shop stewards rapidly reappeared as an important factor in most of the larger establishments.   But the shop stewards' movement of the second World War was in many respects quite unlike its predecessor.   It showed no tendency to develop into a movement of revolt against the Trade Unions—much less into an anti-war movement preaching a revolutionary gospel.   Even though Communists were before long playing a very active part in it, they were for the most part no more disposed than their fellow-workers to stand in the way of the desperate defence measures of 1940 ; and from 1941 they were, as we have seen, most ardent of all in insisting that everything must be subordinated to the war effort. Moreover, the Trade Unions had learnt, by 1940, the wisdom of recognising and seeking to control the shop stewards' organisations instead of making enemies of them ; and there were many fewer unofficial and unrecognised stewards than there had been between 1914 and 1918.

Side by side with the shop stewards' committees there developed, in the major war factories, the Joint Production Committees representing both management and workers.   These bodies were in practice widely different from factory to factory, and met with widely different degrees of success. Their function was not to settle disputes or to act as disciplinary agencies— though attempts were made to use them for these purposes—but to provide for joint consultation upon the best means in each factory (and later in each district, when they were set up on a wider basis) of securing increased output and of minimising friction arising out of war conditions of employment. In general, where managements were willing to make the most of them, they met with considerable success : where, on the other hand, the managements were reluctant to agree to consultation before action, they failed, as they were bound to fail, and output usually suffered.   The Government was somewhat slow to recognise the value of this machinery, and many employers were slower still.   But it made its way gradually, and in general it worked best where the management was favourable and where the closest links existed between the shop stewards' committees in an establishment and the J.P.C.

Of course, the background of this development of the machinery of joint consultation was the scarcity of labour and the imperative need to make the most of such labour as there was.   This scarcity rendered necessary much more stringent measures of compulsion than had been applied between 1914 and 1918.   The conscription of women, for industry as well as for the auxiliary forces, was one great difference ; and in addition drastic powers were taken under the Restriction of Engagements Orders to prevent employers from misusing man-power and under the system of Direction of Labour to compel workers to go where they were needed. Individual workers were specifically directed to particular jobs ; and it became unlawful under the Essential Works Orders for many types of workers to leave the industries in which they were employed, even where some freedom of movement within an industry was allowed. In return for these onerous bindings, it became indispensable to give the workers who were thus restricted improved terms of employment, including in most cases a guaranteed weekly wage ; and the promise of joint consultation was, in one of its aspects, a *quid pro quo* for the novel obligations by which the worker was bound.

Wages, meanwhile, were settled either by direct negotiations between employers' associations and Trade Unions or, in default of agreement, by reference to arbitration. A National Arbitration Tribunal was set up, and dealt with a wide range of industries ; and in special cases other forms of arbitration were invoked. There was, however, from first to last a refusal to lay down any comprehensive " national wages policy," or to take any action that might supersede the established methods of collective bargaining in the various industries and services. In the first instance, employers' and workers' representatives negotiated much as they had done in time of peace ; but if they failed to agree, the recourse was not to the strike or to the lock-out but to arbitration. The position was rather more complicated in industries, such as mining and railway transport, in which the State was in formal control; for in such cases the Government could not always avoid becoming a party to the discussions. This applied particularly to coal-mining—always the most difficult industry from the standpoint of wage-determination. But in most industries the Government kept out as far as it could, only maintaining a steady pressure on the Trade Union leaders to refrain from making large wage-demands, on the ground that, in view of the shortage of consumers' supplies, the effect would necessarily be inflationary and the workers would be unable to reap any benefit, and might indeed find themselves a good deal worse off.

On the whole, the Trade Unions accepted this argument, but attached to it the condition, which the Government on the whole observed, that they could refrain from wage-pressure only as long as the cost of living was not allowed to rise. Thus arose the system of keeping the prices of essential food-stuffs down by increasingly large subsidies, and of controlling rents. But, although by these methods the official cost of living index number was kept practically stable from 1941 (after a sharp initial rise in 1939 and 1940), the actual cost of living rose much more than the index showed. Beer and tobacco were taxed on an enormous scale ; heavy purchase taxes were applied to a wide range of non-food goods, mainly in order to restrict demand ; and there was a margin of uncontrolled goods of which the prices were allowed to rise sharply despite the general powers accorded to Tribunals under the Prices of Goods Act.   Moreover, many workers had to work away from home, and for a long time the price of furnished lodgings was allowed to rise, in many cases to extortionate levels, without any effective checks being applied.

Under these circumstances, the movements of the official cost of living index ceased to give any real clue to the changes in living costs, though wage-rates in a good many industries continued to be determined by it.   Between 1939 (September) and 1945 (average), whereas the cost of living index rose by only 31 per cent., the official index of wholesale prices rose by 66½ per cent. —more than twice as much.   It is probably not far wrong to estimate that during the War the real cost of living rose, despite food subsidies, on the average by as much as 60 per cent.   Meanwhile, average weekly *earnings* as distinct from wage-rates, rose between 1938 and the end of 1945 by about 74 per cent.—men's earnings by 65 per cent. and women's by 85 per cent.   The increases were naturally very unequal in different trades : in general, the war trades and essential civilian industries did best.

Under these conditions, with a large reduction in the supply of goods available for purchase, considerably more was being earned than could be spent ;   and the National Savings Campaign, designed to take purchasing power off the market, was accordingly an indispensable part of the machinery of war finance.   Wage incomes were also subjected to fairly heavy direct taxation, under the system of PAYE (Pay As You Earn), as well as to heavy indirect taxation levied on commodities.   To some extent PAYE undoubtedly acted as a deterrent to production, as it skimmed off—or appeared to the worker to skim off—a high proportion of the return to extra effort ; but this adverse effect became more marked when the War was over, and the war-time stimulus to high output was no longer felt.

On the whole, it cannot be doubted that the entire labour problem was very much better handled during the second World War than it had been during the War of 1914-1918.   This was partly because the problems of public finance and prevention of profiteering were also infinitely better tackled, at any rate from 1940.   There was nothing at all resembling the brazen fortune-making of the first World War.   The wealthier classes were much more heavily taxed ;   and a much tighter control was imposed on company profits.   The severity of the restrictions, which included Excess Profits Tax at 100 per cent., was indeed continually and bitterly complained of by employers ;   but the Labour Party had insisted on it as a condition of entering the Coalition, and without it the acquiescence of the workers in the restrictions on labour could certainly not have been secured.

Of course, despite the general success of the " labour controls," there were muddles and grievances, and strikes did occur.   The muddles were worst in 1940, when the lack of preparedness for war production was made manifest, and a new organisation had to be improvised at breakneck speed.

In this work of reorganisation, Ernest Bevin played a vitally important part, and his management of the " labour front " was as remarkable a feat as any. The chief failure was in the mines, which were not under the Ministry of Labour : it was due mainly to a failure by the Government to bring the coal-mining industry fully under national control and management, and this failure in turn was due to Conservative dislike of anything that might be taken as leading towards nationalisation. The consequence was a system of " dual control," partly by the owners and partly by the Government, which was always breaking down and had the maximum of irritant effect on the miners. If the mines had been firmly nationalised in 1940, instead of being left in an ambiguous status right up to 1946, a great many troubles would have been either avoided or at least very much reduced.

One effect of the War was to add considerably to the power and influence of the Trades Union Congress over its constituent Unions. Congress was the body which, through its General Council, was regularly consulted by the Government on all important labour issues ; and it also sent its representatives to form, with those of the National Confederation of Employers, the Joint Consultative Committees which were set up to advise the Government about labour matters in general and in connection with each of the main departments. Under these circumstances, the Annual Congress and the General Council came to be, more than ever before, policy-forming bodies for the entire official Trade Union Movement. Their policies by no means went un-criticised ; but the " Left Wing " in the Trade Unions, even when it disliked them, was not prepared to challenge them at the risk of any jeopardy to the war effort. Such revolts as there were remained sporadic and on a small scale, and the stoppages arising out of them were usually short. This was partly because, when the malcontents were determined enough and could show a reasonable case, they were more often than not allowed to have a good deal of their way. The War of 1939-1945 was fought on a basis of conciliating Labour, and of letting the Labour Ministers in the Coalition Government handle their own followers. What the workers would not have taken from Neville Chamberlain, or even from Winston Churchill at the height of his war glory, they were prepared to take when Ernest Bevin and the Trade Union leaders urged it in the name of the War against Fascism.

BOOKS

N. Barou. *The British Trade Unions.*
Populus (G. D. H. Cole). *My Dear Churchill.*
Mass Observation. *War Factory.*
International Labour Office. *British Joint Production Machinery.*
Amalgamated Engineering Union. *Report on Joint Production Committees.*
J. B. Jefferys. *The Story of the Engineers.*
M. Heinemann. *Britain's Coal.*
J. H. Wilson. *New Deal for Coal.*
Trades Union Congress. *The T.U.C. in Wartime.*
Trades Union Congress. *Annual Reports.*

3. THE LABOUR PARTY IN WAR-TIME AND AFTER

The political organisation of Labour, unlike the Trade Unions, suffered as a result of the war. In many areas the local Labour Party organisation, for a time, almost fell to pieces. The individual membership enrolled in the local Parties was reduced from 429,000 in 1938 to 219,000 in 1942. Thereafter it climbed back slowly for two years, and then took a rapid leap forward to 487,000 in 1945—the year of Labour's election victory. The reasons for the earlier decline are not difficult to give. For one thing, there was from September 1939 an agreement between the main Parties not to conduct by-elections during the War, and to allow the candidate of the Party holding the seat an uncontested return : so that campaigns were called for only in the fairly rare cases in which an unofficial candidate was put forward. The following month all municipal elections were suspended by Act of Parliament, the local Councils being given power to fill vacancies by co-option. Subsequently, the life of the House of Commons, elected in 1935, was prolonged. Locally, during the critical stages of the " Battle of Britain," many of the local Councils practically went out of action, delegating all their powers to small emergency committees ; but during the later stages of the War the Councils gradually resumed fuller activity, still without elections.

These " electoral truces " made it seem less necessary to maintain the local political machinery in full order, and most of the full-time party agents and officers were called away to other duties. Moreover, both the call-up for the forces and the large-scale migrations of war workers took many members of the Local Labour Parties away from their home districts ; and in many areas evacuation and the *blitz* further thinned the ranks. Comparatively few of the migrant Labour Party members joined the local Parties of the areas to which they removed ; and even apart from this there were great difficulties in the way of holding regular meetings and, when they were held, many were prevented from attending them by the extended hours of work or of absence from home. Both centrally and locally there was too much else to do for political propaganda, in the absence of election contests, to secure any large attention ; and though it was clear that what had been accepted was only an " election truce," and not a " political truce " in any fuller sense, there were some who held that, with a Coalition Government in office, political propaganda was out of place.

The affiliated, as distinct from the individual, membership of the Labour Party did not decline ; but it did not increase at all in proportion to the rise in the number of Trade Unionists. The new members who joined the Trade Unions did not for the most part sign the forms required under the Trade Union Act of 1927 before they could be called on to pay the " political levy." The decline in the proportion of " political " members was especially marked in the great " general labour " Unions, in which so many of the new recruits were enrolled.   This was largely because branch meetings were less regular, and less well attended, and branch secretaries could not find time to solicit signatures : nor were there, in most places, local full-time election agents to urge them on.   It is therefore not at all surprising that, whereas Trades Union Congress membership rose by 2,000,000 between 1938 and 1945, the affiliated membership of the Labour Party rose by only 350,000.   The difference had little or no political significance : the reasons for it were to be found in the general upset due to the war.

The Trade Union Movement was linked to the Labour Party not only through the direct affiliation of individual Trade Unions, but also through the National Council of Labour, reorganised in 1935 to replace the older Joint Board or Council.   The new body represented on the one hand the Trades Union Congress General Council and on the other both the Labour Party's National Executive and the Parliamentary Labour Party.   It was used to make national pronouncements on matters of common concern to the political and industrial wings of the working-class movement.   The Co-operators had been more than once invited to join, but had refused.   The War, however, changed their attitude.   In 1940 they accepted an informal association with the N.C.L., and in 1942 the Co-operative Union, representing the entire Co-operative Movement, formally joined.   Thereafter, national statements were made from time to time in the name of all three " wings."

This arrangement did not affect the position of the Co-operative Party, which by the 1940's had secured the support of most of the larger Co-operative Societies.   Maintaining its separate existence, the Co-operative Party, worked in close association with the Labour Party ; and its M.P.'s on election joined the Parliamentary Labour Party.   In the constituencies the two Parties avoided fighting each other, and, with some friction, reached agreement about the seats to be left to Co-operative candidates.   The arrangements between them were revised and strengthened in 1945 ; and in the Labour Government of 1946 two leading Co-operators, A. V. Alexander and Alfred Barnes, occupied important positions.   In the trading field, Co-operative progress during the second World War was fairly slow, largely because rationing and the ban on opening new businesses checked expansion.   The membership of retail Co-operative Societies rose from about 8,500,000 at the outbreak of war to about 9,500,000 in 1947.

In Parliament, up to the fall of the Chamberlain Government, the Labour Party remained in Opposition, but on terms which pledged it to give full support to the prosecution of the War.   It was heavily under-represented in relation to its support among the electorate ; for there had been a considerable change in popular sentiment since the General Election of 1935.   By itself, it was powerless to throw out Neville Chamberlain ; but it played a leading part in the moves which led up to his supersession by Winston Churchill, and from that time onwards, as we have seen, its leaders held important offices and it took its full share in public responsibility. It must, however, be borne in mind that right up to 1945 the House of Commons itself had a large Conservative majority, and that this majority was in a position to block any measure which it seriously disliked. No doubt the Labour members of the Cabinet could have tried to force the Conservatives' hands by the threat of resignation if it had been seriously meant ; but what would have been the result ? A counter-threat of resignation by Winston Churchill would have compelled them to withdraw, unless they had been prepared to imperil the entire war effort and, in doing so, to lose their hold on the people. In these circumstances, the Conservatives had in the last resort a very wide power of veto upon controversial legislation. They used it, as we have seen, to prevent any effective handling of the problem of the coal mines ; and they also blocked all amendment of the vindictive Trade Union Act of 1927. On the other hand, at some points they were compelled to give way. Ernest Bevin forced through his Catering Wages Act of 1943 in face of strong Conservative opposition, and was also successful in getting his Wages Councils Act—an amended and greatly strengthened version of the Trade Boards Act—on the statute book in 1945. Moreover, the pressure of public opinion in favour of the Beveridge Report on Social Security was so great as to compel the Government as a whole to accept the greater part of its recommendations, and even to advance beyond it at one or two points.

At the Annual Conferences of the Labour Party during the war years, the Party representatives in the Government were always certain of having their essential policies endorsed. The Conference repeatedly rejected collaboration with the Communist Party, even after it had come round to full support of the War. It also, with some hesitation, continued to endorse the electoral truce ; and it supported the Executive's policy of making war upon organisations which were held to be Communist-inspired, or under Communist control. Its main preoccupation, apart from giving support to its leaders in the Government, was with the working out of the policy on which it proposed to fight the General Election that would come after the War. A series of reports on various aspects of policy was drawn up, and received endorsement at successive Conferences ; and in 1944-5 a selection from the long-term programme thus elaborated was cast into the form of a manifesto—*Let Us Face the Future*—on which the Party fought the General Election of 1945. This short-term programme included considerable, but limited, measures of socialisation, covering coal mines, gas, electricity, water, the main forms of inland transport, iron and steel, and the Bank of England, but not the land, which a considerable section of the Party wished to see made public property at an early stage. It also embodied large measures of social security and a comprehensive pledge to take action for the maintenance of full employment and to maintain the controls needed for effective economic planning. About foreign and imperial affairs it was much less precise :

indeed, it became apparent as soon as the Party was put to the test that it had much less clear notions of what it wanted to do in international than in internal affairs.

In 1944, while the War in Europe was still at its height, the Labour Party Conference made clear its determination to fight the first post-war General Election as an independent Party, and to disentangle itself from its coalition with the other Parties as soon as the War was at an end. When, in May, 1945, the German surrender left the War still to be fought to a finish in the Far East, the question arose whether the Coalition should continue for a further period. The leaders of the Labour Party were prepared to remain in the Coalition with a view to an election in the autumn, but rejected Winston Churchill's proposal that it should remain in being until after the end of the War in the Far East, or that a referendum of the people should be held to settle whether it should be thus continued or not. On the rejection of these proposals, the Conservatives determined to rush on the election with the utmost possible speed, in the hope of securing the full benefit of Winston Churchill's prestige as the engineer of victory. The Coalition ended in May, 1945 ; and, until after the General Election of July, power was held by a Conservative Government which did what it could to liquidate the war-time apparatus of economic planning—especially the Ministry of Production, which had become the principal agency of economic co-ordination.

At the General Election, the Labour Party won a remarkable and even startling victory. Whereas in 1931 it had been reduced to a mere handful of 52 M.P.'s, and even in 1935 had returned only 156, in 1945 it won 394 seats, and thus secured for the first time in its history a clear majority in the House of Commons. Indeed its majority of nearly 150, though much smaller than that of the Liberals in 1906, or than the Conservative majorities of 1931 and 1935, gave it ample room for manoeuvre in the new Parliament. The Labour Party did not, however, poll a clear majority of the votes cast. Its vote was roughly 12,000,000, out of 25,000,000 votes cast, on a 76 per cent. poll of the registered electors—a high poll in view of the large numbers away from home at the time of the election. The Conservatives and their allies polled nearly 10,000,000 votes, and the Independent Liberals nearly 2,250,000. The remaining votes were scattered among small groups, ranging from the few Communist and I.L.P. candidates to various brands of Independents.

The Labour victory of 1945 confounded the election prophets, most of whom had expected that, though the Labour Party would win many seats, their gains would fall a long way short of a clear majority. It was widely supposed (but least among those who were most in touch with opinion in the forces) that Winston Churchill's prestige would suffice to carry his Party back to power, despite its evident lack of any constructive programme. In fact, the Conservative campaigners chose to fight on this basis, and put forward very little indeed by way of an alternative to the Labour Party's clearly stated and essentially moderate programme.   Churchill himself, by the violence of his tirades against Socialism and by the virulence of his personal attacks, did what he could to destroy his own value as an electoral asset ; but it is to be doubted whether this made much difference to the result.   Roughly half of the voters had made up their minds that Great Britain needed some sort of a " new deal," and the only Party that appeared to offer any considered and practicable plan was the Labour Party.

This plan was "socialistic " ; but it was not Socialism.   It involved the socialisation of a limited group of key services, and of two great industries, coal-mining and iron and steel manufacture, and therewith a sufficient public control over other industries to make possible the working of a general economic plan with " full employment " as its declared objective.   Beyond that it did not go, though it was clearly stated that the Labour Party's Five Years' Programme was to be regarded as a first instalment, and that a further advance would be made towards Socialism if the Party secured a renewal of its lease of power.   The Labour Party remained in and after 1945 what it had been from its very inception—an evolutionary Party, seeking to advance towards Socialism by gradual stages and without any sharp break from the traditions of British society.   It believed in capturing the State by constitutional means, and then gradually re-shaping it—not, like Marx and the Communists, in overthrowing the capitalist State and putting a new workers' State in its place.   This attitude involved acceptance of the possibility that the next General Election might reverse the verdict, and bring the Conservatives back to office.   The Labour Party leaders accepted that possibility as part of their evolutionary creed, and argued that the Conservatives, even if they did come back, would be unable to undo the achievements of their antagonists. This is not the place to argue the merits of these opinions, but only to state them as an essential part of the contemporary history of the British working-class movement.

During the first year or so from the date when the Labour Government came to power, the pace of legislation was hotter than it had ever been.   It was speedily made plain that the Labour Party fully intended to carry through the domestic programme on which it had fought the election ; and by February, 1947—the time at which these words are being written—it had placed on the statute book a comprehensive social insurance plan, including a complete revision of the system of workmen's compensation.   It had socialised the Bank of England, the system of cable and wireless communication, civil aviation, and the coal mines.   It had introduced Bills for the socialisation of inland transport and of electricity supply, and had announced further measures dealing with gas and other services.   It had postponed, but not dropped, the socialisation of the steel industry, and it was in process of setting up Control Boards of one sort or another for a number of industries that were to be left under capitalist management. It had introduced comprehensive measures for the control and development of agriculture and for town and country planning, including the establishment of " new towns " under public auspices, wider powers of land acquisition, and the complete taking over of the " development value " of undeveloped land. It had begun to tackle the exceedingly difficult housing problem, and had made better headway than had seemed likely during the earlier months. It had passed a momentous Act setting up a comprehensive National Health Service, and had stood up to the violent opposition of the British Medical Association. The list of its measures could be prolonged ; but what has been mentioned is enough to indicate clearly its energy and the wide range of its reforming zeal.

In external affairs, the Government's record was much more mixed. It had felt itself forced by sheer necessity to accept a loan from the United States on exceedingly onerous conditions, fettering its freedom in respect both of monetary management and of bargaining in international trade. It had lined up in the affairs of U.N.O. too often with the United States against the Soviet Union, and had got utterly bogged in its policy in Greece and in the Near and Middle East, not only in Palestine but also in Egypt. It had done badly in its zone of occupation in Germany, though it was questionable how far the blame lay on its shoulders, or how it should rightly be distributed among the four occupying Powers, or at any rate among the three which made the ambiguous and unworkable Potsdam Agreement. In the Far East, it had done well, after a bad start, in Burma, but less well in Malaya ; and in India it had shilly-shallied too long before taking the decisively right step of announcing a definite date for withdrawal. Its colonial policy had been good and sound, as far as it went. But it had failed either to give the needed encouragement at the right moment to the forces of Social Democracy in Western Europe, or to make plain its will to constructive co-operation with the Soviet Union in European affairs. These, I know, are summary judgments ; and only time can prove how far they are soundly based.

Finally, the Labour Government had been definitely shown, by February, 1947, to have planned not too much but too little, and to have underestimated seriously the immediate difficulties of economic recovery. It had been attending to the long-term measures needed for setting the British economic system back on its feet, but had paid too little attention to the pitfalls lying in its immediate path. To say this is not to suggest that any other Party, or a Coalition, would have done the job better : on the contrary, their own records and pronouncements show that Labour's political adversaries would have done very much worse, by planning still less, and by trusting still more to luck.

BOOKS

G. D. H. Cole.   *History of the Labour Party from 1914.*

G. D. H. Cole and R. Postgate.   *The Common People, 1746–1946.*

Labour Party.   *Annual Reports.*

Labour Party.   *Let Us Face the Future* (and other pamphlets).

J. Price.   *Labour in Wartime.*

M. Cole.   *The General Election of 1945* (Fabian Society).

J. E. D. Hall.   *Labour's First Year.*

E. Bevin.   *The Job to Be Done.*

E. Shinwell.   *The Britain I Want.*

H. Morrison.   *Prospects and Policies.*

G. D. H. Cole.   *Fabian Socialism.*

G. D. H. Cole.   *Great Britain in the Post-war World* (1942).

G. D. H. Cole.   *The Intelligent Man's Guide to the Post-war World* (1947).

CHAPTER XII

THE CONDITION OF THE WORKERS IN THE FIRST HALF OF THE TWENTIETH CENTURY

THE nearer the approach to the present, the harder is the task of inducing order into the unsifted mass of facts presented by memory and by current record. In the story of the past, the wood stands out, distinct from the trees ; but the present is all trees in which the wanderer is often lost. In this attempt to estimate the changes in the condition of the workers during the first half of the twentieth century, it is hard to get beyond the crude facts and figures—often, in themselves, elusive and uncertain enough—to any reckoning of their significance.

The task is the harder because the period is sharply broken and, by any estimate, utterly abnormal. The two greatest wars in human history cleave it into four sections, upsetting every traditional method of measurement and making very difficult any precise assessment. In 1947 the effects of *both* Wars are with us still ; for the consequences of the first World War were carried over into the second, and the second is still too near for any confident disentangling of its longer- from its shorter-run effects. Moreover, the idea of a standard of living measurable in terms of the relative movements of wages and prices, on which it used to seem legitimate to base broad conclusions about the direction and extent of social progress, is to-day (in 1947) applicable only subject to reservations so great as to make it almost impossible to draw positive conclusions with any real assurance. It is possible to say, subject to a fairly wide margin of error, how the living standards of the British workers and the broad division of the national income, as well as its amount, changed between 1900 and 1939. But after 1939 the same kinds of measurement can for the most part no longer be applied ; and though certain generalisations can be made on the basis of new and different data, there is no way of joining the new figures on to the old so as to present a continuous curve on a graph. That is why I have had to drop in this revised edition any attempt to represent by graph or table the average movement of real wages, as distinct from money wage-rates, after 1914 I could have carried the estimates on as far as 1939, but only with many misgivings about them. After 1939 they cannot be carried on at all ; and any attempt to calculate a " real wage " figure from the relative movements of the official cost of living index and of the wage-rates index could yield only the most misleading results.

Up to a point, certain of the bare facts are simple enough. In 1896 the long period of falling prices had come to an end, and a slow rise had set in.

Between 1896 and 1914 wholesale prices rose by nearly 40 per cent. and retail food prices by about 25 per cent. Then, with the first World War, came a complete upsetting of the whole price system. Between the outbreak of war in 1914 and the Armistice of 1918 wholesale prices rose by about 135 per cent. and the cost of living by at least 120 per cent. In 1919 the rise was checked ; but in 1920 it was resumed more swiftly than ever. According to the official figures, wholesale prices, at their peak in the spring of 1920, were 225 per cent. above the level of 1913, and the cost of living reached in November, 1920, a peak 176 per cent. above the level of August, 1914. There followed, first for wholesale and then after an interval for retail prices, an extraordinarily sharp fall. For 1921 the average level of wholesale prices was about double that of 1913, and for 1922 less than 60 per cent. above it. Thereafter the fall ceased, and for a time prices became stable within fairly narrow limits. The cost of living meanwhile averaged 126 per cent. above the pre-war level in 1921, 83 per cent. in 1922, and 74 per cent. in 1923, when it too reached for a time a condition of relative stability.

What of wages ? Between 1896 and 1914 money wage-rates rose on the average by 16 or 17 per cent., but most of this rise had taken place by 1900, and wage-rates increased on the average by only about 6 per cent. between 1900 and 1914. Indeed, they were no higher in 1911 than they had been in 1900, and the industrial unrest of the years between 1911 and 1914 raised them by approximately 6 per cent. Thus, as we have seen earlier in this book, the economic position of the workers, as far as it can be measured by wage-rates, had been getting definitely worse ; for retail food prices had risen by 16 or 17 per cent. between 1900 and 1914 and by as much as 25 per cent. between 1896 and 1914—that is to say, from the end of the long period of falling prices in the last quarter of the nineteenth century. During the war years wage-rates still lagged behind prices, standing at the end of 1918 at something appreciably less than double the pre-war levels. In 1919 the position improved, and wage-rates rose by about 20 per cent., in a time of relatively stable prices. They leapt up again in 1920, reaching at the peak a point perhaps 175 per cent. above the pre-war level, and thus almost exactly compensating the average worker for the rise in the cost of living.

Thereafter, in the slump, wage-rates declined, but lagged behind falling, as they had behind rising, prices. At the end of 1921 they were from 110 to 115 per cent. above pre-war level, in 1922 from 70 to 75 per cent., and in 1923 from 65 to 70 per cent. Thereafter they rose, in 1924, and then remained nearly stationary until the defeat of the General Strike in 1926. After that, up to 1929, wage-rates fell, but not sharply, to the accompaniment of a roughly equivalent fall in the cost of living. In 1930 the cost of living began to fall more sharply, and this fall continued as the world crisis developed in 1931 and 1932. During these years wage-rates also fell, but to a considerably smaller extent than prices, so that the purchasing power of those workers who were able to retain full employment improved. By 1935, as the slump passed away, the cost of living was again rising, and by 1936 the relative levels of the cost of living and of wage-rates were much as they had been in 1930. In 1937 both rose sharply : in 1938 the cost of living fell a little, but wage-rates rose, partly on account of re-armament activity. The following year came the second World War.

So far, it is possible to make very rough comparisons. It is, however, necessary to qualify these figures a good deal before drawing from them any general conclusion about the condition of the working class. In the first place, wage-rates are not earnings. In times of prosperity, overtime and high piece-work balances cause real earnings to rise a good deal faster than rates of wages, whereas in periods of depression they fall much lower, not only because these " extras " disappear, but also because discontinuous and part-time employment bring them heavily down. Thus, in the matter of earnings, the average worker was worse off in the bad times than in the good times, even when the change in wage-rates was balanced by changes in the cost of living.

Secondly, averages are in such matters as these apt to be highly mis-leading ; for wages may have risen and fallen very unevenly in different trades. Thus, in the middle of 1925 the wage-rates of printers, tram con-ductors, employees of local authorities, railwaymen (except engine-drivers), painters and builders' labourers, boot and shoe operatives and chemical workers were all 100 per cent. or more above the levels of 1914. On the other hand, skilled engineers were only 45 per cent., shipwrights 35 per cent., South Wales steelworkers 21 per cent., cotton operatives 61 per cent., and iron miners from 30 to 40 per cent. above these levels. These wide differences were, of course, due largely to the different economic position of " sheltered " and " unsheltered " trades. The trades chiefly engaged in export had for the most part cut wages to the bone, whereas in the industries unaffected by foreign competition the workers had been much more successful in retaining some of the gains of the prosperous years. It has, however, to be remem-bered that certain classes of workers, such as railwaymen, were grossly under-paid before the War, and that their large percentage gains still in many cases left their actual wages very low. Similar differences between trade and trade appeared in the great depression of the early 'thirties.

Thirdly, after 1918 there was in most occupations a decrease in working hours, owing to the widespread adoption of a working week of forty-eight hours or less. This meant very different reductions in different trades ; but in almost all the change was fairly considerable. How far the reduction affected output it is hard to say. It was officially estimated, on the basis of comparing the two Censuses of Production, that output per worker was about the same in 1924 as in 1907. The conclusion was drawn that technical improvements had about balanced the fall in working hours ; but it is probable that in 1907, the more prosperous year of the two, a good deal more overtime was worked than in 1924, and the workers were a good deal more continuously employed. Output per man-hour had therefore almost certainly increased appreciably.

Fourthly, wages are not the sole determinant of the standard of living. Between 1900 and 1947 there was a sharp fall in the average size of the family —a factor of course making, whatever its deeper economic consequences, for an improved standard of living where the purchasing power of wages remained unimpaired. There was also a great increase in the social services provided wholly or partly at the public expense. Old Age Pensions, Workmen's Compensation and Health Insurance came before 1914, with Unemployment Insurance for a few trades ; and between 1914 and 1939 there were added almost universal Unemployment Insurance and Assistance and Widows' Pensions, as well as an extension of free schooling. With these went a number of other social measures, or extensions of older measures. Moreover, on the whole, both rates of benefit and conditions of administration were considerably improved, though there were ups and downs and conditions were temporarily worsened both in 1921 and in 1931 under the influence of the cry for " economy " as a means of meeting depression of trade. Workers, of course, helped largely to pay for the improved benefits which they received, both by direct contributions and indirectly through taxation ; but the total effect was certainly some improvement in the standard of life for the main body of the working class, and a considerable increase in security against absolute destitution.

On the whole, then, despite the prolonged slumps of the 'twenties and 'thirties, the workers were considerably better off in 1939 than they had been in 1914, and had much more power, politically as well as industrially, to protect their economic position. Certain important groups, however, including some of the former skilled " aristocrats of labour," such as miners and shipbuilders, had suffered a serious reverse of fortune ; and even in the so-called " sheltered trades " there had been no resumption of the steady advance in the standard of living which had been practically continuous during the latter half of the nineteenth century. In the late 'twenties, before the world economic crisis, whereas wages in the United States had risen in purchasing power by about one-third since 1914, in Great Britain real wages had been standing still. Then came the crisis, involving in all the leading countries both wage-cuts and severe unemployment. But, as we have seen, in Great Britain wage rates fell a good deal less than prices, and the workers' fortunes were very differently affected from district to district, from industry to industry, and as between individuals in regular jobs and those who fell right out of work or could get only casual or intermittent employment, or even none at all.

Another way of attempting to measure the position of the working classes is by estimating, not the level of wages, but the *share* of wages in the total income of the community. Some light is thrown on this question by the calculations of national income and of its distribution made by Professor Bowley and Sir Josiah Stamp for the year 1924 as compared with 1911. According to this estimate wages represented at the two dates about the same proportion of the *home-produced* income of Great Britain—approximately 43 to 44 per cent. This calculation omits in both cases incomes arising out of overseas investment. If these were included the share of wages would be substantially lower, but would be higher in 1924 than in 1911 owing to the loss of overseas investments incurred during the first World War. The actual figures given for 1911 and 1924 are as follows : wages, £800,000,000 and £1,600,000,000 ; real incomes originating at home, £1,868,000,000 and £3,647,000,000 ; incomes from abroad, £200,000,000 and £212,000,000. These estimates, on the whole, agree with the conclusions drawn from the wage figures, and they also serve to show that any *relative* improvement in the position of wage earners as such up to 1924 is imputable almost entirely to the decrease in the tribute drawn by British owners of capital from abroad.

Professor Bowley, in his book on *Wages and Income from 1860*, has estimated that the share of wages in the total national income changed very little between 1880 and 1911, but that there was a considerable rise in what he calls "intermediate incomes"—that is, small salaries and earnings of small farmers and independent workers below income tax level. Professor Bowley puts the share of wages at 40 per cent. of total income (including income from abroad) in the 1880's, at 41 per cent. in the 1890's, again at 40 per cent. between 1900 and 1905, at 39 per cent. from 1906-1910, at 40 per cent. again in 1911, and then as falling off to 38½ per cent. in 1913, not because of a reduction in wages, but on account of a sharp rise in national income as a whole. By 1924, he estimates, the proportion of wages to total national income had risen a little ; but the proportion to *home-produced* national income remained the same as in 1911.

Professor Bowley's estimates cannot be easily carried on beyond 1924, without more detail and qualification than I have room for. It seems best to refer the reader who wishes to go thoroughly into the question to his two main books on the subject, and to use, for the summary purposes of the present chapter, the alternative estimates given by Mr. Colin Clark in his *National Income and Outlay*, published in 1937. Mr. Clark there gives estimates of the share of wages in *home produced* (not in total) income from 1911 to 1935, and presents a separate estimate for salaries. According to his calculations, the following were some of the broad changes in income distribution over this period.

£ millions.	1911.	1924.	1929.	1932.	1935.
(a) Overseas Income . . .	220	280	315	175	215
(b) Home-produced Income . .	1990	3755	4069	3669	4315
Per cent. of (b)					
Share of Wages . . .	39·5	42·1	41·8	42·5	40·5
Share of Salaries . . .	15·6	25·4	26·6	28·3	25·0
Share of Profits and Interest .	33·8	25·1	23·1	18·8	25·4
Share of Rents . . .	11·1	7·4	8·5	10·4	9·1

Mr. Clark's calculations stop at 1935 ; but from 1938 onwards we have the official calculations made by the Government in the annual Budget White Papers issued in recent years. These are in terms of *total* and not merely of home-produced income. For 1938 total income is put at £4,671,000,000 and the respective shares of wages and of salaries at 41·4 and 25·3 per cent. For 1946 the corresponding figures are given as £7,974,000,000 and at 42·3 and 21·0 per cent. ; but in 1946 a good many more workers than in 1938 were in the armed forces, and the proportions of national income going out to the various factors of production cannot be exactly compared with those of 1938.

The main things that stand out from these estimates, for the years up to 1939, are, first, the comparative stability of the share of wages, and secondly the sharp increase in the share going to the salary-earners. This latter, of course, includes salaries of all amounts ; and its rapid rise is due to more than one cause. It is a result partly of the increase in the numbers of clerks, administrators and technicians, both in the public services and in industry, but also partly of the conversion of many more businesses to a joint stock basis and to the diversion of a part of the income previously paid out as profits to the salaries of directors and managers of joint-stock concerns, and to salaried technicians and professional workers. The difficulties in the way of splitting up the amounts paid out as salaries to persons at various levels of income makes it almost impossible to reach an assured statistical conclusion about the changes in class-distribution.

All such calculations are, of course, liable to a large margin of error, and only the most general conclusions can be based upon them. We shall not, however, go far wrong if we describe the position as between wage-workers and capitalists up to 1939, apart from the development of the contributory social services, as having altered somewhat to the dis-advantage of the latter, mainly because of the growth of the class of small salary-earners.

Even though the wage-earners' share in the national income altered but little during the forty years from 1900 to 1939, there were considerable re-distributions among the various sections of the working class, and there was, for most of them, a real and valuable increase in leisure owing to the shortening of the working week. There was, moreover, undoubtedly a great improvement in the position of many of those who had previously been worst off of all—the aged, the blind, the disabled, and the worst-paid and most irregularly employed groups among the wage-earners. The development of social insurance, even if its total effect was largely that of re-distribution of incomes among the working classes rather than between them and the well-to-do, did bring to the lowest strata of all a considerable increase in security ; and such impositions as the Means Test pressed much less on these " bottom dogs " than on unemployed workers who had been used to a higher standard of life. Despite the grave problems of the Distressed Areas, a good deal was done, over a large part of the country, to reduce the pressure of really abject poverty, and to level up from the bottom—though at the same time, as we have seen, some sections of the better-paid skilled workers were being remorselessly levelled down. Moreover, the numbers whose wages increased in purchasing power considerably exceeded the numbers whose real wages declined.

In terms of social welfare as a whole, there was on balance an unquestionable improvement, and the outlook and habits of the main body of the working classes certainly changed a great deal. The working-class consumption of alcohol steadily decreased, though exceedingly high taxation, in part the cause of the decrease, was responsible for an increase in the national drink bill, and made the incidence of the tax system on the workers more severe. The taxes on beer and tobacco, as well as the contributions under social insurance schemes, largely offset the redistributive effects of increased expenditure on the social services. Among the social services, education improved greatly in both quantity and quality. The elementary school improved its methods ; and there was a very rapid growth of public secondary schools increasingly accessible to working-class children. From the foundation of the Workers' Educational Association in 1903, adult education spread fairly rapidly among the workers. It spread much faster after 1919, when new bodies, such as the largely Marxist National Council of Labour Colleges, challenged, but did not retard, the developing activity of the W.E.A.

The N.C.L.C., seeking no aid from public funds such as the W.E.A. and other bodies aiming at " impartial " education received, set out to provide, mainly at a fairly elementary level, classes which assumed the rightness of Socialism and were intended mainly for active workers in the Socialist and Trade Union movements. It repudiated the distinction, drawn by the W.E.A., between " education " and " propaganda ", and attacked the W.E.A. on account of its close connections with the Universities, the Local Education Authorities, and the " capitalist " State. In practice, the two rival movements occupied largely distinct fields. The W.E.A. catered for those working-class, or " near " working-class, students, who wanted a higher education more or less resembling that given to students in Universities or in institutions under L.E.A. auspices—including education in a wide range of cultural subjects which the N.C.L.C. touched little or not at all. The N.C.L.C., which received a large measure of Trade Union support (at least as much as its rival) was much less academic in its methods, and appealed to many who found the W.E.A. methods too " literary ", as well as to those who wanted a definitely propagandist approach. With the growth of the various forms of education went a rapid spread of culture, and a great extension of the reading public. This had the evil effect of largely adding to the power of the millionaire-run Press, to which the *Daily Herald, Reynolds' News* and the few Labour weeklies still offered only an inadequate challenge ; but the good side of the educational advance much more than made up for this unavoidable evil.

The workmen of the 1930's certainly dressed better, probably ate better, were sometimes, but only in a minority of cases, rather better housed, than the workman of 1900. They were on the whole healthier, and their children considerably so. They amused themselves more, especially with the cinema and the wireless, and were altogether less distinguishable in manner, appearance and habits from large sections of the middle classes. It follows that they saved less. The Victorian virtue of thrift had suffered a heavy blow in the days when rising prices made a pound saved shrink rapidly to half its value, and the conditions of the period of extreme uncertainty after 1918 were not such as to encourage the resumption of the habit on the old scale. Moreover, far more than his forebears, the workman of the inter-war years claimed the right to enjoy himself, and was not prepared to live unrelaxed days of labour in order to save himself from destitution in old age. The growth of social insurance also diminished the urgency of the call to put by for a rainy day. Finally, this change of habit certainly applied much more to the rich than to the poor. It was not only or mainly the workman who took to spending to-day what his father or grandfather would have stored up for to-morrow.

The most marked change of all was in the position of the working-class woman. The Women's Sections came after 1918 to be among the best and most active parts of the Labour Party ; the Women's Guilds rapidly increased their influence in the Co-operative Movement ; and in Trade Unions, in educational classes, and in every working-class activity women came to play a steadily increasing part. This change was, indeed, much greater in some places than in others, and on the whole, in this respect, the mining communities for a time lagged behind ; but it was everywhere very great indeed. No less profound was the change in the appearance, the outlook, and the social habits of the working-class housewife or factory girl. Women's political emancipation counted for little directly ; but the change of which it was the outstanding sign was perhaps the greatest of all the changes of the first four decades of the twentieth century.

Politically as well as socially, the working-class attitude to life had undergone a significant change. Not the whole working class, but practically the whole active membership of the organised working-class movement, had become, in a broad sense, Socialist. In 1900 the Socialists had been still a small group ; even in 1914 their hold on the Trade Unions was by no means complete. But after 1918 the Labour Movement as a whole had become practically a Socialist Movement. Mildly Socialist, no doubt ; but definitely it had accepted the Socialist programme offered to it, and, if the Socialists were still preaching to it as to the unconverted, this was because they had found fresh things to preach rather than because it had not accepted their doctrine.

The number of active and well-informed workers in the various sections of the movement had greatly increased. The growth of a Labour Press and the foundation of bodies such as the Labour Research Department (created as a section of the Fabian Society in 1912) and the official Research and Information Departments of the Labour Party and the Trades Union Congress, combined with the multiplication of books and pamphlets dealing with economic and social questions and with the growth of education to increase greatly the common stock of knowledge on these matters ; and the rise of the Labour Party to political influence undoubtedly aided this development. Some political and economic knowledge at least became part of the normal equipment of a much higher proportion of the workers.

And yet ———. If there was a " but," was it not largely because the working class was coming to be judged by far more exacting standards than ever before ? It had staked out a claim to be no longer a subject class, but to take the lead in ruling the world. By this standard it was coming to be judged. It was often alleged that the workman of the 1920's and 1930's lacked the fortitude and determination of his Victorian forebears. Perhaps he did ; but it was not only among the working class that the ostentatious possession of of these often disagreeable qualities had gone out of fashion. Perhaps the generation that came out of the first World War was a degenerate generation, worthy of the scorn of its forerunners. But, after all, what generation ever was not ? It is nearer the relevant truth that ever since 1918 men have had harder problems to face than ever confronted the Victorians. They were becoming, on the whole, perhaps a little better equipped for facing them. But were they well enough equipped ? There lay the doubt ; but there was at any rate a higher average level of acquired intelligence and knowledge than ever before. And these are no mean things.

The first edition of this book was published in 1927 ; and I ended it with the following paragraph, which I reproduce here just as I wrote it twenty years ago :—

" For of one thing at least we may be sure. We have not all time before us. Within a brief space of years it will have been settled whether or not Great Britain is a decaying country, memorable chiefly for her past greatness—a museum and place of pilgrimage for the early historic age of industrialism. At the point to which this history proceeds Great Britain is not standing still ; she is wobbling. She may topple over the edge, or she may make a new civilisation to replace that of which the world's changed conditions have made a misfit and a muddle. In this task, she has, at any rate, to help her, a higher average of intelligence and knowledge than in any generation before. And these, we may hope, are no mean equipment for the task. The working-class movement has, in the years immediately before it, a hard row to hoe ; but, when all is said, it has come through worse things."

That is how I rounded off my history twenty years ago, a dozen years before Great Britain had been drawn into a second World War much more devastating than the first in its long-run effects on the British economy. How have events since I wrote, and especially since 1939, affected the position of the working classes ? Immediately, their relative position has certainly improved. There has been, thanks to the more effective prevention of profiteering and to the less inequitable taxation of the second World War, a sharp reduction in the spendable incomes of the wealthier classes. War has again brought full employment and regular earnings, and though wages have been taxed directly as well as indirectly on an unprecedented scale, the proportion of total spending power accruing to the poorer sections of the people has been greater than ever before. Subsidies have kept the cost of living from rising nearly as sharply as it would otherwise have done ; and, though *average* food consumption has perforce decreased, the bottom third of the population has been fed, right up to 1947, better than it has ever been fed before. The workers have also been able, in general, to save on an unprecedentedly large scale ; and at the same time the new social security measures, based largely on the Beveridge Report, and the introduction of children's allowances have given a considerably greater security against absolute want. The extent of economic inequality has, in fact, been substantially diminished ; and, to that extent, a great social advance has been made.

Yet there are serious factors to be taken into account on the other side. If security has been increased for the individual who is in danger of falling into destitution through unemployment, or sickness, or accident, or old age, there has been as against this a growth of insecurity for the whole people. The new conditions postulate a less unequal sharing of the cake ; but how big is the cake of the future likely to be ? The standard of living of the British people, as it is in 1947, is being sustained only with the aid of large current borrowing—over and above the debts contracted during the war years—from the United States and from Canada ; and it is a plain fact that there is no easy way of restoring British exports to a level high enough to pay for the bare minimum of imports of foodstuffs and materials in default of which the British standards of living must fall, and workers must go without jobs for want of materials to labour upon. This may prove to be only a passing phase ; for, subject to three conditions, British productive capacity should be fully enough to meet British needs at least to the extent of maintaining pre-war standards and of retaining the advances made by the worst-off sections of the people during the war years. These three conditions, however, are all important. The first is that man-power and capital resources shall be rightly directed to the performance of the more urgent tasks, and that there shall be no waste of either, and no military commitments on such a scale as to sap Great Britain's productive strength. The second is that British industry shall be as efficient as it can be made, and that, in order to make it so, there shall be both a large immediate diversion of activity from production for current consumption to the replenishment and modernisation of the capital instruments and a readiness on the part of both labour and management to go all out for high output, even at the sacrifice of cherished prejudices and convictions. Finally, the third condition is that the world shall be in a state and in a mood to receive British exports on fair terms of exchange for the imports that are needed, and that not too many obstacles shall be put in the way of British planning for these processes of exchange.

These are all indispensable conditions ; but of no one of them can it be said that realisation will be easy—much less that it can be taken as assured. This is not the place for an examination of the measures, or of the policies, for which the greatly changed world economic situation of Great Britain calls. I have done my best to examine these problems elsewhere : what is relevant here is to point out that the situation has so changed for the worse that it is no longer possible fruitfully to regard the prospects of the working classes mainly from the standpoint of the distribution of the national income between them and other classes, and that the critical question now is whether Great Britain, having used up a high proportion of its own mineral resources and nearly all its timber, and having followed for a century a policy of dependence on imported food paid for by exports, can continue to sell enough exports to provide for the imports without which the standard of living cannot be maintained. Of course, the need for imports can be diminished to some extent by higher food production at home ; but the cost of this higher food production is still uncertain, and for the most part the dependence on imported materials is bound to continue for as far ahead as it is profitable to look. Throughout the period covered by this book, almost to the very end, · there has been an unspoken assumption that no such difficulties as these need be seriously entertained ; for as long as Great Britian was the " workshop of the world " they did not exist, and even thereafter there was left for some time—indeed right up to 1939—a considerable margin of safety in the form of income due on British investments overseas. The second World War swept this reserve away, and left the entire British economy dependent on two things—its own efficiency in production and the capacity and willingness of the world to absorb its products. On these factors, above all others, the future standards of the British working class, as indeed of the entire British people, must now depend.

BOOKS

A. L. Bowley. *Wages and Income in the United Kingdom since 1860.*

A. I. Bowley. *Studies in National Income.*

A. L. Bowley and J. Stamp. *Three Studies on the National Income (1924–38).*

C. Clark. *National Income and Outlay.*

G. D. H. and M. Cole. *The Condition of Britain (1937).*

The Budget White Papers, annual from 1940.

M. Abrams. *The Condition of the British People, 1911–1945.*

G. D. H. Cole. *The Intelligent Man's Guide to the Post-war World (1947).*

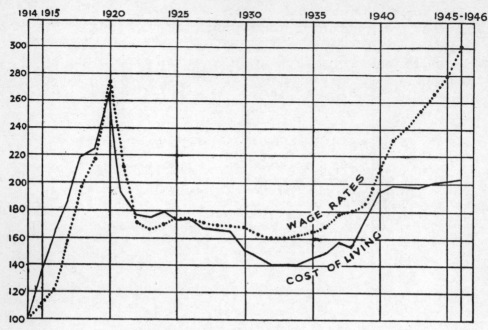

CHART 14.—WAGE-RATES AND COST OF LIVING.

(August, 1914 = 100).

Official Cost of Living Index and Rough Index of Money Rates of Wages at End of Each Year.

NOTE.—The Official Cost of Living Index Figure for 1940 was greatly affected by food subsidies, and cannot be taken as a fair measure of real living costs. The Wage Index is only approximate, and has been compiled by linking together a number of indexes on somewhat different bases. It is meant to indicate only the general trends. It shows only rates, and takes no account of earnings as distinct from rates of wages.

TABLE 10.—WAGE-RATES, PRICES AND EMPLOYMENT, 1900-1914

Date.	Retail Food Prices (London).	Money Wages (excluding Agriculture).	Real Wages (Rates without allowing for Unemployment).	Employment per cent. (i.e., Unemployment reversed).
1900	100	100	100	97
1901	100	99	99	97
1902	101	97	96	96
1903	103	96	93	95
1904	102	96	94	94
1905	103	96	93	95
1906	102	98	96	96
1907	105	102	97	96
1908	107	101	94	92
1909	108	99	92	92
1910	109	100	92	95
1911	109	100	92	97
1912	114	103	90	97
1913	115	106	92	98
1914	117	106	91	97

See Note opposite.

TABLE 11.—EMPLOYMENT AND UNEMPLOYMENT, 1914-1946

Date.	Index of Numbers of Insured Workers in Employment in June (June 1923 = 100).	Insured Workers Unemployed. Yearly Average (thousands).	Insured Workers Unemployed (per cent.).	Trade Union Members Unemployed (per cent.).	Notes.
1914 . . .	—	—	4	3	Outbreak of War
1915 . . .	—	—	1	1	
1916 . . .	—	—	1	—	
1917 . . .	—	—	1	1	
1918 . . .	—	—	1	1	
1919 . . .	—	—	—	2	
1920 . . .	—	691 (Dec.)	5	2	General Unemployment Insurance Act
1921 . . .	—	2,052†	17	15	Coal Dispute
1922 . . .	97	1,637	14	15	
1923 . . .	100	1,344	12	11	
1924 . . .	104	1,205	10	8	
1925 . . .	103	1,340	11	11	
1926 . . .	—	1,505	12	12	General Strike
1927 . . .	109	1,362	10	—	
1928 . . .	107	1,290	11	—	
1929 . . .	110	1,262	10	—	
1930 . . .	106	1,991	16	—	
1931 . . .	102	2,717	21	—	World Crisis
1932 . . .	101	2,829	22	—	
1933 . . .	105	2,567	20	—	
1934 . . .	109	2,171	17	—	
1935 . . .	112	2,027	15	—	
1936 . . .	118	1,749	13	—	
1937 . . .	125	1,482	11	—	
1938 . . .	122	1,801	13	—	
1939 . . .	129	1,408	10	—	Outbreak of War
1940 . . .	—	850	7*	—	Statistics Suspended
1941 . . .	—	292	—	—	
1942 . . .	—	100	—	—	
1943 . . .	151	69	—	—	
1944 . . .	—	64	—	—	
1945 . . .	132	140	—	—	
1946 . . .	126	394	2·5	—	

* First 9 months.   † Average of June and December.

NOTE TO TABLE 10.—If, instead of the figures here used, from the *Abstract of Labour Statistics* and from Mr. G. H. Wood's estimates of Money Wages (in Lord Layton's *History of Prices*), I had used the calculations of Professor A. L. Bowley, published in his *Wages and Income since 1860* since my earlier editions appeared, the figures would be different, but the conclusions much the same. Professor Bowley has calculated a general Cost of Living Index, which shows a rise of only 11 per cent. between 1900 and 1913, as against the rise of 15 per cent. in retail food prices ; but his Index of Money Wages, which takes some account of changing numbers in different occupations and of earnings as well as of rates, shows a rise over the same period of only 5 per cent. The estimate of "real wages" resulting from these alternative series puts the real wages in 1913 at 94 per cent. of that of 1900, as against the 92 per cent. shown in table 10 and in graph 14.

Table 12.—RATES OF WAGES (END OF YEAR)

Date.	Cost of Living Official Index End of Year.	July, 1914 = 100.	Average of 1924 = 100.	Average of 1929 = 100.	Sept. 1939 = 100.	Rough Continuous Index. July, 1914 = 100.
1914 (Aug.) .	100	100				100
1915 . .	135	110–15				112
1916 . .	165	120–25				122
1917 . .	185–190	155–60				157
1918 . .	220	195–200				197
1919 . .	225	215–20				217
1920 . .	265	270–80				275
1921 . .	192	210–15	123			212
1922 . .	178	170–75	99·5			172
1923 . .	177	165–70	98			167
1924 . .	180	170–75	101			172
1925 . .	175	175	101·5			175
1926 . .	175	175	101·5			175
1927 . .	168		99·5			172
1928 . .	167		99			170
1929 . .	166		98·5			170
1930 . .	153		98			169
1931 . .	147		95·5			165
1932 . .	142		94			162
1933 . .	142		94			162
1934 . .	143		95			164
1935 . .	147		96	97		166
1936 . .	151		99·5	100		170
1937 . .	159			105		179
1938 . .	155			107		182
1939 . .	174			110	104	187
1940 . .	196			125	116	213
1941 . .	200*			137	126·7	233
1942 . .	199*			143	132·3	243
1943 . .	199*			150	138·9	255
1944 . .	202*			157	145·6	267
1945 . .	203*			165	153	281
1946 . .	204*			178	165	303

* Professor Bowley's Index of Wages (see his *Wages and Income since 1860* and the issues of the London and Cambridge Economic Service) is calculated on a different basis from the figures used in the above table and in the accompanying graphs. His index attempts to allow for changes in the numbers employed in different occupations, and, because of a shift from worse to better paid occupations, gives the rise in wages as greater than the official estimates which I have used. He does not give any estimates for the years between 1914 and 1924 ; but he gives for 1924 an index number of 194 (1914 = 100), instead of 170-175. He then shows a rise to 196 in 1927, followed by a fall to 183 in 1933, and thereafter by a rise to 190 in 1936. There was undoubtedly a considerable shift away from relatively ill-paid occupations, such as agriculture, into distribution, building and some of the new factory trades ; but it is not easy to say what allowance ought to be made for this factor. The main difference concerns the level of wages in 1924 : there is not much difference between the two estimates of the changes after 1924.

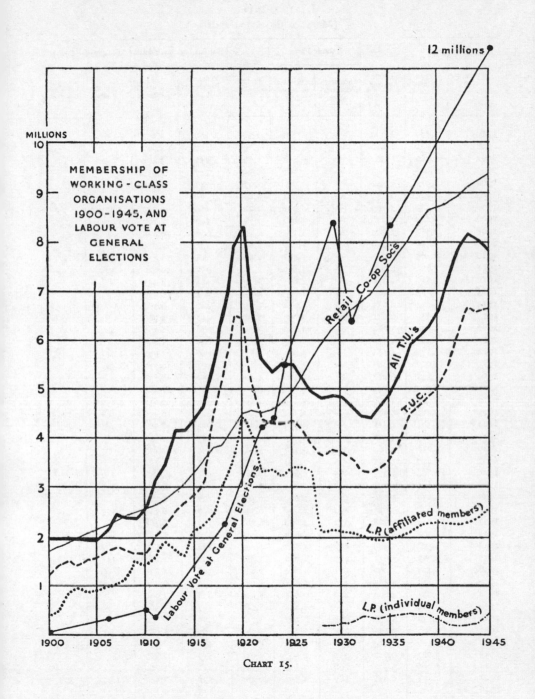

MILLIONS

MEMBERSHIP OF
WORKING - CLASS
ORGANISATIONS
1900-1945, AND
LABOUR VOTE AT
GENERAL
ELECTIONS

12 millions

Retail Co-op Soc's

All T.U.'s

T.U.C.

L.P. (affiliated members)

Labour Vote at General Elections

L.P. (individual members)

CHART 15.

TABLE 13.—MEMBERSHIP OF WORKING-CLASS ORGANISATIONS, ETC.
1900-1946
(Membership in thousands)

Date.	All Trade Unions.	Trades Union Congress [1]	Labour Party.		Retail Co-operative Societies.	Strikes and Lock-outs.		General Elections.	
			Industrial Membership.	Affiliated Membership.		Workers Involved (thousands).	Duration in days.	Labour Vote.	M.P.'s Returned.
1900 .	1,972	1,200	—	376	1,707	189	3,153	63	2
1901 .	1,979	1,400	—	469	1,793	180	4,142		
1902 .	1,966	1,500	—	861	1,893	257	3,479		
1903 .	1,942	1,423	—	970	1,987	117	2,339		
1904 .	1,911	1,541	—	900	2,078	87	1,484		
1905 .	1,934	1,555	—	921	2,153	94	2,470		
1906 .	2,129	1,700	—	998	2,222	218	3,029	323	29
1907 .	2,425	1,777	—	1,072	2,323	147	2,162		
1908 .	2,389	1,705	—	1,159	2,414	296	10,834		
1909 .	2,369	1,648	—	1,486	2,469	301	2,774		
1910 .	2,565	1,662	—	1,431	2,542	514	12,336	506	40
1911 .	3,139	2,002	—	1,539	2,640	952	10,126	371 [4]	42 [4]
1912 .	3,416	2,332	—	1,895	2,751	1,462	38,255		
1913 .	4,135	—	—	— [2]	2,878	664	10,239		
1914 .	4,145	2,682	—	1,612	3,054	447	9,362		
1915 .	4,359	2,851	—	2,093	3,265	448	2,969		
1916 .	4,644	3,082	—	2,220	3,520	276	2,367		
1917 .	5,499	4,532	—	2,465	3,788	872	5,865		
1918 .	6,533	5,284	—	3,013	3,847	1,116	5,892	2,245	57
1919 .	7,926	6,505	—	3,511	4,131	2,591	36,330		
1920 .	8,334	6,418	—	4,360	4,505	1,932	28,858		
1921 .	6,662	5,129	—	4,010	4,549	1,801	82,269		
1922 .	5,614	4,369	—	3,310	4,519	552	19,652	4,237	142
1923 .	5,410	4,328	—	3,310	4,569	405	10,949	4,348	191
1924 .	5,531	4,351	—	3,194	4,703	613	8,361	5,488	151
1925 .	5,522	4,366	—	3,374	4,911	445	7,952		
1926 .	5,218	4,164	—	3,388	5,187	2,751	162,233		
1927 .	4,917	3,875	—	3,294	5,579	108	1,174		
1928 .	4,804	3,673	215	2,077 [3]	5,885	124	1,388		
1929 .	4,855	3,744	228	2,103	6,169	533	8,287	8,365	287
1930 .	4,839	3,719	277	2,070	6,403	307	4,399		
1931 .	4,624	3,613	297	2,061	6,590	490	6,983	6,363	52
1932 .	4,444	3,368	372	2,000	6,760	379	6,488		
1933 .	4,392	3,295	366	1,939	6,917	136	1,072		
1934 .	4,590	3,389	381	1,897	7,203	134	959		
1935 .	4,867	3,615	419	1,958	7,484	271	1,924	8,325	156
1936 .	5,295	4,009	431	2,014	7,808	316	1,830		
1937 .	5,842	4,461	447	2,081	8,085	597	3,410		
1938 .	6,053	4,669	429	2,201	8,405	274	1,330		
1939 .	6,244	4,867	409	2,254	8,643	337	1,360		
1940 .	6,558	5,079	304	2,267	8,717	299	940		
1941 .	7,109	5,433	227	2,259	8,773	360	1,080		
1942 .	7,810	6,024	219	2,235	8,925	457	1,530		
1943 .	8,117	6,642	235	2,268	9,082	557	1,810		
1944 .	8,026	6,576	266	2,407	9,225	821	3,710		
1945 .	7,803	6,671	487	2,552	9·402	531	2,840	11,992	394
1946 .						525	2,160		

[1] Numbers represented at the Congress of the following year.
[2] No figures, because of Osborne Judgment.
[3] Effect of Trade Unions Act of 1927.
[4] December, 1910.

INDEX